CONTEMPORARY MORAL CONTROVERSIES IN TECHNOLOGY

Contemporary Moral Controversies in Technology

Edited by
A. PABLO IANNONE

New York • Oxford
OXFORD UNIVERSITY PRESS
1987

Oxford University Press

Oxford   New York   Toronto
Delhi   Bombay   Calcutta   Madras   Karachi
Petaling Jaya   Singapore   Hong Kong   Tokyo
Nairobi   Dar es Salaam   Cape Town
Melbourne   Auckland

and associated companies in
Beirut   Berlin   Ibadan   Nicosia

Published by Oxford University Press, Inc.,
200 Madison Avenue, New York, New York 10016

Oxford is a registered trademark of Oxford University Press

Library of Congress Cataloging-in-Publication Data
Contemporary moral controversies in technology.
Bibliography: p.
I. Technology—Moral and ethical aspects. I. Iannone, A. Pablo.
BJ59.C63 1987   174   86-5382
ISBN 0-19-504124-0 (alk. paper)
ISBN 0-19-504125-9 (pbk. : alk. paper)

1 2 3 4 5 6 7 8 9

Printed in the United States of America
on acid-free paper

To my father, Nicolás Emilio Iannone,
and the memory of my mother, Marcelina Díaz de Iannone

Whatever be the detail with which you cram your student, the chance of his meeting in after-life exactly that detail is almost infinitesimal; and if he does meet it, he will probably have forgotten what you taught him about it. The really useful training yields a comprehension of a few general principles with a thorough grounding in the way they apply to a variety of concrete details . . . . When I speak of principles I am hardly ever thinking of verbal formulations. A principle which has thoroughly soaked into you is rather a mental habit than a formal statement. It becomes the way in which the mind reacts to the appropriate stimulus in the form of illustrative circumstances. Nobody goes about with his knowledge clearly and consciously before him. Mental cultivation is nothing else than the satisfactory way in which the mind will function when it is poked into activity.

ALFRED NORTH WHITEHEAD
The Aims of Education and Other Essays

Preface

Of one thing we may be sure. If inquiries are to have any substantial basis, if they are not to be wholly up in the air, the theorist must take his departure from the problems that men actually meet in their own conduct. He may define and refine these; he may divide and systematize; he may abstract the problems from their concrete contexts in individual lives; he may classify them when he has thus detached them; but if he gets away from them he is talking about something his own brain has invented, not about moral realities. On the other hand, the perplexities and uncertainties of direct and personal behavior invite a more abstract and systematic impersonal treatment than that which they receive in the exigencies of their occurrence..

John Dewey and James H. Tufts, Ethics

This book has been written in the spirit of the above remarks. It is designed to present a number of contemporary moral controversies in technology, as reflected in various scientific and technological publications, together with discussions in moral theory—ethical theory, moral philosophy, ethics as a branch of inquiry, reflection on morality—that should serve as a background helpful in dealing with these controversies. This background is not meant to offer general statements from which to crank out particular moral injunctions about this or that controversy. The discussions in moral theory are meant, rather, to encourage the application of general statements in moral theory to particular moral controversies in technology so as to help the reader develop skills in reasoning and evaluating both the controversies covered here and others that might arise in the future.

This book is divided into six interconnected parts. The first presents discussions of current technological developments, the conflicting concerns they prompt, and the ethical inquiry occasioned by these conflicts. Part II discusses controversies in technology assessment concerning the role of risk-cost-benefit analysis and that of other methods, as well as the status of technology assessment itself. Part III deals with controversies in technology management about, for example, information technology, gene-splicing, energy, and space technology. Part IV concerns controversies in technology research and development. These range from the issue of freedom of information versus national security to university–corporate research agreements. The fifth part consists of selections on various aspects of the controversies about technology transfer at both the national and international levels. And Part VI presents controversies about approaches to technology policy making.

We have adopted an approach to ethics and technology that, unlike other books on these topics, presents controversies through their discussion in a wide number of scientific and technological, rather than philosophical, publications. They are thus discussed in the language of people involved in technological and scientific activities, and organized according to the categories used by professionals in the fields we discuss. This approach does not place such language and categories beyond critical scrutiny. Indeed, they are worth subjecting to such scrutiny if only because their use may preclude the involvement or understanding of certain constituencies in controversies concerning technology, which would have an effect on whether technology policy making is democratic or not. Accordingly, the language and categories of scientific and technological activities are used here as a way of facilitating the reader's grasp of ongoing moral controversies in technology, not as a way of placing any linguistic use or category beyond critical scrutiny. This contributes to the text the unusual feature of being more easily accessible to those more familiar with the language and categories of scientific and technological activity than with those of philosophy. Philosophical language and categories are introduced in ways that relate them directly to problems raised in the selections, facilitating their understanding.

The selections in this book are recent, most having been published after 1982. Part III, Moral Controversies in Technology Management, has the greatest number of selections, reflecting the much greater number of moral controversies of general concern within this category. However recent, many of the selections deal with controversies that have been developing for more than a decade in the United States and abroad, and that promise to stay with us for quite a while. This is also true of the selections as a whole—they are not about mere fads in technology or matters for discussions in only the United States. Nor is there a slant, pro- or anti-technology. There is no advocacy in this book, though, as a whole, it builds a case for a small set of considerations central for dealing soundly with moral controversies in technology. These are individual and collective consequences, rights, and such pragmatic considerations as the need to do something to resolve the social conflicts partly caused by technology. The relative weight of these considerations depends on the type of case being discussed; this is indicated in the introductory section to each chapter. The introductions provide guidance to the reader and establish the book's basic theoretical framework for discussing what has been said on different sides of the controversies, as well

as for better dealing with them. Recurrent references to this framework give unity to the book and should help readers who are seeking basic tools for dealing with a variety of moral controversies in technology.

The selections are not simplistic, opposing pairs; actual controversies are more complex, as reflected by the inclusion of some selections that explicitly oppose each other but, more often, of selections that only implicitly make presuppositions opposite to those made by other selections, or simply indicate ongoing controversies not addressed elsewhere in the book. The ways in which controversies about matters of technology develop are thus reflected; this should be helpful to anyone interested in becoming better able to deal with controversies as they actually are.

A glance at the Contents makes it clear that, while controversies concerning the particular actions of individuals are not entirely disregarded, there is an emphasis on matters of technology policy. This reflects a greater readiness, if not a trend, to emphasize policy matters in the teaching of engineering ethics, technology ethics, and other science and society courses. Interdisciplinary studies on a wide range of technology policy matters, with significant participation by philosophers, began in about the first half of the eighties, leading those interested in engineering and technology ethics to address policy problems in addition to problems of individual choice, as had mostly been the case earlier. This change was evidenced, for example, at the Third National Conference on Engineering Ethics, which took place in 1985, as well as at a variety of professional meetings in the first part of the decade. Thus, this volume reflects its times, without entirely disregarding more traditional controversies about, for example, the effects of given technologies on such things as the safety and autonomy of workers, and the rights and obligations of industrial management and other employees.

This book is designed primarily for introductory and intermediate level ethics courses; Engineering Ethics and Ethics of Technology; applied ethics courses: Environmental Ethics and Medical Ethics; and technology policy and technology and society courses. It can prove rewarding to those interested in the relationship between applied ethics and ethical theory, in that it provides a wealth of discussions on matters of technology that, singly or jointly, raise and examine significant questions in ethical theory.

This book developed out of my own teaching of various applied ethics courses at the University of Wisconsin–Madison, the University of Texas at Dallas, Iowa State University, the University of Florida, and Central Connecticut State University. It was partly prompted and greatly stimulated by my students' interest in moral problems in technology as well as by their puzzlement about these problems. It also benefited from the many discussions about applied ethics, and about the teaching of applied ethics, that I had with teachers, friends, and colleagues over the past decade. I ought in particular to mention and thank Marcus G. Singer, Jon N. Moline, María C. Lugones, Geoff Bryce,

John Jakovina, Margaret Carter, Robert B. Louden, Kurt Baier, Annette Baier, Richard P. Haynes, Robert J. Baum, Thomas W. Simon, Thomas P. Auxter, Susan Levine, David Braybrooke, my colleagues at Central Connecticut State University, and the readers and editors who helped with the final stages of manuscript preparation and book production, especially Marion Osmun, Wendy Warren Keebler, Ann Gorski, Helen Dimoff, and Cynthia A. Read of Oxford University Press. I would also like to mention and thank the Central Connecticut State University Foundation and the Central Connecticut State University School of Arts and Sciences for providing research funds and access to the Yale University libraries' invaluable resources.

What I owe my wife Mary Kay Garrow for her encouragement and help I cannot possibly repay. I thank her and appreciate the many ways in which she contributed to my thinking through and preparing this book.

New Britain, Conn.   A.P.I.
April 1986

Note to the Reader

This book is designed primarily to be used in courses; but it should also be of help to anyone who wants to do independent reading on contemporary moral controversies in technology. This note is addressed especially to such readers.

There is a General Introduction to the book, as well as an introduction to each part. Both aim to guide the reader in critically and fruitfully thinking about the moral problems raised by the selections in the parts. They do not attempt to provide solutions but, rather, the critical prompting and some basic elements for better dealing with the problems raised. This is done by presenting conflicting claims about the technological issues addressed in the readings, by formulating questions that serve to pose moral problems about these technological matters, and by recurrently pointing to a small set of considerations central for soundly dealing with moral controversies in technology. These include both individual and collective consequences, rights, and pragmatic considerations such as the existence of controversey and even confrontation regarding a variety of technology matters, and the necessity that something be done about this situation. These considerations constitute a basic framework for soundly dealing with moral controversies in technology. It should not, however, be mistaken for a general basis for cranking out injunctions about particular controversies. Rather, it is meant to help the reader develop his or her reasoning and value-appraising skills by encouraging critical discussions of a variety of moral controversies in technology presented in the book. Thus, readers may be helped in developing habits of mind that will enable them to deal better, not only with these moral controversies in technology, but with other such controversies they might face in the future.

Accordingly, I suggest a reading of the General Introduction before reading any section in the rest of the book, and likewise a reading of a part's introduction before reading any section in that part. There is no specific order in which the parts should be read, nor is it necessary to read the whole book in order to understand each section. Greater understanding, however, will be gained from reading the whole book because the parts are interrelated. Further, the order in which the parts are arranged may prove more fruitful than others. The book is organized, first, to provide an understanding of technology ethics and its motivation; then, with this understanding, to address matters of scope and method in technology ethics; next, against this general background, to address moral controversies in special areas of concern; and finally, to synthesize all these factors and address some aspects of a problem that underlies the discussions throughout the book: whether democratic policy making and modern technology are, ultimately, incompatible and what ought to be done about their tensions. An outline of the discussions in the book is then presented.

In reading any of the sections in this book, it is most useful—indeed, it is essential—to read actively, that is, with questions in mind, rather than letting the words pass before one's eyes. Some basic questions one might ask are: What does the author maintain in this selection? What reasons does the author state in support of this position? Are they good reasons? What common opinions go against what the author maintains? Are there any plausible reasons behind those common opinions? Are these reasons better than those the author offers in support of what he or she maintains? Are there even better reasons for still another opinion, which goes against both the common opinions and that of the author? If so, what is *this* opinion and what are the reasons that support it? And, in any case, to what problems are these various conflicting opinions relevant, and what is the significance of these problems?

These questions may seem dizzying to the novice. This is, however, no reason to be discouraged. When moral matters are concerned, thinking well, like singing well, is not something that most of us humans can readily do. To develop the ability to think well about moral matters takes a great deal of practice and reflection. This book is meant to provide conditions conducive to such practice and reflection.

Contents

CONTEMPORARY MORAL CONTROVERSIES IN TECHNOLOGY

1
General Introduction

SENSES OF THE TERM "ETHICS"

In 1974, *Business and Society Review* asked the presidents of 500 of the largest companies in the United States to respond to a number of moral questions about hypothetical cases. One of the questions was posed in the following way:

> A worker in an airplane manufacturing firm's design department is convinced that the latch mechanism on a plane's cargo door is not sufficiently secure and that the door has to be re-designed in order to ensure against the possibility of a crash. He goes to his supervisor with his information and is told that the Federal Aviation Administration has given the legitimate approvals and that he should not "rock the boat." He goes to the president of the firm and gets the same answer.
> Would that worker be justified in taking this information to the news media?[1]

Out of the fifty-one questionnaires sent back to the journal, two had no answer to the question, thirty-five had affirmative answers, and fourteen had negative answers. This disagreement between the respondents indicates a number of things concerning ethics. It indicates, in the first place, that whether the worker's taking information to the media is justified cannot be established simply by consulting the opinions of particular business executives. One can, no doubt, by means of this poll, establish that some business executives' beliefs about the justifiability of the action differ from those of other business executives. This, however, simply establishes the fact that the personal ethics—the morals—of business executives vary, which does not settle the question of what action is right, but does provide a good example of one of the ways the term "ethics" is used: the *personal* sense, in which ethics is a particular individual's beliefs and presuppositions about right and wrong, good and bad, justified and unjustified. This is something a particular person *has*. In the above case, the personal ethics of some business executives include the belief that it would be unjustified for the worker to go to the media. They presumably also presuppose that some considerations, maybe loyalty to one's employer or the financial interest of the airplane manufacturer, take precedence over the risk to the public under the circumstances.

In an attempt to resolve the question of whether it would be right for the worker to go to the media about the plane's latch mechanism, one might consider appealing to an industrial business code. Existing codes, however, provide little or no guidance on the subject, and whatever guidance they may provide is open to the criticism of disagreeing workers, industrial business executives, and members of the public. A group's code of conduct—its mores—does not by itself settle the question of what actions are justified. Any such code, however, constitutes an example of ethics in the *social* sense of the term. In this sense, ethics is a particular group's beliefs and presuppositions about right and wrong, good and bad, justified and unjustified. Ethics in the social sense, accordingly, is something a group—not merely a particular individual—*has,* in that the group has explicitly, however partially, formulated it or predominantly holds it.

When the beliefs and presuppositions constituting a person's or group's ethics are in conflict with those of others, giving rise to disagreements between individuals, groups, or between groups and some of their members, the question of who is right characteristically arises. Indeed, when the disagreements concern matters of technology, they are often sharp, issuing in controversies and even confrontation, and creating an urgency in establishing who is right as well as in acting on the problem of resolving such sharp disagreements. When people engage in critical inquiry about such matters of disagreement, they *do* ethics, rather than simply have ethics, as in the above-described personal and social senses of "ethics." In this latter sense, in which people do, rather than simply have, ethics, ethics is an activity, not simply a set of beliefs and presuppositions. The activity is not identical with, but *about* beliefs and presuppositions, and is often prompted by conflicts among them. Thus ethics becomes a branch of inquiry—moral philosophy, ethical theory, moral theory, or a reflection on morality. It is a critical study with the goal of soundly dealing with problems of right and wrong, good and bad, justified and unjustified that arise in people's lives.[2] When the inquiry seeks to deal effectively with problems concerning matters of technology, it is sometimes called "technology ethics," or "ethics of technology." This book is about technology ethics and is intended to provide introductory guidance in the subject.

KINDS OF ETHICAL PROBLEMS

The latch mechanism case presented above raised the question of whether the worker would be doing the right thing in taking his information to the media. Such a situation involves the rightness or wrongness of a particular individual's action under specified circumstances. It poses an ethical—a moral—problem that is behavioral, in that it concerns an action or piece of conduct. *Behavioral* ethical problems, dealing with the rightness or wrongness of actions, occur quite frequently.

In discussing the rightness or wrongness of the worker's taking the information about the latch mechanism to the media, the question might arise as to whether the worker would be fired as a result of such an action, and whether this would not make the action wrong if the worker has dependents and is their only support. This question is still raised in discussing behavioral ethical problems; but it leads to raising an ethical problem of a different kind, formulated by the question, Ought there to be any protection for workers who publicize information about faulty products manufactured by their employers? The focus of this question is not an action but a policy. The problem it poses is not of behavioral, but of *institutional* ethics. This addresses questions of justifiability in policies, practices, or institutions.[3] The discussions in this book characteristically deal with problems of this kind.

There is yet a third kind of ethical problem that can be raised in discussing the latch mechanism case. The worker who considers the possibility of following the advice of the supervisor and the president of the firm not to "rock the boat" may ask, What is keeping quiet about it going to do to my character? What kind of character traits would such an action tend to instill in me? Are they good traits? The focus of these questions is not policy, practice, or institution, nor is it primarily action. It is, rather, character traits specific to a person, such as courage and kindness—which are to a person's credit, or cowardice and callousness—which are to a person's discredit, and which, together, make up a person's character. Such questions about character traits raise ethical issues we call *ethical problems of character:* problems about the goodness or badness of a person's character, character traits, motives, and attitudes.

ETHICAL PROBLEMS, ETHICAL THEORY, ETHICAL THEORIES

To say that there are three kinds of ethical problems doesn't mean they are not connected with one another. They are, and various selections and discussions in this book illustrate how problems of these various kinds are often raised in an interrelated manner. Yet the kinds are different, and it is a task of ethics as a branch of inquiry to investigate what makes them different, and also to examine whether the kinds of considerations relevant for dealing with ethical problems of one kind—say, institutional—are the same as those relevant for dealing with ethical problems of another kind—say, behavioral. These are but two examples of tasks pursued in doing ethics as a branch of inquiry. They also indicate how some of these tasks, though connected with concrete matters of practical concern, are not simply about one or another particular ethical problem, but about kinds of ethical problems. They are accordingly relatively general in nature and belong at a level of ethics as a branch of inquiry associated with the development of ethical theories, a pursuit that individuals, busy pursuing the pressing concerns of their everyday lives, must often put aside. The help of a sound ethical theory in dealing with the ethical problems often posed by those daily concerns may be more than welcome; for such problems characteristically turn out to be complex, difficult, and urgent; and ethical theories, the products of ethics as a branch of inquiry, are meant to be instruments for dealing with them.

There is, however, more than one ethical theory, and sometimes one ethical theory enjoins what another one proscribes. This raises a further question in ethics: Which theory is sounder and why? In this book, an introduction to these questions and to various ways of attempting to resolve them is provided in the introductory sections to each part, especially to Part III, by referring to the particular ethical problems addressed by the selections presented. In discussing these problems, the introductions formulate various ethical theories involved in the selections, suggest approaches for the critical scrutiny of these theories, and provide examples of ways to approach theoretical points of difference in order to handle intelligently the practical problems discussed in the selections. A careful reading of each part's introductory section should put the reader in a better position to develop sound theories for dealing with ethical problems in technology, and also to apply them to the particular problems treated in the selections—as well as to other such ethical problems they may encounter.

ETHICAL THEORY AND THIS BOOK'S BASIC THEORETICAL FRAMEWORK

To the extent permitted by a selection of readings, we will develop a basic theoretical framework to help readers get started in practicing ethics as a branch of inquiry. This framework is constituted by a few main types of considerations: individual and collective consequences, rights, and pragmatic considerations, as outlined above. The main question we encourage and guide the reader in resolving is, What relative weights do various considerations have in the moral controversy in technology being addressed? The recurrent concern with this question not only gives unity to this inquiry: it should help readers engage, in a structured and productive way, in technology ethics as a branch of inquiry.

As noted in the Preface and the Note to the Reader, neither a pro- nor anti-technology stand is represented in these selections. Nor, indeed, is there a bias for or against any particular technological matter discussed. Again, this is not an advocacy book. Its approach to technology ethics, however, makes no pretense to ethical neutrality; for the considerations that constitute our theoretical framework are the basic elements of an ethical theory that combines considerations of consequences, rights, and the pragmatic instead of relying solely on the desirability of consequences, rights, or the pragmatic in dealing with ethical problems. By contrast with such a unilateral approach, the discussions of the various selections are informed by what can be called "the range hypothesis," according to which ethical problems constitute a range of problems with the following characteristics: At one extreme, individual rights carry much more weight than any other considerations in dealing with problems because, for example, natural rights are significantly and unequivocally at stake in those problems; at the other extreme, consequences carry the most weight because, for example, the very existence and well-being of reasonably good societies is at stake; and, in between, rights and consequences have less decisive weight in themselves, though, fortunately, they often reinforce each other. Sometimes, however, they appear to conflict with each other, constituting hard cases to deal with. All along the range of problems, pragmatic considerations set limits to alternatives that would otherwise have served to address the problems.

Though this volume makes no pretense to ethical neutrality, neither can it be said to be arbitrary. It allows for the use of reason in the scrutiny of its, and alternative, approaches. The guiding introductions will address the question of whether a mixed approach, such as the simple one used here, is preferable to alternative, unilateral approaches. Full-fledged arguments on its behalf, however, belong elsewhere. The reader should keep this in mind, together with the fact that this book encourages not only a critical examination of the controversial technological matters treated, but a critical examination of the very approach used regarding these matters. Dogmatism does not belong in ethics as a branch of inquiry.

NOTES

1. Editorial Survey, "Business Executives and Moral Dilemmas," *Business and Society Review* (Spring 1975), No. 13, p. 52.

2. A very succinct discussion of the senses of the term "ethics" that draws distinctions akin to those found in this section is included in *Morals and Values,* ed. Marcus G. Singer (New York: Charles Scribner's Sons, 1977), 11. By contrast with Singer's, however, the distinctions drawn here do not rely on the notion of a code of conduct, but on the idea of a person's or group's beliefs and presuppositions about right and wrong, good and bad, justified and unjustified—a wider perspective, capable of explaining a code of conduct.

3. Marcus G. Singer distinguishes between problems of conduct and policy in a similar way in *Morals and Values,* p. 5. By contrast with his account, the one here rules out neither a concrete, even personal, aspect in at least some problems of policy, nor the significant effect of solutions on individual conduct.

PART I

TECHNOLOGY, ETHICS, TECHNOLOGY ETHICS

THE RANGE OF TECHNOLOGICAL DEVELOPMENTS THAT PROMPT MORAL CONCERNS

Our times, like all times, are not easy to live in. They are, however, especially complicated, partly because of unprecedented technological developments worldwide. Modern industrial and farming technologies; information technology; recombinant DNA technology; modern health care technology; nuclear technology; and aerospace technology often lead to local, regional, national, and even global consequences, some quite threatening. The increase in atmospheric carbon dioxide is one such consequence. Just as worrisome are the increase in atmospheric fluorocarbons; in haze-causing pollutants and acid rain; the ever-increasing food needs of a steadily increasing world population; the unrelenting proliferation of highly destructive nuclear, conventional, chemical and, some say, biological weapons. Add to these the piling up of nuclear and chemical wastes; the artificial creation and growing production of new organisms that threaten to create new animal and plant diseases, sources of cancer, and novel epidemics; the increasing bureaucratization and expanding technocratic character of values and choices in medical care; the highly concentrated computer storage of sensitive information about ordinary citizens managed by business or government organizations and, too often, easily accessible; and the beginning of the militarization of space. The list keeps growing at an increasing pace, at times not only exceeding expectations, but moving beyond the wildest speculations of fantasy and science fiction.

Such developments have prompted a great deal of discussion as to whether, and to what extent, the technologies that contribute to their existence threaten the privacy, freedom, well-being, self-image, even the very existence of human beings, the well-being of non-humans, the stability of innumerable ecosystems, and the future of planet Earth. Such discussions involve concerns that are, at least in part, moral in that they are relevant to whether certain actions (say, the release of genetically engineered bacteria in the environment) are right or wrong, whether certain attitudes (say, pro-development) are good or bad or particular policies (regarding, say, energy in the United States) are justified or not. And moral concerns characteristically are just about such matters of right and wrong, good and bad, justified and unjustified.

THE LONG-STANDING CHARACTER OF SOME MORAL CONCERNS
ABOUT TECHNOLOGICAL DEVELOPMENTS

The first selection in Part I, Galloping Technology: A New Social Disease, by Jerome D. Frank, though published in article form in 1983, was originally the 1966 Presidential Address to the Society for the Psychological Study of Social Issues, delivered at the meetings of the American Psychological Association. It thus provides a nearly two-decade-old expression of moral concern with technological developments that are of long standing and that, indeed, have shown significant growth since then. The selection also indicates the matters of concern predominant at that time, six years before the creation of the U.S. Congressional Office of Technology Assessment (OTA), an institutional response to those matters and expressions of concern.

OTA, AN INSTITUTIONAL RESPONSE TO MORAL CONCERNS
ABOUT TECHNOLOGICAL DEVELOPMENTS

A current discussion of the social and political process that led to OTA's creation is presented in the second selection, Expertise Against Politics: Technology as Ideology on Capitol Hill, 1966–1972, by Sylvia Doughty Fries. This article not only provides further historical background helpful in understanding the political, economic, and moral concerns of that time, but also provides evidence of the nature and scope of the controversies regarding technology and the different conceptions of technology that were presupposed or explicitly formulated by those taking different sides in the controversies. These conceptions will be addressed later on in Part I and in the rest of the book. It is, however, pertinent here to mention that, rather than take sides by adopting a definition of technology at this point, we will leave the matter open and proceed to discuss a variety of controversial matters that appear to have some claim to be considered instances of technology, in that they are ordinarily considered technological developments. The selections in this book provide ample evidence that the matters of controversy discussed are thus considered. By adopting this approach, it will be possible for the discussions to highlight the issues at stake in the controversies discussed, thus developing reasons for adopting a concept of technology that is sensitive to real issues instead of arbitrarily begging questions of value that should not be begged. This sensitivity is essential if a notion of technology is to be of any use in discussing moral controversies related to technology.

CURRENT PREDOMINANT CONCERNS ABOUT TECHNOLOGICAL
DEVELOPMENTS AS REFLECTED IN OTA's 1983 ANNUAL REPORT

The currently predominant concerns in the United States regarding present trends and future prospects in technology development and use are reflected in the Annual Report to the Congress, January 1 to September 30, 1983, by John H. Gibbons (OTA's director) et al. Some of these matters fall under the general categories of

Jerome D. Frank's 1966 address: "pollution of the living environment, the biosphere; accidents; and drugs," where this last category refers to "new environmental hazards . . . created by the medical profession or, more broadly, the life sciences." The 1983 OTA report includes a section on technologies and management strategies for hazardous waste control, which falls under the category of the "pollution of the living environment." It also includes a section on the role of genetic testing in the prevention of occupational disease, part of the general category that Frank, somewhat misleadingly, calls "drugs". Whether Frank's general categories are adequate for discussing his areas of concern about technology is a question worth raising; the reader is encouraged to pursue it further. It may, however, be more useful here to mention the continuity of concern about technological development over the past two decades and the significant degree to which this concern is moral. We can then proceed to discuss the problems that it has prompted.

MORAL PROBLEMS CONCERNING TECHNOLOGICAL DEVELOPMENTS

Frank formulates moral concerns when he discusses his thesis:

> But "social disease" in my title refers to the . . . old-fashioned medical meaning of the term—namely, illness caused by the conditions of social living. . . . My thesis is that, although the new menaces to life and health may be caused by new machines and poisons, the remedies lie mainly in the realm of human behavior.
>
> In its medical meaning, the term "social disease" referred to illnesses contracted, directly or indirectly, by misbehavior, and therefore blameworthy.

Frank goes on to state that the expression, "social disease" was applied to a number of diseases, among them tuberculosis, which was presumed to result from unhygienic living conditions caused by people who, for this reason, were held blameworthy; he likens this to air pollution caused by current technological developments, and by the uses to which people put these developments.

Moral concerns are also raised in the 1983 OTA report. In his Director's Statement, John H. Gibbons says:

> The rapidly unfolding saga of science and technology was never more apparent than in 1983, and no abatement appears on the horizon. As usual, there is bad news along with the good. The microscopic world of cells, molecules, and solids of various kinds, combined with human scholarship and inventiveness, is yielding improved ways to communicate, save energy and other resources, diagnose and treat disease, better our crops, and entertain ourselves. But it also makes warfare all the more terrifying, undermines privacy, and revolutionizes our workplace in troublesome ways.
>
> While new knowledge merits a lot of investment and attention, existing resources and institutions are also keys to our survival, growth, and quality of life. Therefore OTA devotes considerable effort to analyzing the state and health of such resources, as air and water quality, land productivity, materials, energy, international competitiveness of U.S. industry, the quality and cost effectiveness of health care, and critical areas of national defense.

At least some of this extract is moral in nature, in that it formulates concerns relevant to the rightness of certain actions, the goodness of certain attitudes, or the justification of certain policies. These concerns prompt moral problems because they are in conflict and, in addition, involve conflicts between things like rules, obligations, claims, rights and duties, needs, interests, wants, advantages, desires, attitudes, and traits—precisely the kinds of conflicts that constitute moral problems. One such conflict, for example, pits privacy rights against the organizational advantages of highly concentrated computer storage of information about ordinary citizens. Others pit the quality and availability of work against the advantages of computerizing the workplace, or the advantages of diagnosing, treating, or preventing diseases by means of new developments in genetic engineering or chemistry against the threat to human health and general well-being these developments may pose. Such basic tensions originate moral, or ethical, problems. Since they are all created by conflicting concerns or considerations regarding technological developments, they typically belong to a special area of moral theory: technology ethics.[1]

KINDS OF MORAL PROBLEMS RAISED BY THIS CHAPTER'S SELECTIONS

Though both Frank's article and the OTA 1983 report address moral concerns and problems, the types of concerns and the kinds of problems are, though often related, different from each other. Frank's discussion focuses on consequences of technological developments that may be harmful to individuals or large sectors of society; however, he argues that "the remedies lie mainly in the realm of human behavior"; that the countermeasures employed are ineffective because of perceptual and motivational obstacles; and that though we should be aware of the social repercussions of attempting to deal with those consequences, to conquer the ills caused by technology "requires major changes in . . . attitudes . . . ." The moral emphasis here is on the behavior of individuals, that is, on what they ought or ought not to do, and on the characteristics of individuals—what attitudes or character traits they ought to have.

The OTA 1983 report, by contrast, has a different emphasis. Its suggestions concern policy, its assessments cover "issues that Congress and the country are facing," not problems of individual behavior. These considerations of dominant emphasis in moral problems help us distinguish three main categories: behavioral, educational, and institutional. The moral problems posed by Frank's selection are mainly of two kinds: behavioral, that is, concerning the actions or conduct of particular individuals; and educational, or problems of character, that is, dealing with desirable attitudes, character traits, or overall character. In Frank's discussion, moral problems of character lead to behavioral problems as to what individuals ought to do to develop desirable attitudes or traits so they can deal with the initial ethical problems Frank raises.

Unlike Frank's discussion, the 1983 OTA report poses institutional moral problems: What policies, practices, or institutions are justified in dealing with the mixed blessings conferred by technological development? Note that these consequences are not necessarily caused by bad attitudes or wrong actions, but may well be the results of unavailable technologies (i.e., to improve energy efficiency) and competitive relations in international markets.

Together, then, Frank and the 1983 OTA report provide examples of different kinds of moral problems raised by technological developments, giving us a starting point for a critical examination of various positions on the nature of these problems and morally sound ways of dealing with them. In helping the reader begin to develop an informed position on matters of concern and even controversy regarding problems in technology, their selections and those to come should provide a firm basis for the critical evaluation of moral problems.

SOME CENTRAL ASPECTS OF MORAL PROBLEMS ABOUT TECHNOLOGICAL DEVELOPMENTS

Some central political and conceptual aspects of the moral problems in technological development and their implications are discussed in the second selection of Part I, Expertise Against Politics: Technology as Ideology on Capitol Hill, 1966–1972, by Sylvia Doughty Fries. One problem is whether technological development—conceived as intelligence or expertise that is destined to become predominant in society—undermines a free society by seizing responsibility from its citizens. Pursuing this question, Doughty Fries focuses on the United States, discussing the "record of Congressional testimony of 130 'expert' witnesses on a series of bills" intended to create what eventually became the Congressional Office of Technology Assessment. The author sees the record as evidence that the witnesses, who were politically influential, conceived of technology as expertise or intelligence whose societal predominance was imminent. Many witnesses saw technology as expertise with "exceptional authority over the definition of 'good' government." This latter claim, the author argues, jeopardizes a basic presupposition of democratic politics: that a responsible citizenry is a preeminent condition of a free society.

Whether or not one agrees with Doughty Fries, a host of institutional moral problems is involved in this issue. What position should experts have in a free society? What is their importance in the maintenance of "the quality of life" in a concerned populace? What is "quality of life"? Could it ever conflict with individual freedoms? If so, which should prevail and why? And what freedoms should people have? Most important, how does one determine what these freedoms should be, or how much the quality of life should be preserved or enhanced? A number of these questions regarding policy, practices, and institutions (i.e., institutional moral problems) will be raised and discussed in later sections. Here we point out the interconnectedness of technology, politics, and society and note the effects of each. We also examine problems concerning the viability of policy making options and the determination of values.

MORAL CONTROVERSIES IN TECHNOLOGY

Examination of the social and political aspects of technological development led to the formation of the Congressional Office of Technology Assessment, whose purpose was to recover some control over ongoing technological developments. OTA, however, was simply required to present to Congress somewhat accurate descriptions of various consequences likely to result from alternative technology policies and governmental actions, and to give Congress some sense of the future implications of these technological developments. Questions arose, however, about how to assess alternative policies and governmental decisions. Some thought such assessment required ranking alternative consequences by the use of risk-cost-benefit analysis, but had no objections to the recommendations. Others objected, proposing the political process as an alternative to what they perceived as technocratic social engineering. Still others questioned whether technology assessment could, or even should be apolitical, but were divided as to whether, if not apolitical, it should involve public participation or let power politics prevail.

In discussing the controversies preceding the creation of OTA, Doughty Fries' selection not only provides the historical background of the moral issues raised but also some of the political and logical aspects essential to a productive examination of the positions advanced in Part I and throughout the book. She, for example, describes the heated controversy that took place concerning the role of expertise in technology policy making. Indeed, it still exists. Now, whenever there is a controversy there is sharp opposition of opinions or demands, coupled with disputes, debates, or contentions aimed mainly at establishing the validity of opinions or demands, rather than at mere persuasion. Thus, controversies involve a strong element of dialogue, however heated. And heated dialogue often develops in technological policy making. However, it can turn into outright confrontation without much, if any, dialogue. Things can go awry, with conflicting demands, the use of force, threats, or manipulation being the main, or only, elements involved. Meaningful dialogue, loses its predominance, overpowered by a conflict of wills.

The above characterizations of controversies and confrontations reflect ordinary people's ideas of these terms, and are both theoretically and practically useful ways to distinguish between cases in which both sides in a conflict are still open to reason and discussion and cases where reason and meaningful dialogue have become almost or completely nonexistent.[2]

When a controversy or confrontation about a matter concerning technology is widespread or involves highly influential individuals, it is often societally disruptive, and must be addressed. The remaining discussions in this book will accordingly raise and, to some extent, pursue the question of how controversy or confrontation related to moral problems about technology ought to be approached.

NOTES

1. See Senses of the Term "Ethics" in the General Introduction.

2. For an initial account of controversies and confrontations, the types of problems they pose, and some basic conditions for soundly dealing with them, see my "Nerve Gas, the Common Interest, and Freedom of Inquiry," *Agriculture, Change and Human Values,* ed. Richard Haynes and Ray Lanier (Gainesville, FL: University of Florida Humanities and Agriculture Program, 1983), Vol. 2, pp. 1125–1134. A general account of the same and related topics is being developed in my "Policy and Confrontation. An Essay in the Philosophy of Conflict Government," a project supported by a 1985 Connecticut State University Grant.

2
Galloping Technology: A New Social Disease

JEROME D. FRANK

Jerome D. Frank characterizes the concept of social disease as that of a disease directly or indirectly contracted through misbehavior, and argues that the remedies to the threats posed by the consequences of such modern technological developments as nuclear energy, biotechnology, and, more prosaically, the automobile lie mainly in the realm of human behavior. He further argues that, though attention should be paid to social aspects, combating the ills caused by technology requires major changes in attitudes.[1]

The outstanding characteristic of our time is the headlong rush of technology and science. Scientists and engineers are prying new secrets out of nature and remaking our lives at a breathtaking and ever accelerating rate. The adverse effects on society of their efforts could be referred to as social diseases, although we have preferred the term social issues. Our galloping technology has created or aggravated problems of unemployment, urbanization, racial and international tensions, war, overpopulation, and many others that have been the constant concern of members of SPSSI.

But "social disease" in my title refers to the other, old-fashioned medical meaning of the term—namely, illness caused by the conditions of social living. My particular training has made me sensitive to the direct effects on life and health of man's reckless conquest of the environment, a topic that has been largely neglected by social scientists. The most obvious reason for this neglect is that the problems present themselves as medical or technological. My thesis is that, although the new menaces to life and health may be caused by

new machines and poisons, the remedies lie mainly in the realm of human behavior.

In its medical meaning, the term "social disease" referred to illnesses contracted, directly or indirectly, by misbehavior, and therefore blameworthy. Most commonly, of course, it was a euphemism for venereal disease, but it was also used for illnesses like tuberculosis, presumably contracted by living under unhygienic conditions. These diseases were reprehensible because our forefathers blamed the slum dwellers for the circumstances under which they were forced to live.

Of the social diseases caused by galloping technology, those caused by air pollution might be thought of as analogous to tuberculosis, whereas injuries and deaths caused by reckless driving—a voluntary, pleasurable, but disapproved activity—would be analogues of venereal diseases.

Like their medical counterparts, technological social diseases can be acute or chronic. The most virulent and acute form, which fortunately has not yet broken out, would be modern war. The threat to survival posed by modern weapons is receiving so much ago-

Originally published in *Journal of Social Issues* 22, no. 4 (1983), pp. 1–14. Copyright © 1966 by the Society for the Psychological Study of Social Issues. Reprinted by permission of the Society for the Psychological Study of Social Issues.

nized attention from most of us that there is no need to dwell on it. It may be worthwhile to point out, however, that modern weapons symbolize the reversal of man's relation to his environment, a matter to which I shall return again. For the first time in human history, the chief danger to human survival comes from man himself instead of the forces of nature.

Historians have sufficiently described the horrors of war throughout the ages, but actually weapons were a trivial source of death compared to natural causes until very recently. Even when men tried deliberately to kill each other in war, they succeeded only sporadically and in localized areas. The influenza epidemic in 1918, for example, killed 10 million people throughout the world in six months. Endemic diseases like malaria and tuberculosis took their tolls in millions every year, as did famine.

World War II claimed about 65 million lives in eight years, if one starts with the Japanese invasion of Manchuria, but in that war, as in all others, the great majority of deaths were caused by disease and starvation resulting from the dislocations of society caused by the fighting. World War II was the first in which, even among the fighting men, more died of wounds than disease. As a great bacteriologist has observed: " . . . soldiers have rarely won wars. They more often mop up after the barrage of epidemics. Typhus . . . plague, typhoid, cholera and dysentery [have] decided more campaigns than Caesar, Hannibal, Napoleon and all the inspector generals of history."[2]

Now, just as we have learned to master the major epidemic illnesses and to produce food in abundance for everyone, we have suddenly created a new, more powerful form of death-dealing that can destroy tens of millions of people in minutes and, indeed, could put an end to mankind. If one were mystically inclined, one might suspect that there is some law of nature which states that the danger to human life remains constant, so that as one source diminishes another must take its place.

I shall assume, without any really valid grounds, that humans will shackle the self-created monster of modern weapons before it

is too late. Otherwise there would be no point in continuing with this address, which deals with the causes and cure of chronic forms of technological social disease. These are the subtle, insidious dangers that are the unwanted and incidental by-products of fabulous achievements in raising the level of human welfare. These dangers are at present more apparent in the United States because our society is the most technologically advanced, but in due course they are certain to plague all nations.

The dangers can be grouped into three categories: pollution of the living environment, the biosphere; accidents; and drugs. Let me start with the only brand new danger, of small consequence at present but potentially one of the greatest—the pollution of the biosphere by radioactive products of nuclear power plants.

At this time, twenty-seven nuclear power plants are in operation or under construction, and their number will grow very rapidly. In 1962 nuclear power accounted for only one-half of 1 percent of the total power generated in this country, but it could be as high as 50 percent by the year 2000. And the growth rate is exponential. In absolute figures nuclear power plants produced 500,000 kilowatts in 1960, $1\frac{1}{2}$ million this year, an estimated 5 million by 1970, and 68 million kilowatts by 1980.

Nuclear power plants present three types of danger. The first is a break in the protective casing that encloses the radioactive elements. Such an accident to the reactor in Windscale in England in 1957 is said to have released more radioactivity into the atmosphere than the explosion of an atomic bomb of the Hiroshima type. Another serious potential hazard lies in the possibility of a leak in the transportation and storage of high level radioactive wastes that cannot be safely released. Already some 60 million gallons are stored in underground tanks and, of course, the storage problem will become increasingly serious with each passing year.

The third source of potential danger lies in low level radioactive isotopes. These are now released into the environment under carefully monitored conditions, to insure that the dilution is sufficient to prevent any predictable human exposure above levels believed to be harmful. The trouble is that very little is known about these isotopes, since they have only existed for a few years. So far, none has approached the presumed maximal permissible concentration in humans. However, they raise uncomfortable questions. Even though traces of radioactive isotopes in our tissues may be harmless in the short run, we do not yet know enough about what long exposure to slight doses of ionizing radiation does to living systems to be sure that we are not suffering slow damage. In this connection, deaths from cancer in survivors of the Japanese atomic bombings have only now, after about twenty years, started to show a sharp rise.

A more serious problem is that some living creatures accumulate certain isotopes which become increasingly concentrated as they move up the food chain. For example, algae concentrate radioactive zinc to about 6,000 times that of the surrounding water. The algae are eaten by bluegill fish, in whose bones the concentration is about 8,700 times that of the water. Fortunately, humans do not eat bluegill bones, but who knows what edible tissues will be found to store other radioactive substances in the same way?

Dangers of the same type are created by pesticides. In terms of the amount of chemical per unit of body weight, most pesticides are equally toxic to all living creatures, though immunity for some can be built up in time. They kill insects and not men simply because the former receive enormously greater doses in proportion to their weight. The amount found in human tissues to date is far below the concentration that would cause immediate damage. But certain creatures we eat concentrate pesticides to a fantastic degree. The oyster, for example, accumulates DDT to a level some 70,000 times above that of the surrounding water. This happens because water-living creatures lack the enzymes present in adult humans, that metabolize most of these substances into harmless wastes. It turns out—an example of an unanticipated danger—that babies also lack these enzymes,

so that they would be damaged by much smaller amounts of pesticide than adults.

Furthermore, some pesticides, like radioactive isotopes, cause cancer in animals on repeated exposure, and some are suspected of damaging the germ plasm, so that their deleterious effects, though long delayed, may eventually be very serious.

A more serious, immediate menace to health is atmospheric pollution from factories and automobiles. It is estimated that 133,000,000 tons of aerial garbage are dumped into the atmosphere of the United States each year—more than the weight of our annual steel production. As to its effects on health, a cautious statement is: "A large fraction of our population is now being exposed to significant concentrations of a variety of toxic chemicals. These levels are often a substantial fraction of those which produce acute effects. There is a possibility that our people may be sustaining cumulative insidious damage. If genetic injury were involved, the results could be especially serious."[3] It is estimated that the chances of a man dying between the ages of 50 and 70 from respiratory disease are twice as great if he lives in an air-polluted area than in a clean-air area.

A particularly subtle form of air pollution, which may have the most inexorable effects, is the slow increase in carbon dioxide in the atmosphere produced by industrial use of fossil fuels. This blocks the radiation of heat energy back to outer space, so that the temperature of the earth is gradually rising. The average temperature today is 8% higher that it was in 1890. This of course, could be due to other causes. In any case, if it keeps up, among other unpleasant consequences, it will melt the polar ice caps, flooding the world's seaboards.

The social diseases considered so far have been analogous to tuberculosis—the individual cannot do anything about the noxious agents to which he is exposed. Now let us turn to those that are more analogous to syphilis— that is, they result from a person's own actions, whether deliberate or heedless. This category includes disability and deaths caused by accidents or by drugs. Accidents have become the leading cause of death from ages 1 to 37 and the fourth cause of death at all ages, being exceeded only by heart disease, cancer and stroke. Their prominence obviously results, in part, from the sharp reduction in natural causes of death, especially in the younger age group, but in absolute figures they claim an impressive toll. In 1964, the last year for which figures are available, they killed 105,000 people and injured 10,200,000. The worst offender, of course, is the automobile—or rather the automobile driver. On United States highways a death or injury occurs every eighteen seconds. In 1965, 49,000 people were killed—or almost half of those who were killed in all accidents—and 3,500,000 maimed. I shall return to the question of the causes of this carnage presently, but for the moment wish to pass on to a brief look at the last category of new environmental hazards to be considered. Ironically, these are created by the medical profession or, more broadly, the life sciences.

The worst, fortunately, is only hypothetical so far. Now that biologists have been able to rearrange living molecules, they can create self-reproducing viruses that never before existed. Probably some are doing this in the service of biological warfare, but many are working on such projects purely out of that powerful human urge, scientific curiosity. A Nobel Prize winning biologist views such research with profound alarm. He speaks of the good possibility that these tinkerers will create a new poliomyelitis virus, for example, against which humans have built up no immunity. "Any escape into circulation . . . could grow into the almost unimaginable catastrophe of a 'virgin soil' epidemic involving all the populous regions of the world."[4] He concludes: "There are dangers in knowing what should not be known,"[5] a feeling shared by many atomic scientists. Apparently, splitting the molecule may have consequences as disastrous as splitting the atom.

To return to more mundane but more immediate hazards arising directly from efforts to prolong life and health, floods of new medications are being put on the market.

Despite increasingly stringent laws, some that cause serious damage to health or even death get past the guards. Examples were the contaminated strain of polio vaccine, and, more recently, the malformed babies caused by an apparently harmless sleeping medicine, thalidomide.

Finally, there is the growing menace of drugs that alter states of consciousness, including sedatives, stimulants, mood-lifters and so-called psychotropic drugs such as LSD. Most of these drugs were thought to be harmless when first introduced. Cocaine, barbiturates, dexedrine, and now LSD, to name a handful, were first viewed as great boons to man.

We should have learned by now that no drug powerful enough to cause a change in psychic state is harmless if taken over a long enough period of time or in large enough doses. Barbiturates proved to be superb suicidal agents, dexedrine produces serious psychoses (in one series 83% of those who used this supposedly harmless pep pill for one to five years showed psychotic symptoms), and increasing numbers of sufferers from the acute and chronic ill effects of LSD are appearing in psychiatric emergency rooms.

Hundreds of common drugs, moreover, impair driving ability. One physician found that a group of patients receiving a tranquilizer for ninety days had 10 times more traffic accidents than the population at large. He concludes, glumly, "No matter how strenuously doctors warn patients about drugs and driving, the advice probably wears off faster than the drug."[6]

This reminder that our topic is people, not technology, may serve to conclude this very spotty survey of the new hazards to life and health created by man. I have not even mentioned, for example, water pollution by industrial wastes, the more than 150 poisons that can be found in any household, or the host of new industrial hazards.

The psychological questions I should like to raise concerning this new group of social diseases are, first, why do we not pay more attention to them and, second, why are our countermeasures so ineffective?

The obstacles are both perceptual and motivational. Perceptually, most of the dangers are remarkably unobtrusive. In fact, they are undetectable by the senses. Radioactive isotopes and pesticides in our tissues, and the slowly rising carbon dioxide content of the air cannot be seen, heard, tasted, smelled or felt, so it is easy to forget about them. When they do intrude on consciousness, in the form of eye-burning smog or brown water, in the language of perceptual psychology, they are ground rather than figure. As an authority on air pollution says: " . . . the private citizen is unaware of the fact that the substance he is inhaling may eventually cause cancer of the lungs. He does not associate a bad cough with atmospheric conditions. It may be only on days of particular wind direction that a housewife will be bothered by fly ash on her clothesline; immediately thereafter, she'll forget it. . . . The offensive odors of some industries, the dust on windowsills, the haze that obscures an otherwise beautiful day—all are taken as features of urban living about which nothing can be done. And when the air is clear, the facts of the matter might as well not exist."[7] One is reminded of the old man in Arkansas whose roof didn't leak when it didn't rain.

Occasionally the dangers do spring into focus, as when at least 4000 people died during a four-day London fog in 1952, or when traffic deaths hit the headlines on a holiday weekend, but these occasions are too brief and infrequent to sustain attention.

A further difficulty in identifying the damage to health caused by noxious environmental agents is that illnesses have multiple causes, so in any given case it is hard to single out what really is to blame. If an elderly man with chronic lung disease dies during a heavy smog, who can say for certain that the smog was the cause of death? In other terms, statistical variations in various environmental and internal factors are so great that the true noxious agent may be hidden by them. The problem is analogous to that of detecting evoked potentials on the electroencephalogram. These are spike waves occurring a fraction of a second after the stimulus. They can only be detected by superimposing hundreds of tracings so the random variations cancel each other out.

Finally, although the damage done by environmental poisons is constantly increasing, the increments are very small compared to the base level. So, in accord with a well known psychophysiological law, they do not rise above the threshold of awareness. Humans may be in the same plight as a frog placed in a pan of cold water, which is very slowly heated. If the rise in temperature is gradual enough, he will be boiled without ever knowing what happened to him.

These perceptual obstacles to appreciating the dangers created by technological advances play into strong motives for not doing much about them. The major source of complacency, I believe, is that the new dangers to life and health are tiny compared to the benefits. For example, American industry, the chief source of pollution of the biosphere, produces half the world's goods in addition to a fabulous arsenal of weapons—a technological triumph that could, in a flash, nullify the gains produced by all the others. And our society could not function at all without that space-annihilator, the automobile. Pesticides are mainly responsible for enabling less than 10% of the American population not only to feed the rest too well, but to produce millions of tons of surplus food.

Medical science had prolonged the average length of life in the United States by about 50% in the last half century and has virtually conquered the major epidemic diseases, although this battle is never permanently won. (Recently new strains of resistant malaria have been reported from Vietnam.) And the lives of millions have been made more tolerable by relatively harmless sedatives and anti-depressants.

Surely, it will be said, these huge gains in human welfare (and I have named only a few) far outweigh the relatively minute increases in illnesses and deaths that accompany them.

True, but in absolute numbers over 100,000 accidental deaths a year and the rising death rates from cancer and lung disease are far from insignificant. And even though the immediate danger to health and life may be small, some types of damage are cumulative and some may be irreversible. For example, no one knows how to restore to the water of Lake Erie the oxygen is has lost through a complex chain of biological and chemical reactions set off by industrial wastes, resulting in destruction of its edible fish.

In any case, the rewards yielded by our galloping technology are large, tangible and immediate, and the penalties are remote and contingent. It does not take a learning theorist to know which will determine behavior. The pleasure of a puff on a cigarette far outweighs the probablity that it will shorten the smoker's life by a few years in the distant future. The increased risk of getting killed influences the automobile driver much less than the joy of speeding, especially after a few drinks. And, at the social level, the prospects of increased revenues to a community from a new industry dwarf the hazard to health it might create.

So, everyone is motivated to minimize the dangers, especially when taking them seriously might jeopardize some of the gains. Perhaps this universal underestimation also partly reflects the proverbial American optimism. Even scientists, whose sole task should be to establish the facts, seem to be affected. One is constantly running across new items like: "New tests developed at Pennsylvania State University reveal that pesticide residue in plants is fifty per-cent to a hundred per-cent greater than present tests indicate."[8] Or: "Radioactive caribou and reindeer may pose a health threat to nearly all the residents of Alaska. Scientists previously had believed that only Eskimos living near the Arctic Circle were endangered."[9]

When profits, not merely truth, are at stake, optimism becomes literally blind. One example may suffice. Flourides discharged into the air by phosphate plants in two Florida counties have damaged citrus crops over a radius of about 50 miles, cut production in some groves by as much as 75%, and have resulted in a 20 million dollar reduction in property values. In the face of these facts a spokesman for the Florida Phosphate Council told local citrus growers: "Gentlemen, there's no problem of air pollution in this area that is affecting citrus groves. All you boys have to do is take better care of your groves and you will have no complaints about air pollution."[10]

Since local chambers of commerce wish to attract people to their localities, they join the creators of pollution in minimizing it, so whatever tendency the average citizen has to overlook his slow poisoning is aided by the absence of corrective information. A recent poll of the inhabitants of Nashville, where substantial numbers die every year from heart and respiratory diseases aggravated by heavy air pollution, found that 85% believed it to be a healthy place to live, and less than 3% suggested that measures be taken to reduce air pollution.

Despite these impediments, Americans have at last officially recognized the existence of the problems and taken action to solve them. Congress has appropriated funds for fighting air pollution, water pollution and highway accidents. So, you may ask, what is there to worry about? Unfortunately, in comparison with the size of the dangers, the efforts to combat them are so small as to be pitiable, or laughable, depending on one's point of view. For example, only 130 air pollution control programs are in effect in the nation's 7,000 communities, and most of these are considered inadequate.

The two main sources of air pollution are industry and the automobile. By 1970 there will be 60% more industries pouring pollutants into the air than in 1960, many of them new, so no one knows how toxic they will be. In 1960 74 million automobiles travelled 728 billion passenger miles. In 1980 these figures will be about doubled.

Thus, emission of poisons into the atmosphere would have to be reduced at least 50 percent merely to keep pace with their increased production. To do this would cost an estimated 3 billion dollars a year. Even this would only be about one-half of 1 percent of our gross national product. Actually industry and the government today are spending only about 35 million—that is, slightly over one-tenth as much as would be needed to do a minimal job. To quote an expert: "America of the near future will be filthy and foul, and our air will be unfit to breathe. Indeed, this dark, dangerous era ahead of us is inevitable."[11]

In short, so far, efforts to halt the diseases created by our galloping technology have been too little and too late. That this state of affairs is a pressing social issue seems self-evident, so it is appropriate to ask why it has aroused so little interest among social psychologists. The basic trouble may be that, in contrast to our other concerns such as war, poverty and racial discrimination, this one has no focus and no villains. Ironically, the ills caused by technology are by-products of benevolent efforts to promote the general welfare. It is hard to get indignant over this, and indignation seems to be the initial goad to becoming concerned about a social issue.

Moreover, if one looks about for a focus, one can find only familiar and universal aspects of human nature—such as failure to appreciate the seriousness of dangers that are not in awareness, unwillingness to forego immediate rewards in order to forestall future disasters, and the general inertia of social organizations. We may be dealing with a new manifestation of the illness that, according to the Spanish philosopher, Ortega y Gasset, afflicts all civilized societies and eventually kills them—the desire of the citizens to enjoy the fruits of civilization without putting forth the effort or accepting the discipline necessary to maintain it. Perhaps the last word was really said by Descartes over three centuries ago: "Defects are always more tolerable than the change necessary for their removal."[12]

Lest we throw up our hands prematurely, however, let me suggest some aspects of the problem to which social psychologists might be able to contribute.

One is the American faith in the quick fix. Our history of incredible inventiveness has fostered the belief that some new technological invention can always be devised to correct the evils created by the last one, without causing anyone too much cost or inconvenience. No doubt, new inventions will be required to help combat new dangers, and all of the diseases created by technology have partial technological antidotes. But right now

we have the techniques to sharply reduce such evils as air and water pollution, if only we would apply them, and the most efficient way to relieve many other dangers would be through modifying the behavior of people, not machines.

Traffic fatalities are a case in point. When the disgraceful carnage on our highways finally passed the threshold of awareness, a great cry went up for safer cars, whereas what we need more are safer drivers. Certainly cars could and should be made much safer than they are today, but just consider a few facts. Twenty percent of drivers are involved in 80% of accidents. If they were all kept off the roads, accidents would be sharply reduced at one blow. Many studies have found that in about 50% of fatal accidents one or both of the persons involved had been drinking. And I have mentioned the tenfold increase in accidents found among one group of patients on tranquilizers.

Finally, speeding is involved in nearly 2 out of 5 driving deaths. No amount of tinkering with automobiles will change the fact that the human reaction time is about three-fourths of a second, which means that at 70 miles an hour a car will cover 77 feet or about three car lengths before the driver can even press the brake. So if a driver is tailgating at that speed and the car in front stops suddenly, no safety devices on earth can keep him from crashing, although they could, to be sure, reduce his resulting injuries.

Nor are these considerations merely theoretical. Three New England states have reduced their accident rate to about half the national average simply by enforcing laws against speeding and drunken driving. If to these were added universal driver education courses, and effective measures to keep accident-prone drivers permanently off the roads, traffic fatalities would drop to a negligible level without changing the design of a single car.

Insofar as improved safety features on cars are involved, the human problem has only been pushed one step back to the auto makers. It is much easier to invent safety devices than to get auto manufacturers to install them. No manufacturer can afford the additional cost of making his cars safer unless all his competitors do likewise.

This consideration calls attention to a broad social issue that creates serious impediments to combatting technological sources of damage to health—the competitive orientation of our society. The American social philosophy assumes that competition is the main-spring of social and economic advance. The general welfare is believed to emerge from the interaction of conflicting economic interests. Every American inevitably belongs to several overlapping interest groups, but, by and large, he assigns the highest priority to the one centering on his means of livelihood, whether it be producing or selling goods, working for wages, or selling services. Groups are formed to protect other interests than making money, to be sure, but they do not exert as powerful or pervasive an influence. If an interest does not affect income and offers no dramatic focus for attention, no group will form to protect it, regardless of how vital it may be. It is safer to predict that there will never be a National Association of Air Breathers or an Amalgamated Water Drinkers Union. As a result, efforts to combat the poisoning of the biosphere are bound to receive a low priority. Everybody's business is nobody's business.

Another social issue implicit in technologically-caused ills arises from the fact that they cannot be effectively combatted by local action. The dangers are seldom confined to political units. When they are, as when fumes from a factory pollute the air of a town, the industry involved is seldom locally owned, and so is relatively immune to local pressures. The characteristics of local administrative agencies also impede effective action. If the job of policing water pollution, for example, is assigned to an established agency like the Health Department, it must take its place at the end of the line behind the department's established duties, and must compete for funds and personnel that are usually already inadequate. If a new department is formed, it must battle established agencies, resistant to encroachments on their terrains.

Nor can local communities meet the financial burdens involved in adequate safety measures. A major reason for the success of the federal highway program seems to be that the federal government footed 90% of the bill. It will probably have to assume a similar share of the cost of combatting environmental ills, instead of the meagre 40% it now offers.

And so we find ourselves once again facing in a new guise the perennial problem of the place of government regulation and control in a free society—a manifestation of the inevitable and universal tension between freedom of the individual and the welfare of the group.

In other words, it appears that technologically-caused ills of individuals can be successfully combatted only by correcting the ills of society with which they are intertwined. At this point certain new tools that psychologists have helped to develop may come to our aid.

One is computerized systems analysis. The biosphere is a single system, of which human beings are an integral part. So attempts to modify any aspect of it may have repercussions on the rest, sometimes unforeseen. For example, the introduction of methods to control air pollution might affect patterns of mass transportation and employment, which in turn may influence rates of crime, alcoholism and drug addiction. Computerized techniques of systems analysis, that enable rapid gathering of many types of data and analysis of their interactions, for the first time permit solution of such problems. They analyze the relationships of the different aspects, make it possible to anticipate the effects of various remedies before actually implementing them and provide continuous feedback on the success of the measures finally undertaken. California has pioneered in a pilot application of systems analysis to problems of air and water pollution, mass transportation, and crime, with encouraging results.

To combat the ills caused by technology also requires bringing about major changes in the attitudes of the American people. We would have to learn to view our problems in a broader context—to realize that the quick fix will not work and that adequate solutions require consideration of the social and ethical implications of remedial measures. In addition, we shall have to learn how to cope with a constantly changing environment.

The achievement of both these aims would require drastic and large-scale changes in our philosophy and methods of education. There would have to be more emphasis on general principles, and on learning how to solve problems, and less on sheer information and development of technical skills. It would be necessary to introduce these orientations into the school curriculum from the earliest grades. Their implementation would require full use of new methods of teaching that eliminate the enormous waste motion of traditional methods.

A massive program of adult education along similar lines would also be necessary. Electronic communications media could be used very much more effectively for such a purpose than they are today. Many industrially backward nations are using radio and television to speed the education of their people, as well as for other less worthy aims. Today, educators, political leaders and other molders of the public mind can drop in for a chat, via television, in over 93% of American homes. Attempts to use the educational potentialities of television more fully would run into the same obstacles as any other social innovation. The mere existence of television, however, gives grounds for hope that it will be used to speed the changes in public attitudes required by the changes in the environment.

Lurking behind all the problems I have discussed is a brand new psychological issue, to which I should like to call your attention. It probably concerns philosophers, theologians and poets primarily, but, as psychologists, we cannot be indifferent to it. Let me introduce the topic by taking as a text a comment of a State Conservation Commissioner defending a public utility, one of whose atomic power plants had caused an enormous fish kill by its effluent. He described this mishap as "almost in the vein of an act of God."[13] I do not think he really meant to imply that God is dead and has been replaced by Consolidated Edison. But such a proposition might contain a germ of truth. Our generation is living through the culmination of a struggle between man and nature that began when someone first resolved to sail into the wind, rather than letting currents and breezes carry him where they would. After he learned how to do it, he became able to choose his destination, so he had to develop navigational instruments to tell him where he was and how to reach his goal. From then on, step by step, man has gradually bent the forces of nature to his will, until today, barring only his inability to conquer death, he seems to be nature's master. But let us not become too self-confident. At first the benefits of our assault on the natural environment far exceeded the costs, but now the latter are rapidly mounting. Nature may simply have been biding its time.

The interesting psychological point is that our increasing power over nature has been accompanied by growing despair about ourselves. Playwrights, novelists, poets, philosophers keep hammering away on the related themes that life is meaningless, absurd, a kind of bad joke, and that man is capable only of making himself and his fellows miserable. And these statements find a wide response. Could they spring, in part, from a feeling of terror at our inability to live up to the appalling responsibilities of our new power?

In the past, men could shrug their shoulders in the face of most of the evils of life because they were powerless to prevent them. A misfortune like a fish kill could be blamed on God or Fate. Now there is no one to blame but ourselves. Nothing is any longer inevitable. Since everything can be accomplished, everything must be deliberately chosen. It is in human power, for the first time, to achieve a level of welfare exceeding our wildest imaginings or to commit race suicide, slowly or rapidly. The choice rests only with us.

Perhaps we are realizing that no degree of control over nature can solve basic problems of social living. Our dazzling material triumphs are, rather, a warning that in the end, all depends on improving the quality of our relationships with each other. Without this, all our scientific and technological triumphs may only hasten our destruction.

Man has been characterized as the only creature with an infinite capacity for making trouble for himself, and we seem to be exercising that capacity fully today. It may be some comfort to recollect, with a student of man's origins, that "man is a bad weather animal, designed for storm and change."[14]

Today man is making his own stormy weather. Perhaps it is not too much to hope that the same qualities which enable him to triumph over the destructive forces of nature will enable him to master those he himself has created.

NOTES

1. Presidential address for the Society for the Psychological Study of Social Issues (Division 9 of the American Psychological Association) presented at the meetings of the APA in New York City on September 3, 1966.

2. Zinsser, Hans. *Rats, Lice and History*, Boston: Little Brown, 1935.

3. Abelson, P. H. Air pollution. *Science*, March 26, 1965, *147*, 1527.

4. Burnet, F. M. Men or molecules? A tilt at molecular biology. *The Lancet*, January 1, 1966, 7427, 38.

5. Burnet, 39.

6. Hollister, L. E. *Baltimore Sun*, March 20, 1966.

7. Lewis, H. R. *With Every Breath You Take*. Crown Publishers, 1965, 262.

8. *Medical World News*, October 8, 1965.

9. *AMA News*, January 10, 1966.

10. Lewis, 261.

11. Lewis, 271.

12. Lewis, 221.

13. Wilm, H. G. *New York Times*, May 20, 1965, p. 45, Col. 1.

14. Ardrey, R. *African Genesis*. New York: Atheneum, 1961.

3

Expertise Against Politics: Technology as Ideology on Capitol Hill, 1966–1972

SYLVIA DOUGHTY FRIES

Sylvia Doughty Fries analyses the record of congressional testimony of 130 witnesses on a series of bills to create a congressional office for technology assessment. She finds that most of these witnesses conceived of technology as expertise and appeared to presuppose the impending predominance of technology in society. She also shows that many of these witnesses claimed that technology as expertise had exceptional authority over the definition of good government, and argues that this claim undermines the basic presupposition of democratic politics, that the existence of a responsible citizenry is the preeminent condition of a free society.

Exploration of three thematic problems—the meaning of "technology," technology as historical destiny, and the compatability of technology with democratic politcs—must be a part of any effort to develop an overview of the significance of technology for twentieth-century American ideology. Ambivalence toward technology has become a well-established theme in studies of the mechanization of America. For example, sermons, orations, editorials, and popular lectures of the pre-Civil War era show, according to Hugo Meier, a conscious effort to invest technological progress with democratic legitimacy. Contradiction and anomaly, Leo Marx writes, characterized the attempt of the American literary imagination, from Hawthorne to Fitzgerald, to admit the power of the machine into the moral and symbolic terrain of the country's pastoral heritage.[1]

Nineteenth-century voices and their modern interpreters also reveal considerable confusion over what "technology" meant. The term itself had been in use since the seventeenth century to describe "the practical arts." Scholars commonly infer it from such nineteenth-century American expressions as "inventions," "devices," "engines," "machines," or Amos Eaton's felicitous but more complicated "application of science to the common purposes of life."[2] Not withstanding their confusion over the meaning of the term, both the critics and the champions of technology in the nineteenth century treated it as something that is historically inevitable. Technology may be welcomed or feared, but, by and large, it cannot be resisted. The historical inevitability accorded technological "progress" cannot be less than remarkable, and is certainly problematic, in a society which once perceived (and in some quarters continues to perceive) Divine purpose or democratic destiny as the prime mover in the unfolding of national history.

Thus, nineteenth-century responses to technology posed not one but two ideological questions. The closing of the frontier may have rendered concerns about the fate of "this virgin land" somewhat academic, but it did not settle the political questions of democracy's prospects and national destiny in a technological society. The meaning of "technology," the relationship of technological progress to the nation's historical purpose, and the role of technology in democratic politics—any attempt to appreciate the continuing importance of technology for American ideology must assess whether and how these questions have been resolved.

The heterogeneity of authorship and wide variety of context characteristic of most available commentaries on technology and American society pose, however, serious interpretative difficulties. A less than comprehensive but perhaps more useful approach is to examine closely the perceptions of technology expressed by a fairly homogeneous group of individuals, of some generally admitted public importance, *all commenting in the same elocutionary context*. The record of Congressional testimony of 130 "expert" witnesses on a series of bills to create a Congressional office for technology assessment provides the opportunity for such an analysis.[3] The majority of witnesses whose testimony is explored in this article shared the experience of success and influence in the "hard" and social sciences and engineering in academia and, to a lesser extent, in industry and government. Invited to testify, these witnesses constituted a class of politically influential persons called to interpret technology to a Congress increasingly engaged in making national technology policy.

Analysis of the testimony suggests that machines and devices are no longer fundamentally at issue in twentieth-century discussions of technology. Rather, technology properly refers to a mentality, essentially positivistic in character, whose historical triumph is imminent. Technology thus perceived appears to have been substituted for an otherwise failed sense of history, that is, of logic and purpose in the unfolding of events. The ideological significance of this perception is considerable, for the nature of a society's

historical sensibility determines how it comprehends events in the public world and thus ultimately serves as the basis for its moral and political judgments.

Having substituted an expectation of the historical imminence of technology for a lost core of belief in the ultimate reason of human history, the witnesses tended to claim for technology-as-intelligence, or "expertise," exceptional authority over the definition of "good" government. In so doing, they jeopardized one of the critical assumptions of democratic politics, namely that a responsible citizenry is the preeminent condition of a free society.

The notion that the Congress could make use of systematic efforts to assess the consequences of existing and emerging technologies first surfaced among members of Congress during "purely shirtsleeve" discussions begun in 1964 by a few members and staff of the U.S. House of Representatives Committee on Science and Astronautics and an advisory group from industry and academia. Several times a year, Jerome Wiesner (MIT), James Fiske (Bell Labs), Sam Lehner (DuPont), Guy Suites (General Electric), Don K. Price (Harvard University), Wilfred McNeil (Grace Lines), and General James Gavin (Arthur D. Little) assembled to "brainstorm" with Chairman Emilio Q. Daddario (D–Connecticut), ranking minority member Charles Mosher (R–Ohio), and committee counsel Philip B. Yeager about the best use the Congress might make of science and technology "to attack public problems."[4] Each of the participants recalls that a special sense of urgency prompted their gatherings. They had all been affected by the "emotional movement . . . to protect the environment."[5] In several private meetings and in correspondence, Charles A. Lindbergh had successfully conveyed to Daddario a "fundamental" realization that "the impact of the human mind on life's evolution has been negative," thus "the human intellect . . . to avoid destruction . . . must exercise control over its accumulating knowledge."[6]

The group became sensitive during its meetings to the necessity of distinguishing, for an legislative purpose, between a program that could be perceived as an assault on technological progress per se, and a program to develop what might amount to no more than a diagnostic device for identifying the environmental and social hazards of current and future technologies. The "real spur" toward a descriptive rather than proscriptive emphasis, Yeager recalls, "was the stone wall we ran into from industry in trying to get anyone to talk about it." Would industry react to these efforts in the same way it was reacting to the work of the Environmental Protection Agency or the Occupational Safety and Health Administration, that is, to see the program as one more "stumbling block . . . in the path of private enterprise"? Ultimately, the group articulated a balanced, exploratory approach to the problem, calling it "technology assessment." Neither the public nor Congress was much aware of the proposed Office of Technology Assessment (OTA), observed Mosher, but the professional academic policy scholars and people working in this new . . . rather vogue-ish, discipline of policy analysis . . . they became very much aware of it." Indeed, Yeager reflected, professional policy analysts grew especially warm to the prospect of OTA when it became apparent that it would most likely become "a contract operation rather than an in-house capability."[7]

By Winter 1966, informal conversations had been translated into tentative legislative language and the committee began to receive testimony on technology assessment from expert witnesses, a process that continued from the 89th through the 92nd Congresses, until 1972, when the Technology Assessment Act (PL 92–484) was enacted into law.[8] Meanwhile, interest in technology assessment for the Congress had surfaced in the Senate as well. Largely at the inspiration of Chairman Edmund S. Muskie (D–Maine), the Subcommittee on Intergovernmental Relations of the Committee on Government Operations began to take testimony, also in December 1966, on a resolution "To Establish a Select Senate Committee on Technology and the Human Environment." Most witnesses who testified to either committee were invited on the strength of their profes-

sional reputations or their previous roles in government policymaking, or because they were known to a committee member. "The people invited as witnesses" typically represented "an interest in the question," recalls one staff member, especially when "with a question like this, there is no intrinsic interest by district." Witnesses who had been involved in the House committee's initial exploratory discussions were, as a result, "key witnesses."

Skeptics might suggest that Congressional interest in institutionalizing technology assessment was inspired by the business community's desire to defuse a possible popular backlash against Americn industry. Yet, efforts to interest witnesses from industry in testifying met with only limited success. "They all gave the same reason, which was that they did not really quite understand what we were trying to do," Yeager remembers; industry seemed to view the OTA as just another Federal bureaucracy.[9] Of the witnesses whose affiliations or disciplines could be identified, university-based natural and physical scientists and engineers outnumbered scientists and engineers from industry by roughly 2 to 1. Industry—which had otherwise successfully managed to use Federal regulation as a means of assuring greater stability and predictability in the marketplace than possible with pure, and unruly, competition—appears to have distanced itself from this legislative effort. Not suprisingly, virtually all of *the witnesses endorsed in principle the idea of Congressional technology assessment; but they did not agree on the nature of the "technology" to be assessed.* Numerous witnesses echoed the view of economist Howard R. Bowen who maintained that technology was not simply the "practical application of knowledge derived from the physical and biological sciences," but included "the application of all knowledge." Technology should be seen as the "organization of knowledge for practical purposes" and thus as including not only tools but also linguistics and analytical and mathematical techniques, argued Emanuel G. Mesthene (Director of the Harvard University Program on Technology and Society). Stanley Ruttenberg (U.S. Department of Labor) suggested that "problem-solving techniques" as much as an understanding of nature have been the contribution of science to the engineering, biological, and other technical achievements of modern life.[10] Technology was no longer distinctly represented in the imagery of the dynamo and the locomotive. Clearly, technology as energy and devices was giving way to the notion of technology as effective intelligence.

Some witnesses found the pace at which technology was insinuating itself into modern life to be overwhelming. "We have created in this country," observed a professor of medicine, "the scientific and technological revolution" which has resulted in "skills, techniques, devices and abilities almost beyond belief." Geologist Harrison Brown (California Institute of Technology) found the expansion of technology tantamount to a "fantastic revolution" and, hinting at the notion of technology as irrational force, spoke of it "growing 'like Topsy.' " A sense of rapid acceleration was likewise suggested in the testimony of the U.S. Secretary of Transportation, who called the twentieth century an "era of rapidly advancing progress" with an "embarrassment of technological riches." A process? An accelerating force? Was technology autonomous and self-generating? Anthony J. Weiner of the Hudson Institute implied that it was; he testified that "man's unremitting Faustian striving, impossible to renounce" was likely to "remake both his inner and outer environment." Neither government nor business were ultimately to blame for such disasters as the 1969 Santa Barbara oil spill, argued one witness; rather, the fault lay with "technology itself," which "seems to have a life of its own."[11] Witnesses in the House hearings decried a technology that "has run rampant with virtually no controls placed upon it," and lamented the "almost unbridled development of technology." The image of technology as an autonomous force was clear in the assertion by Stewart H. Udall (then Secretary of the Interior) that "man . . . let his technological efforts . . . move so far ahead of his ability to control [them]," and in a California county

official's complaint that "our technology today is way beyond our ability to use it."[12]

All witnesses agreed that advancing technology (and, they implied, its parent "scientific progress") had hitherto been the principal instrument of humanity's historical ascent from barbarism to civilized enlightenment; but the marvelous inventions of the nineteenth century had acquired an aggregate identity and intelligence of their own, transforming technology into an uncertain and possibly sinister master of human destinies. *Technology assessment was viewed as a means of recovering some control over events. Any viable effort at technology assessment, however, would require the ability to anticipate with some accuracy the future consequences of present action.*

The ability to predict the future in any but the most static, closed universe presupposes some conception of rational historical causation. Otherwise events are either inexplicable or the playthings of Fortuna. But such a conception of history was missing, even by allusion, from the witnesses' testimony. The closest they came was the suggestion that if technology shapes history, then the logic of history is inherently technological, or comprehensible through quantification and mechanical principles or analogies. *The analysis of social forces by "scientific" methods, or by methods resting on measurement and mechanism, would yield laws of change which history then, one supposes, would obligingly obey.*

The environmental critique of modern technology proved to be one of the more ideologically complicated themes of the testimony. Witnesses who, for example, warned of technology's environmental degradations appear to have assumed that a natural landscape could be restored without machinery (or with only a little machinery here and there) and that this could be achieved without significant cost to a large number of ordinary Americans. Also underlying the environmental argument was a set of perceptions about nature which contained internally contradictory views of its plasticity or its self-recuperative powers.

Consider, for instance, the testimony of R. Buckminster Fuller. In describing the earth as a "spaceship," Fuller provided an image of a place no longer the secure dwelling place of humankind but, instead, an isolated and fragile particle in an unforgiving universe. Its ontology was likened to an intricate mechanical contrivance, devoid of spirit, taking its energy not from immaterial life forces— whether animal or divine—but from "synergism," a principle derived from metallurgy. If all the world could be reduced to a mechanism, then the issue was not man against nature, but technology against technology.[13]

Other witnesses revealed a sense of the natural world as a delicate organism whose inner processes could not be accommodated to technology without doing violence to the whole. The most eloquent and informed case for this view was made by Barry Commoner. Describing modern technology as a "system of productivity" which consumes "certain capital goods . . . provided by nature, the environment, and the people who live in it," Commoner warned that "the success of technology is illusory" for it threatens to destroy "irreparably" the capital upon which it depends. Technology, far from being the key to understanding and manipulating the human and natural world, "is intruded on the natural world" in response to some "narrow economic need," resulting in a "myriad of ecological and biological problems."[14]

During the nineteenth century, technological progress might have been heralded as a means of mastering nature for human betterment. The testimony offered during the OTA legislation hearings revealed *not only an altered conception of technology, but contradictory conceptions of nature as well.* The increased complexity of the man-against-nature theme becomes evident when one compares Commoner's remarks with those of a witness from Monsanto Company. In defending the use of pesticides to increase crop yields, Phillip C. Hamm insisted that pesticides constitute only a minor part of pollution.[15] Pollution also comes from nontechnological sources such as animal wastes; and other natural processes can be self-polluting. Implicit in Hamm's comments was the notion that nature is neither necessarily nor

inherently clean, efficient, or benign. The preservation of natural processes is not always tantamount to the protection or enhancement of human life, and some intervention into the natural world—e.g., agricultural technology, irrigation, or flood control—may be excused not only because of human necessity, but also because of nature's resilience in the face of foreign intrusions.

A tendency to see all things as "system," a technologically related concept itself, was evident in this as well as in other aspects of the witnesses' comments on the technology/society/nature relationship. Was nature open and dynamic, able to absorb the random interventions of man without suffering irreversible harm, or was nature a system, organic or mechanical, closed and fixed, one in which human intervention spelled inevitable and perhaps irreparable damage to the fragility of its internal structure? The latter view was by far more common. For example, a typical statement included the characterization that "the earth . . . has a system of its own, a web of life, a system of nature . . . it has its own laws and we are part of that system. And unless we have respect for that system we get in trouble."[16]

Comingled with the concept of the natural world as a closed and fragile system was the view that *what is most worth preserving in nature is its aesthetic or inspirational quality.* One witness (a physicist) asserted, for example, that the globe must be preserved as a "comfortable, aesthetically pleasing environment in which to live," while another (an ecologist) stressed the psychological and inspirational as well as the physiological and biological dimensions of nature. Nature as the scene of human recreation and inspiration also appeared in the Sierra Club representative's call for the preservation of "our most scenic and unique wildlands."[17]

What we have, then, are three views of nature, each with its special ramifications for the proper use of technology. Nature as inspiring wilderness has value in part because of its impalpability. That which can be manipulated rarely inspires, while that which inspires does so in part because of its transcendant qualities. Nature as inspiring wilderness can suffer little intrusion and that intrusion must be limited to the presence of the sensibly engaged observer. Between wilderness and nature as the resilient source of man's provenance lay a vast and confused conceptual terrain occupied by Fuller's "spaceship" and Commoner's vital organism writ large. One could also detect remnants of what Leo Marx has termed the "middle landscape,"[18] embodied in the evocation of "a countryside dotted with new towns and growing rural communities where the benefits of community life are matched by the rich beauty of the countryside—where new industries and factories in rural America provide the necessary economic underpinning for the good life in the country."[19]

Congressional witnesses on technology assessment tended not only to equate technology with all vital intelligence, but also to fail to express a conception of nature which was sufficiently coherent or commanding to serve as a basis for countervailing or non-technological values. Interwoven as well in their testimony was a complicated political issue: assuming that Congress had at its disposal the assessments expected of an OTA, what authority should those assessments have in justifying governmental intervention in the actions of either private enterprise or the public? This issue embodied a more fundamental ideological question: *what is the proper role and authority of expertise in democratic politics?*

No witness claimed that the technological future could be predicted with absolute certainty, but several agreed with Surgeon General William H. Stewart that the probable accuracy of competent "futures" work was high. Carl Madden, speaking for the World Future Society, urged the Congress to undertake the study of alternative futures that it could then rank in order of desirability.[20]

Yet, ranking the desirability of alternative futures would necessarily involve some implicit or explicit measures of relative social value and risk. Engineers and scientists predominated among the witnesses who argued the need to establish "social indicators," or

suggested that "quality of life" could be measured as part of an effort to evaluate objectively the social risks and benefits to be expected from any technological development.[21] The difficulty lay, of course, not in determining whether environmental preservation or "quality of life" were objectives highly prized by Americans, but in determining which objectives should prevail, and on what grounds, when they come into conflict.

Some of the witnesses acknowledged this dilemma of social engineering—that the more difficult task is not how, but to what end[22]—but most spoke as if such a dilemma never existed, insisting instead on "holistic" approaches to technology assessment. The interaction of technology, society, and the environment could be penetrated "holistically," many witnesses claimed, only by those whose mode of analysis was impartial and objective, and whose professional training elevated them above the special concerns of "vested interests." This was, in fact, one of the two most favored solutions to the dilemma of social engineering. Technology assessment and the knowledge upon which it relies should be kept inviolate from the "vested interests" of either business or government and assigned substantially to universities and non-profit research groups, institutions which, presumalby, had no vested interests. The other solution was to challenge the legitimacy of social engineering as an instrument of public power and to rely instead on the political process to resolve complex social questions. The issue was rarely described in such sharp relief, but its presence dominated witnesses' comments on the purpose as well as feasibility of public-sponsored technology assessment.[23]

That "good" public policy rests on scientific foundations was affirmed implicitly by most witnesses when they argued that the natural and social sciences and engineering professions should seek a more influential role in government. Ecology and systems analysis were mentioned most often as the disciplines likely to illuminate the complex relations between man, machine, and nature—understanding of which would be indispensable to effective technology assessment.[24] Congressmen were even offered a preview of what they might expect from the application of one of these new sciences to government: "In the language of systems analysis," volunteered John Dyckman of the University of California's Department of City and Regional Planning, "we have been suboptimizing with tireless efficiency; that is, we have been very good at production of visible, short-run outputs and very poor at sensing the externalities that are thrown off in space and time by these processes." Our individualistic and competitive "socioeconomic system" has led to "heedlessness of the system effects in the social and environmental systems. We have now reached the point where the byproducts of our efficiency have reached such staggering proportions that we are beginning to suffer inefficiencies in the conventional areas of production and distribution from the frictions these byproducts impose [sic]."[25]

Only a few witnesses questioned whether technology assessment could, or even should, be apolitical. The very independence that its supporter advocated would render an office of technology assessment ineffectual, argued Gene M. Lyons (Dartmouth College, Department of Government). Lacking political support, such an organization would be too weak to "challenge the mission-oriented technology supported by both executive agencies and standing congressional committees." Politicians use the information of scientific experts, asserted one witness, only when it suits their political purposes—re-election or public justification, for example—to do so. Their chief obligation is to serve their clients' interests "in good conscience and political safety" and their need for expert advice depends on how they perceive those interests. The limited political usefulness of "sound" policy analysis is especially relevant to the questions of technology assessment, the witness explained, because technology assessment "is at present a non-existent art for which there are no artists." The combination of technologist and social scientist with appreciation for the relevant technology and the political considerations is "rare, perhaps non-existent."[26]

Technology becomes a matter of public policy not because of the technical problems it creates, but because of the social and moral questions it raises, insisted Rev. Robert Brungs (a physicist at St. Louis University). The conflicting values of a pluralistic society inhere in any public assessment of technology. Experts neither have nor should have any special authority to determine which values should prevail. Technology assessment belongs to the people. Another witness shared the apprehension that fundamental questions of value raised by technology would be decided by the few on behalf of the vast majority of society for whom the experts had little understanding and perhaps less sympathy. Harold P. Green (George Washington University) rejected as an "unfounded myth" the notion that "ordinary mortals are incapable of understanding the issues." What divides scientists and engineers from the general public is not the superior wisdom of the former, but "the esoteric jargon of their disciplines."[27]

It is generally acknowledged that the public assessment of technology involves issues of "elite" versus "participatory" politics; most of the solutions proposed involve some type of "mechanism" to give people their say.[28] Yet no mechanism, however well-designed, answered those witnesses who feared technology assessment as just one more vehicle for increased power of "experts" over the lives of ordinary, anonymous Americans. Even if modern life is more complex and more altered by scientific and technological developments than life in previous epochs, does that necessarily mean that public policy must yield to technological values or that "chaos," as Emanuel Mesthene warned, is the only alternative to rule by the technologically proficient?[29] Most witnesses agreed that the public should be involved in technology assessment, but whether or not the public was allowed to participate, or even how the participation of otherwise politically weak and inarticulate groups should be encouraged, was not regarded as the most difficult question. What the Congressional witnesses on technology assessment failed to consider was *why* the public should be involved. If the public spoke, would anyone listen? Or would it suffice merely to have placed public preferences on the record? And what if the desires and anxieties of the many publics to be represented were found to be inexplicable, uneducable, or irreconcilable?

As the hearings testimony makes clear, neither the tension between the machine and a mythical American garden nor a more generalized ambivalence will suffice to describe the ideological impact of technology in twentieth-century America. For these witnesses, testifying in the late 1960s and early 1970s, nature has lost its coherent conceptual or symbolic identity. *That which intruded upon the American moral landscape was nothing so palpable or resistible as machines or devices, but a total mentality.* This mentality was essentially positivistic, one which could recognize validity and effectiveness only in a form of intelligence associated with the methodical and quantitative impulses of conventionally understood science and engineering ("conventionally understood" because the testimony betrays no hint of an awareness of the subjective and social sources of scientific discovery).[30]

One might say were are simply reaping the harvest of nineteenth-century positivism. But *the notion of technology as intelligence also appears to have broken the bounds of formalized inquiry and become* identified with an otherwise failed sense of historical reason and purpose. If confidence in Divine purpose or democratic destiny was one of the casualties of two world wars and the persistence of totalitarianism, then a belief in the historical imminence of technology was one of the survivors.

What the testimony also suggests is that the ultimate importance of the apparent triumph of technology over the historical imagination may be less philosophical that political. The ability to sustain a conviction of the "rightness" of democratic politics is predicated upon an underlying belief in the inherent "rightness" of political processes themselves, a point too often missed by those seeking procedural compromises between specialized knowledge and democratic government in the making of

public policy. Perhaps no one has better appreciated this connection than Charles E. Lindblom, who undertook in the late 1950s to expose the fallacy that such fashionable "scientific" policy planning procedure as operations research, statistical decision theory, and systems analysis would somehow lead to more rational and responsible government.[31] Lindblom characterized these procedures, which were implicated in the notion of technology assessment, as "rational-comprehensive" in method, formalizing decision-making in terms of means-ends relationships.

Few would deny that the measure of a "good" or "rational" policy is the degree to which it attains a specified objective, argued Lindblom. But it is impossible here to agree on objectives, for "limits on human intellectual capacities and on available information set definite limits to man's capacity to be comprehensive." Lindblom proposed, as an alternative, a "science of 'muddling through,' " based upon a continuous process of mutual adjustment to varying advocacy groups in which "policy is not made once and for all; it is made and re-made endlessly." Such a system "can assure a more comprehensive regard for the values of the whole society than any attempt at intellectual comprehensiveness."

Lindblom's skepticism about the possibility, or even desirability, of comprehensive policy planning was echoed by Daniel A. Dreyfus, a Congressional committee staff member. Attempts to "introduce sophisticated policy research into the Congressional decision process" are bound to be futile, argued Dreyfus, for they are, as a matter of policy, bound to be "sterile" of the "personalized political insight" upon which members of Congress must rely if they are to remain "individually responsible to their electorates." He concluded that "responsive and responsible decisions" in the Congress are best based upon the "collective political instincts" gathered in that body. Information enough to feed debate will be assured by "an open Congressional process, a vigilant press and active interest groups."[32] The political world implied in these criticisms of policy planning, however, is likely to be uncertain and unpredictable, to be one in which much could happen that was accidental or inexplicable, one that is, in short, not wholly accessible to technology as intelligence.

The individuals who testified before the Congress on technology assessment between 1966 and 1972 indirectly betrayed a perspective on the American prospect which was devoid of much sense of the nation's history as a rationally explicable course of events leading toward the fulfillment of some higher purpose, such as political freedom or social and economic justice. Technological "progress," welcomed in the nineteenth century as a possible agent of freedom and opportunity, has become transformed into a form of intelligence which was itself transforming history. Only those who could comprehend and acquire that intelligence for themselves had any hope of regulating technology's social and environmental consequences.

Two aspects of this pattern of thought should concern us. First, the subtle displacement of nineteenth-century perceptions of the nation's history as an instrument of Divine purpose or of democratic destiny by the notion of historically imminent technology emptied any remaining historical sensibility of its evaluative content. Our ability to insist upon and to practice notions of equity, decency, and charity in the public world requires a belief that events will justify what may become a lonely or dangerous enterprise. If, however, history has become the creature of technology, and if technology is inherently amoral (as it appeared to these witnesses), then history is amoral. The future belongs to those who can manage technology. But to what end?

Second, these witnesses generally found it difficult to accept unregulated technology as the result of multiple aggregate decisions in the marketplace. Left to itself, observed Harvey Brooks, the marketplace is "rather poor for managing the secondary consequences of innovation."[33] Belief in the economic efficiency of the marketplace is ideologically analogous to a belief in a free and open political process as the most effective way of ensuring that government reflects the

desires of the governed. The many witnesses who denied the ability of the marketplace to manage the "secondary consequences" of technology also thereby questioned the ability, if not desirability, of democratic politics to carry out the prior task of identifying and evaluating those secondary consequences and determining how and by whom they should be borne. The scientists, engineers, and policy professionals who testified appear to have had a low tolerance for the vagaries of the marketplace and democratic politics. Both, their testimony implied, were likely to result in chaos or destruction. Moreover, the witnesses could muster little confidence in the virtue of "muddling through," even if they tried. Lacking a sense of history apart from the triumph of technological intelligence, they could not be sure it would all come out right in the end.

NOTES

The author is indebted to Thomas P. Hughes and Melvin Kranzberg for their initial encouragement of this study, and to Russell I. Fries for valuable suggestions and criticisms. Former Representative Charles Mosher, Representative George E. Brown, Jr., and Philip B. Yeager, Counsel for the Committee on Science and Technology, U.S. House of Representatives, provided many hours of thoughtful discussion. This article is based upon work supported by the National Science Foundation under grant number SOC–7825257. Any opinions, findings, and conclusions or recommendations expressed herein are those of the author and do not necessarily reflect the views of the National Science Foundation.

1. Hugo Meier, "Technology and Democracy, 1800–1860," *Mississippi Valley Historical Review,* Volume 43 (March 1957): 618–640; Leo Marx, *The Machine in the Garden: Technology and the Pastoral Ideal* (New York: Oxford University Press, 1964). Also see John F. Kasson, *Civilizing the Machine: Technology and Republican Values in America, 1776–1900* (New York: Penguin Books, 1975) and Thomas P. Hughes, Ed., *Changing Attitudes Toward American Technology* (New York: Harper & Row, 1975).

2. Eaton quoted in Meier, ibid.

3. The views offered in this article are based on a systematic analysis, quantitative as well as inter-

pretative, of the total testimony taken by the committees of the 89th through 92nd Congresses considering draft and final legislation resulting in the creation of the Congressional Office of Technology Assessment. The author will supply, upon request, the names of all the witnesses, by discipline and institutional affiliation as known, and a simple quantitative analysis of the witnesses' statements topically relevent to the analysis. One of the finest discussions of the use and abuse of evidence in the exploration of attitudes and ideas in history can be found in Quentin Skinner, "Meaning and Understanding in the History of Ideas," *History and theory,* Volume 8 (1969): 3–53.

4. Throughout this article, institutional affiliations or titles of persons involved in the Congressional hearings are given as correct at the time of participation.

5. Quotations are from interviews with Charles Mosher (R–Ohio), held on 10 July 1979, and with Committee Counsel Philip B. Yeager, held on 9 July and 18 December 1979. In addition, the author was kindly granted thoughtful and helpful interviews with George E. Brown, Jr., (D–California) on 18 December 1979, Thomas Moss of Representative Brown's staff on 18 December 1979, Franklin P. Huddle of the Legislative Reference Service, Library of Congress, on 9 July 1979, and Walter Hahn of the Science Policy Research Division, Library of Congress, on 10 July 1979, and Glen P. Wilson, formerly of the staff of the U.S. Senate Committee on Labor and Public Welfare, on 18 December 1979.

6. Charles A. Lindbergh's letter of 1 July 1970 to Emilio Q. Daddario is reprinted in *National Science and Technology Policy Issues, 1979: Part I,* Committee on Science and Technology, U.S. House of Representatives, 96th Congress, 1st Session (Washingotn, D.C.: U.S. Government Printing Office, April 1979), pp. vii–ix.

7. This discussion of the origins of the Office of Technology Assessment is based on the interviews with Charles Mosher and Philip B. Yeager (as cited in note 5 above).

8. For a brief overview of Congressional technology assessment, see *Review of the Office of Technology Assessment and Its Organic Act,* Report of the Subcommittee on Science, Research and Technology of the Committee on Science and Technology, U.S. House of Representatives, 95th Congress, 2nd Session (Washington, D.C.: U.S. Government Printing Office, November 1978). See also Rosemary A. Chalk, "Public Participation and Technology Assessment: A Survey of the Legislative History of the Office of Technology Assess-

ment," Congressional Research Service (Washington, D.C.: Library of Congress, 18 September 1974); Craig A. Decker, "A Preliminary Assessment of the Congressional Office of Technology Assessment," *Journal of the International Society for Technology Assessment* (June 1975): 5–26; and Carroll Pursell, "Belling the Cat: A Critique of Technology Assessment," *Lex et Scientia,* Volume 10 (October–December 1974): 130–142.

9. Interviews with Thomas Moss, Staff of the House Committee on Science and Technology (18 December 1979) and with Philip B. Yeager (9 July 1979).

10. Howard R. Bowen before the Senate Subcommittee on Intergovernmental Relations, 90th Congress, 1st Session, *Hearings on S. Res. 68,* to Establish a Select Senate Committee on Technology and the Human Environment (16 March 1967), p. 45; Emanuel G. Mesthene before the Senate Subcommittee on Intergovernmental Relations, 91st Congress, 1st Session, *Hearings on S. Res. 78,* to Establish a Select Senate Committee on Technology and the Human Environment (4 March 1969), p. 82; Stanley H. Ruttenberg, *Hearings on S. Res. 68* (6 April 1967), p. 209.

11. Philip R. Lee, *Hearings on S. Res. 68* (5 April 1967), p. 194; Harrison Brown, *Hearings on S. Res. 68* (16 March 1967), pp. 58, 65; Alan S. Boyd, *Hearings on S. Res. 68* (6 April 1967), p. 178; Anthony J. Wiener, *Hearings on S. Res. 78* (4 March 1969), pp. 66–67; and W. H. Ferry, *Hearings on S. Res. 78* (24 April 1969), pp. 250–260.

12. Mark Hanson before the House Subcommittee on Science and Astronautics, 91st Congress, 2nd Session, *Hearings on H.R. 17046* (29 May 1970), p. 939; George Pake, *Hearings on H.R. 17046* (28 May 1970), p. 756; Stewart H. Udall, *Hearings on S. Res. 68* (5 April 1967), p. 142; and Langdon Owens, *Hearings on H.R. 17046* (14 March 1970), p. 501.

13. R. Buckminster Fuller, *Hearings on S. Res. 78* (4 March 1969), pp. 2–15; see also Thomas F. Malone, *Hearings on S. Res. 78* (5 March 1969), pp. 133–148.

14. Barry Commoner, *Hearings on S. Res. 78* (24 April 1969), pp. 223–233.

15. Phillip C. Hamm, *Hearings on H.R. 17046* (29 May 1970), pp. 929–938.

16. Barry Commoner, *Hearings on S. Res. 78* (24 April 1969), pp. 222–249; Buckminster Fuller, *Hearings on S. Res. 78* (4 March 1969), pp. 2–33; Thomas F. Malone, *Hearings on S. Res. 78* (5 March 1969), p. 133; David Gates, *Hearings on H.R. 17046* (29 May 1970), p. 855; and Stewart L. Udall, *Hearings on S. Res. 68* (5 April 1967), p. 147.

17. George E. Pake, *Hearings on H.R. 17046* (28

May 1970), p. 757; John E. Cantlon, *Hearings on S. Res. 78* (4 March 1969), p. 70; George Treichel, *Hearings on S. Res 78* (7 May 1969), p. 286.

18. Marx, op. cit., p. 226.

19. Orville Freeman, quoted by George W. Irving, Jr., *Hearings on S. Res. 68* (5 April 1967), p. 160.

20. William H. Stewart, *Hearings on S. Res. 68* (5 April 1967), pp. 193–197; Roger Revelle, *Hearings on S. Res. 298* (15 December 1966), pp. 327–329; Carl H. Madden, *Hearings on S. Res. 78* (7 May 1969), p. 279.

21. Edward Wenk, *Hearings on H.R. 17046* (26 May 1970), p. 103; Myron Tribus, *Hearings on Technology Assessment* (2 December 1969), pp. 67–82; John Holdren, *Hearings on H. R. 17046* (16 March 1970), pp. 604–611; Chauncey Starr, *Hearings on S. Res. 78* (6 March 1969), pp. 177–184.

22. See, for example, Don E. Kash, *Hearings on Technology Assessment* (3 December 1969), p. 132, and Harvey Brooks, statement included in *Hearings on Technology Assessment*.

23. Roger Revelle, *Hearings on S. Res. 298* (15 December 1966), p. 339; Daniel G. Aldrich, *Hearings on H.R. 17046* (14 March 1970), pp. 470–479; James A. Shannon, *Hearings on S. Res. 298* (15 December 1966), pp. 307–318.

24. Gurdon Pulford, *Hearings on H.R. 17046* (16 March 1970), pp. 598–599; Eugene M. Coan, *Hearings on H.R. 17046* (16 March 1970), pp. 576–582; Edward Wenk, *Hearings on H.R. 17046* (26 March 1970), pp. 100–122; Harrison Brown, *Hearings on S. Res. 58* (16 March 1967), pp. 58–70; Alan M. Moorhees, *Hearings on S. Res. 78* (16 March 1967), pp. 153–165; Chauncey Starr, *Hearings on H.R. 17046* (13 March 1970), pp. 343–359; Howard R. Bowen, *Hearings on S. Res. 68* (16 March 1967), pp. 44–57; Alan S. Boyd, *Hearings on S. Res. 68* (6 April 1967), pp. 177–192; P. Willard Crane, *Hearings on S. Res. 78* (5 March 1969), pp. 166–174; John Dyckman, *Hearings on H.R. 17046* (17 March 1970), pp. 630–642; Richard Gordon, *Hearings on H.R. 17046* (29 May 1970), pp. 881–894; James Buzzell, *Hearings on H.R. 17046* (29 May 1970), pp. 863–874; Louis H. Mayo, *Hearings on Technology Assessment* (2 December 1969), pp. 82–118.

25. John Dyckman, *Hearings on H.R. 17046* (17 March 1969), p. 630.

26. Gene M. Lyons, *Hearings on H.R. 17046* (27 May 1970), pp. 126–129; Hugh Folk, "The Role of Technology Assessment in Public Policy," reprinted in *Hearings in Technology Assessment*, pp. 511–518.

27. Robert Brungs, *Hearings on H.R. 17046* (29 May 1970), pp. 913–922; Max Pepper, *Hearings on H.R. 17046* (29 May 1970), pp. 923–928; Harold P. Green, "The Adversary Process in Technology Assessment," reprinted in *Hearings on Technology Assessment*, pp. 352–358.

28. See Rosemary Chalk, op. cit.; Dorothy Nelkin, "The Technological Imperative versus Public Interests," *Society,* Volume 13, Number 6 (1976); Harvey Brooks, "Technology Assessment in Retrospect," *Newsletter on Science, Technology, & Human Values,* Volume 2/Number 17 (October 1976).

29. See John McDermott's review of the Fourth Annual Report for 1967–1968 of the Harvard University Program on Technology and Society, "Technology: The Opiate of the Intellectuals," *New York Review of Books,* Volume 13/Number 2 (31 January 1969): 25–35.

30. Among the best treatments of this aspect of science is Gerald Holton, *The Scientific Imagination: Case Studies* (New York: Cambridge University Press, 1978).

31. Charles E. Lindblom, "The Science of 'Muddling Through'," *Public Administration Review,* Volume 19 (1959): 79–88.

32. Daniel A. Dreyfus, "The Limitations of Policy Research in Congressional Decisionmaking," *Policy Studies* (1976): 269–274.

33. Harvey Brooks, *Hearings on S. Res. 78* (6 March 1969), pp. 178–196.

4

Annual Report to the Congress, January 1 to September 30, 1983–Director's Statement and Year in Review

OFFICE OF TECHNOLOGY ASSESSMENT

This section outlines the major current concerns in the United States regarding present trends and future prospects in technology development. It begins with a statement by OTA's director, John H. Gibbons, indicating OTA's areas of responsibility and intended functions.

DIRECTOR'S STATEMENT

A SENSE OF THE FUTURE IS BEHIND ALL GOOD POLITICS. UNLESS WE HAVE IT, WE CAN GIVE NOTHING EITHER WISE OR DECENT—TO THE WORLD.—C. P. SNOW

By the time this report is printed we'll be well within Orwell's year. Of course Orwell picked 1984 rather arbitrarily—his famous novel was written in 1948 so he simply reversed the last two digits. But it serves to remind us of an enigma—the importance of thinking ahead, yet the impossibility to predict the long-term future of the human enterprise with any precision.

OTA was not created to *predict* the future, but rather to provide a perspective of implications for the future of alternative present actions, and to maintain for Congress a *sense* of the future and implications of emerging developments in science and technology.

The rapidly unfolding saga of science and technology was never more apparent than in 1983, and no abatement appears on the horizon. As usual, there is bad news along with the

good. The microscopic world of cells, molecules, and solids of various kinds, combined with human scholarship and inventiveness, is yielding improved ways to communicate, save energy and other resources, diagnose and treat disease, better our crops, and entertain ourselves. But it also makes warfare all that more terrifying, undermines privacy, and revolutionizes our workplace in troublesome ways.

Since Orwell wrote *1984,* the molecules of heredity have been discovered. The understanding of the splendid and spectacular mysteries of living things is growing at a blistering pace. We now know the complete chemical structure of some viruses, and are within striking distance of determining the total genetic specification of bacteria. The implications of the extraordinary advance in knowledge are a continuing activity at OTA.

While new knowledge merits a lot of investment and attention, existing resources and institutions are also keys to our survival, growth, and quality of life. Therefore OTA devotes considerable effort to analyzing the state and health of such resources as air and water quality, land productivity, materials,

Reprinted from the U.S. Congress Office of Technology Assessment, OTA-A-226 (March 1984).

energy, international competitiveness of U.S. industry, the quality and cost effectiveness of health care, and critical areas of national defense.

It is neither possible nor desired that OTA be the fount of wisdom on such a broad array of topics. Therefore, by design, OTA is organized to catalyze and synthesize information on controversial technical issues and to present the facts and alternative options to Congress. Since these issues are of interest to many different congressional committees OTA acts as a shared, nonpartisan resource for Congress and, through Congress, for the American people.

YEAR IN REVIEW

The assessments carried out by OTA cover a wide spectrum of major issues that Congress and the country are facing. A brief summary of each report published by the Office during the year[1] is presented in this section. The reader is cautioned that these are synopses of reports. They do not cover the full range of options considered or all of the findings presented in any individual report.

Wood Use: U.S. Competitiveness and Technology

The United States could greatly expand its role in world forest products trade over the next decade and become a net exporter of solid wood and paper products before 1990. For the past 30 years, the United States typically has imported more forest products than it has exported. However, because exports have grown faster than imports, the trade deficit has narrowed. This trend is likely to continue.

Global demand for a wide range of forest products is growing rapidly, and the best trade opportunities for U.S. producers appear to be in the paper markets of other industrialized nations, particularly Western Europe and Japan. In contrast to many basic U.S. industries, the forest products industry has distinct advantages over its foreign competitors. It is the most productive and among the most efficient in the world, benefiting from a vast and highly productive domestic forest resource.

To capitalize on international trade opportunities, the forest products industry and the Federal Government probably will have to make concerted efforts to promote exports. Although responsibility for developing foreign markets rests primarily with the private sector, Government action could assist in overcoming trade barriers which currently inhibit the competitiveness of U.S. wood products in foreign markets.

Past Government and private sector concerns regarding a possible domestic timber shortfall no longer seem justifed. Future timber needs, especially for housing but also for other products, probably have been overestimated. The effects of intensive timber management and the ability of wood utilization technology to stretch the wood resource have probably been underestimated.

If current trends toward more intensive forest management continue, domestic needs for wood probably can be met without dramatic price increases. To achieve the full economic potential of U.S. forestlands, however, some changes in policy would be needed, as would an estimated investment of $10 billion to $15 billion in intensive timber management over the next 35 to 50 years.

Although both the Government and private sectors are now investing in intensive timber management, it is unlikely that current trends will lead to full utilization of U.S. forests. Although the Federal Government does provide financial and technical assistance to nonindustrial private landowners, who own nearly 60 percent of the Nation's commercial timberland, this assistance is often limited by budget constraints and is not necessarily targeted to lands most capable of providing increased timber supplies. Greater emphasis on small-scale forestry research, technical assistance, education, and information programs, combined with more accurate channeling of such assistance to the most suitable recipient, could stimulate private forest productivity.

Under the guidance of the National Forest Management Act of 1976, the U.S. Forest

Service periodically prepares programs, for and assessments of the Nation's renewable resources. These programs however, provide little analysis of policies and programs not administered specifically by the U.S. Forest Service, although there are many Federal, State, and local agencies which influence timber supply from public and private lands. The need for increased investments in forest productivity and research and development will be easier to establish with national timber production goals to serve as a guide.

Formulation of forest policy requires up-to-date information about forest acreage, inventories, and growth trends, and realistic assumptions about future demands for forest products. Improvements in the current system for estimating prospective timber supplies and demands are needed if decisionmakers are to have adequate information for design and funding of timber management programs, private landowner assistance, and research needs.

Existing and emerging technologies enable a broad range of wood products to be manufactured from currently underutilized hardwood species and from waste wood material. Expanded research in basic wood chemistry and engineering properties, and research on utilization of hardwoods and waste wood, could increase wood's long-term competitive position relative to other materials, as well as the competitiveness of the U.S. forest products industry. Increased research on hardwood and waste wood utilization could also extend U.S. wood supplies.

Commercial timber production is only one of the many uses for U.S. forestland. Broad-scale intensive forest management may result in increased soil loss, altered wildlife habitat, reduced water quality, and lower soil productivity. The environmental impacts of intensive forestry are not well understood, and further research on its effects will be needed if the practice becomes more widespread.

Significant changes in Federal programs and policies probably are not required to ensure that future domestic forest products needs are met. However, OTA has identified four general policy options which Congress could consider to increase the domestic and international competitiveness of the forest products industry:

1. Encourage research and development of forestry-related and wood utilization technologies, particularly small-scale forestry research suited to the needs of nonindustrial private landowners, basic wood chemistry and physical properties research, hardwood and waste wood utilization, and research on the environmental effects of intensive timber management.

2. Assist exporters through negotiated reduction in barriers to trade, including tariffs, quotas, and nontariff barriers.

3. Promote the use of U.S. wood products and building techniques overseas, using the Foreign Agriculture Service's experience in agricultural export promotion as a model.

4. Improve the quality of information needed for forest policy formulation. The greatest information needs are for up-to-date timber growth and inventory trends and improved forecasting methods which provide decisionmakers with realistic ranges of possible future timber supply and demand.

Industrial Energy Use

For many years to come, energy need not constrain economic growth in the United States. OTA projects that, over the next two decades, investments in new manufacturing processes, a shift to less energy-intensive products, and technical innovation will lead to substantially increased energy efficiency. At the same time, these improvements will increase industrial profitability and competitiveness. As a result, OTA projects that the rate of industrial production can grow considerably faster than the rate of energy use needed for that production.

Corporate investment decisionmaking appears to recognize this link between productivity and energy efficiency. All corporate projects are evaluated in terms of product demand, competition, cost of capital, cost of labor, energy and materials, and Government policy. Energy-related projects are only part of an overall strategy to improve profitability and enhance a corporation's competitive position. OTA has found that corporate capital projects directed solely at improving energy efficiency are not given special status, although energy cost is an important consideration in investment decisions.

OTA examined the four most energy-intensive industries in the U.S. manufacturing sector: paper, petroleum refining, chemicals, and steel. Historical energy use was analyzed, new technologies identified that could improve energy efficiency, and future energy demand projected. In the paper industry, energy use has risen slightly since 1972, but the industry is now more energy self-sufficient. In 1981, the pulp and paper industry generated half of its energy needs from wood residues.

From now through 2000, projections for the petroleum refining industry show a decline in product output, but continued, if only slight, improvement in energy efficiency. Efficiency gains will be offset by a shift to high-sulfur, heavier crude oil feedstock, and a need for additional processing of raw materials to meet market demand for high-octane, unleaded gasoline.

Projections for the chemicals industry indicate an increase in energy efficiency through a combination of technological improvements to existing process equipment, technical innovation in developing new processes, and a shift from commodity chemicals, such as chlorine, to less energy-intensive specialty chemicals, such as pharmaceuticals.

As the steel industry rebuilds to meet foreign competition, production will grow slowly, and will show a large reduction in energy intensity due to greater use of two new processes: the replacement of ingot casting by continuous casting, and the substitution of electric arc furnaces for the blast furnace/basic oxygen furnace combination of traditional steelmaking.

OTA examined four policy options for their effects on industrial energy use. Two options were directed specifically at energy conserva-tion investments, while the remaining two were aimed at stimulating all investment.

OTA's findings suggested that the most effective Government policies to promote the efficient use of energy are not those specifically targeted to energy use, but those that improve the economic outlook and investment climate by lowering interest rates and expanding demand for goods and services. Specifically, OTA concludes that:

• Reduction in capital costs would be the most effective means of stimulating investments that increase energy efficiency. It would also enhance the effect of the recently enacted accelerated cost recovery system [ACRS].

• ACRS depreciation is a positive stimulus to investment, and thus to energy conservation. But, this effect is only significant when industry is profitable and growing.

• Energy investment tax credits at a 10-percent level have little direct influence on capital allocation decisions in large American firms, and thus have little or no effect on energy conservation. However, energy investment tax credits aimed at third-party financing of energy production, such as cogeneration of steam and electricity, would be effective.

• A tax on premium fuels would stimulate investment in energy-efficient processes and products but would also have negative effects. For example, a premium fuels tax would increase the chemicals industry's vulnerability to foreign competition and adversely affect product sales of the petroleum refining industry.

Technology and East-West Trade: An Update

The recent controversies over trade sanctions and export controls have focused attention on the Export Administration Act, whose renewal is now before Congress. *Technology and East-West Trade: An Update,* discusses a range of legislative proposals in terms of four key policy perspectives:

• national security: making Soviet acquisition of militarily relevant Western technology as difficult and costly as possible;
• foreign policy: safeguarding the President's flexibility in using export controls to advance U.S. foreign policy interests;
• efficiency: making the licensing system more predictable, consistent, and efficient to enable U.S. exporters to plan ahead and to increase compliance; and
• trade promotion: reducing trade restrictions, especially foreign policy controls.

Some of these views are mutually compatible. For example, it is perfectly possible to strengthen national security controls while promoting flexibility in foreign policy controls. Some combinations, however, are inherently in conflict. The conflict between national security and export promotion is obvious, but there are others. For example, the very existence of foreign policy controls over exports introduces an element of unpredictability into export licensing, which works against both efficiency and trade promotion.

The perceived importance of national security controls has risen, as evidence has accumulated that the Soviets have a coordinated and effective program to obtain and exploit Western technology for military purposes. Soviet efforts include both legal and illegal transfers. More effective administration and enforcement of existing controls may be more productive than controlling additional items or categories.

While U.S. trade with the U.S.S.R. is small and likely to remain so, it is important for particular sectors (e.g., grain) and firms (e.g., Caterpillar). Retroactive and extraterritorial controls may have an adverse impact on West-West trade, which far exceeds East-West trade in importance to the United States.

The embargoes on grain and oil and gas technology dramatically illustrate the difficulties of a policy of trade leverage against the Soviet Union. The sanctions did hurt vulnerable sectors of the Soviet economy, but probably not enough to make a real economic difference. In fact, although such calculations are highly uncertain, the sanctions may have done more damage to the U.S. economy than the Soviet economy. Nor did they change Soviet behavior. The Soviet Union may even have benefited from the public display of Western disunity following the imposition of the pipeline sanctions, which were applied to preexisting contracts of U.S. subsidiaries and licensees based overseas.

Moreover, tight U.S. export controls require the cooperation of our Allies to have a real effect on the U.S.S.R. Allied cooperation works reasonably well only where there is agreement on what should be controlled. Despite their agreement to conduct policy studies on East-West trade, there is little evidence that the West European countries and Japan will endorse the Reagan administration's position. Their future trade relations with the U.S.S.R. will be shaped more by their own domestic imperatives and worldwide economic forces than by U.S. concerns.

Although the principal issues remain much the same, the stakes in East-West trade have escalated since 1979, when Congress passed the Export Administration Act. Congress was unwilling then to make consistent choices between the goals of national security and export promotion. The result was ambiguous legislation, which has allowed Presidents Carter and Reagan to pursue their own policies, in each case giving foreign policy considerations priority over U.S. export trade.

This report is an update of a more comprehensive OTA report published in 1979.

Role of Genetic Testing in the Prevention of Occupational Disease

Genetic testing in the workplace is an emerging technology that could help reduce occupational disease, but there is concern about its potential misuse. Although none of the genetic tests evaluated by OTA meets established scientific criteria for routine use, existing evidence suggests the value of further research. Routine use of genetic testing, however, would raise significant legal, ethical, and policy questions.

Occupational disease has a serious and far-reaching impact both on society as a whole and on individuals. Genetic testing may be helpful in reducing the incidence of disease resulting from exposure to chemicals and ionizing radiation (e.g., X-rays). The testing encompasses two types of techniques. Genetic screening involves examining an individual for certain inherited genetic traits on the assumption that the traits may predispose the person to disease when he or she is exposed to potentially hazardous chemicals. Genetic monitoring involves examining a group of workers for environmentally induced changes in the genetic material of certain cells in their bodies. The underlying assumption is that the changes indicate exposure to hazardous agents (chemicals or radiation) and that the group may be at an increased risk for disease. The information that might be provided by genetic testing would allow employers or employees to take preventive actions, but some people fear that it could result in employees being unfairly excluded from jobs.

Because of conflicting accounts about the extent of testing in the workplace and the use of the results, OTA surveyed the Fortune 500 industrial companies, the 50 largest private utilities, and 11 major unions representing the largest number of employees in these companies. Of the 366 organizations responding, 6 currently were using one or more tests, 17 used some of the tests in the past 12 years, 4 anticipated testing in the next 5 years, and 55 stated they possibly would test in the next 5 years. Actions taken as a result of testing ranged from informing an employee of potential problems to changing or discontinuing a product. In view of the small number of organizations testing and inherent methodological limitations in the survey, generalization of the results to the entire survey population or U.S. industry as a whole is not warranted.

Although the law has generally not dealt with genetic testing, many existing legal principles are directly applicable to the issues raised by this technology. An employer is responsible for workplace safety, but would not be required to use genetic testing. Under the Occupational Safety and Health Act of 1970, the Secretary of Labor could require genetic testing, if the techniques were shown to be reliable and reasonably predictive of future illness, or could regulate testing, but only in relation to employee health. The act grants no direct authority to protect employees or job applicants from employment discrimination.

Job applicants or employees who were victims of adverse job actions because of their genetic makeup may have some rights under Federal and State antidiscrimination statutes, and, if genetic makeup were considered a handicap, under the Rehabilitation Act of 1973.

Ethical principles provide some guidance for the appropriate uses of genetic testing. Because of the low correlation between genetic traits or genetic damage from exposure and disease, it would be unethical, for instance, for an employer to deny an applicant a job because of test results.

Congress could take a number of specific actions to promote or control genetic testing. The options include funding additional research for the development of more reliable and predictive tests and constraining employment actions that may be taken on the basis of genetic testing.

Technologies and Management Strategies for Hazardous Waste Control

The Environmental Protection Agency's (EPA) regulations do not assure consistent nationwide levels of protection for human health from the potential effects of massive annual accumulations of hazardous waste.

These regulations for hazardous waste management do not effectively detect, prevent, or control the release of toxic substances into the environment, particularly over the longer term. Yet every year 1 metric ton (tonne) of hazardous waste is added to the environment for every individual in the Nation. Moreover, financial restraints and lack of technical resources will make it difficult for States to fulfill their increased responsibility for waste management policy.

Industry and Government are spending $4

billion to $5 billion annually to manage the approximately 250 million tonnes of regulated hazardous waste generated each year. The annual costs are expected to rise to more than $12 billion (in 1981 dollars) in 1990. Some States have stricter definitions for hazardous waste than the Federal program, which regulates about 40 million tonnes annually.

As their responsibilities mount, States fear reductions in Federal support and seek a stronger policy role. States sometimes cannot raise even the required minimum 10 percent of initial Superfund cleanup costs—and they must assume all future operation and maintenance costs.

Because there are no specific Federal technical standards for determining the extent of Superfund cleanup, and because there is an incentive under EPA rules to minimize initial costs, remedial actions may be taken that will prove ineffective in the long term. Much of the $10 billion to $40 billion which will be needed for cleaning up the 15,000 uncontrolled sites of previous disposals so far identified may be wasted. When Superfund expires in 1985, many uncontrolled sites still will require attention. It is estimated that only $1.6 billion will be collected under Superfund by 1985 for cleanup of these sites.

Inappropriate disposal of hazardous waste on land creates the risk of contaminating the environment, including ground water, which could cause adverse health effects and for which cleanup actions are costly and difficult. As much as 80 percent of regulated hazardous waste—some of which may remain hazardous for years or centuries—is disposed of in or on the land.

In addition, millions of tonnes of federally unregulated or exempted hazardous wastes are disposed of in sanitary landfills (meant for ordinary solid wastes) and pose substantial risks. Such exemptions cover all types of hazardous wastes from generators producing less than 1 tonne a month, and other types of waste, such as infectious waste.

Current policies are likely to lead to the creation of still more uncontrolled sites which will require Superfund attention. The unregulated burning of wastes as fuel supplements in

home and industrial boilers may result in toxic air pollutants.

Greater use of alternatives to land disposal could increase industry's near-term costs significantly. However, years or decades from now, cleaning up a site and compensating victims might cost 10 to 100 times today's costs of preventing releases of hazardous wastes.

Federal policies may reduce industry's costs of land disposal by shifting some long-term cleanup and monitoring costs to Government or to society as a whole. The effect may be to retard the adoption by industry of alternatives such as waste reduction and waste treatment.

A key policy issue is: Can unnecessary risks and future cleanup costs be eliminated by limiting the use of land disposal, and by making alternatives to it more attractive?

The Federal regulatory program for hazardous waste management was established by the 1976 Resource Conservation and Recovery Act (RCRA), primarily concerned with the proper management and permitting of present and future wastes; and the Comprehensive Environmental, Response, Compensation, and Liability Act of 1980 (CERCLA), or Superfund, enacted to deal with the many substantiated and potential hazards posed by old and often abandoned uncontrolled hazardous waste sites. The OTA study supports the need for greater integration by EPA of these two programs.

Policy Options
OTA has identified four policy options— beyond maintaining the current Federal program—which could form the basis for an immediate and comprehensive approach to protecting human health and the environment from the dangers posed by mismanagement of hazardous waste:

1. Extend Federal controls to more hazardous wastes, and establish national regulatory standards based on specific technical criteria. Also restrict disposal of high-hazard wastes on land and improve procedures for permitting facilities and deregulating wastes.
2. Establish Federal fees on waste genera-

tors to support Superfund and to provide an economic incentive to reduce the generation of waste and discourage land disposal of wastes; impose higher fees on generators of high-hazard wastes that are land-disposed; provide assistance for capital investments and research and development for new waste reduction and treatment efforts.

3. Study the costs and advantages of classifying wastes and waste management facilities by degree of hazard to match hazards and risks with levels of regulatory control.
4. Examine the need for greater integration of Federal environmental programs to remove gaps, overlaps, and inconsistencies in the regulation of hazardous waste, and to make better use of technical data and personnel.

Key Issues and Findings

• Current monitoring practices and EPA requirements under RCRA—especially for land disposal sites—do not lead to a high level of confidence that hazardous releases will be detected and responsive action quickly taken.

• There are numerous technically feasible management options for hazardous wastes, but they are not being used to their full potential. On the whole, Federal programs indirectly provide more incentive for land disposal than for treatment alternatives that permanently remove risks, or for waste reduction—although technologies are available to reduce waste.

• States are being given increasing responsibilities by EPA without matching technical and financial resources. A lack of State funds often prevents Superfund cleanups. A Federal fee system on waste generators could also be used to support State programs. EPA should make better use of State data and expertise.

• Actions that enhance public confidence in the equity, effectiveness, and vigorous enforcement of Government programs may reduce public opposition to siting hazardous waste facilities. Opposition may also be reduced by improvement in the dissemination of accurate technical information on issues such as waste treatment alternatives to land disposal.

• EPA's risk assessment procedures for selecting Superfund sites and for developing RCRA regulations have serious technical inadequacies that weaken protection of the public.

• Data inadequacies conceal the scope and complexity of the Nation's hazardous waste problems and impede effective control. There is a need for a long-term, systematic EPA plan for obtaining more complete, reliable data on hazardous waste, facilities, sites, and exposure to and effects from releases of harmful substances.

• Wastes can be classified into at least three categories of hazard and, combined with facility classes, might form a technical base for Federal regulatory policies.

Industrial and Commercial Cogeneration

Cogeneration—the combined production of electricity and useful thermal energy—could contribute significantly to reduced costs and greater planning flexibility for electric utilities, and to increased energy efficiency in industrial facilities, commercial buildings, and rural/agricultural areas. But cogeneration's potentially large market will be limited by technical, economic, and institutional constraints. These include the difficulties in using lower cost solid fuels; competition with conservation measures; mismatches between the ratio of need for electric and thermal energy and the ratios typically produced by a cogenerating unit. The high cost of investment capital will limit opportunities further.

To achieve potential long-term benefits for electric utilities, cogeneration systems must use abundant solid fuels and produce high ratios of electricity to steam (E/S). But the available high E/S systems can use only oil or natural gas. Therefore, research and development efforts should concentrate on developing high E/S cogenerators that can burn solid fuels cleanly, and on advanced combustion and conversion systems such as fluidized beds and gasifiers.

Utility ownership could increase the amount of production as well as the reliability of cogenerated electricity. However, such ownership is at a competitive disadvantage because the Public Utility Regulatory Policies Act of 1978 (PURPA) limits qualifying projects to those in which a utility owns less than 50 percent equity. If the PURPA limitation were removed, concerns about the possible anticompetitive effects of utility ownership could be alleviated through careful State review of utility ownership schemes.

For the near term, natural gas will be the preferred cogeneration fuel where the marginal or avoided cost rates for utility purchases of cogenerated electricity are based on the price of oil, and where natural gas is available. In the long term, however, natural gas is likely to be too costly for natural-gas-fired cogeneration to compete economically with electricity generated at central station coal, nuclear, or hydroelectric powerplants.

Cogeneration also must compete for investment capital with conservation, which reduces steam loads—and therefore cogeneration's technical potential—and which often has lower unit capital costs and shorter payback periods than cogeneration.

Costs. The mean capital costs for commercially available cogenerators tend to be 20 to 40 percent lower per kilowatt than central station generating capacity. Also, the relatively small unit size and the shorter construction leadtimes of cogeneration systems mean substantial interest cost savings during construction, and greater flexibility for utilities in adjusting to unexpected changes in electricity demand than the overbuilding of central station capacity.

Electricity Prices. Cogenerators have potentially lower unit costs for generating elec-

tricity than central station powerplants. However, these savings will not necessarily mean lower electricity rates if the price paid to the cogenerator—based on avoided costs—is higher than the utility's retail rates. A price that is less than the utility's full avoided cost, with the difference going toward rate reduction, would share any cost savings from cogeneration with the utility's other ratepayers, but would not provide the maximum possible economic incentive to potential cogenerators.

Interconnection. The primary issues are the utilities' legal obligation to connect generators with the grid, the cost of the equipment, the lack of uniform guidelines, and the uncertain potential for utility system stability problems. Most of the technical aspects of interconnection are well understood, but additional research is needed to determine whether many cogenerators not centrally dispatched will cause utility system stability problems. If PURPA is not amended to require interconnection, and if utilities do not interconnect voluntarily, then the cost of obtaining an interconnection order from the Federal Energy Regulatory Commission could be prohibitive for many potential cogenerators.

Air Quality Impacts. Cogeneration will not automatically offer air quality improvement or degradation compared to the separate conversion technologies it will replace. Rather, its impact will vary considerably from case to case. Adverse local air quality impacts from cogeneration are most likely to occur in urban areas.

NOTE

1. This OTA Annual Report represents a transition from calendar year reporting to fiscal year reporting. It therefore covers the period January 1 through September 30, 1983.

PART II

MORAL CONTROVERSIES IN TECHNOLOGY ASSESSMENT

TECHNOLOGY ASSESSMENT, POLITICS, AND ETHICS

Technology assessment is often a subject of controversy. As some of the selections in Part I have indicated, such assessment, at least by a government agency, is subject to the demands of interest groups, the constraints of law and implementation, criticism of the effort itself, plus the intellectual problems intrinsic to the selection and study of such issues.

Conflicting demands often lead to controversy and even confrontation regarding technology assessment; they raise questions about its effectiveness, objectivity, and ethical soundness. Clearly, technology assessment is not politically or ethically neutral; nor is it carried out by detached, apolitical experts. First, policies, when implemented, affect people's lives. Second, the experts involved, however selfless, informed, and balanced their assessments, are limited by the procedures and criteria of their task. Finally, technology assessment is political, not only because of its consequences and rules, but because it must answer to conflicting interest groups. Thus, technology assessment takes place in a political and ethical environment which affects it, and which it affects.

OTA'S PROCEDURES AND CRITERIA FOR ADDRESSING ITS POLITICAL AND ETHICAL ENVIRONMENT

OTA's procedures and criteria are not insensitive to its political and ethical environment. Indeed, The Status of Technology Assessment. A View from the Congressional Office of Technology Assessment, by Fred B. Wood, gives a current inside view of the procedures and criteria employed by OTA in handling demands, constraints, and criticisms while remaining attuned to its purpose. This purpose, as stated in the selection's first note, provides a point of reference for Part II's discussions of the nature, scope, and validity of technology assessment, as practiced by OTA, or as guided by alternate conceptions of this activity.

According to Fred B. Wood, "OTA is a nonpartisan analytical support agency that serves the United States Congress by providing objective analysis of major public policy issues related to scientific and technological change." OTA, in accordance with its purpose, attempts to attain objectivity in a variety of ways. Among these, Wood mentions the proposal preparation, criteria for proposal authorization, efforts to ensure public participation, and the review of draft assessments by members of OTA, as well as by others with an interest in the subject. At least one of the criteria for proposal authorization, however, has been such a source of concern and criticism that it merits detailed discussion. The following section addresses only a few aspects of this matter, but the reader is encouraged to pursue it further (see the Selected Bibliography).

CONCERNS ABOUT THE USE OF RISK-COST-BENEFIT ANALYSIS

Wood formulates one of the technology assessment criteria used by OTA in the question, "How significant are the costs and benefits to society of the various policy options involved, and how will they be distributed among various affected groups?" This criterion has created great concern and criticism regarding the ways in which costs and benefits should be measured and used in technology assessment. Can they be reliably measured? Should they be used at all and, if so, what constraints, if any, should limit their use? In Comparing Apples to Oranges. Risk of Cost/Benefit Analysis, Barry Commoner, a biologist, argues for one type of constraint in the use of risk-cost-benefit analysis. He first describes one use of this criterion:

> As the concern about the risks of modern technology to people and the environment has been translated into legislation, a basic idea has emerged—that the best way to evaluate such a risk is to compare it with the associated benefits. This is known as risk/benefit assessment. The most recent legislation based on this concept is the Toxic Substances Control Act (TSCA). This act requires that the Environmental Protection Agency (EPA) administrator establish rules for governing the production and use of chemicals which take into account not only a substance's toxic hazards but also "the benefits of a substance for a given use or uses and the availability of less hazardous substances for the same uses." One important section of the TSCA law requires what might be called a meta-cost/benefit assessment. This is a cost/benefit evaluation not only of the substances but also of the EPA decision to regulate it—that is, the social cost of administrative action itself.

As the title of his article suggests, Commoner believes there is a logical mistake in this calculation, namely, that "what should be compared is risk and benefit associated with the *same* substance, not risk (or benefit) of Substance A with the risk (or benefit) of Substance B," let alone the risk (or benefit) of one regulatory action, say, banning red lollipops, with the risk (or benefit) of another, say, banning cigarettes. This criticism reflects Commoner's concern that, because the social costs of banning a substance that is much more dangerous than another might be much greater than the social costs of banning the less dangerous one, the less dangerous substance might be banned while the more dangerous one might not be banned at all. He considers this absurd, and a reason for introducing the above-quoted constraint on the use of risk-cost-benefit analysis in public policy assessment.

WHAT CONSTRAINTS ON RISK-COST-BENEFIT ANALYSIS?

Commoner's criticism of the use of risk-cost-benefit analysis, which either compares the risks and benefits associated with one substance with the risks and benefits associated with another, or considers only those risks associated with one substance but includes the social risks (i.e., likely social costs) of banning or not banning the substance, gives rise to at least the following question: Should social costs never enter the calculation regardless of how disastrous they might be? If so, doesn't this amount to a dangerous tunnel vision in policy making, resulting in a sensitivity to public health, but not to the availability of jobs, or the demands of competent adults for the freedom to risk their health so long as this does not harm others? If these further considerations are involved in banning cigarettes but not red lollipops, what is so absurd about it?

In addressing these questions, it is useful to remember that Commoner's discussion focuses on the risk-cost-benefit approach, which, he thinks, "destroys the logic of the risk/benefit concept." Suppose we grant this, but think that Commoner's highly focused constraint is too insensitive for public policy making, and seek more sensitive constraints. An obvious candidate is to avoid risk-cost-benefit analysis when—even though it might lead to policies beneficial to public health—it would be against the will of individuals who might prefer to smoke cigarettes, or have red lollipops, or both, so long as this does not harm others. And in such a case, one way of avoiding a ban on the less dangerous, but not the more dangerous, substance would be to not ban either. The constraint on risk-cost-benefit analysis involved here would advise, not, as does Commoner, the consideration only of the health effects of one substance, but rather of what people want or have a right to.

This alternative constraint is not necessarily more defensible than Commoner's. Rather, it makes the point that Commoner's objection simply establishes that *some* constraint on risk-cost-benefit analysis must be introduced to avoid such consequences as banning the less harmful but not the more harmful substance *if,* indeed, this outcome is absurd. It does not establish the necessity that Commoner's constraint be introduced, since at least one alternative constraint exists that Commoner has not shown inadequate. Reasons in its favor are that people want, and have a right, to make their own choices between health or jobs, or to decide what health risks to run for the sake of pleasure when no one else would be harmed. These considerations are relevant in assessing policies, and not all of them involve consequences. Considerations of Rights are also part of our theoretical framework, as will become apparent.

TECHNOLOGY ASSESSMENT AND THE PRIVATE SECTOR

The relevance of an appeal to rights as well as consequences in discussions of technology assessment is further supported by the essay, Technology Assessment in Industry. A Counterproductive Myth?, by Vary T. Coates and Thecla Fabian. The authors question the wisdom of extending the use of the phrase "technology assessment" to "parallel, but fundamentally different, corporate planning activities" and conclude that this is a mistake, obscuring the current status of corporate research activities, creating barriers to their future development and improvement, and threatening the public's right to determine its own good by placing decision-making in the hands of corporate executives.

Is it, indeed, good to lift any, let alone all, moral barriers to future development in corporate planning activities by categorizing them as separate from technology assessment, which is centrally concerned with the short- and long-term social consequences of technological developments? Coates and Fabian hold that "So long as industry respects and complies with the constraints imposed by constitutionally sound governmental authority on behalf of the public, it is at least debatable whether industry has a responsibility, or even a right, to make subtle determinations as to what constitutes the long-range public interest." The authors certainly do not believe that corporations should be oblivious to the short-term social impact of their decisions about new technologies or new products. Nor do they believe that corporations should concern themselves with this impact. They leave this matter open, though they are willing to consider that corporations do have an obligation to assess short-term social impact. They do not believe, and argue against the belief, that corporations are obligated, or even have the right, to consider social impact beyond this—for instance, the long term.

This position implicitly raises the question, Are corporations morally responsible in the same ways that individuals are, with their capacity for moral decision making, and accountability for the decisions they make? Coates and Fabian are not concerned with this question (though the reader might be), addressing the issue of overall corporate moral responsibilities or obligations.

Now, that corporations ought not to decide on the public interest gives them no right to disregard the public interest in their corporate planning activities. Not to be paternalistic about the public interest does not establish such a right. If the public's right to determine its own interest has any influence, this must be accompanied by an obligation by individuals or corporations not to disregard this interest, be it short- or long-range.

Coates and Fabian do not deny that corporations should act in the long-range public interest. However, they give reasons that constrain such action:

> [The] judgment that potential, indirect, second order, down-stream impacts of technology are either "detrimental" or "desirable" is incomparably more complex, subtle, and difficult. All the informal adaptations and adjustments that society will make to technological change must be included in this judgment, and it is doubtful that any industry or corporation, from its limited institutional perspective, would be able to identify, much less evaluate, these potential impacts.

Thus, even if corporations have an obligation to consider the public interest in corporate planning, they are unlikely to be able to determine it, since it depends so much on whether or how the public handles technological developments. This point, however, goes beyond providing reasons for the authors' positions; it points to some central constraints on the ways in which technology policy making can be effectively implemented. Let us see how.

If, as appears to be the case, the public has a right to determine its own interest, by itself or through its elected representatives, rather than corporations, it may still be difficult or impossible for the public and its representatives to foresee the long-range public interest regarding a given technological development. A variety of adaptations and adjustments between the public and such developments must take place while a determination of the newly adapted public interest evolves. Rights, consequences, and pragmatic considerations that may rule out certainty about the future are also relevant when dealing with contemporary moral controversies in technology. A central question here is, What relative weight do considerations of consequences, of rights, and pragmatic considerations have in a particular controversy?[1]

NOTE

1. The term "pragmatic" is not used here to mean useful, practical, or expedient, but rather in its philosophical sense: "of or pertaining to pragmatism." See *The Random House Dictionary of the English Language,* ed. Jess Stein et al. (New York: Random House, 1970), p. 1128. Pragmatism is a family of philosophical theories rather than a definite view. See, for example, Arthur Lovejoy, "The Thirteen Pragmatisms," *The Journal of Philosophy, Psychology, and Scientific Method* (now *The Journal of Philosophy*) V (1908), pp. 5–12, 29–39. Pragmatism, as examined in this book, however, is simply a type of theory that assigns a central role to action and mutual adjustments in working out—through critical inquiry and a variety of social interactions—what values take priority in given matters of controversy.

5

The Status of Technology Assessment.
A View from the Congressional Office
of Technology Assessment

FRED B. WOOD

Fred B. Wood's article describes the steps in most assessments carried out by the U.S. Congressional Office of Technology Assessment (OTA). It also outlines various discussions about technology assessment, some published in the United States, some abroad. Wood concludes that the use of technology assessment may have reached a point where it can be used more extensively, both in the development of U.S. and international policies, through the channels of the UN or through implementation in foreign countries.[1]

From an historical perspective, the development of technology assessment (TA) in Congress can be highlighted in four phases. Phase I (1963–1967) was the birth of the TA concept in Congress, starting with the formation of the Subcommittee on Science, Research and Development of the House Science and Astronautics Committee in 1963 and ending with the introduction of H.R. 6698, the first technology assessment bill, on March 7, 1967. During phase II (1968–1972), a consensus on OTA developed in Congress through a long series of studies, hearings, and bills, leading to the enactment of H.R. 10243 and signing of P.L. 92–484 (Technology Assessment Act of 1972) on October 13, 1972. During phase III (1973–1979), an operational role for OTA was created under the direction of OTA's first two directors. This phase included initial efforts to organize OTA, establish program areas, set priorities, and produce credible reports. In phase IV (mid-1979 to the present), the emphasis has been on institutionaliz-

ing the OTA process in Congress and improving OTA's methodology and management. This includes the Task Force work mentioned later and other initiatives of the current OTA Director. These efforts were made possible in part by building on the substantial TA experience accumulated by OTA itself since 1973, by NSF (and its many grantees), and by other TA practitioners and researchers in both the public and private sectors.

On November 30, 1979, the OTA Director established an officewide Task Force on Technology Assessment Methodology and Management. The purpose of the Task Force was to identify and develop ways in which OTA could improve its methodology and management of technology assessment. The Task Force prepared several internal OTA staff reports, and also commissioned a series of external research papers on TA methodology and practice in the United States and in other countries. All but one of the papers described

Originaly published in *Technological Forecasting and Social Change* 22 (1982), pp. 211–222. Copyright © 1982 by Elsevier Science Publishing Co., Inc. Reprinted by permission of the publisher and author.

below are based in whole or in part on the results of the Task Force-sponsored research.

THE OTA ASSESSMENT PROCESS

OTA staff were asked by the Task Force to review and summarize what had been learned from their prior assessment experience. The Task Force found that a detailed description of the OTA assessment process is difficult, since so many aspects depend on project and subject-specific variables. However, on a more general level, the Task Force identified a widely agreed upon series of steps through which most OTA assessments proceed. These steps are listed in Table 5.1 and described briefly below. The description is current as of May 1982 and reflects all Task Force and other recommended improvements implemented as of that time.

Committee Consultation

OTA conducts most of its assessments at the request of one or more committees of Congress. Thus, a continuing dialogue between

TABLE 5.1. Steps through which most OTA assessments proceed

---

1. Consultation with committee members and staffs
2. Proposal preparation and internal review
3. TAB review and approval of proposal[a]
4. Staffing
5. Planning
6. Selecting and convening an advisory panel
7. Ensuring public participation[b]
8. Data collection and analysis
9. Contracting
10. Report writing
11. Review and revision
12. OTA Director and TAB approval of report
13. Publishing
14. Follow-up
15. Close-out

---

[a]TAB = Technology Assessment Board

[b]Public participation occurs at several steps in the assessment process; see text for discussion.

OTA and the congressional committees is essential for OTA so that is keeps abreast of congressional needs and the upcoming legislative agenda, and for the committees to understand OTA's capabilities and expertise. Interaction with client committees occurs at several points in the assessment process—from proposal preparation to follow-up after a report has been published. Such interaction helps ensure that the study will be useful to Congress and that any changes in committee concerns or the policy or legislative context can be accomodated to the extent possible. Requesting committees are provided quarterly status reports on study highlights, e.g., panel meetings held, although the project staff may interact on a more frequent basis. OTA encourages the project staff to provide informal briefings or presentations to the committee staff whenever appropriate through the course of a study. Interim deliverables such as a technical memorandum are included in many assessment plans in order to help committees benefit from key components of a study, e.g., a technology survey, as well as, ultimately, from the final report.

Also, to keep Congress informed of the full range of OTA activities and expertise, OTA provides Members of Congress and their staffs with a periodic (usually twice yearly) booklet on ongoing and new assessment activities. This booklet includes brief summaries of current projects, notices of publications in press, announcements of recently published reports, and lists of selected prior reports.

Proposal Preparation

All OTA assessment proposals include a discussion of the approach and methodology to be used in conducting the study, as well as a description of the problem and study objectives, congressional interest, interim deliverables, schedule, and budget. Proposals are reviewed internally by a cross-divisional OTA Project Screening Committee, and the following points, among others, are considered: congressional committee interest and jurisdiction in specific issues and anticipated use of OTA work product; significant stakeholders (parties at interest); relevant previous OTA experience or studies; related studies by others that have been completed or are in the process; other legislative or executive agencies that could contribute to the study; internal and external staffing requirements; generic description of advisory panel; internal and external review process; and anticipated follow-on activities. All study proposals are coordinated with other congressional support agencies (General Accounting Office, GAO; Congressional Research Service, CRS; Congressional Budget Office, CBO) to avoid duplication of effort and to enlist cooperation where appropriate.

Tab Review

The authorization of specific formal assessment projects and the approval of funds for their performance are the responsibility of the OTA Technology Assessment Board (TAB), whether project requests are initiated by a congressional committee(s), the OTA Director in consultation with TAB, or TAB itself. TAB includes six senators and six representatives divided equally by party, with the OTA Director serving as a nonvoting member. In considering assessment proposals, TAB has established the following general selection criteria:

1. Is this now or is it likely to become a major national issue?
2. Can OTA make a unique contribution, or could the requested activity be done effectively by the requesting committee or another agency of Congress?
3. How significant are the costs and benefits to society of the various policy options involved, and how will they be distributed among various affected groups?
4. Is the technological impact irreversible?
5. How imminent is the impact?
6. Is there sufficient available knowledge to assess the technology and its consequences?
7. Is the assessment of manageable scope—can it be bounded within reasonable limits?
8. What will be the cost of the assessment?

9. How much time will be required to do the assessment?
10. What is the likelihood of congressional action in response to this assessment?
11. Would this assessment complement other OTA projects?

In 1981, OTA worked on more than 30 TAB-approved assessments that, because of their scope and depth, typically require 1–2 years to complete. As of May 1982, 21 TAB-approved assessments were in process, 10 assessments were under TAB review (of final draft report) or in press, and 4 new assessments had recently been approved by TAB.

Staffing

OTA's multidisciplinary staff plans, directs, and drafts all assessments. The relatively small in-house staff of 80–90 professionals spans the spectrum of physical, life, and social sciences, engineering, law, and medicine. Each new assessment is normally assigned a full-time project director from the in-house staff, plus one or two other professional staff, e.g., a senior analyst and research assistant, from existing in-house staff or through new hires. The in-house project team draws extensively on the broad technical and professional resources of the private sector, including the use, where appropriate, of contractors and consultants from industry, universities, private research organizations, and public interest groups. Typically, about one-half of the assessment budget is allocated to in-house staff and one-half to contractors, consultants, and advisory panelists.

The project teams are located in OTA's nine program areas that currently include: energy, materials, international security and commerce, food and renewable resources, health, biological applications, communication and information technologies, oceans and environment, and space, transportation, and innovation. The programs provide administrative support and supervision to the project staffs. OTA encourages cross-program work on specific assessments where appropriate, and identifiable needs for cross-level support and assistance are considered in preparing each assessment proposal. In addition, the OTA Operations Division provides assistance to the project staffs with respect to budgeting, contracting, information retrieval, press relations, publishing, and the like.

Planning

Assessment planning at OTA is a dynamic process. The preparation of an assessment proposal is part of the planning process and may include the convening of a planning workshop. OTA has found such workshops useful in identifying and defining key issues, critiquing a preliminary plan or proposal, identifying major related work completed or in progress by other organizations, involving congressional committees and OTA's sister agencies (CRS, GAO, CBO), and identifying potential contractors, consultants, and panelists. After an assessment has been approved and staffed, a more detailed plan is prepared, although inevitably this plan will change frequently throughout the course of a study.

Perhaps the most important and most difficult aspect is planning the substantive scope of an assessment. Preliminary scoping and issue identification are essential parts of the assessment proposal. But precise definition of study scope and issues usually requires several iterations once a study has been initiated, and is normally a major agenda item for the first project advisory panel meeting.

Planning a high quality and useful assessment can be understood in part as dealing creatively with multiple goals such as the following: 1) the mandate to assess technologies, which requires understanding the technology in depth; 2) the congressional requirement for assessments whose relevance to current problems and policy options is clear; 3) the desire to produce an assessment that covers all major aspects of the subject matter, with all key findings checked and documented; 4) the need to complete the assessment as quickly as possible to meet congressional schedules.

Advisory Panels

For every major assessment, OTA establishes an advisory panel to ensure that the study process and assessment report are objective, fair, and authoritative. Project advisory panels include not only scientists and engineers, but also affected and interested parties from labor, industry, the academic community, public interest groups, State and local governments, and the citizenry at large. These panels help to shape the focus OTA studies, critique studies while in process, and review the reports before they are released. Selection of panelists is very careful and deliberate to ensure that the panel is well balanced in terms of expertise, perspective, interests, geography, and professional and personal backgrounds. The final panel selection is reviewed and approved by the OTA Director. When appropriate, individual members of the Technology Assessment Advisory Council (known as TAAC, established by statute and appointed by TAB) are invited to serve on project advisory panels.

The size of OTA project advisory panels varies, but most panels fall in the range of 12–20 members. Panels normally meet three times during the course of an assessment: initially to review and comment on the study plan, then to review the results of OTA staff and contractor research and discuss report structure and contents, and finally to review and discuss the OTA draft report itself. The role of OTA panels is strictly advisory in nature, and panelists are not expected nor asked to carry out research or draft or "approve" the report. Responsibility for the conduct of the study and the final report rests with OTA. Many OTA assessments also use work groups or workshops as a complement to the advisory panel. Workshops or work groups usually focus on a specific aspect or subset of a larger study, and have a short lifetime, usually meeting only once. This technique has proven effective in obtaining additional subject matter and/or regional expertise.

Ensuring Public Participation

OTA tries to ensure that the views of the public are fairly reflected in its assessments, and that the perspectives of the parties at interest (stakeholders) are taken into account. OTA involves the public and parties at interest in many ways—through advisory panels, workshops, surveys, contracts, formal and informal public meetings, and review of draft reports. Project staff are encouraged to consider ideas, research, and other input from all sources relevant to a specific study. These numerous interactions help OTA to identify and take into account a wide range of public perspectives.

Data Collection and Analysis

An important part of the assessment plan is the selection of data collection and analytical techniques. While most OTA studies use some techniques in common, in general the techniques vary widely depending on the subject matter. Every assessment includes a search of the literature, prior research, and related studies, usually with the assistance of the OTA Information Center which combines traditional library services with the latest in information retrieval technology. Most assessments include a technology and/or policy analysis. The technology analysis may include the current and projected state-of-the-art of the technology, key factors in the development or adoption of the technology, possible effects or impacts of different patterns of deployment of the technology, alternative policies that might be adopted to deal with possible impacts, and the benefits, costs, and uncertainties associated with different policy options. While the technology analysis starts with technology and moves toward policy, the policy analysis starts with policy considerations and moves toward technology. Thus the policy analysis may include the central questions "at issue" in the policy debate concerning the technology, the basic values that are or may be at stake, the main actors, interests, or sectors of society concerned with the issues, their perceptions of the issues, and the most important future choices that may or must be made concerning the technology.

Other analytical techniques vary widely. The Task Force identified the following as having been used at OTA on various studies:

forecasting, survey methods (including written questionnaires, interviews, and statistically designed opinion polls), risk analysis, cost-benefit analysis, social impacts analysis, scenario building, computer modeling, and systems analysis. However, OTA's mandate and resources mean that for most assessments, emphasis must be placed on making use of existing information and the results of prior research conducted by others. Original data collection is generally limited to those areas that are crucial to a particular study and where the necessary data do not exist or are otherwise not available. OTA encourages project staff to thoroughly exhaust all other possibilities, including other Federally sponsored research by or for legislative or executive agencies, academic research, and industrial research. In performing its analytical work for Congress, OTA links and synthesizes the collective expertise from all sectors of the United States. Each year roughly 2000 people from universities, private corporations, State and local governments, and Federal agencies assist OTA in its assessment work. In this manner, OTA avoids duplication of existing work and acts as a catalyst to bring national wisdom to bear on congressional issues.

Contracting

Significant portions of most OTA assessments are carried out through contract research. Contracting permits OTA to obtain the best information and highest caliber expertise available from anywhere in (or outside of) the United States on any subject matter relevant to a specific assessment. However, OTA has found through experience that successful contracting requires that the contract work be very carefully defined and thought through in advance, tied explicitly to the assessment plan and methodology, monitored very closely while under way, and thoroughly reviewed when complete. OTA selects contractors through formal published competition (with a request for proposal, RFP, placed in the Commerce Business Daily, usually for larger contracts in excess of $50,000), formal unpublished solicitation (a letter RFP to qualified bidders), informal competition (for smaller, specialized contracts), and, in some instances, sole source procurement. When appropriate for a specific assessment, a request for statements of qualification and interest (Q&I) is placed in the Commerce Business Daily. In general, OTA discourages unsolicited proposals. The results of contract research are used by OTA project staff along with other sources of information and analysis in preparing the OTA report. Contractor results are generally not published as is, but are carefully integrated into the larger structure of the OTA assessment. However, exceptional quality contractor reports may be published in toto as case studies or background documents, or made available through the National Technical Information Service in Springfield, Virginia.

Report Writing

Since written reports are the major formal product of OTA, the quality of report writing is critically important to a successful study. Writing responsibility is normally that of the project director and designated project staff. Where several people are involved, lead responsibility for specific parts of the report is assigned to each staff member. Working within an agreed upon report outline and perhaps a narrative outline as well, the writers are responsible for integrating material from contractors, panelists, staff, and elsewhere, and ensuring that all material is of high quality, has been checked and documented, and is internally consistent. Given the unique mandate of OTA, and the need for balanced, objective, policy relevant, technically sound, and yet easily understandable reports, OTA has found that report writing can rarely be contracted out. The report represents the ultimate and usually difficult synthesis of issues, technology, impacts, and policy necessary to meet congressional needs. The project staff is usually in the best position to do this synthesis, with the help of program and divisional staff who bring perspective, and, where appropriate, the assistance of an editor with respect to report structure, presentation, and style.

Review and Revision

OTA strongly emphasizes both internal and external review of draft assessment reports. Most reports go through two or three revisions. External review always involves the OTA project advisory panel and a cross section of other individuals and organizations with an interest in the subject matter. External reviewers typically include government agencies affected or involved, private sector stakeholders, public interest groups, and independent researchers and policy analysts. The number of reviewers frequently reaches several dozen, and on occasion, particularly for controversial studies of widespread interest, may total as many as 75 or 100. Internal reviewers include the program and divisional management and, when appropriate, selected OTA staff from other program areas with an interest in or perspective on the subject at hand. In making revisions to the draft report, project staff give serious consideration to all comments received regardless of the source.

OTA Director and TAB Approval

The final draft of every OTA assessment report is provided to the OTA Director for review and, if approved, is forwarded to the Technology Assessment Board for its review. A memo summarizing the review process must accompany the final draft. Prepared by the project staff, the memo highlights the background and history of the study, lists the panelists, contractors, and reviewers, and summarizes the major review comments and OTA response. In this way, both the OTA Director and TAB can gain a deeper insight into and understanding of the study process as well as its substance. TAB review normally takes 10 working days while Congress is in session after which, absent any objections, the report is approved for release subject to final editing.

Publishing

OTA *reports* are the principal documentation of formal assessment projects approved by

TAB for public release. OTA reports are type-set, with illustrations and graphics included when applicable, and printed and sold by the Government Printing Office. OTA *report summaries* (usually chapter 1 of the report) are normally published as a separate document and limited to 28 printed pages in total length (compared to, typically, 200–300 pages for the full report). Summary reports are intended to convey the essence of a study, e.g., findings and conclusions to Members of Congress and their staffs and to the general public, whereas the full report provides the detailed discussion and analysis. OTA *report briefs* are normally limited to about 500 words (the equivalent of two double-spaced typewritten pages) and are intended to be crisp, clear, concise abstracts of the summary. OTA *technical memoranda* are prepared on specific subjects analyzed in projects presently in process. They are issued at the request of Members of Congress who are engaged in legislative actions that are expected to be resolved before OTA completes its assessment. OTA *background papers* contain information that supplements formal OTA assessments or is an outcome of internal exploratory planning and evaluation. The material is usually not of immediate policy interest and does not present options for Congress to consider. Finally, *working papers* are unofficial backup documents, usually prepared by contractors, that are released in typewritten form through NTIS.

During 1981, OTA delivered 14 assessment reports, 11 summary reports, 3 technical memoranda, and 16 background papers to Congress. During the calendar year, the OTA Publishing Office processed over 21,303 (average 58.4/day) separate mail and phone requests for publications. As of March 31, 1982, 25 OTA publications (in whole or in part) had been reprinted by commercial publishers or private organizations. The GPO had sold 151,000 OTA documents during 1981, and NTIS had sold 20,000.

Follow-up

Effective dissemination of study results is an essential part of the assessment process. Thus,

the completion of an OTA report marks the beginning of project follow-up to communicate key findings to both the requesting congressional committee(s) and other committees that might have an interest or jurisdiction in the topic. Requesting committees frequently participate in the public release of OTA reports, either through an OTA press release or a committee press release or both. Each OTA *press release* summarizes the main themes of a report, tells who is releasing it, e.g., OTA, a TAB member, a committee chairman, and how it is being released, e.g., at a press conference or hearing. The press release usually contains comments on the report from several Members of Congress. The entire packet (press release, report brief, summary, and full report) is provided in advance to the requesting and interested committees and selected media representatives. A report brief and summary are sent to all Members of Congress and key congressional staff. The summary includes a tear-out return card to be used for requesting a copy of the full report. After release, packets are provided to key government and private sector officials with an interest in the subject matter and others who participated in the study. OTA encourages the project staff to conduct informal or formal committee briefings and present testimony on the study results, when requested, to attend scientific forums and conferences, and to prepare articles for presentation of findings to peer groups. During January through March 1982, OTA formally testified 12 times before congressional committees and conducted 24 briefings, presentations, or workshops with committee staffs. For technical memoranda and background papers, an OTA *News Advisory* is usually issued to inform the press and others who may be interested in the subject matter. During the first half of fiscal year 1982, OTA averaged about 1200 press clippings received per quarter (or 400 a month) for all types of publications.

Close-out

After a study has been completed and the report published and released, project directors are asked to prepare a "close-out" memo that summarizes who used the report and how, press coverage, follow-up requests and activities, observations on assessment methodology, and the like. In essence, this memo serves as a retrospective summary of key learning for the benefit of new staff and as an ongoing contribution to OTA's institutional development.

OTHER ASSESSMENT APPROACHES

The Task Force also surveyed approaches to TA methodology and management used by others. To do this, the Task Force initially reviewed the results of prior technology assessment technology studies[2] (sponsored primarily by the National Science Foundation) and then commissioned a series of independent research papers. All but one of these are described below.

Management of Technology Assessment

In "A Management Overview Methodology for Technology Assessment," Paul F. Donovan, George D. Gaspari, and Bruce Rosenblum present their view of the management of technology assessment regardless of the subject matter or the specific analytical techniques used. They first list a set of desirable characteristics of TA management and the resulting reports, and then describe the nature of the "focus questions," that are central to this approach. The focus questions serve to define the areas of investigation and become the basis for assignment of staff work, contracting, and the like. Donovan et al. then discuss the four "fundamental concerns" and how any assessment question can be analyzed in terms of its impact on the economy, national security, environment, and social equity and other social concerns. Finally, this paper presents the steps by which a technology assessment could be conducted using this approach. The methodology includes a "fast loop iteration"—to develop focus questions based on a quick cut at laying out key problems and trends, options, and implications—and a "slow loop iteration"—to carry out the study and analysis necessary to answer focus questions. The fast and slow loops work together in a process of successive refinement to produce a final report.

Decision Analytical Technology Assessment

In "A Process for Technology Assessment Based on Decision Analysis," M.W. Merkofer develops a conceptual framework for what he calls "decision-focused technology assessment," and presents a useful illustration based on a previous study of synthetic fuels commercialization. This paper provides a possible methodology for technology assessments where quantitative modeling, explicit specification of uncertainties using probabilities, measurement of risk sensitivity/risk aversion, and sensitivity analysis are feasible and necessary. However, as Merkhofer notes, even where it is "extremely difficult or impossible to quantify adequately all important aspects of a problem, . . . constructing a simple but comprehensive model of the decision provides a framework that forces a disciplined and systematic investigation of relevant issues."

Adequacy of Technology Assessment

In "Thoughts on the Adequacy of Performance of Technology Assessments," Louis H. Mayo presents an approach for the selection of a suitable methodology for the performance of technology assessment. While he concludes that "no particular assessment methodology can be uniformly applied with optimum results" given the wide variety in assessment studies, a concept of adequate assessment performance is needed to help ensure that the methodology selected results in an understandable, credible, and useful product. Mayo lists 10 major distinguishing features of technology assessment whose selection or specification go a long way toward determining whether assessment performance will be adequate or not. These include: the purpose and subject matter of the study; limitations and constraints, e.g., funding, time, available information; technical and policy alternatives; relevant societal context, stakeholders, and decision processes; identification and evaluation of impacts; and presentation of results, e.g., benefit/cost or risk/benefit ratios, impacts/options matrix. Finally, this paper suggests a framework within which any organization conducting assessments can periodically review not only its assessment methodology choices with respect to particular studies, but also its overall performance and that of technology assessment as a part of the ongoing public decision process.

Congressional Technology Assessment

In his paper "On 'Complete' OTA Reports," Lewis Gray summarizes the results of his doctoral dissertation which, by coincidence, was completed at roughly the same time as the OTA commissioned research papers. Gray first reviews the legislative history of OTA. Based on an examination of the various debates, hearings, studies, and bills leading up to enactment of P.L. 92-484 (the Technology Assessment Act of 1972), including the final amendments and compromises, he identifies 13 characteristics of congressional technology assessment. Gray then develops a checklist of components (or contents) of OTA reports that he believes would be "sufficient to guarantee completeness" in the context of OTA's congressional mandate and could be used as a quality control standard. The major elements of the checklist include: a manageably small and jointly exhaustive set of significant, feasible congressional action options; a set of mutually exclusive and practically exhaustive scenarios; a set of opinion or desirability polls of the stakeholders, one poll for each outcome; and a set of objectively obtained numerical conditional probabilities, one for each outcome. The author notes that all elements of the checklist are not individually necessary in every case but do provide a possible guide or standard for the content of OTA reports.

Industrial Technology Assessment

The papers on "How Companies Assess Technology," by James D. Maloney, Jr., and "Technology Assessment in Industry. A Counterproductive Myth?" by Vary T. Coates and

Thecla Fabian, identify many of the same similarities and differences between public and private sector technology assessment. Maloney believes that much of what might be called industrial technology assessment takes place in the context of corporate planning, especially for those firms considering diversification, e.g., new products for new markets. Despite the differences between public and private sector technology assessment (e.g., private TA geared toward profit maximization and corporate decision making, conducted on an ad hoc, flexible basis with a private report; public TA focused on balancing public needs and formulating public policy options, conducted on a formal basis with a public written report), Maloney concludes that technology assessment can help private firms save resources, reduce risks, and increase opportunities.

In contrast, Coates and Fabian argue that the term "technology assessment" should be reserved to describe assessments designed to support public sector decisionmaking. Based on a survey of corporate executives who had attended technology assessment workshops or short courses, she finds that many corporations do conduct analyses that are analagous to public sector TA, yet are inherently different in purpose and scope because they are intended to enhance the viability and strength of the firm rather than to maximize the overall benefits to society. Firms have different, and often conflicting, definitions of TA, and within a single firm, different individuals can be working on the basis of conflicting definitions. Included under the TA rubric may be technology forecasts, market analyses, environmental scans, competitive analyses, and even social audits. Coates concludes that the differences between private and public sector TA need explicit recognition, that one is not a substitute for the other, and that use of technology assessment terminology for comparable analyses intended to assist private sector decisionmaking is undesirable and counterproductive.

International Technology Assessment

The papers on "Technology Assessment in Europe and Japan," by Vary T. Coates and

Thecla Fabian, and "Technology Assessment in Asia: Status and Prospects," by Robert H. Randolph and Bruce Koppel, when read together provide an excellent sense of international TA. The paper by Coates and Fabian presents an overview of TA activities in Canada, Egypt, the Federal Republic of Germany, Great Britain, Israel, Japan, the Netherlands, Sweden, the German Democratic Republic, and Poland. Their survey found that the United States was still the only nation that has a TA organization to serve the national legislature. On the other hand, a number of "exciting and sophisticated" TA activities were identified in established government offices, special government committees, various ad hoc government groups, and nongovernment organizations (centered largely in universities, research institutes, and high technology industries or industrial groups). The implication seems to be that the fact of OTA's existence is in part a reflection of the strength and independence (and political balance) of the U.S. Congress, particularly when compared to other national legislatures.

The paper by Randolph and Koppel quite comprehensively surveys TA in a set of seven Asian countries. The authors found that one country (Japan) had considerable experience with technology assessment and made some independent contributions to TA methodology. Although the other countries (Indonesia, Korea, the Philippines, Taiwan, India, Iran) had experienced little TA in the usual Western sense of the term, they did reveal a wide range of research and decisionmaking activities closely related to TA, suggesting that they may have an important potential for formal TA in the future. Randolph and Koppel conclude that the most important prerequisites for successful development of TA under typical Asian circumstances would appear to be an initiative by or at least support from the highest levels of government, orientation of TA toward established national priorities, and general acceptance of both TA methods and results.

A CONCLUDING NOTE

Perhaps TA methodology and management has reached a threshold where it can be applied more broadly both at home and in other countries. For example, during the first 3 months of 1982, more than 25 officials from 16 countries visited OTA. The countries ranged from Brazil, Mexico, and Uruguay in the Americas, to England, France, West Germany, Portugal, and Sweden in Europe, to Australia, the People's Republic of China, Japan, Sri Lanka, and Thailand in Asia, along with the United Nations. Certainly OTA's charter to provide Congress and the American public with accurate, understandable, and useful analyses of the implications—direct and indirect—of science and technology for current issues and long term problems is relevant to many other countries as well. Such analyses provide a necessary part of the foundation on which effective national and international policy can be built.

NOTES

1. This paper is based in part on research done by or for the OTA Task Force on TA Methodology and Management, the 1981 OTA Annual Report and various other OTA documents. However, it has not been reviewed or approved by the Technology Assessment Board, and the views expressed are those of the author and not necessarily those of OTA. OTA is a nonpartisan analytical support agency that serves the United States Congress by providing objective analysis of major public policy issues related to scientific and technological change.

2. See May 22, 1980, OTA Task Force paper on "Preliminary Results of Phase II A Survey of Non-OTA Assessment Experience" which was distributed to all OTA staff. The following studies were reviewed: Frederick A. Rossini, Alan L. Porter, Patrick Kelly, and Daryl E. Chubin, *Frameworks and Factors Affecting Integration Within Technology Assessments,* Georgia Institute of Technology, Atlanta (December 1978); Mark N. Berg, Jeffrey L. Brudney, Theodore D. Fuller, Donald N. Michael, Beverly K. Roth, *Factors Affecting Utilization of Technology Assessment Studies in Policy-Making,* University of Michigan Institute for Social Research, Ann Arbor (1978); Joe E. Armstrong and Willis W. Harman, *Strategies for Conducting Technology Assessments,* Stanford University Department of Engineering Economic Systems, Stanford, Calif. (December 1977); Alan A. Porter,

Frederick A. Rossini, Stanley R. Carpenter, and A.T. Roper, *A Guidebook for Technology Assessment and Impact Analysis,* North-Holland, New York, 1980; Vary T. Coates, *A Handbook of Technology Assessment,* U.S. Department of Energy, Washington, D.C. (March 1978); Louis H. Mayo, *Monitoring the Direction and Rate of Social Change Through the Anticipatory Assessment Function,* George Washington University Program of Policy Studies in Science and Technology, Washington, D.C. (July 1977); Joseph F. Coates, The Role of Formal Models in Technology Assessment, *Technology Forecasting and Social Change,* Volume 9, 139–190 (1976); Martin V. Jones, *A Technology Assessment Methodology,* Mitre Corporation, McLean, Va. (June 1971); Vary T. Coates, *Technology and Public Policy: The Process of Technology Assessment in the Federal Government,* George Washington University Program of Policy Studies in Science and Technology, Washington, D.C. (July 1972); Vary T. Coates, *Technology Assessment in Federal Agencies 1971–1976,* George Washington University Program Policy Studies in Science and Technology, Washington, D.C. (March 1979); U.S. Congress, Office of Technology Assessment, *Technology Assessment in Business and Government,* Washington, D.C. (January 1977); and James D. Maloney, Jr., Mary Simister, and Daniel Keyes, *Technology Assessment in the Private Sector: An Exploratory Study,* Midwest Research Institute, Kansas City (November 1978).

The one paper not included is Todd R. La Porte, "Technology as Social Organization: Toward Improved Technology Assessments," University of California, Berkeley (September 1981). This paper challenges technology assessors to take an expanded view of technology as social organization. That is, in order to fully and accurately assess the social impacts of a technology, the assessor should consider not just the technical aspects but the resource, e.g., capital investment, logistics, labor, and social requirements, e.g., skills, training, administrative support, for full deployment of the technology. The paper then develops several models and hypotheses about the relationships between technology and social variables.

6

Comparing Apples to Oranges.
Risk of Cost/Benefit Analysis

BARRY COMMONER

Barry Commoner argues that in technology assessment, the use of cost/benefit analysis should be limited to comparing the costs and benefits associated with the same substance, not used to compare the costs and benefits related to one substance with those of another—especially when these include the social costs of banning a substance as compared with those of banning another.

Not long ago there was a curiously symbolic clash between two well-meaning public interest groups, the American Cancer Society (ACS) and the Center for Science in the Public Interest. The subject was lollipops. It seems that certain chapters of the Society were selling lollipops to raise money to fight cancer. Some of the lollipops were red ones, and according to the Center, Red Dye No. 40, which they contained, is a suspected carcinogen. The Center wants the Cancer Society to stop selling the lollipops. The Society has replied: "Until Red Dye No. 40 or any other additive has been declared unsafe and taken off the market, its use in manufactured products is perfectly proper."

Does the ACS think that smoking cigarettes is "perfectly proper" because they have not been taken off the market? Clearly, the Cancer Society would not dream of raising money by selling cigarettes. Apparently, the Cancer Society believes that smoking cigarettes is a more serious risk than sucking red lollipops. But how does one make such comparisons?

As the concern about the risks of modern technology to people and the environment has been translated into legislation, a basic idea has emerged—that the best way to evaluate such a risk is to compare it with the associated benefits. This is known as risk/benefit assessment. The most recent legislation based on this concept is the Toxic Substances Control Act (TSCA). This act requires that the Environmental Protection Agency (EPA) administrator establish rules for governing the production and use of chemicals which take into account not only a substance's toxic hazards but also "the benefits of a substance for a given use or uses and the availability of less hazardous substances for the same uses." One important section of the TSCA law requires what might be called a meta-cost/benefit assessment. This is a cost/benefit evaluation not only of the substance but also of the EPA decision to regulate it—that is, the social cost of administrative action itself.

Although TSCA does not apply to food additives, it is, nevertheless, the most clear-cut statement of the risk/benefit principle and

From *Science for the People* 12, no. 3 (May–June 1980), pp. 9–10. Condensed from "Should This Sucker Get an Even Break?" *Hospital Practice* 14, no. 3 (March 1979), pp. 148, 153, 157. Reprinted by permission of *Science for the People,* 897 Main Street, Cambridge, MA 02139, and by permission of *Hospital Practice.*

it is an interesting exercise to apply it to the red lollipop controversy. Let us assume that a small cancer risk is associated with Red Dye No. 40, and that the dye adds no nutritional or taste value, so has no benefit to the consumer. With the dye in it, however, the lollipop might be said to be more "appealing" than blue ones or yellow ones. Translated, this means that they sell better. Hence the red dye is of benefit to the people that manufacture and sell the lollipops, not to the consumers. However, the hazard associated with the dye is directed toward the consumers of the lollipop, not the sellers. Since environmental regulations are designed to protect people who are exposed to toxic substances rather than the people who manufacture and sell them, it would be reasonable to conclude from this assessment that however small the risk of a toxic effect from the dye, it outweighs the benefits, since there are none. But regulatory action against Red Dye No. 40 could be challenged on the basis of economic and social impact—jobs and profits.

Taking all this into account, how could the Cancer Society, or the rest of us, decide about the relative importance of doing something about cigarettes and red lollipops? How do you compare the importance of controlling one possible carcinogen with another? This is the central question of the growing debate on carcinogens. There is, as yet, no generally accepted logical answer to it; but consider for a moment an *illogical* answer.

Suppose we compare the costs of a regulatory action that might be taken against cigarettes or red lollipops—banning them. Banning cigarettes would wipe out a $6 billion industry (in annual sales), whereas banning even all uses of Red Dye No. 40 would eliminate sales of only a few million dollars per year. Clearly, the social costs of banning red lollipops are much smaller than the costs of banning cigarettes. But this fact would, of course, be a palpably illogical basis for action, since cigarettes are more dangerous. The logical fault is obvious: In a risk/benefit assessment what should be compared is risk and benefit associated with the *same* substance, not risk (or benefit) of Substance A with the risk (or benefit) of Substance B.

Yet this is just what is now being proposed by the chemical industry. We are told that "we do not live in a risk-free world and a balanced policy on carcinogens must take this into account." The American Industrial Health Council (an industry lobby) gives us tables comparing cancer risk with other hazards. The tables tell us, for example, that people who frequently fly the airlines incur the risk of fatality with a probability of .0015% per year; that the comparable risk of cancer from an average medical diagnostic X-ray is .001% per year; that the risk of a fatality from playing football is .004% per year; from canoeing, .04%; and from motorcycle racing, 1.8% per year. The report points out that "Society has chosen not to prohibit any of these activities, or even activities with much higher risks. There are a few activities which pose such a high risk that society has banned them completely (e.g., going over Niagara Falls in a barrel)."

What is the Health Council trying to tell us? Since a 1.8% risk of death per year (motorcycle racing) is acceptable, but a risk of 100% (Niagra Falls in a barrel) is not, do they think we ought to ban a chemical when its risks lies between these two limits?

This logic is reminiscent of a much acclaimed report to the Nuclear Regulatory Commission (and just recently repudiated by it) that decided, on the basis of very elaborate computations, that the risk of being killed by a nuclear reactor accident was about the same as the risk of being hit by a meteorite. Such a "risk assessment" approach destroys the logic of the risk/benefit concept just as surely as does the comparison of the regulatory costs of banning cigarettes and Red Dye No. 40. Its proponents would do well to ponder the moral of the Cancer Society's red lollipops. What counts is the lollipop's risk in relation to the lollipop's benefits. When the dye's contribution to that benefit is zero, the relative risk (however small), becomes, so to speak, infinitely large. This suggests that it may be unnecessary to make elaborate, relative estimates of the risks of many toxic chemicals because, like the color of the lollipop, their benefits are zero.

7

Technology Assessment in Industry. A Counterproductive Myth?

VARY T. COATES AND THECLA FABIAN

The authors argue that the expression "technology assessment" should be applied only to activities aimed at assisting with public sector decisions. To use the term to describe corporate planning studies not only confuses things that often have very little in common, but also casts a negative light on some perfectly good corporate planning practices that do not aim at determining the long-range public interest. They argue that the expression "technology assessment" implies that the long-range public interest ought to be determined in any such assessment and, further, that corporations do not have the obligation or even the right to make such determination.[1]

INTRODUCTION: THE NEED FOR NEW TERMINOLOGY

The term "technology assessment," we will argue, should be reserved to describe a form of policy analysis that is designed to support public-sector decision making and the judicious allocation of public resources through the analysis of potential impacts and consequences to society. The use of the term technology assessment for comparable analyses designed to assist private-sector decision making is, we believe, undesirable and counterproductive. To force-fit the term technology assessment to these activities is to create a Procrustian bed that obscures rather than illuminates, and it tends to cast into a negative perspective some very useful and progressive developments in corporate planning and the exercise of corporate responsibility.

By implying unrealistic and quite possibly undesirable expectations, insistence on the term technology assessment tends to evoke, in industry management, resentment and resistance, both of which become barriers to the development of these desirable management support activities. This resentment and resistance, in turn, may prevent industry from appreciating and making use of the findings of public-sector technology assessments, and from politically supporting this public-sector activity. At the very least, an insistence on using the term technology assessment to query industry about its planning and decision-making techniques tends to confuse those who are trying to respond to these inquiries and to produce data that are nearly worthless or completely misleading.

Public-sector technology assessment was conceived and has evolved over a decade and a

Prepared under a contract with the OTA, U.S. Congress, as part of the activities of the OTA Task Force on TA Methodology and Management. The views expressed, however, are those of the authors and not necessarily those of the OTA or the Technology Assessment Board. From *Technological Forecasting and Social Change* 22 (1982), pp. 331–341. Copyright © 1982 by Elsevier Science Publishing Co., Inc. Reprinted by permission of the publisher and authors.

half to fit the needs of public decision-making and public policy formulation. Public policy formulation rests on the broad responsibility of government to protect and advance the public interest. It requires the sensitive trading off of potential impacts on multiple, competing national objectives, and the balancing of special and group interests and conflicting definitions of the public interest. The function of industry, on the other hand, is to generate the stream of goods and services that respond to society's demands, i.e., demands created by public policy objectives and demands that are created by the exercise of individual freedom and choice.

So long as industry respects and complies with the constraints imposed by constitutionally sound governmental authority on behalf of the public, it is at least debatable whether industry has a responsibility, or even a right, to attempt to make subtle determinations as to what constitutes the long-range public interest. It is true that some potential detrimental impacts of technology may be unequivocally unacceptable, or may obviously fall outside of bounds set formally (in general terms, by public policy) or informally (by simple human morality). We can suppose that imposition of grave, hidden risk to the life and health of consumers, whether or not that risk is covered by existing legal prohibitions and regulations, is unequivocally wrong and that the avoidance of such risk is unequivocally the responsibility of industry. We may also suppose that the unannounced introduction of a serious new pollutant, not yet recognized by laws and regulations, also violates the social responsibility of industry. (However, the acceptance, by both public policy and the general public, of the high mortality associated with the automobile illustrates the fact that even these social imperatives are not clear cut and universal.)

By comparison, the judgment that potential indirect, second-order, down-stream impacts of technology are either "detrimental" or "desirable" is incomparably more complex, subtle, and difficult. All the informal adaptations and adjustments that society will make to technological change must be included in this judgment, and it is doubtful that any industry or corporation, from its limited institutional perspective, would be able to identify, much less evaluate, these potential impacts. Corporations who must account to directors and stockholders have difficulty justifying the extensive use of resources to study indirect impacts that the corporation has no clear responsibility to manage and no "levers" to control.

Problems of public and even internal credibility arise because of the difficulty of avoiding organizational bias. Should the firm's technology assessment be made public, either the judgment and authority of corporate management would be constrained, or the public image of the corporation would be vulnerable to damage. Indeed, aside from these practical considerations, there is the serious question of whether it is more desirable for broad technological initiatives to be stimulated by the corporation's own assessment of potential indirect social impacts and consequences or by societal values, as they are reflected in economic forces that are already shaped or at least bounded by public actions. The former at least raises the possibility that subtle choices and decisions that should be made in public forums would be preempted in corporation board rooms.

Thus, the assumption that industry *should* do technology assessment, in the form evolved to support public decision making, is at least questionable. However, this assumption is implicit in surveys of "the use of technology assessment in industry," including the mini survey reported in this paper. We suggest that the failure of investigators to recognize and deal with this dubious assumption means that much of the information introduced into the public record as a result of such studies has been unreliable and misleading. One of the present authors has strongly suspected this, as she was associated, as an advisor, with several such studies. This suspicion was confirmed as we listened to respondents in this survey struggle to give us realistic and honest answers to questions phrased in terminology with which they were familiar, but [which] did not fit their own terms of reference. In larger and more impersonal surveys, this problem would no doubt be compounded by the strong temptation to answer questions affirmatively that implicitly invite the corporation to present itself as "wearing a white hat." This could and does lead survey respondents to label as technology assessment everything from legally required safety checks to purely profit-motivated market research.

Many corporations do, indeed, conduct analyses that are analogous to public-sector technology assessment, yet are inherently different in purpose and in scope because they are intended to support corporate decision making. While they may be both future oriented and focused on assessment of potential consequences of technological initiatives, their objective is to enhance the long-range viability and strength of the industry rather than to maximize the overall benefits to society.

These studies include, for example, analyses that are intended to help corporate managers ensure that the company:

- respects and complies with the regulatory restraints established by public policy to safeguard the public interest;
- anticipates restraints or liabilities that might be imposed in the future to achieve the evolving objectives of public policy; and
- identifies evolving or changing societal needs and demands so as to identify both future opportunities and possible future constraints on corporation activities

These studies are focused more on the impacts of social change on the company than on the impacts of the industry on society.

In some companies, a form of social benefits accounting, usually known as the "social audit," has also developed. Usually an extension of the annual financial report to stockholders, social audits attempt to display the societal benefits such as employment, participation of employees in community service activities, additional tax revenues, and contributions to charitable and educational programs, etc., created by a company

and by its location in a particular community or region. Social audits usually do not discuss the indirect impacts of the corporation's products or services.

Recently, the Securities Exchange Commission (SEC) promulgated a requirement that "public companies" carry out an environmental audit of their activities in order to protect stockholders from environmental liability. SEC has said that it will require 50 of the largest companies to perform such audits within the next year or two. So far, at least three very large companies—U.S. Steel, Allied Chemical, and Occidental Chemicals—have carried out, or initiated, these environmental audits. As yet we have no information about the scope and content of these audits.

A MINI SURVEY
OF "INDUSTRY TECHNOLOGY
ASSESSMENT"

To get an overview of whether and to what extent technology assessment and related activities were being conducted in industry, we surveyed 27 corporate executives and researchers who had attended technology assessment workshops or short courses. We believe these people were the most familiar with the concept of technology assessment and the most likely individuals to be involved in any ongoing activities within their firms and/or to know of such activities in other firms.

These individuals were sent a two-page questionnaire: those who did not respond in writing were contacted with follow-up calls.[2] We received 23 responses to the original 27 inquiries. Seven of these responses were written replies to the questionnaires: 16 were interviews conducted by phone during the follow-up. Three persons could not be located; and 2 additional responses came from persons recommended by one of the original interviewees.

We also conducted a literature search for topics related to industrial technology assessment. This is not a statistical analysis of the frequency of technology assessment activities within corporations, since the cost of surveying even Fortune 500 corporations would have been well beyond the resources available for this study, and would have been further complicated by the lack of any clear unambiguous definition of technology assessment used by the industries themselves.

Two conclusions emerged from this study. First, technology assessment is not a common or a very familiar concept, even in these corporations. Second, in those firms that did claim to be doing technology assessment, the term was applied to a wide variety of activities and concepts. There are obvious instances of "old wine in new bottles," as marketing studies and technical feasibility studies were hastily relabeled technology assessments.

It would appear that technology assessments, or more precisely, parallel activities that should be differentiated from public-sector terminology assessments, do have a potential role to play in industrial decision making. However, this role will be both different and more limited than the role of technology assessment in governmental decision making. This role will also differ among industries. Certain industries can be expected to use such studies more frequently and to develop more sophisticated techniques than others.

INDUSTRY FAMILIARITY WITH TECHNOLOGY ASSESSMENT

The interviewees were already familiar with technology assessment by virtue of having attended at least one short course or conference. However, we were regularly told by an interviewee that he/she was the only one in the company who had an interest in technology assessment. Many of these people had attended a technology assessment course or workshop at their own initiative; they were supported to the extent of corporate reimbursement for their participation but not encouraged to take further action on establishing the concept within the company.

One corporate official, who had previously spent 10 years as a consultant to Fortune 500 companies, said that he has never encountered technology assessment in any of the

companies he has worked with. He put technology assessment today in the position of strategic planning 20 years ago, guessing that maybe one in 100 corporate officers would have even heard the term.

Several factors seem to contribute to this lack of knowledge about the concept of technology assessment. First, the idea, going back barely over a decade, originated in the field of public policy, and for many of these companies, it is an idea that has never touched any of their activities directly. Second, technology assessment has been very sparsely considered, if at all, in the industry "trade press." Magazines such as *Fortune* and *Forbes,* as well as the more specialized business newsletters, have by and large ignored it. These are the prime sources of general information for the business community. Technology assessment has been written up primarily in articles directed to the scientific and engineering communities or to the public policy community. Those companies whose officers are the most aware of technology assessment are companies that are primarily involved with high technology, innovative activities that carry a high degree of public and governmental visibility.

Respondees showed an interesting split on the complexity of technology assessment itself. There were those who tended to view technology assessment as a common sense technique that was widely used by a variety of companies, but under different names. As one person commented, "I believe *any* major company, of necessity, plans with tools like technology assessment without ever giving them special names." Another felt that it was a fairly straightforward, commonsensical approach to dealing with emerging technologies, and that people in a number of contexts were doing it in bits and pieces without calling it technology assessment.

On the other hand, there were those who considered technology assessment to be too elaborate and rigid a technique to be used by most corporations. At the extreme was one executive from a large company whose viewpoint was that technology assessment was an elaborate process designed to make a great deal of money for consultants. He explained his company's lack of any technology assessment activities by saying, "We voted with our feet; we feel that as a concept, technology assessment is not relevant. . . ."

The companies showing the most familiarity and interest in technology assessment concepts, whether or not they had actually attempted to do studies, appeared to have several characteristics in common. They were engaged in high technology, innovative activities, with a relatively large proportion of their work force trained in some field of engineering or the sciences. These companies tended to see their activities as having a direct effect on the environment or some other aspect of society. Perhaps more importantly, however, they also tended to see themselves as being vulnerable to impacts from outside of the company, particularly from segments of the public or from government regulations. Many of these companies viewed technology assessment solely in terms of trying to anticipate the effects of the outside world on their own activities, rather than anticipating the effects of their activities on factors outside of themselves. One chemical company executive stated this succinctly in explaining the technology assessment activities of the corporate research division, "Research managers spend a great deal of time looking at future trends and trying to identify future opportunities for a high technology chemical company."

Those companies having at least overall familiarity with technology assessment, and the least interest in it, appeared to be companies involved in the manufacture and distribution of basic goods and services, such as food products and household goods. The respondents from these corporations had largely given up any idea of instituting some form of corporate technology assessment, even if they personally considered it a good idea. A marketing executive from one large food company admitted that he did not see any future possibilities for corporate technology assessment activities as being either "terribly realistic or likely" within his corporation; that company was tied to a system of quarterly goals for production and sales that limited

planning to a quarterly schedule. Another executive from a multiproduct corporation felt that the company might use something like technology assessment if they ever decided to introduce a product that was radically different or controversial.

A fair number of firms fell into a "maybe" category. In these companies, there were at least a few people in the firm who had some familiarity with technology assessment but, while the management of the company was not opposed to technology assessment, it was not particularly interested in the concept either. A research engineer with a high technology manufacturing firm, one that produced no consumer products, expressed the idea simply. "They feel they'll get around to looking into it sooner or later." Another person currently involved in technology forecasting indicated that one of the things that could spur interest in technology assessment was a government requirement that it be done.

Overall, corporate awareness of technology assessment appears to be limited to one individual or a small group of people within each corporation, even in these corporations that claim to be doing technology assessment. In some cases, one person has been able to implement some technology assessment activities within the company; in others, their interest remains purely individual. In no case, however, were we able to find a corporation having any sort of a technology assessment process that appeared to be crucial to the decision making of the firm.

WHAT IS "INDUSTRY TECHNOLOGY ASSESSMENT"?

Some firms are beginning to call a broad range of activities "technology assessment." Firms have different, and often conflicting, definitions of the term, and within a single firm, different individuals can be working on the basis of conflicting definitions. In one case, contact was made with two persons, one involved in technology forecasting and the other a corporate planner, within the same branch of the same firm. The technology forecaster maintained the firm was not doing any technology assessment and saw no realistic possibility of its doing any in the near future. He felt that management did not consider such studies cost effective. His colleague, on the other hand, stated that the corporation was doing technology assessment because management considered it important. The studies he referred to as technology assessment appeared to be forecasts of future technologies and their potential for the corporation; they were probably done by the forecaster, who did not consider these efforts technology assessment.

Another respondee listed the following activities as technology assessment: 1) technology forecasts, 2) market analyses, 3) engineering evaluations, 4) site analyses, 5) environmental scans, 6) competitive analyses, 7) economic and business analyses, and 8) other. These studies were done to "help manage the business safely, profitably and avoid surprises," and the major recipients of these studies were the project managers, with department heads and other relevant management also being the targets for such reports. The studies were done regularly and routinely, but as an "integral part of our planning and not something separable or distinct." While some of these activities do contain certain elements of technology assessment, it is apparent that what was done in this case was to take the company's regular planning process and incidental planning tools and relabel the whole thing technology assessment. The activities thus became technology assessments "after the fact."

A number of respondents have identified market assessments and analyses as technology assessment, or the closest thing to technology assessments done by their firms. In most cases, the person was fully aware that such studies did not fit the definition of technology assessment very well. One company executive, for example, said that "the closest thing to technology assessment is . . . trying to predict areas of business opportunity for the future." At the same time, he admitted that the company did "very little in the way of analyzing the effects of their business activities on either society or the environment."

Environmental assessments and environmental impact statements mandated by Federal law were identified by several respondents. An individual from one large industrial laboratory identified a number of studies that he did not consider technology assessments, but that were what he called related activities. These included product safety studies involving the laboratory's own employees, the employees of other firms, and the general public; environmental impact statements; and toxicity studies involving the products.

Several large, technology-dependent corporations have offices or divisions that regularly engage in activities that could be called "inverted technology assessments." These divisions are involved in extensive efforts to anticipate future societal developments for the purpose of analyzing the potential effects of these developments on the firm. One major corporation has a two-pronged approach to this form of industrial technology assessment: 1) a small centralized futurist group reporting to the executive management; and 2) a more short-term project and technology planning office within each of the corporation's several technology areas.

The smaller futurist group had been started by a small group of people within the firm about 5 years ago. It started out by looking at a number of techniques that could be useful in planning for the long-range future of the firm, including futurism, technology assessment, and technology forecasting. The group's interest was oriented primarily toward government, future technologies, and economic factors; the body later was established as a permanent fixture in the company, reporting directly to the top levels of management. Group members presently conduct their own studies, attend seminars and workshops of interest, and produce reports for management. They also conduct brainstorming sessions within the company on such topics as corporate options for coping with the lack of availability of traditional energy sources. They maintain their orientation toward future technological changes, government activities, and economic changes; but they do not cover the social implications of corporate activities (though they do cover the reverse—the effects of social and political change on the company).

This company's second route for industrial technology assessment is the planning function within the technology centers. These centers deal with the various product areas of the corporation and with areas of broad concern, such as energy and the environment. Concerned with both short-term project planning and long-term impacts of their areas of interest, the centers started out being primarily interested in business and economic issues, but have gradually evolved to consideration of the longer term (10–20 years) in areas such as environmental issues. Again, their primary orientation is inward, that is, consideration of impacts on the firm, though they have looked at such issues as the safe disposal of industrial wastes.

Another corporation identified a similar structure within its corporate research division, in which future trends are tracked and then related to future opportunities and hazards for the corporations. Each of the component research divisions attempts trend assessment in its own area for the purpose of planning future corporate activities.

One of our sources said that her corporation had an extensive system to track future social, political, economic, and other developments, and to forecast their effects on her company. However, she was unwilling to provide details beyond the fact that these anticipatory efforts included such issues as energy, environment, taxation, occupational health and safety, and government regulations.

A number of respondents either identified specific instances of technology assessment-related studies or indicated that their companies would, under certain circumstances, be open to the idea of conducting a one-time, ad hoc technology assessment, most probably with the assistance of outside consultants.

A researcher in one Canadian electrical company gave an interesting account of an unsuccessful attempt at contracting out a technology assessment that has apparently left management leery of conducting any further technology assessments (this was the com-

pany's first encounter with the process of technology assessment).

Several years ago the company had hired a contracting firm in the United States to conduct a technology assessment on the effects of rate structures on electricity consumption. The study was intended to examine the ramifications of changing rate structures on the use of electricity, including the social and regulatory impacts. In retrospect, the company was of the opinion that the study fell far short of expectations and that they had been promised much more than was delivered. They did not find the study useful in the decision-making process, and it was consequently forgotten except as a negative incentive to future technology assessments, either in-house or by contract.

When the respondent tried at a later time to propose a much more limited, in-house technology assessment in his own area of expertise (including analysis of such areas as social impact), he met with resistance. The general reaction seemed to be, "This looks interesting, but we don't want to put the time and effort into it." Management seemed to consider technology assessment an unproven quantity, both in terms of the technique itself and in terms of the company's ability to produce a successful outcome and arrive at information useful in the corporate decision-making process.

A defense-related group of one major national research and development corporation is currently conducting one technology assessment-related study, an environment impact statement for the MX missile program. This is a relatively large project being performed by both in-house staff and outside consultants, with emphasis on consultants. Funded by the U.S. Air Force, the project is estimated to be a 10–20 person effort that will last 2–4 years.

In another instance, one respondent wrote,

Because of the nature of our business, we normally have no requirements to perform assessments of our technology developments. That is, being predominantly in the space, communications, and software businesses for the government, we do not become involved with justifying what we do. (Considering

TA in the context of satisfying regulatory requirements, etc.). However, from the technology futures point of view, studies of where our business might go and what problems might be encountered, I feel that TA studies would definitely be helpful. But, until management is incentivized for the long term, support for such work is unlikely unless funded by the government.

This illustrates several fairly common responses. First, technology assessment, even in its inverted form, i.e., consideration restricted to impacts of outside factors on the firm's activities, seems to be a hard concept to "sell" to management, which sees no reason and has no incentive to do it. Second, technology assessment of impacts of the firm's activities on outside factors is often viewed in terms of "justification," or will be done only to the extent necessary to satisfy regulatory requirements.

Some companies did identify sporadic attempts to examine corporate activities in terms of their impacts on broader social issues. These attempts generally paralleled a show of government interest. One chemical company executive stated that whether there is a government policy, the company will generally try to formulate its own policy and/or analyze its activities in terms of that policy. A common example is a company's environmental policy.

Another respondent gave an example of an extensive examination of the projected availability of oil and gas in the near future, and the impacts of that availability on corporate activities. The study was contracted out to an independent engineering firm and resulted in the decision to build a wood-burning cogenerator plant. The wood-burning generator emerged as the most viable option to provide future additional power capacity because it would provide electricity at about half the cost of a traditional generating plant, would serve the community better, and in annual, full-time operation would only use 0.1% of the available wood within a 100-mile radius. Of this amount, a considerable percentage could be purchased from farmers in the form of scrap wood that had no other market value. Obviously, this study did include awareness of impacts on the surrounding community and an effort to include community benefit (as well as corporation benefits) in the analysis. The project, which [was to] cost approximately $30 million and [was to be] brought on line in 1982, was finally approved [in 1980].

Another interviewee said that a technology assessment resulted in the decision not to develop solar cells, but did not give details.

One respondent in a multi-project manufacturing company felt that his corporation would at least consider using technology assessment in the future if the company were planning to enter a new or radically different area of activity. In his opinion, this was the only way the corporation would do any sort of technology assessment, there being little justification for a continuing process of technology assessment within the company.

Aside from specific studies, several respondents have identified a process that might be called informal technology assessment. In some cases this is much closer to the concept of technology assessment as a tool for identifying the second-order impacts of a project or area of new technology than are many of the more formal studies cited.

This informal technology assessment usually involves an individual or a small group of people in an office or division who have taken on the responsibility of staying aware of potential technological changes and their possible impacts on other elements of society. The information is used in their reports and advice to top management without being called technology assessment, and many of these informal assessors have come to the conclusion that their corporations will not put the resources into a formal program of technology assessment. Comments such as the following give some idea of the nature of this informal process of technology assessment: "We do try to bring in social effects, but this isn't a primary thing. It is done on an informal basis. As issues are raised, we try to get the information to the highest level. I've tried to familiarize myself with the issues and to inject this knowledge of social and political factors into the company's decisionmaking." Another comment was, "We try to keep our eyes open and sense emerging trends, but there is no formal group doing technology assessment."

In some ways, this informal type of technology assessment appears to have advantages from the perspective of corporate management. It is a less threatening technique; for instance, a primarily negative assessment presented informally would not seem as dangerous as an officially sanctioned, written report.

Overall, those companies that consider themselves to have engaged in technology assessment have identified a significant number of activities as either assessments or related activities. Some of these are obvious relabelings of conventional corporate practices, such as marketing studies, technical feasibility studies, site planning, etc. Other activities appear to be partial attempts at technology assessment, or more commonly, inverted technology assessment.

THE POTENTIAL OF "INDUSTRIAL TECHNOLOGY ASSESSMENT"

Industrial technology assessment is evolving into a different process from those activities called technology assessment in the public sector. This is not necessarily undesirable, but the two processes should not be confused. Industrial technology assessment, even at its most sophisticated, is fundamentally an analysis of the effects of technological, social, economic, and political change on the industry doing the assessment. Only secondarily, if at all, are industries looking at how their activities affect the external environment.

The largest volume of the effects of an industry's activities on the outside world is probably environmental analysis. This is the area in which corporations have been mandated, in some situations by the government and now specifically by SEC, to analyze certain of their major activities.

There is little incentive in the corporate sphere to conduct further analyses of the effects of corporate activities on the outside world. This would involve putting resources into obtaining information that most firms feel they do not need. As one of the respondents stated, "Corporate officers tend to get infor-

mation that helps them make specific decisions or deal with specific problems. These decisions are first financial, and second, technological. Secondary and tertiary impacts are generally discounted by the corporate world."

Many corporations have trouble perceiving the value of doing even "inverted technology assessment" (impacts of society on the corporation); they see even less benefit in studying the effects, particularly the negative effects, of their planned areas of activity. Many corporate planners do understand that these negative effects can come back to haunt a corporation in the form of public anger and government regulation. But unfortunately, even this sometimes appears to become an argument for using technology assessment activities to identify ways of manipulating public opinion and sidestepping government regulations.

Perhaps what is necessary is an explicit recognition of the intrinsic differences between technology assessment in the public and the private sectors. To the extent that corporate officers can be convinced of the value of "objective" technology assessment in guiding corporate decision making into the most socially desirable options, corporate decision making can become more informed and responsible. However, internal assessments on the part of corporations should not be considered substitutes for technology assessment in the public sector. Indeed, most assessments would be kept from the public if only because they contain proprietary information. We cannot assume that private-sector assessments of future technological options will necessarily be either "objective" or reach conclusions based primarily on the net good for society external to the corporation. That kind of assessment rightly belongs to the public sector.

To the extent that public spirited corporations are willing to take on the task of doing some assessments internally, the collective task will be made easier. In many cases, the corporations themselves will benefit in the long run by avoiding costly mistakes or by identifying truly profitable and socially advantageous courses of action.

However, we do not believe that this sort of analysis will be widely done within the corporate sector in the near future. We argue that to use the term "technology assessment"—a term that whatever its own shortcomings is now firmly attached to public policy impact assessment—to describe parallel, but fundamentally different, corporate planning activities is a mistake. It both obscures the current status of these activities and creates barriers to their future development and improvement.

NOTES

1. A report to the Office of Technology Assessment, U.S. Congress.

2. Many of these people have requested confidentiality and were assured that neither their name nor their company's name would be used without their prior knowledge. They will not be identified here.

PART III

MORAL CONTROVERSIES
IN TECHNOLOGY MANAGEMENT

SENSES OF THE TERM "MANAGEMENT"

To talk of management is, often, to elicit strong responses and confusing controversy. For to some, management is simply a group of technocrats intent on manipulating people for the sake of their own self-promotional, organizational, or class aims. To others, management is merely a group of dull administrators set on running friction-less programs and thereby obstructing all individual creativity along the way. Others think of management as "the best and the brightest"; and still others—less polemi-cally and more generally—think of it as simply the person or persons controlling and directing the affairs of an organization. All these conceptions of management, though sharply different from each other, share one characteristic: they put the emphasis on people.

The term "management," however, can also be used to denote activity, "the act or manner of managing; handling, direction, control."[1] There are, of course, a number of senses in which a person can be said to be managing, handling, or controlling something, or managing to do something. In one sense of the word, a person can be said to be accomplishing something, as in "She is managing to keep ahead of the competition." In another sense, one is said to be taking charge, as in "She is manag-ing the estate." In yet a third sense, when a person or organization is said to be managing, it means continuing to function, progress, or succeed, usually despite hard-ship or difficulty. One can in this sense, for example, say, "People thought we'd go bankrupt, but we're managing." At any rate, the latter conceptions of management emphasize activity, by contrast with the former conceptions, emphasizing persons. In Part III, Moral Controversies in Technology Management, the term "management" is used primarily to refer to activity. Organizational structures and people are involved only insofar as they are a part of carrying out a management activity.

TECHNOLOGY MANAGEMENT AND PUBLIC CONCERN

There are various moral problems that develop in managing technology. Indeed, most of the moral problems and controversies in the area of technology that have prompted general concern appear to arise in regard to its management. In response to this greater level of social concern, Part III has been made longer than the other parts, and includes a number of sections, each devoted to a discussion of controversies concerning a particular type of technology.

MORAL CONTROVERSIES IN INFORMATION TECHNOLOGY

The first selection, The Future of Work: Does it Belong to Us or to the Robots?, by Sar A. Levitan and Clifford M. Johnson, deals with the problem of whether the use of robots and microprocessors in the workplace is likely to lead to unemployment increases and, if so, what ought to be done about it. The authors' position about this likelihood of resulting unemployment increases is optimistic. They say:

> The technology itself may be refined to such an extent that most factory work could be carried out by robots and automated machinery. . . . Yet these theoretical estimates of the potential for automation . . . do not reflect the rate at which the new technology will actually be introduced to the workplace. The pace of innovation will depend on the relative costs of labor and computerized technologies, as well as on broader levels of supply and demand for goods and services.

They argue for this view on the grounds that, first, capital-intensive industries have huge investments in existing facilities, and the wholesale replacement of these would be prohibitive; then, the rate at which such replacement can take place is limited by the time it takes to gather the necessary funds; finally, both consumers and workers tend to resist the introduction of technological devices that would do away with their familiar, human companions at places such as hospitals, where they, as consumers, may seek health care, or the office or assembly line where they work.

However, the fact is that these consumers and workers now have to live with the *prospect* of losing their companions as a result of available technological developments, and of having to resist change, as the authors predict they will. These are the consequences of the mere availability of new technologies and, since they, at the least, increase personal conflict, one must ask, What ought to be done about developments in technology and the new situations their availability creates? Some of the discussions that follow will address this matter.

SOME CRITERIA FOR ASSESSING LIMITED INTRODUCTIONS OF MICROPROCESSORS IN INDUSTRY

The discussion in the first selection in Part III is restricted: it does not consider the problems created by the mere availability of new technologies, and it is limited to the subject of the wholesale introduction of robots and microprocessors to the workplace. It does not discuss their limited introduction. In Workers, Unions, and Industrial Robotics, Thomas L. Weekley treats this theme with reference to industrial settings. He argues that such change need not lead to the loss of jobs, but would likely be at least a cause of displacement: "Workers will face displacement within the plant and possibly in new industries, which may mean moving to other plants or newly opened facilities." Weekley advances various criteria for assessing the introduction of new technologies as they affect the interest of workers. The main ones are, first, whether such innovations would enhance, rather than hinder, job security; second, whether they would help, rather than degrade workers, or confer on them a secondary status; and third, whether this would lead to improved or diminished job safety.

The first criterion provides a basis for Weekley's conclusion that, if the introduction of a certain technology to the workplace would require work force reductions, "Natural attrition, rather than spur-of-the-moment layoffs, should be the only way of reducing the work force." This raises various moral problems and has actually been a significant source of controversy. Should a firm use natural attrition rather than layoffs, even when this would delay its use of a technology, placing it at a competitive disadvantage to other firms already using or about to use the technology? Should it rely on natural attrition alone when most other firms are laying off workers in order to introduce the technology? Does the mere fact that layoffs are the general practice make it morally right for the firm to follow this course? Does it make it excusable? What other circumstances, if any, must exist for the firm's action to be right or at least excusable? If layoffs are morally permissible or excusable in the circumstances, is a firm that uses them to introduce new technology morally required to do anything else? These questions should provide some guidance in exploring the moral implications of this issue, in attempting to formulate alternative criteria, and in trying to establish whether alternative criteria are better than the ones above. They should be kept in mind when discussing moral principles later in this part.

Weekley's second criterion concerns the degradation of workers by the introduction of new technologies: new technologies may break down some jobs requiring skilled workers into small tasks that could be performed by nearly any unskilled person. His criterion rules out such degrading of workers. However, like the first, this second criterion leads to various moral problems and, indeed, to controversy and even outright confrontation. Would this introduction of new technologies actually degrade the workers affected by it? What is it to degrade someone, and what bearing does it have on whether introducing such technology is wrong? Is it wrong under any, or only under some, but not all, circumstances? If the latter, what circumstances are exempt? What should take precedence when conflicts arise, as they indeed do: the availability of jobs, if only at an unskilled level, or the retention of skilled jobs even if this leads to layoffs? Again, these questions are meant both to prompt and provide some guidance for the critical scrutiny of the above criteria. We will return to some of them later on.

A third criterion of Weekley's is safety: "Automated equipment must be safe itself and easily shut off by an operator in case of malfunction. The equipment must be designed to conform to the human operating the equipment, rather than forcing the human to conform to the equipment—for example, to its speed of operation." Though Weekley does not elaborate on this point, this criterion addresses not just a concern for the physical health of workers who might be harmed by the breakdown of hard-to-operate equipment, but also for the mental health of workers who have to concentrate more and more on simpler, repetitive tasks to keep up with the faster pace of the new equipment they must operate.

A moral problem that arises here, which has sometimes caused controversy is, What sort of criteria should be used in establishing whether the pace of a certain piece of equipment is too fast or a threat to the operator's health in any other way? A second such problem and source of controversy is the issue of whether any job-associated health risk is unjustified, or whether any circumstances exist that justify certain health risks. If paint jobs at a car factory pose a threat to workers regardless of safety measures, should robots be used for these jobs, even if this might lead to layoffs; or should workers' jobs be preserved even when unsafe? Should this be a matter for bargaining and negotiation, or should the utter elimination of job-related risks be non-negotiable? This, in turn, raises a further moral problem relating to all three of Weekley's criteria, as well as to many other problems discussed in this book: What is the moral status of bargaining and negotiation in cases of conflicting interests concerning the introduction of technology? Can bargaining and negotiation procedures ever establish what is the morally justified policy concerning technology in the workplace? Or are they simply procedures that, by and large, compromise what is justified? These questions, as well as the others in this section, are worth pursuing carefully and in detail. Though it is not within our scope to engage in a full consideration of them, or attempt to answer them, we will continue to formulate them. Lest the readers feel overwhelmed by the nature and number of questions, it may be helpful to say a few words about the role of such questions.

THE ROLE OF QUESTIONS IN ETHICS AS A BRANCH OF INQUIRY

As is stated in the Preface and Note to the Reader, this book's discussions are not intended to provide solutions to the problems found in the selections or in the discussions. The aim is rather to provoke in the reader the critical interest in, and basic elements for, better dealing with these problems. This is done by presenting conflicting claims about the technological matters discussed in the selections, by formulating questions that pose moral problems about these matters, and by recurrently pointing to a small set of considerations central to dealing sensitively and effectively with moral controversies in technology. These include both individual and collective consequences, rights, and pragmatic considerations. The framework formed by these elements has, to some extent, been developed earlier, and will be further developed in what follows.

Apart from the problems prompting its development, however, our framework is pointless. It must be assessed and used in reference to these problems, which makes it crucial that we formulate them with the greatest possible sensitivity to their various aspects. This can best—if not only—be done by means of questions. Since the problems posed by contemporary moral controversies in technology characteristically involve a variety of matters that relate to each other in complex ways, it is no wonder that the questions formulating the problems turn out to be many and varied, relating to each other in equally complex ways. This may not bring much solace to one seeking ready answers; but it is sound doctrine. After all, there are no answers without questions, and one has little chance of finding answers without asking the right questions, however numerous and complex. A primary aim of this book, then, is to help readers formulate the right questions. Otherwise, moral problems and controversies in technology could not be soundly addressed, nor the theoretical framework developed here be used or assessed. Clusters of questions, as have been recurrently posed serve best to formulate the right questions. Thus we can proceed to discuss the considerations included in our theoretical framework. But let us also keep in mind that, though general in nature, the considerations are not to be mistaken for a set of general statements from which one can simply deduce positions about particular controversies in technology. They are, rather, elements in a framework meant to help the reader develop his or her reasoning and value-appraising skills by encouraging critical discussions of a variety of moral controversies in technology.

TWO EXTREME ETHICAL PRINCIPLES AND SOME CRITERIA FOR ASSESSING THEM

Some of the questions raised so far in Part III are certainly difficult to answer well. In the background of the controversies centering around them, there are often disagreements as to what kinds of reasons are decisive in determining whether the introduction of a new technology is right, or whether policies governing such an action are morally justified. Views advanced from the business sector often appear to imply that the decisive difference in determining if any such action is right, or policy justified, is profitability and growth, with no weight attached to the consequences of the action or policy on job security, status, or the safety of workers except insofar as they affect this profitability and growth. Views advanced by labor, in contrast, often appear to imply that the types of reasons that make a decisive difference concern only the workers' interest, namely, job security, status, and safety, with profitability and growth relevant only to the extent that they help enhance workers' attainment of these things.

Though sharply opposed to each other, these positions often share the presupposition that an action is right or a policy morally justified if it tends to maximize the balance of desirable over undesirable consequences for the members of a certain interest group—a firm or the business sector in one case, a firm's employees or the labor sector in the other—regardless of how great the balance of undesirable over desirable consequences might turn out to be for any other person or group, *unless* this would hinder the above-mentioned maximization of the sector's or group's overall favorable balance of consequences. Otherwise the action is wrong and the policy unjustified. The above amounts to the formulation of a principle, in that it characterizes reasons of a certain type as making a decisive difference in determining what actions are right or wrong, or what policies are morally justified or unjustified. Since it gives overriding predominance to the overall favorable balance of consequences for a sector such as business or labor, or for a corporate person such as a firm, a union, or a political organization, it can accordingly be called the *principle of ethical sectarianism.*

The principle of ethical sectarianism is not entirely unlike the *principle of ethical egoism.* According to the latter, an action is right or a policy morally justified if it tends to maximize the balance of desirable over undesirable consequences for the particular individual who performs the action, or who supports or introduces the policy, regardless of how great the overall balance of undesirable over desirable consequences might be for any other person or group—*unless* this would hinder the maximization of the overall favorable balance of consequences for that person. Otherwise, the action is wrong and the policy unjustified.

The fact that these principles give exclusive importance to the welfare of a particular person or sector raises questions about their validity. Why place such importance on this rather than that person or sector's welfare? This question, which certainly deserves an answer, cannot be answered by an appeal to the above principles. Their assumptions are basically arbitrary. Further, contemporary moral controversies in technology no doubt involve significant conflict but, as stated in Part I, they frequently involve openness to reason and meaningful dialogue, however heated. Such dialogue is often the only viable way of accomplishing anything worthwhile for those involved in controversy, by leading to some arrangement involving sacrifices on all sides, yet reasonably acceptable to the parties involved. The principles of ethical egoism and ethical sectarianism, however, would not enjoin any such arrangements, since these would conflict with the maximization of welfare for those whose advantage must always take precedence in deciding what action to perform or policy to support or introduce. Rather, these principles would enjoin the performance of actions or the support or introduction of policies that would increase conflict and make dialogue and openness to reason impossible in such cases. They are, therefore, not merely arbitrary but also irrelevant, unrealistic, implausible and a sure recipe for disaster—all reasons for rejecting them in favor of more moderate principles, sensitive to the concerns of all involved in a controversy, as well as to the possibility of meaningful dialogue.

Let us clarify the criticisms just advanced. First, these principles tend to be quite irrelevant for dealing with controversy in any way other than through further conflict, a prospect unlikely to deal effectively with any technology controversies. Because they rule out meaningful dialogue, the principles are unrealistic for dealing with most, if not all, contemporary moral controversies in technology. For the positions they enjoin require one to disregard the other side and do not, for the most part, point to feasible options. They are implausible because they conflict with the predominant expectations, moral beliefs and presuppositions of those involved in the controversies, often regardless of the side they represent. Finally, these principles are a certain recipe for disaster because they force the generalization of conflict, which could be catastrophic, while the viable alternative of reducing or containing conflict is not. The above criticisms are based on and exemplify the use of various criteria for assessing ethical principles. Our criteria extend beyond considerations of clarity, coherence, and the extent of the guidance that principles give, though these are no doubt, some of the criteria used in assessing ethical principles.[2] However, the criteria used here include the arbitrariness or lack of arbitrariness of a principle, its relevance in solving ethical problems in ways sought by those addressing the problems, the degree of realism in the guidance it provides, the compatibility of the principle with the expectations, moral beliefs and presuppositions of the parties to the problems, and finally, the consequences of applying the principles. None of these criteria is decisive; each is open to critical scrutiny. Jointly, however, they build a critical case in favor or against a number of principles, though, of course, there are other principles that appear to be mutually incompatible, of which none is easily dismissed on the basis of these criteria. This may be a reason not to dismiss any of the considerations they involve, but to try to formulate a framework that combines them and addresses a variety of moral problems in a sensitive, well-reasoned way. We will develop such a framework to the extent possible.[3]

UTILITARIANISM

The preceding section presented the principles of ethical egoism and ethical sectarianism as being implausible, partly because of the fact that, even when no direct criticism is advanced against the principles themselves, members of labor or of the business sector involved in controversies often honestly reject views that rely on these principles on the grounds that they are cynical and morally insensitive. They further argue that their respective positions on the introduction of technology that might affect job security, status, or safety are supported by the fact that each is likely to maximize the balance of desirable over undesirable consequences for *all* members of society, not simply for the members of a particular sector, let alone individuals arbitrarily endowed with exclusive importance.

Those who take this position often presuppose a further principle, the *principle of utility*. There is a whole array of formulations of this principle. A predominant version is that an action is right or a policy morally justified if it tends to maximize the balance of desirable consequences over undesirable consequences for most members of society. Otherwise the action is wrong and the policy unjustified.

This type of principle is not open to all the criticisms against the two previous ones. But one might object that it is still arbitrary in selecting the majority as that sector whose balance of desirable over undesirable consequences ought to be maximized. Indeed, the principle itself cannot provide an answer to the question of why the majority's welfare should be maximized on each and every occasion. Yet this is a valid moral question. Thus, there is reason to believe that other, nonutilitarian, moral considerations are called for in dealing with problems that the principle of utility cannot address.

Indeed, even if the principle is modified so as to advise that the welfare of all, and not just of the majority, be maximized, it still gives no guidance as to the distribution of such welfare. For example, who should be the beneficiary of certain desirable

consequences included in the maximum balance of desirable over undesirable consequences for all, if this means that one person or sector enjoys them and another does
not? Who should enjoy them? A principle that merely advises the maximization of the
overall balance of desirable over undesirable consequences for all is of no help in the
search for sound answers to this question.[4]

PRINCIPLES OF JUSTICE, DIGNITY, AND RIGHTS

In an attempt to meet these objections, or simply to formulate the principle they rely
on, people sometimes state versions of yet other principles when they discuss matters
of technology introduction likely to affect workers' job security, status, or safety.
These are principles of justice of various kinds, involving such notions of moral rights
as workers' rights to job security, status, and safety, or firms' rights to act so as to
maximize profitability and growth in ways that may sometimes jeopardize jobs, job
status, or job safety. A principle often said to be presupposed by these rights is the
principle of formal justice, which can be formulated in the following way: No one
ought to be treated differently from anyone else, despite the various differences
between individuals, except when one or more of these differences constitutes a good
reason for doing so.

Though this principle is widely presupposed by people in business, as well as in
labor, who engage in discussions about job security, status, and safety threats from
new technology, it still leaves room for a great deal of disagreement. For some argue
that the differences that make the difference, after all, are considerations of profitability and growth, while others argue that they are, rather, job security, job status,
and a minimum of safety. In support of these mutually incompatible positions, still
other principles are often advanced or presupposed in the discussions that arise. One
such principle is often brought up when discussing whether introducing a certain new
technology in the workplace would degrade workers. It is argued that workers are
persons and accordingly ought not to be induced to have jobs that conflict with their
dignity as persons; introducing technology that degrades them by downgrading their
job status or by making them substitutable is to do precisely that. This amounts to
disregarding the respect owed to them simply because they are people, which in turn
violates their rights as people. Involved in this argument is what is sometimes called
the *principle of personality,* and, at other times, the *principle of humanity.* A formulation of this principle is as follows: If an action is right or a policy morally justified,
then it never involves treating persons as merely objects or means, but always, con-
currently, involves treating them as persons or ends.

Considerations of rights associated with an individual's dignity have, no doubt, a
plausible claim to relevance, and even more weight than mere consequences when the
loss of job status is threatened, say, by the introduction of microprocessors in the
workplace, whereas the job and its status would not be threatened if this technology
were not introduced. If they were threatened either way, however, considerations of

consequences would carry significant weight, while the dignity associated with the status of the particular jobs in question would have much less, if any, weight because it would be lost either with or without the introduction of the new technology. One could, of course, argue that it would still be relevant for establishing if any such situation ought to be prevented or eliminated. However, this would address another problem, and is irrelevant to cases in which the situation is, and is likely to stay, as described for quite a while.

The preceding discussion of utilitarianism, justice, dignity, and rights in connection with controversies in which the matters of concern are significantly open to bargaining and negotiation provides support for three general points. First, happiness alone does not establish what actions are right and what policies justified when dealing with the moral problems raised. Rather, happiness without the abuse of anyone does—that is, happiness that is not attained in disregard of anyone likely to undergo loss or injury thereby.[5] Second, determining what such happiness will turn out to be cannot always be done beforehand, independently of the dialogue, bargaining, and negotiation between those affected. After all, those affected should, if possible, have a say in establishing what would amount to abuse. It should also be kept in mind that, as indicated in Part II, those affected may themselves not be able to give a reliable answer beforehand to the question of what would constitute an abuse. To do so, they may also have to engage in dialogue, bargaining, negotiation, and interaction with other affected parties, and examine the technological developments at issue for a while. The third point, which is supported by the preceding discussion, is that considerations of justice are not independent of the process just described, or of considerations of happiness. After all, why would justice matter if it had nothing to do with how people would be affected?[6] It would be irrelevant to the problems, which are prompted by real concerns about how people would be affected, say, by the introduction of microprocessors in the workplace. As indicated above, however, justice is not irrelevant, in that it sets constraints on mere considerations of consequences for individuals, societal sectors, or even the majority, which would, and do, lead to abuses.

These three points concerning the mutual constraints of happiness and justice, and the role of dialogue, bargaining, negotiation, and interaction in working out the details of such constraints provide further grounds for the basic theoretical framework developed in this book. It combines considerations of consequences, considerations of rights, and pragmatic considerations in accordance with the range hypothesis, in which the relative weight of these various types of considerations varies depending on the ethical problem being addressed. A central question in each case is, accordingly, What is the relative weight of the various considerations in this case?, not What rights are involved in this case?; What would bring about the greatest balance of desirable over undesirable consequences for all affected in this case?; or even What will work in this case? The answer to that central question may sometimes have to be worked out, through bargaining, negotiation, and some limited interaction with the proposed changes, by those affected.

THE SCOPE OF CONFLICTING INTERESTS

In the preceding discussion, we emphasized such things as conflicting values, principles, and interests. But what is the actual scope of these conflicts? To what extent are
they only surface conflicts, which will disappear once further circumstances are considered? In his Social Choice in the Development of Advanced Information Technology, Richard E. Walton takes the position that the actual scope of the conflicts is
narrower than one might suspect. He first describes some common consequences of
introducing microprocessors in offices: "If the technical system decreases skill requirements the meaning of work may become trivial, and a loss of motivation, status and
self-esteem may result." But some of those who lose motivation, status or self-esteem
counterattack the system. Walton also says, "If the system increases specialization
and separates the specialty from interdependent activities, then jobs may become
repetitive and isolated, and fail to provide workers with performance feedback." This,
he adds, produces alienation and conflict. Finally, "If the system increases routinization and provides elaborate measurements of work activity, job occupants may resent
the loss of autonomy and try to manipulate the measurement system."

Of course, this is not to say that all consequences of introducing new technology in
the workplace must be undesirable: "Technology *can* be guided by social policy, often
without sacrifice of its economic purpose. . . . sometimes the *unplanned* consequences
are positive." Walton mentions that sometimes more jobs turn out to be upgraded
than downgraded, that resulting work schedules may accommodate, rather than conflict with, human preferences, that new careers may be opened up, and that operators
may be brought closer to, rather than isolated more from, the end product. The two
main points he makes are that these consequences can be brought about by the
decisions of human beings and that they are often beneficial, rather than detrimental,
to the interests of business firms. Indeed, he indicates that the workers' loss of
motivation, status or self-esteem, their alienation and the conflicts that go with it, and
their resentment at their loss of autonomy in the workplace and concomitant attempts
at manipulating systems measuring their work activity constitute serious obstacles to
the efficient pursuit of business interests. New office information technology, Walton
states, "either can exacerbate the problem of white-collar disaffection or can be part
of the solution. Technology can either constrict human development or promote it."

Far as this approach may go toward dealing with the conflicts between firms and
their employees regarding whether and how to introduce a new technology in the
workplace, conflicts are likely to remain, and questions like those formulated above
still seem likely to retain some practical relevance, if only because the conflicts involved are not always simply—if at all—between interests, but are also, if not only,
conflicts of values, principles, ideals, obligations, and the like. Some of these can be
explored with the help of a further set of questions, prompted by the three readings
just discussed: What is the basis of the self-esteem people develop as a result of their
jobs? Is it merely the fact that they have a job? Is it, rather, the fact that they have a
job that takes skill to perform? Is it that their job takes skill to perform, and that no

technological device is likely to be introduced to do the same job because of lack of funds, despite the technological capability for producing it? Or do people develop such self-esteem only when their job takes skill and no technological device, given current trends in technological development, could be produced that could ever do the same job? In other words, is people's self-esteem based on the fact that they are not substitutable because the technology is not, nor likely to be, available to substitute for them? If it is available, then self-esteem will not be secured by any agreement guaranteeing that no such technology will be introduced; for so long as the technology is currently possible, it makes people, in principle, even if not in practice, substitutable. Having made this point, we can proceed to question the grounds on which people currently base their self-esteem and consider whether substitutability should make a difference. This is yet another line of inquiry the reader can puruse in subjecting these selections and discussions to critical scrutiny.

THE DISCUSSIONS SO FAR AND THE DISCUSSIONS AHEAD

Let us now turn to the remaining selections in this part and consider them in the light of the principles and moral considerations just discussed. Let us especially keep in mind the basic theoretical framework this book has so far developed in connection with controversies about the nature of current technological developments, the moral concerns they prompt, and the type of inquiry they motivate (Part I); about technology assessment status and methods (Part II); and about information technology in the first section of the current part. We have seen that these controversies and the problems they pose provide reasons for considering this framework central for dealing with the above contemporary moral controversies in technology. The further controversies and problems these pose, which will be addressed in the remainder of this book, provide reasons for considering this framework equally central in dealing with controversies in areas that range beyond those just mentioned, such as gene-splicing, energy, and space technology; it can also be applied to areas other than technology management.

In examining the selections and discussions that remain, it should be of help to keep in mind, for example, that the discussion of risk-cost-benefit analysis in Part II is informed by considerations of consequences which, whether the sole or main components of technology assessment, turn out to be utilitarian considerations. Similarly, it should be of help to bear in mind the central place of considerations of justice and rights in controversies concerning the compatibility of bringing microprocessors into the workplace with workers' self-esteem, dignity, and the rights this confers. Whether these considerations are the main or only ones considered in technology assessment, they are somewhat limited in that, as we have stated, they may prevent situations in which jobs and status might be threatened by new technology, but by themselves they are of little help when such a situation has developed and, with or without the new technology, jobs or their status are threatened. The theoretical framework we have developed does not reduce all or most relevant considerations to consequences or to rights, but includes the range hypothesis, according to which these, as well as pragmatic considerations, carry different weight depending on the moral problems addressed. Thus this framework is not only more sensitive than the alternatives to the variety characteristic of contemporary moral controversies in technology and the problems they pose, but is also closer to the various ways those involved in the controversies think about them and, consequently, more readily applicable than the alternatives to these controversies. Though the weight and scope of each consideration is not generally spelled out for every situation by the framework, it should help avoid exaggerations and omissions that could result from not considering all relevant types of considerations, and foster an awareness of the varying relevance and weight of the considerations, depending on the controversy addressed.

MORAL CONTROVERSIES IN GENE-SPLICING TECHNOLOGY

The second section in Part III begins with Development of the National Institutes of Health Guidelines for Recombinant DNA Research, by Bernard Talbot, who states: "The benefits of recombinant DNA research are already many; the risks remain hypothetical. . . . But because of concern about possible dangers of recombinant DNA molecules, scientists working in this field have from the beginning spearheaded discussions of safety." Talbot proceeds to describe the development of the NIH guidelines in response to the initial concerns and the subsequent recommendations of scientists and laymen. He mentions that "scientific support for the changes that have been made in the guidelines over time has come in part from risk assessment experiments supported by the NIH," and discusses throughout the guidelines with reference to the risks and benefits of recombinant DNA technology. This brings up the various issues in the risk-cost-benefit analysis controversy discussed in previous parts. It also raises a number of questions concerning ethical principles. Should risk-cost-benefit analysis be used as an exclusive criterion for assessing such activities as DNA research, thereby presupposing some form of utilitarianism? The discussion so far provides some reasons in support of a concern, though not of an exclusive concern, with consequences. The question just formulated would, then, appear to have a negative answer. A further question arising at this point, however, is whether any use of risk-cost-benefit analysis is compatible with considerations other than consequences and, if so, what this use is.

One such use might involve two steps: first, establishing, on the basis of the political process, of appeals to rights, or of a combination of these, what risks to life, health, or the environment ought not to be run; and second, using risk-cost-benefit analysis to establish what policy would be best within the constraints of the limits set in the first step.[7] Now, however morally acceptable any such approach might be, would it work without somehow reintroducing risk-cost-benefit analysis in the first stage? Would it be reliable? What should take precedence, reliability or a less precise political process informed by appeals to rights? What arrangement would be in accord with a morally acceptable balance between these various considerations, and what would this balance be?

Robert L. Sinsheimer, in his Genetic Engineering: Life as a Plaything, asks three questions about gene-splicing technology akin to those just formulated: "Is it safe, Is it wise, Is it moral?" In response to the question, "Is it safe?", his position is close to Talbot's so long as the short run is concerned: "If we can keep the developments open to public scrutiny, then I believe in the short-term it probably is." By contrast with Talbot, however, when the long run is concerned, Sinsheimer is hesitant to rely on the fact—if it is a fact—that the risks of gene-splicing technology remain hypothetical. He is concerned with the long-term consequences: "We cannot really predict whether our genetic tinkering might unwittingly lead to novel and unexpected hazards." This leads to the other two questions: Is genetic engineering technology wise? Is it moral? Sinsheimer does not answer these questions. He indicates, however, that in using such technology, human beings are commiting themselves "to assume responsibility for the structure and cohesion of the animate world," which "requires the continuous input of human intelligence," and that such a commitment might be unwise. He also poses the question of whether there is something morally objectionable in using a technology that may well weaken people's reverence for life, inadvertently preclude human creativity, change people's notion of what it is to be a human being or, at any rate, a human being free from defects, and even undermine all sense of human dignity and respect for human beings.

Sinsheimer's recurrent theme is that public scrutiny is central to protect "the larger view," which includes the various long-term concerns and the significant moral values just indicated. This theme is also present in David L. Bazelon's Governing Technology: Values, Choices, and Scientific Progress. In discussing policy-making problems, Bazelon argues that, since biotechnology policy decisions involve difficult value choices, public debate is needed to have "reason to hope that erroneous decisions can be changed in light of new information or changing preferences." Such a debate calls for "full disclosure of values and uncertainty," and though such disclosure would no doubt risk public misunderstanding and opposition, it would be grounded on "the right of the public to make basic value and risk choices." Whatever delays and other undesirable consequences such disclosure might lead to, Bazelon states that they are overriden by this public right.

Bazelon's position points back to the problems discussed in previous parts, especially to whether quality-of-life concerns can ever override people's freedoms in a free society and, if they can, what procedures ought to be followed in establishing what quality-of-life concerns override what freedoms. Should one only rely on the opinions of the experts to establish these? Should the concerns of the public be listened to in this process? Should representatives of the public also have decision-making power in the process? What will work, while also addressing considerations of rights and of consequences? Previous discussions in this book have indicated some reasons for not relying exclusively on expert advice. Though the discussions pointed to dialogue, bargaining, and negotiation as central elements in a sound consideration of consequences, rights, and their respective relevance and weight in certain cases, they have not, however, specified any details of the ways in which it would be justified to engage in them. This will be partially addressed in upcoming sections. But whatever the justified ways of relying on public, together with expert, advice turn out to be, the preceding discussion provides further support of our basic theoretical framework by indicating that not merely consequences, rights, or expedience, but a combination of all three is relevant, indeed essential in addressing moral controversies in gene-splicing technology.

MORAL CONTROVERSIES IN HEALTH CARE TECHNOLOGY

The problems just discussed are not peculiar to recombinant DNA technology. David Hellerstein, for example, addresses these issues in Overdosing on Medical Technology. He says, "We may soon face a day when all our hospitals will be filled with very ill people whose physical existence can be prolonged almost indefinitely but whose quality of life will be intolerable." To prevent this from coming about, he suggests instructing students in how to listen to patients' concerns, attempting to change the attitudes of physicians already out of school by holding "conferences . . . in which the questions of technological overkill are discussed concerning specific cases" and, first and foremost, instituting technology evaluation teams. He accordingly addresses the above-mentioned institutional problem of how to justify the combination of expert advice with public concerns in assessing and making decisions about the uses of technology. Hellerstein suggests that, in a health care setting, teams "could be composed of an internist, an intensive-care specialist, a psychiatrist, a nurse, and a few patient advocates." Just as with recombinant DNA technology, then, problems in health care technology have led to suggest that the public should have a say, as well as decision-making power, on what technology may or may not be used in specifiable circumstances.

Hellerstein realizes that "some doctors may perceive this kind of team as a threat to their own authority or as a potential source of embarrassment." The moral problem— indeed, the controversy—that arises about this centers around the following question: Should the experts' opinions be all that is relied upon in establishing whether to use available health care technology in given circumstances, or should the public have some say and even vote on the matter? The controversy regarding this question often involves implicit appeals to different moral considerations. The view that the public should have a voice and even vote on the matter is sometimes based simply on a concern with avoiding undesirable consequences for patients, coupled with a belief that only they or patients' advocates can be relied upon to establish what consequences are indeed undesirable for the patients.

At other times, however, those who favor bringing the public into the medical technology decision-making process do so out of a concern with the patients as persons, and thus deserving of respect, which requires giving significant weight to their wishes when deciding whether available technology ought to be used in treating them. By contrast with the former considerations of consequences, these are considerations of rights based on dignity and the respect it calls for. To this, one must add the pragmatic considerations of whether instituting such a team will work and how, once instituted, the team will affect the concerns of those involved with rights and consequences. What makes the latter two considerations pragmatic is primarily the fact that they can only be significantly addressed through the process of setting up the team and trying to make it work, and not beforehand. In order to address them beforehand, one would have to decide for the public and, as already stated, there are reasons not to do so.[8] The framework developed in this book for dealing with controversies that pose problems of this type is further strengthened by its relevance to the considerations involved in the above discussion for, by contrast with accounts that rely decisively on either consequences or rights, regardless of the problems posed, it makes room for assessing the relative weight of these various considerations, depending on the problem. The framework also reflects better the mixed considerations—pragmatic, rights, and consequences—that, to judge by the various selections in this book are characteristically appealed to by those involved in controversies.

Another issue that concerns the expanding use of medical technology is the rising cost of health care. This is addressed by H. David Banta, Anne Kesselman Burns, and Clyde J. Behney, in Policy Implications of the Diffusion and Control of Medical Technology. The authors' position is that "concerns about medical technology transcend the cost issue." As evidence by this, they mention the fact that "many felt that risks were not adequately considered when the benefits of a new technology were estimated by physicians and others." This is reminiscent of the concerns stated previously regarding the widespread use of recombinant DNA technology, and echoes also some of the concerns of David Hellerstein's "Overdosing on Medical Technology." Are they, however, well grounded? One of the authors' aims is to point to what research has shown about the soundness or lack of soundness of these concerns. They believe this research indicates that "acquisition of medical technology was more likely to result from the actions of hospital administrators and selected hospital-based or hospital-oriented physicians than by demands of patient-admitting community physicians."

A related issue in this article is the effectiveness of mechanisms in regulating medical technology adoption, and the wisdom of the policies that foster the use of such mechanisms. With respect to this, the authors discuss the 1974 National Health Planning and Health Resources Development Act, which was based on the requirement that institutions seek a certificate of need before they could make large capital investments. Banta, Kesselman Burns, and Behney also discuss programs to control cost increases. In summary, they state that "little basis can be found in the available literature for determining wise policy toward technology adoption." Besides this shortage of information on setting incentives that will positively affect technology use, the authors mention other factors affecting the current use of medical technology: "(1)decision making . . . is scattered among thousands of individual physicians, health policymakers, and other individuals; (2)the effects of any changes . . . in the adoption and especially in the use of medical technology will benefit some of parties at interest and will harm others; and (3)there is shortage of information on medical technology's benefits, risks, and costs. . . ." They state that clinical and policy decisions are appropriately based on a large number of factors, many of which are more important than analytical results; but that a greater and more sensitive use of assessment results might in some situations help in making better decisions. This, again, raises questions about the proper role of risk-cost-benefit analysis in reaching such decisions. Should it have any? If so, what should it be? Questions also arise about the proper way of dealing with the conflicting factors involved in medical technology policy making. What form of public participation should it involve?

WILLINGNESS TO PAY, WILLINGNESS TO SELL, AND RIGHTS

The issue of whether risk-cost-benefit analysis should have any role in technology policy decisions concerning health care leads us to question whether its risks, costs, and benefits can be reliably measured and, if so, how. In his Measuring Elusive Benefits: On the Value of Health, John Mendeloff outlines ways of measuring risks, costs, and benefits that, he argues, are needed by policy makers dealing with matters of health care. He takes a more favorable position toward the use of risk-cost-benefit analysis in medical technology policy making than do the authors of the previous article.

> Skeptics may reasonably caution that analysts tend to oversell the contribution that quantitative analysis can make. But while critics of mindless quantification do not lack ammunition, it is at least as easy to be mindless without looking at the numbers. Whatever methodology, policymakers do need information and tools that will allow them to consider more explicitly, either quantitatively or qualitatively, what it is that people value about their programs, and how their worthwhileness can be assessed.

Mendeloff certainly does not hold that risk-cost-benefit analysis is, by itself, sufficient for reaching decisions. He knows that "analysts have frequently posed issues as if they could be resolved in a cost-effectiveness framework, when, in fact, they cannot." He argues, however, that valuation is inevitable and that the unavoidable question is what and how to value.

Searching for a method for finding a reliable answer to this question, he says, "We can start by construing the valuation problem in terms of three questions: (1) What factors should influence the valuation? (2) How much should each factor influence it? (3) From what benchmark should these variations be measured?" He answers these questions by outlining a survey strategy and the need for "multiple approaches, including more studies of willingness to pay." Mendeloff, however, has no objections to the willingness-to-pay criterion. His only concern is what questions should be included in the suggested survey in order to "really tap how much individuals would be willing to pay."

This, however, raises a moral problem. For the question arises, Is willingness to pay the morally or even logically appropriate criterion to apply when dealing with matters of health? Some have argued that it is not, because it places those whose opinions are used in determining what individuals would be willing to pay in order to prevent a certain health risk in the role of mere consumers.[9] Instead, the argument goes, the question should place them in a different role, say, that of a citizen or of a trustee of one's own and others' health, and of all other things that matter in people's lives. The questions to ask should, accordingly, aim to determine, not what individuals would be willing to pay for their health, but what they would exchange their health for. It should be added that, at least when others' or everyone's health is concerned, the questions should attempt to determine what the individuals *as trustees* would exchange it for. This would not demean people by treating them merely as consumers, ruled solely by self-interest and price. It would also treat them as persons—indeed, as persons with features that qualify them to be entrusted with the interest of others and of the public at large.

This argument points back to considerations of dignity, respect, and rights. It also provides a further starting point for a critical scrutiny of the principle of utility, which, some argue, involves thinking of everyone as a consumer—an exaggeration with undesirable consequences, such as preventing sensitivity in the handling of problems and controversies the principle is supposed to help resolve in a sound and sensitive way. One might add that the opposite exaggeration, not considering persons as consumers under any circumstances, also leads to undesirable consequences of the same type. The *mixed* approach we have developed, however, is free from such consequences. But the criterion used in developing surveys that might be helpful in employing a mixed approach should not be willingness to pay in matters of health and the environment, but one that places people in a role such as of trustees, not of consumers. One such criterion is the willingness to sell, outlined above, which could be used to introduce more precision in the first step of the procedure outlined previously, in discussing moral controversies in gene-splicing technology. It could do this because it is based on considerations of rights, it can be used in the political process, and it introduces constraints on the scope of the risk-cost-benefit analyses used in assessing alternative policies, which would not then be evaluated in terms of imaginary bids between consumers.[10]

MORAL CONTROVERSIES IN SPACE TECHNOLOGY

A concern with treating persons as persons, rather than as objects, or as trustworthy moral agents rather than as merely self-interested individuals is perhaps nowhere harder to come by than when matters of space technology are involved. This is reflected by the selections on this topic. The first, The New Arms Race: Star War Weapons, is a briefing paper by the Union of Concerned Scientists. It describes various proposals for using directed energy for defensive purposes and points to problems in the defense system envisioned. The most threatening of these may well be that, since the ABM weapons envisioned would have only a few minutes to identify the target and execute an attack, "human participation would be eliminated from the process." The decision to attack would be delegated entirely to machines.

Other objections raised against the development and deployment of said defensive systems are that they would lead to a massive buildup of offensive, as well as defensive, weapons by both the United States and the USSR, that it would be highly destabilizing, that it would violate the U.S.–USSR 1972 treaty, which explicitly outlawed ABM systems of the type currently being explored by the United States, and that it would be tremendously expensive. At least on the surface, these are all considerations of consequences.

As regards the legal consequences, The Militarization of Space and International Law, by Allan Rosas, points out that the 1972 U.S.–USSR ABM treaty, the only bilateral treaty formally in force, defines ABM systems in a way that

> is not unequivocal, as the description of an ABM system ("a system to counter strategic ballistic missiles or their elements in flight trajectory") is followed by a reference to the fact that such systems are "currently consisting of" ABM interceptor "missiles," ABM launchers and ABM radars (article II). While this wording suggests that directed-energy weapons *are* included in the prohibition, the matter is somewhat complicated by an Agreed Interpretation stating that the two parties agree that in the event ABM systems based on other physical principles are created in the future, specific limitations on such systems and their components would be subject to consultations.

Rosas, however, argues that the official U.S. position, which appears to be that directed-energy weapons, too, are included, is the correct one; but that even with this interpretation, the treaty does not preclude fixed ground-based ABM systems or the development and testing of directed-energy or other weapons systems intended, for example, as anti-satellite (ANSAT) systems. Further, it is not clear whether the treaty's prohibition of air-based and space-based ABM systems includes research.

Rosas summarizes various initiatives and attempts at demilitarizing outer space, and argues that disarmament is possible, that it is urgent not only for the sake of curbing the arms race in a new environment, but also because of the risk that the militarization of outer space will upset the strategic balance between the two powers. What has been, and should not be, disregarded is common security, not simply the international law in force.

Rosas's article points to a lack of political will to demilitarize outer space. The article by the Union of Concerned Scientists states that the only hope for a lasting and durable peace between the superpowers is persistent arms control that builds on the successful negotiations of the past. What is stopping such developments? In response to this question, Rosas mentions that, in his testimony before a subcommittee of the U.S. Senate on May 18, 1983, Kenneth L. Adelman, Director of the Arms Control and Disarmament Agency, spoke of a dilemma facing the U.S. administration: it must "balance the desire to limit threats to U.S. satellites against the desire to be able to take actions against Soviet satellites that could cost American lives in situations far short of all-out war." The question likely to arise is whether any such situations can remain stable and not develop rapidly into all-out war; and further, whether they should be given the significance that is attributed to them. The discussion appears to center around the risks and threats to common security, which are considerations of consequences, perhaps not even utilitarian but, rather, belonging to the principle of ethical sectarianism discussed at the beginning of Part III.

Should the above discussion include any other approach? Are any of the considerations relevant to the militarization of space moral? What reference group's common security is morally relevant here: The United States? The United States and its allies? The nations of the earth? What, if any, are the minimum conditions for establishing the relevance of moral discourse to policy and decision-making problems such as the militarization of space and the arms race? These are some of the questions that might prove useful in dealing with contemporary moral controversies in space technology. The theoretical framework in this book, which involves considerations of consequences, rights, and pragmatic considerations, leaves room for the possibility that, in some situations, mostly or only rights, consequences, or pragmatic considerations may be decisive. This is not incompatible with the possibility that only considerations of consequences may be morally significant in the case of the militarization of space.[11] What it does, however, rule out is a sectarian concern with just the United States, or the Soviet Union, or any one block, so long as there is room for meaningful dialogue and controversy, and the openness to reason, however heated, has not turned into sheer confrontation involving mostly a conflict of wills between the powers involved. At this point, at least one of the minumum conditions for the relevance of moral discourse, the dialogue, which makes bargaining and negotiation possible, would begin to be threatened. This threat, plus the fact that the impossibility of negotiation offers little but the prospect of disaster for all, provides a reason for reestablishing a dialogue if it should break down, and to preserve it if it is still being carried out, regardless of how heated it or the controversy may be.

The third article in this section, Space Commercialization, by the National Science Foundation, lists the possibilities in space commercialization and raises the various issues and choices concerned. It explains that the federal role will be of critical importance for any significant commercial development of space, and points to the conflicting context within which commercialization must be pursued. This context, made painfully clear by the 1986 Challenger space shuttle accident, is constituted by the main objectives of the U.S. space program: to maintain U.S. world leadership for security and economic purposes, together with the pursuit and support of a workable research program in order to attain these objectives. One question that arises here is whether, and how, both objectives are mutually compatible, and compatible with the moral values predominant in the United States. Even if they are compatible, are there any moral reasons why one objective should be given priority over the other, or why yet other objectives should be given priority over both objectives of the U.S. space program? A helpful approach to dealing critically with these questions might be to compare the U.S. space program objectives with the objectives of a somewhat analogous program: the U.S. energy program, and its role in shaping nuclear energy development. This task, however, is beyond the scope of this work, which will deal, in the next section, simply with energy technology controversies in their current form. What the theoretical framework of this book would indicate, however, is that the above objectives must be pursued in accordance with the need for dialogue because of the disastrous collective consequences a breakdown is likely to cause. This is one case in which collective consequences have significant weight and, indeed, support the preservation of conditions under which moral discourse is viable or, if they are not present, make their development imperative. In other words, here collective consequences constitute relevant reasons of weight even when moral discourse has broken down. However, when the conditions under which *moral* discourse is viable break down, considerations such as rights, and of a fair distribution of consequences have no weight, since they are relevant only when conditions under which moral discourse is viable are present.[12]

MORAL CONTROVERSIES IN ENERGY TECHNOLOGY

The first selection in this section is Better Energy Security, by Amory B. Lovins and L. Hunter Lovins. The authors argue that most U.S. energy systems, which are highly centralized and complex, are, by the same token, highly vulnerable, and therefore pose a "growing threat to American prosperity, liberties, and even lives." They also argue that there is an alternative that is cheapest, best for jobs and the environment, and also capable of resilience. This is efficient energy use, with more diverse, dispersed, and renewable energy resources, such as wind-powered generators and even local gas turbines. The authors report that these are already being tried by a great number of individuals and communities and that, as a result, "since 1979 the U.S. has gotten more than a hundred times as much energy from savings as from expanded supplies, and more new supply from renewables than from any or all nonrenewables."

This position is supported in the second selection, The Trouble with Fusion, by Lawrence M. Lidsky. The author, who has worked on plasma physics and fusion-reactor technology for 20 years, is professor of nuclear engineering at M.I.T., Associate Director of the Plasma Fusion Center, and editor of the *Journal of Fusion Energy*. He sets the tone for his article with the following introductory statements:

> The technically advanced nations of the world will spend over $1 billion this year in the quest for controlled thermonuclear fusion power. . . . Now the solution of the scientific problem appears to be almost within our grasp, and many assume that with it will come . . . virtually unlimited, environmentally safe energy. But that outcome is unlikely. Instead, the costly fusion reactor is in danger of joining the ranks of other technical "triumphs" such as the zeppelin, the supersonic transport, and the fission breeder reactor that turned out to be unwanted and unused.

Lidsky compares fusion, as currently pursued, with fission, and concludes that fusion fares poorly in comparison because of the much higher percentage of fusion energy released in neutrons, which travel much further than most fission products. Also, the significant radioactivity resulting from fusion would create problems of complexity, reliability, and size, and could easily be used to manufacture atomic weapon materials. The high radioactivity resulting from fission, by contrast, would involve problems and dangers of a lesser magnitude, including "problems of disposal and reactor safety" that, Lidsky thinks, will be eventually solved. His suggestion is to attempt to develop neutron-free fusion: "We have no guarantee that an answer exists. But we know that if it does, it can meet the original goal of the fusion program— universally available, inexhaustible, environmentally benign power." This solution would, if successful, address some of the concerns raised by Amory B. Lovins and L. Hunter Lovins. It is questionable, however, that it would address the concern with vulnerability that is tied to the centralization of energy production in the United States, or the concern for jobs. At any rate, both selections discuss energy production mainly by reference to the consequences of producing it in one way or another.

But are any considerations other than consequences relevant? A person prone to emphasizing the role of individual rights in assessing alternative technologies might think so. Indeed, such a person might appeal to rights, arguing that centralized energy production would not simply be highly vulnerable but, more important, would unjustifiably limit the choice that persons, *as persons,* are entitled to. These limitations could range from the market choices for individual energy use to an individual's ability to change this situation by concentrating energy production in the hands of a corporate sector, namely, the power companies. Do individuals have the right to be free from such limitations and, if so, in what circumstances and to what extent do these rights override considerations of consequences? In pursuing this question, the reader might find it fruitful to use the willingness-to-sell criterion as a constituent of the theoretical framework developed for dealing with contemporary moral controversies in technology.

Lidsky's selection mentions the connection between fusion energy production technology and nuclear arms. This connection is no doubt worthy of critical attention. Does it make fusion technology morally objectionable? If so, why? Is it simply because nuclear arms themselves are morally objectionable, or is the technology objectionable because it would facilitate the proliferation of nuclear arms and their use by a wider number of states, and even by terrorists? Robert P. Churchill's discussion of Nuclear Arms as a Philosophical and Moral Issue may help us in dealing with some of the above questions. He asks, "Given quite reasonable beliefs in the need for self-defense against an adversary with nuclear arms, what is the moral justification for threatening to use our nuclear weapons to deter him from aggression?" In addressing this question, Churchill discusses the theory of just war, according to which, "if it is necessary for a nation's leaders to threaten annihilation in order to protect innocent civilians from unjust attacks, then it is morally obligatory that this threat be made." He argues that, in the case of nuclear deterrence, this theory leads to a moral dilemma in that what is wrong to do is also wrong to threaten; also, counterforce deterrence, that is, the targeting of strategic nuclear weapons only against nuclear installations, conventional military bases, and isolated economic objectives instead of against population centers will not do away with the dilemma. Churchill further dismisses the defensive systems previously discussed in this section on the grounds that they would be destabilizing and would not be capable of eliminating the strategic need for at least some offensive systems, which is what they are meant to eliminate entirely.

The alternative Churchill offers is nonviolent self-defense, which would seek to deter aggression by making it clear that the social life of the unarmed nation could not be controlled if an invasion were to take place because of the civilian resistance that would develop. He states that those who oppose it should try to show the moral inadequacy of civilian resistance. Here, it might be useful to pursue the question of whether civilian resistance would work even if the potential invader had no interest in preserving the unarmed nation or even its territory, but only in getting the enemy out of its political and economic way. In any case, significant considerations in assessing this suggestion are pragmatic: Will nonviolent self-defense work? In what type of country will it work? Are the risks it involves overridden by the dilemma Churchill points out? Other considerations have to do with consequences: Is nonviolent self-defense any less likely to be destabilizing than the alternatives? If not, and if the dilemma Churchill describes is indeed a dilemma and not just an apparent one, this would provide a further reason to attempt to approach the controversy through dialogue, and to resolve it as soon as possible. For if, as the dilemma indicates, policy makers dealing with the nuclear arms race are caught in a moral inconsistency, it may simply be a sign that, at the international level—the context in which these policy makers must deal with the arms race—the role of reason, and thus of moral discourse, becomes irrelevant. If such, indeed, is the situation, then whatever the remaining role of reason and moral discourse at other levels turns out to be, they cannot but enjoin actions aimed at creating conditions in which reason and moral discourse would be relevant.

MORAL CONTROVERSIES IN MATERIALS TECHNOLOGY

The matters of controversy addressed in this section's selections are in part related to those discussed in the preceding sections. Radioactive wastes and the policy problems they pose are the subject of I. Peterson's Radwaste Program: A Delay in Plans, and are closely related to the issues of energy production technologies previously discussed. Some of the consequences of war are dealt with in Janet Raloff's Agent Orange: What Isn't Settled. These consequences, however, do not concern nuclear weapons use but the military use of toxic substances and the effects of exposure to those chemicals on the troops and even the children of the troops who were supposed to be helped by these chemicals.

By contrast with these two selections, John P. Mascotte's Technology and the Environment. Who Pays the Piper? is about the issues of materials such as asbestos, which harm human health or the environment, and have been widely used for non-military purposes. Mascotte thinks the twenty-first century's leading public health problem will be environmental accidents and disease, and he holds that this problem cannot simply be addressed through the courts, letting victims sue for punitive damages on the basis of strict liability criteria. He suggests that meritorious victims should be quickly and fairly compensated by disbursing available payments from a voluntary fund created by congressional action as well as through negotiated contributions from manufacturers, suppliers, installers, their insurance companies, and possibly the federal government. This position raises a number of questions about strict liability in particular, and the purposes and limits of the law in general. Is one purpose of the law to ensure compensation to victims of technological products manufactured in accordance with all applicable standards existing at the time of manufacture? If so, who should compensate the victims? Should manufacturers be required to compensate the victims even if the deleterious effects of the products were unforeseen and unforeseeable at the time of manufacture; if they exercised due care in trying to establish the products' safety, even going beyond the required standards? Would this be a morally justified way of correcting unintended and unforeseen misfortunes? What should be done when various manufacturers are known to have unintentionally and unforeseeably introduced a product that, say, 10 years later harmed a number of people; when it is not possible to trace the particular manufacturer that sold the item that has harmed a victim seeking compensatory damages? Is a policy that would hold any one of the manufacturers liable under such circumstances morally justified?

These questions may or may not apply to the asbestos industry, but they do to a significant number of cases in which manufactured materials or the consequences of their manufacture unforeseeably turned out to have deleterious effects on human health. This makes them pertinent to problems of technology policy. Should the morally justified policies in such situations be like those described above, that is, regulatory, involving at least an element of coercion rather than simple governmental intervention as in policies involving subsidies or tax breaks? Is, for example, the alternative Mascotte suggests morally more defensible? Why or why not? This leads to a further question, informing the whole book: What should be done about matters of technology policy, such as those discussed in this part and, indeed, throughout, given the existence of controversy and even outright confrontation about them? Our theoretical framework is intended to help address this question in a manner sensitive to the whole range of problems posed by such moral controversies and confrontations; it may also help establish the relative weights of consequences, rights, and pragmatic considerations for each problem. Pragmatic considerations may, for example, advise negotiation in dealing with some of the above environmental controversies. The above question will be addressed further, especially in Part VI, Governing Technology: Morally Assessing Aproaches to Technology Policy Making.

NOTES

1. *The Random House Dictionary of the English Language,* ed. Jess Stein et al. (New York: Random House, 1970), p. 870.

2. For a related discussion of tests of an ethical theory, see Marcus G. Singer, *Generalization in Ethics* (New York: Atheneum, 1961), p. 8.

3. These criteria are not unlike those used in branches of inquiry other than ethics.

4. For a discussion of a nonpredominant version of utilitarianism that is more defensible than the predominant ones discussed here, see *Ethics in the World of Business* ed. David Braybrooke, (Totowa, NJ: Rowman & Allanheld, 1983), especially pp. 55–56 and 480.

5. This is similar to Braybrooke's position (p. 199).

6. This is the other side of the first point. It is also made by Braybrooke, who does not, however, appear to give bargaining and negotiation the central role they have in the theoretical framework developed here. For a short but insightful discussion of bargaining, negotiation, and related procedures for dealing with conflicts, see Brian Barry, "An Outline of Social Decision Procedures," *Political Argument* (New York: Routledge & Kegan Paul, 1965), pp. 85–91. For an excellent discussion of the role of interaction in social problem solving, see Charles E. Lindblom and David K. Cohen, *Usable Knowledge* (New Haven: Yale U.P., 1979), pp. 19–29.

7. For a discussion of this use of risk-cost-benefit analysis, see M. Baran, "Cost-Benefit Analysis: An Inadequate Basis for Health, Safety and Environmental Regulatory Decision Making," *Ecological Law Quarterly* 8 (1980), p. 443.

8. Section II, introductory section.

9. This point is made by Mark Sagoff, in "At the Shrine of Our Lady of Fatima, or Why Political Questions Are Not All Economic," *Ethics and the Environment,* ed. Donald Scherer and Thomas Attig (Englewood Cliffs, NJ: Prentice-Hall, 1983), p. 223.

10. The willingness-to-sell criterion is used here not simply to refer to what anyone would sell something for. It refers to what a *trustee* of that thing would be willing to sell it for when acting within the requirements of the role of trustee. This point is not, or not clearly, made in the otherwise excellent discussion of willingness to pay and alternative criteria by Mark Sagoff, "Ethics and Economics in Environmental Law," *Earthbound,* ed. Tom Regan (New York: Random House, 1984), pp. 147–178.

11. This point is akin to Virginia Held's contrast between the suitability of deontological and teleological frameworks for different types of moral problems. See Virginia Held, "*The Political 'Testing' of Moral Theories,*" *Midwest Studies in Philosophy,* ed. Peter A. French et al. (Minneapolis: University of Minnesota, 1982), 7, pp. 356–357.

12. The position here is not unlike that of Thomas Hobbes on justice in a state of nature. For a useful account of this position, see Kurt Baier, "The Supremacy of Moral Reasons," *The Moral Pont of View* (New York: Random House, 1965), chap. VII, sect. 3, pp. 148–157(abridged edition). See also Singer, "State of Nature Situations," pp. 152–161.

8

The Future of Work: Does It Belong to Us or to the Robots?

SAR A. LEVITAN AND CLIFFORD M. JOHNSON

The authors' position is that it is unlikely that the use of robots and microprocessors in the workplace will lead to unemployment. They hold that supply and demand will slow down the pace of innovation because, first, capital-intensive industries have huge investments in existing facilities and their wholesale replacement would be prohibitive; second, the rate at which such replacement can take place is limited by the time it takes to gather the funds necessary; and finally, innovations will be resisted by both consumers and workers.

Today, futurists are discussing the onset of a sweeping technological revolution, one which would rival or surpass the Industrial Revolution of the 19th century in importance. This envisioned social order has been given many names—"postindustrial," "technetronic," or "information society." At the center of this flurry of interest in technological change is the microprocessor. While computerized automation has been theoretically feasible for more than a decade, large and expensive computer systems could produce cost savings only in the most massive industrial settings, and automated machinery could not be easily adapted to serve various production functions. Now, with the development of the microprocessor, these obstacles have been overcome and the potential uses of computerized machinery at the workplace have dramatically increased.

Microprocessor technology is best symbolized by the silicon chip, a miniaturized system of integrated circuits which can direct electrical current and, thereby, generate vast computational power. A silicon chip the size of one square centimeter can perform millions of multiplications per second, and has the capacity to store the texts of the Declaration of Independence, the Constitution, and a few chapters of the Federalist Papers. Technological advances are expected to result in at least a fourfold expansion of these capabilities within a decade, so that the microprocessors of the future will be extremely powerful computers on a single silicon chip or combination of chips. The reduction in size is astounding—today's hand-held programmable calculators have more computational power than the first full-scale computers built during World War

Reprinted from *Monthly Labor Review* 105 (September 1982), pp. 10–14. The *Monthly Labor Review* is a publication of the U.S. Department of Labor Statistics. Adapted from *Second Thoughts About Work* (Kalamazoo, Mich.: W. E. Upjohn Institute for Employment Research, 1982) and reprinted by permission.

II, computers which could have been "hand held" only by juggling 18,000 different vacuum tubes.

This miniaturization of computer technology is particularly important because it has been accompanied by dramatic cost reductions, making microprocessors economically competitive in a wide range of industrial applications. Once designed, silicon chips can be mass produced at a very low cost, and even further price declines are anticipated as volumes rise. As a result, a calculation which cost 80 cents to perform in the early 1950's costs less than one cent today, after adjusting for inflation. The combined reductions in size and cost of microprocessor technology have triggered renewed interest in prospects for automation and in the broader possibility of a wholesale transformation of modern society driven by these new technological capabilities.

The silicon chip is particularly important to economical automation because it provides the basis for fully integrating computer and machine. In industrial settings, the microprocessor makes possible the development of manufacturing machinery with unique adaptability. The great majority—at least 75 percent—of all manufactured goods fall into the category of shorter, lower-volume production runs, with only the most basic industries continuing to fit the mass-production stereotype. Technological advances in microelectronics, therefore, were an essential precondition to widespread automation, and the expanding use of reprogrammable machinery has triggered today's intense debate regarding the future of industrialized societies.

The potential impact of microprocessors is heightened by their seemingly endless number of applications. This new technology promises to alter not only the factory, but the office as well. Sophisticated word processors and computerized information storage and retrieval systems are becoming increasingly cost-effective, and because this new technology does not require knowledge of specialized computer languages, their growing use may raise traditionally low productivity among office workers. These office innovations are considered qualitatively different

from previous office equipment which "mechanized" or "automated" routine tasks. While memory typewriters made an office worker's tasks easier, emerging computer technologies may change the means by which information is transcribed and made available to others. Again, only with the silicon chip has this decentralized use of computer technology at an affordable cost become possible.

"ROBOT REVOLUTION" COMING

The use of the microprocessor to automate production functions is epitomized by the development of the robot. Prior to the last decade, robots were confined to the domain of children's stories and science fiction—their practical and efficient application in work settings was virtually inconceivable given the state of computer technology. The silicon chip has thrust robots from fantasy to reality, and the technology is being pursued with remarkable speed and vigor. A number of top computer companies are now considering entry into the robot market, and several large U.S. corporations have made commitments to purchase robots which are already available. The use of robots in manufacturing has nearly quadrupled between 1979 and 1981, and most analysts expect the sales curve to shoot higher during the next few years.[1] Most importantly, microprocessors seem to be in a prime position for the implementation of "learning curve pricing" strategies in which firms lower prices in anticipation of rising volumes and declining unit costs. The entry of large computer companies into the robot market could ensure this aggressive marketing stance and trigger a sharp rise in robot sales by 1990.

Today's robots bear little resemblance to the creations of screenplay writers and science fiction authors. Rather than some form of mechanical humanoid, industrial robots are characterized by mechanical arms linked to reprogrammable computers. An exact definition of a robot, as distinct from other automated machinery, eludes even industry representatives. The Robot Institute of America, an industrial trade group, stresses that it is the "reprogrammable and multifunctional" character of the robots which is unique, allowing them to perform a variety of tasks.[2] And the emerging versions of robots are varied—the more extravagant include a "bureaucratic robot" which stamps signatures on letters, a robot "nurse" to assist handicapped persons in wheelchairs, a robot "janitor and guard dog" for the home, and "talking robots" which would advertise products or give job training to illiterates. Microprocessors are revolutionizing design methods for the development of new manufactured goods, and have become an integral part of nearly all modern research equipment so as to expedite lengthy data analysis.[3] Innovations such as voice-sensitive computers which can directly transcribe dictation into written text may be marketable within just a few years. It is this diversity of applications for microprocessor technology which distinguishes it from less significant innovations, and which has led futurists to predict a societal transformation "comparable with the agricultural revolution that began about 10,000 years ago, and with the industrial revolution."[4]

HOW FAR . . .

There is little consensus as to where the "robot revolution" is heading and how far it will go. The technology itself may be refined to such an extent that most factory work could be carried out by robots and automated machinery. For example, a study conducted at Carnegie-Mellon University asserts that the current generation of robots has the technical capability to perform nearly 7 million existing factory jobs—one-third of all manufacturing employment—and that sometime after 1990, it will become technically possible to replace all manufacturing operatives in the automotive, electrical-equipment, machinery, and fabricated-metals industries.[5] Yet these theoretical estimates of the potential for automation, which reach as high as 65 to 75 percent of the factory work force, do not reflect the rate at which the new technology will actually be introduced to the workplace. The pace of innovation will depend on

the relative costs of labor and computerized technologies, as well as on broader levels of supply and demand for goods and services. Predictions of this nature are infinitely more difficult than abstract assessments of future technological capabilities.

The automobile industry offers an interesting case study, because it is probably the first manufacturing industry to aggressively pursue the use of robots in automated processes. The push toward automation in the auto industry is a response to both rising labor costs and growing concerns for quality control and competitiveness in international markets. Auto manufacturers already find it possible to operate robots for $6 per hour, well below the $20 per hour required for the pay and benefits of a skilled worker in 1981.[6] General Motors, aware of the growing use of robots by Japanese auto makers, predicts that by 1987, 90 percent of all its new capital investments will be in computer-controlled machines.[7] A 1980 survey conducted by the American Society of Manufacturing Engineers predicted that robots will replace 20 percent of existing jobs in the auto industry by 1985, and that 50 percent of autombilie assembly will be done by automated machines (including robots) by 1995.[8] Even the United Auto Workers anticipates a 20-percent decline in membership by 1990 and has successfully obtained advance notice and retraining rights from auto manufacturers in a growing effort to gain protection from sweeping automation. Yet, few of these estimates include any consideration of the extent to which capital shortages confronting robot manufacturers and purchasers may limit the speed with which the new technology is adopted.

Projections of the impact of microprocessors on office employment are even more problematic, with analysts more frequently predicting the number of office jobs "affected" rather than eliminated by automation. The Carnagie-Mellon study argued that 38 million of 50 million existing white-collar jobs would eventually be affected by automation, while a vice president for strategic planning for Xerox Corp. offered the more conservative guess of 20 to 30 million jobs affected by

1990.[9] There is a general agreement that office technologies will be changing rapidly, but little indication of whether the result will be reduced office employment, shifts in future employment growth, or simply higher levels of productivity in white-collar settings.

A 1982 study prepared for the International Labour Office found that microelectronic technology has not caused widespread displacement of office workers, but perhaps only because of the impact of poor economic conditions on the rate of diffusion of the new technology in office settings. Selected case studies of the banking and insurance industries suggested that new job opportunities were being created, but the skills made redundant by new technologies were generally inappropriate for those emerging opportunities. The report stressed that this trend poses special threats to employment prospects for women, and called for additional education and training efforts to close the "skill gap" caused by the use of microprocessors in office jobs.[10]

Perhaps the greatest fears that automation will lead to widespread unemployment have been voiced, not in the United States, but in Western Europe. For example, two British authors have predicted nothing short of the collapse of work as a social institution in an era of microprocessors:[11]

It is impossible to overdramatize the forthcoming crisis as it potentially strikes a blow at the very core of industrialized societies—the work ethic. We have based our social structures on this ethic and now it would appear that it is to become redundant along with millions of other people.

In West Germany, studies of the impact of automation on future employment levels commissioned by the Bonn government projected that the number of jobs in 1990 will at best be marginally above 1977 levels—a pessimistic view in light of anticipated population growth. The issue of technology induced unemployment increasingly is capturing the attention of West European leaders, and unions in Italy, Germany, and elsewhere are responding with demands for shorter workweeks to protect employment levels. Perennial fears that ma-

chines would replace workers have never been fulfilled, but European futurists insist that it will be different this time.

. . . AND HOW FAST?

While the impact of automation in the past has been offset by the emergence of new industries and by growth in the service sector of the economy, these avenues for employment growth may indeed be less open in an era of microprocessors. The electronics industry, which supports this computerized technology, certainly will experience rapid growth in the coming decade, but a 1979 survey of the world electronics industry prepared for the Organization for Economic Cooperation and Development revealed that the internal use of its own technology will keep employment growth in this sector to a minimum.[12] It is this "reproductive" potential of computerized technology—the prospect of robots building robots—which challenges traditional patterns of employment growth through new industries. And to the extent that the microprocessor will affect service as well as manufacturing industries, even the recent trend of expanding service employment may fail to provide jobs.

In spite of these relatively unique characteristics of microprocessor applications, predictions of immediate and massive job losses tend to ignore the market forces which slow the pace of technological change. As stressed in recent research by the Bureau of Labor Statistics, many factors limit the speed of diffusion of technological change and thereby mitigate possible employment implications. The size of required investment, the rate of capacity utilization and the institutional arrangements within industries all can act as "economic governors" which slow the adoption of automated technologies.[13]

Virtually all capital-intensive industries have a massive investment in existing plant facilities, and they cannot afford to squander these resources through the wholesale replacement of working machinery. More importantly, the financial constraints on capital formation necessarily limit the rate at which new technologies are introduced. In this context, Joseph Engleberger, president of Unimation, Inc. (the Nation's largest robot manufacturer), has dismissed predictions of galloping automation, noting that even the replacement of 5 percent of all blue-collar workers in Western industrialized nations would require investments totaling $3 billion in each of the next 40 years.[14] While microprocessor technology may be promising in its flexibility and potential efficiency, industries must be able to afford the new acquisitions in order to use them.

A less tangible but perhaps equally important force limiting the expansion of computer technology lies in the attitudes of both workers and consumers. While a computer may be able to diagnose medical problems, its bedside manner may be less than comforting. Similarly, word processors and telephone answering systems may alter clerical roles, but most executives will not want to forgo the convenience offered by their personal secretaries. People can hear the best music in the comfort of their homes, but flock to concert halls to hear lesser performances. Even on the assembly line, where robots may be perfectly suited for production processes, the aversion of managers and workers to such unfamiliar companions may hamper their smooth and rapid assimilation at the workplace. These psychological barriers cannot be factored into equations of economic efficiency, but they are likely to slow the pace of technological change nonetheless.

WILL WORKERS BECOME OBSOLETE?

The picture which emerges when the functioning of capital markets and work organizations is considered is one of evolutionary rather than revolutionary change. With annual sales of robots well below 10,000 in a labor force of more than 100 million, it will be some time before computerized technologies make a major dent in aggregate employment levels. This perspective is emphasized by Robotics International, a professional group which polled 100 users and manufacturers of robots. Based on the responses, the group concluded that robots are likely to replace 440,000 rather than a million workers by 1990, and that all but 5 percent of the displaced workers would be retained rather than dismissed.[15] The relative lack of union concern in the United States over aggregate job losses through automation also stems from this belief that the pace of innovation has been exaggerated. William Winpisinger, president of the International Association of Machinists, has argued that the replacement of human skills with computerized machinery will occur slowly and that a shortage of skilled workers will remain our most pressing manpower problem.[16] No doubt, unions will continue to seek guarantees of job security in some industries, and collective bargaining may gradually extend to include management investment decisions.

In the more distant future, no one can be sure where new employment growth will occur. Expectations of a workless society still linger; as described in one forecast.[17]

Earning a living may no longer be a necessity but a privilege; services may have to be protected from automation, and given certain social status; leisure time activities may have to be invented in order to give new meaning to a mode of life that may have become economically useless for a majority of the populace.

The literature in recent decades has been replete with speculations on how people would cope with the loss of meaningful work roles, or how society would allocate and distribute wealth in the absence of strong ties between work and income.[18] Even for those who reject such forebodings, the belief in continued employment growth admittedly contains as much faith as foresight.

Still, there seems little likelihood that the worker will become obsolete in the foreseeable future. In one sense, past waves of automation have created dislocation, but it has been distributed throughout the labor force in the form of benefits and social progress—shorter workweeks, more vacation time, longer training and education, earlier retirement, child labor laws, and welfare and unemployment payments. We can expect this trend to continue, particularly as labor seeks assurances of job security. Assuming a healthy rate of economic growth during a period of innovation and increasing automation, it is also likely that levels of aggregate demand will support the emergence of new goods and services. Rising expectations alone will cause Americans to translate productivity gains into higher standards of living instead of less work, a pattern which has held for centuries. The period of adjustment which lies ahead may not be painless, but it seems that work is here to stay.

NOTES

1. "Robots Join the Labor Force," *Business Week,* June 9, 1980, p. 62; and Joann S. Lublin, "As Robot Age Arrives . . . ," *The Wall Street Journal,* Oct. 26, 1981, p. 1.

2. Otto Friedrich, "The Robot Revolution," *Time,* Dec. 8, 1980, p. 75.

3. Gene Bylinsky, "A New Industrial Revolution is on the Way," *Fortune,* Oct. 5, 1981, pp. 106–14; and Barnaby J. Feder, "The Automated Research Lab," *The New York Times,* Oct. 27, 1981. p. D1.

4. Herman Kahn, William Brown, and Leon Martel, *The Next 200 Years* (New York, Morrow, 1976), pp. 8; 20–24.

5. Lublin, "As Robot Age Arrives . . . ,"; and "The Speedup in Automation," *Business Week,* Aug. 3, 1981, p. 62.

6. *Congressional Record* (daily edition), Dec. 10, 1981, p. S14908.

7. Harley Shaiken, "Detroit Downsizes U.S. Jobs," *The Nation,* Oct, 11, 1980.

8. Fred Reed, "The Robots Are Coming, The Robots Are Coming," *Next,* May/June 1980, p. 32.

9. "The Speedup in Automation."

10. Diane Werneke, "Microelectronics and Office Jobs: The Impact of the Chip on Women's Employment," report prepared for the International Labour Office, 1982, pp. 115–24.

11. Clive Jenkins and Barrie Sherman, *The Collapse of Work* (London, Eyre Methuen, 1979), p. 182.

12. Mich McLean, "Sector Report: The Electronics Industry," background study prepared for the Organization for Economic Cooperation and Development, in *The Technical Change and Economic Policy* (Paris, OECD, 1980).

13. Richard W. Riche, "Impact of new electronic technology," *Monthly Labor Review.* March 1982, p. 39.

14. Reed, "The Robots Are Coming."

15. Lublin, "As Robot Age Arrives . . . ."

16. William W. Winpisinger, "Correcting the Shortage of Skilled Workers," *The AFL–CIO American Federationist,* June 1980, p. 21.

17. Theodore J. Gordon and Olaf Helmer, "Report on a Long-Range Forecasting Study," in *Social Technology* (New York, Basic Books, 1966), pp. 81–82.

18. James S. Albus, *People's Capitalism: The Economics of the Robot Revolution* (Md., New World Books, 1976); and Colin Hines and Graham Searle, *Automatic Unemployment* (London, Earth Resources Research Ltd., 1979).

9

Workers, Unions, and Industrial Robotics

THOMAS L. WEEKLEY

Thomas L. Weekley argues that the introduction of robots in industry need not be a matter of losing jobs; but it is likely to involve displacement. He takes the position that new technologies should enhance, rather than hinder, job security, help workers rather than degrade them, and increase, rather than decrease, job safety.

The United Auto Workers'(UAW) Union began in the 1930s. When did this union first address new technology? Is new technology a new question? Obviously it is not. This issue was first addressed in the 1930s, and in 1935 the United Auto Workers' first convention talked about many of the issues that are still being talked about today. The terms used were "standardized wages," "economic security," "company profit," and so on, terms still familiar today. We are facing the same problems. They are more complex, but they are still the same problems. Management's striving for profits has always conflicted with the union's drive for protecting working men and women—not only their benefits, but their security on the job. In the 1950s this really became more of a problem, and new technology and technological advances began to be especially addressed.

HISTORICAL BEGINNINGS

In a talk before a joint session of Congress on 17 October 1955, Walter Reuther gave testimony that outlined not only the union's position but some of his predictions for the future, predictions that proved to be very

accurate. What he predicted in the 1950s and his reasoning have since become the basis for the UAW's position on new technology. At that time, a type of industrial revolution had begun, bringing a changeover to fixed automated pieces of equipment, such as turnovers[1] and merry-go-rounds,[2] things familiar in the plant today. Such pieces of equipment have been implemented in great numbers since the 1950s.

The many types of automation currently in the plant—other than the new type of robots or pieces we refer to as robots—really began in the 1950s. Walter Reuther was asked what the effect on the UAW membership would be as time went on. He said to keep in mind one thing, which holds true today as well: "Robots cannot buy cars and neither can people that are not working." There is a built-in security in our society. If people are not working, they do not have money and cannot purchase cars; therefore the companies cannot make a profit. For this reason companies must face the fact that they have a social commitment to provide jobs, if for no other reason than to maintain their own profits. Reuther went on to negotiate contract provisions that addressed exactly those issues he predicted. The negotiated

From *Annals of the American Academy of Political and Social Science* 470 (November 1983), pp. 146–151. Copyright © 1983 by the American Academy of Political and Social Science. Reprinted by permission of Sage Publications, Inc.

gains created jobs by allowing members time off while at the same time the plants could continue to be operated full-time. There would not be a drop in production but an actual increase, even though workers were spending less time in the plant.

CONTINUED PROGRESS

Succeeding UAW presidents, Leonard Woodcock and Douglas Fraser, continued in that direction, coming up with new types of benefits and proposals to reduce work time and create jobs while at the same time providing security and increased productivity. In the 1970s automation took a leap forward, and new types of automation began to be used. Such equipment was mainly used for tedious, competitive, or dangerous jobs. The then healthy economy's demand for more and more cars hid or masked any effect of this increase in new technology in the replacement or displacement of workers, because there was a constant increase in the demand for cars. There was also a constant increase of new facilities. People were put in those new facilities to operate the new equipment, and generally automation was accepeted just as it had been in the 1950s, as a benefit not only to management but to the worker as well.

CURRENT EFFECTS

In the 1980s the United States faces another stage in the evolution of automated equipment, one that is going to affect every area of the employment market requiring more advanced equipment. The Japanese invasion has taught us that we will have to automate if we are to remain competitive on a world basis. As a society we will have to address the fact that in their design, production, and inspection areas management will have to turn out a better quality product by designing a better quality product, and by allowing people on the floor to have more input on problems in production.

Union and nonunion members alike are now threatened by the advance of new technology. The recent decrease in car demand and the present shape of the economy have brought into focus the fact that as automation comes into the plant, people are going to be displaced. People may not necessarily be laid off as a direct result of automation, for there is always attrition in the work force—people retire or leave for one reason or another. But some people will be displaced, moved from their jobs. Displacement can move people into higher-paid jobs, jobs in semiskilled areas, but the negative side of the coin is that displacement can force people to seek jobs in other industries. Jobs are going to be created because of automation, but at the same time workers will face displacement within the plant and possibly in new industries, which may mean moving to other plants or newly opened facilities.

SUGGESTED SOLUTIONS

What are unions doing about the influx of automation? What are unions going to do about automation that can be reprogrammed without being torn out, simply by pushing buttons or changing a particular tape? The UAW is addressing these problems, and the following is a review of the recent resolution—involving much discussion of new technology—passed at the February 1982 Skilled Trades Conference, a policy-setting body within the union.

1. The UAW must insist that contracts assure workers' income and employment security.
2. There must be advance discussion before the implementation of any type of automated equipment.
3. The new technology designs must be subject to bargaining in order to develop systems that help workers rather than degrading them or placing them in secondary status.
4. Layoffs caused by the introduction of technological advance or change must be prohibited.
5. UAW craftworkers should be assigned to perform all the necessary skilled work.
6. There should be regular and periodic information meetings, informing mem-

bers and keeping local representatives updated on developments in new technology. Much work has been lost to salary units in the past because either local leadership within the plant or international representatives at one time or another just agreed and allowed such work to go out, feeling that members were no longer qualified to do it. This resolution addressed that issue directly.

7. The use of computers must not be allowed for time study or disciplinary methods within the plant.

These are just some of the areas addressed by the Skilled Trades Conference. The Production Conference, another policy-setting body that met in February 1982, addressed the same types of issues, which are becoming critical and which in the years ahead the UAW will have to address.

Each succeeding contract since the 1930s has addressed the problems of the future. Subcontracting, productivity, job creation, and so on are not only benefits but also issues that affect UAW membership. Job loss and job creation benefits are not new; they have been with us all along. The resolutions outline some specific areas that must be addressed, but in addition the Skilled Trades Department of the UAW has staff members that attend various tool shows, seminars and colleges, and investigate developments in new technology. The UAW wants to know what new types of equipment our membership is going to be facing, and at the same time to be able to advise local unions on who should perform the resulting new types of work. The union should be well versed as to the type of tools that are going to be necessary in order to troubleshoot and maintain the equipment. When going into negotiations, the union can then assure that such equipment will be provided in the tool cribs, or that equipment will be purchased by the company for use by members or as replacements for tools being used now. There are also interstaff study committees throughout the international union that have prepared for upcoming negotiations and that address problems specifically in each area.

PREPARATION FOR THE FUTURE

The UAW is preparing to face the future. Automation is going to continue, but workers have to be prepared to share in the benefits it can bring. The process should not be one-sided: jobs will be lost to automated processes unless all concerned parties continue to address this issue. There will be fewer production facilities in the future. Moreover, robots and optical sensing equipment are beginning to move into the next labor grade of jobs. In the past robots could perform only simple pick-and-place types of operations. Now optical sensing can actually inspect parts coming down the line, signaling a robot to reject certain parts and to stack, crate, or package other parts.

The totally automated factory, though controversial and an attention-getter, is not a reality. There will always be jobs that have to be performed, such as packaging, loading, and in some cases transporting; such jobs may eventually be of a much higher nature technically than those currently performed, but there will always be someone who has to troubleshoot the equipment. Will the troubleshooters have to be all-around general mechanics, trained in both mechanics and electronics? Not necessarily; there will have to be teams of specialists on such jobs. We still believe that the individual craftsman will be needed in the future, and that is the direction we will be following as a union.

One problem with the coming of automation is the issue of security. Security can really be the only basis on which workers can continue to accept automation in the plant. The issue has been addressed in the past but will need special attention in the future. There have been temporary setbacks in current programs of paid personal holidays, which allow random time off and create jobs in the plant; but this is still a long-term union goal. The holiday program accomplishes several objectives: it allows management to continue to use the plant; it provides additional jobs because of those needed for replacement; and at the same time the union gets the benefit of added leisure time for its membership.

Another issue for the future is lifetime employment guarantees: companies point at the lower wages of the Japanese, but they do not consider the fact that the Japanese are in many cases guaranteed a future with the companies they work for. Retraining for more highly skilled jobs is another necessity, along with protection of work that was at one time in unit.

THE SKILLED WORKER

A short article from a newspaper in Southfield, Michigan,[3] near the heart of the auto industry, outlines some of the problems facing the skilled work force, which must be addressed:

People who create the miracles of modern industrial life are given little esteem by the society they serve. . . . How can it be that the kind of work that creates the hallmark of advanced society is scorned by the same society . . . ? The industrial revolution has changed our world. With the advent of the factory, a relentless process of deskilling began. Skilled craftsmen were a problem for factory owners because they could force higher wages simply by withholding their specialized knowledge from the workplace. Employers could end this dependence by breaking jobs down into tasks small enough that anyone could learn them, thus eliminating the need for craftsmen. . . . Without the need for special skills, any worker could perform any part of the assembly process with only a short training period. . . . Blue Collar workers . . . are not subject to such a measurement of output.

THE SEMISKILLED AND NONSKILLED WORKER

Not only will our society have to address the replacement or infiltration by automation of semiskilled or production-type operations; there is also going to be a management tendency to break down further some skilled classifications and skilled job operations, and wherever possible to assign these jobs to less skilled groups. There will have to be advanced agreement by UAW members on installation. Design of equipment must take into account the safety element not only for those who work on the equipment, but also for those who operate it. Automated equipment must be safe in itself and easily shut off by an operator in case of malfunction. The equipment must be designed to conform to the human operating the equipment, rather than forcing the human to conform to the equipment—for example, to its speed of operation.

SUMMARY

Security of workers must be a top priority, safety must be assured, and there must be advance discussion and communication before the implementation of automation. Introduction of any automation must be timed so as to benefit workers. Natural attrition, rather than massive spur-of-the-moment layoffs, should be the only way of reducing the work force. Such a policy would share out the benefits a booming car market provides the companies: companies would still have to provide employment and job guarantees for people when the economy restricts the demand for cars.

Workers understand that the industry needs automation to remain competitive, but this must not happen at the expense of their livelihood. Workers must share in the benefits of new technology. Society as a whole must face the fact that for America to continue to prosper, people have to work. That consideration in and of itself is going to force America to face the responsibility of providing jobs of some nature. Those jobs may ultimately be work performed at home on a small computer unit tied to the workplace, or some other method, but there will have to be some way of providing employment for people if America is to continue to grow. That is a simple economic fact. The UAW is in the forefront, ahead of any other union in this country, in addressing these issues. As an international union, the UAW plans to stay abreast of technological advances. The union has worked very closely with Carnegie-Mellon University and other universities in the Midwest on studies of automated equipment and its effect in the future. We have also maintained a close connection with the Society of Manufacturing Engineers/Robotics Institute of America. The UAW plans to continue addressing these issues, making sure that its members reap some of the benefits that the new types of automation will bring.

NOTES

1. A turnover is automation that takes a panel from a particular press or welding operation and turns the panel over for work to be done on the other side as it goes down an assembly line.

2. A merry-go-round is an automated section at the end of a line where large pieces, such as roof bodies or frames, are stacked on a circular, traveling conveyor and then are unloaded, as they turn around, onto racks or other types of storage devices.

3. *Southfield Eccentric,* 8 Oct, 1981, Copyright © 1981, Observer & Eccentric Newspapers. Reprinted with permission.

10

Social Choice in the Development of Advanced Information Technology

RICHARD E. WALTON

The author argues that the concern with workers' autonomy, health, and self-esteem caused by advanced information technology in the workplace should not, need not, and probably will not lead to actual conflict between these workers' concerns, on the one hand, and economic aims, on the other.

For the past few years the author and his associates have been studying the implications of advanced information technology for white-collar work, and how social criteria might be employed to guide development in this area. Here they will suggest why social criteria *should* be employed, why they *can* be employed, and why it is increasingly likely that they *will* be employed, based on this research and its findings. Some of the issues that arise when people try to apply social criteria will also be outlined.

Extensive automation of white-collar work has become possible because of two types of technological advances. The first is an explosive growth in computer power per unit of cost—on the order of tenfold increases every four or five years. The second advance is in telecommunications, making it possible to achieve unprecedented movement and integration of electronic information. Consider also two economic facts: (1) the annual growth rate of capital per employee in offices has lagged behind that in manufacturing, and (2) office overhead costs have risen rapidly in

recent years. These factors combined to make an extraordinary variety of new applications economically feasible. Experts regard information technology as the most dynamic sector of technical innovations.

IMPLICATIONS FOR WORK AND PEOPLE AT WORK

The first proposition is that the new information technology has profound implications for the nature of work performed by clerical, professional and managerial personnel. The potential impact on the workplace may be greater than any earlier wave of new mechanization or automation to hit industry. Thus, the human stakes are high.

The new technical systems differ from those of prior generations, particularly because their relationship to human systems has become more pervasive and complex—and more important. Earlier systems utilized large computers, performed a limited number of separate functions, relied upon batch-processing, and were tended by special full-time opera-

Reprinted from *Technology in Society*, 4, pp. 41–49. Copyright © 1982, Pergamon Press, Ltd. Reprinted by permission of Pergamon Press, and the author. This article also appeared in *Human Relations* 35 (Dec. 1982), pp. 1073–1084.

tors. The newer technologies utilize a network of large and small computers and embrace many activities within a given system, often crossing departmental boundaries. Managers, professionals and clerical personnel are required to interact *directly* with computer terminals, often as an integral part of their responsibilities. And, because these systems are on-line, the relationship between the user and the system is more immediate. Thus it is not surprising that the newer systems have the potential for affecting more employees in more ways than ever before, and for influencing work and communications patterns at higher executive levels than previously.

The studies conducted by the author and his colleagues have covered a number of different applications, including the following three:

1. Electronic mail terminals were placed on the desks of thousands of managers and support personnel in a large firm. This innovation affected the nature of vertical and horizontal communications, access to executives at different levels, and decision-making processes, and it modified somewhat the contents of the jobs of those who used the tool.
2. A procurement system was installed in a large company, embracing buyers and their clerical support, as well as personnel in the receiving and accounts payable departments. The system made it possible to monitor more closely the performance of purchasing agents, changed the interdepartmental patterns of accountability for errors, and created more tedious clerical work.
3. A telephone company automated its local repair bureaus, employing information technology to test phone line automatically, to monitor the status of all repair orders in the bureau, and to provide telecommunication linkage with service representatives who received subscriber complaints at a new centralized office. Before automation, these service representatives were located at the local repair bureaus.

Looking more closely at this application, in the *repair bureau,* the new technology re-duced the number of personnel and decreased skill requirements. The "test man" is a case in point. In the past, the test man's job was a professional one, with a high-status dress code of "starched white shirts and ties." Mastery required innate ability and experience. Today the testing function is becoming increasingly automated, and the test man's skills and knowledge have become technologically obsolete. The persons who held those positions, therefore, have suffered psychologically and economically.

The new system also dramatically affected personnel in the new *centralized answering facility.* The service representatives felt that they had become physically and informationally isolated from other steps in the process of satisfying the customers whose complaints they take. The central facility takes complaints for local bureaus in several states, and the answering personnel neither learn what happens to a particular complaint nor know the people in the bureau to which they pass along the complaint. Service representatives cannot determine the status of repair work and, therefore, either cannot respond to customers who call back or have to provide customers with meaningless promises about delivery of service. This has led to tension and mutual fault-finding between the service representatives and the repair personnel. In this, and many other respects, the technical system helped to produce "unhealthy" jobs—jobs which failed to meet normal human needs for knowledge and control of the workplace. The result was employee alienation and defective problem-solving.

Not all of the human side effects of these and the other systems studied were negative; this point will be discussed shortly. But the negative human consequences that were found were significant—and largely predictable. The following behavioral generalizations describe some of the common organizational consequences of office applications of the new microprocessor technology.

If the technical system decreases skill requirements the meaning of work may become trivial, and a loss of motivation, status and self-esteem may result. This was a common occurrence. In some circumstances, those who suffered counterattacked the system.

If the system increases specialization and separates the specialty from interdependent activities, then jobs may become repetitive and isolated, and fail to provide workers with performance feedback. Such jobs produce alienation and conflict.

If the system increases routinization and provides elaborate measurements of work activity, job occupants may resent the loss of autonomy and try to manipulate the measurement system. The fact of measurement itself can put excessive pressure on individuals and can strain peer relationships.

IMPACT OF TECHNOLOGY VARIES AND CAN BE INFLUENCED

The second proposition here is that technological determinism is readily avoidable. Technology *can* be guided by social policy, often without sacrifice of its economic purpose. Information technology is less deterministic than other basic technologies that historically have affected the nature of work and the people at work.

True, the side effects described above were generally negative, but sometimes the *unplanned* consequences are positive. In each of the areas listed below, the effects were not inherent in the technology. The directional effects resulted—to an important degree—from particular choices made in design or implementation.

- Work systems based on the new technology often require less skill and knowledge, but sometimes these new systems result in more jobs being upgraded than downgraded. System design can influence that outcome.
- The technical system can increase the flexibility of work schedules to accommodate human preferences, or it can decrease flexibility and require socially disruptive work schedules.
- New systems often contribute to social isolation, but sometimes they have the opposite effect. Similarly, they often

separate an operator from the end result of his or her effort, but occasionally they bring the operator into closer touch with the end result. Seldom are these planned outcomes, but they *can* be.

- These systems sometimes render individuals technologically obsolete because of changed skill and knowledge requirements, but they also open up new careers.
- New technology can change the locus of control—toward either centralization or decentralization.
- New information systems can change—for better or worse—an employee-typist into a subcontractor opening a terminal out of his or her own home.

The problem is that those who design applications and those who approve them currently make little or no effort to anticipate their human effects. Thus positive organizational effects are likely to be accidental, as are negative ones.

Why is computer-based technology becoming less deterministic, allowing planners more choice?

First, the rapidly declining cost of computing power makes it possible to consider more technical options, including those that are relatively inefficient in the use of that power.

Second, the new technology is less hardware-dependent, more software-intensive. It is, therefore, increasingly flexible, permitting the same basic information-processing task to be accomplished by an ever-greater variety of technical configurations, each of which may have a different set of human implications. For example, one system configuration may decentralize decision-making; another may centralize it. Yet both will be able to accomplish the same *task* objectives.

TRENDS FAVOR THE EXERCISE OF SOCIAL CHOICE

The third proposition is that a number of factors could produce an industrial trend in which human development criteria would be applied to the design of this office technology. The author has not yet observed such a trend. But a social revolution affecting work in the manufacturing plant gathered momentum during the 1970s, and the most natural extention of this social revolution to the office would be a movement to seize upon this new office technology and shape its development.

Managements—and unions, where workers are organized—are increasingly acting to modify the way blue-collar work is ordered and managed. And the changes are explicitly in the interest of promoting human development as well as task effectiveness.

The work improvement movement began in the United States and Canada and in some European countries in the early 1970s, after several years of sharply increasing symptoms of employee disaffection. Symptoms included costly absenteeism and sabotage, and the media labeled the general phenomenon "the blue-collar blues."

Over the past decade attention has gradually shifted from symptoms to solutions. Work reform in plants throughout the United States and Canada has grown steadily, and the trend appears to be taking the path of the classical "S" growth curve. Today the rate of growth in these experiments continues to increase annually, suggesting the steeper portion of the curve is being approached.

Work reform reverses many practices launched with the industrial revolution in which tasks were increasingly fragmented, deskilled, mechanically paced, and subjected to external controls. The current trend combines specialized jobs to create whole tasks, integrates planning and implementation, and relies more on self-supervision.

THE "QUALITY OF WORK" ENDEAVOR

A particularly striking illustration is provided by General Motors (GM) and the United Automobile Workers (UAW), who have jointly sponsored "Quality of Work Life" (QWL) activities in over half of GM's facilities. Over the course of a decade, political support for QWL activities within each of these organizations grew to a point where such activities

have become the official policy of the dominant coalition within each organization.

For GM management, policies that favor human development produce a more committed workforce; moreover, these policies have come to be regarded by many managers as morally right. For the UAW, these same policies promote industrial democracy and advance unionism. For the workforce, such policies allow some discretion where there had been none; they afford human dignity where it had been absent; and they increase the employees' voice in matters that affect them.

The aims of this social revolution are *not* radical in the sense that they challenge either the ownership structure of industry or the basic legitimacy of professional management's current role in deciding where to allocate resources. In this respect, the social revolution in North America differs from some of the forms of industrial democracy developing in Europe.

Some related North American trends *do* have an impact on the ownership structure of smaller enterprises. Professor William F. Whyte and his colleagues at Cornell have documented the experiences of employee-owned enterprises. Moreover, the addition of UAW President, Douglas Fraser, to the Chrysler Corporation Board of Directors is a step toward labor participation in major decisions about resource allocation. But these developments are not typical of the social revolution referred to here.

The value and behavior patterns which characterize this social revolution have a significance beyond the workplace. More research is needed, but the studies with which the author is familiar confirm his observation that, when individuals are able to use a broader range of skills and abilities in their work, they tend to see themselves as capable of making a larger variety of contributions to their communities. And, when people are afforded a voice in, or influence over, matters that affect them at work, they will expect the same sort of participation in other social settings.

In short, human development at work

creates pressures on other institutions to promote similar development. Conversely, human constriction at work is conducive to human constriction in other societal settings.

These observations have been illustrated in a number of American manufacturing plants started in the 1970s in which the governing philosophy has emphasized human development. Self-supervising work teams were set up, requiring workers to solve technical and social problems. Members were encouraged to take initiative, to express themselves, and to make constructive use of conflict. The skills and self-confidence gained at work were then exercised in the family setting.

For example, their new work roles raised the consciousness of women employees in working class families and many of them undertook to change their decision-making roles at home from passivity to activity, and to move their marriage-role relationships from subordinacy to equality. Many male workers in these innovative plants practiced their own listening skills at home, again with implications for the human development of family members.

THE MOMENTUM OF THE 1970S

Why did this revolution in the manufacturing plants gather momentum during the 1970s? Several forces led to change, at least in North America. One factor, which was mentioned earlier, was the acute rise in worker disaffection during the early part of the decade; this was not unrelated to the unrest that was prevalent in the cities and on college campuses.

Then, during the middle 1970s, it became increasingly apparent that American industry was losing its competitiveness in international markets. Management started looking for better ways to utilize human resources and recognized that it would have to meet more of the needs and expectations of its employees. Unions—fearful about the loss of jobs to foreign competitors—increasingly joined in this venture.

Recently American managers—by now somewhat humbled by their own lackluster industrial performance—have shown a strong interest in Japanese techniques—techniques which also happen to be consistent with Quality of Work Life innovations already developing at home.

No change comparable to that just described is yet under way in the American office. Some clerical workers have been the target of Quality of Work Life activities, especially in large insurance and banking organizations. But, for the most part, there is little activity in this area. Ironically, where quality of life has been improved for blue-collar workers, white-collar workers in the same facility often feel neglected by comparison. This feeling of neglect is shared by lower-level managers and professionals, as well as clerical personnel.

Concern within these white-collar groups is growing as national surveys confirm a decline in job satisfaction among middle managers. Recently white-collar groups have found themselves almost as vulnerable to massive force reduction as blue-collar workers. In steel, automotive and rubber companies, for example, tens of thousands of white-collar employees have been cut.

Management is beginning to recognize that it does not tap the fund of skills and knowledge of these white-collar groups. Recently "quality circle," or participative, problem-solving teams have been introduced into white-color workplaces, often with beneficial effects on human development. Still no major pattern of positive social change has emerged affecting those who work in offices.

Now new office technology based on the computer-on-a-chip enters the scene. This new technology either can exacerbate the problem of white-collar disaffection or can be part of the solution. Technology can either constrict human development or promote it.

Although not yet constituting a trend, a significant development is the recent agreement entered into by the American Telephone and Telegraph Company (AT&T) and three unions (including the Communications Workers of America), representing 700,000 employees. The unions and the company have established joint committees to discuss plans for new technology at least six months before new equipment is introduced and to analyze the potential human implications, including job pressures and job organization.

In Europe there *is* an established trend for companies and unions to enter into "technology agreement," giving unions and employees an opportunity to modify new technology before it is introduced. The AT&T agreement covers unionized employees, who are mostly blue-collar workers, but the idea probably will be extended to the company's white-collar workforce as well.

IMPLEMENTING SOCIAL CHANGE

The idea that technology has a social impact certainly is not new. Social scientists have long argued that technology can dramatically affect individuals, institutions, and society as a whole. Managers who introduce new work technologies have long appreciated that there will be organizational side effects. But this knowledge has had little influence on the introduction of new work technology.

In the past, considerations of the human impact of innovation have led merely to efforts to overcome workers' resistance. These efforts have emphasized implementation methods, including communication and training, and employment assurances. But efforts to ameliorate the impact, should increasingly extend upstream to the design stage itself and affect the design of hardware, software, and management operating systems.

In the past, where human criteria have been considered in the design of work technology, they have centered on narrow factors, such as ease of learning, operator fatigue, and safety. The criteria should be extended to include a broader array of human needs—for autonomy, for social connectedness, for meaningful work, for effective voice.

But in order to exercise social choice in the significant sense that has just been described, one must break new methodological ground. Some ways in which this should be done are as follows:

1. Organizations need explicit normative models, by which designers can judge what human effects are to be considered

good, bad, or neutral, and which ones are especially salient. An organizationally specific model would be based both on general knowledge about human development, and on an understanding of the particular circumstances of the company.

2. Designs should not be approved until an "organizational impact statement" has been prepared and reviewed. The first step would be an examination of the requirements for a proposed technical system. This would clarify the first-order social consequences of the system—how it changes the degree of specialization, locus of control, or skill requirements. The next step would be a prediction of second-order consequences, such as motivational effects, social conflict, and human development. This would require the perspectives of behavioral disciplines not currently involved in systems projects.

3. One needs practical methods for involving those who will eventually use and/or be affected by the system. While "user involvement" in systems development has been a widely endorsed concept for more than a decade, in practice users seldom report that they have been meaningfully involved.

4. System development should be approached as an evolutionary process. This contrasts with a more typical assumption that the design can and should be completely conceived before implementation. This methodological recommendation is based on the finding that the human impacts of complex information systems are *dynamic,* in the sense that their effects change over time; for example, some initially negative reactions disappear as tasks are mastered, and some initially positive reaction decline as novelty wears off. Complicating the picture is the fact that effects are *reciprocal* in the sense that the employee will react to the technical system; for example, user reactions may affect the quality of inputs to the system and, in turn, the functionality of the system.

5. The final recommendation here is that

significantly greater effort must be devoted to evaluation of the operational system, and this evaluation must comprehend social effects as well as economic and technical achievements.

These methodological proposals have an additional implication: management should assign a fraction of every development budget to be used to explore the human implications of these systems, and then it should act upon the knowledge derived from these explorations.

People are only beginning to learn how to exercise social choice in the course of technological development. There are still relatively few instances in which designers have paid explicit and comprehensive attention to potential impacts on human systems. In Europe there is growing experience with trade unions which have insisted on being involved in evaluating new computer-based technology before it is installed in the workplace. Two Cornell professors have developed a model for design and implementation of word-processing systems that attend to social dimensions.[1] In the United Kingdom, Enid Mumford and her associates have developed a participative approach to the design of systems which affect clerical groups.[2] These are pioneering efforts, and though their achievements may be instructive, they are by no means definitive.

CONCLUSION

To summarize: Applications of the new information technology should be guided by human-development criteria; they can be so guided, and now there is a decent probability that they will be. If this new work technology is to be shaped by social criteria, it will be necessary to gain new implementation "know-how," and a rich field will be opened for basic and applied research.

The design and implementation of advanced information technology poses major organizational problems, and these problems must be dealt with. These innovations also represent the most important opportunity available in the 1980s for the introduction of constructive changes in clerical, professional and managerial work.

First, a few pioneering organizations, and then a larger number of progressive ones will exploit this opportunity. The introduction of this technology offers the chance to rethink the organization and management of professional and clerical work in the office . . . analogous to the way green-field plants created an opportunity to pioneer new approaches to managing factory work.[3]

The 1980s will be a period of trial and error as man learns how to exercise social choice in systems design. Academic institutions can contribute to the analysis and dissemination of these experiences, but only if some management, systems developers, and unions choose to lead the way in this uncharted field.

NOTES

1. Lodahl, Thomas M. and Lawrence K. Williams, "An Opportunity for OD: The Office Revolution," *OD Practitioner,* December 1978.

2. Mumford, Enid and Don Henshall, *A Participative Approach to Computer Systems Design* (London: Associated Business Press, 1979).

Mumford, Enid and Mary Wier, *Computer Systems in Work Design* (London: Associated Business Press, 1979).

Hedberg, Bo and Enid Mumford, "The Design of Computer Systems" in Enid Mumford and H. Sackman, eds., *Human Choice and Computers* (Amsterdam: North-Holland Publishing Company, 1975).

3. Walton, Richard E., "Work Innovations in the United States," *Harvard Business Review,* July–August 1979.

11

Development of the National Institutes of Health Guidelines for Recombinant DNA Research

BERNARD TALBOT

The author states that, although the risks of the recombinant DNA technique remain hypothetical, scientists working in the field have spearheaded discussions of its safety. These led to the National Institutes of Health (NIH) Guidelines for Recombinant DNA Research, initially issued in 1976, significantly revised in 1978, and regularly revised about every three months since then. The author discusses how they work and why they are valuable.

Deoxyribonucleic acid (DNA) makes up the genetic material of all cells and determines hereditary characteristics. Recombinant DNA is a technique, first reported[1,2] in 1972, that allows the transfer of genes from cells of one species to cells of another species in the laboratory.

Figure 11.1 depicts a recombinant DNA experiment. At the upper left of the diagram is a bacterial cell containing chromosomal DNA and some small, circular loops of DNA called "plasmids." These plasmids can be isolated from the bacterial cell and cut open by an enzyme known as a restriction endonuclease. At the upper right of the diagram is another cell that can be from any species—bacteria, fly, frog, or man. The DNA of this cell can also be extracted and treated by a restriction endonuclease to yield pieces of DNA. When the material from both cells is mixed in a test tube, one of the products is a plasmid from the bacterial cell that carries a piece of DNA from the other cell. As indicated at the bottom of the diagram, this recombinant DNA can be inserted back into a bacterial cell. When the "host" cell divides, the recombinant DNA will be duplicated along with the cell's chromosomal and plasmid DNA, and each daughter cell will receive a copy.

In such experiments, the foreign DNA inserted into a bacterium will usually amount to one gene or less, while the bacterium already contains thousands of bacterial genes. Thus the technique is not producing cells that are half bacteria and half frog, but rather is producing bacteria that contain—in addition to all other normal DNA—less than one part

Reprinted from *Public Health Reports* 98 (August 1983), pp. 361–368. *Public Health Reports* is the official journal of the U.S. Public Health Service–U.S. Department of Health and Human Services.

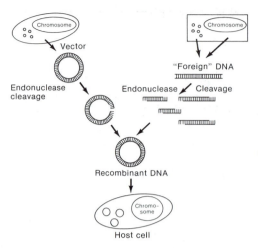

Figure 11.1. A recombinant DNA experiment. A small loop of DNA from a bacterium (upper left) is cleaved by an enzyme and mixed with similarly treated DNA from another cell. The opened bacterial plasmid takes up a piece of the "foreign" DNA, forming a recombinant DNA plasmid that is then inserted into a "host" bacterium. When the host divides, each daughter cell will receive a copy of the recombinant DNA as well as the host's genetic material.

in a thousand of additional DNA that originally derived from another species.

USES OF RECOMBINANT DNA TECHNOLOGY

By introducing a particular piece of DNA into a bacterium and then culturing the bacterial cells, one can produce large amounts of the desired DNA segments for study. This technique has been, and continues to be, widely used, in thousands of laboratories throughout the world, to produce DNA that scientists then analyze to determine the precise structure of specific genes. Such studies have led to a major finding about the organization of DNA in eukaryotic cells: the existence of "intervening," or "intron," sequences.[3-5] Much new information is arising from recombinant DNA experiments that is currently of great importance in basic biomedical research, and that promises to be of still greater

importance in the future diagnosis, treatment, and prevention of many diseases.

If the inspired recombinant DNA in the cell is transcribed into messenger RNA (ribonucleic acid) and then translated into protein a whole new range of possibilities opens up. Major successes have been reported in the past few years, leading to the production by bacteria of mammalian proteins such as somatostatin,[6] insulin,[7-9] growth hormone[10,11] and interferon.[12,13] Techniques are being perfected to increase the yields of bacterial production of such proteins. Theoretically, any protein can be made in bacteria. Recombinant DNA promises to yield huge amounts of such scarce products as biologically active peptides[14] and viral antigens for use as vaccines,[15-17] at much lower cost than can be achieved today.

Outside the pharmaceutical industry, many other uses for micro-organisms into which recombinant DNA has been inserted are being explored. Among these uses are:

- Chemical production—inserting genes into bacteria so that they can synthesize various industrially important organic chemicals, such as ethylene oxide and ethylene glycol.
- Energy production—inserting genes into bacteria to enable them to convert plants or sewage into methane, methanol, ethanol, hydrogen, or other compounds that could be burned as fuels.
- Metal extraction—inserting genes into bacteria to aid in the extraction of desired metals from ores.

There has been intense press interest in the industrial uses of micro-organisms into which recombinant DNA has been inserted.[18-24]

Beyond the insertion of recombinant DNA into micro-organisms, a whole other class of uses, just beginning to be explored, involves the insertion of recombinant DNA into higher organisms. There have already been numerous instances of recombinant DNA's being added to, and expressing protein products in, the cells of higher organisms in tissue culture. A future goal is the insertion of nitrogen fixation genes into agriculturally important plants, eliminating the need for fertilizers. Ultimately, it should be possible to alter the genetic constitution of higher animals and man to cure inherited disorders.

SAFETY CONCERNS

The benefits of recombinant DNA research are already many; the risks remain hypothetical. Recombinant DNA experiments have now been performed for over 10 years, and millions of recombinant DNA clones have been produced in thousands of laboratories throughout the world. To date, no actual hazard has been demonstrated. But because of concern about possible dangers of recombinant DNA molecules, scientists working in this field have from the beginning spearheaded discussions of safety.

Both the promise and the possible hazards of recombinant DNA were discussed at a 1973 Gordon Conference. Those present voted that a letter be sent to the National Academy of Sciences and be published,[25] suggesting that the academy "consider this problem and recommend specific actions or guidelines."

In response to this initiative, the academy formed a committee of distinguished scientists, chaired by Dr. Paul Berg of Stanford University. These scientists prepared a letter[26] that appeared simultaneously in *Science, Nature,* and the *Proceedings of the National Academy of Sciences.*

First, the letter proposed that "until the potential hazards of such recombinant DNA molecules have been better evaluated or until adequate methods are developed for preventing their spread, scientists throughout the world join with the members of this committee in voluntarily deferring [certain] experiments." This request by scientists for a voluntary "moratorium" on such work while questions of public safety were further evaluated was widely hailed in the press.

Second, the letter proposed that the National Institutes of Health (NIH) establish an advisory committee for "devising guidelines to be followed by investigators working with potentially hazardous recombinant DNA molecules."

Third, the letter called for an international conference of scientists, which was held in February 1975 at the Asilomar Conference Center in California. There were 150 attendees from 15 countries, plus members of the press who gave the meeting wide, immediate coverge. Two journalists subsequently wrote books on the conference.[27,28] The final conference report[29] recommended proceeding with most recombinant DNA experiments, using appropriate "physical containment" and "biological containment" (discussed in detail below).

THE NIH GUIDELINES

The first meeting of the NIH Recombinant DNA Advisory Committee (RAC)—formed in response to the letter of Berg and his associates—was held the day after the Asilomar conference. (Minutes of all RAC meetings are available from the Office of Recombinant DNA Activities, NIH, Bldg. 31, Rm. 3B10, Bethesda, Md. 20205.) After a series of meetings, the RAC in December 1975 adopted its proposal guidelines for recombinant DNA research carried out with NIH funding. When the NIH Director at the time, Dr. Donald Fredrickson, received the proposal, he called a meeting of his Director's Advisory Committee, to which he invited many distinguished scientific and public representatives. (The full transcript of this February 1976 meeting, and all letters of comment on the proposed guidelines, form the bulk of Volume 1 of what is now a seven-volume massive public record[30–36] of the history of the NIH guidelines. The first five volumes in this series can be purchased from the Superintendent of Documents, U.S. Government Printing Office, Washington, D.C. 20402, or viewed in some 600 public libraries of the GPO depository system. Volumes 6 and 7 are available from the Office of Recombinant DNA Activities at NIH.) Following an analysis of the comments and suggestions received at the February 1976 meeting and afterwards, Fredrickson addressed a number of questions to the RAC for discussion at its April 1976 meeting. After an analysis of the RAC's responses, Frederickson decided on the final form of the NIH guidelines, promulgated in July 1976.[37]

The original guidelines included a list of prohibited experiments and described in great detail four sets of special practices, equipment, and laboratory installations that defined four levels of physical containment: P1, P2, P3, and P4 (Figure 11.2). P1 corresponds to the microbiology diagnostic laboratories, existing in all hospitals, where infectious micro-organisms isolated from patients are grown and analyzed. P2 adds more practices and equipment—most important, the use of biological safety cabinets for certain operations. P3 adds still more special practices, equipment, and laboratory installations; most important, the entire laboratory is operated with an inward air flow, as though it were a giant hood. P4 laboratories have many special engineering features. All experiments are confined to air-tight biological safety cabinets, and scientists perform their work through glove ports. In addition, a whole of secondary barriers exists.

P1 to P4 are levels of physical containment; however, a major advance resulting from the Asilomar conference was the concept of biological containment— the use, in experiments, of micro-organisms with limited ability to survive outside the very special conditions that are maintained in the laboratory. Most recombinant DNA experiments at present are being done with the harmless bacterium Escherichia coli, strain K-12. Its use, together with that of certain specified plasmids or bacteriophage viruses into which the foreign DNA is inserted, constitutes what is called the EK1 level of biological containment. By further modifying E. coli K-12 to render the bacteria much less likely to survive, were they to escape from the laboratory

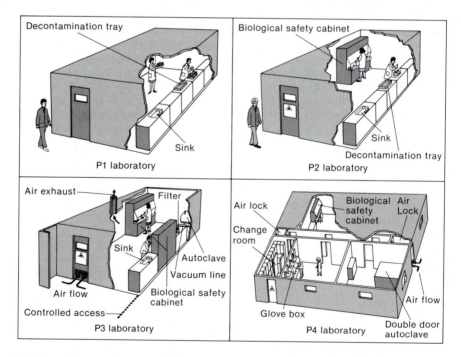

Figure 11.2. These diagrams illustrate the four levels of physical containment specified for various types of recombinant DNA experiments by the NIH guidelines. The P1 level is that of a hospital microbiology laboratory. Each higher level adds more special practices, equipment, and installations, culminating in the P4 laboratory with its air-tight biological safety cabinets and experiments performed through glove ports.

(for example, by making them dependent for survival on certain nutrients that are supplied in the laboratory but that do not occur in significant concentrations in nature, and by making the modified bacteria sensitive to sunlight and to bile acids), and by requiring data on survivability to be submitted to NIH and approved by the RAC, one arrived at what were called the EK2 and EK3 levels of biological containment.

Having defined four levels of physical containment and three levels of biological containment, the guidelines then went on to specify levels of physical and biological containment required for each of many different kinds of experiments. Finally, the guidelines discussed the roles and responsibilities of the scientist, his or her university, the university's institutional biosafety committee (which in most cases already existed to oversee other potential hazards), and the NIH.

After their promulgation in 1976, the NIH guidelines were adopted by other Federal agencies. (The three major Federal agencies funding recombinant DNA research are NIH, the National Science Foundation, and the Department of Agriculture.)

In July 1976, Senators Jacob Javits and Edward Kennedy wrote to President Gerald Ford, urging that "every possible measure be explored for assuring that the NIH guidelines are adhered to in all sectors of the research community." In his reply to the two Senators, President Ford described the creation of the Federal Interagency Advisory Committee on Recombinant DNA Research. This committee has met periodically since 1976 and consists of members from all Federal agencies that either fund or might regulate recombinant DNA research. In 1977, the committee recommended new national legislation to extend the NIH guidelines to private industry.

In the first session of the 95th Congress, which lasted through 1977, 16 different bills on the topic of recombinant DNA were introduced, and extensive hearings were held. More than 100 witnesses appeared before the Senate Subcommittee on Health and Scientific Research; the Senate Subcommittee on Science, Technology, and Space; the House Subcommittee on Health and Environment; and the House Subcommittee on Science, Research, and Technology. There was great disagreement on a number of provisions of the proposed recombinant DNA bills, and none ever reached the floor of the full House or Senate. There is, therefore, no national law making the NIH guidelines mandatory for private industry.

In the absense of national legislation, a number of States and localities have acted. In Cambridge, Mass., in 1976, the city council called for a 6-month moratorium on all P3 and P4 research at Harvard University and the Massachusetts Institute of Technology while an appointed experimental review board studied the problem. The board consisted of a former Cambridge mayor and owner of a heating oil business, a community worker, a hospital nurse, an engineer, a practicing physician, a social worker, and a professor of urban policy. None of the members knew anything about recombinant DNA before they were appointed. They heard more than 75 hours of testimony and finally issued their report in January 1977, recommending that recombinant DNA research be allowed in Cambridge, basically under the NIH guidelines, with a few added restrictions. The report was adopted by the Cambridge city council in February 1977. Other local jurisdictions that have made the NIH guidelines mandatory are Princeton, N.J., Amherst, Mass., Waltham, Mass., Berkeley, Calif., and Emeryville, Calif. New York State and Maryland have also enacted such legislation.

DECEMBER 1978 GUIDELINES REVISION

In December 1978 a revision of the NIH guidelines was issued. The revision involved many steps. First, the RAC worked, at a number of meetings during the spring of 1977, to produce draft revisions. A workshop held in Falmouth, Mass. in June 1977[38] led to a consensus of experts that E. coli K-12 is a harmless organism and cannot be converted into a pathogen by the insertion of recombinant DNA. Revised guidelines proposed by the RAC were published in the Federal

Register in September 1977[39] and sent out widely for public comment. At the NIH Director's Advisory Committee meeting in December 1977, many witnesses gave their views of the proposed revisions. Additional scientific meetings were held, focusing especially on the risks of recombinant DNA experiments involving viruses[40] and plant pathogens.[41] Then, after much further analysis, a new set of proposed revised guidelines was published in July 1978. This document,[42] which amounted to 136 pages in the Federal Register, had three parts: the new proposed guidelines; a "decision document" explaining in detail the proposed changes and the reasons for them, as well as why certain suggested changes were not adopted; and an environmental impact assessment. The document was mailed to more than 2,500 persons who had communicated their interest in the issue to NIH, with a 60-day period allowed for public comment; 170 responses were received. In addition, a public hearing was held in September 1978, chaired by the General Counsel of the Department of Health, Education and Welfare.

After careful analysis of all comments received, the revised guidelines were promulgated on Dec. 22, 1978,[43] accompanied by a new decision document and an environmental impact assessment. Some of the major changes in the December 1978 guidelines, as compared with the original, were:

1. In general, experiments were assigned lower levels of required containment.
2. Certain classes of experiments deemed of the lowest potential hazard were exempted entirely from the guidelines.
3. Increased representation was mandated on local institutional biosafety committees (which oversee recombinant DNA research at individual institutions) and on the RAC.
4. Procedures were built into the guidelines for changing them in the future.

The RAC had originally been a 14-member committee composed entirely of scientists. At the RAC's own suggestion, two laymen were added to the committee in 1976:

a professor of government and a bioethicist. At the time of the 1978 guidelines revision, the RAC was expanded to 25 voting members, with the requirement that at least 6 members "be persons knowledgeable in applicable law, standards of professional conduct and practice, public attitudes, the environment, public health, occupational health, or related fields." Also, scientists representing many different backgrounds were added as members, and all relevant Federal agencies were given nonvoting membership. Now 15 agencies are represented, including the National Science Foundation, Department of Agriculture, Environmental Protection Agency, and Occupational Safety and Health Administration.

Local institutional biosafety committees also underwent an expansion as a result of the 1978 guidelines revision. Membership on each of these committees must now include at least two persons, not affiliated with the institution, who represent the interests of the surrounding community with respect to health and protection of the environment.

SUBSEQUENT GUIDELINES REVISION

Perhaps the major change in the December 1978 guidelines was that a process was built into them for further change. Anyone wishing to suggest a revision of the guidelines may submit it to NIH. It is then published in the Federal Register, at least 30 days before a regular meeting of the RAC, for public comment. The suggested revision and all written comments received are considered by the RAC at an open meeting; members of the public wishing to speak on the subject are given the opportunity to do so. Following the discussion, the RAC votes on whether or not to recommend the revision. After the meeting, the responsible Federal official (before June 1981 this was the NIH Director; since then, the responsibility has been delegated to the Director of the National Institute of Allergy and Infectious Diseases) promulgates his final decision on the RAC recommendations in the Federal Register. In this fashion, the guidelines have been incrementally modified approximately every 3 months between[44-56] December 1978 and August 1982 (Copies of the most recent revision, and of any future ones, can be obtained from the NIH Office of Recombinant DNA Activities.)

The major differences between current guidelines and those issued in December 1978 are:

1. Many more classes of experiments are exempted entirely from the current guidelines.
2. In general, covered experiments are assigned lower levels of required containment under the current guidelines.
3. The current guidelines lessen requirements for prior approval of many classes of experiments.
4. The current guidelines have been reorganized and simplified.

The guidelines continue to be mandatory for institutions receiving NIH funding. Certain experiments continue to require prior review by the local institutional biosafety committee, and some experiments also require prior approval by NIH.

RISK ASSESSMENT

Scientific support for the changes that have been made in the guidelines over time has come in part from risk assessment experiments supported by the NIH. In April 1979, NIH issued a proposed plan for a program to assess risks of recombinant DNA research.[57] Following review of the proposal by the RAC and analysis of public comments received, a final plan was issued in September 1979.[58] A risk assessment workshop was held in April 1980,[59] and a proposed update of the risk assessment plan was issued in September 1980[60] and made final in June 1981.[61] A new proposed update was issued for public comment in December 1982.[62]

THE GUIDELINES AND THE PRIVATE SECTOR

The original NIH guidelines dealt only with institutions receiving Federal funds for recombinant DNA research and said nothing about the private sector. In the absense of legislation mandating compliance by industry with the guidelines, NIH provided a means for voluntary compliance. A new section—Part VI, "Voluntary Compliance"—was formally added to the NIH guidelines in January 1980, following its endorsement by the Federal Interagency Advisory Committee and the RAC.

Under Part VI, private companies may register experiments with NIH, seek clarification of the guidelines, and receive NIH certification of new host-vector systems. (Part VI also specifies how NIH will protect proprietary information voluntarily submitted to it.) In addition, private companies may submit information about the membership of their institutional biosafety committees to NIH, which will verify that the committees meet the requirements of the NIH guidelines. (To date, 51 companies have registered their committees with NIH.)

The 1978 guidelines stated that certain recombinant DNA experiments involving more than 10 liters in volume required prior approval by the NIH Director. A number of proposals to exceed 10 liters were voluntarily submitted by industry to NIH for review, were recommended for approval by the RAC after careful study, and were finally approved by NIH. These proposals included large-scale production of human insulin, growth hormone, somatostatin, and interferon. In April 1980 NIH issued physical containment recommendations for large-scale recombinant DNA work.[63]

SUMMARY

Recombinant DNA techniques are a major scientific advance, used widely in biomedical research and increasingly in industrial applications. Benefits of these techniques are being produced in thousands of laboratories throughout the world, while scientific data along a number of lines indicate that the potential hazards were initially overestimated. The NIH Guidelines for Recombinant DNA Research provide widely accepted safety standards, continuously evolving in response to the recommendations of scientists and laymen.

NOTES

1. Jackson, D. A., Symons, R. H., and Berg, P.: Biochemical method for inserting new genetic information into DNA of simian virus 40, circular SV40 DNA molecules containing lambda phage genes and the galactose operon of *Escherichia coli*, Proc Natl Acad Sci USA 69: 2904–2909 (1972).

2. Cohen, S. N., et al.: Construction of biologically functional bacterial plasmids in vitro. Proc Natl Acad Sci USA 70: 3240–3244 (1973).

3. Breathnack, R., Mandel, J. L., and Chambon, P.: Ovalbumin gene is split in chicken DNA. Nature 270: 314–319 (1977).

4. Tonegawa, S., et al.: Cloning of an immunoglobulin variable region gene from mouse embryo, Proc Natl Acad Sci USA 74: 3518–3522 (1977).

5. Tilghman, S. M., et al.: Intervening sequence of DNA identified in the structural portion of a mouse beta globin gene. Proc Natl Acad Sci USA 75: 725–729 (1978).

6. Itakura, K., et al.: Expression in *Escherichia coli* of a chemically synthesized gene for the hormone somatostatin, Science 198: 1056–1063 (1977).

7. Villa-Komoroff, L., et al.: A bacterial clone synthesizing proinsulin. Proc Natl Acad Sci USA 75: 3727–3731 (1978).

8. Goeddel, D. V., et al.: Expression in *Excherichia coli* of chemically synthesized genes for human insulin. Proc Natl Acad Sci USA 76: 106–110 (1979).

9. Baker, R. S., et al.: Preliminary studies of the immunogenicity and amount of *Escherichia coli* polypeptides in biosynthetic human insulin produced by recombinant DNA technology. Lancet II (8256): 1139–1142 (1981).

10. Goeddel, D. V., et al.: Direct expression in *Escherichia coli* of a DNA sequence coding for human growth hormone. Nature 281: 544–548 (1979).

11. Stebbing, N., et al.: Biological comparisons of natural and recombinant DNA-derived polypeptides. *In* Insulins, growth hormone, and recombinant DNA technology, edited by J. L. Gueriguian. Raven Press, New York, 1981, pp. 117–131.

12. Nagata, S., et al.: Synthesis in *E. coli* of a polypeptide with human leukocyte interferon activity. Nature 284: 316–320 (1980).

13. Derynck, R., et al.: Expression of human fibroblast interferon gene in *Escherichia coli*. Nature 287: 193–197 (1980).

14. Shine, J., et al.: Expression of cloned beta-endorphin gene sequences by *Escherichia coli*, Nature 285: 456–461 (1980).

15. Burrell, C. J., et al.: Expression in *Escherichia coli* of hepatitis B virus DNA sequence cloned in plasmid pBR322. Nature 279: 43–47 (1979).

16. Pasek, M., et al.: Hepatitis B genes and their expression in *E. coli* Nature 282: 575–579 (1979).

17. Kupper, H., et al.: Cloning of cDNA of major antigen of foot and mouth disease virus and expression in *E. coli*. Nature 289: 555–559 (1981).

18. Shaping life in the lab. Time, Mar. 9, 1981, pp. 50–59.

19. DNA's new miracles. Newsweek, Mar. 17, 1980.

20. Weaving new life in the lab. Life, May 1980.

21. Cloning gold rush turns basic biology into big business. Science 208: 688–692 May 16, 1980.

22. Biotechnology: research that could remake industries. Chemical Week, Oct. 8, 1980, pp. 23–38.

23. DNA can build companies too. Fortune, June 16, 1980.

24. On the brink of altering life. The New York Times Magazine. Feb. 17, 1980, pp. 16–80.

25. Singer, M., and Soll, D.: Guidelines for DNA hybrid molecules. Science 181: 1114 (1973).

26. Berg, P., et al.: Potential biohazards of recombinant DNA molecules. Science 185: 303 (1974). Nature 250: 175 (1974). Proc Natl Acad Sci USA 71: 2593–2594 (1974).

27. Wade, N.: The ultimate experiment. Walker and Company, New York, 1977.

28. Rogers, M.: Biohazard. Alfred A Knopf, New York, 1977.

29. Berg, P., et al.: Asilomar conference on recombinant DNA molecules. Science 188: 991–994 (1975).

30. National Institutes of Health: Recombinant DNA research, vol. 1. GPO Stock No. 017-004-00398-6. U.S. Government Printing Office, Washington, D.C., August 1976.

31. National Institutes of Health: Recombinant DNA research, vol. 2. GPO Stock No. 017-040-00422-2 (supp: Environmental Impact Statement, GPO Stock No. 017-040-00413-3), U.S. Government Printing Office, Washington, D.C. March 1978.

32. National Institutes of Health: Recombinant DNA research, vol. 3. GPO Stock No. 017-040-00429-0 (apps.: GPO Stock No. 017-040-00430-3). U.S. Government Printing Office, Washington, D.C., Sept. 1978.

33. National Institutes of Health: Recombinant

DNA research, vol. 4. GPO Stock No. 017-040-00443-5 (apps.: GPO Stock No. 017-040-00442-7). U.S. Government Printing Office, Washington, D.C., Dec. 1978.

34. National Institutes of Health: Recombinant DNA research, vol. 5. GPO Stock No. 017-040-00470-2. U.S. Government Printing Office, Washington, D.C., March 1980.

35. National Institutes of Health: Recombinant DNA research, vol. 6. U.S. Government Printing Office, Washington, D.C., April 1981. Available from Office of Recombinant DNA Activities, NIH, Bethesda, Md.

36. National Institutes of Health: Recombinant DNA research, vol. 7. U.S. Government Printing Office, Washington, D.C., December 1982. Available from Office of Recombinant DNA Activities, NIH, Bethesda, Md.

37. Recombinant DNA research—guidelines. Federal Register 41: 27902–27943, No. 131, pt. II, July 7, 1976.

38. Gorbach, S. L.: Risk assessment of recombinant DNA experimentation with *Escherchia coli* K-12—preceedings of a workshop held at Falmouth, Massachusetts. J Infect Dis 137: 613–713, May 1978.

39. Recombinant DNA research—proposed revised guidelines, Federal Register 42: 49596–49609, No. 187, pt. III. Sept. 27, 1977.

40. U.S.-EMBO workshop to assess risks for recombinant DNA experiments involving the genomes of animal, plant, and insect viruses. Federal Register 43: 13748–13755, No. 63, pt.III, Mar. 3, 1978.

41. Report of a workshop on risk assessment of agricultural pathogens. Federal Register 43: 33174–33178, No. 146, pt. IV, July 28, 1978.

42. Recombinant DNA research—proposed revised guidelines. Federal Register 43: 33042–33178, No. 146, pt. IV, July 28, 1978.

43. Guidelines for research involving recombinant DNA molecules. Federal Register 43: 60080–60131, No. 247, pts. VI and VII, Dec. 22, 1978.

44. Recombinant DNA research—actions under guidelines. Federal Register 44: 21730–21736, No. 71, pt. II, Apr. 11, 1979.

45. Guidelines for research involving recombinant DNA molecules. Federal Register 44: 42914–42917, No. 141, pt. IV, July 20, 1979.

46. Recombinant DNA research—actions under guidelines. Federal Register 45: 3552–3556, No. 12, pt. VI, Jan. 17, 1980.

47. Guidelines for research involving recombinant DNA molecules. Federal Register 45: 6718–6749, No. 20, pts. V and VI, Jan. 29, 1980.

48. Recombinant DNA research—actions under guidelines. Federal Register 45: 25366–25370, No. 73, pt. IV, Apr. 14, 1980.

49. Recombinant DNA research—actions under guidelines. Federal Register 45: 50524–50531, No. 147, pt. II, July 29, 1980.

50. Recombinant DNA research—actions under guidelines. Federal Register 45: 77372–77409, No. 227, pt. VI, Nov. 21, 1980.

51. Recombinant DNA research—actions under guidelines. Federal Register 46: 16452–16457, No. 48, pt. II, Mar. 12, 1981.

52. Guidelines for research involving recombinant DNA molecules. Federal Register 46: 34454–34487, No. 46, pts. II and III, July 1, 1981.

53. Recombinant DNA research—actions under guidelines. Federal Register 46: 53980–53985, No. 210, pt. V, Oct. 30, 1981.

54. Recombinant DNA research—actions under guidelines. Federal Register 47: 13308–13310, No. 60, pt. III, Mar. 29, 1982.

55. Guidelines for research involving recombinant DNA molecules. Federal Register 47: 17166–17198, No. 77, pts. II and III, Apr 21, 1982.

56. Guidelines for research involving recombinant DNA molecules. Federal Register 47: 38040–38068, No. 167 pts. II and IV, Aug 27, 1982. (Editor's Note: As of this writing, the most recent revision of the guidelines appeared in the Federal Register 51: 16958–16985, No. 88, pt. III, May 7, 1986.

57. Proposed plan for a program to assess the risks of recombinant DNA research. Federal Register 44: 19302–19304, No. 64, pt.III, Apr. 2, 1979.

58. Program to assess the risks of recombinant DNA research—final plan. Federal Register 44: 53410–53413, No. 179, pt. IV, Sept. 13, 1979.

59. National Institute of Allergy and Infectious Diseases meeting. Federal Register 45: 12496, No. 39, Feb. 28, 1980.

60. Program to assess risks of recombinant DNA research—proposed first annual update. Federal Register 45: 61874–61878, No. 182, pt. II, Sept. 17, 1980.

61. Recombinant DNA research—final plan for a program to assess the risks. Federal Register 46: 30772–30778, No. III, pt. II, June 10, 1981.

62. Program to assess risks of recombinant DNA research—proposed second annual update. Federal Register 47: 55104–55109, No. 235, pt. III, Dec. 7, 1982.

63. Recombinant DNA research—physical containment recommendations for large-scale uses of organisms containing recombinant DNA molecules. Federal Register 45: 24968–24971, No. 72, pt. II, Apr. 11, 1980.

12

Genetic Engineering: Life as a Plaything

ROBERT L. SINSHEIMER

Robert L. Sinsheimer asks of gene-splicing technology, Is it safe? Is it wise? Is it moral? He asserts that though it appears to be safe in the short run, it is not at all clear that it is also safe in the long run; that it would be unwise and, indeed, morally objectionable to act as if it were safe in the long run; and that public scrutiny—not only scientists' scrutiny—is central to bringing the larger view into the assessment and decision-making process.

In a process almost as old as the earth, a huge panoply of organisms has evolved. The process has been one of chance and selection, and the star player has been the gene. For 3 billion years, natural changes in the number, structure, and organization of genes have determined the course of evolution.

We have now come to the end of that familiar pathway. Genetics—the science of heredity—has unlocked the code book of life, and the long-hidden strategies of evolution are revealing themselves. We now possess the ability to manipulate genes, and we can direct the future course of evolution. We can reassemble old genes and devise new ones. We can plan, and with computer simulation ultimately anticipate, the future forms and paths of life. Mutation and natural selection will continue, of course. But henceforth, the old ways of evolution will be dwarfed by the role of purposeful human intelligence. In the hands of the genetic engineer, life forms could become extraordinary Tinkertoys and life itself just another design problem.

Genetic engineering is a whole new technology. To view it as merely another technological development may make sense for those who invest in its commercial exploitation. But such a view is myopic for anyone concerned with the future of humanity. I want to consider three major areas of concern that will surely arise from this new technology. The first is the transformation of the science of biology itself. The development of molecular genetics is a transition as profound for biology as the development of quantum theory was for physics and chemistry. Until recently, biology was essentially an analytical science, in which researchers undertook the dissection of nature as observed. Genetic engineering now furnishes us with the ability to design and invent living organisms as well as to observe and analyze their function. If we consider the significance of synthesis to the science of chemistry, we can perhaps envision the importance of this development for the science of biology.

A NEW BIOLOGY

The new techniques open the door to a detailed understanding of the form and organization of genetic structures in higher organisms, of the control of gene expression, and

Originally published in *Technology Review* (April 1983), pp. 14, 15, and 20. Copyright © 1983. Reprinted with permission from *Technology Review*.

of the processes of cellular differentiation. Out of such knowledge will come a new biology that gives us the means to intervene in life processes at the most basic possible level.

The impact of this new biology on the practical and technical arts—the second area of development—will be profound. With this technology, human ingenuity could design agricultural crops that thrive in arid zones or brackish waters, that provide better human nutrition, that resist disease and pests. Human-designed crops, adapted to the needs of efficient agricultural technology, could leap ahead of their natural parasites and predators.

In chemistry, microorganisms could be programmed to carry out the complex organic synthesis of new pharmaceuticals, pesticides, and chemical catalysts. Other organisms could be programmed to degrade chemical compounds and reduce environmental pollution. In animal husbandry, the prospects seem equally bright for designing disease-resistant, fast-growing, nutritious animal forms. In medicine, we envision the synthesis of antibiotics, hormones, vaccines, and other complex pharmaceuticals. But these achievements, almost certainly feasible, will pale before the potential latent in the deeper understanding of biology.

Control over gene expression will provide a whole new array of therapies for genetic disorders. And that introduces the third domain of consequence and the most profound. With the decline of infectious diseases, genetic disorders are now increasingly the source of ill health. Diabetes, cystic fibrosis, sicke-cell anemia, and Tay-Sachs disease all stem from well-recognized genetic defects. The possibilities of human gene therapy—replacing the "bad" gene with the "good"—are extraordinary.

THE DARKER SIDE

It is not hard to sense the excitement, the challenge, the promise in all these ventures. But is there a catch? Is there a darker side to this vision as we have come to see in other new technologies? Some of us believe there may be—that life is not just another design problem, that life is different from nonlife. Just as nature stumbled upon life some 3 billion years ago and unwittingly began the whole pageant of evolution, so too the new creators may find that living organisms have a destiny of their own. They may find that genetic engineering has consequences far beyond those of conventional engineering.

As we become increasingly confident that this technology can, in fact, be achieved, there are a few major questions to be asked: Is it safe, is it wise, is it moral?

First, is it safe? If we can keep the developments open to public scrutiny, then I believe in the short-term it probably is. We can monitor the hazards of any new product we introduce into the biosphere and can probably cope with any immediate, untoward consequence.

For the long-term, however, I am considerably less sure. Life has evolved on this planet into a delicately balanced, intricate, self-sustaining network. Maintaining this network involves many interactions and equilibria that we understand only dimly. I would suggest that we must take great care, as we replace the creatures and vegetation of earth with human-designed forms, as we reshape the animate world to conform to human will, that we not forget our origins and inadvertently collapse the ecological system in which we have found our niche.

Through intensive study, we have learned of the different pathogens that prey on humans, animals, and major crops. But we have a very limited understanding of the evolutionary factors that led to their existence. We have limited knowledge about the reservoir of potential pathogens—organisms that could be converted by one or two or five mutations from harmless bugs into serious menaces. And thus we cannot really predict whether our genetic tinkering might unwittingly lead to novel and unexpected hazards.

More broadly, is it wise for us to assume responsibility for the structure and cohesion of the animate world? Do we want to engineer the planet so that its function requires the continuous input of human intelligence? Do we want to convert Earth into a giant Skylab?

LIFE AS OUR PLAYTHING

What happens to the reverence for life when life is our creation, our plaything? Will we have species with planned obsolescence? Will we have genetic olympics for homing pigeons or racing dogs? Will we have a zoo of reconstructed vanished species—dinosaurs or sabretoothed tigers—or as-yet unimagined species? Genetic engineering will inevitably change our sense of kinship with all our fellow creatures.

Will the extinction of species mean much when we can create new ones at will? Until now, we have all been the children of nature, the progeny of evolution. But from now on the flora and fauna of Earth will increasingly be our creations, our designs, and thus our responsibility. What will happen to our nature in such a world?

The most profound consequence of this technology is its application to humankind. The impetus to employ genetic engineering on the human race will come, I believe, out of our humanitarian tradition. Genetic engineering will be seen as just another branch of surgery, albeit at the most delicate level. Since we now know that many sources of human misery are genetic in origin, the urge to remedy these defects and even eliminate their transmission to succeeding generations will be irresistible. Thus, these changes will become part of the human genetic inheritance—for better or worse.

Having acquired the technology to provide genetic therapy, will we then be able to draw a line and restrict human genetic experimentation? How will we define a "defect"? And how will we argue against genetic "improvement"? Or should we? Will we even stop to consider the morality of what's being done?

The extent to which our more specifically human qualities—our emotions and intellects, our compassion and conscience—are genetically determined is not yet known. But geneticists cannot escape the dark suspicion that more is written in our genes than we like to think.

What will happen if we tamper with our physical or mental traits, given the complexity of human development and behavior? Such banal qualities as height or weight can surely affect one's identity, and good health has its own concomitants. How many of our greatest artistic works have been produced by the afflicted or the neurotic?

I suspect human genetic engineering is repugnant to many people because they think its purpose is to impose an identity upon a descendant, to replace the sport of Nature with models of human fancy.

In some sense, education is an attempt to impose an identity. An educational system demands adherance to values of attention, concentration, delayed gratification, and so on. Mere literacy, while enlarging freedom by opening new worlds of knowledge, destroys the freedom of innocence. Yet clearly we have long decided that the virtues of literacy outweigh any drawbacks. University literacy is regarded as good and mandated in most societies. Might there be similar genetic characteristics that we would come to regard as a universal good?

Cloning can be seen as an extreme effort to impose a particular identity—a particular character—upon a descendant. But all human genetic engineering will move us toward that extreme.

GENETIC LOTTERY

Genetic engineering is the ultimate technology, for it makes plastic the very user and creator of that technology. This new tool makes conceivable a vast number of alternative evolutionary paths. We may even be able to adapt humankind to varied technological regimes.

Will we try, for instance, to breed—or mutate—people fit to work in special environments? Miniature people to travel in space or live on our overpopulated Earth? Will we create people resistant to carcinogens, radiation, and pesticides to work in chemical factories, nuclear plants, and farms? Or, alternatively, will we breed people who are better able to tolerate cytotoxic drugs should they contract cancer? What intellectual abilities, psychological strengths and life-spans would we choose?

I hope it is clear that the whole character of human life is at issue. To use a simile: Life has been a game, like cards, where each of us seeks to make the best of the hands (or genes) dealt to us. Shall it become a game like football, a collective strategy in which people play assigned roles in a coordinated plan? Or might it become more like a card game with a rigged deck, with more aces and fewer treys. If so, who designates the aces?

How will people react when they realize that their very genes are the product of a social decision? Will they rebel against such predestination? Will they become sullen and passive? Or will our descendants be proud they were each "planned," not the product of a genetic lottery but the recipient of the best inheritance our culture could devise at the time? How will they then react should a better model become available during their teens?

To what extent should we consciously leave a place for the element of chance in human affairs?

I suspect there is no turning back from the use of this awesome knowledge. Given the nature of our society, which embraces and applies any new technology, it appears that there is no means, short of unwanted catastrophe, to prevent the development of genetic engineering. It will proceed. But this time, perhaps we can seek to anticipate and guide its consequences.

TAKING THE LARGER VIEW

I believe the university is the place to address and analyze the social consequences of technological innovation. Yet even in academia, pressures for immediate results distract researchers from the quest for deeper understanding. Indeed, a salient characteristic of our increasingly secular society is its emphasis on the short-term payoff. We must try to avoid this myopia in developing this new technology. We must seek to protect the larger view.

Among other things, we must insist that university research continue to be available for public scrutiny in the open scientific literature, that it not be secreted as proprietary information and industrial know-how. We must also insist that private funding directed toward patentable and profitable inventions does not grossly exceed public funding directed toward the general increase of knowledge, including an understanding of possible hazards.

I would suggest that what we sorely need now is a new group of trained professionals to mediate between scientists and engineers on the one hand and citizenry on the other. Such professionals should be practicing scientists more broadly educated in our humanistic traditions. They would be trained to understand the potential implicit in this new technology, able to balance the ethos of environmentalists with the concerns of those who cherish civil liberty, able to perceive the imperatives of a technological society and still bear in mind that technology exists to serve. They would remember that the human species is very diverse, that it encompasses both a Mahatma Gandhi and an Adolf Hitler.

Ecclesiastes tells us that "he that increaseth knowledge increaseth sorrow." The modern version might be "he that increaseth knowledge increaseth power." Western society has become, in a sense, an extraordinary machine for converting knowledge into power.

Human beings, of course, are sprung from the same DNA and built of the same molecules as all other living things. But if we begin to regard ourselves as just another crop to be engineered, just another breed to be perfected, we will lose our awe of humanity and undermine all sense of human dignity.

13

Governing Technology: Values, Choices, and Scientific Progress

DAVID L. BAZELON

Bazelon compares biotechnology to previous technologies, argues that, like them, biotechnology will both promise benefits and threaten harm, and reviews the roles of the judiciary and Congress in dealing with this new technology. He concludes that, since biotechnology policy decisions involve difficult value choices, public debate is needed in order to realistically hope that mistakes can be corrected in the light of new information.

Freud once praised the wonders of modern technology for enabling him to speak with his children living hundreds of miles away. On second thought, he noted that—were it not for the damn modern railroad—his family would not be so far away in the first place.

As a federal judge for more than three decades, I have developed a similar ambivalence toward new technologies. In my private life I enjoy the tremendous benefits that technological progress has brought. On the bench, however, I frequently hear the pleas of persons for whom a particular form of progress represents an onerous burden.[1] That perspective constantly reminds me that technological progress has its costs, and those costs rarely fall equally on us all. The burdens of progress are allocated—explicitly or otherwise.

My observations of earlier technologies make me confident that biotechnology will be a similarly two-sided coin. The promise of biotechnology offers hope to the most destitute people on earth. Through its miracles we can conceive of winning the eternal struggle against hunger and disease.[2] At the same time, the application of biotechnologies carries with it risks that are difficult to define, much less to assess. Many uses of biotechnology will involve the release into the open environment of life forms not currently found in nature. The effects of such microorganisms on the surrounding environment cannot be predicted with certainty—and might be catastrophic. In the event of disastrous consequences, moreover, it is likely that many people will be harmed who had little to gain from the use of the technology in the first place.

In short, the development and use of biotechnology involves decisions about what risks are worth taking for whose benefit. Competing values, each of which is held dearly when considered alone, must be traded off against each other. Selecting these trade-offs is invariably difficult because it forces us to expose priorities which, for a variety of reasons—political or otherwise—we would prefer were left unexposed.[3] In such circumstances, it is tempting to structure the decision-making process in a way that hides the

Reprinted from *Technology in Society* 5, pp. 15–25. Copyright © 1983, Reprinted by permission of Pergamon Press and the author.

clash of values. Methods of choice can be used to create an appearance either that we have avoided making a decision or that it was easy because the proper choice was clear. Both of these approaches are suspect, and the first is pure illusion.

When faced with a promising, but risky, technology, there is no such thing as a non-decision. Prohibiting the technology can preserve the status quo, but at a sometimes devastating cost to those who could have benefitted from it. Postponing a choice is sometimes less devastating, yet frequently entails other costs.[4] Both time and additional information can be expensive resources, and investing in them involves trade-offs as well.

Because difficult issues cannot be avoided, decision-makers frequently camouflage their choices as value-neutral ones. The desired appearance is often achieved by delegating decisions to institutions that convey an appearance of objectivity. A common example is the reliance on the workings of free market forces. But the determinations of the marketplace reflect its values, which a priori are no more neutral than any others.[5] I am reminded of the story of the elephant who shouted, "Everyone for himself!" as he stood in front of a pile of grain among a flock of chickens.

The appearance of value neutrality is also often created through the quantification of competing values to enable comparison of them in an "objective" manner.[6] It is a marvelous trick—simply paint the apple orange, then pick the fairer fruit—but an illusion at best. At bottom, all the difficult decisions about biotechnology will rest on value-laden assumptions, priorities, and predispositions. Shall we release into the ocean a bacteria that cleans up oil spills? What effect will it have on fish? Who gives a damn about fish? I prefer white beaches—though I do have a tender spot for salmon. Uncertain risks coupled with unpleasant trade-offs—but decisions need to be made. Who shall make them, and how?

THE DECISION-MAKERS

Many scientists feel that the regulation of science should properly be left up to the individual scientist. As the publisher of *Scientific American* once wrote, "A scientist can accept no authority but his own judgment and conscience. . . ."[7] If outside interference is to exist at all, according to this view, it should come exclusively from within the scientific community. For only those peers understand the complex issues sufficiently to assess them rationally.

That view predominated until relatively recently. Scientific and technological progress was seen as inevitable and inherently desirable, and we marvelled at the fantastic rate of technological advance. Since World War II, however, government, science and technology have become increasingly interdependent. The reasons for this symbiosis are several. First, the costs of projects, such as constructing an atomic bomb and exploring the universe, are so enormous that only the government has the resources to foot the bill. With funding inevitably comes some supervision. Second, we have become increasingly conscious of the adverse effects that frequently accompany technological developments. Decisions about whether to beat those costs inevitably involve value choices. Such choices certainly fall beyond the exclusive domain of scientists and engineers. Although their expertise is essential for assessing the costs and benefits of particular innovations, it provides no special qualification for determining the appropriate balance between the two.

Scientists frequently object to outside scrutiny, and their complaints are not frivolous. It costs a lot to pay the salaries of the bureaucrats who look over the scientists' shoulders. Moreover, such surveillance can, of course, impede or even stifle research. Many scientists would prefer to return to the prior "unregulated" research environment. They assert that the government should avoid imposing health and safety measures on society, or better still, get out of the risk-control business altogether.[8]

Such suggestions frequently confuse the health-risk problems with the agencies and regulations created to deal with them. Society has always regulated health risks—and always will. Long before regulatory agencies, our system of private lawsuits served to control risk-taking—to encourage some activities and discourage others. In a sense, one cannot really "deregulate" these activities. One can only redistribute their benefits and burdens.[9] Biotechnology can be promoted, for example, by relaxing research regulations and shielding scientists from liability arising out of its use. Likewise, biotechnology can be discouraged by extending the reach of private lawsuits in an attempt to redress indirect harms caused by its use. When an unnatural life form is released into the environment, for example, who shall be liable for harms it may cause— the scientist who developed it, the company that produced it, the customer who relased it, or all of them? And what sorts of harms should they be liable for?

REGULATION IN COMMON LAW

If agencies and legislatures fail to address the risks of biotechnology—either to deter them or compensate their victims—the courts will likely do so, perhaps even more vigorously, in deciding private lawsuits. I can easily imagine the effects of biotechnology producing expansive doctrines in the common law of nuisance and tort. There are many modern examples of the common law evolving to enable private lawsuits to address the harms of new technologies. Tort actions for cancer, for example, have encountered many obstacles because of difficulties in establishing causation, and the fact that cancer frequently develops many years after exposure to carcinogens, when much of the evidence needed to establish liability has been lost. In responding to this problem, the California Supreme Court recently permitted a cancer victim to sue a group of manufacturers of the hormone DES, even though she did not know which one had produced the specific drug that had injured her.[10]

Regulation through the common law has many drawbacks. It has a substantial impact on science, technology, and the economy generally. It "regulates" and constrains just as surely as an agency does. It can cause researchers to follow a variety of unnecessary practices, simply to avoid lawsuits. It also imposes extremely high costs in damages, insurance, and attorneys' fees. Morever, judicial regulation cannot provide the consistency, rationality, or political responsiveness offered by a consciously designed and clearly articulated legislative solution. A courtroom is not the place to decide such complex and controversial issues of fact and policy. And judges are not the appropriate persons to decide them.

The problem is not just that these scientific issues are complicated; courts have long grappled with complicated issues in reviewing actions by the FCC, SEC, ICC, CAB, and scores of other governmental regulatory agencies. These more traditional administrative matters, however, involve issues with which all judges have at least a speaking familiarity. Increasingly, the caseload of our courts involves challenges to federal administrative action relating to the frontiers of technology. Expanding health and safety regulations and increasing citizens' suits have drawn the courts into such difficult questions as: What level of exposure to known carcinogens is safe for industrial workers?[11] Shall we ban the Concorde SST,[12] DDT,[13] or lead in gasoline?[14] How shall society manage radioactive wastes?[15] I dare say that most judges do not have the knowledge and training to assess the merits of competing scientific arguments involved in these issues, and that it is hardly a task for on-the-job training.

More important, regulation through common law doctrines places decisions concerning appropriate trade-offs among competing values in the hands of judges. As an independent branch of government lacking in political accountability, the judiciary should feel reluctant to play this role. I know that I do. I realize that such a role is, to a certain extent, inevitable in a common law system such as ours. But the evolution of the common law through judicial innovation creates fewer problems of legitimacy when that evolution occurs in small increments over a long period of time. Such evolution is more likely to reflect a consensus of values and to permit legislative intervention when it frustrates the majoritarian will.

In recent years, however, the rapid advancement of powerful technologies has created new legal problems on a scope and at a rate that overwhelms the ability of the common law to respond in a coherent, legitimate manner. The nature of the technological risks at stake cannot be addressed sensibly on a case-by-case basis. Many harms, particularly those to the environment, take years to manifest and often cannot be traced to their sources. Those damages must be addressed through regulation to prevent harm rather than litigation to redress it. Control of such risks cannot be left to the ad hoc value choices of judges through possibly inconsistent determinations at trial.

The temptation to place difficult value choices on judges is particularly great concerning ethical questions which, because they seem less complex, seem more within the competence of judges. Advances in the biological sciences have already presented several such questions and are sure to generate many more. Questions concerning the legal definition of death, a patient's right to die, a patient's right to demand treatment such as *in vitro* fertilization, all present difficult moral questions in a technological context. Biotechnology presents similar ethical questions arising out of, for example, the foreseeable potential to alter the genetic make-up of man.[16] Although perhaps few persons would object to tampering with genes to eliminate tragic birth defects, who should define a birth defect? If we have the capability to make everyone six feet tall, should we do so? Should our tampering with the "natural order" deprive someone who would otherwise be of unusual intellect of his privileged position?

ETHICAL VERSUS TECHNICAL ISSUES

Some of these issues present questions of constitutional law, which the judiciary must decide. For the most part, however, judges are not the appropriate persons to decide such issues. In the context of the courtroom, moreover, ethical questions tend to be avoided in favor of the technical issues involved. In the recent controversy over the patentability of living microorganisms,[17] for example, the legal arguments have focused on the intended coverage of patent laws and the distinction between an invention and a living organism.[18] Little debate has considered the moral question whether to extend the concept of proprietary rights to commercial use of new life forms.

Government regulation will not necessarily eliminate the problems I have mentioned concerning regulation through private lawsuit. But it may obviate the courts' need to confront many intractable risk problems and ethical dilemmas. If Congress has consciously made an ethical choice concerning a particular technology, if it has weighed the scientific evidence, assessed the economic effects, and tested the political winds concerning a particular risk, *or* if it has delegated these tasks to a regulatory agency, specifying the procedures, policies, and standards to be applied, then courts will more readily defer to those legislative decisions.

Although the appropriate role for the courts in the regulation of biotechnology is limited, it is nevertheless important. It consists principally of judicial oversight of actions by administrative agencies. In playing that role, however, courts and judges must recognize the implications of their institutional strengths and limitations. It makes no sense to rely upon the courts to evaluate the scientific and technological determinations of agencies. There is perhaps even less reason for the courts to substitute their own value preferences for those of the agency, to which the legislature has presumably delegated the decisional power and responsibility. The limits of judicial competence in technical fields and the judiciary's lack of political accountability preclude these roles.

The contribution that courts can make in this process is in monitoring the decision-making processes of agencies to make sure that they are open, thorough, and rational.[19] In this role, courts rely on their institutional strengths. The independence of the judiciary, which delegitimizes judicial choices among competing values in the first instance, is an advantage in the role of monitor. Likewise, lawyers are very familiar with the rights of interested parties to be heard, requirements of notice, openness, and disclosure. These concepts form the core of the administrative process. The legal training of the bench and bar—although wholly inadequate for evaluating scientific evidence—is good preparation for overseeing that process.

THE NEED FOR PUBLIC DEBATE

The goal of judicial oversight is to facilitate peer review and legislative and public oversight. By forcing an agency to articulate the factual basis and rationale of its decisions, they can be evaluated by other experts in academe, government, and industry. Individuals and groups that differ with the agency's value choices can make their views known in the various public forums. Such public debate gives reason to hope that erroneous decisions can be changed in light of new information or changing preferences.

The need for public ventilation of difficult value choices reminds me of an extraordinarily painful experience that I had many years ago at the University of Washington School of Medicine. I had been invited to sit in as an anguished group of doctors, confronted by the mind-boggling cost and limited availability of life-saving renal dialysis, sentenced some of their patients to death so that others could live.[20] A pair of massive oaken doors hung tightly closed in the background. After the doctors had made their horrifying choices, one anxiously asked me if I had any suggestions. Feeling impotent in the face of these awesome moral dilemmas, I could offer only one thought. "See those doors over there," I said. "Keep them open. Let the public know how you have made these decisions. Show the public your assumptions, your uncertainty, and your value choices. Let them share your burden."

When I have told this story at other times, many people have pointed out that when horribly difficult choices must be made, there may be value in not knowing how it is done.

Should a person sentenced to die because of a shortage of renal dialysis machines have to face the added trauma of knowing why he was not chosen to live? Must he be told that it was because he was old, or poor, or uneducated, and considered less "valuable" than other candidates for treatment?

Such an argument is only persuasive to me if one assumes that certain decisions are fixed, when, in fact, they are not. One must assume, for example, that the number of available renal dialysis machines is set in concrete. In fact, that number reflects an allocation of society's resources away from other uses. Can we really assume that, if the public understood the impact of their decision and the choices it implies, they would not make a different choice? Might not the public decide to build one less nuclear warhead in order to save a certain number of individuals who happen to have defective kidneys? Unless we know that the answer to that question is negative, we must not encourage the public to remain uninformed.

Having argued for full disclosure of values and uncertainty, I realize that institutional pressures often militate against this approach. Uncertainty is messy. It detracts from the simplicity of presentation, ease of understanding, and uniformity of application. To focus on uncertainty is to invite paralysis. To disclose it is to risk public misunderstanding or opposition. Such unattractive possibilities encourage policymakers to ignore uncertainties and compensate for them by, for example, making intentionally inflated estimates of risk. They might incorporate extremely conservative assumptions about the shape of a dose-response curve for low levels of a harmful agent. But such tactics do not erase the uncertainty inherent in many decisions, and an added safety margin may tilt the balance away from the best alternative. The goal is accurate forecasting to enable a comparison among alternatives. Where scientific estimates are highly tentative and filled with uncertainty, those uncertainties must be fully disclosed and considered as part of the package.

CONSIDERATION OF UNKNOWNS

I do not mean to suggest that public oversight should impede agency action in the face of uncertainty. For some activities, the magnitude of potential harm and the probability of its occurrence may be essentially unknown. That is certainly the case concerning much research in biotechnology and the application of it. Many risk estimates depend upon future contingencies of human behavior or other highly complex and unpredictable variables. Historical experience may be totally lacking, as it was when biotechnology first began. Even the best risk estimates are subject to an unknown degree of residual uncertainty and may thus overstate or understate the dangers involved. And many times an agency must act in circumstances that make a crap game look as certain as death and taxes. In such situations an agency need only disclose the uncertainties that it faces and explain why action is necessary in spite of such risk. As long as the agency satisfies the level of certainty required by Congress, the courts should not interfere.

When scientists participate in the public debate over biotechnology—as I hope that they will—they must keep in mind the specific role that they play. They are not, unless so designated, the policymakers. Their role is not to make conclusions concerning the appropriate trade-offs among risks, but rather to make clearer what the estimated trade-offs are. What the public needs most from any expert, biologists included, is his wealth of intermediate observations and conceptual insights adequately explained. Decision on the ultimate questions must be left to the public decision-making process.

My experience with the regulatory system suggests that scientists are uncomfortable in this role. Scientists who appear in the public arena all too often focus on little more than making conclusory pronouncements. Either they omit any real discussion of underlying observations and methods of inference—or they drown such discussion in a sea of jargon. To paraphrase Lewis Carroll, they use "labels as shrouds rather than guides." The tell us a particular innovation is safe, rather than *how* safe and *why*. They ignore the basic fact that a conclusion that a technology is "safe" reflects a host of value choices about the relative importance of such diverse concerns as the health of a particular industry or company, the severity of the problem addressed by the technology, and the value of the things that the technology might harm. Just as a doctor's decision to send a patient home from the hospital might be influenced by overcrowded conditions in the hospital, a biologist's recommendation that a particular microorganism can be safely released into the environment may be affected by considerations independent of the risk that the release might cause harm.

In short, conclusory statements are of little use in making ultimate decisions that must be left to the public arena. Policy questions are multi-dimensional. They involve scientific, moral, and social judgments. Conclusory statements cannot be digested by the decision-making process. Simply put, they fail to provide the facts that the public needs to mix with its moral and social judgments. Scientists must recognize the right of the public to make basic value and risk choices.

MAKING DECISIONS OPENLY

As an interested observer of the biotechnology controversy, the development of the NIH Recombinant DNA Research Guidelines strikes me as an optimistic example of how decisions on controversial issues can be made openly.[21] At the time that work on the Guidelines began, the situation in biotechnology had all the ingredients for developing into an impassioned political stalemate. From the scientists' perspective, the principle of free scientific inquiry was at stake over a technology that may be the most powerful tool ever devised for biological advance. From the public's perspective, biotechnology involved the release of new life forms into the environment with potentially catastrophic consequences—a fact that many of the researchers acknowledged in 1973 when they adopted a self-imposed moratorium on certain kinds of research. These conflicting interests created strong pressure to gloss over the potential risks and convince the public not to be interested.

Instead, the public was invited to participate in the development of guidelines for regulating the research. At the opening of a public hearing on the Guidelines, Dr. Fredrickson, Director of the NIH, observed, "Recombinant DNA research brings to the fore problems of public scrutiny of the process and the progress of basic science. . . . Procedural safeguards with a full exploration of relevant facts and possible alternatives must be the hallmark of the scientific process, if we are to retain the trust and the whole-hearted support of society."[22] In addition to public participation, the NIH developed an environmental impact assessment in compliance with the National Environmental Policy Act of 1969.[23] The assessment gave thorough consideration to the environmental effects of research to be conducted under the Guidelines.

In retrospect, it seems that the initial Guidelines and the concern that produced them were over-reactions. The dangers appear less catastrophic, and controlling them less difficult, than at first imagined. But the process has shown itself very flexible in meeting changed perceptions of risk. The Guidelines have been continuously reconsidered, and many have been revised or removed.[24] Public hearings concerning possible changes have been held at every stage. This process continues apace.

Critics of public participation will point to the delays that it causes to suggest that public involvement should be kept to the minimum. It is possible, for example, that the NIH Guidelines could have been written more expeditiously if they had been developed with greater secrecy. I suspect, however, that the later the public had been asked to participate, the greater their sense of suspicion would have been. The willingness of scientists to describe their uncertainties, to allow public participation and comment, has produced considerable good will toward biotechnology. Despite some early sensationalism, I think

that the public has performed responsibly. The Guidelines seem to have produced an outcome that allows research in biotechnology to continue in a manner that scientists can live with and that the public finds worthwhile.

The regulatory experience of biotechnology contrasts sharply with the history of relations among the public, the government, and industry concerning nuclear power.[25] That history has been shaped in part by a continued insistence by industry and the regulators that the issues involved are beyond the grasp of the public. To prevent the public from creating obstacles to the new technology, the regulating agencies have continuously tried to restrict public participation. When mistakes have been made—and inevitably they have been— the public's disappointment is reinforced by their lack of involvement. This feeling has certainly hampered the ability of the NRC to provide the public with assurances that it has adequately considered the safety-risks of nuclear power. The fact that many mistakes of the past had been foreseen by public groups whose warnings were ignored has added fire to the public's cynicism. The resulting uneasy atmosphere has hampered the growth of both nuclear technology and the nuclear power industry.

THE REQUIREMENT OF OPENNESS

It follows, therefore, that openness is in everyone's best interest. When issues are controversial, any decision will fail to satisfy large portions of the community. But those who are dissatisfied with a particular decision will be more likely to acquiesce in it if they perceive that their views and interests were given a fair hearing. If the decision-maker has frankly laid the competing considerations on the table—so that the public knows the worst and the best—he is unlikely to find himself accused of high-handedness, deceit, or cover-up. Scientists cannot afford, for the public will not tolerate, the handling of these vital matters in a manner that invites public cynicism and distrust.

In the final analysis, the requirement of openness and candor in controlling risky technologies reflects our society's democratic values. Power in the society resides with the people. The freedom enjoyed by scientists and industry to explore is given by the public and can be taken away. In this sense, the prerogatives of a technology depend upon the public good will. False reassurance, unjustified confidence, and hidden agendas will only encourage the public to exercise its ultimate veto power. Our people have always been prepared to accept risks and pursue the greater good of society. Progress can hardly be achieved any other way. It was Thomas Jefferson who once said, "If we think the people not enlightened enough to exercise their control with a wholesome discretion, the remedy is not to take it from them, but to inform their discretion."[26] Choices will be made despite uncertainty and despite their social disruptions and dislocations. To preserve the good will on which biotechnology depends, however, society must be informed about what is known, what is feared, what is hoped, and what is yet to be learned.

NOTES

1. See e.g., Keene v. Insurance Co. of North America, 667 F. 2d 1034 (D.C. Cir. 1981) (asbestos); American Federation of Labor v. Marshall, 617 F. 2d 636 (D.C. Cir. 1979), *aff'd in part, vacated in part sub nom,* American Textile Mfrs. Institute, Inc. v. Donovan, 452 U.S. 490 (1981) (cotton dust); Environmental Defense Fund, Inc. v. Ruckelshaus, 439 F. 2d 584 (D.C. Cir. 1971) (DDT).

2. See Krause, "Is the Biological Revolution a Match for the Trinity of Despair?", *Technology in Society* 4:4 (1982).

3. See generally Calabresi and Bobbitt, *Tragic Choices* (1978), discussing different methods societies use to make "tragic" choices.

4. See Environmental Defense Fund, Inc. v. Hardin, 428 F. 2d 1093 (D.C. Cir. 1970) (reviewing agency inaction rather than action).

5. Perhaps most significantly, market determinations reflect an existing distribution of wealth. See Calabresi and Bobbitt *supra* note 3, at 81-129 (discussing methods of modifying market allocation systems and the flaws of such modifications).

6. This approach is seen most clearly in attempts at cost-benefit analysis. The flaw with such analysis in many contexts is well known. It stems from the difficulty of identifying and quantifying many costs and benefits; the inevitably arbitrary nature of valuations of human life or health; the problem of interpersonal and intergenerational comparisons of utility; and many others. See P. Schuck, *Regulation: Asking the Right Questions,* 11 Nat'l J. 711 (1979); National Academy of Sciences, *Decision Making for Regulating Chemicals in the Environment* 39–44 (1975) (report prepared by the Natinal Research Council); E. Quade, *Analysis for Public Decisions* 25–26 (1975).

7. Sinsheimer and Piel, *Inquiring Into Inquiry: Two Opposing Views,* Hastings Center Report, August 1976, at 19 (statement by Piel).

8. In 1976 the National Science Foundation asked directors of leading American research institutions for their views on the state of American science. A recurring response was an objection to excessive regulation of scientific activities, and to bureaucratic "meddling" in the scientific domain. See National Science Board, National Science Foundation, *Science at the Bicentennial: A Report from the Research Community* 63–69 (1976). In the words of one participant in the study, "the ever increasing bureaucracy . . . will in the not too distant future completely eradicate our Nation's world position in research and technology." *Id.* at 66 (response of the Director of Los Alamos Scientific Laboratory).

9. See L. Friedman, *A History of American Law* 409–27 (1973) (arguing that the common law of torts changed during the industrial revolution in order to protect emerging industries from some forms of liability); M. Horwitz, *The Transformation of American Law* (1977) (same); but see Schwartz, *Torts Law and the Economy in Nineteenth-Century America: A Reinterpretation* 90 Yale L.J. 1717 (1981) (arguing that nineteenth century tort law did not favor industry).

10. Sindell v. Abbott Laboratories, 607 P. 2d 924, *cert. denied sub nom.* E.R. Squibb & Sons, Inc. v. Sindell, 449 U.S. 912 (1980) (cancer victim permitted to sue six of 200 DES manufacturers because six defendants constituted 90% of the market).

11. Industrial Union Department, AFL-CIO v. American Petroleum Institute, 448 U.S. 607 (1980) (benzene).

12. See Environmental Defense Fund, Inc. v. Coleman, No. 76–1105 (D.C. Cir. May 19, 1976) (unreported).

13. See Environmental Defense Fund, Inc. v. Ruckelshaus, 439 F. 2d 584 (D.C. Cir. 1971).

14. See Ethyl Corp. v. EPA, 541 F. 2d 1 (D.C. Cir.) (en banc), *cert. denied,* 426 U.S. 941 (1976).

15. Natural Resources Defense Council, Inc. v. NRC, 547 F. 2d 633 (D.C. Cir. 1976), *rev'd sub nom.* Vermont Yankee Nuclear Power Corp. v. Natural Resources Defense Council, Inc., 435 U.S. 519 (1978).

16. See e.g., President's Commission for the Study of Ethical Problems in Medicine and Bio-medical and Behavioral Research, *Splicing Life: A Report on the Social and Ethical Issues of Genetic Engineering with Human Beings,* ch. 3 (1980).

17. See Diamond v. Chakrabarry, 447 U.S. 303 (1980).

18. *Id.* at 309–10. The Court explicitly refused to consider the policy issues raised by the parties, saying that they should "be addressed to the political branches of the Government, the Congress and the Executive, and not to the courts." *Id.* at 317.

19. For several years my colleagues on the D.C. Circuit and I have engaged in a lively debate about the standards that should govern judicial review of administrative action in scientific areas. See, for example, the five separate opinions in Ethyl Corp. v. EPA, 541 F. 2d 1 (D.C. Cir.) (en banc), *cert. denied,* 426 U.S. 941 (1976), in which our court upheld regulations issued by the EPA Administra-tor requiring annual reductions in lead content of gasoline. In large part, the debate has focused on the extent to which judicial review should examine only agency procedures followed in taking an action or whether it should also review the substance of the action. Compare Bazelon, *Coping with Technology Through the Legal Process,* 62 Cornell L. Rev. 817 (1977) with Leventhal, *Environmental Decision-making and the Role of the Courts,* 122 U. Penn L. Rev. 509 (1974).

20. For additional discussion of this allocation system, known as the "Seattle God Committee," see Calabresi and Bobbitt, *supra* note 3, at 187–188.

21. For a more complete history of the develop-ment of the guidelines, see Perpich, "Industrial Involvement in the Development of NIH Recombi-nant DNA Reseach Guidelines and Related Federal Policies," 5 *Recombinant DNA Technical Bulletin* 59 (June 1982).

22. *Id.* at 60.

23. 42 U.S.C. § 4321 (1976).

24. See 43 *Fed. Reg.* 33042–33178 (July 28, 1978) (proposed revisions); 43 *Fed. Reg.* 60080–60105 (1978) (final revisions).

25. For a richly detailed account of the nuclear power controversy, see S. Tolchin and M. Tolchin, *Dismantling America: The Rush to Deregulate,* ch. 6 (Boston: Houghton Mifflin Company, 1983).

26. Letter from Thomas Jefferson to W.C. Jarvis (September 28, 1820), reprinted in 7 *Writings of Thomas Jefferson* 177, 179 (H. Washington, ed., 1855).

policy issues
moral/ ethical issues

14
Overdosing on Medical Technology

DAVID HELLERSTEIN

David Hellerstein asserts that advanced health care technology threatens to lead to a situation in which hospitals will be filled with very ill people kept alive but miserable for a long time. To prevent this, he suggests instructing students in how to listen to patients' concerns; attempting to change the attitudes of physicians by holding conferences on questions of technological "overkill"; and, most of all, instituting technology evaluation teams, each including an internist, an intensive-care specialist, a psychiatrist, a nurse, and patient advocates.

A few years ago, when I was in medical school, I spent a long Sunday afternoon squeezing bags of blood. I was on Surgery service then, and had half a mind of becoming a surgeon—I loved the cutting and sewing, the urgent rush to the operating room, and the feeling of omnipotence that came from excising disease and suturing together what was left.

This particular Sunday, an old alcoholic was brought into the emergency room, nearly dead. His name was Kalicki (all the names in this article have been changed), and his bloated belly was rigid. His body had all the stigmata of the end-stage boozer—beef-red palms, dilated webs of veins across his stomach, spidery bursts of broken blood vessels on his face and chest. There seemed to be no question of what to do. The excited voices of residents and nurses filled the emergency room, as intravenous lines were started, blood was drawn, and catheters passed into stomach and bladder. Soon old Kalicki was in the operating room. His belly was shaved and prepped, and in a few minutes the surgeon had made an incision along the line of his ribs.

Kalicki's insides were a confusion of old scars and adhesions. With each slice of the surgeon's scalpel, each movement of a blunt probe, new blood bubbled up black from within. The electric bovie, which usually stops bleeding with its cauterizing jolt, only brought forth new oozing. Kalicki's pressure began to drop; the intravenous lines were opened wide. His pressure kept falling. The blood bank was notified of the state of emergency, and soon soft plastic bags of blood began to arrive. Plastic tubing was uncoiled, new lines were started in the arms and neck, and in a few minutes what seemed like a forest of weird maroon fruit with long purple stems hung over the table. Yet Kalicki's blood pressure stayed low.

That was when they told me to drop the

Reprinted from *Technology Review* (August–September 1983), pp. 13–17. Copyright ©1983 by David Hellerstein. Reprinted by permission of *Technology Review* and the author.

retractor I had been holding and grab a bag of blood in my gloved hands. And to squeeze. I squeezed. I squeezed like hell. I must have squeezed a dozen bags until my hands went limp. Then somebody else took over, pushing hands together to force blood through the limp plastic tubing, frantically fighting to replace the deluge on the table. Of course it didn't work. Every suture put inside Kalicki's belly to stop the bleeding only brought new blood softly pumping to the surface. Finally, after 30-odd units of precious blood had traveled through Kalicki's leaky system, the chief surgeon said to stop. And everyone stood there in that stainless steel and tile room, gowned and gloved, as the pressure fell and Kalicki died. By the time somebody went to tell Kalicki's son, it was 7:30 at night; the day was gone. The son was not much surprised. Really, he said, it was for the best. The family had been expecting this for years.

That was it. Or almost it. A few weeks later, in the monthly morbidity and mortality conference, somebody brought up Kalicki's case, and mentioned a paper about the regrettably high incidence of uncontrollable bleeding in end-stage cirrhosis of the liver. Our chief commented that as soon as he made the first cut, he knew he wouldn't be able to stop the bleeding. But once he'd started, what choice did he have?

POINTLESS DISPLAYS OF TECHNIQUE

The events of that afternoon have stuck with me. Even without them I doubt I'd have been a surgeon, but they did cast a pall on the whole endeavor. What had looked so heroic now seemed bullheaded and pointless, a display of technique for its own sake.

At first such displays seemed peculiar to surgery, but as I finished medical school and began my internship and residency I began to see the same sequence of events played out over and over indifferent settings—in internal medicine, pediatrics, neurology, and oncology. Time after time we'd be there, in situations with no hope of survival. What I was seeing, I realized finally, was not an isolated phenomenon but something pervad-

ing the contemporary practice of medicine in America.

Certainly there are some situations where the motives for continuing aggressive treatment are more or less rational. If there is a slight hope of recovery, it's always difficult to stop treatment. And in an emergency, it's often better to act first and question later. Sometimes there are educational reasons for making a vigorous push—so interns and residents-can learn to deal with the failure of multiple systems. Other times there's a need to experiment with a new drug or technique. Still other times I think there's a vague fear that lawyers might be sniffing around for malpractice possibilities or that an outraged family member might turn up after the fact. And in still other situations, unethical practitioners may perform extra tests for their own financial gain. But in many terminal situations, the barrage of testing and treatment continues without any apparent reason. The machinery of the hospital, once set in motion, just continues rolling.

These are the most baffling situations. For some reason we doctors don't seem to know how *not* to treat, how not to make the first cut, how to stand back and let nature have its way. To decide not to treat the pneumococcal pneumonia in a dying patient seems like negligence—even it it may be mercy. To leave a cancer drug on the shelf seems like a crime.

To some degree, this obsession with technology reflects a bias of our culture. But to blame this situation solely on our culture would be futile. It would also be a mistake, because the problem has as much to do with the habits of the medical profession as anything else. Over the past century, medicine has grown from being a relatively passive clinical discipline with an emphasis on the observation of disease into a scientifically based profession dedicated to the collection of data, the close monitoring of organ function, and above all the aggressive treatment of disease. The medical profession embraces—indeed, endorses—technology with little critical examination. It rewards overtesting and overtreating. And worst of all, it has trained an entire generation of doctors—mine—in certain attitudes and thought patterns that are often detrimental to patient care.

My own experience was a textbook example. I received my training in a medical center that prides itself on delivering highly specialized, state-of-the-art care. But along with my excellent formal education in high-tech medicine came a number of informal lessons that often led to bad treatment.

TECHNOLOGY PAYS

One was the lesson of our patients' lab sheets. Every day, a new computerized record of all lab tests would be put into all the patient's charts; it was a record of all tests done since the person entered the hospital. By the time someone had been in the hospital for a few weeks, this record could amount to 30 or 40 pages. The sense one got from this was that it would be a good idea to order a whole new set of tests every day—to check against the day before.

A second lesson—which I occasionally wish I had learned better—was that technology pays. Technology gets people grants, promotions, tenure. The surest way to power in a medical center is to ally oneself with technology. I can think of one resident in my psychiatry program who has learned this lesson particularly well. When he heard that our medical center was about to get an NMR scanner, an experimental diagnostic device, he learned as much as he could about the new machine and its possible relevance to psychiatry. He became instrumental in writing up protocol for research on the new machine and in supervising the research. This affiliation has given him power—the power to control access to this device—and will eventually enable him to publish a stream of research papers that can only increase his standing among other psychiatrists.

In addition, technology reimburses its followers well. The anesthesiologist makes more than the pediatrician, and the internist who performs more procedures to make a diagnosis makes more money than the internist who does only a few.

A third lesson, not explicitly stated but obviously followed in practice, was that virtually everyone should be treated. Instead of acknowledging that one patient might stand a chance of being cured while another might only have his or her terminal pain relieved, our approach was that we should try to do everything for everybody. It was extremely difficult for us to step back and ask what our overall goals should be or even more important, to find out what the patient might want.

The same lessons, apparently, are still being taught today. In the first major review since 1932 of what doctors study for their M.D. diploma, a panel of the Association of the American Medical Colleges (AAMC) found that medical students are being swamped by science and technology at the expense of basic healing skills. "Specialization and the rapid rate of advancement of knowledge and technology may tend to pre-empt the attention of both teachers and students from the central purpose of medicine, which is to heal the sick and relieve the suffering," was how the AAMC panel phrased it.

Aside from doctors' attitudes, another reason for the excessive use of technology has to do with its consumers—patients and their families. Technology often serves the purposes that religious ritual once did. Better than prayers or candles or offerings, technology conveys hope. For the dying patient, the lab test and the CAT scan are symbols of recovery, and the administration of drugs or futile emergency operations brings a certain degree of relief. For the family, there is also some consolation in the thought that everything that can be done is being done. "Intensive care" sounds like love, so the dying patient is surrounded by monitors and catheters and respirators.

HIDING BEHIND MACHINES

Technology is often used as a distraction as well—to avoid painful and difficult issues. During my internship, this happened with an old man dying of stomach cancer. Mr. Johnson came to my hospital floor in a terminal state. But before we'd let him die, we did an enormous workup: CAT scans of body and head, x-rays of soft and hard tissues, collections of all available body fluids. He spent days in radiology waiting for these tests. He was sure we'd cure him; he had great faith in medicine. He'd already gone through one regimen of anticancer drugs with no effect; we gave him a second, experimental regimen. When that failed, a third course was begun. The most difficult thing to recall in retrospect is his suffering, not only the pain of his disease but the long waits for tests and his extreme pain from the corrosive chemotherapy. He'd cry when the futile medication went through his IV. Only in the last day or so did he realize that it was having no effect, and then he began screaming that we were killing him. There was no way to console him.

He was wrong, of course—we weren't killing him, but we weren't doing him any favor either. We were just adding to his expense and suffering, misleading him with technology. Probably we, his doctors, were misleading ourselves too; the oncologists I was working with knew full well they couldn't save Mr. Johnson, but nobody could admit it. And that's the problem. Despite all the promise of medical technology, in the crucial moments, many of us are ashamed to admit how woefully inadequate it remains.

Technology serves still another function: that of communication. There is no language anymore for sitting by the bedside; the doctor has no time for waiting and consoling. More and more, the monitor's beep and squeal replaces the doctor's voice. The sounds of communication in the hospital are not English words but the respirator and the CAT scan. Many patients, like Mr. Johnson, are falsely reassured by these sounds, only to learn too late that they mean nothing.

Whether serving as communication, ritual, habit, or evasion, medical technology fulfills often fundamentally dishonest purposes. It is expensive, wasteful, and not infrequently inhumane to communicate through machines. And it may not even improve doctors' ability to diagnose disease, according to a recent study by physicians at Boston's Brigham and Women's Hospital. The study was conducted to determine whether the new diagnostic hardware was making autopsies obsolete as a way of helping doctors learn from their mistakes. The investigators studied the results of 100 post-mortem examinations performed at their hospital in 1960, 1970, and 1980, and they found that the percentage of diagnostic errors was about the same in each of the three time periods. So much for the infallibility of technology.

LEARNING HOW TO LISTEN

What, then, can be done to remedy this addition to machines, this technological fix? Ironically, sheer cost is forcing policymakers on the state and federal level to act. Already, five states have devised their own hospital-reimbursement plans based, for the most part, upon fixed fees for services. The Reagan administration is proposing a similar package that would replace the traditional Medicaid reimbursement system with one that establishes, in advance, prices for 467 specific diagnoses. If a hospital spends less than the set Medicaid price, it gets to pocket the difference, creating an incentive to hold costs down. However, under this system, hospitals may end up denying patients care beyond a certain arbitrary limit. Particularly needy patients may suffer, and I don't believe this approach will make doctors more selective in their use of technology.

Any truly effective changes must come from the medical profession itself. And the place to start is at the beginning—by changing the values taught in medical school. The AAMC panel has wisely concluded that students must be taught to pay attention to treating minor problems, compiling patient histories, and using fundamental instruments such as the stethoscope. I would also suggest instruction in how to deal with terminally ill patients and their families, how to rely less on tests and more on diagnostic judgment, how to listen to patients' concerns. Such courses should be required, beginning in medical school and continuing through the clinical years of training.

Furthermore, we should attempt to change

the attitudes of doctors already out of school. Many practitioners, in an effort to keep up with the bewildering pace of clinical research, regularly attend conferences and read two or three professional journals a week. Why not hold conferences, sponsored by individual hospitals or medical associations, in which the questions of technological overkill are discussed regarding specific cases? Answers to questions such as what tests are unnecessary and at what point treatment should be abandoned become increasingly important as newer technologies emerge, as we implant artificial hearts as well as kidneys, as the prospect of artificial livers becomes less fantastic. We may soon face a day when all our hospitals will be filled with very ill people whose physical existence can be prolonged almost indefinitely but whose quality of life will be intolerable.

THE TEAM APPROACH

I also think it essential that we get directly into the medical arena to affect decisions as they are being made. Most hospitals have professional groups that evaluate patient care, but these "utilization review" committees are not very effective in dealing with the problem of overtreatment. They basically want to make sure that some kind of active treatment—or testing—is under way; they don't look too closely at whether it's really necessary. In fact, these committees may sometimes encourage a frenzy of overactivity among doctors who don't even know whether a particular patient should be hospitalized.

What I propose instead is the team approach—a group of medical professionals who would go on regular hospital rounds to evaluate the use of technology in patient care. Such a team could be similar to the "pain team" I know of at one hospital that evaluates the best approach to relieving the pain of terminal cancer patients. The team includes an internist, a neurologist, a psychiatrist, a social worker, and a nurse. Similarly, a "technology evaluation team" could be composed of an internist, an intensive-care specialist, a psychiatrist, a nurse, and a few patient advocates. Team members would work with doctors and patients to help them decide on reasonable treatment goals and on the best use of medical technology. Such teams could help restore medical technologies to their proper role as useful, but fallible, tools. Some doctors may perceive this kind of team as a threat to their own authority or as a potential source of embarrassment. But I think many would welcome the support in making difficult clinical decisions.

One final example. At the end of my internship, an elderly man, a Mr. Stone, came to my floor with severe heart failure. Despite high doses of all the right medications, his body filled up with excess fluid. He was almost unable to breathe; only by giving him intravenous Lasix, which increases the flow of urine, could his lungs be kept clear. I was shocked when his cardiologist, Dr. Evans, took me aside one afternoon to recommend that I stop giving Lasix. Dr. Evans said that Mr. Stone was not enjoying life anymore, that he was very unlikely to make it out of the hospital, that he, Dr. Evans, had discussed intensive care and dialysis with the Stones and they had decided against that kind of intervention, and that Mrs. Stone was suffering because of her husband's protracted illness.

I can't see it, I said—it's just a few squirts of Lasix every day. So I continued. Mr. Stone kept getting heavier and had more trouble breathing. Mrs. Stone was sitting at his bedside every day, suffering. So one day I decided that I was being ridiculous and did what Dr. Evans suggested. Mr. Stone died. Mrs. Stone cried and thanked me and went home.

I knew I'd done the right thing yet I felt strange, because I knew that if I *wanted* to I could have kept his heart going for quite a long time. It was very unsettling, after the kind of training I'd received, to just stand aside and let nature have its way.

15

Policy Implications of the Diffusion and Control of Medical Technology

H. DAVID BANTA, ANNE KESSELMAN BURNS, AND
CLYDE J. BEHNEY

The authors state that medical technology has become a controversial national policy issue, largely because of rising national health expenditures and their relation to medical technology. They argue that concerns about medical technology transcend the cost issue, and that the available evidence, though scarce, indicates that acquisition of medical technology is more likely to result from the actions of hospital administrators and selected hospital-based or hospital-oriented physicians than by demands of patient-admitting community physicians. In this context, the authors discuss the Medicare program and make suggestions for its reform.

Technology has become a visible and much-discussed issue in the United States during the past few years. Medical technology has also become controversial, in part because of this broader concern about technology and in large part because of the rapidly rising costs of health care.

What is technology? Galbraith[1] defined it as "the systematic application of scientific or other organized knowledge to practical tasks." Thus technology is more than hardware and, in fact, is pervasive in our society and in our health care system. The Office of Technology Assessment (OTA) defines medical technology as "the drugs, devices, and medical and surgical procedures used in medical care, and the organizational and support systems within which such care is delivered."[2] Medical technologies may also be categorized by their purposes, including prevention, diagnosis, treatment, and rehabilitation. In this article, we will focus on drugs, devices, and procedures, but many of our statements will also apply to system technologies.

Medical technology has become a policy issue largely because of the rising costs of medical care. National health expenditures have risen at an average annual rate of about 13 percent over the past 15 years, twice the rate of general inflation. Health expenditures as a percentage of the gross national product have risen from 4.4. percent in 1950 to almost 10 percent in 1981.[3] These dramatic increases have led to a search for the causes and have also spawned a variety of government and private programs aimed at slowing the rate of increase.

The search for underlying causes has been somewhat successful. Economists have demonstrated that technology, broadly construed, accounts for up to half the cost increases of recent years.[4] However, the exact source of

Originally published in *Annals of the American Academy of Political and Social Science* 468 (July 1983), pp. 165–181. Copyright © 1983 by the American Academy of Political and Social Science. Reprinted by permission of Sage Publications, Inc.

the increase has not been well characterized. Is it due to expensive procedures, such as computed tomography (CT) scanning and coronary bypass surgery? Is it due to the proliferation of many small changes, such as the hundreds of tests available in the usual modern clinical laboratory? What is the contribution of physician incomes? These and many other questions remain to be effectively addressed.

Concerns about medical technology transcend the cost issue. While medical technology has clearly made major contributions to health, the benefits of specific technologies are not always so clear, especially in recent years. The triumphs of previous decades seemed to encourage a nearly unquestioning acceptance of new technology. However, many medical technologies introduced during the past few years have come under increasing questioning.

Some medical technologies have been widely used and then abandoned as ineffective, and the risks of technology are gaining increasing attention.[5] Many feel that risks were not adequately considered when the benefits of a new technology were estimated by physicians and others.

Further, in an era of obviously limited resources, costs are increasingly viewed in relation to benefits or effectiveness. The application of the formal techniques of cost-benefit and cost-effectiveness analysis have gained increasing prominence.[6] Some economists have described the basic problem with medical technology as an increasingly small marginal benefit for an increasingly large marginal cost.[7] This is obviously more difficult to deal with than lack of benefit.

Attempts to control the rate of increase of costs and adoption of medical technology have largely been regulatory. A wide range of state and federal government programs have been aimed at this purpose. One important federal undertaking has been the health planning program, with its ability to deny certificates-of-need to institutions that want to make large capital investments. Another keystone attempt is the professional standards review organizations (PSRO) program, in which physician services in hospitals paid for by Medicare and Medicaid are reviewed for appropriateness. While these programs have had many positive results, they have failed to achieve what has come to be seen as their primary goal: controlling costs. This failure has led to attempts, partially successful, to abolish both programs.

In this article we first discuss the available knowledge on the factors that facilitate or impede the adoption and use of medical technology. We focus on public policy mechanisms that have been developed to affect these processes. We then discuss the Medicare program, whose costs have become perhaps the predominant health issue politically. In our final section we discuss some of the implications of possible changes in policies toward medical technology.

DIFFUSION OF MEDICAL TECHNOLOGY

The development, diffusion, and use of medical technologies have been described as including at least seven steps.[8]

- discovery, through research, of new knowledge, and relation of this knowledge to the existing knowledge base;
- translation of new knowledge, through applied research, into new technology, and development of strategy for moving the technology into the health care system;
- evaluation of the safety and efficacy of new technology through such means as controlled clinical trials;
- development and operation of demonstration and control programs to demonstrate feasibility for widespread use;
- diffusion of the new technology, beginning with the trials and demonstrations, and continuing through a process of increasing acceptance into medical practice;
- education of the professional and lay communities in use of the new technology;
- skillful and balanced application of the new development to the population.

This seven-step sequence offers a logical model for understanding the development process; but medical technologies, like others, emerge from a process that is far less systematic and certainly less linear than that which this model depicts. It is nonetheless useful and convenient to discuss development and diffusion using this framework. The stages are presented schematically in Figure 15.1. The right-hand side of the figure is the typical S-shaped diffusion curve. The diagram below the curve indicates the complexity of the process.

RESEARCH AND DEVELOPMENT

Medical advance rests on an expanding foundation of knowledge about the biological mechanisms that underlie the normal functioning of the human body and its malfunction in disease. Much of this knowledge is acquired through basic, or nontargeted, biological research. Applied research, on the other hand, is aimed at the creation of solutions to problems in prevention, treatment, or cure of disease. Targeted development of a technology begins when knowledge derived from research, including epidemiological and social science research, is sufficient to support the effort.

There are considerable differences in development, depending on the type of technology. Drugs develop from a basic knowledge of organic chemistry, pharmacology, and human pathophysiology. Devices develop out of the physical sciences and engineering, but such development also requires biological knowledge. Procedures are typically developed by practitioners, often academicians, who have patients available to them. Procedures are combinations of different types of technology, and the development of these can be quite complex.

Biomedical research and development are supported by a number of institutions. Expenditures on biomedical research and development represent more than 3 percent of the health expenditures in the United States, amounting to an estimated $7.9 billion in 1978.[9] The federal government provides about two-thirds of this total, and the National Institutes of Health (NIH) controls more than two-thirds of the federal expenditure. Most of the federally sponsored research is carried out in universities and medical schools. In the private sector, industry invested about $2.4 billion in 1978, mostly through pharmaceuti-

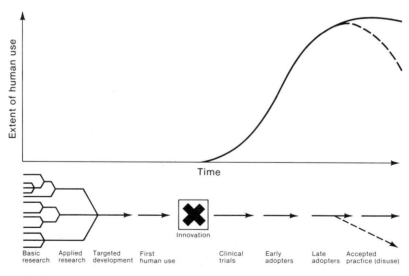

Figure 15.1. A scheme for development and diffusion of medical technologies. [*Source:* Office of Technology Assessment, *Development of Medical Technology: Opportunities for Assessment* (Washington, DC: Government Printing Office, 1976)].

cal manufacturers. In addition, more than 2000 firms are involved in developing and marketing medical devices and instrumentation, and they invest several hundred million dollars in biomedical research and development. The federal government is the prime supporter of basic research, while industry investment is almost entirely in applied research and technology development.

We need to know more about the processes of biomedical research. Available knowledge is not very helpful in distinguishing between successful and unsuccessful innovation. There have been few studies of failed innovations. Marginally useful, expensive technologies are developed, while unmet needs abound.

ADOPTION OF MEDICAL TECHNOLOGY

The process by which a technology enters and becomes part of the health care system is known as diffusion. It has two phases: the initial period during which the decision is made to adopt the innovation, and the subsequent and continuing period encompassing the decisions to use the innovation. Research has focused on adoption, as have government policies. However, use may be only tenuously related to adoption, so it will be discussed in a separate section.

Little empirical research has been done on the diffusion of medical technologies, and much of that is purely normative. There seems to be a tacit assumption in much available research that adoption of an innovation is desirable. Early research on diffusion grew out of sociology,[10] but much recent research has been done by economists.[11] The classical S-shaped curve presented in Figure 15.1 is the pattern followed by the diffusion of such technologies as intensive care units and cardiac pacemakers.[12] (Figure 15.2.) However, Warner[13] has described a variant in the case of chemotherapy for leukemia—the "desperation-reaction model" (Figure 15.3). A first phase of rapid diffusion seems to occur because of the provider's sense of responsibility to the patient and because of their mutual desperation faced with a life-threatening situation. This is related to what Fox[14] has called

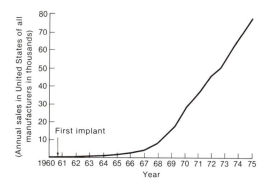

Figure 15.2. Cardiac Pacemaker. (*Source:* Medtronic, Inc. Redrawn by the Office of Technology Assessment. Reprinted with permission.)

"scientific magic," a part of which is the tendency of medical practitioners to favor vigorous treatments and to be staunchly hopeful even when a positive outcome is unlikely. Since most studies of diffusion of medical technologies were done years ago, before third-party reimbursement was widespread, findings may not be generalizable to medical technology today.

Before adoption or rejection can occur, knowledge about a technology must be communicated. In the medical area only drugs have received the attention of researchers investigating communication flow.[15] Research on drugs led to the description of a two-step model, in which information flows initially to those physicians who are opinion leaders. Through informal channels the opinion leaders then transfer information to their followers.[16] Sources of information have been little studied. One study indicated that physicians specified drug detail men as their most important source of information on new drugs.[17] How results of evaluations of technology affect adoption has not been studied. It is clear that the amount and quality of communication from researchers to practitioners are problems.

A number of factors have been identified as influencing adoption. These include characteristics of the technology, complexity of understanding and using it, and observability or visibility of the results.[18] Characteristics of

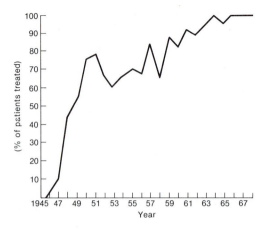

Figure 15.3. Chemotherapy for Leukemia. (*Source:* Warner, "A 'Desperation-Reaction' Model of Medical Diffusion"; redrawn by the Office of Technology Assessment. Reprinted with permission.)

the adopter, including a cosmopolitan outlook, have been stressed.[19] Large, complex, acute care hospitals with medical school affiliations have been found to accept innovations readily.[20] Almost all studies of adoption have dealt with institutions such as hospitals, and little is known about other institutions or about practice situations.

Much of the research assumes physician dominance in decision making.[21] When there is concern about the slowness of change, physician conservatism is blamed. When premature adoption of technology is seen as the problem, physicians are considered to be uncritical and technology hungry. Considerable homogeneity is assumed among physicians. Greer[22] has questioned these assumptions through research, still in progress, in the Milwaukee area involving 362 focused interviews of those involved in the health care system, including 201 physicians. She found that community practitioners are generally not interested in gaining influence in the hospital and have little effect on technology acquisition. Acquisition of medical technology was more likely to result from the actions of hospital administrators and selected hospital-based or hospital-oriented physicians than by demands of patient-admitting community physicians.

From the standpoint of public policy the key question concerns the characteristics of the environment that affect adoption.[23] These factors are most manipulable and include financing methods, market conditions, and government programs. There is little question that the growth of third-party payment is related to increases in medical technologies and medical expenditures.[24] The extent of insurance and the methods of payment used promote the adoption of expensive hospital technologies and inhibit the adoption of preventive, rehabilitative, and ambulatory ones. Existing fee-for-service schedules reward the provider generously for diagnostic and curative services involving high technology. For example, a recent analysis showed that while gastroscopy costs the physician about $40 to $50 to provide, Blue Shield pays up to $240 for the procedure in California.[25] Since the 1960s, as mentioned before, the government has assumed an ever greater role in protecting the public and attempting to rationalize technology through formal regulation. In recent years interest has been growing in using government programs such as Medicare to channel technological adoption. In part this is based on a perception that professional self-regulation has failed.

A key regulatory program that certainly influences adoption is the drug regulation program of the Food and Drug Administration (FDA). FDA is required to approve all new drugs as efficacious and safe before they are marketed, and in 1976 its authority was extended to medical devices. FDA processes affect, and generally slow, the adoption of technology. A considerable body of research has confirmed that there is a lag in the licensing of drugs in the United States relative to other countries and that this lag can be attributed in part to FDA.[26] However, since many technologies have diffused prematurely, it is not clear whether this delay is a good or a bad thing.

Since 1974, with the passage of the health planning act, federal policy has tended to emphasize controlling or slowing diffusion of technology both for cost containment and for efficiency. The major power of the planning program has been to require that institutions seek a certificate-of-need before they can make large capital investments. The effect of this program is not known. In an early study of certificate-of-need laws, Salkever and Bice[27] reported reduced hospital expenditures on beds but unchanged overall hospital investment. Apparently when hospitals were faced with greater control over the number of their beds, they channeled their investments to other technologies. Cromwell and his colleagues[28] found that certificate-of-need laws appeared to reduce adoption rates for expensive technologies that were already in widespread use—such as X rays, cobalt, and radium therapies—but did not affect other technologies examined. The health planning legislation was not found to correlate with interstate differences in the adoption of CT scanners.[29]

States too have attempted to control cost increases. A number of states have developed programs of prospective reimbursement or rate regulation, in which rates of payment are set in advance of the time period in which they will apply. The theory is that if revenue is limited and choice among technologies is necessary, physicians and hospitals might reduce or forego the use of technologies that have low marginal efficacy, that duplicate others, or that have less costly alternatives.[30] The effect on technology adoption of prospective reimbursement to hospitals has been mixed, perhaps reflecting the different forms of prospective reimbursement.[31] However, a recent analysis by Cromwell and Kanak[32] found that rates of technology diffusion in states with mandated rate setting were definitely lower than elsewhere. Complex services diffused at only about three-fourths the rate in states with rate setting as compared to a random national sample of hospitals. Likewise Wagner and her colleagues[33] found that prospective reimbursement seemed to affect the number of units of a technology adopted, although it may have had little effect on the decision to adopt or not to adopt. The New York program, perhaps the most stringent in the country, was found to have a consistently negative effect on the adoption of three

cost-raising technologies and positive effects on the adoption of cost-reducing technologies.

Overall, although some findings are suggestive, little basis can be found in the available literature for determining wise public policy toward technology adoption.

USE OF MEDICAL TECHNOLOGY

While there is obviously some relation between adoption and use of technology, no clear-cut relation has been demonstrated. It has been shown that hospital beds tend to be used regardless of health problems or the nature of a geographic area.[34] It also appears that the ready availability of laboratory tests, promoted by automation, has stimulated a rapid increase in the number of laboratory tests done.[35] However, Cromwell and his colleagues[36] reported that nonprofit hospitals in Massachusetts used certain diagnostic equipment at only 50 to 60 percent of capacity.

It is surprising that the relation of patient need to technology use has not been demonstrated to be a powerful determinant.[37] Even for clearly defined technologies addressed to clear-cut medical conditions, use varies remarkably. Wennberg and Gittelsohn[38] found that rates of common surgical procedures vary greatly in small areas of New England, for example, even when the areas are contiguous and similar in makeup.

As mentioned previously, the nature of physicians, their training, and their role in society are important factors in technology use. The sociological literature on professionalism and on physician dominance is of course large. Physicians are professionals and are granted a high degree of autonomy.[39] The physician acts as an agent of the patient and attempts to provide the best possible care, regardless of cost. With full insurance coverage, so that the patient pays little or nothing for a procedure directly, and in a system that rewards technology use with both profits and prestige, physicians have strong reasons to use technology.[40] The development of specialties has also affected technology greatly. Specialties have developed in response to professional, technological, and economic interests in the past[41] and will most likely continue to be responsive to such forces. For example, the United States is faced with a potential excess supply of physicians.[42] Physicians could respond by entering specialty practice and maintain their incomes by using specialized technologies more intensively.

Malpractice [litigation] apparently encourages wide use of such technologies as skull X rays,[43] electronic fetal monitoring,[44] Caesarean sections,[45] and clinical laboratory testing.[46] The dynamic nature of malpractice has been little studied. An overemphasis on technology and a correspondingly diminished human concern on the part of the physician can dehumanize medical practice. Such dehumanization has been found to be associated with high rates of malpractice litigation.[47]

The involvement of a profit-making industry certainly affects the use of technology. The drug and device industries spend a great deal to promote use of their products.[48] As mentioned previously, physicians list agents paid by drug firms as their most important source of information about drugs.

The institutionalization of medicine also affects technology use. In fact, evaluations of prepaid group practices that have shown fewer hospitalizations and less use of expensive technology were one of the important forces leading to the health maintenance organization (HMO) strategy of the 1970s, and this same area of evaluation is now encouraging the competitive strategy that is the latest policy buzzword. In part bureaucratization has been seen as a counterforce to physician autonomy. However, institutionalization of medical practice dilutes the physician's commitment to the interests of the patient and may lead to a loss of the caring function of medicine.[49] The result could be increased malpractice claims, a corresponding increase in technology use, and so forth.

Payment for services has already been stressed as a key factor. Fee-for-service payment to physicians and cost reimbursement to hospitals reward providers for providing more services. Existing relative fee scales reward physicians more lucratively for time spent

using sophisticated technology than for such human factors as counseling.[50] The extent of insurance is also important. The spectacular rise in the use of ancillary services such as laboratory testing is related to specialization, extent of insurance, and payment method. From 1968 to 1971 one study indicated that more intense use of nine such medical services accounted for about 40 percent of the increase in hospital operating costs.[51]

While the reimbursement system could be used more actively to control use, the major public program addressed to this area has been the professional standards review organization (PSRO) program, established in 1972. PSROs review hospital services, including a few technological services, such as CT scanning. The effects of PSROs on adoption and use of technologies is not known. Evaluations have focused on cost savings from the program and have apparently shown that the program costs approximately as much as it saves.[52] However, the effects of the PSRO program on quality have not been examined.

In summary, use of technology has been little examined, and even more than with adoption, the knowledge available is just not sufficient for the development of sound public policy.

EVALUATION OF MEDICAL TECHNOLOGY

Questions concerning benefits of certain medical technologies and benefits in relation to costs have made evaluation, or what has been called technology assessment, a prominent topic. The key element of assessment is the evaluation of efficacy—benefit—and safety. The most powerful technique for assessing efficacy is the randomized controlled clinical trial (RCT), and it is no accident that this method has received increasing prominence.[53] The major supporter of such clinical trials is the National Institutes of Health, which invested about $135 million in 1979—about 5 percent of its budget.[54] Other investments are small. Government support for studies of cost and cost-effectiveness are dramatically smaller.

From the perspective of this article, the key

task is to assure that research is done in such a way that it can be used for policymaking on medical technology. Such assessments could be done for purposes of utilization review, for planning research programs, or to influence health planning decisions. Recently reimbursement decisions have had more visibility than other uses of information. However, original research is not very useful for policymaking purposes, for policymakers have neither the time nor the training to interpret it. It is necessary to synthesize the results of research, sometimes including other information—such as clinical judgment—to make the results accessible and understandable to policymakers.

A modest move in this direction was made in 1978 with the passage of legislation to establish the National Center for Health Care Technology.[55] The center was given a relatively small budget to support original evaluations of medical technology, and was charged with doing syntheses and with advising the Medicare program on coverage decisions. In 1981 the center was abolished by the Reagan administration budget cuts.

USE OF THE MEDICARE PROGRAM TO CONTROL MEDICAL TECHNOLOGY

In 1980 federal expenditures under Medicare were $36.7 billion.[56] The federal share of national health expenditures has risen continuously, largely because of the Medicare program, whose growth has been close to 20 percent per year for the past few years. In 1965 federal funds were the source of 13.3 percent of national health expenditures. By 1980 the federal share had more than doubled to 28.7 percent, with total public funds accounting for 42.2 percent of national health expenditures.

Medical technology is probably more important as a source of cost increases in the Medicare program than it is in the broader system. Medicare clients on average are older and sicker than the general population. Every type of technology—with the exception of obstetrical and, possibly, preventive interventions—is more often applied to elderly people

than to the general population. In 1980 those over the age of 65 accounted for 11.2 percent of the population but 31.4 percent of health care costs—$68.4 billion.[57] Both percentages are expected to rise significantly in the future. This has led Congress and the Medicare program itself to examine the role of medical technology in Medicare costs and the possibility of controlling costs through managing medical technology.

Changes in the Medicare program related to medical technology may be approached in several ways. One approach is to focus on individual technologies. However, this approach is inherently limited because of the vast number of technologies and the decentralized nature of the program. Another approach is to change the demand for technologies by increasing the financial involvement of consumers under the program. This approach has the particular problem of discouraging services that may be needed by the subject.[58] Finally, it is possible to change the ways in which hospitals and physicians are paid in order to change the incentives for these providers to provide technologies.

For the long term the most promising alternative seems to be prospective reimbursement, whereby rates are set prior to the period during which they apply. The incentives for technology adoption and use vary with the method selected. For example, paying per day, as under the current cost-based system, gives hospitals incentives to increase patients' lengths of stay. Similarly, paying per service encourages overuse, particularly for high-cost technologies. Paying per discharge, which was mandated by Congress for use in Medicare in fiscal year 1983 by the Tax Equity and Fiscal Responsibility Act of 1982, removes the incentive to provide more technologies. The administration presented a legislative proposal to Congress to develop a system based on this principle in December 1982.[59] Congress modified the proposal but passed it into law in April 1983. Under that law, payment to hospitals will be based on so-called diagnostic-related groups (DRGs). In theory once a payment rate is established for each type of discharge or diagnosis, there is an incentive not to increase the provision of technolgies above the payment amount.

Although hospital payment is changed under the DRG plan, the issue of physician incentives remains, since they are not included in the proposed system. Controlling technology in hospitals could result in an increasing movement of technologies out of the hospital and into physicians' offices or other settings. Anecdotes indicate that such a shift may already be under way.

Payment to physicians raises another set of pertinent issues. As noted earlier, the standard for fee-for-service reimbursement provides an incentive for physicians to increase technology use, because the use of additional services can increase their revenues. Even within the current fee-for-service system, the incentive to provide more and more expensive technologies might be reduced by adjusting the reimbursement fee more often and on a rational basis—such as on the basis of what the technology actually costs, rather than on its historical prevailing charge. Of course, that would require amending the Medicare law, which requires "usual, customary, and reasonable" fees.

To the present, the main policy question dealing with individual technologies is whether they should or should not be covered in the Medicare program. This has required a determination of efficacy and safety. As noted before, the National Center for Health Care Technology gave advice to the Health Care Financing Administration on such coverage decisions. With the demise of the center, this function is continuing in the new Office of Health Technology Assessment—in the Public Health Service—with a lower level of funding and staff. As previously noted, this approach is inherently limited. However, linked with active manipulation of the fee and reimbursement system, it could become a more powerful tool.

DISCUSSION

The country is now debating the future of the Medicare program. At issue are its goals, its role in federal government costs, its effect on health status and health resources, and, as previously indicated, on the ways in which costs might be reduced with minimal effect on benefits and quality of care. As decision makers and analysts become more sophisticated about the role of medical technology in costs and quality of care, increasing attention will be paid to techniques for changing incentives for its use. Nevertheless a difficult, and common, policy predicament will confront them. They will find that controlling the adoption and use of medical technology is difficult at best. At the same time they will become even more aware of the need for control. The following discussion considers both sides of that predicament.

Difficulties in Controlling Technology

Most of the difficulties involved in attaining a more appropriate use of medical technology stem from the interaction of three coexisting factors: (1) decision making in our pluralistic and largely private-sector-oriented health care system is scattered among thousands of individual physicians, health policymakers, and other individuals; (2) the effects of any changes brought about in the adoption and especially in the use of medical technology will benefit some of the parties at interest and will harm others; and (3) there is a shortage of information on medical technology's benefits, risks, and costs, and on how to set incentives that will positively affect its use.

The first two factors imply that conflicting forces are set in motion by most decisions. The third implies that in many cases we cannot know in advance what changes in use of technologies we should move toward, or what policies will set desired changes in motion.

The system also helps to explain the behavior of policymakers. In the United States the system of government that structures policymaking—and thus affects the ability to make successful changes in the Medicare program—is political, not scientific or rational. Decisions are intended to be made by the people or by their representatives. People have no innate responsibility to look at the broad consequences of their actions. It is in human nature to be self-interested and biased.

The delivery of health care remains largely a private-sector activity, and government influence over it is relatively small. Health care is associated with large profits and financial rewards, as well as prestige. It is often seen as a right, which further circumscribes possible actions. Finally, it is an area in which values and ethics play a large part, limiting the role of rationality in planning or decision making.

Underlying all other factors is public demand for medical technology. The public would not translate its perceptions of illness into visits to physicians if they did not have faith in the technology of the medical system. The role of the press and of the medical profession itself in promoting this faith is important.

The Importance of Improved Technology Management

Despite the difficulties in moving toward more appropriate use of medical technology, an effort to do so is critical for a number of compelling reasons.

The most important reason is that there is a limit to the resources that can be spent in any one area of national life. That limit is decided upon through intricate combinations of economic, social, and political considerations. We seem to be reaching such a limit in health care, and particularly in the Medicare program. Faced with a limit on spending for health care or in Medicare, the country in effect will be operating on a fixed budget.

We have already begun, in measures described previously, to try to control the costs of the Medicare program. However, controlling costs requires attention to what opportunities will be foregone, and we lack fundamental information on what is useful and what is not. Furthermore, even for some technologies that have undoubted efficacy, the public seems to be developing misgivings about widespread use. Life-extending technology can be cited here.

Finally, all medical technology is associated with risks. These risks must be balanced against expected benefits, but such decision making is hampered by the lack of information.

We do not suggest that a formal system be developed to monitor all decisions, specify the assessment results available or needed, assure the use of existing data, and initiate needed studies. Such a rigorous, mechanistic system is neither possible nor ideal. Policy analysis is not science; the use of results is even less so. Clinical and policy decisions are appropriately based on a large number of factors, many of which are more important than analytical results.

However, there are situations in which increased and more sensitive use of assessment results might lead to improved decisions. Coverage of technologies under Medicare, and the design and implementation of modified reimbursement schemes are examples of potentially fruitful areas.

In conclusion, it is important to reemphasize that the Medicare program should not be viewed in isolation from the policy questions now being raised about medical technology's benefits and costs. The quality of care provided and the costs associated with the financing of that care are intimately connected to the ability to reach judgments about the value of specific technologies and to set up a payment process that will encourage appropriate use of technologies.

NOTES

1. John Kenneth Galbraith, *The New Industrial State* (New York: New American Library, 1977), p. 31.

2. U.S., Congress, Office of Technology Assessment (OTA), *Assessing the Efficacy and Safety of Medical Technologies*, GPO stock no. 052-003-00593-0 (Washington, DC: Government Printing Office, 1978), p. xii.

3. Department of Health and Human Services, Public Health Service, *Health U.S. 1981*, DHHS pub. no. (PHS) 82-1232 (Hyattsville, MD: DHHS, 1981), p. 195, Table 60.

4. Stuart Altman and Robert Blendon, eds., *Medical Technology: The Culprit behind Health Care Cases* (Hyattsville, MD: National Center for

Health Services Research and Bureau of Health Planning, 1979), pp. 27–30.

5. U.S., Congress, OTA, *Strategies for Medical Technology Assessment,* GPO stock no. 052-003-00887-4 (Washington, DC: Government Printing Office, 1982), pp. 91 ff; see also H. Fineberg and H. Hiatt, "Evaluation of Medical Practices," *New England Journal of Medicine,* 30(20):1986 (15 Nov. 1979).

6. OTA, *Strategies for Medical Technology Assessment,* pp. 91 ff.

7. Louise B. Russell, *Technology in Hospitals: Medical Advances and Their Diffusion* (Washington, DC: Brookings Institution, 1979), p.4.

8. President's Biomedical Research Panel, *Report,* DHEW pub. no. (OS) 76-500 (Washington, DC: Government Printing Office, 1976), p.7.

9. *Health U.S. 1981,* p. 215, Table 78.

10. Everett M. Rogers and Floyd Shoemaker, *Communication of Innovations: A Cross-Cultural Approach* (New York: Free Press, 1971), p. 100.

11. Russell, *Technology in Hospitals;* see also Kenneth E. Warner, "Treatment Decision-Making in Catastrophic Illness," *Medical Care,* 15:19 (1977).

12. U.S., Congress, OTA, *Development of Medical Technology; Opportunities for Assessment,* GPO stock no. 052-003-00217-5 (Washington, DC: Government Printing Office, 1976), p. 76; see also Russell, *Technology in Hospitals,* pp. 41 ff.

13. Kenneth E. Warner, "A 'Desperation-Reaction' Model of Medical Diffusion," *Health Services Research,* 10:369 (1975).

14. Renee C. Fox, "The Human Condition of Health Professionals" (Lecture presented at the University of New Hampshire, 1979).

15. Arnold Kaluzny, Diana Barhyte, and George C. Reader, "Health Systems," in *The Diffusion of Medical Technology,* ed. Gerald Gordon and G. Lawrence Fisher (Cambridge, MA: Ballinger, 1975), p. 29.

16. Christian P. Tannon and Everett M. Rogers, "Diffusion Research Methodology: Focus on Health Care Organizations," in ibid., p. 51.

17. H. Dowling, *Medicines for Man* (New York: Knopf, 1970), p. 174.

18. Tanon and Rogers, "Diffusion Research Methodology."

19. Ann L. Greer, "Advances in the Study of Diffusion and Innovation in Health Care Organizations," *Milbank Memorial Fund Quarterly/Health and Society,* 55:505 (1977).

20. C. Perrow, "Hospitals: Technology, Structure, and Goals," in *Handbook for Organizations,* ed. J. March (Chicago: Rand McNally, 1965).

21. Ibid.

22. Ann L. Greer, "Deus ex Machina: Physicians in the Adoption of Hospital Medical Technology" (Unpublished manuscript, Urban Research Center, Milwaukee, WI, 1981).

23. Gordon and Fisher, eds., *Diffusion of Medical Technology.*

24. Committee on Technology and Health Care, *Medical Technology and the Health Care System* (Washington, DC: National Academy of Sciences, 1979); see also Russell, *Technology in Hospitals.*

25. Jonathan A. Showstack, Steven A. Schroeder, and Howard R. Steinberg, "Evaluating the Costs and Benefits of a Diagnostic Technology: The Case of Upper Gastrointestinal Endoscopy," *Medical Care,* 19(5): 498 (May 1981).

26. Leonard G. Schifrin and Jack R. Tayan, "The Drug Lag: An Interpretive Review of the Literature," *International Journal of Health Services,* 7:359 (1977).

27. David S. Salkever and Thomas W. Bice, "The Impact of Certificate-of-Need Controls on Hospital Investment," *Milbank Memorial Fund Quarterly/Health and Society,* 54:185 (1976).

28. Jerry Cromwell et al., *Incentives and Decisions Underlying Hospitals' Adoption and Utilization of Major Capital Equipment* (Boston, MA: Abt Associates, 1975).

29. U.S., Congress, OTA, *Policy Implications of the Computed Tomography (CT) Scanner: An Update* (Washington, DC: Government Printing Office, 1981).

30. H. David Banta, Clyde J. Behney, and Jane Sisk Willems, *Toward Rational Technology in Medicine* (New York: Springer, 1981), p. 88.

31. Applied Management Sciences, *Analysis of Prospective Reimbursement Systems: Western Pennsylvania,* Prepared for the Department of Health, Education and Welfare, Office of Research and Statistics (Silver Spring, MD: Applied Management Sciences, 1975); see also William L. Dowling et al. *Prospective Reimbursement in Downstate New York and Its Impact in Hospitals—A Summary* (Seattle: University of Washington, 1976).

32. Jerry Cromwell and James Kanak, "The Effects of Prospective Reimbursement Programs on Hospital Adoption and Service Sharing," *Health Care Financing Review,* 4(2):67 (Dec. 1982).

33. Judith L. Wagner et al., *A Study of the Impact of Reimbursement Strategies on the Diffusion of Medical Technologies* (Washington, DC: Urban Institute, 1982), pp. 6–8.

34. Milton Roemer and Max Shain, *Hospital Utilization under Insurance* (Chicago: American Hospital Association, 1959).

35. OTA, *Development of Medical Technology: Opportunities for Assessment.*

36. Cromwell et al., *Incentives and Decisions.*

37. Russell, *Technology in Hospitals.*

38. John E. Wennberg and Alan Gittelsohn, "Health Care Delivery in Maine, Patterns of Use of Common Surgical Procedures," *Journal of the Maine Medical Assocation,* 66:123 (May 1975).

39. Eliot Freidson, *Profession of Medicine* (New York: Dodd, Mead and Co., 1970).

40. Kenneth E. Warner, "Effects of Hospital Cost Containment on the Development and Use of Medical Technology," *Milbank Memorial Fund Quarterly/Health and Society,* 56:187 (1978).

41. Rosemary Stevens, *American Medicine and the Public Interest* (New Haven, CT: Yale University Press, 1971).

42. U.S., Congress, OTA, *Forecasts of Physicians Supply and Requirements,* GPO stock no. 052-003-00746-1 (Washington, DC: Government Printing Office, 1980).

43. Russell S. Bell and John W. Loop, "The Utility and Futility of Radiographic Skull Examination for Trauma," *New England Journal of Medicine,* 284:236 (1971).

44. H. David Banta and Stephen Thacker, "Assessing the Costs and Benefits of Electronic Fetal Monitoring," *Obstetrical and Gynecological Survey,* 34:627 (1979), supp.

45. Helen Marieskind, *An Evaluation of Cesarean Section in the United States* (Washington, DC: Department of Health, Education and Welfare, Office of the Assistant Secretary for Planning and Evaluation/Health, 1979).

46. Steven A. Schroeder and Jonathan A. Showstack, "Financial Incentives to Perform Medical Procedures and Laboratory Tests: Illustrative Models of Office Practice," *Medical Care,* 16:189 (1978).

47. Department of Health, Education and Welfare, *Report of the Secretary's Commission on Medical Malpractice* (Washington, DC: DHEW, 1973).

48. Milton Silverman and Philip R. Lee, *Pills, Profits, and Politics* (Berkeley, CA: University of California Press, 1974).

49. David Mechanic, "The Growth of Medical Technology and Bureaucracy: Implication for Medical Care," *Milbank Memorial Fund Quarterly/ Health and Society,* 55:61 (1977).

50. Steven A. Schroeder and Jonathan A. Showstack, "The Dynamics of Medical Technology Use: Analysis and Policy Options," in *Medical Technology: The Culprit behind Health Care Costs,* ed. Altman and Blendon, p. 178.

51. Michael Redisch, "Hospital Inflationary Mechanisms" (Paper presented at the Meeting of the Western Economic Association, Las Vegas, NV, 1974).

52. Department of Health, Education and Welfare, Health Services Administration, Office of Planning, Evaluation, and Legislation, *PSRO: An Evaluation of the Professional Standards Review Organizations* (Washington, DC: DHEW, 1977); Department of Health and Human Services, Health Care Financing Administration, *Professional Standards Review Organization 1979 Program Evaluation* (Washington, DC: DHHS, 1980); Congressional Budget Office, *The Effects of PSROs on Health Care Costs: Current Findings and Future Evaluations* (Washington, DC: Government Printing Office, 1979).

53. A. L. Cochrane, *Effectiveness and Efficiency* (Abingdon, England: Burgess and Sons, 1972); see also OTA, *Strategies for Medical Technology Assessment.*

54. OTA, *Strategies for Medical Technology Assessment.*

55. Seymour Perry, "The Brief Life of the National Center for Health Care Technology," *New England Journal of Medicine,* 307:1095 (24 Oct. 1982).

56. Robert M. Gibson and Daniel R. Waldo, "National Health Expenditures, 1980," *Health Care Financing Review,* 3(1):48 (Sept. 1981).

57. Wendell E. Primus, "Financing Medicare through 1975," *National Journal,* 1 May 1982, p. 789.

58. U.S., Congress, OTA, *Medical Technology under Proposals to Increase Competition in Health Care,* GPO stock no. 052-003-00892-1 (Washington, DC: Government Printing Office, 1982).

59. Carolyne K. Davis, Testimony before the House Committee on Energy and Commerce, Subcommittee on Health and the Environment, 22 Nov. 1982; see also Richard S. Schweiker, *Report to Congress: Hospital Prospective Payment for Medicare* (Washington, DC: Department of Health and Human Services, 1982).

16

Measuring Elusive Benefits: On the Value of Health

JOHN MENDELOFF

The author argues that questions about the value of health in health and safety policy making cannot be easily resolved by appealing to analytic methods alone. He suggests that the costs and benefits to be used in one analytic method, cost-benefit analysis, could be soundly established by means of surveys focused directly on the questions that health and safety policy makers face. These, he suggests, could be indirectly based on a willingness-to-pay criterion.

Although pressures are mounting for public policy makers to judge whether medical and health programs are worth what they cost, proponents of economic analysis have had to confront several major hurdles.[1] First, the effects of such programs on health are often so uncertain as to make valuation irrelevant. Second, any attempt to place a monetary value on the saving of lives and limbs is morally repugnant to many people, and the behavior of elected officials usually reflects this aversion. Third, significant analytic difficulties impede agreement about what valuations to use: for example, how should we value the prevention of risks on the job versus risks at play, risks to the rich versus risks to the poor, risks to the young versus risks to the old, or risks in the present versus risks in the future? This paper wrestles with some of the most troublesome valuation questions. Although it cannot claim to provide answers, it does present a strategy for attacking the questions. The information learned could help policymakers to improve the choices they make.

THE INEVITABILITY OF VALUATION

Is it really important to address these valuation issues? Certainly, an argument can be made that doing so is not only politically naive but also analytically unnecessary. The chief point in that argument is often that cost-effectiveness analysis can be done without considering questions of valuation. Typically, the analyst will show that if the policy maker is considering a policy that prevents 100 deaths for a million dollars, an alternative exists which would prevent 120 deaths for the same cost (or the same number of deaths for a lower cost). As long as the costs of the two programs are the same and we overlook possible complications such as distributional differences, then such an analysis can be very helpful. Indeed, cost-effectiveness studies can usually tell us what policy option to choose if we have a fixed budget constraint and if we agree on the effect we want to maximize.

Unfortunately, analysts have frequently

Reprinted from *Journal of Health, Politics, Policy and Law* 8, no. 3 (Fall 1983), pp. 544–580. Copyright © 1983 by the Department of Health Administration, Duke University. Reprinted with permission of the publisher.

posed issues as if they could be resolved in a cost-effectiveness framework, when, in fact, they cannot. For example, the recent recommendation that Pap smears to detect cervical cancer should be performed only once every four years (instead of annually) was based largely upon a comparison of the marginal cost-effectiveness of different screening programs for several types of cancer:[2] this criterion would be appropriate if the funds for screening for cancer were fixed; but they are not, and thus a program of more frequent screening could be preferable even though it involved a higher cost per cancer detected. The key question is how much we value preventing the cancers that more frequent screening detects. Or consider the oft-cited observation that, because OSHA's health standards appear to prevent deaths at more than ten times the cost that highway safety programs do, we could prevent more than ten times as many deaths for the same cost by reallocating funds from OSHA regulation to highway safety. In the absence of either a clear budget constraint or a rule for valuation, OSHA leaders could plausibly retort that the disparity suggests that we should spend more on highway safety, not that we should spend less on OSHA. (Or, as we discuss below, they might claim that society places a higher value on preventing occupational cancer deaths than highway fatalities[3]).

Even when policymakers are working within a budget constraint, valuation issues must be confronted. For example, state highway officials in California report that they hear considerable clamor for median barriers to prevent head-on collisions. Their own calculations show that a greater emphasis on removing roadside obstacles would have more impact on reducing accidents and fatalities—particularly since median barriers actually cause some accidents when drivers who might have briefly and safely wandered over the median strip and back instead bounce off it and collide with other cars.[4] Should these officials use their budget to achieve some maximum measure of accident damage prevented, which itself requires a method for comparing the relative value of different types

of injuries and combining that with property damage? Or should they instead set budgetary priorities based on some concept of how much citizens would value the reduction in risk? Since most drivers seem to feel that they have much less control over head-on collisions than they do over running off the road, they may very well place a higher value on reducing the former. If we could show that they were poorly informed about the actual dangers they faced from the two hazards, and that they would be likely to change their views if they were better informed, we might easily choose to maximize "public health" rather than the value of risk reduction.

In fact, despite the overall statistics, for *most* drivers the risk of a head-on collision could indeed be greater than the risk of running off the road. The higher overall rate for the latter could reflect the experience of a subgroup of drunk drivers—i.e., some people run off the road rather frequently; most never do. If so, in this case the implication would be that the priority placed on median barriers might certainly reflect informed and rational preferences. More generally, this example suggests a third possible basis for resource allocation: majority rule. Thus, even if removing roadside obstacles would prevent more accident costs, and even if the subgroup of drunk drivers placed an extremely high value on reducing risks, the majority might decide that priority should be accorded to those risks that its members worried about the most. Operating within their budget constraint, highway planners have to decide what measure of benefit to use for allocating resources.

HOW DO WE MEASURE?
WHAT DO WE CARE ABOUT?

Choosing proper measures of health effects is a crucial issue for economic analyses. At least four factors need to be considered:

1. *The hazard* (e.g., is it understood, or mysterious?) and the context in which it is encountered (e.g., how voluntarily is the risky activity undertaken?).
2. *The health damage* (e.g., is there great pain and lengthy suffering? Does it in-

volve a risk of death as well as of disability?).

3. *The people at risk* (e.g., are they young or old, rich or poor, risk-seeking or risk-averse?).

4. *Timing* (e.g., how far in the future do the health effects occur?).

All of these may affect how an individual values the reduction of a particular risk to himself or herself. They may also affect how much we are willing to pay to reduce risks that *other* people face: the extent of external caring may vary considerably depending upon the context. Whether to care about others and how much to contribute to them are inescapably ethical questions, ones which analysis can contribute relatively little to answering.

The last three factors listed above have all been addressed in the literature on indices of health status, which has its roots both in traditional health planning and in clinical decision-making.[5] Clinicians constantly face problems of weighing relief from one disease against drug side effects, or against some risk of death on the operating table. A key development in that literature has been the concept of the discounted "well year" or the "quality adjusted life year" (QALY), to which we will return below.

The major development in more direct efforts to value health effects has been the challenge to the "human capital" approach by the "willingness to pay for risk reduction" (WTP) framework.[6] The former measures losses due to illness by totting up medical expenses and the discounted stream of lost earnings. Not only do the results of this approach relegate the lives of the very old and the very young to irrelevancies, but the approach itself has not been justified by the normal economic standard by which goods are valued—the preferences of consumers and citizens as expressed by their willingness to pay. Advocates of WTP sidestep the obvious objection that almost no one would give up his life, no matter how much you paid him, by stressing that the issue is how much people would pay for reductions in the *risk* of harm. The common knowledge that everyone stops

short of adopting every possible risk-reduction measure makes this argument quite plausible. Of course, like the human capital approach, willingness to pay raises the dilemma that preventing harm to the rich confers greater benefits than preventing harm to the poor. But, as we discuss below, policymakers are free to reject this particular implication.

Despite its conceptual liabilities, the human capital approach is still used to value fatality reduction in many benefit-cost studies. Its continued use is explained largely by its ability to produce a dollar figure through an easily understandable and straightforward process. In addition, it can usually be relied upon as a conservative (i.e., low) estimate of benefits. The willingness-to-pay approach, however, has by now also generated many estimates of the value of risk reduction.[7] Almost all of them rely on studies of the labor market, using econometric methods to determine whether workers are paid more—other factors being equal—for jobs with higher risks. The answer is usually yes, and from these figures the value placed on risk reductions can be calculated. For example, if among a group of workers the pay increases by $300 a year for jobs which carry a risk of death one in a thousand greater than the average risk, then the inference can be drawn that a group of 1,000 workers would have to be paid an extra $300,000 a year to accept the extra risk that, on average, one of them would die. Eliminating that extra risk— and thus preventing one death—would be worth $300,000 to the workers because they would be willing to give up that much in wages. In this manner, results from several hundred thousand dollars per fatality to several million have been calculated.

Controversy still surrounds this approach, due both to concerns about the econometric techniques and to skepticism about how much information workers have about risks. Yet (if the experience with the human capital approach is any guide) now that some numbers exist, the willingness-to-pay method is likely to get increasing use in benefit-cost studies.

To the extent that they are internally valid, these WTP studies probably tell how much a group of men with a mean age in the early forties values reductions in the risk of accidental death on the job. Yet, as acceptance of the WTP approach grows, these numbers are likely to be injected into contexts where they are not totally appropriate; it will be necessary to be sensitive to the likely biases that result. As a practical matter, it will be impossible to make empirical estimates of willingness to pay in each and every risk-context. Therefore, it becomes important to understand which characteristics of a risk are most likely to affect how we value reducing it. At least in theory, the labor-market WTP calculations might be a benchmark for making adjustments for these factors. Some economists have suggested that the context in which risks are encountered will rarely have much effect on how much one would actually pay to reduce them; but a number of studies indicate that many characteristics of a risk do influence judgments about the "acceptable" level of that risk.[8] However, translating those findings into clear guidance for policymakers has proven difficult.

Although the health status literature fails to address the issue of the contexts in which risks are faced, it does provide a possible basis for comparing health programs. But for practical use, a concept like the discounted QALY requires some simplifying assumptions. One analysis suggested the following set: (1) "that all individuals assign the same QALY values to equivalent circumstances of age and health condition"; (2) "That QALYs returning to different individuals should be weighted equally"; and (3) "that their preferences are such that QALYs received in different years should be discounted at a constant rate." The authors conclude: "Given these assumptions, the appropriate measure for the output of a health program is the total gain in discounted QALYs it provides to all members of the population."[9]

The remainder of this paper reviews some of the complications lurking in these assumptions: the ethical problems with maximizing QALYs, the conflicts between equity and efficiency, the question of whether some years should be valued more highly than others, and the rationale for discounting life-years. It concludes with a discussion—in light of both political and analytical dilemmas—of how these complications ought to be treated by policymakers, and a suggestion that surveys could help them to address valuation problems.

FAIRNESS AND ADJUSTMENTS FOR THE QUALITY OF LIFE

If two programs each prevent twenty deaths, but one leaves its beneficiaries as quadriplegics while the other leaves them with broken arms, we would clearly prefer the latter. We care about the quality of life as well as its length. The assumption that people have similar judgments about the relative importance of different health conditions is not strictly, or perhaps even loosely, true—as, for example, in the case of loss of a leg to a football player versus the same loss to a physicist. For public policy makers, however, the relevant issue is whether identifiable, politically relevant groups differ in their preferences. Based on a panel study of 867 households, one group of researchers concluded that differences among groups (on race, religion, and sex) did exist, but that they were too small to be a cause of concern. Group differences accounted for less than 1 percent of the variance in preference ratings.[10]

When we are talking about comparisons of programs to help a single group, we are on relatively firm ground in maximizing QALYs. But suppose we are comparing a program that helps men versus one that helps women, or blacks versus whites, or blue-collar workers versus white-collar workers. In each case, the former have shorter expected lifespans, and thus a lower expected "ability to benefit" from programs which improve the chance of having an average lifespan. For ethical reasons, we would probably prefer to use a common expected lifespan, even though such a tactic raises the problem of *whose* expected lifespan to use as the common benchmark. And in practice, if we discount years, the problem will often become inconsequential, because the present value of an extra five or ten years at the end of the lifespan is small.[11]

Not so amenable to the balm of discounting

fairness
equal standards for equals
should you provide safety
according to ability to pay?

162   MORAL CONTROVERSIES IN TECHNOLOGY MANAGEMENT

is a comparison between programs for groups with significantly different current levels of wellness. The clearest case would compare life-extending programs for well people [with] programs for paraplegics, or for people with kidney disease, diabetes, or arthritis. We certainly need to consider quality of life, because we care about preventing morbidity and disability as well as mortality.[12] On the other hand, most of us would probably not choose to devalue the extension of life for those people who are already sick or disabled. Indeed, one could make an argument for going beyond "equal treatment" to "compensatory treatment"—i.e., placing a higher value on the number of their years so as to compensate for the lower quality of those years. In a sense, this goes beyond the principle of lifespan equality to the principle of "equality of QALYs." My own speculation is that such a step would exceed the sacrifice in well-years that most of us are willing to make for the sake of such equality: the sense of fairness does not extend to giving the disadvantaged person more actual years than the non-handicapped.

Do these arguments extend to the impact of age per se? The elderly person will have a lower expected benefit than the young from any measures that place a value on the normal remaining lifespan; however, this "discrimination" is one that everyone must suffer, and therefore seems much more likely to be perceived as fair. Still, not everyone accepts this view. For the allocation of scarce life-extending technology, one philosopher has defended the view adopted by the Federal Artificial Heart Panel—that only the criterion of "medical needs" should count; otherwise, or within that category, selection should be by lot.[13]

EFFICIENCY AND EQUITY: ONE MAN, ONE LIFE?

Should QALYs returning to different individuals be weighted equally? As a nation, we have largely adopted a policy that access to medical care should not be rationed by ability to pay. In practice, we do not forbid some people from using their own money to fly around the country to consult top experts, as others cannot; but we do provide a fairly high minimum for services considered to be medically necessary. It would be inconsistent to treat other inputs to health differently than we treat medical care. This concern with equity would be violated if the government—using the rationale that airline passengers were, on average, wealthier and willing to pay more for reducing risks—required a higher standard of safety on airlines than on buses.[14]

Ignoring differences in willingness to pay will, of course, be inefficient. In the case of a classical public good like clean air, once it has been provided to one person in a neighborhood, it costs no more to provide it to everyone; all share the same quality of air, even though they may have differed in how much they would have been willing to pay to attain it. Assuming that the level of provision is determined by the median demand group, and in the absence of a tax system based on willingness to pay, people with high or low demands will have suffered a loss, as compared to a system in which they could purchase clean air directly. Thus, while safety on a particular airplane is inescapably a public good—all passengers necessarily share the same level of safety—requiring the same level of safety in all modes of transportation (or requiring a universal standard of medical care) in a sense *creates* a public good, and creates efficiency losses in the process.

For low-income groups (presumably including a disproportionate share of low-demand people), we have relied on Medicare and Medicaid payments to provide something close to one class of medicine. Suppose, however, that we required the poor to get high-quality care, but refused to help them pay for it. In some regulatory programs, in fact, we do just that. For example, requirements for safer (and thus more expensive) ladders are not accompanied by subsidies to the poor, some of whom might have preferred a less safe but cheaper product.

The prospect that persons with low demand can be made worse off when we ignore individual willingness to pay is a strong

creating a public good
can create efficiency losses

argument for using the WTP approach. Then, as a second step, we can bring in considerations of equity to help determine how much our society is willing to pay to reduce a certain risk. Unfortunately, this approach is difficult to defend publicly; the concept of *willingness* to pay becomes tainted whenever people feel that it reflects individual or class differences in *ability* to pay—as, of course, it often does. If the concept of willingness to pay is to be retained in health policy analysis, as it should be, then it must be wealth-neutral with respect to individuals.

For high demand groups, the losses imposed by a too low standard of protection can be reduced when supplements can be purchased privately. People can install smoke detectors to supplement the fire departments, keep a big dog to supplement the police, and air condition their houses or move to a less polluted area to get cleaner air. The efficiency loss will depend upon how cost-effective these private methods are as compared to the public methods of protection. (For example, perhaps both crime and costs would decrease if we laid off police and subsidized German shepherds.)

In practice, losses to high-demand groups may not be a serious inefficiency. In addition to the ability to supplement the public level of protection provided against a particular risk, people are often able to substitute among risks. If the costs of lowering air pollution and its resultant risk of chronic lung disease is higher than you would choose to pay, then you can choose to achieve the desired risk reduction in some other way—e.g., by changing your diet, exercise, or smoking habits so as to reduce your risk of heart or lung diseases. The evidence that these and other behaviors have the largest identifiable impact on longevity reveals the substantial opportunities for substitution.[15]

As other writers have observed, although most of the things that a person can do to reduce risks of death do not cost money, that does not mean that class differences are not involved. Victor Fuchs has emphasized that individual differences in rates of time preference may play a significant role in determining the adoption of healthful practices.[16] Viewing both healthful behavior and education as investments with distant payoffs, Fuchs notes that both will tend to be larger among people who use lower discount rates. This view would help to explain why educational attainment is consistently found to be the most important determinant of health practices. An alternative explanation emphasizes financial expectations: people who expect a poverty-stricken old age may not believe that living long enough to experience it is worth much of a sacrifice. This explanation has some plausibility, but several weaknesses. First, it is plausible that elderly people's sense of well-being is related to how great a *decline* in living standards they experience; often this decline is greater for higher-earning people.[17] Second, some survey evidence shows that blacks are much more likely than whites to express a desire to live to a very old age (although, like evidence on suicide, the data may be heavily influenced by cultural rather than directly economic factors).[18] Most importantly, health status itself, rather than wealth, appears to be the chief determinant of older people's satisfaction with life.[19] But, if initial low income causes a failure to invest for the future (including failure to invest in healthful behavior), wealth would still play an important indirect role. Older people may have become less healthy, and thus less desirous of a long life, because of the indirect effects of wealth on healthful behavior.

Compared to the middle class, poor people are likely to use higher discount rates for health investments, just as they do for more direct economic investments.[20] As noted above, ignoring differences between rich and poor in willingness to pay for health creates inefficiencies. When programs with distant payoffs are at issue, these differences in WTP will be compounded if we use different discount rates. Yet if we fail to use them, it will be the inefficiencies that are compounded. Nevertheless, the same equity rationale used above to argue for valuing all well-years equally would suggest that a uniform discount rate is desirable as well. What that discount rate should be remains one of the most perplexing issues analysts face, and we will return to it later.

DIFFERENT VALUES FOR DIFFERENT PARTS OF THE LIFESPAN?

Up to now we have not mentioned the issue of *when* in the lifespan the added years occur. Some have argued that preventing deaths early in the lifespan should be our top priority, based partly upon the large number of years that are typically lost with the death of a young person, but also upon the view that preventing the loss of this part of life deserves a higher priority.[21] This latter rationale would lead us to place a higher value on adding ten years to the life of a 20-year-old than to that of a 60-year-old.

What evidence is there that these views are widely held? One national survey found that 56 percent of the sample believed that ensuring a healthy life until the age of 70 deserved priority over prolonging life past 70; 21 percent believed the reverse, and 18 percent were neutral.[22] In another survey, over 400 Los Angeles County adults—about equal numbers of blacks, Japanese-Americans, Mexican-Americans, and whites—were asked which of the following deaths seemed most tragic and which seemed least tragic: an infant's death (up to 1 year); a child's death (around 7 years old); a young person's death (around 25 years old); a middle-aged person's death (around 40 years old); and an elderly person's death (around 75 years old).[23] In interpreting the answers, it seems reasonable to assume that the more "tragic" a death is, the greater the value people would place on preventing it.

All groups except the "whites" thought the 25-year-old's death was most tragic, but the death of the 7-year-old (the whites' choice) ran a solid second. When it came to least tragic, the elderly person's death was the overwhelming choice, followed by the infant's death. None of the other ages got more than 5 percent of the choices. An analysis of the respondents by age group (20–29, 40–59, 60+) showed that the youngest adults, who were much more likely to have infants or

young children, also were much more likely to perceive death at age 7 as the most tragic (38 percent compared to 27 and 21 percent for the two older groups respectively). However, the older groups both gave the top priority to the 25-year-olds, even though the oldest group's children were more likely to be 40. Perhaps some people give priority to the youngest of their direct descendants, which could explain why the elderly still tended to choose age 25, the age of many of their grandchildren.

While we would be obtuse to ignore the role of protective feelings toward one's progeny, it seems evident that a more abstract judgment is present as well. I know of no data that break down these opinions by parental status or age of children, but I believe that even older adults who chose not to have children would call elderly deaths the least tragic.

Given the shortcomings of the existing data, it may make more sense to start by asking what people care about. Bioethicist Daniel Callahan approached this issue by asking what a "natural death" was and concluded that it occurred at a point in the lifespan when several conditions were met: "(1) One's lifework has been accomplished; (2) one's moral obligations to those for whom one has had responsibility have been discharged; and (3) the death will not seem to others an offense to sense or sensibility or tempt others to rage at human existence." He also included a fourth condition, the absence of unbearable and degrading pain.[24] Although objections can be raised as to the language and the items themselves—for example, do most people really have a lifework they want to complete—the list does point in the right direction.

Society has some direct economic and social concern with an individual's death. The refutation of the human capital approach as the proper basis for valuing life should not blind us to the real differences in the economic consequences for society when a young person dies. Yet, in developed nations, we have the luxury of relegating these effects to a secondary place. What appears to matter most to individuals is the loss of life's experiences and ties. Many of the most important—marriage, raising children, launching a career—occur in the years after about 20 and continue until the obligation to support children wanes, an age which has increased for some with delays in having children.

Critics of WTP often correctly note that the studies may capture only the WTP of the person at risk, not of others who may care about him. However, when the other people draw upon the same resource pool as the person at risk (e.g., when the other person is the spouse of the person at risk), their joint valuation on reducing risk to one of them may be no higher than the WTP of either one of them individually, and could be lower.[25] Similarly, a person with children might reduce his willingness to pay for increased longevity in order to ensure that bequests will be available for them. Having no money, children are unable to add to the willingness to pay for risk reduction for their parents. But the children will eventually have income of their own; their inability to borrow on it can be laid to imperfections in capital markets. Thus a case can be made on efficiency grounds for societal supplements to the risk-reduction measures (for the parents) that parents of young children would support on their own.

Benevolence provides another reason for supporting such supplements. To refuse to acknowledge its relevance, and thus to claim that only the willingness to pay of those directly at risk should be counted, is too narrow a perspective. Yet it is also important to recognize that benevolence is both limited and selective. Overall, for example, health programs and hospitals receive about $6 billion a year in charitable contributions. While not paltry, this amounts to only $75 per household. If we compare the distribution of charitable giving to associations dealing with different diseases (see Table 16.1), it is apparent that the share going to combat diseases afflicting children and youth far exceeds their contribution to total mortality rates, to the number of people afflicted, and to most other measures of health loss.[26] The recent advertising campaign by the Arthritis Foundation to show that children as well as the elderly suffer from that disease illustrates the expectation that public support is enhanced when the disease is linked to children. Of course, many factors probably explain organizational variations in fundraising success, including differences in skill at tapping latent support. Nevertheless, it seems safe to conclude that benevolence is most important

Table 16.1. Giving to national health agencies, 1979[a]

Agency	Donations	Age of onset of disease
American Cancer Society, Inc.	$142,128,732	Old age
American Heart Association	82,933,148	Old age
The National Foundation	65,170,640	Birth defects
Muscular Dystrophy Association, Inc.	65,016,996	Childhood
National Easter Seal Society	52,000,000	Birth defects
American Lung Association	47,000,000	Elderly
Planned Parenthood Federation of America, Inc.	35,000,000	—
National Association for Retarded Citizens	34,465,963	—
National Multiple Sclerosis Society	27,242,099	Young adulthood
United Cerebral Palsy Association, Inc.	24,888,956	Childhood

[a]Some organizations (e.g., the Red Cross) specifically asked to be excluded from the list. The agencies included here are the ten receiving the largest donations.

Source: Giving USA, 1980 Annual Report, American Association of Fund-Raising Counsel, Inc.

when we talk about the death and illness of the young.

Although they overlap considerably, it may be useful to distinguish between losses due to cutting ties to others and losses due to missed experiences. Death at 20 or 25 often occurs before adult ties and responsibilities have been established. The loss is the lost chance to establish oneself. Death at 35 or 45 also involves some lost chances, but differs because it terminates so many outstanding responsibilities.

As Jonathan Glover noted in his book *Causing Death and Saving Lives,* the existence of ties to others supplies one argument against simply maximizing life-years.[27] If one person loses 40 years and two others lose 20 each, the latter case involves two sets of severed ties and the losses that go with them. Finally, we should also note the grief felt by parents whose child dies before they do, especially if the death occurs during the years when parents are most closely tied to the child.

It is hard to imagine how we could measure the effects of these circumstances on how years of life are valued. With adults, we could ask them to consider trade-offs among different periods in the lifespan that were spent in a complete coma (ignoring medical costs). How many months in a coma at age 25 would they be willing to endure in exchange for avoiding twelve months of coma at age 20? The coma question may roughly capture the importance of ties and responsibilities that are lost with death, but it does not adequately simulate the impact of missed life experience. A ten-year coma beginning at age 20 may postpone marriage and career until the next decade, but not totally wipe them out the way that death would. A thirty-year coma beginning at age 20 would have a very different effect. When we talk about life experiences, it may be that small changes in years often lack significance. We may be willing to grant that a 30-year-old deserves priority over a 60- or even a 50-year-old, but not be willing to distinguish between a 30-year-old and a 35-year-old.

Thus, although not much evidence is available, we can construct an argument that different periods of the lifespan are valued

differently. Elderly years are valued least. Infancy also seems to get low ranking, because parents' ties to the infant are still developing. For various reasons, periods between infancy and old age all have some claim for special concern, perhaps especially from about age 5 until age 50. Discerning differences within that span or deciding how much of a priority those years warrant over other years are tasks which cannot easily be performed now.

Under these conditions, it would probably be unwise to try to develop quantitative formulae for adjusting estimates of years (or well-years) added to account for the different values of different parts of the lifespan.[28] In the absence of useful evidence about how people make these trade-offs, the analyst has little to offer the policymaker beyond the insight that "prime" years do seem to count for more, and a demonstration of how the results differ depending on just how much more we value them.

In 1975, about 25 percent of all deaths occurred before age 65. From 1900, this represented an average rate of decline in early death of 0.5 percent a year. The Surgeon General's report, *Healthy People,* which sets health goals for 1990, calls for a reduction in early deaths to 18 percent, a continuation of that historical rate of progress.[29] This objective seems feasible; indeed that is probably one reason it was chosen. The continuing reduction in early death will reduce its relative importance as a social problem.[30] Yet, as it continues to become less common, it seems certain that its occurrence will evoke an even greater sense of unfairness and tragedy, and thus that the marginal benefit of prevention of early deaths will increase over time.

TIME PREFERENCE AND DISCOUNTING[31]

A recent study of proposals to screen school-age children for high cholesterol concluded that the cost per life-year saved was $3,400 to $6,600—if the costs and effects were discounted at 5 percent. At a 10 percent rate, since the costs come early and the effects late, the cost per life-year soared up to $60,000.

With no discounting, the per-life-year cost was only a few hundred dollars.[32] How we discount can clearly affect the relative and absolute attractiveness of health programs. In practice, some studies have not discounted; others have discounted health benefits at a lower rate than other effects; several others have discounted all costs and benefits at the same rate, although they vary on what that rate should be.

The fundamental reason we discount is that money now is worth more than money later, because it can be invested. One thousand dollars now is worth more than $1,000 next year because the former can be invested to grow to more than one thousand next year. For an individual, then, it obviously makes sense to discount at the rate at which money would grow in its best alternative use. Governments too have the same rationale for discounting; but choosing the appropriate rate becomes more difficult. Some economists urge that government use the expected return on those funds in private-sector investment as the basis for the discount rate. After all, they argue, if the return would be higher in the private sector, the public project is reducing future wealth. In contrast to this "opportunity cost" approach, others argue that the proper basis for discounting is really social preferences for consumption between one period and another.[33]

The opportunity-cost approach seems inappropriate if the effects being discounted cannot, in fact, be invested to produce future wealth. Although health can contribute to material wealth, and in poorer countries health investments are justified primarily on those grounds, in the U.S. public emphasis on the health of children and the elderly suggests that avoiding losses in production is not the major rationale behind public policy. Benefits should be measured by how much people would be willing to pay to reduce risks of harm. This measure would be consistent with the human capital approach only if people values their lives and others' solely for the goods they produced. This is not the case, however, and most studies of willingness to pay suggest that the human capital method

would amount to less than half of individuals' valuations.

If we do not rely on the opportunity-cost method to establish the discount rate for health benefits, what are the alternatives? Weinstein and Stason have argued that "the reason for discounting future life years is precisely that they are being valued relative to dollars and, since a dollar in the future is discounted relative to a present dollar, so must a life year in the future be discounted relative to a present dollar." They acknowledge that this argument assumes that "life years are valued the same in relation to dollars in the present as in the future."[34]

This argument for discounting can be illustrated by considering an individual who would be indifferent between enjoying perfect health for the next year, or receiving $1,000 now but being slightly ill for the year. Similarly, faced by the same choice the following year, he would again be indifferent between $1,000 or mild illness. If this person could invest the $1,000 at 10 percent, then he ought to be indifferent between the prospect of perfect health the following year or receiving $911 [1,000/(1 + 0.1)] now. Health next year has a lower present value than health this year.

This argument suggests that the reluctance to discount life-years in the same way we discount other goods is merely a reflection of the reluctance to place a monetary value on them. The appropriateness of the usual discounting methods becomes apparent once we do place such a value on them—and since we all realize that implicitly, if not explicitly, we do place a money value on them, any special treatment for discounting is incorrect. If the benefits to society of improved health are the gain in production and the avoidance of medical costs, then clearly these should be discounted using the same rate that we use for other resources, whether costs or benefits.

Although Weinstein and Stason do not stipulate what the discount rate should be, they do argue that it should be the same for both costs and effects. This position is persuasive if the issue is when to spend the money. In the example above, suppose that we could either spend $1,000 now to get the health improvement in year 1 or spend that same amount next year to get the health improvement in year 2. Unless we discount the health effects at the same rate as the costs, spending the money in the later year would be preferable. Discounting health effects at a lower rate than costs lead us to the absurd conclusion that it will always be worthwhile to continually postpone a program. This conclusion follows because each postponement reduces the present value of the costs more than the present value of the benefits.[35]

However, suppose that the issue is spending money *now* for health effects in either year 1 or year 2. If the health effects have no investment value, then the only basis for assessing their relative attractiveness in the two years is the time preferences of the population affected. Economic theory assumes that, although individuals can differ in rates of time preference for consumption, they will all equate their marginal rate of time preference with the interest rate they face. If you can invest funds for a year with a guaranteed rate of return of 25 percent, then it clearly pays for you to borrow funds (to make that investment) at any interest rate up to 25 percent, no matter how much lower your rate of time preference may be. This point seems to have little relevance, however, for calculating the present values of a month of pain this year versus a month of pain next year.

The conclusion that the discount rate for health effects should largely be based upon individuals' time preferences does not really seem much different from the conclusion that quality adjustments should be based upon individuals' preferences about quality of life. Unfortunately, useful empirical determinations of time preferences will be difficult to arrive at. Indeed, it is possible that different aspects of health may be discounted differently. For example, non-fatal conditions have two main dimensions, disability and discomfort. We can ask whether people prefer disability later to disability now, or discomfort later to discomfort now. While we expect people to want to postpone unpleasantness, it is not obvious that they would have the same

time preference regarding both discomfort and disability. When we try to measure these dimensions over time, we could use measures of both intensity (how bad the disability, how intense the pain) and duration. In addition, of course, people often accept higher risks of death to gain reductions in pain or disability. When we turn to mortality, we find that time preference cannot be distinguished from attitudes toward risk. The only plausible measurement question is: "How much added risk of death would you accept now for added years of life in the future?"[36]

One of the few empirical studies addressing time preferences for health involved asking fourteen cancer patients what number of assured years of life would be equivalent to a 50 percent change of dying now and 50 percent chance of surviving 25 years (their maximum expected lifespan).[37] Perhaps the most important finding was the diversity of the answers suggesting that some would prefer surgical treatment (with its higher initial risk but longer life expectancy) and others would not. The mean choice was five years, which implies a 14 percent discount rate. The median of 3.5 years equates to about a 20 percent rate. (Note that a choice of 12.5 years, halfway between 0 and 25, would have implied a 0 percent discount rate; or, viewed in terms of attitude toward risk, it would imply risk-neutrality. The shorter certainty equivalents imply that later years are weighted less heavily.) If government were trying to decide what treatments to fund, then the types of preferences expressed by these individuals would be the proper conceptual basis for calculation. However, this study is a good example of the difficulty of eliciting preferences, and we must be reluctant to generalize on the basis of its particular results.

We can reject the view that costs and health effects must be discounted at the same rate, but it is hard to say what the proper rate for the latter should be.[38] One contributing problem is that with such non-fungible qualities as life-years, distinguishing between how they are valued and how they are discounted becomes difficult. For example, good health may be particularly valuable to some people during the years when their children are growing up; but because their observed choices already represent discounted valuations, our observations will not allow us to isolate each factor.

A final point, drawing on the study of cancer patients, is that it may turn out that—assuming the two approaches were mutually exclusive—eliciting preferences from patients would be less satisfactory than relying on doctors' judgments. In addition to the pitfalls in the quantitative methodology, patients may lack a good understanding of the qualitative consequences of the treatments, whereas doctors, who have gone through the decision-making process many times, may know how often (and which kind of) patients regret their decisions.[39] However, when we turn to government regulatory policy, there is no analogue to the experienced physician. Where can the public policy maker turn for help?

GUIDANCE FOR GOVERNMENT?

To the limited extent that government agencies explicitly measure the costs and outcomes of health programs, they usually describe the cost per life saved or, more precisely, the cost per fatal accident or cancer averted. Would any other measure of outcomes be analytically preferable and politically feasible? Should the Office of Management and Budget ask for the cost per QALY, discounted at 5 percent? The answer, of course, depends upon whether other measures are more valid indicators of the characteristics that most people care about. We may agree that a factor like the number of years

should count, but find no consensus about *how much* it should count.

Consider how our assessment of health benefits would be affected by the factors we have examined above. If past practice with benefit-cost analysis is any guide, quantifiable factors drive out qualitative factors. Thus the discount rate would be weighted more heavily than "quality" and stage-of-life concerns. The critical role that discounting can play is readily apparent from Table 16.2. If we discount life-years at a zero or low rate, we implicitly give strong weight to the qualitative factors, because they are highly (but not perfectly) correlated with life-years. If we use very high discount rates, we essentially revert to weighting all deaths equally.

The choice of the discount rate also crucially determines how we transform "value-of-life" assessments derived from labor-market studies to a cost per life-year. If we take a range of $500,000 to $2,000,000 as the valuation placed on industrial deaths at age 41, the translation to value per life-year for the 31 years lost varies as shown in Table 16.3. It is interesting to note that, according to this interpretation of the labor-market figures, the more short-sighted one thinks workers are, the higher the value that they can be inferred to place on each year of life. Thus, if a group of one thousand 41-year-old workers would demand an extra $500,000 to accept the annual added risk that one of them would die that year, and if their discount rate were 15 percent, each year lost would be valued at $76,000. A 5 percent rate would imply a life-year valuation of $32,000. These figures can be compared with several cost-effectiveness estimates of medical prob-

Table 16.2. Considerations that affect how we value preventing the deaths of the young and the old

Adjustment factors	Death of a 25-year-old	Death of a 60-year-old
Benchmark—number of deaths	Equal	
Number of years lost	Favors	Disfavors
Quality declines with age	Favors	Disfavors
Early years more precious	Favors	Disfavors
Contribution to human capital	Favors	Disfavors
Contribution to lifespan equality	Favors	Disfavors
Discount the future	Disfavors	Favors

Table 16.3. Death at age 41: The implied value per life-year for the 31 years lost depends upon the valuation and the discount rate

Discount Rate	At a $500,000 value for life	At a $1,000,000 value for life	At a $2,000,000 value for life
0%	$16,000	$ 32,000	$ 64,000
3%	25,000	50,000	100,000
5%	32,000	64,000	128,000
10%	52,000	104,000	208,000
15%	76,000	152,000	304,000

lems, shown in Table 16.4, where the costs and life-years are both discounted at 5 percent.[40]

More striking is a comparison with estimates for most OSHA standards, where costs per fatal cancer averted usually begin around $3 million.[41] Using the assumptions of disease at age 55 after a 25-year latency, a $3 million cost translates to $790,000 per life-year at a 5 percent discount rate. After adjusting for special concerns we have about occupational settings and cancer, it is still necessary to ask whether such spending accords with our standards for fairness—equal treatment of equals—or for efficiency.

IN SEARCH OF A METHODOLOGY FOR VALUING RISK REDUCTIONS

What strategies should researchers pursue in order to generate findings about how risks are valued that will be useful to policymakers? We can start by construing the valuation problem in terms of three questions: (1) What factors should influence the valuation? (2) How much should each factor influence it? (3) From what benchmark should these variations be measured?

Answers to the first question are relatively easy to find. All of the issues we have discussed—number of years, stage in the lifespan, etc.—as well as characteristics of the risk-context (e.g., voluntariness) have strong claims for consideration. We saw that the difficulties multiplied when we tried to address the second question. Is fifteen years

after age 60 worth more than ten extra years at age 30? Lack of evidence about people's preferences leaves us unable to answer questions about the relative worth of different lifesaving programs, except in the rare case when one option is better than the others in every respect—i.e., involves more years, more prime years, years that are nearer in the future, risks that are more involuntarily borne, etc.

If we could establish how much more or how much less in percentage terms citizens valued the prevention of a furniture-fire death compared to a death from pollution-induced pulmonary disease, we would have made great strides. With such an interval scale, we would know whether current programs were properly ranked, and whether the differentials were too small or too large in percentage terms; we would still not know, however, what the absolute levels of spending should be, nor the absolute size of the proper differentials among programs. To answer these questions we would still need to answer the third question posed above. Thus, if we knew how much the prevention of an occupational accident fatality was valued in dollars, and we knew how much more or less in percentage terms of people valued preventing furniture-fire deaths and air-pollution deaths, we could derive dollar values for all of them.

The method of estimating the value of risk reduction directly from behavior, as in the studies of labor-market risk premiums, obviates the need for this three-step procedure. However, although future studies of this sort are welcome, a strategy of relying primarily on them seems misguided. The first reason is simply that it will be very difficult to make such estimates for other types of risks.[42] For the workplace studies, fairly accurate measures of accident probabilities are known to the researcher (and can be plugged into the regression equation), and the people at risk can plausibly be expected to have some knowledge of them. In cases of occupational health and air pollution, the dose-response curves are uncertain in the minds of experts and, a fortiori, in the minds of the people at risk. Estimates of market behavior will be

Table 16.4. Cost-effectiveness of health programs: Some representative studies

Medical condition	Program evaluated	Cost per year of life added[a]
Hypercholesterolemia	Changing diets	$ 4,200–$15,000
Hypertension	Screening and treatment	$10,500–$22,500
Coronary disease	Coronary care units	$ 4,500
	Mobile coronary care units	$ 6,400
End-stage renal disease	Facility dialysis	$33,000
	Home dialysis	$21,000
	Transplantation (with facility dialysis of failures)	$18,000–$27,000
Tuberculosis	Screening children	$37,500–$135,000
Phenylketonuria	Screening neonates and dietary treatment	$ 7,500
Phenylketonuria	Follow-up screening of initially negative screenees	$45,000
Breast cancer	Screening with physical exam by trained lay-people	$ 6,000
	Screening with mammogram (marginal effect)	$49,500
Measles	Immunization	$ 3,100

[a]1980 dollars, discounted at 5 percent.

Source: Donald M. Berwick, Shan Cretin, and Emmet Keeler, *Cholesterol, Children, and Heart Disease: An Analysis of Alternatives,* pp. 272–3. See this book (which presents these figures in 1975 dollars discounted at 5 percent) for specific references to the various studies.

even less reliable than those from the keenly disputed studies of workplace accidents. A second shortcoming of studies of the behavior of those at risk is that they ignore the willingness to pay of those not at risk: while trivial in some cases, this external caring may be substantial in others.

Rejecting estimates derived from market behavior as our main strategy, we turn next to the strategy of estimating the value of each element that counts in our preferences, and then aggregating these values. In essence, the QALY measure falls within this strategy, which requires answers to the second question we posed above. What rules should we adopt for counting years, for judging quality, for discounting, and for assessing risk-contexts?

Measurements of health status or quality, based on citizen preferences or expert judgments, are the subject of a large literature, and further progress in addressing these issues is certainly possible. One strategy would be to present individuals with sets of data on such variables as number of years added, stage of lifespan when added, and years from the present when first added, and then to ask them to rate each set with either a cardinal or interval scale. With that judgment, a regression would compute the coefficient for each of the three independent variables. These coefficients could then be used to predict any new combination that came along.

Several problems are evident here. First, how much confidence would we have in people's judgments when asked for cardinal or interval comparisons of the value to them of 10 life-years five years hence at age 50, versus 20 life-years ten years hence at age 60? Second, this example still leaves out the potentially critical issue of risk-context. Third, it does not relate the judgments to monetary standards which can be compared with costs.

For clinical decision-making, doctors do need fine-grained categories for comparing symptoms. However, for many public and environmental health and safety decisions, it may be wiser to ask questions directly about what we care about, rather than attempting to calculate separate coefficients for each risk factor and then to aggregate them. That second strategy may still be essential if we want to predict the value of lifesaving for a very large number of programs. But for public health and safety, even rough judgments for a few of the major programs could be very valuable. Moreover, asking for overall judgments about recognizable programs like preventing highway deaths and workplace cancers seems less likely to encounter cognitive difficulties than asking more abstract questions about trade-offs.

Fischoff and his colleagues have shown that it is possible to get people to rank risks on an interval scale.[43] Although their work has generated important insights, its usefulness for policymaking is limited by its focus on the concept of "acceptable risk." Respondents were asked how much higher or lower the levels of acceptable risk were for many different activities ranging from nuclear power generation through skiing and police work. To the extent, however, that policy determinations about risks depend upon weighing the costs and benefits of reducing them, some notion of marginal benefits needs to be supplied.

Of course, in the absence of WTP behavior that can be examined, people could simply be asked for their WTP for different risk-reduction programs. (The only study to rely on this method to date has been a study of WTP for improved emergency services for reducing the risk of dying after a heart attack.[44]) The primary defect of this method (aside from the possibility of strategic behavior) is that individuals are believed to be insensitive to differences in low-probability events. However, it is not apparent why this defect necessarily affects survey responses any more than it would studies of behavior (e.g., buying safety equipment). A research program should be designed to compare surveys of WTP with the answers derived from the approach suggested below.

It seems important not to ask people directly to place dollar figures on the value of lifesaving. Instead, we should tell respondents that government now spends funds to prevent a certain type of fatality (e.g., deaths due to cars running into roadside obstacles); then ask them whether, compared to the amount that government spends to prevent a fatality in that program, the government should spend (or require consumers to spend, if the program is regulatory in nature) more, less, or the same on each of a list of specified programs—e.g., reducing occupational accident deaths, heart-attack deaths that could be prevented by better emergency services, pollution-induced pulmonary disease deaths, furniture-fire deaths, etc. If the respondents indicated that more (or less) spending would be justified in any of these cases, they could then be asked to specify how much more or less, in percentage terms.

Methodological problems with this approach again include the possibility that people would not give consistent answers to the "how much" question. Answers could easily be biased by presenting categories for the respondents to choose from (e.g., + 50%, + 100%). Answers are also likely to depend upon the assumptions people make about the cases: Do the auto accidents involve drunks? Were the furniture fires caused by smoking in bed? Were the workers receiving compensation? Were the air-pollution victims very old? It would be illuminating to understand the assumptions that guide people's judgments. That could be done in preliminary studies by asking people why they made the judgments they did. Particularly if mistaken assumptions are common, each risk-reduction program could be accompanied by a brief description of whatever the salient facts are (e.g., the average age of victims, the latency period, or the percentage which are alcohol-related). The extent to which answers change as the facts presented are altered could then be monitored. Thus, although we need not try to estimate coefficients for each element in the valuation equation, and although the crux of this approach is to ask for overall judgments, we cannot avoid looking into the decision process in order to examine how informed the choices are. Cues and biases are inevitable in deciding what facts constitute relevant information, but attempts to impose norms of consistency or rationality on the views people express should be carefully curbed.[45]

The sort of interval scale that this approach should provide would be valuable for many policy purposes; but an absolute value on risk reductions would also be useful. For instance, if one of the risks in the survey were death from occupational accidents, it might be possible to use the findings of empirical labor-market studies as a benchmark. Thus, if the value placed on preventing one type of death was $800,000, and people said that only half as much should be spent to prevent another type of death, then the value to be placed on that death would be $400,000. The utility of such a benchmark is limited, however, by the ten-fold variation in estimates from labor-market studies. Moreover, the survey asks for judgments about the relative amounts that *society* should be willing to pay. The labor-market studies ask about the WTP of the individuals at risk. If there is a significant WTP for reducing those particular labor-market risks by people who are not subject to them, then the social WTP—which should properly serve as the benchmark—will be higher than the empirical estimates. Again, however, because of the large disagreements among the empirical studies, precision about the extent of external caring in this case hardly seems worth achieving.

The lack of a clear relation between WTP and individuals' relative valuations may cause real quandaries when we try to aggregate them into social valuations. For example, the valuations are likely to vary among individuals. Suppose that 50 percent of the population believe that twice as much should be spent to prevent death X as death Y, and the other 50 percent believe just the opposite. The outcome would be that the two risks would be weighted equally. Suppose, however, that members of the first group—whether because of greater wealth, greater risk-averseness, or a lower initial probability of survival—were willing to pay more for risk reduction—e.g., perhaps their true ratio for the X:Y was $1 million:$500,000, while the second group's was $200,000:$400,000. In such case, equal

weighting would obviously misstate the true collective demand for risk reduction.

We may be prepared to ignore these distortions to the extend that wealth differences lie at their root. The higher WTP of people with a lower probability of survival may not be a serious problem as long as we are comparing different prevention problems, rather than comparing prevention with treatment programs.[46] Differences in attitudes toward risk may pose the greatest problem. Risk-averseness is likely to be associated with a relatively large value placed on reducing less voluntary risks as compared to more voluntary ones. Risk-averse people may also place a high absolute value on risk reductions. If these assumptions are true, then equal weighting would tend to understate the value placed on reducing less voluntary risks.

The most important difference in valuation may be between those who are subject to a particular risk and those who are not. Do people exposed to workplace carcinogens place a higher relative value on preventing a death from that cause than people who are not at risk in the same way? If they do, then the overall relative judgments generated by the survey method will depend, in part, on the number of people who face each risk. For example, suppose that compared to the base risk $X = 100$, Group A, (which faces risk Y, but not risk X) values the prevention of risk Y at 400, while Group B (which faces X but not Y) values it at 200. If 75 percent of the people are in Group A, the average value on preventing Y is 350. If 75 percent are in Group B, the average value is 250.

Certainly, in a market context we expect people to pay more to reduce risks that they do face than risks that they do not face. The survey asks for normative judgments about how much *ought* to be spent for one program compared to another. Economists are skeptical that such questions really tap how much individuals would be willing to pay. It is probably true that the answers that will emerge through the two procedures will be different, but that does not mean that one is wrong. The survey question could be reworded to emphasize the individual's cost:

"Suppose that government spends a certain amount of your tax dollars to remove roadside obstacles so as to prevent a certain number of deaths due to cars running off the highway. Compared to that amount (call it 100 units), would you be willing to have more, less, or the same amount of your money spent (either as a taxpayer or as a consumer) to prevent the same number of deaths from these other kinds of hazards?" This rewording, however, would still not address the basic fact that WTP measures the actual willingness of people to incur the opportunity cost, while the survey only asks, "*If* these measures were undertaken, what relative weight should be placed on them?" The latter question raises the issue of the fairness of different claims to resources. You may not be willing to spend anything personally to reduce a risk that you do not share, but you still may agree that government should spend more of your tax dollars to reduce that risk than to reduce a comparable risk that you do face.

A further complication is that whenever there is a "we" who are paying to help "them," the issue of whose preferences policymakers should count arises. Take the issue of time preferences. Suppose that a group of workers has high discount rates, and thus places a current value of only $30,000 on preventing a fatal cancer 25 years in the future. (Note that, with a 15 percent discount rate, such cancer prevention saves only 3 percent of the discounted life-years saved by preventing an immediately fatal industrial accident. In those terms, even if the latter were worth $1 million, the cancer prevention would indeed be worth only $30,000.) If those preferences were represented in collective bargaining, the workers would give up no more than that amount to win the preventive measure. Suppose the public feels that the workers are shortsighted, and therefore establishes regulations costing up to $1 million per future cancer averted. If the workers end up paying for the improvements, they will have been made worse off. But if the public pays the costs, then it seems proper that their preferences should prevail. It will be true that the workers would be better off receiving the

public's contribution in cash and spending it on something else, but that would not satisfy the motivation for the giving—to reduce occupational health risks.

Attempts to explore the survey strategy proposed here should identify more clearly the extent of the methodological problems. They also promise insights that can be helpful to policymakers. The problems identified here suggest, however, that expectations should be modest. Recent research repeatedly emphasizes the lability of preferences and the crucial impact of how questions are framed.[47] These are facts that must be lived with and taken into account, not problems that can be solved. Their existence argues for multiple approaches, including more studies of willingness to pay. Skeptics may reasonably caution that analysts tend to oversell the contribution that quantitative analysis can make. But while critics of mindless quantification do not lack ammunition, it is at least as easy to be mindless without looking at the numbers. Whatever the methodology, policymakers do need information and tools that will allow them to consider more explicitly, either quantitatively or qualitatively, what it is that people value about their programs, and how their worthwhileness can be assessed.

NOTES

For their contributions to this paper the author would like to thank Nathaniel Beck, James Bush, Peter Cowhey, Ann Linda Furstenberg, Peter Goldschmidt, John Graham, Sandy Lakoff, Monica Paskvan, Paul Slovic, Tracy Strong, and James Vaupel. Financial Support from the UCSD Academic Senate is gratefully acknowledged.

1. On the growth of cost-effectiveness studies of medical care, see Office of Technology Assessment, *The Implications of Cost-Effectiveness Analysis of Medical Technology* (Washington, D.C.: U.S. Government Printing Office, August 1980).

2. David Eddy, *Screening for Cancer: Theory, Analysis, and Design* (Englewood Cliffs, N.J.: Prentice-Hall, 1980), pp. 245–246, 254.

3. However, see John D. Graham and James W. Vaupel, "The Value of a Life: What Difference Does It Make?" *Risk Analysis* 1 (March 1981): 89–

95. They found that the breakeven value per life saved was either below $170,000 or above $3 million in all but 11 of the 57 policy choices they examined, and concluded that within a broad range the valuation on lifesaving usually does not alter the policy implications. Of course some valuation is still required to draw policy implications. Also, as they would agree, if we could tally the costs of foregone liberty, the valuation on lifesaving required to justify some of the "cheap" programs would probably jump. For a very rich discussion of liberty issues, see James W. Vaupel and Philip J. Cook, *Life, Liberty, and the Pursuit of Self-Hazardous Behavior,* Institute of Policy Sciences and Public Affairs Working Paper, Duke University, Working Paper »8781 (August 1978).

4. Interviews by the author with officials of the California State Highway Department.

5. A recent review of both theoretical and empirical work on health status indexes appears in *Health: What Is It Worth?,* ed. Selma Mushkin (New York: Pergamon Press, 1979); the contribution by Joseph Lipscomb is especially relevant to attempts to integrate WTP into health policymaking. A shorter review is provided by Milton Weinstein in "Economic Evaluation of Medical Procedures and Technologies: Progress, Problems, and Prospects," in *Medical Technology;* National Center for Health Services Research, DHEW No. (PHS) 79–3254, September 1979.

6. Jan Paul Acton, "Measuring the Monetary Value of Lifesaving Programs," *Law and Contemporary Problems* 40 (Autumn 1976): 46–72, provides a review of the two approaches.

7. Robert S. Smith, "Compensating Wage Differentials and Public Policy: A Review," *Industrial and Labor Relations Review* 32 (April 1979): 339–352; and Martin J. Bailey, *Reducing Risks to Life* (Washington, D.C.: American Enterprise Institute, 1980).

8. Baruch Fischhoff, Paul Slovic, and Sarah Lichtenstein, "How Safe is Safe Enough: A Psychometric Study of Attitudes Toward Technical Risks and Benefits," *Policy Sciences* 9 (1978): 127–152. R. A. Brown and C. H. Green also report that a contextual factor—whether people felt that fires were the fault of those at risk—heavily influenced responses to questions about allocating resources for fire safety. See "Threats to Health and Safety: Perceived Risk and Willingness to Pay," *Social Science and Medicine,* 15C:67–75.

9. Richard Zeckhauser and Donald Shepard, "Where Now for Saving Lives?" *Law and Contemporary Problems* 40 (Autumn 1976): 14–15.

10. Robert M. Kaplan, J. W. Bush, and Charles

C. Berry, "The Reliability, Stability, and Generalizability of a Health Status Index," American Statistical Association, *Proceedings of the Social Statistics Section,* 1978.

11. For example, if we compare 60-year-olds with 20 years of life expectancy with those with 15, the present value of that five-year difference is 2 years if we discount at 5 percent, and less than 0.8 years if we discount at 10 percent.

12. This paper shares the all too common shortcoming of focusing almost exclusively on mortality and ignoring morbidity. For useful correctives, see Leon Kass, "Regarding the End of Medicine and the Pursuit of Health," *The Public Interest,* no. 40 (Summer 1975), pp. 11–42; and Ernest Gruenberg, "The Failures of Success," *Milbank Memorial Fund Quarterly* 55 (Winter 1977): 3–24.

13. James F. Childress, "Who Shall Live When Not All Can Live," in *Ethics and Health Policy,* ed. Robert M. Veatch and Roy Branson (Cambridge, Mass.: Ballinger, 1976). An excerpt from "The Totally Implantable Artificial Heart: Economic, Ethical, Legal, Medical, Psychiatric, and Social Implications," by the Artificial Heart Assessment Panel, National Heart and Lung Institute, is included in this collection.

14. For an interesting discussion of safety as a public good, see Lester Lave, "Safety in Transportation," *Law and Contemporary Problems* 32 (Summer 1968): 512–535. For a recent discussion which examines the ethical problems posed by the inefficiencies of valuing all lives equally, see Thomas Schelling, "Economic Reasoning and the Ethics of Policy," *The Public Interest,* no. 63 (Spring 1981), pp. 37–61.

15. Nedra B. Belloc and Lester Breslow, "Relationship of Physical Health Status and Health Practices," *Preventive Medicine* 1 (1972): 409–421. Risks, however, are rarely perfect substitutes; and, as Thaler and Gould emphasize, there is no way (with the possible exception of organ transplants) for a very sick person to make an exchange with someone else for better health. See Richard Thaler and William Gould, "Public Preferences Toward Life Saving: Should Consumer Preferences Rule?" *Journal of Policy Analysis and Management* 1 (Winter 1982): 223–242.

16. Victor Fuchs, "Time Preference and Health: An Exploratory Study," Working Paper »539, August 1980, National Bureau of Economic Research, Cambridge, Mass.

17. Reviewing studies of "adjustment" to retirement, Harold L. Sheppard writes that "Level of retirement income has been found to be crucial, but few, if any, studies have used retirement income as

a percentage of pre-retirement income as a more refined variable involved in adjustment." See Sheppard, "Work and Retirement," in *Handbook of Aging and the Social Sciences,* ed. Robert H. Binstock and Ethel Shamas (New York: Von Nostrand Reinhold Company, 1976), p. 304.

18. See Richard A. Kalish and David K. Reynolds, *Death and Ethnicity: A Psycho Cultural Study* (Los Angeles: University of Southern California Press, 1976), p. 99.

19. See Reed Larson, "Thirty Years of Research on the Subjective Well-Being of Older Americans," *Journal of Gerontology* 33 (1978): 109–125.

20. See Richard H. Thaler and H. M. Shefrin, "An Economic Theory of Self-Control," *Journal of Political Economy,* April 1981, pp. 402–405. One study they cite, based on purchases of room air conditioners, implied discount rates of below 10 percent for families with incomes about $35,000; 17 percent for the $25,000 group; 27 percent for $15,000; and 39 percent for $10,000.

21. James Vaupel, "Early Death: An American Tragedy," *Law and Contemporary Problems* 40 (Autumn 1976): 73–121. A somewhat longer version appears in *The Prospects for Saving Lives: A Policy Analysis,* Duke University, Institute of Policy Sciences, May 1978.

22. The survey was conducted by Policy Research Incorporated (Baltimore, Md.) for "A Comprehensive Study of the Ethical, Legal, and Social Implications of Advances in Biomedical and Behavioral Research and Technology," for the National Commission for the Protection of Human Subjects of Biomedical and Behavioral Research. The disaggregated data on age were sent to me by Dr. Peter Goldschmidt of PRI.

23. Kalish and Reynolds, *Death and Ethnicity,* pp. 33–34.

24. Daniel Callahan, "Natural Death and Public Policy," in *Lifespan,* ed. Robert Veatch (San Francisco: Harper and Row, 1979), p. 164. The essay by Veatch is also quite interesting.

25. Zeckhauser and Shepard, "Where Now," pp. 33–34.

26. For figures on amount and distribution of charitable contributions, see *Giving USA,* the 1980 Annual Report of the American Association of Fund Raising Counsel, Inc. (New York).

27. Jonathan Glover, *Causing Death and Saving Lives* (New York: Penguin, 1977), pp. 221–22.

28. In his essay in *Lifespan,* Robert Veatch speculates about the possible formula for assessing contributions to lifespan equality. For example, each year could be weighted by $[1 - Y/70]$, so that the first year of life $(Y = 1)$ would get almost

full weight, while the 65th would get almost none.

29. U.S. Public Health Service, *Healthy People: The Surgeon General's Report on Health Promotion and Disease Prevention, 1979* (Washington, D.C.: G.P.O., 1979). The fall in rates to 1990 was calculated by the author by aggregating the goals for all of the age groups below 65. Vaupel calculated the long-term rate of decline in early death in the studies cited in note 22.

30. James Freis, "Aging, Natural Death, and the Compression of Morbidity," *New England Journal of Medicine* 303 (17 July 1980): 130–135.

31. The argument in this section was developed jointly with Nathaniel Beck.

32. Shan Cretin, "Cost/Benefit Analysis of Treatment and Prevention of Myocardial Infarction," *Health Services Research* 12 (Summer 1977): 174 ff.

33. Although the distinction is not always easy to maintain, this discussion focuses on intragenerational rather than intergenerational issues. As Nathaniel Beck and Talbot Page have argued, the latter more clearly center on the ethical question of what does the present generation want to bequeath to future generations.

34. Milton Weinstein and William Stason, "Foundations of Cost-Effectiveness Analysis of Health and Medical Practices," *New England Journal of Medicine* 296 (31 March 1977): 716–721. In another article, Weinstein notes the apparent paradox that while discounting life-years is controversial, once we agree to place a money value on those years, no one has argued that they should not be discounted like other money values; see Weinstein, "Economic Evaluation," p. 61.

35. Emmett B. Keeler and Shan Cretin, "Discounting of Non-monetary Effects," Rand Corporation Working Draft WD-841-HHS, December 1980.

36. A. J. Cuyler discusses this feature of "standard gamble" approaches in *Measuring Health: Lessons for Ontario* (Toronto: University of Toronto Press, 1978), pp. 92–93.

37. B. McNeil, R. Weichselbaum, and S. Pauker, "Fallacy of the Five Year Survival in Lung Cancer," *New England Journal of Medicine* 299 (21 December 1978): 1397–1401. For another attempt at eliciting preferences, see Joseph S. Pliskin, Donald S. Shephard, and Milton C. Weinstein, "Utility Functions for Life Years and Health Status," *Operations Research,* January–February 1980.

38. For a discussion of discounting, which shares the spirit of this one, see Lester Lave, *The Strategy of Social Regulation* (Washington, D.C.: Brookings Institution, 1981), pp. 41–45.

39. Paul Slovic made this argument to me about the possibly superior performance of a physician. However, I doubt that McNeil would claim that such procedures should actually be incorporated into medical practice, rather, her studies highlight differences that doctors should at least be sensitive to.

40. See Donald M. Berwick, Shan Cretin, and Emmett Keeler, *Cholesterol, Children, and Heart Disease: An Analysis of Alternatives* (New York: Oxford University Press, 1980), pp. 272–273.

41. For a review of OSHA costs, see Ivy Broder and John Morall III, "The Economic Basis for OSHA's and EPA's Generic Carcinogen Regulations," a paper presented at the Research Conference of the Association for Public Policy Analysis and Management (Boston) 23–25 October 1980.

42. Some non-workplace studies have been conducted. See Glenn Blomquist, "Value of Life: Implications of Automobile Seat Belt Use" (Ph.D. dissertation, University of Chicago, 1977). For a review of air pollution studies, see A. Myrick Freeman III, *The Benefits of Environmental Improvement: Theory and Practice* (Baltimore: Johns Hopkins University Press, 1979).

43. Fischhoff, Slovic, and Lichtenstein, "How Safe is Safe Enough."

44. Acton, "Measuring the Monetary Value," pp. 64–70.

45. For a recent review of methodological issues (and their substantive implications) see Baruch Fischhoff, Paul Slovic, and Sarah Lichtenstein, "Lay Foibles and Expert Fables in Judgments About Risk," in *Progress in Resource Management and Environment Planning,* Vol. 3, ed. T. O'Riordan and R. K. Turner (Chichester: Wiley, 1981).

46. Thaler and Gould ("Public Preferences") show why we should expect people who know that they have lower initial probabilities of survival to be willing to pay more for an absolute increment in the probability of surviving. This disparity provides another basis for possible conflicts between maximizing "lives saved" and WTP.

47. Amos Tversky and Daniel Kahneman, "The Framing of Decisions and the Psychology of Choice," *Science* 211 (30 January 1981): 453–8.

17

The New Arms Race: Star Wars Weapons

UNION OF CONCERNED SCIENTISTS

This article describes various proposals for using directed energy for defensive purposes and points to problems in the defense system envisioned: Machines instead of humans would make the decision to attack; the system would lead to a massive build-up of offensive, as well as defensive, weapons by both the United States and the USSR; it would be highly destabilizing; it would violate the 1972 U.S.–USSR ABM treaty; and it would be tremendously expensive.

On March 23, 1983, in a televised address to the nation, President Reagan called on "the scientific community which gave us nuclear weapons" to turn its talents toward the goal of freeing the world from the threat of nuclear war. He called for the development of defensive technologies that would provide the means of rendering nuclear weapons "impotent and obsolete."

Such a prospect is alluring, but can it be achieved? Is it possible to develop a technical fix to the arms race? These questions cannot be answered with certainty, yet it appears that the goal set out by President Reagan is not attainable. Insurmountable technological and political obstacles will prevent us from developing an effective "shield" against nuclear weapons. Most important, even the effort to build and deploy these "defensive technologies" could spur a dangerous new phase of the arms race.

THE STAR WARS VISION

The Soviet Union now has approximately 7,500 strategic nuclear weapons with which it could destroy America. The United States in turn has some 9,500 such weapons to deter the Soviets from ever initiating a nuclear attack. Due to their unprecedented destructive power, these arsenals set the framework for what is commonly called "mutual assured destruction" (MAD): If one side launches its weapons, the other will retaliate, and both sides will be destroyed. This precarious "balance of terror"—though flawed in many ways—has helped to maintain stability between the superpowers for more than three decades.

The president, a group of his advisors, and a handful of others now lay claim to a "vision of the future" in which exotic new weapons offer an escape from MAD. Through the

From Star Wars Weapons, Union of Concerned Scientists Briefing Paper, August 1983. Reprinted with permission from the Union of Concerned Scientists.

development of anti-ballistic missile (ABM) systems on earth and orbiting in space, they believe that the U.S. could effectively intercept and destroy Soviet nuclear weapons launched against the U.S. or our allies. In this way, they suggest, we would no longer need to threaten the Soviet Union with a devastating retaliatory attack.

The futuristic technologies that evoke this hope for an ABM defense involve the use of "directed energy," with lasers and particle beams being the principal candidates. Briefly, the following are the major proposals for using directed energy for defensive energy for defensive purposes.

CHEMICAL LASERS: THE DARPA TRIAD

A laser is a device that creates a beam of energy composed of a single wavelength of radiation. The beam can take the form of visible light or invisible radiation like X-rays or infrared radiation. There are many different laser devices, and different forms of laser beams generated, yet all possess one thing in common: They have the potential to inflict damage to a distant target at the speed of light. This feature makes the laser beam an obvious candidate for a weapons system.

To create a laser of sufficient strength to act as a weapon system would require large inputs of energy, which has been a problem in development efforts. One energy source being tried is that of highly reactive chemicals. The Defense Advanced Research Projects Agency (DARPA) is attempting to develop a space-based-chemical laser weapon. One of its programs, called TRIAD, is comprised of three separate research projects: ALPHA, developing the laser itself; TALON GOLD, developing the means of picking out and tracking fast-moving distant targets, because an effective laser weapon needs near-perfect accuracy over great distances; and LODE (Large Optics Demonstration Experiment), developing a very large, durable, lightweight mirror to focus and aim large lasers.

If and when the three parts of the TRIAD are perfected, they would be integrated into an operational laser battle station and placed into orbit via the space shuttle. Dozens, perhaps hundreds, of these orbiting battle stations would have to be placed into space to ensure that enough of them were strategically positioned at all times to target Soviet ICBM fields. Proponents of TRIAD claim that if the Soviets initiated a nuclear attack against the United States, these weapons would detect the missiles and start shooting them down.

II. EXCALIBUR: THE X-RAY LASER

Lasers can also be generated by other sources of energy. One such alternative is being pursued under the code name "Excalibur" at the Lawrence Livermore National Laboratory. It involves the use of small nuclear explosions to "energize" a laser.

When a nuclear device is detonated, massive quantities of X-rays are produced. Scientists working on Excalibur are trying to harness these "clouds" of X-rays for the purpose of attacking enemy ICBMs. They believe this could be done by "pumping" the X-rays through lasing rods to produce focused X-ray energy beams. If these beams were produced in space, they could, theoretically, be targeted against Soviet missiles in flight.

The proponents of Excalibur call for a "pop-up" deployment scheme. When an enemy missile attack appeared imminent, the U.S. would launch dozens—perhaps hundreds—of X-ray laser battle stations into space atop missile boosters. Each U.S. battle station would track rising Russian ICBMs with its 40–50 laser rods. This tracking would be done with information gathered by U.S. military satellites. The sensor equipment aboard these satellites would have to distinguish real missiles from decoys, and transmit the data to ground stations for processing. Ground-based computers would make an immense number of calculations needed to plot the Soviet ICBM flight trajectories, and would transmit that information back to the computers on board the battle stations. When the laser turrets were all aligned, the command would be given, the nuclear device in each weapon would explode, and the X-ray beams would deliver crippling blows to their targets. After this occurred, the battle stations would themselves be destroyed by the nuclear blasts.

III. THE HIGH FRONTIER

The High Frontier proposal, first presented by the Heritage Foundation in 1982, calls for a multi-layer approach to strategic defense. Two layers would be space-based, and a third would be ground-based. The first layer would consist of 432 orbiting battle stations, each armed with 40–50 non-nuclear kill devices. These weapons would be equipped with infrared sensors to home in on Soviet missiles and destroy them by direct collisions. The second layer would involve directed-energy battle stations similar to TRIAD and Excalibur.

In the High Frontier plan, the first two layers would "thin out" the Soviet attack, leaving fewer weapons for the third layer—a ground-based system—to contend with. The ground-based layer would consist of weapons surrounding U.S. missile silos, for example, swarms of projectiles or rocket-powered interceptors that would be launched to destroy the incoming ICBMs.

IV. PARTICLE BEAMS

The particle beam is another form of directed energy now being pursued by the U.S. Department of Defense for possible ABM applications. Particle beams differ from lasers in that they are composed of streams of atomic or subatomic particles rather than light waves. To create such an energy beam, particles are injected into a large machine called a particle accelerator that accelerates the particles to nearly the speed of light. If formed into a narrow beam, these particles could deliver a damaging blow to a target.

The advocates of particle beam weapons offer deployment schemes similar to that of TRIAD. The weapons would be fashioned into orbiting battle stations and placed "on patrol" in outer space. At the sign of a Soviet ICBM launch, these space-based particle accelerators would generate and direct beams of energy to disable the Soviet missiles.

V. ORBITING MIRRORS

Another ABM plan now being proposed envisages enormous mirrors placed in space to target and focus laser beams generated on the ground. Such mirrors would be stationed permanently in orbit, or "popped up" (as with Excalibur) upon warning of an attack. As many as 100 ground-based laser stations would be dispersed across the continental United States. When a command to attack was given, the mirrors would be aimed, the laser beams would be transmitted into space and bounced off the mirrors to intercept the enemy ICBMs. If everything worked according to plan, the missiles would be destroyed, and the U.S. would escape from the damage the Soviet ICBMs would otherwise inflict.

FLAWS IN THE STAR WARS VISION

Space-based ABMs are now being considered at high levels of the U.S. government. These various schemes are alluring, but would they work? None of these systems has been built, and all face enormous technical hurdles. In fact, as the following list suggests, the technologies needed for these proposed space weapons may *never* exist.

• For laser weapons to be effective against ICBMs, they would require targeting capabilities far beyond anything ever accomplished. The lasers would have to maintain near-perfect accuracy long enough to inflict damage upon targets traveling at more than 10,000 miles per hour, up to 3,500 miles away. A senior Pentagon weapons designer compared this targeting challenge to that of "being on top of the Washington Monument, shooting a rifle, and hitting a baseball on top of the Empire State Building."

• No mirror ever built comes even close to meeting the requirements necessary for an ABM laser weapon. The mirror might have to be 40 to 50 feet across, whereas the largest laser mirror built to date is less than six feet in diameter. The mirror would have to withstand enormous temperature changes. Anything short of perfect reflection would result in destruction of the mirror by the laser itself.

• A successful anti-ballistic missile defense would require immense battle-management capabilities. Hundreds of space weapons, each capable of delivering hundreds of energy beams or non-nuclear kill devices, would have to be aimed at some 1,000 targets in the course of only five to eight minutes. (After this short period, the enemy missiles would begin releasing their multiple warheads and the number of targets would increase by a factor of up to ten.) Computers capable of accomplishing this sort of massive, instantaneous data processing do not exist.

• Kill verification would be extremely difficult. Several seconds could pass before an attacked missile strayed from its anticipated trajectory. In a situation where targeting and retargeting must occur with lightning speed, time would be of the essence. The weapon would be of little value if target destruction could not be assured.

• Since the ABM weapons would have only a few minutes to identify the target and execute an attack, human participation would be eliminated from the process. Automatic weapons would require an entirely new generation of "smart" technologies, machines with "artificial intelligence" capability to engage in a space warfare mission independently. As a research analyst for the U.S. Department of Defense has observed, "We would have to delegate the decision-making to the weapon system itself and we have had no experience in that type of operational system."

• Particle beam ABMs would face additional obstacles. Building a particle accelerator small enough for deployment in space may not be possible. Finding a suitable energy supply for such a weapon will be difficult. The actual physics of particle beams, moreover, may not allow them to be aimed effectively in space.

As formidable as these technological obstacles may be, one might assume that they could

still be mastered. Three or four decades ago, few would have believed that we would place astronauts on the moon. Some space-weapons advocates claim that President Reagan's call for these exotic ABMs is analogous to President Kennedy's call to put a man on the moon. The fallacy of this comparison is obvious. The moon did not try to defy our attempt to conquer it with technology. The Soviets will.

THE SOVIET RESPONSE

The U.S.S.R. will not sit idle while the United States develops a means to render its nuclear arsenal ineffective. Immediately following President Reagan's call for futuristic defense systems, Soviet leader Yuri Andropov responded sharply: "The Soviet Union," he said, "will never allow them to succeed." The Soviets will develop countermeasures to ensure the effectiveness of their nuclear weapons. Indeed, the United States, anticipating Soviet development of such ABMs, is working on at least six countermeasures of its own: (1) warheads that fly erratically toward their targets; (2) warheads that confuse radar tracking abilities by releasing clouds of metal from their tips; (3) decoys that behave like warheads and thus work to saturate the defense; (4) hardened and reflective materials that would blunt the effect of lasers; (5) rotating missiles that would disperse laser beam energy; and (6) warheads that emit smokescreens as a shield against lasers.

In addition to such countermeasures as these, the Soviets could also be expected to shift a larger portion of their arsenal towards terrain-hugging cruise missiles, low-flying bombers, and depressed-trajectory ballistic missiles—none of which could be destroyed by space-based ABMs. In fact, the Soviets are in the process of building weapons with such evasive capabilities. Likewise, the U.S. could expect a massive Soviet buildup of offensive weapons as a hedge against an ABM defense.

DEFENSE OR OFFENSE?

All the proposed ABM systems described above would have inherent offensive anti-satellite (ASAT) capabilities that would be highly destabilizing. Satellites are extremely fragile systems that would be much easier to shoot down than enemy missiles. For this reason, the deployment of space-based ABM systems by the United States and the Soviet Union would create an unprecedented threat to the command, control, and intelligence satellites of each country.

Fearing that its enemy could destroy its "eyes and ears" in the skies, each side would adopt hair-trigger postures that increase the risk of nuclear war. If a military satellite (or, for that matter, one of the orbiting battle stations) suddenly stopped functioning, it could be interpreted as the beginning of an attack. A computer malfunction, a collision with a piece of space junk, or a faulty instrument reading on earth might be mistaken as an act of war. Because these systems would be functioning autonomously, World War III could be initiated without anyone knowing it.

Even the mere prospect of ABM deployment could spark hostilities. The imminent deployment of ABMs could tempt an enemy to attack suddenly and decisively to disarm its opponent. Suppose the Soviets believed the U.S. was about to develop a defensive "shield" against nuclear weapons. In a moment of crisis, seeing that their offensive arsenal might be neutralized in the event of war, the Soviets might launch a first-strike attack before it was "too late." Failure to do so, in the view of some military leaders, might mean "submission" to the U.S. The U.S. could be expected to think along similar lines in response to a Soviet ABM defense.

The fact that these ABM systems would be less than 100 percent effective also creates a first-strike incentive. The nation that launched first would have the advantage of contending with the enemy's diminished retaliatory nuclear forces.

VIOLATING THE ABM TREATY

In 1972, the United States and the Soviet Union signed a treaty that explicitly outlawed ABM systems of the type that is now being explored by the U.S. government. To proceed with space weapons would require the abrogation of this treaty, even though most arms control analysts believe the ABM Treaty to be the single most important achievement of U.S.–Soviet negotiations over the past two decades. The ABM Treaty laid the foundation for all subsequent talks to reduce the offensive arsenals on both sides. If the ABM Treaty is abandoned, any incentive to scale back offensive weapons will be undermined. Both sides will want massive offensive arsenals to ensure penetration of their opponent's defense.

When the superpowers decided to forgo an ABM competition, they did so with the understanding that such ABM systems: (1) would fuel an offensive arms race; (2) would make a first strike more probable; (3) may not work; and (4) would be very costly. These arguments remain as valid today as they were in 1972.

The ABM space weapons would also be tremendously expensive. According to one ABM advocate, a comprehensive space-based defense program would require a $200 billion investment, and an additional $50 billion in annual maintenance costs. In 1982, the Pentagon estimated that a "damage denial" system would cost about $500 billion. Considering the number of battle stations projected in some of these schemes—and the fact that hundreds of space shuttle trips might be required to place them in orbit—it is obvious that the cost of these weapons would be astronomical—easily in the hundreds of billions of dollars.

We all wish that the "balance of terror" that looms over us could be wiped away. Raising false hopes about the promise of a technological panacea, however, will not end the nuclear arms race. If anything, the quixotic pursuit of "Star Wars" technology will drive the arms race to a new level of intensity, adding a new and dangerous dimension to the U.S.–U.S.S.R. rivalry. The only hope for a lasting and durable peace between the superpowers is persistent arms control that builds on the successful negotiations of the past.

18

The Militarization of Space and International Law

ALLAN ROSAS

Allan Rosas argues that deployment of directed-energy defensive systems would not appear to violate the 1972 U.S.–USSR ABM treaty, but that common security, not just international law alone, should be considered in assessing these systems, which threaten to upset the strategic balance between the two powers.

1. MILITARY SPACE SYSTEMS[1,2]

Military systems utilizing in some form or another space as a theater of operations may be roughly divided into *space-based* and *ground-based* systems. Satellites, of course, belong to the former category but they require ground-based stations as well. Anti-satellite weapons may be either space- or ground-based. The U.S. space shuttle illustrates the difficulties in making a sharp distinction between the two categories.

Military space systems can also be classified according to their "agressive" nature. Extremes are on the one hand satellites used for the verification of disarmament agreements and on the other hand space-based bombs and missiles targeted on earth. The following chart (Table 18.1) starts from systems of primarily indirect use in military attack and ends up with outright weapon systems. A rough dichotomy is in this regard maintained between military support systems (S) and weapon systems (W). Examples are provided of systems already in use or planned to become operational in the near future.

The altitudes of military *satellites* range from some 100–150 km (many photographic reconnaissance satellites) to the geostationary orbit of some 35,000 km (many early-warning, remote sensing and communication satellites). The latter are probably out of reach for the *anti-satellite* (ASAT) systems currently developed. The U.S. ASAT Thor rocket with a nuclear warhead was dimantled in 1975. The Soviet tests with a "killer" satellite using conventional explosives reportedly involved the actual damaging of the target satellite in March 1981. The U.S. Miniature Homing Intercept Vehicle system (MHIV), planned to be ready for use around 1987, is a small conventional vehicle launched with a rocket from an F-15 aeroplane.[3]

The U.S. *space shuttle* is claimed to be a mere space transportation system carrying civilian and military payloads but it may have an ASAT or other attack capability as well.[4] Studies are carried out on the feasibility of other types of re-usable space vehicles.

The laser and other *directed-energy* weapons might have a role both as space-based or ground-based ASAT systems and ballistic

From *Journal of Peace Research* 20, no. 4 (1983), pp. 357–364. Reprinted by permission of the International Peace Research Institute. This article is a slightly revised version of a paper presented at the 42nd Pugwash Symposium on the Arms Race and International Law, Helsinki, February 10–12, 1983.

Table 18.1

	"Aggressive" nature	Space-based	Ground-based
	Reconnaissance, early-warning, weather and remote sensing satellites	Various systems in use by many states	Ground stations
S	Communications, navigation satellites	Communication satellites of four states, U.S. NAVSTAR system (1988)	Ground stations
	Satellite transport systems with attack capability	U.S. space shuttle	U.S. space shuttle
	Anti-satellite systems (ASAT)	USSR "killer" satellites (tests since 1968), directed-energy weapons(?)	U.S. Thor (1964–75) U.S. air-based MHIV system (1987?)
W	Ballistic missile defence (BMD)	Directed-energy weapons?? Conventional weapons??	(ABM systems, only USSR site operational), directed-energy weapons??
	Bombs and missiles targeted on earth		(1CBMS, including FOBS)

S = support systems, W = weapons.

missile defence systems (BMD). The military feasibility of these weapons is still highly uncertain, however.[5] Space-based BMD laser weapons would be directed against attacking enemy missiles immediately upon launch. Studies have also been undertaken on space-based conventional BMD weapons.

The development of ASAT weapons has led to the initiating of various satellite survivability measures for the defence of one's own satellites such as the hardening of satellites and the use of reserve satellites and decoys.

The ABM and ICBM systems mentioned in the chart in brackets are not space systems proper. The Fractional Orbital Bombardment System (FOBS) tested by the Soviet Union comes closer to a space system in that the intercontinental ballistic missile is placed in orbit, albeit a partial one.[6]

2. INTERNATIONAL SPACE AGREEMENTS

The main treaty regulating the exploration and use of outer space is, of course, the 1967 Treaty on Principles Governing the Activities of States in the Exploration and Use of Outer Space, Including the Moon and Other Celestial Bodies. The Treaty was preceded by UN General Assembly resolution 1884 (XVIII) of 1963, in which states were called upon not to station in outer space nuclear weapons or other kinds of weapons of mass destruction.[7]

Although the 1967 Treaty broadens the scope of the 1963 resolution it does not provide for a complete demilitarization of outer space. Article 4 of the Treaty reads as follows:

States Parties to the Treaty undertake not to place in orbit around the earth any objects carrying nuclear weapons or any other kinds of weapons of mass destruction, install such weapons on celestial bodies, or station such weapons in outer space in any other manner.

The moon and other celestial bodies shall be used by all States Parties to the Treaty exclusively for peaceful purposes. The establishment of military bases, installations and fortifications, the testing of any type of weapons and the conduct of military manoeuvres on celestial bodies shall be forbidden. The use of military personnel for scientific research or for any other peaceful purposes shall not be prohibited. The use of any equipment or facility necessary for peaceful exploration of the moon and other celestial bodies shall also not be prohibited.

Without going here into all the problems of interpretation raised by this article it should be noted that the concept of weapons of mass destruction in paragraph 1 encompasses besides nuclear weapons chemical and bacteriological and probably also radiological weapons but apparently not, for instance, laser and other directed-energy weapons (which are discriminate rather than indiscriminate in character).[8] It should be noted moreover that the Treaty only prohibits the *stationing* of such weapons in space, not their testing, development or deployment on earth nor perhaps, even the deployment of ground-based nuclear systems designed for use against space objects (cf. the above-mentioned U.S. ASAT system in use 1964–1975). The prohibition on placing weapons of mass destruction "in orbit around the earth" has not been interpreted by the United States to include the above-mentioned Soviet FOB system.[9]

Paragraph 2 of the article dealing with the moon and other celestial bodies provides for a more complete demilitarization although certain loopholes remain. It should be noted that this paragraph, but not paragraph 1 on outer space in general, speaks of the use of celestial bodies "exclusively for peaceful purposes." The reference to "peaceful purposes" appears in the preamble, too, but not in other substantive articles. Even if certain other provisions of the Treaty must also be taken into account (notably articles 1, 3 and 9) it is difficult to interpret the Treaty as prohibiting all military activities in outer space, notably in orbit around the earth. Furthermore, the United

States has asserted that "peaceful" merely means "non-aggressive," not necessarily "non-military."[10]

After 1967 international space agreements have also been concluded on the rescue of astronauts and the return of objects launched into outer space (1968), the international liability for damage caused by space objects (1972) and the registration of objects launched into outer space (1975).

The relevance of these conventions for the prevention of the militarization of space is marginal, however. Of more concrete relevance in this regard is the 1979 Agreement Governing the Activities of States on the Moon and Other Celestial Bodies. This Agreement, not yet in force,[11] reaffirms the demilitarization of celestial bodies contained in the 1967 Outer Space Treaty and contains certain supplementary details in this regard (article 3).

Moreover, there are some disarmament agreements which restrict the military use of space in some respects. In this context mention may be made of the Partial Test Ban Treaty of 1963, prohibiting nuclear tests, inter alia, in outer space, and the ENMOD Convention of 1977 on ecological warfare, prohibiting also certain environmental modification techniques affecting space.

Of the bilateral agreements between the Soviet Union and the United States, mention should be made of the 1972 ABM Treaty, the 1972 Interim Agreement on the limitation of strategic offensive arms (SALT I), the 1974 Threshold Test Ban Treaty, the 1976 Peaceful Nuclear Explosions Treaty and the 1979 SALT II Treaty. All these agreements—of which only the 1972 ABM Treaty is formally in force—contain a prohibition on interfering with the national technical means of verification of the other Party. The prohibition— which is not absolute[12]—is intended to cover satellites used as a means of verification (notably reconnaissance satellites).

In view of the current discussion on the possible role of space-based directed-energy weapons as BMD systems it is to be noted that the 1972 ABM Treaty also prohibits the development, testing and deployment of sea-based, air-based, space-based and mobile land-based ABM systems (article V). However, the definition of ABM systems in the Treaty is not unequivocal, as the description of an ABM system ("a system to counter strategic ballistic missiles or their elements in flight trajectory") is followed by a reference to the fact that such systems are "currently consisting of" ABM interceptor "missiles," ABM launchers and ABM radars (article II). While this wording suggests that directed-energy weapons *are* included in the prohibition, the matter is somewhat complicated by an Agreed Interpretation stating that the two parties agree that in the event ABM systems based on other physical principles are created in the future, specific limitations on such systems and their components would be subject to consultations.[13]

There have been voices claiming that the listing of ABM systems in article II of the Treaty (ABM missiles, launchers and radars) is meant to be exhaustive and that directed-energy weapons are not covered by the Treaty.[14] However, this interpretation seems to bypass the fact that the purpose of the Agreed Interpretation is "to insure fulfillment of the obligation not to deploy ABM systems and their component except as provided in Article III of the Treaty." The emphasis seems here to be on possible problems in the application of the limitations on *fixed land-based* ABM systems contained in Article III[15] rather than on the prohibition on the development, testing and deployment of other ABM systems. The official U.S. position appears to have been that directed-energy weapons, too, are included in the prohibitions and limitations of the ABM Treaty.[16] It is submitted that this interpretation is the correct one.

Even with this interpretation, however, the development of space-based directed-energy or other BMD systems is not entirely precluded under the ABM Treaty. First of all, the Treaty does not prohibit the development and testing of fixed ground-based ABM systems (note the difficulties in distinguishing between the development of ground-based, air-based and space-based directed-energy weapons). Secondly, it is not clear that the prohibition on

the "development and testing" of air-based and space-based ABM systems includes research. Thirdly, the ABM Treaty does not prohibit the development and testing of directed-energy or other weapons systems intended, e.g., for an ASAT role.

Finally, reference may be made to the 1971 Agreement between the Soviet Union and the United States on measures to improve the U.S.A.–USSR direct communications link ("Hot Line") and the Agreement on measures to reduce the risk of outbreak of nuclear war between the two countries in the same year (Nuclear Accidents Agreement). Certain provisions in these agreements may be interpreted as prohibitions on interference with the Hot Line satellite systems and possibly with early-warning satellites.[17]

3. LOOPHOLES AND LACUNAE IN THE TREATY SYSTEM

Although a variety of military space options are prohibited under international agreements in force, notably the 1967 Outer Space Treaty and the 1972 ABM Treaty, a number of loopholes and lacunae remain to be filled if space is to be completely demilitarized. Among those military systems with possible space application which are *not* expressly prohibited under written agreements mention may be made of the following:

• ground testing and development of weapons of mass destruction, even those designed for use in space (however, nuclear tests must be underground and bacteriological weapons are prohibited under the 1972 Convention)
• ground deployment of such weapons (with the exception of bacteriological weapons)
• testing, development and deployment (also in space) of directed-energy and conventional weapons designed for an ASAT role (however, ASAT weapons may not as a general rule be *used* against verification of Hot Line satellites)
• research on directed-energy and conventional weapons designed for BMD use (however, the actual development of such

weapon systems may be prohibited under the 1972 ABM Treaty)
• the placing of conventional bombs and other similar weapons (including directed-energy weapons) in orbit around the earth
• the use of observation, communication and navigation satellites for military purposes.

While the above activities are not expressly prohibited, one can envisage additional prohibitions or restrictions being deduced from the general principles expressed in existing agreements in combination with principles of general international law (customary law). Thus, the preamble of the 1967 Outer Space Treaty refers to the exploration and use of outer space "for peaceful purposes," while article 1 states that the exploration and use of outer space shall be carried out "for the benefit and in the interest of all countries." According to article 3 the states parties shall carry on activities "in accordance with international law, including the Charter of the United Nations, in the interest of maintaining international peace and security and promoting international cooperation and understanding."[18]

Though not devoid of legal relevance, these and other similar lofty statements are not likely to check the military R & D of the great powers to any considerable extent. The space powers should still be constantly reminded of the spirit and, indeed, the wording of the 1967 Treaty as well as other relevant agreements. If actual weapon systems (directed-energy or conventional) were to be deployed in space there might be a reaction from the international community entailing an argumentation along the above lines. In this context it is also to be noted that there is a new rule of international humanitarian law imposing certain restraints upon states in the study and development of new weapons. According to article 36 of Protocol I of 1977 additional to the Geneva Conventions of 12 August 1949, the states parties shall "in the study, development, acquisition or adoption of a new weapon, means or method of warfare . . . determine whether its employment would, in some or all circumstances, be prohibited by this Protocol or by any other rule of international law applicable to the High Contracting Party."[19]

The focus in this provision upon the use of weapons in times of armed conflict brings us to a general problem concerning the application of the above agreements relating to space *in time of war*. Traditionally, it has been held that the outbreak of war as a general rule cancels or suspends the treaties in force between the belligerents, except those concluded especially for war.[20] With the outlawing of the use of force there has been an adverse trend and the present situation is far from clear.[21] The agreements relating to space do not contain any express provision on the matter. Their language seems to suggest that the drafters have had primarily peace-time relations in mind. However, we would suggest as a starting point for an analysis that the 1963 Partial Test Ban Treaty, the 1967 Outer Space Treaty and the bilateral U.S.A.–USSR agreements remain in force during armed conflict. This is even more true with respect to the 1977 ENMOD Convention and the 1979 Moon Agreement. According to article 3, paragraph 2, of the last-mentioned Agreement "any threat or use of force or any other hostile act or threat of hostile act on the moon is prohibited." According to paragraph 3 of the same article the parties shall, inter alia, not place "or use" weapons of mass destruction on or in the moon. Though not referring explicitly to the applicability of the Moon Agreement in time of armed conflict, these provisions seem to indicate that such applicability is intended.[22] This aspect of the law governing outer space deserves further examination.

4. DISARMAMENT TALKS

After the failure of the efforts aimed at a total demilitarization of outer space in connection with the 1967 Treaty, Italy in particular has put forward initiatives in this regard.[23] A paragraph (80) on the prevention of the arms race in outer space was included in the Final Document of the 1978 UN General Assembly special session devoted to disarmament. In

1978–1979 the Soviet Union and the United States held bilateral talks on prohibiting or restricting ASAT weapons. Referring to the situation in Afghanistan the United States broke off these and some other bilateral arms control talks.[24]

In 1981 the question of the conclusion of a treaty on the prohibition of the stationing of weapons of any kind in outer space was, on the initiative of the Soviet Union, included in the agenda of the UN General Assembly.[25] Since spring 1982 the question has been discussed in the Committee on Disarmament (CD). While the thrust of the Soviet initiative is on the prohibition of the *stationing* of *weapons* in space, the Western European states have emphasized the importance of prohibiting *ASAT systems*. The two approaches overlap but do not coincide, as the stationing of other than ASAT weapons, too, would be prohibited under the Soviet proposal (e.g., space-based BMD systems) whereas the Western states have referred to prohibitions or restrictions on the ground development of ASAT weapons as well.[26]

The militarization of outer space has also been a source of concern for the UN Committee on the Peaceful Uses of Outer Space (COPUOS). Efforts to place the question of the prevention of an arms race in outer space on the agenda of the Committee have not been successful so far.[27]

The question received considerable attention at the second UN space conference (UNISPACE 82) in Vienna in August 1982.[28]

Finally, mention should be made of the 1978 French initiative for the establishment of an international satellite monitoring agency. The question has been explored in a UN study of 1981.[29]

5. PROSPECTS

Outer space offers an example of an arms race arena where disarmament measures would still be possible as many military systems are still in the research or testing stage. At the same time disarmament is urgent not only for the sake of curbing the arms race in a new environment but also for the apparent risks that the militarization of outer space entails for the strategic balance between the great powers.

But at the same time we seem to be witnessing the classic situation of failure to grasp the moment when it is at hand. The arms race spiral is not showing many signs of weakness. This is not to say that the development is irrevocable. But there is an apparent lack of political will for disarmament in space on the part of one of the great powers, the United States. Contrary to some of its Western allies, this power has shown no enthusiasm for urgent arms control measures.[30] Instead, there are many indications that it in reality opposes such measures. In his by now well-known address on national security of 23 March 1983 President Reagan referred to the possibilities of developing new BMD systems.[31] Apparently he had primarily in mind space-based laser systems.[32] The President announced that he had directed "a comprehensive and intensive effort to define a long-term research and development program to begin to achieve our ultimate goal of eliminating the threat posed by strategic nuclear missiles." As explained above, such a program would be in contravention of the 1972 ABM Treaty only if it implied the "development" or "testing" of other than fixed land-based BMD systems or the deployment of fixed land-based systems in excess of the restrictions imposed upon such systems in article III of the Treaty.[33]

While many Western European states have pressed for the banning of ASAT systems, considering the fact that the Soviet Union has tested killer satellites since 1968, the position of the United States has been more reserved since the suspension of its bilateral talks with the Soviet Union in 1978–79. One reason may be that the forthcoming MHIV ASAT system is calculated to achieve a higher military efficacy than the Soviet killer satellites.[34] In his testimony before a subcommittee of the U.S. Senate on 18 May 1983, Kenneth L. Adelman, Director of the Arms Control and Disarmament Agency, also referred to the threat posed by present and prospective Soviet satellites.[35] According to him, there is a dilemma as to whether agreements that would restrict the ability of the United States to "deal with" such satellites are in its national security interest. The U.S. administration has thus to "balance the desire to limit threats to U.S. satellites against the desire to be able to take actions against Soviet satellites that could cost American lives in situations far short of all-out war."

The prospects for instant disarmament agreements relating to outer space thus seem rather bleak. There may be some hope for disarmament, however, if the negotiations especially on strategic (Salt–Start) and intermediate-range (INF) nuclear forces make headway. Also the on-going review of the 1972 ABM Treaty seems to be of vital importance.

Unfortunately, there is not much international lawyers acting in that capacity can do to reverse the trend. Whether a solace or not, it is a fact that the arms race in outer space has by and large taken place *within* the framework of existing international agreements. What has been disregarded is a conception of common security more than international law in force.

NOTES

1. See, e.g., Bhupendra M. Jasani and Maria A. Lunderius, Peaceful Uses of Outer Space—Legal Fiction and Military Reality, *Bulletin of Peace Proposals* 1980, pp. 57–70; Outer Space—A New Dimension of the Arms Race, SIPRI symposium. London 1982; FOA-tidningen (Försvarets forskningsanstalt), tema: rymdteknik och säkerhetspolitik, juni 1982.

2. See, e.g., Thomas H. Karas, Implications of Space Technology for Strategic Nuclear Competition, The Stanley Foundation, Occasional Paper 25. Muscatine, Iowa 1981.

3. On recent ASAT technology see Svein Melby, Anti-Satellite Weapons, the Strategic Balance and Arms Control, NUPI-rapport nr. 69 (Norsk Utenrikspolitisk Institutt). Oslo 1982, pp. 27–96.

4. Melby, op.cit. pp. 41, 51. Cf. Walter D. Reed and Robert W. Norris, Military Use of the Space Shuttle, *Akron Law Review* 1980, pp. 670–672.

5. For scepticism in this regard see, e.g., Kosta Tsipis, Laser Weapons, *Scientific American,* December 1981, pp. 35–41.

6. See, e.g., Ivan A. Vlasic, Disarmament

Decade, Outer Space and International Law, *McGill Law Journal* 1981, pp. 151–152.

7. For the preparatory work on the 1967 treaty see, e.g., Nicolas Mateesco Matte, *Aerospace Law.* London-Toronto 1969, pp. 105–111, 263–268; Fariborz Nozari, *The Law of Outer Space.* Stockholm 1973, pp. 34–37.

8. E. Anthony Fessler, *Directed-Energy Weapons. A Juridical Analysis.* New York 1979, pp. 56–60.

9. Fessler, op. cit. pp. 61–62. The unratified SALT II-treaty (article IX) would prohibit the parties from developing, testing or deploying "systems for placing into Earth orbit nuclear weapons or any other kind of weapons of mass destruction, including fractional orbital missiles."

10. See, e.g., I. H. Ph. Diederiks-Verschoor, Die Bedeutung des Begriffs 'friedlich' im Weltraumvertrag von 1967, Beiträge zum Luft- und Weltraumrecht, Festschrift zu Ehren von Alex Meyer. Köln 1975, pp. 301–306.

11. The Moon Agreement had in February 1983 been ratified by four states only. (Editor's Note: In January 1985, the agreement had been signed by 11 States—Austria, Chile, France, Guatemala, India, Morocco, Netherlands, Peru, Philippines, Romania and Uruguay—and ratified by Austria, Chile, Philippines, Netherlands and Uruguay.)

12. According to article XII, paragraph 1, of the ABM Treaty each Party shall use national technical means of verification at its disposal "in a manner consistent with generally recognized principles of international law." According to paragraph 2 of the same article each Party undertakes not to interfere with the national technical means of verification of the other Party only on the condition that they are "operating in accordance with paragraph 1 of this Article."

13. The text of the Agreed Interpretation in Fessler, op. cit. pp. 70–71.

14. Fessler, op. cit. p. 71. In a Dutch intervention in the First Committee of the UN General Assembly in 1981, it is stated that BMD directed-energy weapons "are apparently not covered by the definition of ABM systems in that Treaty," UN doc. A/C.1/36/PV 23, p. 32.

15. It is to be recalled that article III allows under certain conditions two ABM system deployment areas involving a maximum of 100 launchers and missiles each (since 1974 one deployment area only has been allowed).

16. U.S. Fiscal Year 1983, Arms Control Impact Statements. Washington 1982, pp. 141–42.

17. See in particular article III of the Nuclear Accidents Agreement, whereby the parties "under-

take to notify each other immediately in the event of detection by missile warning systems of unidentified objects, or in the event of signs of interference with these systems or with related communication facilities, if such occurrences could create a risk of outbreak of nuclear war between the two countries."

18. On the provisions of the Outer Space Treaty affecting the military use of space see, e.g., Stephen Gorove, Arms Control Provisions in the Outer Space Treaty: A Scrutinizing Reappraisal, *Georgia Journal of International and Comparative Law,* 1973, pp. 114–123; Diederiks-Verschoor, op. cit. pp. 301–306; Marko G. Markoff, Disarmament and "Peaceful Purposes" Provisions in the 1967 Outer Space Treaty, *Journal of Space Law* 1976, pp. 3–22; Fessler, op. cit. pp. 48–52.

19. See Allan Rosas, Conventional Disarmament—A Legal Framework and Some Perspectives, in: *Militarization and Arms Production,* edited by Helena Tuomi and Raimo Väyrynen. London and Canberra 1983, pp. 261–262.

20. See, e.g., L. Oppenheim, *International Law, A Treatise. Vol. II.* Seventh edition edited by H. Lauterpacht. London 1965, pp. 302–306.

21. See, e.g., D. P. O'Connell, *International Law, Vol. I.* Second edition. London 1970, pp. 268–271.

22. We are not aware of explicit comments on this question. Cf. Simone Courteix, L'accord régissant les activités des États sur la lune et les autres corps célestes, *Annuaire française de droit international* 1979, pp. 210–211; Bin Cheng, The Moon Treaty: Agreement Governing the Activities of States on the Moon and Other Celestial Bodies within the Solar System other than the Earth, December 18, 1979, *Current Legal Problems* 1980, pp. 222–223; D. Goedhuis, Conflicts in the Interpretation of the Leading Principles of the Moon Treaty of 5 December 1979, *Netherlands International Law Review* 1981, pp. 22–26, 27–28.

23. See, e.g., the memorandum presented by Italy to the Committee on Disarmament, CD doc. CD/9 (26 March 1979).

24. See, e.g., Melby, op. cit. pp. 103–105.

25. UN doc. A/36/192.

26. See resolutions 36/97 C and 36/99 of the UN General Assembly of 1981, CD documents CD/272, CD/274, CD/320 and CD/329 and the UN Press Release DC/1140 (21 April 1983).

27. See the Reports of the Committee on the Peaceful Uses of Outer Space 1979 (UN doc. A/34/20), p. 31; 1980 (A/35/20), paras. 22–24, 67; 1981 (A/36/20), para. 68.

28. See also the report of the Seventeenth United Nations of the Next Decade Conference, Maintaining Peace in Outer Space, Cooperstown, New York, June 19–24, 1982. The Stanley Foundation, Muscatine, Iowa 1982.

29. UN doc. A/AC.206/14 (6 August 1981).

30. See, e.g., the statement by the representative of the United States in the First Committee of the UN General Assembly in 1981, UN doc. A/C,1/36/PV 5, pp. 71–72.

31. President Reagan's Speech on National Security, 24 March 1983.

32. See, e.g., Newsweek, April 4, 1983, pp. 14–20.

33. President Reagan states explicitly that the measures taken were "consistent with our obligations under the ABM Treaty."

34. Melby, op. cit. p. 47, notes that "in spite of several uncertainties, there are indications that this ASAT weapon will achieve a much greater capability than is the case for the Killer Satellites."

35. Testimony before the Subcommittee on Arms Control, Oceans, International Operations and Environment of the Committee on Foreign Relations of the U.S. Senate, by Kenneth L. Adelman, Director U.S. Arms Control and Disarmament Agency, May 18, 1983.

19
Space Commercialization

NATIONAL SCIENCE FOUNDATION

According to this article, the role of the private sector in U.S. space policy will be constrained not only by the large and long-term capital investments involved, but by the scientific, political, and national security objectives of the U.S. space program. Any realistic strategy for encouraging space commercialization must involve the federal government, at least in the initial development stages. But early and effective private sector involvement in space technologies could help determine promising, exploitable research directions and also ensure the development of services and systems that meet the criteria of commercial operation.

The commercial exploitation of space has, in recent years, become a topic of serious policy consideration for a number of reasons. Foremost among them is a belief that after more than two decades of an active space program, it is time for the sizable national investment in space to pay off to an even greater extent than it has to date. Given current constraints on the Federal budget, coupled with the Administration's active reassessment of the proper relationship of government and business, an increased focus on the role played by the private sector in facilitating the economic growth and well-being of the United States is sure to continue. Such fundamental policy considerations will have an impact on all commercialization and technology transfer decisions, including those pertaining to space.

There is little argument regarding the desirability, in principle, of commercializing space activity whenever and wherever feasible. The contribution of satellites to the development and expansion of our communications capability serves as an encouraging example of the payoffs possible from timely R&D efforts and industrial involvement in exploiting technological developments. However, a number of basic problems surround the transfer of any given space technology or activity to the private sector. The problems become especially troublesome if commercialization is understood to mean private sector ownership rather than some such hybrid arrangement as Federal ownership and private management or the creation of a publicly funded corporation. In all areas of space activity, one of the key questions is: What constitutes a reasonable risk for industry and a fair burden for taxpayers in the development of space technologies that will serve multiple purposes for the Nation?

Consideration of what space activities can be commercialized and how, and what the appropriate government/industry relationship should be, cannot be separated from other important considerations imposed by the multiple objectives of U.S. space policy. Although a prominent and responsible private sector role in space is one of the implicit

Reprinted from National Science Foundation, *Emerging Issues in Science and Technology, 1981. A Compendium of Working Papers for the National Science Foundation* (Washington, D.C.: National Science Foundation, 1982). The National Science Foundation is responsible for providing primary assistance to the president's science adviser in the preparation of the *Annual Science and Technology Reports to the Congress,* for which the papers in the *Compendium* were written.

objectives of that policy, the role needs to be evaluated and understood in relationship to other goals important to national well-being. The attempt to meet those various goals may at times create dilemmas and constraints for enhancing the role of the private sector.

AN OVERVIEW OF U.S. SPACE POLICY

U.S. space policy has sought to achieve a wide range of objectives, including national security, U.S. economic and political leadership, international cooperation, commercialization, and scientific progress. The initial premise of implementing a space program with a large civil component was that the undertaking was of great benefit to the Nation and thus was worthy of large-scale public support. That premise has been elaborated in the National Aeronautics and Space Act of 1958 and its amendments.

Entry into space has necessitated the development of new technologies to conquer and to utilize effectively the advantages and opportunities presented by the new environment. It has also required the creation of an entirely new infrastructure where none previously existed. Parallels to this situation can be found throughout U.S. history where, at crucial points, the Federal Govermment played a pivotal role in underwriting the Nation's development by subsidizing particular industries, especially in trade, railroad construction, and land development.

The large task of creating a space infrastructure to support technological development has been influenced primarily by military and national security objectives, although the creation of the infrastructure has fulfilled other purposes as well. The advance of communications and information technology has been important for national security reasons and for maintaining U.S. leadership in key high-technology areas. Remote sensing, like satellite communications, provided many areas of the world with otherwise inaccessible services, established the United States as world leader in the field, enhanced international cooperation, and provided information on world resources vital for planning, economic development, national security, and public benefit. Finally,

the space shuttle has been developed to serve both civil and military needs. It, in particular, is perceived as playing a vital national security role.

THE INTERNATIONAL CONTEXT

The crafting of a long-term investment program in space in an era of budgetary constraints will be complicated considerably in the years ahead by discussions and rulemaking on space in the international arena. Far from being esoteric and of interest to only a few nations, space issues have evoked worldwide concern and involvement well beyond the members of the "space club," those nations with active space programs.

Experience with some issues recently discussed at the World Administrative Radio Conference—for example, the Moon Treaty, direct broadcast satellites, and solar power satellites—points to a determination on the part of the world community, and particularly third world nations, to design a set of rules that would preserve and set aside opportunities for latecomers. Negotiating rules that establish a predictable and reasonable framework for the continued development of space while preserving the flexibility necessary to respond to changes and challenges in the space environment and to encourage private industry's involvement is one of the most important political and economic challenges of the next decade. The ability of the United States to respond constructively to pressures to explore and exploit the Moon, for example, or to build space manufacturing facilities to process resources originating from space will depend on a clarification of rules governing the extraction of space resources and a framework of international cooperation and even collaboration in space.

AN OVERVIEW OF PUBLIC AND PRIVATE SECTOR ROLES IN SPACE COMMERCIALIZATION

While a fundamental belief in the benefits of a major public investment in space has served as the basis for all space development activities, the evidence for a profit, from a cost accounting perspective, resulting from the Nation's space investment is difficult to pinpoint. Many more years may be required before a reasonable assessment can be made. Only in one area, communications, can the short-term tally be shown to justify the initial investment. Although the eventual commercial benefit of space development is incalculable, it is nonetheless thought by many to hold great promise. However, any intensified private sector role in space development will have to be premised on the existence of a space program that is long range, diversified, and founded on a strong science and technology base. Appropriate Federal decisions and strategies concerning private industry's role first must focus on the commercial opportunities being created by the Nation's space program.

The range of private sector involvement and the forms some commercial ventures have taken vary a great deal. Complete private sector ownership and operation has been achieved only in satellite communications and may possibly, though with far greater difficulty, be achievable in remote sensing. Space development has, however, promoted private sector participation as contractor and supplier, as developer of secondary services (for example, value-added processing of remote sensing imagery), and as transfomer of space technologies into new commercial ventures and applications.

Unfortunately, the public debate on commercialization and space frequently casts the Federal Government and private industry as antagonists. The fact is that broad-based Federal space policy has not been the antagonist; it is, rather, the basis of commercial profit from space. Once that is understood, the key issue for the future becomes not how to remove the Federal Government from the picture but how to develop or define the most positive and appropriate role government can play in the commercial development of space technology and space systems.

CANDIDATE ACTIVITIES FOR COMMERCIALIZATION

Although the initial investigations of civilian uses of active communications satellites were done by American Telephone and Telegraph Company (AT&T), the National Aeronautics and Space Administration (NASA), in the early sixties, pioneered geosynchronous communications satellites. Since then, many other types of space activity have been developed and now are viewed with varying degrees of optimism as candidates for future commercialization. For example, remote sensing has been, for the last few years, the focus of intensive scrutiny, both within and outside of the Federal Government, to determine whether transfer of any portion of its operational responsibility to the private sector is feasible and, if so, under what conditions. Such other space activities as shuttle operations or space manufacturing are recognized as somewhat more distant candidates for commercialization if the proper circumstances prevail.

Three major categories of space activities, each with varying potential for commercial exploitation are discussed briefly below:

- space-assisted communications and information services,
- space conveyance, and
- space industrialization.

There are obvious differences in the maturity of these activities and the possibilities for their technical exploitation. Other dimensions on which the activities covered by these categories differ include the availability of ready or plausibly developable markets, the relationship of the technology to national security and other public policy concerns, the constraints that could be imposed by the international political environment, the investment of capital required, and the risk any public or private investment would entail.

Space-Assisted Communications and Information Services

The two space activities with the most immediate commercial application, satellite communications and remote sensing by satellite, are essentially land-based activities in which satellites play a crucial role in recording or relaying information from one point on the earth's surface to another. In neither case, however, has industry assumed a leadership role without aid. In both cases, the role of the Federal Government has been important, though in varying degrees, and, in the case of remote sensing, successful transfer to private ownership has yet to occur.

Satellite Communications

The communications satellites pioneered by AT&T in the late fifties and by NASA in the early sixties lent themselves to immediate and highly successful commercial exploitation. Indeed, the extraordinary growth of the domestic and international communications satellite industry has made it logical to point to its success story as a model for future space commercialization efforts. However, the relatively easy success of satellite communications may have been more an exception than a pattern. The single most important factor accounting for this success was the existence of an already well-developed market served by an established private industry. Communications is the only area, thus far, where that condition has existed with respect to applying space technology to commercial operation.

Nevertheless, even the highly positive market conditions were not sufficient in and of themselves to ensure the long-term commitment of private sector involvement and take-over without some Federal assurances. Thus, during the Eisenhower Administration, private industry was initially reluctant to assume all the initial risk of developing satellite communications without assurances that the government would provide launch services for any new technology developed and would not enter into direct competition with private sector development. Later, under the Kennedy Administration, Congress perceived it in the national interest to have the technology implemented and decided to enter into the communications satellite business by passing the law creating a quasi-private, quasi-public communications satellite corporation, COMSAT.

More recently, advances in communications and information technology and continued development of receptive markets have resulted in a period of rapid growth, diversifi-

cation of services and service providers, and high profits in the communications and information industries. Both established carriers and newcomers have, in an environment of deregulation and increased competition, moved to take advantage of and promote the opportunities made possible by technical advances in those industries. Currently, the principal challenges confronted by the industry are the limitations on the radio frequency spectrum, the availability of space in the geostationary orbit, and the restrictions (for example, a priori planning for frequency and orbit use) that could be imposed by international bodies regulating both resources.

Clearly, the existence of a strong private sector communications industry with large, well-established markets, by which the technology could be readily exploited, was of fundamental importance to the success of commercialization efforts. The technological advances made possible by NASA research and development served, in effect, to extend at a propitious time the reach and scope of a service already being supplied by other means. More recent strategies for exploiting new communications technologies have not required a public demonstration model and initial investment of public funds. However, strategies used by private firms to provide innovative telecommunications and information services may be indicative of the types of institutional arrangements needed if other space activities are to be successfully commercialized. Specifically, the creation of Satellite Business Systems, combining the resources of three large companies (IBM, COMSAT, and Aetna), has raised the question of what resources, both institutional and financial, are required to reduce anticipated market risks to acceptable levels. That, in turn, may have some implications for antitrust considerations and the direction that targeted deregulation may have to take.

Remote Sensing

After satellite communications, remote sensing from space appears to be the most promising of the space activities for near-term commercialization, although current budget battles may render such commercialization moot. The technology used to sense the earth from space to estimate crops, map terrain, and make inventories of resources has been available on a demonstration, quasi-operational basis for approximately a decade. The utility of the imagery from the resource-sensing satellites of the Landsat series is widely acknowledged, although its ultimate benefits cannot be estimated accurately in dollar amounts. Over 100 nations have purchased Landsat data from the Earth Resources Observation Systems (EROS) data center operated by the Department of the Interior, and 13 have bought their own earth stations to be able to receive Landsat data directly from the satellite. Domestically, several Federal Government agencies rely routinely on Landsat data to conduct a portion of their business, and State and local governments have similarly increased their reliance on satellite imagery. Through contract arrangements with the federally operated program, first with NASA and now with the National Oceanic and Atmospheric Administration (NOAA), private activity to date has focused primarily on building satellites for the Federal Government and on providing value-added services to other, mostly private clients by enhancing Landsat imagery.

In the wake of increasing administration and congressional interest in assessing the feasibility of transferring operational responsibility for remote sensing to the private sector, specific mechanisms need to be explored both by the Federal Government and by private firms. Past efforts to devise plausible strategies for that transfer have encountered some difficulties. Remote sensing, especially in its quasi-operational phase, has never been a self-sustaining enterprise, and returns on the purchase of data have not come close to matching the costs of operation.

Unlike satellite communications technology, remote sensing has not emerged within the context of an established and growing market served by a well-developed and thriving industry. In fact, the technical and market risks associated with satellite communications pale by comparison to the problems confronted by remote sensing. The need to develop markets while simultaneously defining the parameters of an internationally competitive and commercially sustainable system is quite a challenge. The uncertainties are reinforced by other, international factors. Among them is competition from the French remote-sensing satellite, SPOT, now slated for implementation in 1984–1985. That system's development and operations will be supported by the French government, and its performance may make some of the capabilities of the U.S. system obsolete. The international rulemaking process might impose restrictions inimical to commercial expansion of the collection and dissemination of data, causing an additional problem. Even if the U.S. Government makes no attempt to recover development costs (and none is likely), it is difficult to conceive of a single industry being willing or able to shoulder all the investment risks required for operational transfer.

Within this context, efforts to maximize private sector involvement may require both compromises and imaginative institutional solutions. The primary issue may be not whether a private company can successfully operate the system but, rather, what entry conditions must be considered to reduce the overall risk of initial investment to acceptable proportions without, at the other extreme, presenting an outright handout. If the Federal Government decides that continued U.S. leadership in remote sensing is a worthwhile national goal, new institutional arrangements to achieve that goal will have to be sought. It is currently thought that continued, but decreasing, public support during the transition period will be the case. One possible solution would be for the Federal Government to launch Landsat-D if private industry agreed to take over its operational responsibility.

Space Conveyance

Technology has now made two types of conveyance to space possible: the expendable rocket and the reusable space shuttle. The intention of U.S. space policy has been that shuttle services would, once developed, be relied upon for the transfer of objects and human beings to orbit. However, the future is likely to allow purchases of transportation to space to choose from a variety of options, including the shuttle, the French rocket Ariane, U.S. rockets, and even launch by a domestic or foreign company, for example, OTRAG, a German-based, private rocket development company, or its American counterpart, Space Services, Inc.

Rocket Launch Service

Future U.S. deemphasis of traditional rocket launch systems as a consequence of encouraging shuttle use has not dampened interest, both domestic and international, in the commercial possibilities of rocket launch services. Based on the continued demand for space conveyance (especially for commercial communications payloads), the French government decided that a launch capability priced competitively with shuttle fees could become a successful commercial venture. That belief in the continued competitiveness of expendable rocket launches may have been well placed. Delays in NASA's shuttle program have generated concern among potential launch customers so that some customers, to ensure delivery of their satellites into orbit at required times, have made inquiries of the French. The attractiveness of the traditional launch method has also been enhanced by the escalating costs of the shuttle program and the expectation that future operational costs could sharply outstrip initial expectations.

U.S. private enterprise is also taking on the calculated risk that traditional launches will remain a profitable alternative for some purposes. Thus, Space Services, Inc., a private company based in Texas, tested its first rocket in mid-1981. Although the first test proved unsuccessful, it was, nonetheless, the opening shot of a venture intended to provide cheap, reliable launches as an alternative to government-sponsored systems. The endeavor of Space Services, Inc., is particularly noteworthy in that it is a rare example of a private company deciding to proceed in a space activity without initial government assistance.

How successful private efforts to develop a space launch capability will be is not clear. Even though the launch technology is well established and accessible, adequate standards of reliability and control may require more of an investment and higher fees for service than initially imagined. Nevertheless, a cautious prediction might be made that rocket launches under private commercial sponsorship will eventually become a fixed part of the menu of space services available to those who require them, provided no undue obstacles are presented by domestic or international law. One potential domestic obstacle is whether the Federal regulatory structure is applicable to private launches from U.S. territory.

Space Shuttle

The new U.S. Space Transportation System (STS), based on the shuttle, opens up the possibility of a new era in space. The shuttle is a reusable vehicle that can deliver and retrieve payloads as well as serve as a temporary in-orbit base for operations, experimentation, and repairs. More than an alternative launch vehicle, it is capable of transporting larger satellites into orbit than conventional rockets can, and it is highly maneuverable.

Although probably not realistic in the near future, private sector operation of the shuttle has always been an option under consideration. Proponents point out that once STS is established it ceases to be the object of research and development, except in the case of refinements to the technology. The appropriateness of NASA's continuing role as the system's operator may, therefore, be an issue if a strict interpretation of NASA's charter as one that confines the agency to an R&D role is taken.

As a practical matter, however, a reasonable strategy for the private takeover of STS operations or even a portion of them is difficult to devise. First, STS was developed for joint civilian and military use. Not only is the shuttle expected to carry civilian and military payloads, but it has been proposed that the two launch sites and at least a portion of mission control will be used in common.

Second, the enormous cost of the entire system makes duplication for commercial purposes unlikely in the foreseeable future. The cost of the system was a primary consideration for the dual use and, therefore, by extension, argues against the possibility or advisability of disaggregating the system into civil and military components.

Thus, devising plausible strategies for commercializing (i.e., promoting private ownership or operation of STS) becomes difficult. The multipurpose approach, strongly focused on serving national security requirements, frustrates possible notions of reserving portions of the system for private sector development. Assuming a willingness on the part of a single company or, more realistically, a consortium, to invest the $1 billion needed to purchase shuttle technology, questions would still remain aobut how a private orbiter could be integrated into the existing operational scheme. A time- or cost-sharing scheme might be one solution. Equally puzzling is the question of how a privately owned vehicle would fit as a user of an integrated Federal facility.

If the nature of STS precludes even limited private ownership, a long-term alternative strategy might include a gradually expanding private role achieved by leasing STS to a private operator through a GoCo (government-owned, contractor-operated) arrangement. The GoCo concept is well established as an acceptable arrangement by which private contractors operate key facilities for the Department of Defense. Assuming the establishment of a management and operations scheme adequately responsive to national security requirements and assuming, as well, an increased economic viability for STS, this kind of limited commercialization of the shuttle might be possible.

Space Industrialization

The cluster of activities described under the rubric of space industrialization is a far more distant, long-term component of the space development program. If those activities were to reach fruition, they could eventually enhance the commercial relevance of STS and provide a rich potential for private industry's involvement. As in the preceding cases, however, realizing that potential will no doubt hinge on maintaining a broad-based, federally funded space program that establishes a plausible investment and risk climate for the private sector.

Materials Processing in Space
Materials processing in space offers the possibility of using the low-gravity and high-vacuum environment of space to produce certain classes of alloys, pharmaceuticals, glasses, semiconductors, and superconductors. Initial space experiments with materials processing took place in rockets that simulated the environment of space. Future experiments are slated to use the shuttle to deliver payloads into orbit and retrieve them.

With the inception of NASA's Materials Processing in Space (MPS) program, there was a clear and immediate perception of the need for private involvement from the outset to ensure the most favorable circumstances possible for systematic commercialization. The programmatic approach of MPS could be construed as a deliberate mechanism to correct the long, drawn out experience of attempts to commercialize remote sensing. The two central elements of the MPS program were the establishment of a solid processing research base and early industrial involvement. In addition, the establishment of cooperative international research activities and the development of nongovernment facilities of national stature for independently funded space research reinforced the vitality of the program.

NASA's creative thinking yielded some early positive signs of industrial interest. For example, McDonnell Douglas Company and Johnson & Johnson entered into a joint agreement with the space agency for a materials processing experiment to be flown on the shuttle. Thus joint venture commits the two parties to provide specific materials and services (shuttle transportation and integration by NASA, the experiment by McDonnell Douglas and Johnson & Johnson), but no money will change hands. This agreement mechanism could be a great facilitator in the future of joint public and private projects.

Sustained commercial development of this kind will require the continuation of the NASA MPS program, continued availability of such creative institutional arrangements as the joint venture described above, and reliability of STS for delivery and retrieval of experiments and, eventually, marketable payloads on a reasonably predictable production schedule. Further expansion of MPS into a permanent, stable, fully developed industrial venture must, however, be viewed as belonging to a more distinct future when and if the unfolding of a comprehensive space industrialization capability becomes possible.

Solar Power Satellite

Many of the general observations made about materials processing also apply to the possible development and commercial operation of a solar power satellite (SPS) system. Such a system entails the development of some means to capture solar energy in space, transmit it to earth, and convert it into electricity. The most likely system now proposed would place solar panels in space to beam solar energy to earth through microwave transmission. SPS differs from MPS in several crucial respects that, taken together, indicate that the development of solar power from space may not be feasible in the near future. SPS would require a prior substantial development of the space infrastructure—a manufacturing capability and large, flexible, platform construction. In other words, the viability of SPS is dependent upon a broadly developed space capability. The impetus for the establishment of such a capability is directly related to R&D costs and how those costs relate to the availability of alternative energy sources. Development of the SPS system will also be affected by international rulemaking. Decisions about microwave transmission of solar energy to earth were set aside in an atmosphere of some controversy at the 1980 World Administrative Radio Conference. It is clear that despite steadily rising costs of terrestrial energy sources, the space-based solution is still a long way from becoming a cost-effective, environmentally acceptable reality.

Space Mining

Although clearly a long-term future development, space mining has already been the subject of vigorous public debate. Terrestrial resources no doubt will remain adequate for the foreseeable future. Yet the eventual exhaustion of particular terrestrial minerals may one day make mining the Moon and other planetary bodies more attractive, especially if building in space becomes a reality.

Like the previous issues, space mining will require certain prior conditions, for example, the continued development of a broad space capability, an increased need on Earth for space-derived materials, a feasible risk situation for private industry, and an acceptable international framework.

Questions concerning the international framework have assumed an early and urgent significance because of the Moon Treaty. Formally titled "Agreement Governing the Activities of States on the Moon and Other Celestial Bodies," the treaty was drafted in the U.N. Outer Space Committee and was submitted in 1981 to individual nations for ratification. Lack of clarity in key provisions governing the exploitation of lunar resources and the consequent controversy raised questions about whether the treaty could provide an environment appropriate for active private sector pursuit of space mining.

ISSUES AND CHOICES

The objective of maintaing U.S. world leadership for national security and economic purposes, the many objectives of the U.S. civil space program since its conception, and the broad requirements of maintaining a workable research and technology base for a sustained space capability form a complex and sometimes conflicting context within which to pursue commercialization.

Nonetheless, several factors point to the possibility of a more active future involvement by the private sector in space activities. First, left to itself, technical development and refinement can be extended indefinitely, and those involved can demonstrate a reluctance to "freeze" the state of the art for purposes of general transfer and use. From this perspective, it is argued, focusing on the "readiness" of technology developed under Federal auspices can be misleading and distract from the central issues, which are the receptivity of the market for the technology or technical system and the technology's commercial feasibility.

Second, a primary source of space-related R&D is to enhance the position of the United States in international trade and to sustain competitiveness and, wherever possible, leadership in technical areas. Early industrial involvement or even primary responsibility for the activity is essential to the achievement of that purpose and the successful accomplishment of commercial adaptation. Where private sector involvement is most appropriate, technologies can be developed with an explicit eye toward existing and potential markets, and system requirements can be defined to meet common denominator standards of reliability and service delivery instead of being geared to exciting but perhaps commercially inappropriate technical advances. Early and effective private sector responsibility could thus be perceived as playing a crucial role in selecting, from a range of possibilities, those activities that are clearly marketable profitably, thereby obviating the extended and costly pursuit of those technological alternatives where the ultimate economic payoff is questionable.

Finally, the nature of the U.S. political economy plays an important role in defining the most appropriate modes for adapting technological innovations and improvements stemming from Federal research and development activities to new commercial purposes. The traditional role of the private sector as an independent, self-motivating, creative producer of goods and services provides scant legitimacy to the Federal Government in the role of market developer, sales agent, and, at times, even R&D performer. In effect, the Federal Government is relatively less effective as a vendor than a private company in commercializing and exploiting an ongoing, profitable endeavor.

However, any realistic strategy for encouraging commercialization must recognize that Federal involvement in the initial phases of developing a space program is not antithetical to a private sector role but, rather, is often a prerequisite for such a role. The experience of the last 20 years has demonstrated the reluctance of industry to undertake the risk of assuming ownership and operation of innovative space systems or initial responsibility for the required basic research.

Thus, encouragement of greater industrial involvement in space and in other high-risk technology areas may be achieved by a coherent cluster of policies that enhances the attraction of unusually long-term investments in select areas where development is judged to be in the national interest. The risks may be further attenuated by the pursuit of innovative institutional arrangements—for example, joint ventures, public/private corporations, consortia for research, development, and even operation of space technology, and the like. That kind of policy framework could relieve the Federal Government of at least a portion of the financial burden it now assumes in underwriting the initial development of space activities.

However, it would be unrealistic to expect industry either to assume primary responsibility for civil space development or even to take, unaided, the first steps in assuming ownership of major space systems. From both perspectives, the Federal role will be of critical importance. The key elements of that role will continue to be, as they were in the past, responsibility for long-term R&D and the delineation of a policy framework that encourages private participation and responsibility in partnership with the Federal Government. Strategies used in the past clearly will require careful reassessment with an eye toward limiting the extent and duration of

Federal involvement in areas that could benefit from an earlier and more extensive private sector role. Ultimately, effective private involvement in a variety of space technologies could help rationalize the costs of R&D deemed appropriate for public support; help determine fruitful, exploitable directions for space research; ensure an expeditious development of relevant markets; ensure the development of services and systems designed to meet criteria of commercial operation; and, perhaps, contribute in a variety of ways to reducing the total amount of public support now needed for space activities.

20

Better Energy Security

AMORY B. LOVINS AND L. HUNTER LOVINS

The authors argue that most of the U.S. energy systems are highly centralized and complex and, as a consequence, highly vulnerable. They argue that a cheaper alternative, which is also best for jobs and the environment, is efficient energy use along with more diverse, dispersed, and renewable energy resources such as wind-powered generators and even local gas turbines.

Nearly a tenth of America's energy comes from imported oil. Much of that oil hangs by a thread. That's the good news. The bad news is that nearly all of the *other* 90-odd percent of the nation's energy is equally vulnerable—easily disrupted by accident, natural disaster, or terrorism. A few people could shut off three-fourths of the natural gas to the eastern United States in one evening without leaving Louisiana. Domestic oil systems are at least that fragile. Electric grids are even more so.

Most U.S. energy travels hundreds or thousands of miles. It depends on the split-second timing of computer-controlled networks which link incredibly complex multi-billion-dollar machines. National policy has intensively promoted such systems as a replacement for foreign oil, without realizing that they were at least as vulnerable. The energy industries spend a Treasury subsidy of more than $10 billion a year building an energy system so centralized and complex that a handful of people can turn off the country. Policies meant to increase our energy security are reducing it, undermining the mission of our Armed Forces.

This growing threat to American prosperity, liberties, and even lives is real. Centralized energy systems have lately been attacked in 26 states and 40 foreign countries. Such attacks are occurring weekly. They are becoming more frequent, intense, and sophisticated. Terrorists already know that modern energy systems are among the softest targets. It is time the public and politicians knew it too—and found out what they can do about it.

For there is an alternative. The energy options that are cheapest (and best for jobs and the environment) can also be inherently resilient. The best buys—efficient energy use and appropriate renewable sources—can meet the energy needs of a dynamic economy, save trillions of dollars, and make major failures of energy supply *impossible*.

The first step toward energy security is to wring far more work out of our energy. Modest improvements in the efficiency of cars and buildings could more than eliminate U.S.

Originally published in *The Christian Science Monitor*, June 28, 1982. Reprinted by permission of the first author.

oil imports in this decade—before a power plant or synfuel plant ordered now could deliver any energy whatever, and at a tenth of its cost.

But efficient energy use also makes failures more graceful and correctable. If the heating system fails in January in your superinsulated house in Minnesota, you won't know it for weeks, and then only because the indoor temperature will slowly drift down from 72 degrees to 62 degrees or at worst the upper 50s—but no lower, so neither you nor your pipes can freeze. The body heat from a few neighbors seeking refuge will bring the house back up to 72 degrees; extra children will overheat it.

Likewise, in a 50-mile-per-gallon car you could continue normal driving for weeks just on the gas in its own tank. A comparably efficient transportation system could run for a year on the oil stored here and there between wellhead and gas pump—whereas today, if a major pipeline to a refinery is cut, refining shuts down in a few *days*. Efficient energy use can thus stretch stored fuel long enough to fix what's broken or to improvise new supplies.

More diverse, dispersed, renewable energy sources can improve normal reliability and be virtually uninterruptible. A man who powers his Northern Plains house with wind recently reported that he was watching the evening news on television and saw that his whole area was blacked out. He went outside and looked. Sure enough, all his neighbors' lights were off. So he came back in and watched TV some more to see when his neighbor's lights would come back on.

Decentralized supplies saved Holyoke, Mass. from the 1965 Northeast blackout. A quick-thinking engineer cut off the city from the collapsing grid and ran it instead on a local gas turbine. The money saved by not having to black out Holyoke paid off the capital cost of the power plant in four *hours*. Likewise, when a 1980 thunderstorm blacked out West Chicago, a gas station which, hours earlier, had installed its own bank of solar cells was the only station pumping gas.

Millions of individuals and thousands of communities are already mobilizing their own resorces to save money, stop the hemorrhage of energy dollars out of the local economy, and insure against energy cutoffs. As a result, since 1979 the U.S. has gotten more than a hundred times as much new energy from savings as from expanded supplies, and more new supply from renewables than from any or all nonrenewables. As the President's corporate socialism erodes true energy security, local initiatives and market economics are starting to restore it—piece by piece, from the bottom up.

21
The Trouble with Fusion

LAWRENCE M. LIDSKY

Lawrence M. Lidsky discusses the shortcomings of fusion as currently pursued, as contrasted with fission. He argues that there may be an alternative, namely, neutron-free fusion, which might meet the goal of the fusion program: universally available, inexhaustible, environmentally benign power. He accordingly suggests that fusion research seek to develop this alternative.

The technically advanced nations of the world will spend over $1 billion this year in the quest for controlled thermonuclear fusion power. This program has been sustained for 30 years with steadily mounting commitments of money and the dedication of an international group of scientists and engineers. Our knowledge of the related physics has grown enormously in the effort. Now the solution of the scientific problem appears to be almost within our grasp, and many assume that with it will come that technological Holy Grail: virtually unlimited, environmentally safe energy. But that outcome is unlikely. Instead, the costly fusion reactor is in danger of joining the ranks of other technical "triumphs" such as the zeppelin, the supersonic transport, and the fission breeder reactor that turned out to be unwanted and unused.

The dominating goal of the fusion program is to produce a reactor fueled by deuterium and tritium, isotopes of hydrogen containing one and two extra neutrons. This choice of fuel greatly eases the problem of achieving an energy-producing fusion reaction, but the choice also has features that make it far more difficult to turn that energy source into a useful power plant. The most serious difficulty concerns the very high energy neutrons released in the deuterium-tritium (D-T) reaction. These uncharged nuclear particles damage the reactor structure and make it radioactive. A chain of undesirable effects ensures that any reactor employing D-T fusion will be a large, complex, expensive, and unreliable source of power. That is hardly preferable to present-day fission reactors, much less the improved fission reactors that are almost sure to come.

When these drawbacks become more widely realized, disillusionment with the existing fusion program will weaken the prospects for other fusion programs, no matter how wisely redirected, for decades to come. But such a result isn't necessary. The public has shown that it is enlightened enough to support long-range scientific research without a clearly defined near-term goal; witness the support for expensive research on high-energy physics. Furthermore, other nuclear reactions such as the fusion of protons with lithium or boron produce either fewer neutrons or none at all. A reactor based on these fuels would be far preferable to existing fission reactors.

Of course, we do not know how to build a reactor to ignite such "advanced" fuels. Indeed, we know that neutron-free reactions cannot be ignited in the magnetic bottles

Originally published in *Technology Review* (October 1983), pp. 33–44. Copyright, 1983. Reprinted with permission from *Technology Review*.

developed for D-T and, unfortunately, little of the physics painstakingly developed for D-T fusion will apply. There is no clear path for an alternative scheme, and not coincidentally almost no support. As a result, only a few researchers are at work in the field. But it is clear that if we can build a reactor employing neutron-free fuels, we can avoid the enormous, probably insurmountable, problems posed by deuterium and tritium.

How could highly motivated and intelligent people get themselves into such a difficult situation? A fundamental reason concerns the difference between scientists' and engineers' view of what it means to solve a problem. Although they are usually able to agree on the definition of a "good problem," scientists and engineers often have different perspectives as to what constitutes a "good answer."

Good problems challenge our abilities to the limit but ultimately are solvable—that is they are not so difficult that the time spent is wasted. In both science and engineering, the greatest satisfaction accrues to those solving a problem first, even though "better" (simpler or more complete) answers are often found later. In science, such answers can coexist peacefully and are usually mutually illuminating. However, engineering answers must meet economic and social demands from the start, and fundamentally different answers rarely coexist for long.

Fusion is a textbook example of a good problem for both scientists and engineers. Many regard it as the hardest scientific and technical problem ever tackled, yet it is nonetheless yielding to our efforts. We have made substantial scientific progress, and the advances in fusion-system engineering have been astounding. We have developed superconducting magnets that dwarf ordinary laboratory magnets. Today's particle beams are nearly a million times more powerful than those available at the beginning of the program. We routinely fill huge devices with ionized gases at temperatures of tens of millions of degrees and use lasers to measure their properties. The fusion program has stretched our abilities to the utmost, and we have responded.

The fusion program was, from its inception, dominated by scientists. In the best tradition of science, we chose the most promising target—D-T fusion—out of the dauntingly complex areas of thermonuclear physics, and we concentrated on it. We may well achieve that goal, which would be a scientific triumph. But the scientific goal turns out to be an engineering albatross. From the engineering point of view, we should have started from the answer and worked backward.

The second reason why intelligent and motivated people were led astray in fusion research is common to government programs that must compete annually for funds. There is a strong temptation to choose a near-term answer over a more rational long-term answer, even though this choice precludes reaching the ultimate goal. The alternative would be the much more difficult task of developing support for a long-range program through persuasion and education. There is a related disinclination to adjust established plans, even if perceptions change. Indeed, it is considered dangerous even to admit uncertainty in a highly visible public program. Once established, an explicit goal, such as generating commercially competitive electricity from D-T fusion, is not easy to change.

As a result, the Office of Fusion Energy of the U.S. Department of Energy has promised that it will, early in the next century, demonstrate the production of large amounts of power via D-T fusion. Producing net power from fusion is a valid scientific goal, but generating electricity commercially is an engineering problem. The requirement is to develop a power source significantly better than those that exist today, and D-T fusion cannot provide that solution. Even if the fusion program produces a reactor, no one will want it.

THE SCIENCE OF FISSION AND FUSION

Fusion and fission power both have their roots in nature's tendency to favor the nuclear moderate: the elements of intermediate weight are energetically preferred—that is, the elementary particles forming the nucleus are more tightly bound. As a result, energy can be released either when heavy nuclei are split (fission) or light nuclei are joined (fusion). Fission is far easier to achieve than fusion. Several atoms with heavy nuclei, such as uranium-235 and plutonium-239, are on the verge of splitting spontaneously; adding a single nuclear particle causes instantaneous fission. The nucleus splits into smaller fragments, releasing energy and several neutrons. These neutrons, because they are electrically neutral, can easily penetrate the electric barriers surrounding uranium and plutonium nuclei to cause additional fissions. This, of course, is the so-called "chain reaction."

The problems with fission almost all stem from the smaller fragments of the original nucleus. We have no control over which of the hundreds of different fission products are formed, and, unfortunately, many are noxious, radioactive, toxic, or corrosive. These fission products are primarily responsible for the problems of reactor safety, including waste disposal and even the possibility of a meltdown.

Although fusion is conceptually simpler than fission, it is technically much more demanding. The root of the problem is that there is apparently no equivalent of the fission reaction that is induced by uncharged neutrons. All the nuclei that must be brought together for fusion are positively charged and, therefore, repel each another. This repulsive force between nuclei increases rapidly with increased atomic charge and becomes prohibitive for even moderately large atoms. Thus, it appears that fusion fuels must be chosen from among the lightest elements—hydrogen, helium, lithium, beryllium, and boron. But despite the relatively small number of light elements, more than 100 fusion reactions are possible.

Common to all is the fact that the reacting particles must be raised to very high energies (that is, must be very hot) to overcome their mutual electrical repulsion and approach close enough to fuse. Even at these very high energies, the particles are much more likely to bounce off each other at random angles—to "scatter"—than to fuse. Energy is conducted out of the system in this process. Thus, energy must be used to ignite fusion and to replace the energy continuously lost by the hot fuel. Obviously, the energy produced by the reaction must exceed the required input if the reactor is to be of any use.

But merely producing a net positive power output is not enough; achieving a high enough power *density* is also crucial. Power density refers to the rate of energy production per unit of reactor volume. Fusion will almost certainly have a lower power density than fission and therefore will require a larger plant to produce the same output. Suppose a fusion plant had to be 10 times as big—and therefore, likely ten times as costly—as a present-day fission plant to produce the same amount of power. Given the already intolerable costs of building fission plants, that would hardly be economically feasible. These issues of producing net energy and achieving a high enough power density are the dominant themes of fusion.

HOW FUSION FUELS WORK

The choice of deuterium and tritium as fuels early in the fusion program evolved quite naturally. Deuterium is a nonradioactive isotope of hydrogen that, as mentioned, has one extra neutron in the nucleus. In nature approximately 1 out of every 6,500 hydrogen atoms is deuterium. Thus, it is abundant—after all, there is a lot of hydrogen in seawater—and separating it from ordinary hydrogen is straightforward because of the substantial disparity in the masses.

The first reaction seriously considered for fusion power plants was simply the self-fusion of deuterium—the D-D reaction. Deuterium reacts with itself to produce either helium-3, a stable but extremely rare isotope of helium, or tritium, the triply heavy isotope of hydrogen with two extra neutrons in the nucleus. These reaction products can themselves react with deuterium to produce even more energy than comes from the D-D reaction itself. Thus, a deuterium-fueled fusion reactor could, and almost certainly would, recycle and burn both

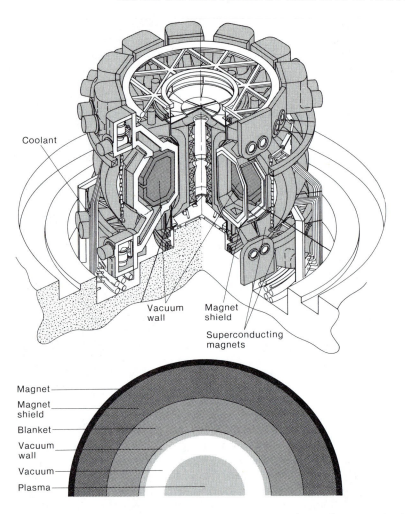

Figure 21.1. The schematic cross-section of proposed fusion reactors (bottom) has remained essentially unchanged from one proposed in a 1961 textbook. In the most likely scheme, called the "tokamak" (top), the tubular reactor is curved to form a torus (or doughnut). Temperatures in the plasma where fusion takes place would approach 150,000,000° C. The inner surface of the vacuum (or first) wall encircling the plasma will be subjected to intense heat and bombardment by damaging neutrons from the reaction. The "blanket" containing lithium, outside the first wall, absorbs these neutrons to "breed" tritium for fuel. The engineering will be complicated by the fact that lithium reacts explosively with air and water. On the reactor's exterior, the superconducting magnets that contain the plasma must be cooled almost to absolute zero. Hence the shielding to protect them from the extreme heat. Despite the potential for problems in such a reactor, hands-on repair will be impossible because of radioactivity. All in all, the proposed fusion reactor would be a large, complex, and unreliable way of turning water into steam.

the tritium and helium-3 in the so-called D-T and D-He^3 reactions.

Calculating the energy available from this complex series of reactions is the first problem assigned to students in my introductory course in controlled fusion at M.I.T. If they do their work properly, the students find out that the energy released by fusing the deuterium in

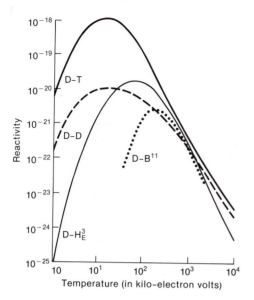

Figure 21.2. The fusion of deuterium (D) with tritium (T) is 100 to 1,000 times more reactive than the fusion of combinations involving helium-3 (He^3), protons (p), or boron-11 (B^{11}). In other words, a D-T-based power plant would yield 100 to 1,000 times more energy than an identical plant using the other fuels. That is why almost all research has focused on D-T fusion. However, the energetic neutrons it releases would damage and induce radioactivity in the reactor structure.

one cubic meter of seawater equals that released by burning 2,000 barrels of crude oil. Every single cubic kilometer of ocean water therefore contains as much energy as the world's entire known oil reserves, and there are more than a billion cubic kilometers of water in the oceans. This astounding finding—in effect, an inexhaustible source of energy—shows why tens of billions of dollars have been spent and hundreds of scientists have devoted their entire careers seeking to tap this extraordinary energy source.

Unfortunately, making D-D reactions occur is extraordinarily hard, but there is an alternative. The tritium by-product that would be recycled in the D-D reactor is a far better fuel when mixed with deuterium than is deuterium itself. Not only is more energy released, but the combination of deuterium and tritium is 100 times more reactive than a simple mixture of

deuterium. In other words, in similarly engineered reactors, a system fueled with deuterium and tritium will produce at least 100 times as much energy as one fueled by deuterium alone. Thus, as soon as scientists realized how difficult fusion was to achieve, they almost unanimously agreed that developing the D-T reactor should be the first goal of the fusion program. This scientific goal was well justified, and no one seriously questioned it as an engineering goal at the time.

One of the first issues posed by the D-T fusion reaction was how to supply sufficient tritium. Tritium is radioactive, with a relatively short half-life of 12.4 years, and therefore it exists only in minute quantities in nature. Luckily, the neutron emitted in D-T fusion can react with an isotope of lithium to produce tritium and even release additional energy in the process. Though nothing compares with the vast store of deuterium in seawater, the world's lithium resources are enough for several thousand years of energy production. The lithium-neutron reaction resolves the tritium-supply problem. However, it introduces additional engineering difficulties.

FUSION REACTORS: LARGE AND COMPLEX

The severity of the technical problems associated with the D-T reaction was not fully understood in the early years of the fusion program. But these difficulties have gradually been revealed by the extraordinarily detailed series of conceptual reactor designs produced under Department of Energy (DOE) funding over the last decade. The object of these studies is to describe a plausible fusion reactor based on the underlying physics and reasonable extrapolations of the technology. Of course, no one can be certain exactly what a D-T fusion reactor will look like. Nevertheless, several difficult questions that might seem to depend on this knowledge can already be answered. In particular: will a fusion reactor be simpler or more complex, cheaper or more expensive, safer or more dangerous, than a fission reactor? The answers depend only on the broad outlines of future reactors.

The main fusion reaction will take place in a

gas-like plasma in which deuterium and tritium atoms are so energetic—so hot—that the
nuclei have lost their electrons. The temperature of this gas will probably exceed
150,000,000° C. This plasma cannot be contained by physical walls, not only because no
material could withstand the heat, but also
because walls would contaminate the plasma.
Instead, the plasma will be bottled within a
vacuum by magnetic forces.

Four-fifths of the energy from the D-T
reaction is released in the form of fast-moving
neutrons. These neutrons are 15 to 30 times
more energetic than those released in fission
reactions. The first wall surrounding the
plasma and vacuum region will take the brunt
of both the neutron bombardment and the
electromagnetic radiation from the hot
plasma. This first wall is expected to be made
of stainless steel or, better, one of the
refractory metals such as molybdenum or
vanadium that retain their strength at very
high temperatures.

In colliding with this wall, the neutrons will
give up some of their energy as heat. This heat
must be removed by rapidly circulating coolant to prevent the wall from melting. After
being piped out of the reactor, the heated
coolant is used to produce steam and generate
electricity.

Many of the collisions between neutrons and
atoms in the first wall actually knock the atoms
forming the metal out of their original positions. Each atom in the first wall will, on
average, be dislodged from its lattice position
about 30 times per year. Obviously, this causes
the structure of the metal to deteriorate.

A few of the neutrons colliding with atoms
in the first wall will have the beneficial effect
of dislodging some neutrons from the atomic
nuclei. These dislodged neutrons, plus the
original ones generated by the fusion, pass
through the wall and into the so-called "blanket," which contains lithium in some form.
Here, the bulk of their energy is used to
produce heat, which also is used to create
steam for generating electricity, and eventually the neutrons are absorbed by the lithium
to "breed" tritium.

Lithium itself poses serious engineering

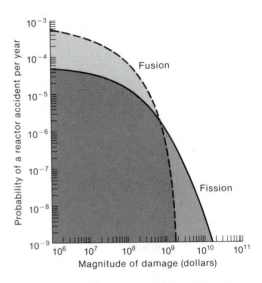

Figure 21.3. The worst possible accident for a
fusion reactor would destroy only the power plant
itself—a minor hazard compared with the possibility of a meltdown in a fission reactor. However, a
fusion reactor would be far more complex and
prone to minor accidents. Since the fusion reactor
would be too radioactive for hands-on repair, any
accident could pose grave financial consequences
for utilities. (The general shapes in the diagram are
correct; however, the actual numerical values are
uncertain and should not be taken literally.)

problems. It is an extremely reactive chemical: it burns violently when it comes in contact
with either air or water and is even capable of
undergoing combustion with the water contained in concrete. The lithium may be either
in liquid form or in solid compound. Liquid
lithium blankets produce substantially more
tritium and allow it to be more easily removed. However, the need to handle large
amounts of this metal in liquid form leads to
technical complexity and poses safety hazards.

The tritium-breeding region has other engineering requirements. It must be designed in
such a way that the structural materials, as
contrasted with the actual lithium, capture a
minimum of neutrons. Also, the operating
temperature must be high enough so that the
coolant, when piped outside the reactor, can
generate steam efficiently.

Outside the blanket, powerful magnets must provide the magnetic fields to contain the plasma. These fields will exert enormous forces on the magnets themselves, equivalent to pressures of hundreds of atmospheres. If made from copper wire, these magnets would consume more power than produced by the reactor, so they will have to be superconducting. Superconducting magnets, cooled by liquid helium to within a few degrees of absolute zero, will be extremely sensitive to heat and radiation damage. Thus, they must be effectively shielded from the heat and radiation of the plasma and blanket.

Temperatures within the fusion reactor will range from the highest produced on earth (within the plasma) to practically the lowest possible (within the magnets). The entire structure will be bombarded with neutrons that induce radiation and cause serious damage to materials. Problems associated with the inflammable lithium must be managed. Advanced materials will have to endure tremendous stress from temperature extremes and damaging neutrons. The magnetic fields will exert forces equivalent to those seen only in very high pressure chemical reactors and specialized laboratory equipment. All in all, the engineering will be extremely complex.

A working fusion reactor would also have to be very large. This conclusion is based on fundamental principles of plasma physics and fusion technology. To begin with, because of the properties of magnetic fields, a fusion reactor must be tubular. There is still dispute as to whether this tube should be bent into a toroidal (doughnut) shape, as in the device known as the "tokamak," or kept as a long, straight tube with end plugs, as in the device known as the "tandem mirror." However, the main conclusions as to the size and complexity of a D-T reactor are independent of this choice.

The first wall of the reactor encloses the plasma. The best theories available suggest that the radius of the plasma must be at least two to three meters if the fusion reaction is to be self-sustaining. Even if a breakthrough in physics were to allow a smaller plasma, separate engineering requirements would prevent the radius of the first wall from being appreciably less than three meters. These requirements arise from the need to avoid excessive differences in power density.

For the neutrons to be slowed enough in the lithium to effectively breed tritium, the blanket surrounding the first wall must be between half a meter and one meter thick. The radiation shield outside the blanket must also be between half a meter and one meter thick to protect the supercooled magnets. Finally, the superconducting magnets and their structure will add another meter each to the radius. That gives a total radius of at least five meters for the plasma and the tube surrounding it.

In a tokamak reactor, this tube—over 30 feet across—would be bent into a doughnut-like shape at least 75 feet in outer diameter. As a power plant, this is somewhat larger than today's fission reactors and substantially more complex. If the energy density of the fusion plant turned out to be lower than that of a contemporary fission plant, as seems likely, then all this size and complexity would produce less power—hardly an economic proposition. But even if the power density were comparable, the D-T fusion reactor would, like today's fission plants, be a large and costly power source, producing thousands of megawatts of electricity. Detailed studies, some costing millions of dollars, aimed at deducing the smallest plausible size for a D-T fusion reactor all come to this same discouraging conclusion.

Such a large reactor would not meet the needs of utilities. Plagued by financially crippling cost overruns on fission reactors, managers are loathe to invest several billion dollars in any single plant, fission or fusion. Smaller plants, such as coal plants with scrubbers, are much easier to finance, not only because the investment is far lower, but also because the final cost is predictable. And if a small plant breaks down, the effects on regional electricity production are much less serious. Thus, utility managers find large plants undesirable.

Suppose fusion reactors could be built despite the inherent difficulties of size and complexity. Another critical engineering problem would still have to be faced. That is the matter of heat transfer—the way in which heat is removed from the reactor structure by the circulating coolant. The history of much large-scale power engineering has been dominated by the effort to achieve ever higher temperatures and heat-transfer rates. High temperatures imply high efficiency, and high heat-transfer rates imply high power density. Because these goals are so desirable, heat-transfer systems have been pushed close to their limits. Above these limits, materials either melt or fail from excessive stress caused by heat. Additional gains are coming only slowly.

Consider heat transfer in fission and fusion reactors. In today's typical light-water reactor (LWR), heat is generated by fission in fuel pins containing uranium. The heat is then transferred to the coolant at the surfaces of a relatively large number of small-diameter pins. This arrangement provides a larger surface area to transfer heat than, say, a single large fuel cylinder. Indeed, by decreasing the diameter of the pins even further (but increasing their number to keep the amount of uranium unchanged), the total surface area available to transfer heat would be further increased. Thus, the actual heat-transfer rate through any given square inch of surface on a fuel rod is not critical. Sufficient heat can always be removed merely by increasing the total area.

This strategy does not work in a fusion reactor. The heat-transfer surface is limited to the inside of the wall surrounding the plasma, and the relatively small surface area of this wall cannot be increased without further increasing the size of the reactor. In fact, bigger reactors need *larger* heat-transfer rates. Thus, the actual heat-transfer rate per square inch must be extremely large and cannot simply be reduced by a design change.

Suppose a fission reactor and a fusion reactor were built with equivalent heat-transfer rates. Knowing this, one can calculate two other critical engineering factors: the flux of neutrons at the heat-transfer surface, and the overall power density of the reactor. The neutron flux should, of course, be as low as possible, because it damages the reactor structure and makes it radioactive. And the power density should, and mentioned, be as high as possible, so that a reasonable amount of power will be produced in a reactor of a given size.

On these counts, a comparison between current LWR fission reactors and the somewhat optimistic fusion designs produced by the DOE studies yields a devastating critique of fusion. For equal heat-transfer rates, the critical inner wall of the fusion reactor is subject to 10 times greater neutron flux than the fuel in a fission reactor. Worse, the neutrons striking the first wall of the fusion reactor are far more energetic—and thus more damaging—than those encountered by components of fission reactors. Even in fission reactors, the lifetimes of both the replaceable fuel rods and the reactor structure itself are limited because of neutron damage. And the fuel rods in a fission reactor are far easier to replace than the first wall of the fusion reactor, a major structural component.

But even though radiation damage rates and heat-transfer requirements are much more severe in a fusion reactor, the power density is only *one-tenth* as large. This is a strong indication that fusion would be substantially more expensive than fission because, to put it simply, greater effort would be required to produce less power.

FUSION'S BENEFITS

Given all of fusion's liabilities, why are we working so hard on it? The universal availability of fuel has provided a strong motive to develop fusion, and it does promise some other substantial advantages over fission. To begin with, fusion generates much less radioactivity than fission, and there is no long-term storage problem for radioactive wastes. A fusion reactor would create a lot of tritium, which is radioactive and hard to contain. However, tritium's biological effects are relatively benign—it does not tend either to concentrate or to linger in living organisms— and it emits relatively weak radiation. After a short period of operation, the radioactivity

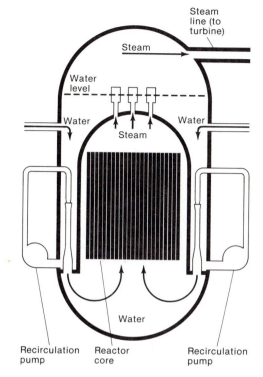

Figure 21.4. In a fission reactor, heat from the reaction is released through the surfaces of thousands of fuel rods. Additional surface area to transfer heat can be created by providing more fuel rods but making them thinner. However, in fusion plants, the 150,000,000° C plasma is encircled by a "first wall," the surface of which cannot be increased in any practical way. (If the encircling wall is made bigger, then the larger plasma creates even more heat.) Thus, as much energy as possible must be transferred through each square inch of the first wall. Unfortunately, improvements in heat-transfer rates are coming only slowly.

from neutrons bombarding the structure of a fusion reactor itself would greatly exceed the feeble radioactivity of the tritium.

But even the radioactivity of the structure will be composed primarily of nonvolatile isotopes. By contrast, a substantial amount of the radioactivity in fission reactors is in the form of volatile gases that can escape if the containment structure is breeched. To further minimize the radioactivity associated with

fusion, reactor designers can choose structural materials that do not become strongly radioactive when bombarded by neutrons. A fusion reactor of stainless steel would have 300 times less radioactivity than a fission reactor of the same power output. A fusion reactor based on a vanadium structure would be 10 times better yet. In other words, it seems possible to build a fusion reactor with 3,000 times less radioactivity than a fission reactor producing the same amount of power.

The radiological difference between fission and fusion is even more striking in the production of long-lived wastes. There is nothing in the fusion reactor comparable to the fission fragments or the plutonium in fission reactors. Plutonium is extremely hazardous and its radioactivity is very long-lived, with a half-life of 24,100 years. After a 100-year storage period, the radioactive waste produced by a stainless-steel fusion reactor would be 1 million times less hazardous than that produced by an equivalent fission reactor. And there would be no need to store the waste of a fusion reactor with a vanadium structure even that long. A well-designed fusion reactor could completely eliminate the problem of storing long-term waste.

The fact that a fusion reactor does not require long-term waste storage seems a clear advantage. But it is less significant than would first appear, for we have tended to exaggerate the waste-storage problems of fission reactors, primarily because of ill-considered decisions early in their development. Early schemes for disposal of fission wastes had to be inexpensive to allow the reactors to compete with conventional power plants fueled by inexpensive oil. Early schemes for disposing of the wastes—dumping them on the ocean bottom or injecting them into underground strata—were certainly cheap. However, these schemes were so clearly inadequate that the fission community did its reputation lasting damage by advocating them.

Although the public is still concerned about the disposal of radioactive waste, the economic situation is now completely changed. Fission products can be safely stored, as is routinely done in Europe now. To be sure, such processes are not inexpensive. For example, one technique consists of sealing intact fuel elements in welded metallic canisters and storing them in mined granite cavities. If better techniques for storage should become available, the wastes can be retrieved. The costs of such relatively expensive disposal still play only a small role—less than 10 percent—in the total price of power. Public perception changes slowly, but the time scale under consideration is long. Waste disposal will eventually be considered a difficult but not insurmountable problem.

The matter of safety is difficult to weigh so concretely. Current analyses show that the probability of a minor mishap is relatively high in both fission and fusion plants, because both contain many complex systems. But the probability of small accidents is expected to be higher in fusion reactors. There are two reasons for this. First, fusion reactors will be much more complex devices than fission reactors. In addition to heat-transfer and control systems, they will utilize magnetic fields, high power heating systems, complex vacuum systems, and other mechanisms that have no counterpart in fission reactors. Furthermore, they will be subject to higher stresses than fission machines because of the greater neutron damage and higher temperature gradients. Minor failures seem certain to occur more frequently.

Comparing the probability of more serious accidents is harder, partly because that issue is the subject of such heated debate concerning fission reactors. But the probability of major accidents affecting public safety will certainly be substantially lower for fusion reactors. Indeed, the hypothetical worst-case accident of a fission reactor—catastrophic meltdown with release of fission products—has no equivalent in fusion. The fusion reactor simply does not contain enough radioactive material.

Thus, fusion reactors will have a higher probability of small accients but a much lower probability of major accidents. This at first appears to be a strong argument for fusion, but consider Three-Mile Island. This accident, thought by some to have sounded a death knell for the fission industry, may have had equally damaging consequences for fusion. Although no one was physically injured in the TMI accident, the utility owning the reactor was mortally wounded financially. The multi-billion-dollar plant was put out of commission because it was too radioactive to repair. From a manager's standpoint, all systems that are too radioactive for hands-on maintenance are equivalent: if something major breaks, it is unrepairable. Although there is much less radioactivity in a D-T fusion reactor than in a fission reactor, it is still so high that contact maintenance would be impossible. And a D-T fusion reactor would be far more likely than a fission reactor to require repairs.

The analysis of safety factors comes down to this: While the public is primarily concerned about major catastrophes, power-plant operators are also fearful of less threatening accidents that could cause serious financial problems. In respect to these, fusion is at a disadvantage. If this factor is added to the reactor's high initial cost, large size, and poor power density, D-T fusion becomes an unacceptable financial risk. The public perception of fusion as ultimately safer than fission cannot nullify this.

Furthermore, in a broader sense the safety of a D-T fusion reactor would depend on its being used responsibly. One of the best ways to produce material for atomic weapons would be to put common, natural uranium or thorium in the blanket of a D-T reactor, where the fusion neutrons would soon transform it to weapons-grade material. And tritium, an unavoidable product of the reactor, is used in some hydrogen bombs. In the early years, research on D-T fusion was classified precisely because it would provide a ready source of material for weapons. Such a reactor would only abet the proliferation of nuclear weapons and could hardly be considered a wise power source to export to unstable governments.

A major driving force behind fusion has been the promise of abundant fuel. Indeed, the fusion program was originally justified not on safety grounds—fission's safety was not widely doubted then—but because of the expected rapid depletion of uranium reserves. But this is no longer a major concern. One reason is the declining demand for additional fission power and hence for the uranium to fuel it. The earth's reserves of uranium are now known to be large enough to supply fission reactors for at least 50 to 70 years without fuel reprocessing.

There has also been a breakthrough in the technology for removing uranium from seawater. A Japanese consortium is starting up a pilot plant that uses an efficient filter to trap and concentrate the extremely dilute uranium in seawater. This technology will make available virtually unlimited supplies of uranium at a cost at most 10 times the current (depressed) price for conventionally mined uranium. The cost of nuclear fuel is so small a fraction of the total cost of generating electricity that the new technology would increase electricity prices only negligibly. The same oceans that could supply fusion fuels can also supply fission fuel; the abundance of deuterium for fusion ceases to be a compelling argument.

DIM PROSPECTS FOR D-T FUSION

In retrospect, it is not totally surprising that fusion should fare so poorly in comparison with fission. The problem is simply that in fusion, 80 percent of the energy is released in neutrons with an energy of 14 million electron volts (MeV) that travel about 50 centimeters. In fission, less than 3 percent of the energy is released in neutrons, and these have an energy of only 1 to 2 MeV. Most of the fission products are highly charged nuclei that travel less than .001 centimeter before coming to rest.

Thus, while the major radioactivity from fission is contained within the fuel pins, the major radioactivity from fusion would damage the reactor structure and create problems of complexity, unreliability, and size. While fission's numerous wastes pose problems of disposal and reactor safety, fusion's neutrons could easily be used to manufacture material for atomic weapons. It is hard to see why a utility in need of additional generating capacity would purchase a D-T fusion reactor instead of a contemporary LWR fission reactor. And as far as most utilities are concerned, even the LWR no longer seems a good choice.

The early history of the fission program was similar to current experience in the fusion program—except that success in fission came too easily. As soon as we found a concept that worked reasonably well, powerful forces drove that machine, the LWR, to prominence. We did not take the time to test, modify, and finally choose the "best" nuclear reactor among many competitors.

Now we know that safer, smaller, and probably cheaper fission reactors can be built. In fact, reactors could be small enough to be assembled in a factory and shipped via truck, reactors so safe that no operator error or even loss-of-coolant accident could cause release of radiation. The dreaded meltdown would also be impossible in these small, "modular" reactors. Such a reactor has been operating for 15 years in Germany. To be sure, this kind of reactor would probably not be the best choice in a world in which uranium was scarce and reprocessing and fuel breeding were necessary. But we do not live in such a world. Unfortunately, the resounding crash of the LWR has prejudiced the possibility of a new beginning for fission reactors.

The only real hope for fusion is to take the long view ignored in the fission program. Neutron-free fusion is a quintessential example of a high-risk, high-gain area of physics that *might* also provide a good answer to an engineering problem. We have no guarantee that an answer exists. But we know that if it does, it can meet the original goal of the fusion program—universally available, inexhaustible, environmentally benign power. Perhaps we should not be greatly troubled that our first attempt to develop such a marvelous thing will not be the success we had hoped. We can go on to seek a better alternative.[1]

NOTE

1. [Editor's note: The following information appeared as a caption in the original article The Trouble with Fusion.]

Neutron-free fusion: Almost all of the lighter elements are capable of entering into fusion reactions in which the nuclei of atoms are combined and energy is released. The prime candidates for power-producing reactions are based on two isotopes of hydrogen: protons (p), which are the standard hydrogen nuclei; and "heavy hydrogen," or deuterium (D), which has a neutron attached to the proton. The nuclei of the hydrogen isotopes have the lowest possible electric charge—one positive charge. Thus, they require lower energies to be brought together for fusion reactions than other nuclei with larger positive charges.

The original proposal for fusion was to produce power through the self-fusion of deuterium—the D-D reaction. This reaction produces, with equal probability, either the light helium isotope with two protons and a neutron (He^3) or the heaviest hydrogen isotope, tritium (T), with one proton and two neutrons. Both reactions release energy, generally measured in millions of electron volts (MeV).

$$D + D \rightarrow He^3 + n + 3.2 \text{ MeV}$$
$$D + D \rightarrow T + p + 4.0 \text{ MeV}$$

These reaction products can themselves react with deuterium and will either be "burned" in place or recycled.

$$D + T \rightarrow He^4 + n + 17.6 \text{ MeV}$$
$$D + He^3 \rightarrow He^4 + p + 18.3 \text{ MeV}$$

Because the fuel for the last two reactions is generated in the first two, only deuterium need be supplied externally. The final reaction products—ordinary helium and hydrogen—are benign, but the energetic neutrons can damage and induce radioactivity in the structure of the reactor.

Fusion based on *any* fuel cycle containing deuterium produces undesirable neutrons. The reason is this: Most of the deuterium can be made to "burn" in a desired reaction—for example, the benign D-He^3 fusion above, to produce ordinary helium, a proton, and energy. But some of the deuterium in the mixture will also collide with itself, producing neutrons and radioactive tritium; further collisions with the tritium will produce more neutrons.

Fuel cycles based on protons tend to produce far lower amounts of neutrons. The lithium-6 reaction

$$p + Li^5 \rightarrow He^3 + He^4 + 4.02 \text{ MeV}$$

is often considered because of the low charge of both constituents. But it is not completely neutron-free. A product (He^3) can react with Li^6 to produce neutrons via a low-probability, but nonetheless troublesome, side reaction.

From an engineering point of view, the boron-11 reaction

$$p + B^{11} \rightarrow 3He^4 + 8.68 \text{ MeV}$$

is nearly ideal. Neither the fuel *nor* the end products are radioactive. Furthermore, no neutrons capable of inducing radioactivity are produced.

Because all the products of the boron-11 reaction are charged, they could theoretically be harnessed to generate electricity directly, without the inherent waste of generating steam to run a turbine. However, the high electric charge of boron (it has 5 protons) makes the task of designing an energy-producing system very difficult.—*L.L.*

22

Nuclear Arms as a Philosophical and Moral Issue

ROBERT P. CHURCHILL

The author argues that attempts to apply the doctrine of just war to the question of whether nuclear deterrence is morally justified leads to a moral dilemma: although nuclear deterrence seems justified as self-defense, there are compelling reasons for concluding that threats of retaliation are immoral. He discusses alternative deterrence policies, such as defensive weapons systems, argues against them, and proposes nonviolent national defense as a possible solution.

Philosophical reflection about the problems of nuclear armament and deterrence give rise to three kinds of questions: (1) logical and conceptual questions about nuclear strategy; (2) questions about the effects of nuclear technology on the meaning of humanity and our visions of life and death; and (3) moral or ethical questions about justifications for the use or threatened use of nuclear weapons.

An important role for philosophical analysis lies in scrutiny and criticism of the main concepts involved in deterrence and the assumptions underlying the arms race. What is the logic of the classical *para bellum* doctrine, which offers the paradox that the best way to ensure peace is to prepare for war? What is the meaning of "defense" and "security" in the nuclear age? What does "strategy" really mean when any use of nuclear power renders one liable to a massive counterattack? There is presently much disagreement among strategists preparing war scenarios over the proper criteria for rational decision making under uncertainty. Some defense analysts employ models of rationality imported from economics and game theory to describe the risks and options facing world leaders. A crucial task for the logician is to examine the wisdom of extending game theoretical criteria of rationality, such as the concept of utility maximization, to the situations of deterrence strategy.[1]

A second and different category of questions concerns the meaning of human life under the cloud of nuclearism. Secretary of War Henry Stimson declared, at the dawn of the nuclear era on 31 May 1945, that the making of the atomic bomb "should not be considered simply in terms of military weapons, but as a new relationship of man to the universe."[2] What is this relationship? And what is man's responsibility to the biosphere that sustains him and without which future generations will be impossible?[3] What is the phenomenon of psychic numbing that makes so many of us unable to contemplate sudden annihilation, and this strange double life that comes with the realization that all we have ever known or loved could be extinguished in a moment?[4] How has it come about that homicide has been bureaucratized and terror

Originally published in *Annals of the American Academy of Political and Social Science* 469 (September 1983), pp. 46–57. Copyright, 1983 by the American Academy of Political and Social Science. Reprinted by permission of Sage Publications, Inc.

so easily domesticated in our lives?[5] These are among the philosophical questions to be asked about a world suddenly threatened with nuclear holocaust.

However, the issues that continue to receive most philosophical attention concern the morality or immorality of deterrence policies and the question whether the just-war doctrine can justify a national defense based on threats of massive retaliation. John Bennett forcefully stated the problem when he called on us to explain how we can live with our consciences knowing that our leaders are prepared to kill millions of children in another nation if worse comes to worse.[6]

MORAL QUESTIONS

If we maintain deterrence, must we live with a troubled conscience? This article will attempt an answer, and will discuss the moral case for and against nuclear deterrence—in particular, the morality of the deterrence proposals that presently guide our defense strategies, and the justifiability of these policies given reasonable beliefs that because of the uncertainties and dangers of the world, it is necessary to prepare a defense against aggression. Thus for the purposes of this discussion I presume that (1) some form of deterrence is necessary as a national defense, and (2) however we solve our defense problems, we must do so unilaterally, without expecting cooperation from the USSR, or any other adversary, on a nuclear freeze or multilateral disarmament. Of course these assumptions may be false; in fact I hope they will soon prove to be so. But it is certainly not now known that they are false, and starting with a worst-case analysis allows me to frame the issue as sharply as possible. Given quite reasonable beliefs in the need for self-defense against an adversary with nuclear arms, what is the moral justification for threatening to use our nuclear weapons to deter him from aggression?[7]

In evaluating answers to this question, I presuppose familiarity with the basics of deterrence theory. In addition the inquiry will be limited to cases in which the problem of aggression is most extreme, and therefore

justifications most plausible. Thus while American strategists have often contemplated possible uses for nuclear arms in a "diplomacy of violence,"[8] I am concerned only with nuclear weapons as deterrents to direct attack upon the United States or its allies. For this purpose, strategic nuclear weapons exist as a second-strike capability that ensures U.S. ability to inflict unacceptable suffering upon the USSR even after sustaining an all-out nuclear attack. It is the threat of this retaliatory second strike, combined with the adversary's perceptions of the credibility of threats to use it, that produces the deterrent effect. As the political scientist Michael Walzer has said, "deterrence works by calling up dramatic images of human pain."[9] The object of the offense is not the adversary's armed forces so much as his mind.

DOCTRINE OF JUST WAR

What moral justification, if any, can there be for a policy of deterrence that rests the risk of mutual annihilation upon each superpower's perception of the other's intentions? Some theologians and ethicists do believe that such second-strike deterrence policies are not only morally permissible but morally obligatory. Their arguments are drawn from a venerable tradition of reflection and moral suasion. The doctrine of just war concerns warranted uses of force or violence as a necessary means to secure a just cause: if it is necessary for a nation's leaders to threaten annihilation in order to protect innocent civilians from unjust attack, then it is morally obligatory that this threat be made.

Many contributions have been made to the doctrine of just war, but its classic formulation is generally attributed to St. Augustine.[10] St. Augustine reasoned that war is always an evil in the sense of being a human calamity, and violence in its nature is always evil. However, war viewed as a necessary measure, undertaken as the only means of defending the innocent from unjust attack, is not sinful. Under severe necessity, the lesser evil of violent resistance to injustice is the morally preferable act, tragic but not wicked.

How much does the doctrine of just war justify? It starts with the assumption that the rightness of the resistance depends upon the cause for which the war is fought. It also presupposes that the violence threatened or employed is required as the only recourse. The doctrine will therefore justify only wars waged in self-defense or for the protection of the innocent. Moreover, the cause must be backward-looking, war waged only because of something intolerably unjust done by the adversary. This means that the doctrine will not justify war waged on the basis of forward-looking consequential or utilitarian grounds, even if this were a preventive or preemptive strike on a belligerent planning an attack. Thus the doctrine justifies nuclear deterrence only insofar as threats to retaliate are necessary to prevent unjust assault.[11]

Is the threat to retaliate really necessary? The familiar but dreadful truth is that we cannot be guaranteed that a nation capable of making a nuclear threat will not use it to its—perceived—advantage. In fact the effects of an adversary's use of a nuclear advantage would be so devastating that it is an intolerable risk, however small the probability of actual use. Consequently any nation confronted by a nuclear adversary, whatever the ideologies or adversary relationship involved, and capable of developing its own nuclear armaments, will find the reasons for seeking—relative—safety in a balance of terror compelling. Against an enemy willing to use the bomb, or perceived to be willing, self-defense is impossible by any means short of threatened retaliation. It therefore makes sense to say that the only compensating step is the awful threat to respond in kind.[12]

Thus despite the monstrosity of the threat, deterrence averts a graver danger and thereby meets the test of necessity for just war. Much evidence also shows that despite the danger of instability, deterrence works. The Soviets believe in deterrence, and as David Holloway's research shows,[13] there is no evidence to suggest the Soviets believe either that they can win a nuclear war, or that victory in a global war would be anything other than catastrophic.

JUS AD BELLUM AND JUS IN BELLO

Despite the air of morality given to nuclear deterrence by the doctrine of just war, there are strong reasons for believing that retaliatory threats may not be justified after all. Even if war or preparations for war are justified as measures of restraint, the instruments of enforcement are so faulty that further constraints upon the waging of war must be imposed. The most important of these are restraints on the means of pursuing the just cause. In effect the doctrine insists upon the distinction between *jus ad bellum*, the morality of going to war, and *jus in bello*, moral choice in the selection of the tactics and instruments of warfare. Among the principles of *jus in bello*, three are directly relevant to nuclear deterrence: (1) the immunity of noncombatants from direct attack; (2) the use of the least amount of force necessary to restrain or neutralize the aggressor effectively; and (3) the rule of proportionality, which asserts that there must be due proportionality between the end to be accomplished by a military action and the unavoidable harm inflicted in its pursuit.

It is in connection with the principles of *jus in bello* that charges of the immorality of nuclear deterrence arise. Threatening civilian populations completely disregards the distinction between combatants and noncombatants. Deterrence requires that millions be threatened as a means to influence the decisions of a few leaders. Thus deterrence requires that we treat human life as a mere object of policy and a means rather than an end. The theologian Paul Ramsey draws the analogy of deterring reckless automobile drivers by tying babies to the front bumpers of their cars. He points out that this would be no way to regulate traffic even if it succeeds in regulating it perfectly, for "such a system makes innocent human lives the *direct object* of attack and uses them as a mere means for restraining the drivers of automobiles."[14]

In response to Ramsey's argument by analogy, Michael Walzer maintains that the moral wrong of actions that harm the innocent is not a reason also to condemn actions that only threaten to risk harming.[15] Ramsey's innocent babies are not only exposed to terrible risks but also forced to endure a terrifying experience that is an actual harm. But nuclear deterrence, according to Walzer, imposes threats that do not restrain us or deprive us of our rights:

We are hostages who lead normal lives. It is in the nature of the new technology that we can be threatened without being held captive. This is why deterrence, while in principle so frightening, is so easy to live with. It cannot be condemned for anything it does to its hostages . . . it involves no direct or physical violation of their rights.[16]

Yet even if nuclear deterrence does not violate the rights of its hostages, it is nevertheless immoral. It commits a nation to a course of retaliation, since if a nation bluffs its adversary may learn this through espionage. But if deterrence does fail, and the opponent launches an attack, there would be no rational or moral reason to carry out the threatened retaliation. Indeed the leaders of the stricken nation would have conclusive moral reasons not to retaliate. Retaliation would punish the leaders who committed this unprecedented crime and would prevent them from dominating the postwar world; but it would accomplish no deterrent effect while massacring millions of innocent civilians in the attacking nation, and in other nations, would set back postwar recovery for the world immeasurably, and might even render the earth unfit for human survival.

IMMORAL THREATS

The immorality of nuclear deterrence lies in the threat itself, not in its present or even likely consequences. Paul Ramsey also recognizes this point: "Whatever is wrong to do is wrong to threaten, if the latter means 'means to do'. . . . If counter-population warfare is murder, then counter-population deterrence threats are murderous."[17]

Since it would be wrong to retaliate, and through moral intuition we know it to be wrong, then it cannot be right for us to intend to do it. Indeed moral systems depend upon

some version of the so-called wrongful intentions principle: to intend to do what one knows to be wrong is itself wrong.[18] The necessity of this principle is obvious from reflection about our moral experience and is not denied by any major system of morality.[19]

Yet it might be objected that U.S. leaders intend not to annihilate Soviet citizens but to preserve peace. Thus by threatening to kill, they intend not to kill. This objection contains elements both of error and of truth. When these are sorted out, the intention to retaliate is still immoral, although certainly not as wicked as a direct and unconditional intention to kill.

In objecting that it is not immoral to intend retaliation, one may be confusing "intending an action" with "desiring the outcome of that action." Ordinarily an agent will form the intention to do something because he desires doing it either as an end in itself, or as a means to other ends.[20] In the case of nuclear deterrence, however, the intention to retaliate is entirely distinct from any desire to carry it out. In fact the intention to retaliate is entirely consistent with a strong desire not to apply the sanction. Thus while the object of our leaders' deterrence intention is an evil act, it does not follow that in adopting that intention, or even desiring to adopt it, they desire to do evil, either as an end or as a means.

While the absence of a desire to kill is important, it is not sufficient to exculpate our national leaders for the intention to retaliate. What counts in establishing the immorality of their intentions are the preparations they make to retaliate, the signals they send to the adversary, and courses of action that may leave their hands tied and make retaliation almost automatic. These plans and actions underscore their willingness, in order to deter aggression, to accept the risk that in the end they will apply the sanctions and allow the world to be consumed.

The objection that it is not immoral to intend massive retaliation may also be based on the claim that the U.S. intention is entirely conditional upon the behavior of the adversary. We are intending not to attack, but to launch a strike only if the opponent attacks.

Such conditional intentions seem strange because they are by nature self-extinguishing: the purpose of forming the intention to retaliate is to prevent the very circumstances in which the intended act would be performed.[21] Nevertheless the wrong intentions principle applies to conditional just as to unconditional intentions. When a terrorist hijacks an airplane at gunpoint and threatens the lives of his hostages, the immorality of his threat is not canceled by its being conditional upon the behavior of the officials he seeks to coerce. The same is true of nuclear deterrence. In addition to the leaders who decide to launch a first strike, millions who have no part in the decision will die or suffer. Thus one does not significantly change the immorality of the threat to kill innocent persons by making it conditional upon the actions of national leaders.[22]

A MORAL DILEMMA

Where we have persuasive moral reasons both for and against the same action, we have a moral dilemma. We must either accept our obligations to defend the innocent, in which case we threaten retaliation, or we do not threaten retaliation, in which case we abandon hope of effectively protecting the innocent. Thus it is both morally wrong for our government to commit us to a policy of massive retaliation involving immoral threats, and at the same time morally wrong not to do so. Walzer seems entirely correct when he says that "nuclear weapons explode the theory of just war."[23]

This moral dilemma surrounding nuclear deterrence policy is intolerable. But by what means can we escape from it? We could show that the dilemma does not really exist by denying one of its horns. We might marshal new arguments to show that there are moral reasons we had overlooked but which justify threats of nuclear retaliation. A second possibility is to show that there is a nuclear deterrence strategy that evades moral censure. Ramsey has asserted that just war can support a counterforce deterrence strategy.[24] His argument is especially important because

since 1973 counterforce strategy has become the officially preferred nuclear strategy in the United States.[25]

COUNTERFORCE DETERRENCE

Ramsey argues that it is possible to prevent nuclear attack without threatening to strike population centers in response. Strategic nuclear weapons can be targeted against nuclear installations, conventional military bases, and isolated economic objectives. This strategy could have the same deterrent effect as the conventional countervalue strategy, because although only military objectives would be targeted, a consequence of retaliation would inevitably be the unacceptable loss of millions of collateral civilian deaths.

However, the civilians likely to die would be the incidental victims of legitimate military counterstrikes. Herein lies the alleged moral superiority of counterforce strategy. These civilians are not hostages whom we have formed the—conditional—intention to kill. These collateral damages would be justified as an unavoidable consequence of a justifiable response; hence it is also justifiable to intend—conditionally—such a response.

Nevertheless there are serious difficulties with Ramsey's argument. First, could a retaliatory counterforce strategy really deter a first strike? Deterrence works only if the defender threatens unacceptable harm, and in recent years there has been much speculation that with evacuation, hardened industrial sites, and civil defense, the Soviets might escape with as little as 10 million casualties—judged to be an "acceptable loss" by some defense consultants.[26] Thus the danger of collateral damage is likely to deter only if the threatened damage would be very great indeed, disproportionate to the value of the military site targeted. The proportionality rule bars use of the doctrine of just war to justify any number of civilian casualties on the grounds that although these casualties were unavoidable, we did not intend to kill them since we did not really aim at them.

Ramsey's response is to maintain that in nuclear deterrence, proportionality is to be measured against the value not of a particular military target, but of world peace itself.[27] But how are we to reckon proportionality between the—certain—loss of human life and any—uncertain—increase in world peace? World peace is obviously an end we value very highly, but does this mean that, according to Ramsey's logic, the more highly we value peace, the more lives we may threaten so long as any actual deaths would be only collateral? If this is what Ramsey means, then the word "collateral" has lost most of its meaning and "proportionality" has been defined so broadly as to void the rules of just war.[28]

In any event, Ramsey's proposal does not overcome the problem of immoral threats. Since we know that counter-force strategy will deter aggression only if the threat to the civilian population is very great, and since we intend these threats to deter, it follows that we have formed the conditional intention to bring about their deaths after all. Like other deterrent theorists, Ramsey wants to prevent nuclear attack by threatening to kill very large numbers of innocent people, but unlike other deterrent theorists, he expects to kill these people without aiming at them. However, we might as well aim at them, if we know that a direct and necessary consequence of our attacking military targets would be their death.[29]

RENOUNCING RETALIATION

Counterforce deterrence provides no real solution to our moral dilemma, but there may be a second means of escape. This would involve denying the alternatives presumed in formulating the dilemma. It had been assumed, not without reason, that we must either accept our obligations to defend the innocent, in which case we threaten retaliation, or we do not threaten retaliation, in which case we abandon hope of effectively defending the innocent. But is it not possible to meet our obligations of self-defense and protection of the innocent without threatening nuclear retaliation? An affirmative answer has been offered: we develop a technological capacity for self-defense that does not require

threats of massive retaliation against the adversary.

On the evening of 23 March 1983 this proposal was dramatically presented to the American people by President Reagan. The president asked, "What if free people could live secure in the knowledge that their security did not rest upon the threat of instant U.S. retaliation to deter a Soviet attack, that we could intercept and destroy strategic ballistic missiles before they reached our own soil or that of our allies?"[30] The inference he knew we would draw is that such a system of self-defense would remove the moral opprobrium surrounding present deterrence policies. Such a system, if it could work, might also inaugurate a new era in strategic nuclear deterrence, a technological solution to the problem of vulnerability created by nuclear technology in the first place.

Could such a purely defensive strategy work, and would it really eliminate the need to make immoral threats? The development of new antimissile weapons would be destabilizing and might dangerously increase the risk of a preemptive Soviet strike. In the game of deterrence, the adversary's perceptions of our intentions are what ultimately count. And the Soviets are not likely to trust our claims that the new devices are purely defensive. Soviet leaders would correctly reason that since such weapons could knock out Soviet missiles sent in a second strike, it might increase U.S. capacity to prevail in a nuclear war. At present, the Soviet deterrent to a U.S. first strike is massive retaliation, and Reagan's proposed antimissile defense would effectively eliminate that deterrent threat. Consequently the Soviet's increased vulnerability would cause them to fear the possible sense of adventurism that knowledge of this edge might give our leaders.

An antimissile defense system would also consign the United States to the spiraling costs of a runaway antiarms arms race. The history of the arms race since 1945 suggests that the new defensive systems would be quickly matched by technological breakthroughs designed to overwhelm or outmanuever them.[31]

More important still is the following consideration. Suppose the Soviets continue to arm; then in the event of an attack, we could never be sure our antimissile system would completely neutralize their offensive weapons. Even a very low rate of failure during an all-out attack would result in horrendous losses, perhaps even annihilation. Thus it is clear that the threat of a retaliatory second strike must remain as the unexpressed but final recourse if the United States is to deter aggression with nuclear arms. The point is that Reagan and our national security managers know we would need to hold onto our second-strike forces as an insurance policy, and that is why the president's proposal seems so deceitful. By attempting to push the immoral threat of retaliation away from the light of debate and analysis, our leaders hope will overlook its hideous reality. The Soviets also know we would keep a second-strike insurance, and that is why these so-called defensive antiballistic weapons would be perceived by them as offensive.

MORAL FAILURE OF
NUCLEAR DETERRENCE

Nuclear deterrence as practiced by the superpowers fails the test of morality; its appearance of moral respectability arises from close association with perceptions of dire emergency. A stopgap effort at conflict containment or postponement, it does not resolve international conflicts by removing their cause, nor does it bring about changes that lessen the danger of clashes. By exchanging immoral threats, the superpower players merely push the real problems into the background, taking the position that no solution at all is preferable to the risk of escalating a conflict that could lead to a nuclear exchange. In fact nuclear deterrence may well be self-defeating over the long run. Although real security no longer exists, our national security managers relentlessly seek to instill a sense of security in us by pursuing actions that objectively increase the danger: they build more and deadlier weapons.[32]

Furthermore, since nuclear deterrence requires credible threats that weapons may be used, its success diminishes its own credibility, and efforts to reassert its credibility threaten to bring about its failure. The runaway arms race is due only in part to worst-case analyses on both sides and current methods of weapons procurement;[33] it is also a product of the constant need to underwrite deterrence with the image of Armageddon. Since perceptions of our preparation for self-protection and of our willingness to retaliate are directly correlated, nuclear deterrence will require greater efforts to ensure the survivability of our nuclear forces. What better way to communicate the seriousness of our intent than to commit a staggering proportion of the federal budget to the development of new weapons? President Reagan argued that defense budget cuts "will send a signal of decline, of lessened will, to friends and adversaries alike."[34]

Both President Reagan's proposal and Paul Ramsey's approach attempt to overcome the immorality of nuclear deterrence by making changes in strategic uses of nuclear weapons. Is there a common error in the assumption that deterrence is equivalent to military, and especially nuclear, defense capability? Neither deterrence nor self-defense is necessarily equivalent to threatening military might, and it may be this fact that a solution to the problem of self-defense must recognize.

NONVIOLENT NATIONAL DEFENSE

Deterrence connotes retaliation but this association is not logically part of the concept. As Thomas Schelling has indicated, deterrence occurs whenever a potential enemy is persuaded to abandon a certain course of activity because he sees that it is in his own self-interest to do so.[35] Thus deterrence is essentially a process of persuasion, and the method that persuades most clearly deters most effectively.

Nobody understands this fact more emphatically than the advocates of nonviolent national defense or civilian resistance. Here is offered an approach to defense that escapes the moral dilemma. It takes seriously the obligation to defend the innocent, and its advocates claim that it would deter aggression; moreover it would overcome occupation and oppression if deterrence were to fail.[36]

Civilian resistance focuses upon the defense of a nation's basic social institutions, culture, and ideological beliefs by training the civilian population in organized nonviolent resistance and noncompliance. In addition to protecting human lives, a national defense must successfully protect a way of life: the institutions, rights, and principles that form the stable framework for life and provide a group with an organized expression of conscious preferences and commitments.[37] Civilian resistance therefore seeks to deter aggression by making it clear to any potential invader that he could not control and dominate the political and social life of the nation he seeks to invade. He would see that military occupation would not by itself give him political control and would not be experienced by the population as defeat; rather it would mean an extension of the contest of will and ideology.

Gene Sharp, a leading advocate of civilian resistance, asks us to reflect about the conditions that are most likely to create a nuclear attack.[38] Who fears and expects a nuclear attack the most today, and who expects one the least? It is precisely the nuclear powers who fear a nuclear attack the most, and this fear of attack, or of defeat in a major conventional war, may itself be the overriding temptation for a superpower to launch a first strike. Civilian resistance, which unlike nuclear forces can be used only for defensive purposes, would remove that danger and thereby reduce the chances of annihilation. In addition, while there remain some circumstances under which a nuclear attack might seem rational, given present deterrence policies, there appear to be no circumstances under which a nuclear attack on an unarmed nation would appear rational. It will surely be objected that civilian resistance could not save a nation from a maniacal opponent. However, since no one can predict what a maniac would do, there is no more reason to suppose that he would respond rationally to nuclear threats than that he would pointlessly devastate an unarmed and unthreatening country.

Walzer has objected that while nuclear deterrence depends upon inspiring fear in the adversary, in nonviolent defense the adversary would experience no fear, but at best only guilt, shame, and remorse. "The success of the defense [would be] entirely dependent upon the moral convictions and sensibilities of the enemy soldiers."[39] But this presumption appears mistaken. First, it has frequently been noted that inhibitions of a political, social, and cultural nature are normally more decisive than fear in holding back the hand on the trigger.[40] Second, there is no reason to suppose that nonviolent deterrence must depend more than nuclear deterrence upon the moral sensibilities of the adversary. All deterrence policies must depend upon the adversary's calculations that the costs of aggression would outweigh the benefits, and this would be true no less for nonviolent defense than for nuclear deterrence.

The case for nonviolent defense has not been completed, but serious and intelligent criticism has also hardly begun. Civilian resistance has not received the attention it deserves. It may turn out that a nonviolent national defense would be impossible, or if possible, less acceptable morally than nuclear deterrence. But nonviolent defense is not foolish on its face, nor is it merely pacifism or unilateral disarmament under a different guise.[41] Its apparent moral superiority to nuclear deterrence obligates us to give it our careful attention. Indeed if threats of nuclear retaliation are morally permissible, then they are permissible only because deterrence is absolutely necessary, and nuclear threats are the only means of effecting this deterrence. Thus even those who argue for the moral superiority of nuclear deterrence, if they are earnest and sincere, must attempt to demonstrate the moral inadequacy of civilian resistance.

NOTES

1. See Philip Green, *Deadly Logic* (Columbus: Ohio University Press, 1966); and Robert P. Wolff, "Maximization of Expected Utility as a Criterion of Rationality in Military Strategy and Foreign Pol-

icy," *Social Theory and Practice*, 1:99–111 (Spring 1970).

2. Quoted by Robert Jay Lifton and Richard Falk, *Indefensible Weapons* (New York: Basic Books, 1983), p. 66.

3. See Jonathan Schell, *The Fate of the Earth* (New York: Avon Books, 1982), pp. 99–178.

4. Lifton and Falk, *Indefensible Weapons*, pp. 3–127.

5. Henry T. Nash, "The Bureaucratization of Homicide," in *Protest and Survive*, ed. F. P. Thompson and Dan Smith (New York: Monthly Review Press, 1981), pp. 149–60.

6. "Moral Urgencies in the Nuclear Context," in *Nuclear Weapons and the Conflict of Conscience*, ed. John C. Bennett (New York: Charles Scribner's Sons, 1962), p. 109.

7. This discussion also presupposes that moral principles are relevant to issues of war and national defense. Anyone who doubts this should see Richard A. Wasserstrom, "On the Morality of War: A Preliminary Inquiry," in *War and Morality, ed. R. A. Wasserstrom (Belmont, CA: Wadsworth Pub., 1970), pp. 78–101: and Michael Walzer, Just and Unjust Wars* (New York: Basic Books, 1977), pp. 3–20.

8. Thomas C. Schelling, "The Diplomacy of Violence," in *Peace and War*, ed. Charles Beitz and Theodore Herman (San Francisco: W. H. Freeman and Co., 1973), pp. 74–90.

9. See *Just and Unjust Wars*, p. 269.

10. See selections from his *The City of God*, in *War and Christian Ethics*, ed. Arthur F. Holmes (Grand Rapids: Baker Book House. 1975), pp. 61–87, and Ralph Potter, "The Moral Logic of War," in *Peace and War*, ed. Beitz and Herman, pp. 7–16. Modern versions of the doctrine have a variety of theoretical bases. Barrie Paskins and Michael Dockrill, *The Ethics of War* (Minneapolis: University of Minnesota Press, 1979). pp. 191–245, derive the doctrine from Kantian ethical principles, although they deny its justification of nuclear deterrence. In *Just and Unjust Wars*, Walzer develops a version of the doctrine that is independent of any particular theological or ethical position.

11. See David Wells. "How Much Can the Just War Justify?" *Journal of Philosophy, 66:819–29 (Dec. 1969)*.

12. Walzer, *Just and Unjust Wars*, pp. 272–73.

13. *The Soviet Union and the Arms Race* (New Haven, CT: Yale University Press, 1983).

14. *The Just War* (New York: Charles Scribner's Sons, 1968), p. 171.

15. *Just and Unjust Wars*, pp. 270–71.

16. Ibid. But perhaps nuclear weapons can be condemned for their psychological effects on hostages. For a discussion of the psychological evidence, see Lifton and Falk, *Indefensible Weapons*, pp. 48–52, 54, 68, 77.

17. "A Political Ethics Context for Strategic Thinking," in *Strategic Thinking and Its Moral Implications*, ed. Morton A. Kaplan (Chicago: University of Chicago Center for Policy Studies, 1973), pp. 134–35.

18. Gregory S. Kavka, "Some Paradoxes of Deterrence," *Journal of Philosophy*, 75:285–289 (June 1978).

19. Ibid.

20. Kavka, "Paradoxes of Deterrence," p. 291.

21. Kavka, "Paradoxes of Deterrence," p. 290.

22. But see Kavka's objection to this argument, ibid., p. 289.

23. *Just and Unjust Wars*, p. 282.

24. *The Just War*, pp. 285–366.

25. James Fallows, *National Defense* (New York: Vintage Books, 1981), pp. 141–45.

26. See the testimony before the Senate Foreign Relations Committee or Retired General Daniel O. Graham, former director of the Defense Intelligence Agency, as quoted in Fallows, *National Defense*, pp. 145–146.

27. *The Just War*, p. 303.

28. Walzer, *Just and Unjust Wars,* p. 280.

29. I certainly agree that threatening to kill 10–20 million civilians by counterforce retaliation is not as immoral as threatening to kill 60–100 million by countervalue retaliation, other things being equal. But this reduction in the immorality of the threat can be achieved in a more straightforward way simply by cutting back on our overkill capacity, so that retaliation would be less massive.

30. *Washington Post*, 24 Mar. 1983, p. A12.

31. For a discussion of the arms race and the futuristic weapons defenses envisioned by some analysts, see Ground Zero, *Nuclear War: What's In it for You?* (New York: Pocket Books, 1982), pp. 72–82, 199–211.

32. Lifton and Falk, *Indefensible Weapons*, p. 25.

33. Mary Kaldor, "Disarmament: The Armament Process in Reverse," in *Protest and Survive*, ed. Thompson and Smith, pp. 134–82.

34. *Washington Post*, 24 May. 1983, p. A1.

35. *The Strategy of Conflict* (Cambridge, MA: Harvard University Press, 1960) pp. 6ff.

36. Anders Boserup and Andrew Mack, *War without Weapons* (New York: Schocken Books, 1975); B.H. Liddell Hart; *Defence of the West* (New York: Morrow, 1950): idem, *Deterrent or Defence* (New York: Praeger, 1960); H.J.N. Horsburgh,

Non-Violence and Aggression (London: Oxford University press, 1968); Adam Roberts, ed., *Civilian Resistance as a National Defence* (Baltimore: Penguin Books, 1969); and Gene Sharp, *The Politics of Non-Violent Action* (Boston: Porter-Sargent, 1973).

37. Horsburgh, *Non-Violence and Aggression,* p. 106.

38. "National Defense without Armaments," in *Peace and War,* ed. Beitz and Herman, P. 360.

39. *Just and Unjust Wars.* p. 334.

40. Boserup and Mack, *War without Weapons,* p. 176; Green, *Deadly Logic,* p. 201.

41. Unlike many proposals for unilateral disarmament, nonviolent defense responds to the need for deterrence; and unlike traditional versions of pacifism or passive resistance, it advocates nonviolent force and coercion. On the concept of nonviolent coercion, see Judith Stiehm, *Non-violent Power* (Lexington, MA: D. C. Heath, 1972).

23

Radwaste Program: A Delay in Plans

I. PETERSON

This article, written in early 1984, describes some of the problems currently being faced by the Department of Energy in developing a sound plan for managing radioactive waste from nuclear power plants, namely, the "mission plan."

With the release of the first draft of its "mission plan" for managing radioactive waste from nuclear power plants, the Department of Energy (DOE) late last month took another small but important step toward building the nation's first permanent repository for highly radioactive waste. And, only one year after the passage of the Nuclear Waste Policy Act that set the program in motion,[1] squirming DOE officials find themselves caught in the straightjacket of a tight, congressionally mandated schedule and already facing delays and complaints. They concede that the program's goal of having a permanent repository operating by early 1998 may not be met.

Robert L. Morgan, acting director of DOE's civilian radioactive-waste management office, said recently, "We are concerned about the very optimistic timetable . . . [but] we will dispose of whatever waste we receive, in whatever form, beginning in 1998." To ensure that some kind of facility will be ready on time to accept nuclear waste shipments from utilities, the mission plan, which outlines DOE's thinking on how the department intends to meet its obligations, calls for a parallel program to design and find a site for a "monitored retrievable storage" (MRS) facility. If Congress approves the construction of such a facility for temporary storage of high-level nuclear waste, it will serve as a backup in case the permanent repository is unfinished.

Compared with the special conditions needed for a permanent, geological repository—which will be sunk deep into a suitable rock formation—the requirements for an MRS facility are less stringent. According to the plan, acceptable MRS sites could probably be found in any state. One possible scheme involves sealing radioactive waste into special casks that are then stored in a field of dry wells or in large surface vaults. Depending on its capacity, an MRS facility could cost as much as $2 billion. Next month, DOE hopes to publish a draft of its criteria for selecting potential MRS sites.

Some critics question whether DOE's concept of an MRS facility as an elaborate temporary storage system actually meets the

Originally published in *Science News* 125 (January 7, 1984), p. 5. Copyright 1984 by Science Service, Inc. Reprinted with permission from *Science News,* the weekly newsmagazine of science.

intent of the Nuclear Waste Policy Act. The act clearly states that MRS is an option for "long-term storage" with continuous monitoring "for the foreseeable future" that allows the possibility of recovering the stored material for later use.

Commenting on the mandated schedule, Rep. Morris K. Udall (D-Ariz.), who was instrumental in getting the nuclear waste legislation through Congress, said at a recent DOE public meeting, "We were not all-knowing when we set those dates." He suggested that the timetable provided a way of assessing the program's progress, and if necessary, the law could be "bent a little to get the job done." Udall said, "We gave the states and the public a powerful and direct role in decisions that will shape the program in the next 15 years." Much of the uncertainty in the schedule depends on how DOE responds to that input. DOE's effort is still not well organized, Udall noted, partly because the nuclear waste program has been without a permanent director for almost a year and most of the other senior positions are filled on an "acting" basis.

The first major delay in the program occurred in the process of coming up with guidelines for recommending a site as the location for a permanent repository. These guidelines, due last July were finally forwarded to the Nuclear Regulatory Commission (NRC) for review late in November. The six-month delay came about because of extensive revisions that had to be made after DOE received about 2,000 comments on its original proposal. State representatives, in particular, complained that they should have been consulted earlier in the process. The experience with the guidelines led DOE to issue its proposed mission plan in draft form before it officially appears in the Federal Register next spring. Officials expect that this could save time by settling many issues before public hearings take place.

Although NRC has not yet completed its review of the selection guidelines for a permanent repository site, DOE is planning to nominate as early as this month at least five sites for detailed environmental assessments. They will be selected from the nine

sites that DOE has studied so far and will represent a wide range of different types of rock, including salt, basalt and a "welded" volcanic ash called tuff.[2] Any sites not meeting the guidelines will be eliminated from further consideration.

"Every site has significant opposition," said DOE's Michael J. Lawrence. "Obviously, people wouldn't like to have this facility near them." Local opponents are already preparing arguments that include technical reasons why the nominated sites are unsuitable.

Morgan admitted that the current selection process does not identify the best possible site in the country for a geological repository. The department has to be satisfied with finding an acceptable site that meets all the requirements, he said. "The utilities and the taxpayers do not have the funds to find the *best* site," Morgan said. Just drilling a test shaft and characterizing a site thoroughly could cost $100 million. To meet the schedule, DOE had to go with sites already known, he said. This eliminated granite, for example, as a medium for the first repository.

Utilities with nuclear reactors are worried not only about where they will store their used fuel as on-site storage pools fill but also about how DOE is spending their money. The entire civilian nuclear waste management program is funded by a special levy of one-tenth of a cent for every kilowatt-hour of energy generated by nuclear power, which adds up to about $400 million a year. In return for the fee, DOE last June signed 70 contracts with 56 different organizations, including 46 utilities, promising to provide for the eventual disposal of their nuclear wastes.

Representatives of the nuclear industry have questioned DOE's ability to control the cost of the program. "Is the money being well-spent?" asked Edwin Wiggin of the Atomic Industrial Forum, headquartered in Bethesda, Md. He worried about the cost of delays due to "political and social matters" rather than technical problems and because of the tendency of DOE's national laboratories "to research a problem to death." Wiggin said, "Most of the basic research has been accomplished. We can make a mistake in looking for the perfect answer when an 'adequate' answer is enough."

DOE is being closely watched not only by the states, Congress and the nuclear industry but also by NRC. NRC's John G. Davis said, "We see ourselves as the public's advocate for safety." What isn't clear yet is how easily NRC will get the information it needs in order to evaluate DOE's plans and to license the construction of a permanent repository.

The mission plan describes the nuclear waste program as a "high-risk undertaking." Because many of the activities must be performed in a certain sequence, a delay in meeting one milestone may delay the start of a subsequent activity, the plan says. J. William Bennett, one of the DOE officials responsible for establishing the geological repository, commented, "It will not be an easy matter to implement [the plan]" The year 1983 was both hectic and frustrating, yet a lot was accomplished, he said; 1984 looks even more busy.

NOTES

1. SN:1/1/83, p. 6.
2. SN: 5/21/83, p. 329.

24

Agent Orange: What Isn't Settled

JANET RALOFF

Janet Raloff discusses the settlement between Vietnam War veterans and the chemical manufacturers of Agent Orange. This product was an herbicide used widely by the U.S. Air Force during the Vietnam war to defoliate ground cover protecting enemy troops, and is said to have caused deleterious effects on the health of the troops exposed to it, as well as of their children. This article focuses on what was not settled: the issues that would have clarified legal prospects for a host of other cases involving civil suits seeking reparation for injuries due to toxic substances. It discusses approaches adopted by those involved in the suits as of mid-1984.

In January 1962, President John F. Kennedy gave his approval to begin Operation Ranch Hand in Vietnam—an Air Force program to defoliate ground cover protecting enemy troops. In 9 years of aerial spraying, Ranch Hand rained an estimated 19 million gallons of chemical herbicides over between 10 and 20 percent of the South Vietnamese landscape. Of several herbicides deployed, Agent Orange proved to be the Air Force favorite: U.S. planes doused the Asian country with 11 million gallons of it.

Today, thousands of U.S., Australian and New Zealand troops who served in Vietnam during the period of aerial spraying are claiming that exposure to these herbicides has harmed them, and in some cases their children as well. Prevented by the Supreme Court's *Feres* decision from suing the U.S. government, the veterans and their families brought suit instead against the seven chemical firms that manufactured under military contract Agent Orange and its dioxin-tainted cousins— Agents Pink, Green, Purple and Orange II. But in a surprise development last week, a tentative settlement was reached between the veterans and the chemical manufacturers. Coming on the eve of final jury selection in the 5-year-old suit, it averted what many had been predicting would have been the most complex case ever brought before a U.S. jury.

Though the compromise agreement promises to settle some of the litigants' long-standing complaints, it also promises to leave unresolved quite a few more. Interestingly, those issues left unsettled are precisely the ones in which the legal and scientific community are most interested, because they would have clarified legal prospects facing a host of other equally nightmarish cases involving "toxic torts"—civil suits asking remedies for injury from toxic substances.

In fact, although it is unlikely, the case could still go to trial. Many details of the proposed settlement are still to be ironed out, such as how a claimant establishes he or she deserves compensation; how much will be paid out for any particular problem; whether there's a ceiling on how much an individual may be compensated; and if there is not

Originally published in *Science News* 125 (May 9, 1984), pp. 314–317. Copyright © 1984 by Science Service, Inc. Reprinted with permission from *Science News,* the weekly newsmagazine of science.

enough money to go around, who gets priority in receiving funds. Once these and other pertinent details are agreed to, all parties of the suit will have an opportunity to voice objections in a hearing expected to occur within the next 60 to 90 days. If their objections are not satisfied, class members may pull out of the settlement. And among the conditions that prompted the chemical companies to initially agree to the accord was a proviso permitting them to pull out if the number of plaintiffs who choose to opt out "is substantial."

The chemical companies only agreed to the arrangement because they expected it would indeed *settle* any legal claims by the more than 15,000 known class-action members. Veterans who had chosen not to become a party to the class action—and prior to the settlement, several had—retained the right to sue separately over their alleged injuries. If the number of individuals ultimately expected to bring independent suit against the defendant chemical companies became too large, the value of the settlement—in limiting the defendants' litigation costs—would diminish substantially.

But why would the veterans opt out? As it now stands, the defendants have agreed to set up a "trust fund" with a starting kitty of $180 million. Accruing interest at a rate of roughly $60,000 daily, the fund is expected to eventually amass almost $250 million in disbursable funds. The number of claimants, however, is expected to number in the tens of thousands. If 20,000 veterans or family members with derivative claims (for miscarriages or birth defects allegedly deriving from a veteran's exposure) established justifiable claims, there would be only an average of $12,500 available for each—not much considering today's health costs. If 50,000 awards were made, there would be a mere $5,000 for each. So a veteran or group of veterans believing they could win higher claims by suing individually may choose to opt out. If enough do, the still fragile settlement agreement could fall apart.

Yet even if the settlement holds up, it will have left a number of the most important legal questions unanswered. And it may have been

the intention of doing just that which most motivated the defendants' decision to settle.

Explains trial law authority Paul Rothstein of the Georgetown University Law Center in Washington D.C., "one of our frustrations in cases like this is that you seldom get a decision" because the parties decide to settle out of court. In an interview with *Science News* weeks before the settlement was announced, Rothstein predicted the Agent Orange accord. Why? "The industry may not want to push some of the questions here to a decision because it could [risk getting] bad law out of it," he said.

Rothstein was referring to the fact that the significance of the Agent Orange suit was expected to go far beyond the question of whether veterans deserved to be compensated for injuries they claim had been caused by herbicides. Had it gone to trial, the case stood not only to be a catalyst in the resolution of several important legal ambiguities, but also in the creation of new law.

Specifically, the case was expected to redefine the type of litigation for which class action is deemed appropriate. Second, it would have tested the reach of the *Feres* doctrine in cloaking the government and its contractors from litigation over personal injuries. Manufacturers were watching the case for the creation of precedents affecting product liability law. And finally, the entire science community was watching to see how the judicial system made use of the confusing scientific record amassed on dioxin toxicology. If the requirements for establishing injury causation[1] had been substantially relaxed, and all parties to the case knew this was a possibility, it would have had a direct bearing on how subsequent toxic torts were resolved—from those involving asbestos to leaking toxic waste dumps.

Why did the plaintiffs choose to settle, especially after asking for a trust fund involving 10 or more times the amount to which they ultimately agreed? According to Washington attorney and product liability expert Victor Schwartz, they probably realized "that there was very little predictability as regards how this case would come out. I see this case as one where the plaintiffs could have walked away with absolutely nothing because of the very difficult causation problem: A fundamental of tort law—one no court has moved away from—requires tying the product to injury."

He is not alone in believing the veterans would have a tough time establishing that exposure to dioxin caused their injury. In fact, of the many questions in this case, this would likely have proven the hardest to answer because the scientific record on dioxin toxicology is so equivocal.

The litigants are claiming a wide spectrum of health effects from their exposure to the herbicides—including cancer, liver damage, peripheral nerve problems, chloracne, and birth defects. In a 46-page "complaint" filed with the U.S. District Court in New York City, the litigants alleged that the chemical companies that manufactured Agent Orange and related phenoxy herbicides for use in Vietnam breached their contract with the military by supplying a defective product—specifically, that the chemicals were adulterated with an unauthorized toxic contaminant, 2,3,7,8-tetrachlorodibenzoparadioxin (TCDD). They also contended that the chemical companies never warned the military of the contaminant nor its potential for human harm—even though the manufacturers "knew or should have known" about the contaminant's presence and toxicity.

The defendants were charged with criminal negligence, with fraud, with breach of both implied and expressed warranties and with a legal tenet known as "strict liability." And because they allowed their products to be distributed in containers that did not identify the manufacturer, the defendants were asked to share responsibility for health effects suffered by TCDD-poisoned servicemen in proportion to the market share that each firm's products represented.

For their part, the chemical companies — Dow Chemical, Monsanto Co., Diamond Shamrock Corp., Uniroyal Inc, T.H. Agricultural and Nutrition Co., Thompson Chemical and Hercules Inc.—claim that scientific data do not support the contention that these herbicides are causally related to the health effects that have been cataloged thus far among the veterans and their families.

TCDD is now universally regarded as the most toxic of the chlorinated dioxin family's 75 members. In fact, TCDD is frequently termed the most toxic chemical made by man. But is it? TCDD has been demonstrated to kill 50 percent of those guinea pigs to which it has been administered at doses as small as 0.6 to 2 micrograms (μg) per kilogram of body weight.(A microgram is a millionth of a gram.) However, for the monkey the minimum dose required to kill 50 percent of the animals tested is closer to 70 μg. And in industrial accidents where humans have been exposed to proportionately equal or greater doses, there have been no deaths immediately traceable to the exposures, and little sign of disease beyond chloracne, a potentially disfiguring disease marked by acne-like eruptions that can persist, despite medical treatment, for 15 years or more.

James Saunders, a physician and toxicologist who directs biomedical research in Dow Chemical's health and environmental sciences division, tells of one 1964 accident at the company's Midland, Mich. facilities where TCDD exposures in some of the 61 affected workers are now roughly estimated to have been "some considerable number of micrograms—500 μg or so." If true, those doses are roughly equivalent to five times the lethal dose for guinea pigs.

Though they were put through a battery of medical tests at the time, the workers apeared to have suffered no adverse health effects other than chloracne; 49 workers developed the disease. Because animal studies had suggested the liver might be a target organ for TCDD, a liver biopsy was performed on the worker most exposed in the accident; it was negative. "There were no objective medical findings in any of these individuals with the exception of chloracne," Saunders says, "which leads us to believe that man is less sensitive to dioxin than other animal species."

Moreover, Saunders points out, the waste chemicals to which workers were exposed in the Dow accident contained TCDD levels tens of thousands of times higher than those found in Agent Orange. That, taken together with data from other industrial accidents, he says, suggests the comparatively small exposures that undoubtedly occurred in Vietnam are unlikely to have produced the type of long-term health effects that have been reported by the litigants in this suit.

Other assessments of TCDD, however, emphasize its potential danger. Last month the National Institute for Occupational Safety and Health (NIOSH) reported in the Centers for Disease Control (CDC) publication *Morbidity and Mortality Weekly Report* that it was recommending "TCDD be regarded as a potential occupational carcinogen . . . based on studies that demonstrate the carcinogenicity of TCDD in rats and mice." The report also mentioned animal studies that had shown the chemical to be a teratogen, threat to immune-system functioning and source of blood problems.

An Air Force study of Ranch Hand participants recently reported indications of suspicious symptoms among the men it studied.[2] What's more, a study reported last year at the International Symposium on Herbicides and Defoliants in War, in Ho Chi Minh City, Vietnam, cited elevated numbers of birth defects among North Vietnamese children whose fathers had fought in South Vietnam[3] —and presumably were exposed to the TCDD-contaminated defoliants. (It should be noted, however, that the toxicology community is somewhat skeptical of this study based on its methodological design.) Finally, a Jan. 27 report in *Morbidity and Mortality Weekly Report* by CDC announced that the agency had decided to consider TCDD greater than 100 parts per billion in residential soil to be "a level of concern"

Though exact levels of TCDD in Vietnamese soil were never quantified, estimates made by the Air Force suggest a single dose of Agent Orange might have resulted in concentrations roughly 100 times lower than those the CDC described as being "of concern."

In its newer epidemiological study, however, the Air Force admitted that "the average Ranch Hander was substantially exposed to the herbicides and dioxin (relative to other military personnel in the Republic of Vietnam) on almost a daily occupational basis.

Exposure calculations have estimated that an average Ranch Hander in his tour received, at a minimum, 1,000 times more exposure to Agent Orange than would an average un-clothed man in an open field directly beneath [the] spraying aircraft."

If Ranch Handers were most exposed to Agent Orange, were they also—of all Vietnam veterans—the most injured by it? Evidentally not. Surprisingly, there were no Ranch Handers among the five veterans and seven derivative cases that were to have been presented in this class action. The cases chosen were supposed to be not only representative of the thousands of cases not highlighted, but also the best cases the lawyers could identify linking Agent Orange and illness.

The chemical companies had intended to play on the absence of Ranch Handers in their defense. If the most exposed are not the most injured, then maybe something else is responsible for the veterans' problems, the defendants were going to argue.

Donald Frayer, claims manager for Dow Chemical's legal department, notes for example that there were 100,000 cases of malaria among the Vietnam troops. Not only has malaria been implicated in a form of cancer—Burkitt's lymphoma—but also Dapsone, the medicine initially used to treat the particularly resistant form of malaria encountered in Vietnam, appears to have caused a disease of the blood marrow in at least 16 men, he says. (Eight of them died.) Another 70,000 troops in Vietnam were hospitalized for skin conditions. And, says Frayer. "that was estimated to be about one percent of the dermatological problems that they [the troops] had." He also points out that "about 20,000 men were hospitalized for hepatitis, which today is considered a possible factor in liver cancer."

Frayer says Dow had planned to argue that if Vietnam veterans have special medical problems, "these are all candidates for consideration"—along with Agent Orange —as possible predisposing factors.

Explains one lawyer representing veterans who had chosen to opt out and have their cases tried independent of the class action,

"This is probably one of the few very strange cases where delay benefits the plaintiffs. Normally, in this situation, delay benefits the defendant." There are at least eight major epidemiological studies looking at Vietnam veterans exposed to TCDD and Agent Orange that are expected to release new findings within the next 5 years. Realizing how shaky their case would be today trying to link TCDD with disease causation in the veterans, several lawyers advised their clients to sit back and await results of these upcoming studies rather than risk all by going to court too early as part of the class action.

If the jury had decided that none of the representative cases in the class action had proven their illness was attributable to the herbicides, all other members of the class would have lost their case too. Owing to the equivocal scientific record on which their proof of disease causation would have to have been made, the plaintiffs may have decided to accept a smaller sum than they considered ideal as a hedge against going home without anything to show for their efforts.

As Schwartz puts it: "Juries are not, in my experience, as plaintiff-oriented as lay people think." He points out that this case was hardly a classic product liability action where someone had injured his foot in a lawnmower. Schwartz maintains that a good defense should have been able to convince the jury that in times of war—as some have likened the Vietnam conflict—the standards of civilian accountability may have to be suspended. "And even if there were fault involved, a good defense could be made to shift responsibility onto somebody else"—like the government, he says.

Which brings up an important point, namely what it would have taken to win the suit. If some or all of the plaintiffs had

Table 24.1. Dioxin-tainted herbicides used in Vietnam

Name	Chemicals	When used	Amounts used (gallons)	TCDD level (parts per million)
Agent Orange	50/50 mix of n-butyl esters of 2,4-D and 2,4,5-T (2,4,5-trichlorophenoxy-acetic acid)	1965–70	10,646,000	2
Agent Orange II	50/50 mix of n-butyl ester of 2,4-D and isooctyl ester of 2,4,5-T	1965–70	a	2
Agent Purple	50/30/20 mix (by weight) on n-butyl ester of 2,4-D, n-butyl ester of 2,4,5-T, and isobutyl ester of 2,4,5-T	1962–65	145,000	33
Agent Pink	60/40 mix (by weight) of n-butyl ester of 2,4,5-T and isobutyl esters of 2,4,5-T	1962–65	123,000	66
Agent Green	100% n-butyl ester of 2,4,5-T	1962–65	8,200	66

a Although 900,000 gallons were delivered, the Department of Defense is not sure how much was used; if any, it was "negligible."

succeeded in proving to the court that their problems indeed stemmed from herbicide exposures, would the chemical companies be held responsible?

To be guilty of negligence, Rothstein says, it makes a difference whether the chemical companies knew their products were contaminated with a harmful chemical. According to Frayer at Dow (Dow was the military's leading supplier of Agent Orange), the defense was prepared to argue that the levels of TCDD in Agent Orange—when it was made for the military—were below the limits of detection; therefore, the defendants did not knowingly sell a harmful product.

However, to be guilty under "strict liability," the defendants need not have known their product was dangerous. All that must be proven is that their products caused harm. This was, in fact, expected to be the plaintiffs' strongest argument in the suit.

According to Joseph Page, an authority on product liability at the Georgetown University Law Center, "If you can call [TCDD] an inherent part of the product, something that's unavoidable . . . then [liability] becomes a question of whether you gave adequate warning" to the buyer or user. "If you knew or should have known and didn't give adequate warning, you could be liable," under strict liability, he says. However, he points out, "If you didn't know and couldn't have known—and of course didn't give any warning—and then side effects developed, in most states [those harmed] would not be able to recover" compensation for injury.

Even that is not an iron-clad defense, however, Page notes that in the asbestos case *Beshada vs. Johns Manville,* the New Jersey Supreme Court recently held that lack of knowledge was irrelevant: harm alone justified responsibility under strict liability.

Frayer says the defendants could also have pointed to evidence suggesting the government did not use their herbicides properly. If the defendants can prove that, "then they have a defense," Rothstein says, because "there's a well-known defense to product liability that if the product is not used in accord with the manufacturer's instructions or recommendations, then the manufacturer is not liable."

However, even if the government did not misuse the product, the manufacturers might still have avoided legal responsibility for any harm their products caused if the court allowed them the "government contractor defense." This evolving, and not fully tested, defense claims that contractors who make a product to government specifications should have a right to the same immunity from prosecution that the government has under *Feres.*

Frayer says that to shore up their claim to immunity from prosecution, the chemical manufacturers could have shown evidence proving that the government was every bit as aware as the manufacturers were of the herbicides' dioxin content, of dioxin's toxicity, and of the inevitability of TCDD trace contamination in these herbicides.

But clinching each side's decision to settle in this case, Schwartz believes, was trial judge Jack Weinstein's announcement that he intended to use this case as a catalyst for developing a *federal* tort law, (Tort law deals with civil remedies for wrongful acts other than breach of contract.) The Erie Doctrine says that a federal court adjudicating a tort case is supposed to use the same state-developed law as would a state court if it were trying the case. But Weinstein—renowned for his courage in charting new legal waters—argued that because no one state's law was clearly most applicable in this obviously national suit, it was probably time to evolve the law.

As both sides knew well, appellate courts frequently overturn innovations such as new laws. And if the case were overturned on appeal because of the law applied, a new trial would be required, effectively doubling the costs of this already enormously expensive litigation. Moreover, since plaintiffs' lawyers are paid a percentage of their clients' awards—and therefore get paid only if they win—the idea of a second trial for no additional pay (and no guaranteed pay at that) was undoubtedly a sobering prospect during the settlement negotiations.

Tackling such a complicated case as this

today is like gambling in Vegas, Schwartz says: No one goes into it certain of a win. Seen in that light, the settlement offered everyone the only guarantee for some success. The plaintiffs got a mechanism set up for instituting compensation. The defendants were offered an expedient end to a lawsuit that had already cost them millions and would have cost them many times the settlement amount had they lost. Moreover, the herbicide manufacturers were able to extricate themselves without admitting guilt.

NOTES

1. SN: 11/19/83, p. 330.
2. SN: 3/3/84 p. 132.
3. SN: 9/3/83, p. 156.

25

Technology and the Environment. Who Pays the Piper?

JOHN P. MASCOTTE

John P. Mascotte states that in the twenty-first century, the leading public health problem will be environmental accident and disease. He argues that this problem cannot be dealt with simply through the courts, with victims suing for punitive damages on the basis of strict liability criteria. He suggests that meritorious victims should be quickly and fairly compensated by payments from a voluntary fund created by congressional statute with money derived through negotiated contributions from manufacturers, suppliers, installers, their insurance companies, and possibly the federal government.

Thank you very much for the invitation to speak to you today. The Executives' Club of Chicago is widely known as one of the top forums in the country for the serious discussion of major issues and that is why I am particularly pleased to be here. I want to talk to you about a growing concern of mine and what I hope will become a growing concern of opinion leaders around the country.

I speak of the unexpected, unpredictable, undesirable side effects of technology. The costly, painful, unfair, sometimes calamitous side effects—in human terms—of a technological society caught up in a worldwide competitive race for markets, jobs, profits and the achievement of other national goals.

I didn't come here today to make an anti-technology speech. Quite the contrary. Technology is not our enemy. In fact, it may be ironically true that only technology itself— properly applied —can save us from the undesirable side effects of technology. But our understanding of technology and how to control it, and predict its side effects, is the problem we must master.

Until recent years, Americans have taken a benign view of technology. And well they might, for American industry, as the prime manager of technology, has given us the most advanced and wealthiest society on earth. Until the early 1960's—outside of science-fiction films—we virtually ignored technology's impact on the environment. More recently, however, such problems as brown lung disease, Love Canal, Three Mile Island, kepone, and now asbestosis have become synonymous with unnatural and unexpected events that have undermined public confidence in our ability to manage technology safely.

Over the last decade or two, new laws and regulations have come into our lives to help protect us from dangers. Some of these laws and regulations may have gone too far. But, by and large, the basic laws on the books are needed and effective, and are backed up by a

Originally published in *Vital Speeches of the Day* 49 (January 15, 1983), pp. 220–223. Reprinted by permission of *Vital Speeches of the Day*.

court and jury system that has generally served us well over the years.

Asbestos-related disease, one of technology's unfortunate side effects, is a medical, social and economic problem of far-reaching consequences that has been coming on quietly for over thirty years. It takes decades for the disease to manifest itself. We are not prepared to handle this kind of problem, and the way we are handling it today is making the problem worse.

What we must ask ourselves is this: Can our present court/jury system respond to the challenges of asbestosis, and other similar environmental health problems, which may strike us in the future? Some of us are convinced that the current system cannot respond fairly and quickly to those who are victimized by this tragedy.

Let me examine this issue by giving you some necessary technical background on this difficult situation. Asbestos is a mineral whose unique properties permit its use in more than 3,000 commercial, industrial and personal products. It is an important and probably indispensible part of the modern industrial economy. There is, however, a substantial body of evidence that serious and harmful effects arise from its misuse. It is known to be a causative or contributive factor in certain respiratory and gastrointestinal diseases. It has been estimated that at least 5.6 million persons have been exposed to asbestos and may be at risk—and some say that this number may be conservative. There is no way to calculate how many may die and how many millions of others may suffer disability and a substantially reduced span of life.

Persons suffering from asbestos-related disease are now resorting to that all-American remedy, the lawsuit, in ever increasing numbers. One company alone estimates their current number of lawsuits at about 17,000 in 1982; and this company expects another 32,000 lawsuits in the next twenty-years. Now that's just one company! And in most cases, more than one manufacturer is being named as a defendant. Litigation is expected to continue at a high rate until about the year 2,010 before diminishing largely as a result of industry's growing ability to handle asbestos more safely.

The long-term cost of this litigation is now estimated by one study at $40 to $80 billion at 1980 dollar values. Some 260 involved insurance companies will pay claims through workers compensation or product liability coverage but it will represent only a fraction of the total eventual cost. And hundreds of millions of dollars more are, and will be, sought from asbestos manufacturers and other companies perhaps involved in the form of punitive and other damages.

I would be remiss if I did not mention that some claimants—according to one asbestos manufacturer I talked to—have "insubstantial or marginal claims and a fair number are highly questionable." Those situations, of course, must be carefully screened.

It is interesting to note that the nation's trial lawyers, a group who could be expected to oppose any proposal to circumvent the court/jury system to solve this problem, is beginning to understand the major predicament we are facing.

From the California Trial Lawyers publication, the FORUM, comes the following quote: "The enormity of the litigation, in terms of the numbers of claims now pending throughout the country and those expected to enter the system, raises grave problems. There are obviously not enough courtrooms in the world to accommodate the trial of each of these filings, should court and counsel fail to arrive at a mechanism for large-scale disposition of cases."

As you may know, The Manville Corporation, Unarco and Amatex have recently asked for the protection of a bankruptcy court. Moreover, under the prevailing tort system, all parties contributing to an injury are jointly liable for damages. Some courts have continued to process cases against these Chapter 11 companies. If the result is to shift their liability to other defendants, then the domino-effect could force many others into bankruptcy as well.

This growing wave of litigation—if not handled in a more sensible way—will have far-reaching consequences for American industry, for the legal system and for the government. Its most immediate impact, as you might imagine, is upon our legal system. More courts, judges, personnel and equipment will be needed to handle these cases and public money will pay for them.

Product liability law is very complex, because the laws of fifty different states are involved. The costs of litigation—for plaintiff and defendant—therefore, will be extremely heavy.

A lawsuit may seem like a costly, even wasteful remedy, given the meager amount of insurance available to compensate the victims of asbestos-related disease. But as the circumstances now dictate, there is no other remedy at hand. The victim may have been exposed to the disease forty years ago, his employer may no longer exist as a legal entity, or it may have merged with a successor corporation. *The problem for the victim has been, and continues to be, to find someone to accept responsibility— the manufacturer, the distributor, the general contractor, the installer, the insurance company, the government—somebody!*

The search for additional responsible parties goes on at a feverish pace. Courts of appeal in many jurisdictions are beginning to consider this litigation. To no one's surprise, they are coming to widely varied judgments and they are beginning to expand liabilities in the face of the inadequacy of the available insurance coverage. They have created some novel concepts of liability that threaten the established understanding of what constitutes the law, and what the rights and responsibilities of manufacturers, suppliers and consumers will be.

My point at this meeting today is to suggest that our institutions—mainly the law and our legal system—are inappropriate mechanisms to use in handling the tide of litigation that is, and will be, generated by asbestos-related disease.

If we were designing a new system that would work rationally, efficiently and fairly for all, how would it work? How might it be created?

In considering the question, we find the following elements are probably necessary to any workable solution:

1. We start with the victims themselves. We must remember the terrible cost being paid by those people afflicted and their families. This cost is economic and psychological, as well as physical. The present system, when it delivers justice, is costly, inefficient and, above all else, painfully, if not cruelly slow. Justice Holmes once said that "justice delayed is justice denied." How prophetic those words must be to thousands of victims, many in their 60's or older, who urgently need help now.

2. We should seek at all times the equitable and uniform treatment of asbestos victims. The present fault system of litigation is a lottery—some win and some lose— often seemingly unrelated to the merits of an individual's case. Settlements may have to do with the peculiarity of local law or even the skill of individual plantiff's counsel or even the whim of a jury.

3. One of our principal objectives ought to be the conservation of available financial resources. It's clear that liability for asbestos-related disease is enormous and that available insurance coverage is limited. The present court/jury system dissipates those resources. For example, defendants and insurance companies are conservatively paying out $2.00 in expenses for every $1.00 put into the hands of the victims, and the $2.00 in expenses does not include the cost to the public in providing judges, juries and other court expenses.

4. And as a corollary to that, we should devise a special system or trusteeship that makes for an efficient distribution of available money to the victims. *The amount of money now devoted to offensive and defensive litigation is staggering.* I say this not as a criticism of the plaintiff's attorney. I do not entirely share the view, particularly among some in the insurance industry, that there would be no problem but for the greed of the plaintiff's counsel. There are some offenders, true, but the trial lawyers did not create the present system, any more than the insurance

companies did. *What we must do now is focus on the problems of the victims and devise a system that delivers promptly the benefits they are entitled to receive.*

5. Another objective of a more efficient, workable system would be an end to most litigation: because it may be destructive of the victim's best interests; because it is weakening the courts and legal system; and because the search for responsible persons to sue is leading to broader use of litigation, and to novel and unsound theories of legal liability. Such a new system, however, would recognize that there would always be some differences of opinion which must be resolved by litigation.

6. And lastly, our objective should also be the conservation of Manville, and other involved companies, and the protection of the rights of their shareholders, workers, suppliers and creditors. Justice is a two-edged sword . . . a set of scales . . . and the rights of all parties must be considered in these proceedings.

The petitions by Manville and others seeking the protection of a court in a Chapter 11 bankruptcy is, at the very least, one of the legal novelties generated by the problem of asbestos-related disease. I find the position of Manville's management, that the viability of the company is threatened by overwhelming asbestos claims, a compelling one. Manville's estimates of its potential future liabilities, backed by an independent study, is—if accurate—frightening. Moreover, corporations are being sued for punitive damages on the basis of what they allegedly knew, or should have known, about the hazards of asbestos thirty or forty years ago.

It cannot be in the public interest for companies to be liquidated to find the money to pay these claims. This is like killing the goose that lays the golden egg. The shareholders, workers, creditors, and suppliers of these companies also have rights to be honored. I earnestly believe that the time has come to end this legal scramble and get on with the main task of compensating meritorious victims as quickly and fairly as possible.

And so the question arises, how might this be done?

We, at Continental, believe that the time has come to take asbestos-related disease out of the fault system. This is the only way to bring this litigation nightmare to an end. It is the only way we can conserve the available financial resources—of the asbestos manufacturers and their insurance companies—in order to more fully help the victims.

This means no-fault handling—a worker would need only to prove that he was exposed to asbestos and that he currently manifests the symptoms of disease.

We believe that compensation should cover all the victim's medical expenses; that he should also be compensated for lost or reduced earnings, pain and suffering, and some amount for foreshortened life span, and that he should be compensated for reasonable legal expenses.

What the victims need then is a special fund, created by Congressional statutory action, which would be a vehicle for the disbursement of available funds promptly to all meritorious asbestos-related cases. The fund should have a board of trustees representing the spectrum of involved parties. This voluntary fund would derive its money from negotiated contributions from asbestos manufacturers, suppliers and installers and their insurance companies, and possibly the Federal Government.

We do not rule out responsibility for the Federal Government. A large proportion of persons affected by asbestos-related disease are shipyard workers whose work was carried out for the government in a government-controlled workplace. And remember, a war was on when most were exposed. It is also a fact that the public is already paying part of the victim's expense through Medicare, Social Security and public assistance. If we properly understand the full ramifications of the asbestos disease problem, resources of both the private and the public sector may be needed as we consider the long-term costs involved.

Congress has been considering several legislative remedies. Congressman George Miller's bill HB5735, "The Occupational Health Hazards Compensation Act," we see as a reasonable vehicle for removing asbestos compensation from the fault litigation system. We support the concept of this legislation as a practical and necessary step toward a long-term solution to this problem.

Such health hazards as asbestos, and the toxic substances found at Love Canal recently, are but two examples of the potential for environmental disruption that are the by-products of our accelerating technology. These problems will always be with us. Our challenge, obviously, is to learn to do a better job of managing technology and its potentially damaging side effects.

Since the 1960's we have learned much about environmental pollution; however, it's apparent that these recurring environmental problems are undermining American faith in industry's ability to manage technology in the public interest. This loss of faith is having growing political consequences. We require the great benefits of technology, so we must help the American public recognize that these benefits do not come without risk and cost.

As we look forward to the twenty-first century, we must contemplate a future where environmental accident and disease may well be the leading public health problem. We solved the public health problems of tuberculosis, poliomyelitis and other dread diseases but we need to know more, through research, to understand and forecast environmental disease before a frightened public decides that public health can be assured only by public control of all technology. And they have a right, I believe, to insist on public control if we in business and industry do not listen more carefully and get our act together.

MORAL CONTROVERSIES IN TECHNOLOGY RESEARCH AND DEVELOPMENT

FREEDOM OF INQUIRY, NATIONAL SECURITY AND OPEN SOCIETIES

New policies in technology research are often a source of controversy and open confrontation. In this respect, they do not differ from other technology policies. Research policies, however, have a characteristic effect that distinguishes them from the others: they can become divisive issues in colleges and universities. In the first selection of Part IV, Secrecy in Science: A Contradiction in Terms?, Lois R. Ember discusses one such issue: secrecy constraints on research and development of new technologies. Ember outlines the legal and political background that led to the Executive Order on Security Classification, which was being revised when the article was written, in 1982.[1] She comments: "The fourth draft of the executive order sends a chilling message to government classifiers: When in doubt, classify.

"Among its features, the . . . draft executive order:

• Lowers the minimum standard for classification by eliminating the requirement of 'identifiable' harm to national security.
• Requires rather than permits classification of any information which meets the minimum standard.
• Eliminates the 'balancing test' which requires a weighing of public interest in disclosure against the asserted harm to national security when public access to classified information is requested.
• Eliminates specific prohibitions against classifying basic scientific research information and other privately developed ideas that do not use or reveal classified materials."

These features of the executive order indicate that a number of mutually conflicting interests underlie the problems the Executive Order addresses: the U.S. interest in security is, for example, in conflict with the public interest regarding access to information on the research and development of new technologies. Also, the U.S. interest in vigorous research and development of such technologies, which requires a significant freedom of exchange of information, conflicts with its interest in controlling the results of such research and development, which calls for secrecy.

A moral question at the center of the controversy is, What policy regarding secrecy in research and development of new technologies is justified in present world circumstances? This raises the methodological and moral question of how one would go about answering it. Rosemary Chalk addresses the latter problem in her commentary on the NAS Report. This report was the outgrowth of discussions by a panel charged by the National Academy of Science with examining the various aspects of applying controls to scientific communication, and with suggesting how to balance competing national interests so as to best serve the general welfare. Chalk states that the panel could have proceeded in either of two ways: it could have asked, How much openness is desirable and what risks, including military risks, should a nation accept to maintain its open character?; or it could have asked, What controls should be introduced to avoid running certain military risks, assuming that they are undesirable. The NAS panel, Chalk argues, asked the second question, thereby accepting "a set of unstated premises about the military's right to dictate how national security interests should be protected in times of national conflict." Chalk acknowledges that the NAS panel "identified four major benefits" resulting from national policies that encourage openness: "national resiliency, effective political authority, a responsive democracy, and adaptation to changing circumstances." The panel, however, "emphasized . . . that costs to military strength resulting from a policy of openness are also high." In this regard, Chalk raises a number of issues related to ethics as a branch of inquiry: "Are these costs comparable? If so, what criteria should be used to determine which costs are acceptable? Are both costs restorable over the same time frame, or is one set of interests more vulnerable than the other?" Further questions suggested by this discussion may prove fruitful in a critical approach to this selection: Are the above questions adequate for dealing with balancing the conflicting interests involved? Or are they too abstract? Should the existence of controversy about attempts to control scientific communication for the sake of national security be a factor in assessing proposed policies, or even approaches for establishing what policies are justified? Should the fact that, though there is no war, the international situation has worsened and détente is gone make a difference? This is related to the discussion in Part III concerning the need for meaningful dialogue, however heated, in order to preserve the conditions under which considerations of rights —including rights to exchange information freely—are relevant, and life can flourish without oppression.[2]

FREEDOM OF INQUIRY, TRADE SECRETS, PATENTS, AND COPYRIGHTS

All selections in this part deal with conflicts between the interests of inquiry and other interests that, in two of the selections, are military. The other selection, however, emphasizes the constant tension between the interests of inquiry and economics. This emphasis is clear in the title, University/Corporate Research Agreements. The author, Peter Barton Hutt, states that there is no conflict between the goals of universities and those of corporations, but there is a permanent tension between theoretical research and a market economy; that basic research is always in a precarious position and, in order to undertake scientific research, one must make some accommodation to those who are willing to fund it. According to the author, the "real issue . . . is how far the university should bend in order to obtain research funds, and where it should draw the line." Most of the article is devoted to answering this question as regards, for example, patents, trade-secret information, and the assignment of copyrights.

This is another instance in which the need for meaningful dialogue, bargaining, and negotiation is central in working out the differences between various interests. For not only is it often the case that differences cannot be worked out beforehand, but often it is impossible to know beforehand what these differences are! Especially when new technologies are concerned, the participants themselves often have not established what their interests actually are, and thus they must engage, not only in bargaining and negotiation, but in interaction with the technologies and research concerns involved in order to determine what is important to them.[3] These considerations reflect the pragmatic element in the basic theoretical framework. It may accordingly be fruitful, with this framework in mind, to reflect on the selection with the help of the following questions: How should the interests of researchers, the public, and corporations be balanced against each other in dealing with such matters? Should property rights serve to balance these interests? What are property rights, and on what grounds and through what procedures can one establish how far the property rights relevant to research activities extend? Can the interests of researchers, universities, and corporations involved in research in new technology projects be balanced simply by referring to their nature and the relation to the projects of the researchers, universities, and corporations involved? Or should, for example, the fact that there *is* controversy and even confrontation about establishing a balance make a difference? The latter question informs the discussions in Part IV just as the more general question—Does the fact that there is controversy and confrontation make any difference in technology policy making?—informs the discussions in the book as a whole. In addressing the above questions, two more arise: If the fact that there is controversy and confrontation about matters of technology does make a difference, what difference does it make? And what, if any, should be the role of bargaining and negotiation in dealing with this situation? As we have argued in previous parts, and will discuss in further detail in Parts V and VI, bargaining and negotiation are crucial to effective and morally acceptable technology policy making. At any rate, it should be helpful to keep the above two questions in mind when critically scrutinizing Part IV's selections.

NOTES

1. After years of debate, the U.S. Congress finally approved a four-year extension of the 1979 Export Administration Act during the last week of June 1985. The Act had expired in September 1984. For reactions to this legislation and previous developments connected with it, see *Science News* (July 6, 1985), p. 5; (December 8, 1984), p. 358; (February 25, 1984), p. 117; (June 4, 1983), p. 357; (April 24, 1983), p. 218; (October 9, 1982), p. 229; (March 27, 1982), p. 218; and (October 17, 1981), p. 252.

2. Though the notion of flourishing without oppression has not been mentioned in previous parts of this book, it was involved in their discussions, as it is really a specific concern within the relations between considerations of happiness, of rights, and pragmatic considerations discussed in Part III.

3. This point is not peculiar to technology research and development controversies. It is rather frequent in a variety of technology controversies. See, for example, the discussion in the introduction to Part III.

26

Secrecy in Science: A Contradiction in Terms?

LOIS R. EMBER

Lois R. Ember discusses the controversy between scientists and engineers, who argue that secrecy can stifle inquiry in their areas, and government officials, who argue that national security requires secrecy controls. The article outlines the legal and political background of the controversy, and focuses on the Executive Order on Security Classification, which was being revised at the time the article was published, in 1982.

Last year six of the nine Nobel Prizewinners in science were Americans, a clear sign of the country's scientific pre-eminence. In the future, fewer Americans will be able to scale those heights, some researchers claim, if the Reagan Administration, in the name of national security, erects legal and regulatory barriers to the free exchange of scientific information.

The barriers—some in place, some now being revised—long have been on the books. But over the past few years some have been invoked in novel ways and others are being redrafted to subject more types of information to regulation and classification. In isolation none have drawn the ire of the scientific community. But taken together, they have evoked cries of consternation from a vocal minority of researchers, some supported by their universities or professional societies.

These cries of concern for scientific enterprise have been muted and infrequent. Yet one government official, who has asked not to be named, calls scientists "emotional brats." He says, "The image of an embattled, power-less, and divided academic community hold-

ing the high ground against a unified government juggernaut is just not accurate."

True. Neither side is organized. Scientists and engineers have yet to define the limits beyond which they believe government standardization, oversight, and regimentation could stifle innovation. The government has yet to articulate its legitimate concerns by defining clearly how much security damage results from normal scientific communication of basic, unclassified research.

Until recently, the scientific community has not heard from those within government who understand that free discourse is the lifeblood of creative science—the alchemy that transmutes science into technology and technology into products that enhance the nation's security. Instead it has heard vague danger signals being sounded by defense and intelligence hardliners and echoed by the President's science adviser.

A CALL TO ARMS

Last year the Defense Department released its "Soviet Military Power" brochure, which

Reprinted from *Chemical and Engineering News* 60, no. 17 (April 5, 1982), pp. 10–17. Copyright © 1982 American Chemical Society. Reprinted with permission of the American Chemical Society.

alleges that the Soviets have an overpowering military advantage—an advantage that has been aided, in part, by the American scientific community through exchanges, meetings, and "professional/open literature." Last January, Adm. Bobby R. Inman, Deputy Director of the Central Intelligence Agency, warned scientists at an American Association for the Advancement of Science meeting that "there will be pressure for legislation to stop the hemorrhage of the nation's technologies."

A month later, in a *New York Times* interview, the President's Science Adviser George A. Keyworth II echoed Inman: "Nobody is talking about putting a wrench on the nut of academic freedom. But there is a real hemorrhage of technology flowing to the Soviet Union."

Still another-month later, CIA Director William J. Casey said that American R&D—and western technology in general—"has contributed to the increased accuracy, sophistication, precision, power, and countermeasure capability of the Soviet arsenal. . . . We found that scientific exchange is a big hole." And Defense Secretary Caspar W. Weinberger played his variation on this theme; "The Soviets have organized a massive, systematic effort to get advanced technology from the West" to support their military buildup. "Merely reading the full range of technical literature openly published gives the Soviets the ability to repair and maintain products they have acquired illegally," he added.

Academic researchers might have noted, then forgotten these remarks had they not been accompanied by government efforts to contain the flow of technical information in the name of national security. For example:

• A novel interpretation of export control rules that allowed the Commerce Department to exclude Eastern bloc scientists from meetings on computer bubble memories and laser fusion technologies.
• The use of export controls by the departments of State and Defense to limit the access of foreign nationals—scientists and students—to university laboratories performing unclassified research.

• An unprecedented, voluntary scheme cajoled from academic cryptologists by Adm. Inman last year when he headed the supersecret National Security Agency, under which researchers submit papers on code making and breaking to NSA for review before submitting the papers for publication. This year, he called for an extension of this system to a broad range of disciplines.
• A draft executive order on security clasification that, if signed by the President in its present form, would, some feel, catch basic scientific research in its wide net.

Instead the remarks and actions by national security-minded government officials have prompted protests from scientists at prestigious universities and the adoption of a sweeping resolution by the AAAS council opposing "governmental restrictions on the dissemination, exchange, and availability of unclassified knowledge." Other professional groups, including the American Chemical Society, are monitoring the issue closely and lending support to a National Academy of Sciences' effort to find an accommodation. A dialogue between university representatives and the Defense Department over security controls on science is under way, and similar communication is being sought with the departments of Commerce and State.

At the same time, Commerce is in the process of revising its Export Administration Regulations (EAR) and State is redrafting its International Traffic in Arms Regulations (ITAR). Both sets of rules will control the export of militarily critical technologies (including some research now being conducted on university campuses) to U.S. adversaries. The rules have been long in the revision process. The agencies realize that if they are written too broadly they could raise Constitutional issues, and if they are applied too stringently they could hamper scientific enterprise.

"We don't want to intrude unnecessarily on the free exchange of ideas. It's conterproductive. On the other hand, we don't like to see some of our best applied research going out the door where it can come back to haunt us," says Stephen Bryen, Assistant Secretary of Defense for International Economics, Trade, and Security Policy.

Until recently the clash between academia and government has been more emotional than reasoned—knee-jerk responses to a fluid, ill-defined situation. Scientists who cherish academic freedom may have overreacted from uncertainty. The government has yet to define what it means by national security, which, "once unpinned from physical security and war," warns George Washington University law professor Mary Cheh, "becomes hard to confine." Also, the government has yet to explain what it means by basic research, applied research, and technology. Officials slide freely from one term to another, confounding academic researchers. University researchers have yet to be told which disciplines are critical to the military and, thus, sensitive. Some definitions may evolve from the many ongoing dialogues if the government doesn't hold to Inman's belief that: "Specified details about why information must be protected are, more often than not, even more sensitive than the basic technical information itself."

On the other hand, by making fitful stabs at implementing a new protectionist policy, government officials may have overreacted out of zeal. Building on efforts begun under former President Jimmy Carter, the Reagan Administration seems intent on using trade, including technology transfer, as a strategic weapon to check the growth of the Soviet economy and military might. Academic scientists are pawns in this game.

The 1980 Presidential election brought both a change in political parties and a philosophical shift in world view. The death of détente again raised the heinous specter of Soviet military prowess stalking the globe. According to the Administration this military might is sustained by U.S. technology acquired by the Soviets through stealth and study. Stealth—the clandestine acquisition of hardware and know-how or the legitimate purchase through third countries of the Western Alliance. Study—the reading of the open scientific and technical literature; attentive ears at conferences and seminars; and advance study at pre-eminent universities. Indeed, some government officials argue that the very openness that U.S. researchers thrive on and the dynamic scientific enterprise demands is crippling our national security and hampering economic prosperity.

There are valid points being made on both sides of the issue. The thorny problem is finding the appropriate balance between security derived from secrecy and security derived from progress.

Rep. George E. Brown Jr. (D.-Calif.), a member of the House Science and Technology Committee, insists, however, that "there is no security for our country through the repression of the development of new knowledge. Our only protection comes from our pre-eminence in developing new, basic knowledge and new technologies."

However, "the tendency in this Administration toward restricting the flow of scientific and technological information is merely part of a larger world view with which I fundamentally disagree—the inevitability of a conflict between the good guys (us) and the bad guys (the Soviets)," Brown explains. If the U.S. continues down this repressive path, Brown thinks, it will become the "mirror image" of the Soviets, ultimately snuffing out the most important aspects of scientific creativity and technological innovation: the inspiration and motivation to develop.

According to Brown, "the existing boundaries of secrecy are probably greater than they need to be for any rational protection of our core national security interests." Indeed, "the breadth of what can be done under existing regulation is very great," he says. And he is puzzled by the Administration's efforts to change existing regulations. It already has been shown that "they can be used to prohibit almost anything," Brown says.

CONTROLS AT HAND

But in some cases, the changes have been mandated by Congress to accommodate an altered concept of what needs to be controlled. For example, the Commerce Department has the dubious distinction of promoting trade while, at the same time, prohibiting the export of "sensitive" technologies. Commerce administers the Export Administration Act of 1979 through its implementing Export Administration Regulations and a Commodity Control List. With the exception of munitions, which are controlled by a separate law, all exports, including the transfer of "technical data," are prohibited unless authorized by a Commerce Department license or regulation.

The 1979 Act shifts the emphasis from controlling the export of individual products to controlling the export of the skills, techniques, and know-how associated with classes of critical technologies. The Act also shifts the focus to "active" mechanisms of transfer such as technical exchanges, seminars or workshops, and training agreements. To accommodate these shifts, Commerce is in the process of revising EAR and the Commodity Control List. The latter will incorporate some of those technologies on the Defense Department's classified Militarily Critical Technologies List.

Even without revision, the definition of technical data is so broad and the list of commodities controlled so extensive that a wide range of information can be curbed. In 1980, Commerce invoked EAR to exclude Soviet scientists from meetings on bubble memories and laser fusion. It also has used the rules to monitor the activities of foreign graduate students.

Under the Arms Export Control Act of 1976, the State Department maintains a Munitions List and via the International Traffic in Arms Regulations (ITAR) prohibits the import or export of items on this list unless a license is obtained. "Technical data" is on the list and is so broadly defined that even domestic publication or presentation of unclassified data is swept under its control.

ITAR has been used to ban Eastern bloc scientists and engineers from meetings in the U.S. and to ban foreign graduate students from some courses in computer science, physics, and engineering. ITAR also has been invoked in an attempt to restrict the publication of nongovernment cryptology papers.

Table 26.1. Government's cornucopia of information controls

1. Export Administration Act of 1979. Commerce Department controls nonmunition, sensitive technologies, including technical data, through Export Administration Regulations and a Commodity Control List.
2. Arms Export Control Act of 1976. State Department controls munitions and munition-related technical data via International Traffic in Arms Regulations and a Munitions List.
3. Atomic Energy Act of 1954. Classified and nonclassified information on nuclear weapons and nuclear energy is considered "restricted data" and is "born classified"; that is, it is a government secret until affirmatively declassified.
4. Inventions and Secrecy Act of 1951. Applications to Commerce's Patent and Trademark Office are reviewed by defense agencies. If publication of the patent is judged harmful to the national security, a secrecy order is issued on the invention, which becomes a government secret for one year. Orders are renewable each year.
5. Executive order on security classification. Now being revised, the draft order, among other things, lowers the minimum standard for classification and removes specific prohibitions against classifying basic scientific research information.

A nonbinding 1978 opinion from the Department of Justice found ITAR provisions unconstitutional because they established prior restraint on publication of cryptographic information developed by scientists in the private sector. This opinion, however, is the likely genesis of Inman's successful call for a *voluntary* prepublication review system.

Under both ITAR and EAR, information in the public domain is exempt from export controls. But how can new ideas get into the public domain if government can use export controls to prevent publication or communication of private, unclassified ideas? Narrowing the scope of the regulations is one answer, and supposedly the ongoing revision processes in State and Commerce are expected to do this.

Although the export regulations pose a potential threat to academic freedom, the Atomic Energy Act of 1954 is an actual threat to such freedom. However, the government has, on the whole, enforced the law in an "enlightened" manner and rarely has forced public confrontation, Harold Green, Professor Emeritus of George Washington University's National Law Center, told an AAAS meeting in January.

Under provisions of the Act, almost all information, classified, or not, on nuclear weapons and nuclear energy is considered "restricted data," and is a government secret as soon as it is conceived. And as the 1979 *Progressive* case demonstrated, even declassified information reworked in a new combination by a private individual is "born classified."

The *Progressive* case is one of the few instances when the Department of Energy (descendant of the Atomic Energy Commission) has sought to push matters to judicial confrontation. DOE tried to prevent *Progressive* magazine from publishing an article on how the hydrogen bomb works. All the material for the article was in the public domain. But DOE argued that the "reworked" information was not declassified and was, therefore, restricted data. An appellate court agreed and suppressed publication. The decision became moot when similar information was published elsewhere. Eventually *Progressive* published the article.

However, the court ruling still stands and is the first prior restraint on publication order ever issued. Whether the ruling would have been upheld by the Supreme Court is uncertain. In another prior restraint case, the Pentagon Papers case, the Supreme Court ruled that the papers would not cause immediate, direct, and irreparable harm, conditions that must be satisfied to justify infringement of First Amendment rights. Publication was allowed, and no perceivable harm was dealt the U.S.

Still not satisfied with the sweeping reach of the Act, this Administration sought and won an amendment to the DOE appropriations bill that allows the Energy Secretary to regulate the flow of unclassified or declassified information relating to nuclear weapons or facilities. Persons disclosing restricted information can be fined civil penalties of up to $100,000.

Success generates imitators, and laws are no exception to this rule. A cousin to the Atomic Energy Act has been dropped into the House hopper. H.R. 109, introduced by Rep. Charles E. Bennett (D.-Fla.), would extend the born-classified concept to militarily critical technologies—ideas as well as hardware.

For more than 30 years, the government has had control over private ideas through a legislative vehicle called the Invention Secrecy Act of 1951. This law allows defense agencies to review applications submitted to Commerce's Patent and Trademark Office to determine whether publication of the patent "would be detrimental to the national security." If a positive finding is made, a secrecy order is issued; the invention becomes a government secret for one year, with continuous renewals possible. The law provides for an appeals mechanism and for an appeals mechanism and for "just compensation" to the inventor.

According to law professor Cheh, the secrecy provisions of the law have never been challenged on First Amendment grounds. Some legal commentators, she says, believe that if so challenged, the law would be declared unconstitutional, an infringement of freedom of speech.

The government has no specific statutory authority to control the dissemination of nongovernment cryptographic research. Instead, it has relied on ITAR and the Invention Secrecy Act. Under the latter, secrecy orders were issued on an encryption device invented by University of Wisconsin professor George I. Davida and on a voice scrambler developed by three private inventors. Attendant publicity got both orders lifted. Adm. Inman, then head of NSA, said the order on the Davida application was a bureaucratic error; he never explained why the second order was lifted.

Several House committees and the private Center for National Security Studies, headed by Morton H. Halperin, are trying to focus the glare of publicity on a draft executive order on security classification. The draft as written reverses a 30-year trend toward reducing classified information. As in the two cryptologic cases, these groups hope that publicity will force the Administration to moderate its stance. The fourth draft of the executive order sends a chilling message to government classifiers: When in doubt, classify.

Among its features, the Reagan Administration's draft executive order:

• Lowers the minimum standard for classification by eliminating the requirement of "identifiable" harm to national security.
• Requires rather than permits classification of any information which meets the minimum standard.
• Eliminates the "balancing test" which requires a weighing of public interest in disclosure against the asserted harm to national security when public access to classified information is requested.
• Eliminates specific prohibitions against classifying basic scientific research information and other privately developed ideas that do not use or reveal classified materials.

Thus the executive order paves the way for government efforts to control the spread of scientific information generated by private individuals and institutions. "The government has two ways to handle sensitive information," Allan R. Adler, an attorney with the Center for National Security Studies, says. "It can classify it or restrict foreign dissemination through export controls. The executive order lowers the threshold standard for classification and could be used to classify information now being restricted by export controls."

Law professor Cheh agrees with Adler. She explains: "If an individual seeks a license to export technology—and recall that "export" may include simple domestic or foreign publication of information—such information may be said to be 'under the control of the U.S. government' and thus subject to the proposed executive order. If it concerns 'the vulnerabilities or capabilities or systems, installations, projects, or plans relating to the national security,' the information can be classified as secret or confidential. Almost any information can fall under this heading."

Cheh also believes that the order may have the nonsalutary effect of increasing the num-

Table 26.2. NAS panel on scientific national security issues

Dale R. Corson, Chairman; physicist, President Emeritus, Cornell University
Richard C. Atkinson, Chancellor, University of California, San Diego
John Deutch, Dean of Science, Massachusetts Institute of Technology
Robert H. Dicke, Einstein Professor of Physics, Princeton University
Edward Ginzton, President, Varian Associates, Palo Alto, Calif.
Mary Good, Vice President, UOP Inc., Des Plaines, Ill.
Norman Hackerman, President, Rice University
James R. Killian, President Emeritus, Massachusetts Institute of Technology
Franklin Lindsay, Chairman, executive committee, ITER Corp., Lexington, Mass.
Richard A. Meserve, Covington & Burling, Washington, D.C.
Wolfgang K. H. Panofsky, Director, Stanford Linear Accelerator Center, Stanford University
William J. Perry, Hambrecht & Quist, San Francisco
Samuel C. Phillips, Vice President and General Manager, TRW Energy Products Group, Los Angeles
Alexander Rich, Sedgwick Professor of Biophysics, MIT
John D. Roberts, Provost, California Institute of Technology
Charles Slichter, University of Illinois, Urbana-Champaign
Michael I. Sovern, President, Columbia University
Elmer B. Staats, Washington, D.C.

ber of invention secrecy orders issued (currently about 300 are issued each year). It also may encourage "efforts to extend the 'born classified' concept of the Atomic Energy Act to privately developed technological information," she says.

The proposed order also allows for reclassification of previously declassified information. Adler asks: "What does this mean to someone developing a private idea using information that had been affirmatively declassified but has now been reclassified?"

That question and many others never have been answered by the Administration. Both the Justice Department and the National Security Council declined to send witnesses to hearings on the executive order before the House Subcommittee on Government Information and Individual Rights, chaired by the Oklahoma Democrat Glenn English.

Adler says the Administration is in the process of reviewing comments on the draft and, with some changes, "could issue the order within the next two weeks." One committee staff member says that even if the order is issued substantially unchanged, Congress is unlikely to take any action to redress any problems statutorily this year.

OTHER CONTROL MECHANISMS

As all-encompassing as the laws and administrative controls previously mentioned appear to be, the government has other vehicles at its command to control the exchange of scientific information. One is the State Department-sponsored, NAS-administered scientific exchange program. Another is the voluntary censorship program wrestled from cryptologists last year by NSA.

The scientific exchange programs between the Academy of Sciences of the U.S.S.R. and NAS have been going on quietly for years. And for years NAS, without questioning, has been passing along to host universities the State Department's restrictions on visiting scientists. But this February, Stanford University balked publicly at rigid restrictions placed on topics that Soviet robotics expert Nikolay V. Umnov would be allowed to discuss with scientists at Stanford and three other universities. Stanford said it would host Umnov's visit if the restrictions were altered, and the university was absolved from policing Umnov's off-campus activities.

The State Department placed the restrictions on Umnov's visit as a result of its review process for determining if or how to issue a visa to the Soviet scientist. Foreign Service Officer James Jatras says, "From our point of view there is nothing in the Umnov case that represents any change in past policy, no tightening of restrictions. The only thing about the Umnov case is that Stanford reacted publicly."

For its public protest, Stanford got a "clarification" of the State Department-imposed strictures. Umnov would be allowed access to "research intended to result in openly available documents, or for presentation in lectures, seminars, or other academic forums," and Stanford would not have to monitor his off-campus activities. Given this clarification Stanford said it would host Umnov's visit.

Still it is not clear whether Umnov will be allowed to visit U.S. universities. According to Jatras, State still is reviewing the universities' replies "to see if we have a basis for an agreement or if there are still problems." Umnov has not yet applied officially for a visa. And even if he does, Deputy Assistant Secretary of Commerce for Export Administration Bohdan Denysyk says his agency "is looking into requiring an export license of Stanford and other universities" for Umnov's visit. And, he adds, "Based on current sanctions against the Soviet Union because of Poland, we likely will not issue a license."

Stanford reports, perhaps with some glee, that even as the Umnov brouhaha continues, another unnamed Soviet expert on walking machines is "quietly working" at Stanford "with the full knowledge of the State Department."

And with some chagrin over its past role as an unthinking messenger, NAS says that designated staff officers will review restrictions proposed by the government to determine whether they are "workable and compatible with the general procedures for conducting unclassified research in an academic environment."

Another mechanism which can be used to keep science secret is funding. In the name of national security, the National Security Agency asked that the National Science Foundation turn funding of cryptographic research over to it. NSF appeared ready to concede to NSA's request when a respected cryptographer balked. The foundation's spine stiffened somewhat: It still funds academic cryptographic research, but NSA can review and comment on applications.

NSA was more successful in another effort. Concerned that free dissemination of cryptographic research could enable other countries to harden their codes and make it more difficult for NSA to eavesdrop, as well as make it easier for other countries to crack America's cryptosystems, Adm. Inamn, then NSA's director, asked the American Council on Education to form a public cyrptography study group in 1980. The group was charged with devising a mechanism that would prevent a clash between national interests and scientists' First Amendment rights to perform research and publish their results.

A year later the group recommended a voluntary system of prior restraint. Researchers, on a voluntary basis, could submit their papers to NSA for review prior to publication in scientific journals. This was an unprecedented concession by private citizens to a government not at war.

The University of Wisconsin's Davida, who was one member of the study group, objected. In a dissenting opinion he wrote that, "the effects of withholding basic or applied research results relating to cryptography would handicap researchers, not only in data security, but in computer science and engineering and allied areas. . . . The long-term consequences would no doubt be harmful to the nation" and its national interests. And by national interests, Davida includes the protection of private, civilian information—computerized financial and medical records, electronic fund transfers, and even electronic mail.

Elsewhere Davida has written that the group's concession to NSA could serve as a precedent for NSA forays into the control of information from other disciplines, and as a precedent for future legislation. Davida tells C&EN that he "has been vindicated by Inman's remarks" at the AAAS meeting in January.

Indeed for Inman—who surfaces from the intelligence community infrequently and then is very circumspect—those were intemperate remarks. He allowed as how the voluntary censorship of cryptography research papers was working well: 25 papers had been submitted to NSA, which found no problems with any of them. But then he implied that such a

system should be extended to a broad range of other research with military or even economic implications for national security.

Inman's suggestion is that security-minded government agencies receive research proposals or papers during "the peer review process (prior to the start of research and prior to publication)" to review them for "potential harm to the nation." He ticked off fields in addition to advanced weapon design and cryptography that could be candidates for such review: "computer hardware and software, other electronic gear and techniques, lasers, crop projections, and manufacturing procedures."

The debate between government and scientists could take the form of a "nice intellectual dialogue," Inman said. But then he warned the scientists that once the public becomes enraged by the massive "hemorrhage" of sensitive technologies to the Soviets, Congress could overreact by passing repressive legislation. "I think the tides are moving, and moving pretty fast, towards legislative solutions that are likely to be more restrictive, not less restrictive, than the voluntary" system taken with cryptology.

VOLUNTARY CONTROLS

Before scientists too quickly embrace the voluntary approach to prior restraint, they ought to consider this: The cryptology system never has been tested. And it's a good thing it hasn't because the mechanism for resolving disagreements has not been put in place. The five-member advisory committee, whose members were to be selected by the NSA director and the President's science adviser from a list of nominees provided by NAS, does not exist. NAS president Frank Press tells C&EN that he would want to be helpful, but he would have a problem providing a list of names to the science adviser. That action, Press says, "would imply that we endorse the process without us having taken part in the deliberations that led up to it."

And scientists also ought to consider this: Government can control more information under a system of voluntary prior restraint than the courts are likely to allow it under a legislative scheme.

Court rulings on Constitutional questions of free speech or, in this case, legislated prior restraint schemes to protect national security fall under the "clear and present danger" doctrine. The courts have ruled that laws regulating free speech "have to be narrowly tailored," law professor Cheh explains. For a law to be upheld by the courts, the government would have to show that the information communicated presented the danger of direct, immediate, and irreparable harm.

Furthermore, Cheh points out, in those cases in which "secrecy controls over private information have become public"—as in the *Progressive* case and the two cryptographic invention secrecy orders mentioned earlier— "the government has been unable to substantiate alleged threats to national security."

It is Cheh's view that Inman and those like him in government are keen on voluntary schemes because it saves them from going to Congress "and having to fight in that public arena." And if they can extract voluntary schemes from the academic community they can garner more control over a wider variety of information "than any court would sustain, even if legislation were passed," she says.

SUBTLE DEFENSES NEEDED

In a cogent study for the Defense Advanced Research Projects Agency entitled "Selling the Russians the Rope?", Rand researcher Thane Gustafson argues that "critical military technologies" may have to be controlled on a case-by-case basis, as they are now, to prevent "clear and immediate military use of American technology by the Soviets." But more "subtle defenses" are needed for those channels of technology transfer that are the normal modes of exchange used by university researchers and which offer only "indirect military advantages" to the Soviets, Gustafson contends.

Certainly for some research areas, and for some prescribed period of time, voluntary controls may be a salutory "subtle defense" mechanism. But the defense and intelligence communities are going to have to come to the academic community with convincing reasons for such constraints on what to date has been a successful unfettered enterprise.

And one of the forums the national security-minded officials can use is the NAS committee set up to study the issue of possible regulation of the dissemination of scientific and technical information. As NAS President Press explains, the panel will review both basic and applied academic research areas for which the government claims damage to national interests if results are disseminated widely through graduate-level seminars, publication, and other normal channels of communication. The committee, he says, "would like to understand what kind of research areas are critical in this sense." But the panel also will examine "damage to our ability to maintain a world leadership position in these areas if we control them," Press adds.

Attempts to control what Gustafson calls "active" transfer mechanisms and what academicians consider normal academic freedom "may inhibit unimpeded and rapid international communication of technical skills and information at a time when the U.S. is moving from the position of a dominant supplier of leading technology to that of a beneficiary of foreign advances, and is therefore increasingly dependent upon free exchange," Gustafson writes.

In fact, as a result of a recent recommendation of a Defense Science Board Panel, the Defense Department is working with the Association of American Universities to set up task forces which will develop guidelines for the dissemination of information resulting from DOD-sponsored research in a few, very specific technologies. These guidelines will serve as alternate solutions to excessive classification and too restrictive export control laws.[1]

The Defense Science Board recognized an essential truth, most vividly explained by Gustafson: "Regulation, however well-intentioned, introduces screens and filters between the perception of an opportunity for innovation and the inspiration and incentive to take advantage of it." If the U.S. intends to maintain its technological lead, he writes, it should first remain a country of "good innovators." And he warns: "We should beware lest we hobble ourselves, as the Soviet system has so clearly succeeded in doing in the greater part of its industry."

Parts of the Pentagon seem to have heard the message. "We must maintain the proper balance between two competing objectives," says Francis B. Kapper, Director of Military Technology Sharing in the Defense Department. "The need to push and exploit technologies to their maximum must be balanced against the need to control the unauthorized release of militarily critical technologies to our adversaries," he explains. But extending the born-classified concept to the basic sciences would be a "tragic mistake," Kapper says. And yet he, too, believes that university researchers may have to accept prior restraint of publication in some militarily sensitive research areas.

Kapper's boss, Undersecretary of Defense for Research and Engineering Richard DeLauer, however, says that he doesn't "advocate any prior restraints unless they are part of the contractual relationship, I'm trying move away from an adversarial approach." And indeed he is seeking guidance from universities. In turn, DOD plans to provide universities with a clear set of national security concerns, and criteria for recognizing militarily critical technologies.

The mechanism for achieving these goals was suggested to DeLauer by the Association of American Universities and the Defense Science Board: Form a university-defense forum. DeLauer did, naming himself and Donald Kennedy, president of Stanford University, cochairmen of the panel. The group will work on a broad range of issues affecting the DOD-university relationship—training, facilities and instrumentation, the whole crumbling infrastructure of academic sciences—but its first charge will be to look at technology transfer and export controls.

DOD, for the most part, would like to rely on voluntary arrangements with universities and on their sense of patriotism, explains Assistant Secretary for Defense Stephen Bryen. That is, once universities understand the Pentagon's criteria and concerns they will decide what to publish, and even whether foreign nationals should be allowed to study in certain disciplines.

DeLauer believes, and he is supported by the recently released Defense Science Board study, "University Responsiveness to National Security Requirements," that too much emphasis has been placed on technology loss via normal scientific communications channels and too little focus has been placed on the deteriorating state of academic science and engineering.

Still there are those in the defense agencies who readily cite an FBI estimate that the Soviets get as much as 90% of their intelligence from open sources, including normal scientific communication. They also refer to the fact that at least 30% of the graduate students in engineering, mathematics, and computer sciences are foreign nationals (and therefore potential transfer conduits). They agree with Commerce Deputy Assistant Secretary Denysyk that the "scientific exchanges are one-sided," in favor of the Soviets. And they concur with CIA director Casey that "we send scholars or young people to the Soviet Union to study Pushkin poetry; they send a 45-year-old man out of their KGB or defense establishment to exactly the schools and the professors who are working on sensitive technologies."

Might these officials be taking a parochial view, engaging in tunnel-vision? NAS president Press thinks so. "We have a shortage of Soviet experts in this country. If there is any country we should know more about in terms of institutions, how things work, how good they are, what their weaknesses and strengths are, it is the Soviet Union. It is important for us to know about [these things] as it is for us to know about their military systems. And so I think we are pretty smart to send social scientists to the Soviet Union." Press also argues that in recent years the scientific exchanges between the two countries have not been one-sided, that the U.S.S.R. has not gained more than it gave.

After its study is completed, the NAS committee looking at these issues may be able to quantify—no matter how imprecisely—the damage to national security from normal scientific discourse, although DOD's Bryen says that "it is very difficult to document." Scientific communication is "one transfer mechanism, perhaps not a major one, but certainly not an unimportant one," Bryen contends.

In one case, Bryen says, DOD has "done an absolutely thorough analysis of the loss [via the open literature] of information, technical data, and know-how for producing armor-piercing weapons." Over a 10-year period, mostly in the 1960s, "we estimate that the Soviets and Eastern Europeans got 40% of the design know-how for their armor-piercing (antitank) weapons from the open U.S. literature, mostly unclassified research papers and patent information." Most of this research was applied rather than basic: how to go about making the shaped charge or packing the explosive, Bryen says. And by using U.S. sources, the Soviets developed more effective antitank weapons five years sooner than they otherwise would, Bryen contends, which means the U.S. has to "push up its planning and funding to develop countermeasures."

So what can DOD do to prevent similar losses in the future? "We aren't interested in taking Draconian measures," Bryen says. For basic research, DOD probably will rely on voluntary restraint. For applied research, of which DOD has several categories, DOD will rely on more tightly written contracts, which could include classification clauses, and the State Department-implemented ITAR.

The Pentagon has asked that certain militarily critical technologies be incorporated in the revised ITAR, and be controlled via licensing. According to Bryen, among the items DOD would like to see controlled are: very large-scale integrated circuits; certain metallurgical processes, superalloys in particular; isothermal forging; certain types of high-speed computers; computer design and software having military applications; and genetic engineering that can find military application.

Bryen also says that DOD is searching for a solution that is halfway between the unclassified and classified paths—an option that would allow universities such as Stanford, which by charter cannot accept classified research, to perform research for DOD, but without freely disseminating the results. Bryen calls this "DOD proprietary" research, and he says the report of results would go only to DOD. This is akin to arrangements universities have with industry, Bryen points out. DOD is seeking counsel from its university advisers on this concept, he says.

Bryen also says that the Pentagon is working on a prototype decision-making aid—using the semiconductor field as a model system—that would help DOD decide what aspects of a research project to classify. "We are not aiming at just stamping secret or something. That doesn't serve any great purpose. We are looking to be as precise as we can, and we are seeking expert advice now," he says.

COMMERCE TRIES TO NARROW CONTROLS

The academic community also is waiting to see how precise the Commerce Department's revised export control regulations are going to be. Commerce's effort last year "raised Constitutional questions," A. R. Cinquegrana, Justice Department Deputy Counsel for Intelligence Policy, says. But he adds that Commerce, cognizant of the academic community's concerns, did try to exclude formalized classroom instruction and basic research from strict controls.

According to Commerce Deputy Assistant Secretary Denysyk, the current version of the export-adminstration regulations exclude products and technical information in the public domain, basic research that has no applicability to a controlled product, and open classroom instruction. Even the list of items now requiring a license is being whittled down so that those technologies that are not considered to be militarily critical (and will not be on the revised Commodity Control List) will not be controlled, Denysyk says.

Denysyk says he hopes to have the regulations out by July, "but that's approximate right now," he concedes. An employee in an executive branch agency who has seen some of the revised regulations says that "they are not being well defined." Fuzzy definitions raise the specter of Constitutional questions, which may cause Commerce to delay issuing the rules. July might be optimistic.

Commerce not only is trying to sharpen and narrow its control. It also is attempting to include definitions of "proprietary, technical data" that it will control, and clarify the types of U.S. exporters, including universities, subject to control.

For example, Denysyk says that organizers of "closed conferences at which proprietary, technical data are discussed in the presence of communist country attendees" will need an export license. "A university professor will need an export license if he is doing research on robotics, and robotics is controlled commodity, and he has a graduate student from the Soviet Union working on the project, and he wishes to publish proprietary information that is not in the public domain," Denysyk explains. Also likely to be controlled and to require licenses are such sensitive, dual-purpose (commercial/military) technologies as cryptography, superalloys, and gas turbines, he says.

Commerce, Denysyk says, has yet to define these sensitive technologies, although he suspects that there may be about nine general categories of technologies. Certain to be among the general groups are biology (genetic engineering), lasers, computers, microelectronics, aerospace, and manufacturing processes.

"From my perspective," Denysyk says, "it makes no sense to have regulations applied to only one sector of our society. They should apply across the board to all U.S. exporters. If universities are exporting technical data, they should also have the same restrictions placed on them as does U.S. business. What we are really trying to control is proprietary technical data in specific technologies. We are not trying to restrict free speech at all, even in those controlled technologies; we are simply

trying to restrict to whom the data are communicated, and that, we feel, is a valid right of government."

How Commerce's export regulations and the State Department's ITAR are constructed—whether they respect the different natures of the academia and business communities—will determine whether they protect "a valid right of government" or infringe on First Amendment rights.

In February 1981, five university presidents, including Kennedy of Stanford, wrote the Secretaries of Commerce, State, and Defense of their "grave concern" about attempts to extend export controls to academia. They warned that tourniquets of control on the "free flow of information among scientists and engineers would alter fundamentally the system that produced the scientific and technological lead that the government is trying to protect and leave us with nothing to protect in the very near future." NAS president Press believes that that sentiment is felt widely on campuses across the U.S.

To get a better picture of that sentiment, AAAS is polling 100 leading representatives of the scientific and engineering community, seeking their views on the whole realm of issues coalescing under the rubric national security and secrecy in science. The poll will be studied by AAAS's Committee on Scientific Freedom and Responsibility, which also will review a background paper written by member Harold Relyea, senior specialist with the Congressional Research Service. Relyea is trying to develop criteria that could be used to balance scientific freedom against national security concerns, AAAS staff officer Rosemary Chalk says.

Through symposia, position papers, resolutions and elegant broadsides by executive officer William D. Carey, AAAS is striving to clarify the "important issues at stake in the debate," Chalk says. But because the debate is in a state of flux, because the government's position won't be known until it issues regulations, and because the construct of those rules could be shaped by the many ongoing dialogues, AAAS views its role now as educational and informative rather than advocatory. Other professional societies are taking the same tack.

The earlier, more polarized positions taken by the government and the academic community—characterized, a Congressional Research Service specialist laughingly says, by the Albanian proverb "never trust a man with two holes in his nose"—have eased. There are now many structured opportunities for each side to clarify its position. But like insects caught up in a mating dance, it is uncertain whether the two sides will be able to consummate a viable compromise.

The academic community must remember that every Administration has sought to stem leaks and staunch the flow of information. It must however, remind this Administration of the dismal failure of an earlier attempt to prevent nonclassified information from reaching foreigners. In the 1950s, the Office of Strategic Information was spawned by McCarthyism and snuffed out by Sputnik.

NOTE

1. *Chemical and Engineering News* (March 15, 1982), p. 6.

27

University/Corporate Research Agreements

PETER BARTON HUTT

The author discusses the ongoing changes in the relations between universities and corporations in the area of genetic engineering, and the conceptual and moral problems such changes involve. He argues for the need to balance the interests of researchers, the government, and corporations in dealing with these problems, and suggests ways of effecting this with regard to such matters as patents, trade secrets, and copyright ownership.

Universities and corporations have engaged in productive cooperative enterprise for decades.[1] It is thus surprising that, with the impressive new advances in biotechnology, the nature and content of these joint enterprises have recently come under public scrutiny.[2] There is nothing inherent in biotechnology that alters traditional issues that have been raised by these joint ventures for decades, nor is there anything inherent in the nature of a university/corporate agreement that differs fundamentally from a contract between two commercial enterprises.

In light of the increased public attention given to these relationships, however, it is appropriate to review both the conceptual premises on which they are based and also the specific patent issues that they must address. This article addresses both aspects of the matter. The author's thesis is that these agreements, properly constructed, can result in substantial mutual advantages for both parties, as well as for the broader public interest, without harming any fundamental academic, corporate, or social values.

ACADEMIC FREEDOM AND CORPORATE PROFITS

No one can quarrel with the general statements made by university presidents about the essential open and altruistic nature of our great academic centers of learning.[3] A university must indeed exist to foster free inquiry and free exchange of ideas.

Nor can anyone quarrel with the general statements made by corporate officials about the essential profit motive of our great corporate enterprises.[4] A corporation must indeed offer goods or services that will be purchased by the public, at an acceptable rate of profit, or it will shortly disappear.

There is, fortunately, no conflict between these two admittedly different goals. Academic freedom and corporate profits have coexisted and been mutually beneficial for decades. The academic world has educated most corporate officials and has conducted much of the basic research, which has been developed into marketable products by corporations. In turn, corporate profits have been sources of great endowments, yearly gifts, and other funds on which universities depend for their continued existence.

A university must realize that it is one thing to provide an open forum for ideas, but quite another to engage in the enormously expensive type of basic research that characterizes biology and most of the other sciences today. To get from the former to the latter, one needs large sums of money. Since a university cannot conduct basic scientific research without substantial funds, it must forthrightly address the question whence those funds will come and under what limitations.

Because tuitions cannot realistically be raised to cover any significant level of basic research, a university is left with three sources of funding for basic research: the Federal government, private industry, and philanthropy. Of these three potential sources, one would be hard-pressed empirically to argue that any imposes greater restrictions or more onerous limitations than the others. At times, each can be frustratingly parochial and demanding.

Alexis de Tocqueville recognized the problems of financing basic research in *Democracy in America*.[5] He stated that aristocratic societies gave precedence to pure or basic scientific research. In a democracy, however, the profit motive leads inexorably toward emphasis on the application of science in everyday practical terms. He thus argued that "people living in a democratic age are quite certain to bring the industrial side of science to perfection anyhow and that henceforth the whole energy of organized society should be directed to the support of higher studies and the fostering of a passion for pure science."

A PERMANENT TENSION

There is a permanent tension, which will never be overcome, between theoretical research and a market economy. It is the experience of many universities that philanthropical institutions closely resemble industry in their demands for practical applications of science, and Congress is not far behind. As long as Congress is in session, in fact, support for basic research is at peril. Thus, basic research is always in a precarious position.

The pressures on the Federal government to increase its limitations and requirements for funding basic scientific research, rather than to reduce them, have existed for many years and are unlikely to abate in an era of reduced economic growth. In the Spring 1978 issue of *Daedalus,* the author catalogued existing public criticism of Federal support of basic scientific research that has come to his attention in the past several years, and urged the importance of dealing forthrightly with the fundamental reasons why the Federal government should fund such research at universities.[6] Unless and until these public criticisms are adequately met, further erosion in public support for such funding could occur.

The author personally supports major government funding of basic research at universities with a minimum of governmental intervention. He firmly believes that de Tocqueville was right. His concern is that this view—which is shared by most scientists—is not sufficiently shared or understood by the public and its elected representatives.[7]

Thus, like most things in life, one cannot reasonably view academic freedom to pursue scientific research as an absolute principle. Any university that insisted on absolute academic freedom, without any limitations or restrictions, would be obligated to decline most governmental, philanthropic, and corporate funding. The only absolute freedom one has is to think. In order to undertake scientific research one must make some accommodation to those who are willing to fund it.

The author does not find this troubling. Indeed, required research, to be conducted in the so-called real world of competition and limitations, may well be healthier than if true scientific and academic freedom existed in a vacuum. It requires individuals to probe their own motives, to make value choices that are often difficult, to strengthen resistance to the temptation to surrender precious academic principles, and perhaps thus to make better choices and ultimately to produce better research. None of our other most precious freedoms—speech and religion, to name just two—is wholly unfettered.

The real issue, in practical terms, is how far

the university should bend in order to obtain research funds, and where it should draw the line. The author would never suggest a wholly pragmatic approach. Some principles must remain paramount. On the basis of substantial experience, however, the author concludes that neither corporate enterprises nor the Federal government has any interest in destroying the concept of academic freedom. Both have an active interest in promoting academic research and an abiding loyalty to their own academic roots and heritages and thus are, in most instances, quite accommodating. The kinds of limitations that are sought by private enterprise are not as inherently in conflict with a university's principles of academic freedom as many in academia fear. If a rule of reason is used on both sides, the relationship should enrich both rather than provoke confrontation.

ACADEMIC COMPETITION

In this context, it is necessary to recognize that some of the statements of university presidents about the wholly altruistic nature of universities have been unduly sweeping and pretentious. For those of us whose eyes were first opened by *The Double Helix*,[8] who have witnessed the various cheating scandals in science at major academic institutions,[9] and who have read the public accounts of the race for a Nobel prize between two eminent scientists,[10] those protestations of purity and simplicity do not ring true. While universities can indeed be free marketplaces of ideas, they can also be as motivated by competition as the most cutthroat retailer.

Thus, the contention that commercial developments occurring in recombinant DNA research have drastically altered the tendency towards secrecy in university scientists simply has not been proved. Certainly, Watson and, more recently, Schally and Guillemin would put many corporate entrepreneurs to shame.

It is simply not necessary for either universities or corporations to change their fundamental natures in order to enter into productive research agreements. One need only recognize that universities are not and never

have been absolutely open and unrestricted, and that corporations are not and never have been operated solely to make a profit. Where good faith is involved in negotiations between decent people, there is an enormous middle ground on which they can meet.

There are unquestionably compelling reasons counselling against a university directly operating a business. Faculty members must indeed make basic choices in their careers. Once again, however, the author finds it more difficult than many academic administrators to set any bright line between permitted and forbidden faculty involvement with private enterprise.

In Europe, from which the U.S. derives its university tradition, there has always been a very close relationship between private enterprise and the universities. People frequently serve in dual capacities. In the U.S., eminent scientists like Carl Djerassi have successfully bridged the university/corporate gulf without harming either side.

Nor are many of the current university guidelines on this subject as clear as their drafters intended. Some, for example, would prohibit a professor from serving as director of a corporation, even though that same professor could properly serve as a consultant one day a week—involving an amount of time far in excess of that which would be expended in the capacity of director, and undoubtedly much greater remuneration. In short, universities run the risk of establishing the same kind of arbitrary rules that academia distrusts so thoroughly when they are imposed by the Federal government and that invite easy evasion.

One must, on the other hand, be fully mindful of concerns about conflicts of interest. Open disclosure of all faculty consulting and research arrangements provides an excellent solution. But if this is a solution for exposing excesses and thus promoting voluntary self-regulation respecting such relationships, why should it not apply equally to directorships and other types of faculty/corporate relationships? Public disclosure in academia can be as important in assuring wise judgment in such relationships as the Freedom of Information Act[11] and the Government in the Sunshine Act[12] have been important in encouraging good government.

LICENSING OF PATENTS

Perhaps no aspect of university/corporate agreements has engendered greater discussion than exclusive licensing of patents. The purpose of a university, as all will agree, is to promote the public interest. Experience teaches that, in the area of patents, the public interest can in most instances only be promoted by exclusive licenses. This was the conclusion of the 1968 report of the General Accounting Office (which certainly is not known for ignoring the public interest or giving away government property), which recommends exclusive licenses for NIH patents[13] and, more recently, the Patent Amendments of 1980.[14] In this competitive market economy, private enterprise will not invest funds to develop ideas that can be copied with impunity. Without exclusive licenses, important inventions may remain undeveloped and thus unavailable to the public.

This does not mean, of course, that methods cannot be found to make certain that exclusive licenses are not abused. Reservation of march-in rights can readily serve this purpose.

Similarly, contracting for the exclusive services of a faculty member—where that enables the faculty member to conduct research that otherwise would be impossible—should not automatically be condemned as bringing improper proprietary motives within the university. This implies that money will clearly corrupt faculty members into doing things that they otherwise would not do. To reach this conclusion, one must have a very poor opinion of the faculty. A more optimistic approach would be to suggest that, in return for reasonable conditions, faculties be given increased freedom to pursue research of a nature in which they are deeply interested and committed to and which may lead to important advances in public health. It is, in short, a matter of how one wishes to view it. University direction and control over research done

under an exclusive contract can, of course, be maintained.

It is inevitably the academic humanist, rather than the academic scientist, who most distrusts all university/corporate agreements. Perhaps this is a function of the fact that scientists are far more likely to be approached to enter into such agreements.

Nowhere is the diversity of views on this subject more evident than in the distinction that is often drawn in university policy between faculty rights to copyrighted and patented material. Copyrights (which most often are generated by a university's humanists) are routinely assigned to the authors, whereas patents (which most often are generated by a university's scientists) are routinely assigned to the university. The different handling of these rights is best attributed to historical reasons than to any principled distinction.

CORPORATE FUNDING AND PATENT ISSUES

Corporate funding of scientific research at a university immediately raises important patent issues. These issues are complicated by the fact that, in most instances, the corporate-funded research is conducted simultaneously with, and perhaps as an integral part of, similar research that is funded by the Federal government. In entering into any university/corporate agreement, therefore, it is essential that the full implications of the arrangement be thought out in advance and reduced to writing.

This requires that both parties have established policies on these matters and are willing to incorporate them into a written contract. While the issues raised by such contracts may be slightly different, in a few instances, from the issues posed by a contract between two commercial enterprises, they are more similar than many people realize and in large part reflect standard contract principles and sound common sense.

Scientific research at a university may at any time lead to an invention that can be the subject of a patent. If that research is funded by the Federal government, the Patent

Amendments of 1980 and OMB Circular A-124[15] govern the legal obligations and rights of the inventors and the university respecting any invention. If the research is funded by a corporation, the legal obligations and rights of the inventors and the university respecting any invention are governed by the contract between the university and the corporation.

In the case of scientific research funded in whole or even in the smallest part by Federal funds, the university must comply with the obligations imposed by the Patent Amendments of 1980. As interpreted by OMB, these requirements are not overly burdensome. It is important, however, that these obligations be incorporated in a written university policy in order to fully inform the faculty and students about them. It is also important that they be reflected in any university/corporate research agreement to avoid misunderstanding and confusion about the implications of any related Federal funding.

In the case of a contract between the university and a corporation, the university has greater discretion where no part of the research also depends on Federal funds. Policy must be developed to shape the wise and consistent use of that discretion. It is equally important that a written university policy fully inform the faculty and students about the university's intent respecting such contracts to avoid misunderstanding.

The following issues often arise when inventions are made in the course of scientific research. University policy and university/corporate agreements should provide clearly written rules to resolve them.

Reporting of Inventions

The 1980 Amendments and the OMB Circular contain explicit requirements respecting reporting of inventions by a university to a government agency that is funding research at the university. The obligations of faculty members and students to report inventions to the university (and of the university to report such inventions to the government) should be spelled out in university policy.

Basically the same issues arise under a contract for scientific research between a corporation and a university. The contract should make clear whether the researchers have any obligation to report any invention to the university and should state whether the university, in turn, has any obligation to report such invention to the corporation.

Determination of Inventor

Once an invention is made, the identity of the inventor(s) must be promptly determined. This is often a complex issue in the context of collaborative scientific research. A university policy on this matter should designate a specific office within the university to make the initial determination based upon a review of all the pertinent facts (as well as to carry out other university functions respecting patents). An appeals mechanism should be established within the university, with the ultimate decision resting in a faculty committee or a specific university official. There is no need, however, to include any aspect of this procedure in any contract for scientific research with the Federal government or with a corporation.

Ownership of Inventions

When a student, member of the faculty, or other individual connected with a university makes an invention, the question arises whether the individual(s) or the university, or both, owns the rights to that invention. Most university patent policies provide that the university owns or has the right of first refusal to the invention, and that the individual(s) may own the invention only if the university declines to take ownership. Under the 1980 Amendments, the university owns any invention funded by the Federal government (with limited exceptions). When research is funded by a corporation, the contract can provide either that the university or the corporation will own the invention.

The person who owns the invention will be responsible for any patent application. Under the 1980 Amendments, the university must inform the Federal agency about any invention within 2 months after the inventor discloses it to the university. The university then has 12 months from the date it learned of the invention to determine whether or not to retain title to the invention. If it concludes not to retain title, the Federal agency will obtain title. The university must establish rights to the invention throughout the world or convey those rights to the Federal agency. In order to implement these provisions, the university must require, by written agreement, that its employees disclose all inventions and execute all patent applications and other similar documents as required by the 1980 Amendments and the OMB Circular. This obligation of the university can be discharged through a written university policy.

The same issues arise in a contract with a corporation. University policy and standard provisions should also be developed for such contracts.

Inventions Under Faculty Consulting Arrangements

In virtually all universities there is a written or implied agreement that faculty members may consult with corporations and other groups for specified portions of their time (e.g., 20% or one day per week). Faculty members may also work on inventions on their own time (i.e., at night). University policy should establish what time is the faculty's own time (e.g., weekends and vacations) and whether inventions made outside of university time are subject to the same, or different, rules respecting university/faculty reporting, ownership, and royalties. Any contract governing a faculty consulting arrangement with a corporation should reflect this policy.

Waiver of Patent Rights by the University

Although, as a general rule, the university will usually assert ownership of a patent, in some instances the university may choose to waive the rights to a patent. University policy should specify that, under those circumstances, the university's right to the patent will revert to the inventors. In any contract between a corporation and a university, a specific provision should be included to cover this eventuality.

Separation/Commingling of Private/Government Research Projects and Funds

Under the 1980 Amendments, any invention conceived or reduced to practice utilizing any government funds is automatically subject to the provisions of those Amendments and, thus, to some government rights. Some corporations are willing to permit the commingling of corporate and government research projects and funds, with the result that the 1980 Amendments will apply to any resulting invention. Other corporations may insist upon complete separation of such projects and funds, so that any invention resulting from corporate funding will not be subject to any government rights under the 1980 Amendments.

Any contract between the university and a corporation should deal specifically with the issue of separation/commingling of private and government projects and funds. If the university is unwilling to separate such projects and funding, the contract should so state. If the university is willing to separate such projects and funding, the contract should so provide and specify how it will be accomplished. The contract might also provide, in the event of such separation, that the cost of implementing procedures to assure such separation will be borne by the corporation.

If separation is provided, the contract should also include a provision respecting the rights of the parties in the event that separation is unsuccessful and the 1980 Amendments become applicable to an invention also funded by the corporation. In all contracts, it would be wise to explicitly recognize that the 1980 Amendments are applicable if government funds are used in the conception or reduction to practice of any invention, in order to avoid the criticism made by the General Accounting Office of the Massachusetts General Hospital/Hoechst contract.[16]

Control of Research

In the course of any scientific research, questions will arise respecting the exercise of scientific judgment about both the general direction and the specific details of the research involved. Which research opportunities to pursue (and how to pursue them) could be a subject of disagreement. This will seldom occur in Federally funded research. It is more likely to occur in research funded by a corporation. The contract between the corporation and the university should, therefore, explicitly state how such matters will be handled.

In most instances, the university will insist upon exercising final judgment on such matters. It may be appropriate, however, to permit the corporation to express its views before the university makes a final decision in order that the university may have the benefit of all possible considerations and to assure a good working relationship.

Trade-Secret Information

The potential receipt of confidential trade-secret information ordinarily should not arise under Federally funded research grants, but could arise pursuant to a contract with a corporation. Some universities are willing to protect the confidentiality of such information. If the university concludes that, as an entity, it has no means of policing the secrecy of confidential information, it should consider including in the contract a provision stating that it will not receive information subject to confidentiality restrictions. Individuals within the university who are working under specific corporate contracts may then enter into separate confidentiality agreements with the corporations to the extent necessary for the conduct of the research. Any special equipment (e.g., a locked file) or procedures could be paid for by the corporation.

Publication and Public Presentation of Research Results

Scientific research inevitably leads to the development of information that the researcher will wish to make public through oral discussion or written publication, but that, if disclosed, may have adverse patent implications. Public disclosure of such information merely triggers the one-year time period for filing of a patent under United States law, and thus poses no significant issue in this country. Under some foreign laws, however, a patent application must be filed before any public disclosure of the invention, and thus such disclosure may preclude foreign patents.

Where the research is funded by the Federal government, the OMB Circular provides that the university must disclose to the government, at the time that it informs the government about the invention, whether a manuscript describing the invention has been submitted for publication and, if so, whether it has been accepted for publication at that time. At any time thereafter, the university must inform the government if any such manuscript is accepted for publication. This allows the government to make certain that foreign patent rights are protected.

In the context of a contract between a university and a corporation, considerably greater discretion is permitted. It would be wise to include explicit provisions respecting not only submission of manuscripts for publication, but also oral disclosure at scheduled symposia or seminars and even spontaneous oral discussions. Reasonable provisions can be found that will protect both academic freedom and the interests of the corporation in preserving patent rights. A copy of any manuscript can be provided to the corporation when it is submitted for publication, which will, in virtually all instances, be several weeks before it actually appears in print. The corporation can be informed about scheduled presentations at seminars or symposia when such presentations are, in fact, scheduled; this, in virtually all instances, will be more than a month in advance. The possibility of spontaneous oral presentations can sometimes be foreseen (e.g., at scheduled seminars or symposia on the general subject matter), in which case the corporation can be forewarned, but if it is not foreseen, the corporation can be informed immediately thereafter so that appropriate steps can be taken to protect patent rights.

No perfect system can ever be established, but reasonable provisions such as these will take care of the vast majority of situations without encroachment on academic freedom or corporate interests.

Exclusivity of Patent Licenses

Under the 1980 Amendments, if the university obtains a patent to an invention funded by the Federal government, the university has the option of granting exclusive or nonexclusive licenses. Ordinarily, potential licensees will be interested in licenses only if they are exclusive for at least minimum periods of time. It was for this reason that Congress explicitly provided that exclusive licenses would be permissible. The 1980 Amendments include specific provisions designed to prevent abuse of an exclusive license, including reservation of a nonexclusive license in the government and government march-in rights.

Where the university conducts research pursuant to a contract with a corporation, the corporation typically will wish to include in the contract a provision stating that any patent resulting from the research will be licensed exclusively to the corporation, subject, of course, to any government limitations and rights resulting from commingling of private and Federal funds. Ordinarily, a corporation will be unwilling to fund research without this type of provision.

The university may conclude that it has a moral obligation to assure itself that any invention resulting from research conducted on its premises and with its resources is used for the public good. Accordingly, various types of mechanisms can be considered to prevent any abuse of such an exclusive agreement. One method is to limit the breadth of the exclusivity to particular types of products or to the line of business of the corporate enterprise involved, thus assuring that any invention could be the subject of noncompeting licenses in other fields that might otherwise go unexploited. This approach raises difficult issues of definition and implementa-

tion, however, and the time that must be spent in negotiating such provisions, tailored to each individual contract, may be excessive.

A second approach, which circumvents these problems, is to grant an exclusive license, but to include in it required reports respecting commercialization of the license and a reservation of march-in rights for the university where commercialization is not achieved, but is thought feasible by the university. By incorporating this standard process in each such contract, there is virtually no expenditure of time and effort at the time of the execution of the contract, or until such time as commercialization is found inadequate. The latter approach is, therefore, thought by many to be a more cost-effective way of assuring that the university's obligation to the public interest is fully protected.

Royalty Split Between the Government/Corporation and the University/Inventor

Under the 1980 Amendments, all royalties from a patent obtained from government-funded research are given to the university. There is no recoupement by the government.

In a contract between a university and a corporation for scientific research, the future royalty rights, respecting potential inventions not yet conceived or reduced to practice, are typically resolved. A percentage of sales is usually specified as the royalty for the university. On occasion, the corporation may wish to place a cap on the royalties to be paid in any year or to be paid as a total amount.

Royalty Split Between the Inventor(s) and the University

University policy should determine how the royalties from any invention will be utilized. This is entirely a matter of judgment within the university and should be included in a written university statement of policy, but it is not a subject for inclusion in any contract for scientific research with the government or a corporation.

One or more individuals may be the

inventor(s). They may include undergraduate and graduate students as well as faculty and even visiting faculty or people wholly outside the university. A determination must be made whether only faculty, or also students and others, will participate in the royalties, and how those royalties will be divided if there is more than one inventor. It must also be decided whether those royalties will continue to be paid if the individuals should later leave the university and, if so, at the same or at a reduced rate.

The split of royalties among all the inventors as a group and the university must be decided. The disposition of the university's share of the royalties also must be determined. Some or all of the university's share of the royalties might be designated for future research in the department in which the invention occurred.

Use of Name of University or Researcher

The names of the university and the researcher(s) are valuable assets. Their use by a corporation may enhance the marketability of a product resulting from the research. The contract should prohibit such use or should permit it under specific conditions.

Copyright Rights

In addition to potential patents, the research can lead to potential publications, which are subject to copyright rights. The government does not assert any interest in copyright rights or royalties of this nature. In any contract between a corporation and a university, the copyright ownership and the rights to royalties from any copyrighted materials should be specified.

COMPLEX ISSUES IN A COMPLEX SOCIETY

While these may seem like complex issues, they cannot be avoided by any university in today's complex society. The intelligence and productivity of the university faculty make it inevitable that patentable ideas will emerge,

and thus that these issues must be confronted. Corporations, recognizing the public value of sound new ideas generated by the faculties of our great universities, will inevitably seek them out. The public will benefit from these joint ventures, because it is only through commercial enterprise that the most important university-generated ideas can be fully utilized for the public good.

NOTES

1. E.g., L. E. David and D. J. Keyles, "The National Research Fund: A Case Study in the Industrial Support of Academic Science," *Minerva* 12 (1974), p. 207; National Commission on Research, *Industry and the Universities: Developing Cooperative Relationships in the National Interest* (1980); J. W. Servos, "The Industrial Relations of Science: Chemical Engineering at MIT, 1900–1939," *ISIS* 71 (1980), p. 531; and C. E. Kruytbosch, *Academic-Corporate Research Relationships: Forms, Functions, and Fantasies* (Washington, DC: The National Science Foundation, 1981).

2. For information on such agreements, see "Government and Innovation: University-Industry Relations," hearings before the Subcommittee on Science, Research and Technology of the Committee on Science and Technology, US House of Representatives, 96th Congress, First Session (1979); C. E. Krutybosch and D. B. Weisz, *Notes on Practices and Policies in Selected Federal Mission R&D Agencies Concerning University-Industry Research Relationships* (Washington, DC: The National Science Foundation, 1980); B. J. Culliton, "Biomedical Research Enters the Marketplace," *New England Journal of Medicine* 304 (May 14, 1981), p. 1195; "Commercialization of Academic Biomedical Research," hearings before the Subcommittee on Investigations and Oversight and the Subcommittee on Science Research and Technology of the Committee on Science and Technology, US House of Representatives, 97th Congress, First Session (1981); B. D. David, "Profit Sharing Between Professors and the University?" *New England Journal of Medicine* 304 (May 14, 1981), p. 1232; W. Lepkowski, "Research Universities Face New Fiscal Realities," *Chemical and Engineering News* (November 23, 1981); D. Kalergis, *The Role of the University in the Commercialization of Biotechnology* (Charlottesville, VA: University of Vir-

ginia School of Law, 1981); "The View from the Whitehead Institute. *SIPIscope* 10:2 (March–April 1982); J. L. Teich, *Inventory of University-Industry Research Support Agreements in Biomedical Science and Technology,* National Institutes of Health (January 1982); W. Lepkowski, "Academic Values Tested by MIT's New Center," *Chemical and Engineering News* (March 15, 1982); "University/Industry Cooperation in Biotechnology," hearings before the Subcommittee on Investigations and Oversight and the Subcommitee on Science, Research and Technology of the Commitee on Science and Technology, US House of Representatives, 97th Congress, Second Session (1982).

3. E.g., D. C. Bok, "Business and the Academy," *Harvard Magazine,* May–June 1981; A. B. Giamatti, "The University, Industry, and Cooperative Research," *Science* 218 (December 24, 1982), p. 1278.

4. T. D. Kiley, *Licensing Revenue from Universities—Impediments and Possibilities,* Genentech Corporation, December 15, 1982.

5. A. de Tocqueville, *Democracy in America,* Vol. 1, part 1 (1840), ch. 10.

6. P. B. Hutt, "Public Criticism of Health Science Policy," *Daedalus,* Spring 1978.

7. E.g., the three Congressional hearings cited in note 2 supra.

8. J. Watson, *The Double Helix* (1968).

9. "Fraud in Biomedical Research," hearings before the Subcommittee on Investigations and Oversight of the Committee on Science and Technology, US House of Representatives, 97th Congress, First Session (1981); and W. Broad and N. Wade, *Betrayers of the Truth* (1983).

10. N. Wade, *The Nobel Duel* (1981).

11. 81 Stat. 54 (1967) and 88 Stat. 1561 (1974), 5 U.S.C. 552.

12. 90 Stat. 1241 (1976), 5 U.S.C. 552b.

13. General Accounting Office, *Problem Areas Affecting Usefulness of Results in Government-Sponsored Research in Medicinal Chemistry,* Rep. no. B164031(2) (August 12, 1968).

14. 94 Stat. 3025 (1980), 35 U.S.C. 200 et seq.

15. *Federal Register* 47 (February 19, 1982), p. 7556, superseding *OMB Bulletin* no. 81.22, *Federal Register* 46 (July 2, 1981), p. 34776, which had provided for interim implementation of the 1980 Amendments. For an extensive analysis and discussion of the impact of the 1980 Amendments and the OMB Circular, see Advisory Committee to the Director of the National Institutes of Health, *Cooperative Research Relationships with Industry* (October 1981).

16. General Accounting Office Letter Report no. B-204687 (October 16, 1981).

28

Commentary on the NAS Report

ROSEMARY CHALK

Rosemary Chalk argues that the NAS 1982 report on scientific communication/national security failed to address the question of what military risks a nation should run for the sake of openness, and asked, instead, what minimum controls were necessary to avoid running military risks. This, she argues, amounted to a failure to confront the central conflict in the controversy involving scientific communication and national secruity, thus implicitly accepting a questionable assumption about the military's right to dictate how national interests should be protected in times of national conflict.

The National Academy of Sciences' report *Scientific Communication and National Security* presents an attractive but incomplete solution to a political problem that contains irreconcilable social choices. It also provides an interesting example of how a "technical fix" can be used in the interactions of science and politics. The report emerged from a process in which a select group of scientists and policy-makers translated politically divisive issues into a set of cost-benefit questions based on unstated assumptions. Those questions were then substituted for the policy conflict itself and, in the process, changed the terms of the debate.

The report emerged from the discussions of a nineteen-member panel chaired by Dale Corson, President Emeritus of Cornell University. Appointed by the National Academy of Sciences (NAS) in May 1982, the panel met several times during Summer 1982 with governmental officials and with representatives from various scientific and educational groups. Initially commissioned as a one-year study, the final report was prepared and published about six months after the panel was formed.

The panel was charged by the NAS

. . . to examine the various aspects of the application of controls to scientific communication and to suggest how to balance competing national objectives so as to best serve the general welfare.

The original goals therefore were to identify the various social interests at stake in the scientific communication/national security debate ("to balance competing national objectives"), to formulate a set of objectives which would promote the national interests in this debate ("best serve the general welfare"), and to suggest ways in which alternative forms of information controls would promote or weaken the common good.

Political debate on these issues has centered on competing views over how U.S. national security interests should be fostered and protected. One school of thought—represented primarily by those associated with

From *Science, Technology, and Human Values* Volume 8, no. 1 (Winter 1983), pp. 21–24. Copyright © 1983 by the Massachusetts Institute of Technology and the President and Fellows of Harvard College. Reprinted by permission of John Wiley & Sons, Inc., and the author.

scientific and educational interests—argues that openness is an essential feature of our national strength, and that openness should be protected even though the United States might "lose control" over state-of-the-art information in selected scientific or technical fields. Those who share this concern believe that openness in science is both an end in itself—part of traditional American respect for freedom of speech—and a means to enhancing greater scientific productivity and creativity, economic growth, and education. These factors in turn not only contribute to the advancement of military strength but also independently foster a broader foundation for national security. Those who advocate controls—primarily persons with ties to the defense and/or intelligence communities— argue that without military strength there is no national security and that increased attention should be given to maintaining U.S. control over advanced technology. To foster military superiority, therefore, the Federal government should restrict (and certainly should not aid) the transfer (or "leakage") of advanced technologies or information about those technologies to adversary nations. From the perspective of the advocates of control, even though state-of-the-art information may at times result from university research, such information should be restricted, whatever its source.

It is possible to imagine two approaches that could resolve these differing views. One approach, based on the issue of openness, could carefully review how openness either fosters or weakens national security. Asking how much openness is desirable would explore how much risk a nation should assume to maintain its open character in the face of possible losses to its military strength. Such a review would involve both a critical assessment of how concepts of national security are defined, and an examination of how competing interests between openness and military strength relate to this concept.

A second approach could be derived from the concerns of those who advocate the need for stronger controls. Rather than looking at openness as a central issue, the focus instead

would be on protecting military interests, and would include analysis of threats resulting from unwanted technology transfer. Concerns about openness, or other cultural values, then become "satellite issues" ringing this central question.

From my perspective, the assignment given to the NAS panel was to seek a balance between these competing approaches. What the panel actually did, however, was to accept the latter model as the sole framework for their study, as is clear from their own re-statement of their charge:

In order to determine how and where controls might further the national welfare, it is necessary to balance many factors, including the military advantage from controls, their impact on the ability of the research process to serve military, commercial and basic cultural goals, and their effects on the education of students in science and technology.[1]

The central feature of the NAS study was therefore the issue of "controls" rather than openness. The panel did not attempt to develop a model based on the issue of openness. Instead it sought to derive a formula that would be responsive to the terms of the problem as presented by the defense and intelligence agencies, and yet would impose minimal damage or costs upon their own research and education interests:

[The panel sought] to develop solutions that will provide maximum benefits, both in terms of maintaining the health of the U.S. scientific enterprise and safeguarding national security, while incurring minimum national costs.[2]

Such an approach translated the national policy debate between openness and military controls into a problem of minimizing the impact of military objectives on other national interests. The translated problem was then substituted for the policy debate itself.

From the outset, the panel looked at the question of technology transfer only in a military context. Once the members were convinced that some undesirable transfer of technical goods and information had occurred, they explored how the controls sought by the Department of Defense could be developed without seriously damaging the research and education functions of the university. In the process, the panel accepted a set of unstated premises about the military's right to dictate how national security interests should be protected in times of national conflict:

All parties have an interest in . . . research . . . and in educating . . . scientists and engineers. *These objectives must fit,* however, within a system that enables the government to classify work under its sponsorship . . . and that enables the university to select only work compatible with its principal mission.[3] [emphasis added].

"Fitting" research and education activities into a national security context, without also addressing such activities in a context based on openness, created a major source of bias within the panel discussions. As a result, the panel did not fully explore the benefits of openness, except as a "cultural factor" that might be harmed by military controls. A notable exception to this approach is the following paragraph, which clearly identified some of the benefits:

The Panel believes that the costs of even a small advance toward government censorship in American society are high. The First Amendment's guarantee of free speech and a free press help account for the resiliency of the nation. If political authority is to be exercised effectively, there must be trust in government on the part of those affected—a trust that is promoted by openness and eroded by secrecy. Openness also makes possible the flow of information that is indispensable to the well-informed electorate essential for a healthy democracy. Openness also strengthens U.S. institutions by allowing comparison with the performance of others and nurturing adaptation to changed circumstances.[4]

The panel thus succinctly identified four major benefits that result from national policies encouraging openness: national resiliency, effective political authority, a responsive democracy, and adaptation to changing circumstances. It noted that the costs of reducing these benefits are high. The report emphasized, however, that costs to military strength resulting from a policy of openness are also high.

Are these costs comparable? If so, what criteria should be used to determine which costs are acceptable? Are both costs restorable over the same time frame, or is one set of interests more vulnerable than the other? Unfortunately, the NAS panel made no effort to grapple with these questions. Instead, it chose an apporach that arbitrarily placed priority on reducing damage to U.S. military interests. As a result of this bias, the report seems more concerned about the scientist who slips into areas of military concern than about military interests that may spill over into the working environment of the scientist. For example, the report noted that "scientists working at the research frontier are closer to military applications than they may have intended to be" and that some "scientists may . . . extend their research into applications of technology with military relevance." In many cases this may well be the situation, but the report nowhere acknowledged the possibility that the reverse may also be true— that is, that military concerns may be reaching beyond the technical products of scientific work into the processes of science itself: from the *what* to the *how.* Instead, the reader is left with the image of the unsuspecting scientist, poor fellow, who stumbles into areas of military application and, as a result, needs guidance.

Having translated the national security/ scientific communication debate into a problem of undesirable technology transfer, the NAS panel then proceeded to develop a set of specific recommendations. First, it reviewed the extent and nature of technology transfer from the United States to the Soviet Union, drawing on briefings primarily from classified sources within the Department of Defense and the intelligence agencies. When presented with evidence of technology "leakage," the panel concluded that "there had been transfer of U.S. technology of direct military relevance to the Soviet Union from a variety of sources." They did not seek to assess how much transfer may benefit other interests, but accepted such transfer as a serious threat in itself.

The Panel then asked whether this transfer involves a significant amount of research from university sources or the open scientific literature, and concluded:

... there is a strong consensus that scientific communication, including that involving the university community, appears to have been a very small part of this transfer up to the present time. Open communication on [sic] basic research results ... has, however, contributed to the scientific knowledge base of the Soviet Union as well as to that of other nations.

Finally, the Panel asked whether any areas of university research should be restricted because of their benefit to the Soviet Union. They concluded that "limited restrictions short of classification are appropriate" for some "narrow gray areas," and then outlined four criteria that officials should consider in deciding when to impose government controls:

The Panel recommends that no restriction of any kind limiting access or communication should be applied to any area of university research, be it basic or applied, unless it involves a technology meeting *all* the following criteria:

- The technology is developing rapidly, and the time from basic science to application is short;
- The technology has identifiable direct military applications; or it is dual-use and involves process or production-related techniques;
- Transfer of the technology would give the USSR a significant near-term military benefit; and
- The U.S. is the only source of information about the technology, or other friendly nations that could also be the source have control systems as secure as ours.[5]

The panel's narrow interpretation of its task is evident in the sole emphasis on military interests. I believe that the list would have been strengthened if the panel had added a fifth consideration requiring the military benefits of restricting sensitive information to be balanced against the costs of depriving non-military groups (e.g., the general public) of the data. This consideration would urge an assessment of the non-military value of the information deemed to be sensitive to national security concerns, and would require a true balancing of national security interests: that is, weighing a perceived military edge against factors that directly contribute to national vitality and strength. For example, new information about the medical treatment of tropical diseases could conceivably fall within the criteria outlined by the panel. Would these criteria apply to a new development in genetic engineering which could have some application to bacterial or chemical warfare? Restricting such information in times of military conflict is at times considered to be appropriate. To do so in times of peace, however, requires stronger justification than the simple acknowledgment that the information may contribute to the military strength of an adversary nation.

The press commentaries that appeared in the wake of the NAS study were disappointingly superficial. Both major newspapers and scientific news magazines emphasized the extent to which the NAS report agreed or did not agree with the government's assessment of the need for controls. The *New York Times* (1 October 1982) reported that "there has been 'substantial and serious' leakage of American technology to the Soviet Union," but that "open scientific communications and exchanges, particularly the activities of universities, played 'a very small part' in the leakage." *Science* magazine (15 October 1982) echoed this theme, emphasizing that the NAS report validated the belief that universities were only a small part of the larger problem of unwanted technology transfer. The *Science* article reported that the NAS "failed to find evidence that leaks of technical information from universities or other research centers have damaged the national security." Neither article addressed the issue of how concerns about undesirable technology transfer had obscured the importance of questions related to the value of openness in science and in American society.

When the panel translated its charge of identifying and balancing competing national interests into a task of determining how the information controls sought by government officials could be imposed with minimal damage to university and research interests, the creation of a "gray zone" of restricted data was inevitable. Technology transfer, rather than the development of competing views over what actions best promote national security, emerged as the critical problem. As of the writing of this commentary, there has been no public assessment of the costs to national strength when the values of openness and public communication traditionally associated with American scientific work are compromised as a result of new strategic policies that place heavy reliance upon technical innovation as a primary measure of military superiority. Given the short time-frame of the study, the temperature of the debate, and the fact that the Department of Defense was the major client for the NAS report, it may have been unrealistic to expect that the panel would seek to conduct an open-ended review of the competing interests at issue in this debate. We could have expected, however, that such studies not be framed as broad-based efforts to foster the common good when the participants accepted at the outset a one-sided approach to the problem at hand without independent critique of the terms of the definition of the problem to be addressed. As a result, it is necessary to maintain a healthy skepticism toward efforts that present short-term fixes to problems rooted in historical conflicts. Choices between the strengths of an open society and the strengths of military efficiency are difficult ones to make, because they are based on competing political and social perceptions of what combination of interests best promote the common welfare. Developing criteria to assist in the resolution of these choices is a task that still remains.

NOTES

1. National Academy of Sciences, *Scientific Communication and National Security* (Washington, D.C.: National Academy of Sciences Press, 1982), pp. 11–12.

2. *Scientific Communication*, p. 16.

3. *Scientific Communication*, pp. 4–5.

4. *Scientific Communication*, p. 50.

5. *Scientific Communication*, p. 5.

PART V

MORAL CONTROVERSIES IN TECHNOLOGY TRANSFER

SCOPE OF TECHNOLOGY TRANSFER

"Technology transfer" is often thought of as applying only to matters concerning the diffusion to developing countries of technologies invented elsewhere. It does, no doubt, cover these matters, but it covers others as well. This is evidenced by the fact that those in government, industry, or academia involved in the assessment and introduction of technology policies often think of technology transfer in broader terms. Besides the first type of technology transfer, the range of this activity includes the diffusion of technologies from highly technologically developed countries to other highly developed countries; and, judging from the third selection in Part V, it is sometimes thought to apply to the diffusion of technologies from one to another region within the same country as well.

TECHNOLOGY TRANSFERS TO DEVELOPING COUNTRIES

Part V's first selection, The Transfer of Technology, by Carl Dahlman and Larry Westphal, deals with technology transfer of the first type described. The acquisition of technological capacity can occur in a variety of ways. The authors point out that, though the methods most often discussed "are those where foreigners play an active role and provide information in an immediately operational form—direct foreign investment, turnkey projects, licensing, know-how agreements, and technical service contracts," there are other "very important channels of technology transfer." These are channels " in which foreigners play a passive role, and . . . locals acquire the knowledge and . . . translate it into technology. . . . These channels include sending nationals for foreign education, training, and work experience; consulting foreign technical literature; and copying foreign processes and products." The central moral problem that arises here is whether any such technology transfer is justified and, if so, under what conditions. The authors outline a traditional argument used in support of unrestricted technology transfer, and proceed to criticize it and discuss criteria for assessing any such transfer. The argument is roughly this: Technology is a good that, once produced, is neither depleted nor diminished in value through use. The cost of technology transfer is zero. Overall, then, technology transfer would contribute to maximizing the welfare of technology's potential users. There should be no restrictions on the maximization of welfare. Hence, there should be no restrictions on technology transfer, and technology should be available to all potential users without charge.

This argument involves an appeal to a form of the principle of utility. We have discussed some of the limitations of several major versions of this principle previously. The authors, however, do not take issue with the principle. Indeed, much of their discussion is based on an analysis of costs and benefits which would be compatible with some form of utilitarianism. The authors' criticism is that free diffusion preempts markets that the innovators might have served, thus possibly removing the incentive to innovate. This simply points to a possibility; but the possibility places the burden of further proof on the above utilitarian argument in support of free-for-all technology transfer. For any transfer to be justified on the said utilitarian grounds, it would have to be false that the transfer would, as a whole and relatively soon, lead to a lessening in technology improvements for all. But often it appears to be true.

PATENTS, PRICES, AND APPROPRIATE TECHNOLOGIES

The attempted solution to free technology transfer has been the use of patents. This, however, has led to high, sometimes excessive, prices for technology as a result of the innovators' exercise of their proprietary rights, embodied in patents restricting the technology's use, as well as of consumer ignorance of the technology's real value. The authors describe the resulting problem:

> High prices for technology and restrictions on its use are the basis for many developing countries' call for an international code of conduct on the transfer of technology and a revision of the international patent system. But no satisfactory agreement has been reached on either. Why? Because of the inherent conflict of interests between the suppliers and the demanders, which mirrors society's fundamental dilemma between the need to stimulate the creation and the need to encourage the diffusion of technology.

The authors point out that, in dealing with this problem, it should be kept in mind that objectives can be attained in a variety of ways, and that not technology by itself, but a technology that would serve these objectives is what should be sought, whether it already exists or needs to be created: "Concern with appropriate technology extends beyond choices among existing alternatives to address the possibilities of creating new technologies."

In accordance with these conditions, plus the argument that "few would argue that foreign technical knowledge should be eschewed, so the issue ultimately concerns the division of labor between foreigners and locals in transposing technological knowledge into concrete form." Dahlman and Westphal list several factors they consider central for establishing appropriate ways of acquiring elements of foreign technology:

> First, the costs and terms at which elements can be obtained from abroad may be affected by the competition among alternative sources of supply and the negotiating power of the recipient, including the degree of government support. The second factor is the technological capability of the recipient and stage of development of [the] local technological

infrastructure. The third is the size of the market for which the technology is to be applied.

These are largely economic considerations. The authors appear to leave a door open to other, noneconomic considerations when they state, "There are trade-offs—involving risks, short- and long-term considerations, and private versus social costs and benefits—between attempting to supply some of the elements locally and importing them." Even if noneconomic considerations are involved, however, these are still described in terms of costs and benefits, and as subject to trade-offs for the sake of one goal, assumed to be desirable: technological development along the lines of foreign technical knowledge. This position may well be valid; but it raises the moral question of whether any such technological development is always desirable. The authors do not question that it is—only some of the ways in which technology may be acquired. A further moral question is raised by the above position: Are all considerations—economic or noneconomic—involved in technological development subject to trade-offs, or are some not appropriate for trade-offs at all? These questions point to conflicts between considerations of consequences and considerations that are not, or not primarily, of consequences. As was previously discussed, especially in Part III, to find solutions to some of these conflicts it is crucial that those affected engage in meaningful dialogue, bargaining, negotiation, and interaction with each other and, to some extent, with the technologies at issue; thus the relative weights of the various issues involved can be established. This may take time and cause impatience, but it is often the only way of finding out what conflicting interests are involved from the start or are prompted in the process. Sometimes not just the solutions, but the conflicts themselves need to be defined by those affected. The pragmatic considerations that constitute part of our theoretical framework are sensitive to this aspect of conflicts concerning new technologies.

THE APPROPRIATE TECHNOLOGY MOVEMENT

Malcolm Hollick's What Is Appropriate Technology? is a review of various conceptions of technology and the resulting social arrangements considered desirable by individuals and groups that have criticized, over the past decade, the dominant technologies and their impact on society. The author points out that these conceptions fall under two main categories: those prompted mainly by a concern with developing countries, and those mainly concerned with the quality of life and environmental and resource problems in the United States, some countries in Western Europe, and Japan. There is, however, enough unity between these two categories of the so-called "appropriate technology (AT) movement, provided that those who advocate the mass production of AT gadgetry for developing countries and/or view AT merely as a necessary way station on the road to western-style development are excluded. To a large extent the visions of Third World development then merge with those of the future of the West in a unified image of a desirable society."

Malcolm Hollick discusses the basic values of the appropriate technology

movement—cultural diversity and individual freedom, decentralization and self-sufficiency, nonalienating work—in the light of the writings of their exponents as well as
critics. In doing this, he raises a number of moral questions to be used in assessing
technologies and the societal arrangements thaty accompany them: Is small always
beautiful? If not, when is it? At any rate, how small is small? Does this depend on
technological, social, or environmental circumstances? How, and in what specifiable
circumstances, does it depend on them? Is rural self-sufficiency always desirable?
Should it be? Should all sectors of economic activity be amenable to craft production?
Is decentralization always possible? Is it desirable whenever it is possible? How should
those affected proceed in dealing with these questions?

Hollick thinks the complexity of dealing with so many hard questions constitutes
both a weakness and a challenge in the appropriate technology movement:

> Maybe the time has come to try to develop a theory of appropriate technology
> that . . . permits a blend of big, small, and middling. Such a theory would have to be
> built upon a deep understanding of human needs—both individual and social—that could
> accommodate wide cultural variations. It would have to include sufficiently specific crite-
> ria that the appropriateness of any particular technology could be assessed, but avoid the
> totalitarian implications of state determination of appropriateness or needs.
>
> This is a massive task which may be beyond the bounds of possibility. . . . Neverthe-
> less, even failure could prove to be very valuable in clarifying the nature of a "technology
> as if people mattered."

The task is massive indeed, and even more massive than some of Hollick's words
would indicate. For by seeking a technology "as if people mattered"—a worthy and
plausible aim—one may be giving people priority over everything else. However, this
view has come under criticism from those concerned with the rights or well-being of
such nonhumans as animals, giving rise to various moral questions: Should people
always take precedence over everything else?[1] If so, is this simply because they are
human? What if there were nonhuman persons? Should they be disregarded? Or
should people take precedence because they are rational? But not all of them are. Is
it, then, because they all belong to the kind of being that is generally rational?[2] If so,
why should this characteristic make such a difference? If it does not, which characteristic might? Suppose that the capacity to feel pain or undergo suffering is appealed to
instead. In such a case, not only people or humans, but at least many animals other
than humans, are entitled to have their well-being, or possibly rights, balanced against
the well-being or rights of humans whenever there is an interspecies conflict. Whatever the answers to these questions, they arise in a context in which the claims made
on behalf of the welfare or possible rights of nonhumans, as we know them, must be
settled by humans acting as trustees of such nonhumans.[3] For their judgments would
carry no weight if they acted in any other capacity. And since the questions to be
settled cannot realistically be brushed aside, whatever theoretical framework is found
adequate for resolving these matters must make room for humans acting as trustees or
stewards, and not simply as consumers. These considerations, stated previously, are
thus extended to moral controversies arising in technology transfer, thus providing

further support for the use of the willingness-to-sell criterion discussed in connection with the evaluation of health risks, costs and benefits in Part III—another criterion in our framework.

TECHNOLOGY TRANSFER AT HOME

The third selection in this chapter, Technology Transfer: That's What It's All About, by Robert R. Irving, deals with technology transfers between different regions or sectors of one country. He asks: "What are the factors that oppose technological change in industry?" In answer to this question, he cites the fear of change on the part of those who manage and work in powerful industrial empires, the companies' fear of being guinea pigs, the competitive inclination to develop better technologies in one's own firm rather than introducing technologies from elsewhere, the fear that the technologies considered have not been sufficiently tested, and the apprehension created by so much talk of the failures that, after all, often are the effects of misuse.

These fears, however, can be addressed by pointing to various factors that might facilitate technology transfers in industry. Irving, for example, mentions the presence of a person who is greatly interested in the technology, capable of actively overseeing its introduction and operation in the firm acquiring the technology; its funding, and the stability of its implementation throughout the process of introducing the technology. Another factor is great support for the new project by such a person's superiors. In any case, all such technology transfers call for a great deal of effort and practical, as well as intellectual, flexibility on the part of the firms and managers involved. The author offers a number of examples of the unwillingness to change of individuals ranging from old-timers, for whom the new technology would pose too many adaptational demands, to design engineers, who are very satisfied with their last project and see little need to substitute it with a new one.

These examples of obstacles to technology transfer in industry raise a pressing moral question akin to others already raised in this book: Should people always adapt to machines and new technological developments; or should such developments always fit the preferences or inclinations of the people involved, from managers to design engineers? A question of this type was, for example, discussed in Part III, where the discussion was concerned with how much, and under what circumstances, should factory and office workers below the managerial level adapt to new technology in the workplace? And, as indicated in the first two selections in this part, the concerns involved in the above questions are also prompted by technology transfers into developing countries, as well as by technological development in highly technological societies such as the United States, Western Europe, and Japan. These concerns focus on the dignity and self-esteem of persons *as persons*—what they think they and their lives ought to be like; what they feel about ongoing changes, given the social circumstances; the likely consequences of rejecting technological options; their own interaction with the technologies that have been tried; and who favors or opposes such technologies. As has been argued, the fact that these concerns are significantly involved in controversies about the matters of technology in question serves to establish their relevance and determine their relative weights in dealing soundly with the controversies. The further fact that these concerns are involved in controversies about a wide variety of technology matters, ranging from the local context of a factory, an office or a hospital to the international and transregional context of technology transfer and international competition, serves to establish that these concerns are not merely relevant but central for soundly dealing with the controversies. As we have indicated all along, the basic theoretical framework developed throughout articulates these concerns in ways that indicate how to establish relative weight, depending on the controversy addressed—the willingness-to-sell criterion, bargaining procedures, or overall limitations based on likely collective disastrous consequences. This wide-ranging articulation of relevant concerns further supports the framework.

NOTES

1. For discussions of this point, see, for example Peter Singer, "All Animals Are Equal," *Philosophic Exchange,* 1, No. 5 (Summer 1974); and his "Animals and the Value of Life," *Matters of Life and Death,* ed. Tom Regan (New York: Random House, 1980); and Tom Regan, *All That Dwell Therein: Essays on Animal Rights and Environmental Ethics* (Berkeley: University of California Press, 1982).

2. This position has been taken by Stanley Benn, in *Nomos IX: Equality,* ed. J. Roland Pennock and John W. Chapman (New York: Atherton Press, 1967), p. 71.

3. For a good discussion of the notion of such stewardship, see John Passmore, *Man's Responsibility for Nature* (New York: Charles Scribner's Sons, 1974), pp. 28–40.

29

The Transfer of Technology—Issues in the Acquisition of Technological Capability by Developing Countries

CARL DAHLMAN AND LARRY WESTPHAL

The authors see the problems of technology transfer to developing countries as manifestations of society's fundamental dilemma: the need to stimulate the creation and the need to encourage the diffusion of technology. They take the position that this issue ultimately concerns the division of labor between foreigners and locals in transforming technological knowledge into concrete form, and list a series of factors that should be taken into account in establishing the best ways of acquiring various elements of foreign technology.

Throughout history, the assimilation of technologies invented elsewhere has been central in raising living standards. The modern era differs from previous epochs in that, although there are greater disparities now in technological levels among countries, there is also greater ease of communication and transportation. These differences have enhanced both the perceived and the real gains from acquiring foreign technologies—hence the increasing prominence of technology transfer in discussions of development.

Market failures in the creation and the diffusion of technology are at the heart of the international debate about technology transfer. Technology has characteristics of a public good in that, once produced, it is not depleted through further use by others. It is usually presumed that the cost of transferring technology is zero and that additional uses of the technology do not detract from its value. On those grounds, achieving optimal welfare requires that technology be available to all potential users without charge. This argument is the basis for claims that developing countries should have free (or cheap) access to developed countries' technology. But free diffusion preempts markets that the creator might have served, and may thus remove the incentive to innovate. The patent system permits the diffusion of technology while attempting to protect the proprietary rights of the innovator. In exercising these rights, technology suppliers seek to restrict use of the technology so as to maximize their returns. Control over the supply, plus the buyer's ignorance regarding the true value of technology, can lead to excessively high prices.

High prices for technology and restrictions on its use are the basis for many developing countries' call for an international code of conduct on the transfer of technology and a revision of the international patent system. But no satisfactory agreement has been

From *Finance and Development* Volume 20 (December 1983), pp. 6–9. Reprinted by permission of *Finance and Development*.

reached on either. Why? Because of the inherent conflict of interests between the suppliers and the demanders, which mirrors society's fundamental dilemma between the need to stimulate the creation and the need to encourage the diffusion of technology.

Many governments in the developing world have adopted "defensive" measures—that is, measures that control contractual technology transfers—in order to redress the bargaining asymmetry and protect the development of local technological capabilities. Although such regulations have helped reduce the price and improve the terms of the contractual inflow, they may also have affected the character of the foreign technology that can be imported. Foreign technology suppliers are unwilling to sell when they consider the returns too low. Moreover, direct foreign investment is often the only means of obtaining access to closely guarded technological assets. It is also not clear that regulating formal inflows has stimulated the development of local capabilities. Such development requires technological effort on the part of local firms, which is not ensured by regulation of or protection from technology imports.

WHAT IS TECHNOLOGY?

Technology is a method for doing something. Using a method requires three elements: information about the method, the means of carrying it out, and some understanding of it. Much of the confusion about what technology transfer is arises from trying to identify one or two of the elements as technology. Information and means can be transferred, but understanding can be acquired only by study and experience. Information embodied in blueprints, operational manuals, and technical books is transferable, as are physical means, such as capital goods. But both physical means and information are worthless unless the recipient knows how to use them, which involves the knowledge of a technology's potential and—most important—some experience in its use.

The transfer of information or means is not the same as the acquisition of technological capability. The ability to use technology effec-

tively comes from a person's (or organization's) understanding, and the degree of understanding required is related to the objective sought in employing the technology. For example, full comprehension of the potential of photography may call for some knowledge of optics and chemistry, but this knowledge is not necessary to take standard snapshots. Moreover, all technologies are elements of larger systems, and the presence or absence of other technologies has a major impact on what has to be acquired to accomplish the objective sought. For example, developing and printing capabilities are not needed to take snapshots, but they may be required where these services are not locally available.

Technological capability is not an end in itself. Objectives can be achieved in various ways and the selection of the best way requires a strategy. Optimum strategies for choosing and acquiring particular elements of technologies vary across countries, sectors, firms, and individuals, according to their needs and characteristics. These obvious considerations are too often neglected in discussions of technology and development.

CHOOSING A TECHNOLOGY

For most activities in most industries, no single technology is best for all circumstances. Local requirements and factor endowments vary widely—both among developing economies and between them and the developed economies. As well as differing in their relative use of capital and labor, alternative technologies also use different intermediate inputs and produce outputs that are not strictly identical in all respects. These characteristics affect a technology's suitability for individual situations. Although definitions of appropriate technology vary, a core characteristic is that it makes optimum use of available resources. The conventionally prescribed method for choosing among alternative technologies is to evaluate their associated benefits and costs, using prices that properly reflect relative scarcities. The best or most appropriate technique is that which has the highest net benefit.

Lack of local capability to identify needs and to search for and assess different technologies is often responsible for the selection of inappropriate techniques. In turn, government policies—such as those leading to distortions in factor prices—can induce producers to search for technologies that are, in fact, inappropriate. Monopolistic market structures and excessive protection from imports can, by unduly raising prices, destroy rational incentives to search for the most cost-effective technology. In addition, producers may anyway fail to respond to market signals, and base their choices on criteria that are independent of economic forces, such as seeking the newest or most sophisticated technology regardless of cost.

The implementation of an appropriate choice often requires complementary investments in local skills to make the optimum use of available resources. To the extent that these skills can be augmented, they need not impose absolute constraints on the selection of what would otherwise be appropriate technologies. Labor and management abilities can be upgraded through investments in human capital formation, for example, or local machinery repair and production facilities for spare parts can be developed.

But concern with appropriate technology extends beyond choices among existing alternatives to address the possibilities for creating new technologies. Technological change in the developed economies has resulted in modern technologies that are urban-based, large-scale, capital-intensive, and whose requirements for capital and intermediate inputs are often import-intensive. Likewise, the characteristics of the outputs produced by these technologies are sometimes ill-suited for developing economies. Nonetheless, because of their high productivity, modern technologies are frequently most appropriate. But modern and older technologies alike can be adapted to conditions in developing economies. Whether changes are warranted depends on their costs relative to the expected benefits.

ACQUIRING TECHNOLOGY

Less developed countries typically obtain many elements of technology from more developed countries. But there are various combinations of foreign and local contributions. Information, means, and understanding can be (1) provided by foreigners who retain ownership; (2) purchased from foreigners; or (3) acquired through indigenous efforts to translate foreign technological knowledge into specific methods. And technology can be transferred with varying degrees of human capital accumulation and institutional development.

At one extreme, a package consisting of all the elements is transferred, with indigenous involvement limited to an unskilled labor force—as with direct foreign investment, or to operating the technology—as with "turnkey" projects. (In the latter case, a foreigner contracts to provide all the elements needed to design and establish a production facility in the local environment, but ownership is local.) At the other extreme the underlying knowledge is assimilated and then used to create the necessary elements. The knowledge can be acquired through education, experience, experimentation, research, or purchase.

The modes of technology transfer that are most often discussed are those where foreigners play an active role and provide information in an immediately operational form—direct foreign investment, turnkey projects, licensing, know-how agreements, and technical service contracts. But modes in which foreigners play a passive role, and where locals acquire the knowledge and later translate it into technology, are very important channels of technology transfer. These channels include sending nationals for foreign education, training, and work experience; consulting foreign technical literature; and copying foreign processes and products.

In discussing what is acquired through technology transfer, it is useful to distinguish three broad types of capability: production capability—that required to operate a technology; investment capability—that required to expand existing productive capacity or to establish new capacity; and innovation capability—that required to develop new methods of doing things. There is often an implicit notion that technology transfer gives the recipient the first two if not all three types of capability. That is rarely the case. The capability to operate a technology is different from the ability to develop the means of implementing it. Similarly, having the capability to implement a technology is different from having the capability to create a new one.

Production capability is not achieved by passively importing technology. It requires local participation and considerable indigenous effort to master the technology's use. Research shows that in most cases where the technological elements are imported as a "black box," the recipients are not able to take full advantage of it because they do not understand how or why the black box operates as it does. This hampers their ability to improve productivity or to adapt to changing circumstances—such as shifts in input prices or demand patterns—that affect how it is best used.

The understanding that underlies production capability is also an important aspect of the capabilities to invest and to innovate. Thus the accumulation of low-production experience can provide the understanding necessary to carry out some, but not all, of the tasks involved in investment and innovation. For example, plant engineers may acquire some capability in plant design, spare parts production, and adaptation of existing technology from experience in breaking bottlenecks, maintaining equipment, and solving production problems. But it is unlikely that they will acquire a capability in basic plant design, capital goods manufacture, or the creation of radically new technologies. The background and experience necessary to carry out many of these tasks is different, and the relevant capabilities tend to be developed in specialized entities, such as process engineering firms, capital goods producers, and technological research institutes.

Part of the increase in local capabilities acquired through transfers spills into related activities. For example, the capabilities gained from establishing one industry can enable greater indigenous participation in subsequent transfers of related technologies, increasing their effective assimilation. The accumulation of such experiences can also

lead to the creation of specialized firms which, in turn, permits greater local participation in future transfers. More generally, the increased capability contributes to an economy's capacity to undertake independent technological efforts, including replication or adaptation of foreign technologies as well as creation of new technologies.

But unless carried out with the explicit objective of doing so, some modes of technology transfer do not provide the experience that is critical to the development of indigenous technological capability. Tasks involving project design and the manufacture of capital goods, for example, which could be performed locally, may be carried out by foreigners. This precludes local learning through experience—experience that may be directly relevant to the industry's subsequent development. Moreover, project costs may be higher; cheaper local services may not be used; and intimate knowledge of local conditions, required to optimize project design and to take advantage of available raw materials, may be ignored.

IMPORTED OR DOMESTIC TECHNOLOGY?

Any project entails much iterative problem solving and experimentation as the original concept is refined and given practical expression. Important elements of the technology appropriate to the project are developed through applying existing technological knowledge and engineering principles to specific local circumstances. There may even be some minor innovations or adaptations in the technology being implemented. Whether the elements of technology should be obtained locally or from abroad ought to depend on the relative costs and benefits involved. Few would argue that foreign technical knowledge should be eschewed, so the issue ultimately concerns the division of labor between foreigners and locals in transposing technological knowledge into concrete form.

An economy's capacity to provide the necessary elements depends on the stage of development of the relevant sector and those closely related to it. Firms engaged in well-established activities may often acquire technology locally—either through their own efforts or through the diffusion of expertise from other domestic firms. Hiring personnel with expertise from previous work experience plays an extremely important part in the diffusion of knowledge among firms, as does the interchange of information among suppliers and users of individual products, especially for intermediate products and capital goods.

Firms in new or relatively new industries can rarely take advantage of previous local experience or the diffusion of expertise or information from other domestic firms. Such firms are likely to find it more cost-effective to rely initially on foreign technological "packages" in the form of direct foreign investment and turnkey contracts. As a country develops its technological capability, it can disaggregate these packages to import more cheaply or efficiently only those elements that it cannot obtain locally.

The relative merits of different ways of acquiring various elements of foreign technology depend on several factors. First, the costs and terms at which elements can be obtained from abroad may be affected by the competition among alternative sources of supply and the negotiating power of the recipient, including the degree of government support. The second factor is the technological capability of the recipient and stage of development of the local technological infrastructure. The third is the size of the market for which the technology is to be applied.

There are trade-offs—involving risks, short- and long-term considerations, and private versus social costs and benefits—between attempting to supply some of the elements locally and importing them. A rational firm is unlikely to use inexperienced local engineering services or untested capital goods, for example, unless their use brings long-run developmental benefits that more than compensate for the greater short-run risks and higher costs of using such local inputs. The social benefits from increasing technological capability generally exceed the private gains

that an individual firm can expect to capture. There are many avenues along which technological capability can move to other firms, and not all of these are controlled by the firm that finances the initial acquisition. This discrepancy between private and social value often leads to underinvestment. Moreover, firms may value the private benefits that they do capture at less than their true social worth, or consider that the cost of securing them exceeds the true social cost.

Furthermore, firms may opt for more expensive monopolistic sources of foreign technology, such as those that confer a well-known brand name, because such sources confer monopoly power. There is then a convergence of interests between the domestic firm and the foreign supplier since the domestic firm can offset the promise of domestic monopoly profits against the excessive price paid. Thus, the motives that give rise to technology imports can sometimes conflict with social objectives. In turn, where imports are consistent with social objectives, domestic firms may prefer importing technology without considering ways of increasing domestic technological capability. Even the simplest form of participation—intelligent observation of activities carried out by foreigners—entails a cost to firms.

STRATEGY OVER TIME

The central issue of strategy is how to build upon what can be obtained from abroad to stimulate the development of local capability in selected areas. For many reasons, timing is of critical importance. Since all capabilities cannot be developed simultaneously, and since the accumulation of any one capability takes time and experience, the sequence in which various capabilities are developed is crucial. And the required capabilities change as a firm or country matures, because of changes in existing capabilities, and because of changes in market conditions.

If the market is small and growing slowly, so that investments in new plants are infrequent, the best strategy may be to acquire only production capability—say, by importing a turnkey plant, with the training required to adjust the operation as necessary. But if the market is large or growing rapidly, it may be economic to acquire some investment capability. Furthermore, if technology is changing rapidly, it may be desirable to insure the capability to assimilate new advances quickly or even to innovate new products or processes. Or a decision may be made to rely on direct foreign investment in dynamic areas where it would be too costly to keep up with rapid world technological developments.

In this context, the strategy of Japanese firms is instructive. During the 1950s and 1960s, when they were technologically far behind firms in the then developed nations in almost all areas of industrial technology, they actively and unabashedly imported foreign technology. The means to accomplish this included commercial contracts, such as licensing and know-how agreements and turnkey plants, as well as copying products, getting training overseas, making visits to foreign plants, and studying foreign technical literature. In areas in which they wanted to excel, they sought to understand the underlying principles rather than simply to import technological "black boxes." Thus, Japanese firms allocated specific local research and development efforts to acquire this understanding. Further, they used the import of technology as a starting point and focused the bulk of their efforts on understanding, adapting, and improving the technology. In particular, they focused on increasing the quality of products and on reducing production costs. In the 1970s, and even more now in the 1980s, Japanese firms have devoted more attention to basic research and innovation. Their strategy has changed as their capabilities have evolved.

There are various situations in which it may be cost-effective to develop basic product and process knowledge as an element of local innovation capability. These include instances when foreign technology is not appropriate or does not exist for the needs at hand, when it can be obtained only at excessively high costs or is unavailable because of monopoly supply restrictions, or when the size of its potential market is large enough to justify the cost of developing it locally because of the gains from successive applications. Efforts to acquire substantial innovation capability may pay off by reducing future costs and providing greater flexibility to adapt to changing circumstances. The difficulty of assessing these returns, together with differences in sensitivity to technological considerations, may explain why firms in the same industry exhibit vastly different levels of technological effort.

Because of market failures and externalities in the creation, diffusion, and choice of technology, there is an important role for government incentives and other interventions in fostering the effective use of technology. The objectives of such policies include inducing the choice of the socially most appropriate foreign techniques; importing technology on the best possible terms; ensuring adequate local participation designed to increase domestic technological capability; and promoting, where appropriate, the use of local rather than foreign sources. Some of these aims can be achieved through defensive measures, but others can only be attained by positive steps, such as building up local physical and human technical infrastructure.

It is not always clear how to design and implement policy measures most effectively. While defensive steps are not enough, positive measures are not always successful. For example, many research institutes have been poorly integrated with production needs. In addition, measures to support and encourage local technological effort have frequently worked at cross purposes with other elements of industrial and trade policies. As a result, firms, even those owned by the state, have often not responded to technologically oriented policies. Another difficulty is how to foster the development of technological capability in different domestic sectors, while minimizing the costs to the users—often other industries—of temporarily shutting out more efficient foreign sources or making access to them more costly. And perhaps more important than specific policy measures is the establishment of an environment that sensitizes firms to technological considerations and stimulates them to develop greater techno- logical capability to improve their overall performance.

Technology is multidimensional. Many dif- ferent capabilities are required to assess, select, assimilate, use, adapt, and create it. Elements of different technologies already exist in the developing world. Sometimes a completely new technology is not needed, but rather an improvement on existing technologi- cal elements or a complement of new ele- ments imported from abroad and adapted to local conditions. Countries may follow differ- ent paths toward the acquisition of the tech- nology they need, paths that involve varying degrees of openness to foreign technology and of reliance on foreigners rather than locals to transform technical knowledge into concrete form. Not much is known about the relative merits of the different paths, because little attention has been focused on economic per- formance along these paths. There is much to learn about the best strategies. The perfor- mance along the path matters. So do the targets. There is an inherent difficulty in that the targets are constantly shifting as the future unfolds and new technologies are developed. The only recipe for success is pragmatism based on constant monitoring of performance and of the possibilities opened up by new technological developments.

30

What is Appropriate Technology?

MALCOLM HOLLICK

Malcolm Hollick reviews the literature expressing the diverse set of interests and philosophies that have come to be called "the appropriate technology movement." He discusses its main general areas, as well as its central values: cultural diversity and individual freedom; decentralization and self-sufficiency; and unalienated work, and argues that the time may have come to develop a more precise, realistic, and nontotalitarian theory of appropriate technology, one that gives clear guidance concerning particular technology transfer problems.

MOVEMENT OR MELTING POT?

Many groups and individuals in the last decade or so have been critical of modern technology, but have advocated changes rather than abandonment. Their diversity of interests and philosophies is reflected in the variety of labels chosen to describe their proposals: appropriate, intermediate, alternative, radical, self-help, democratic, people's, progressive, low cost, autonomous, soft, utopian, liberatory, non-violent, convivial, and more. Within this *pot-pourri* can be identified two broad divisions: those whose prime concern is with the problems of developing countries, and those who are more interested in the "quality of life," environmental, and resource problems of developed nations. Each claims that its ideas are relevant to the other, but few groups have combined them successfully, probably because of the very different socioeconomic situations in which they are interested.

Developing Countries

The term "intermediate technology" was coined by Schumacher[1] "to signify that it is vastly superior to the primitive technology of bygone ages, but at the same time much simpler, cheaper, and freer than the super-technologies of the rich." The key criterion was that it should create jobs at a small fraction of the capital investment required for western technology, but still increase labor productivity relative to traditional techniques used in developing countries. However, traditional techniques vary from region to region, so that what is "intermediate" in one country may be traditional in another. For example, the ox-drawn plough is an intermediate technology in much of Africa, where it replaces the hand-hoe, but is traditional in the Middle East and Asia.[2] Despite Schumacher's insistence that it should employ the "best of modern knowledge and experience," the term "intermediate technology" has fallen from favor because of its connotations of "second best." It also has been criticized for implying a technological fix for development problems, separate from the social and political factors involved. Thus, Schumacher's Intermediate Technology Development Group calls its journal *Appropriate Technology*.

"Appropriate" is perhaps the most commonly used term, but it has not been without its critics. Jequier[3] pointed out that it is value-laden, because it implies both that all else is "inappropriate" and that appropriateness is a quality which can be engineered into a particular technology. He claimed that "appropriateness lies less in the specific design features of a particular piece of hardware than in the broadness of the evaluation criteria which underlie its development and application." To illustrate this point Jequier used the concepts of internal and external appropriateness, which are closely related to those of internal and external costs and benefits in economics. Thus, a large steel mill operating close to capacity and producing high-quality steel at a profit is internally appropriate in engineering and cost-accounting terms. However, it may be externally inappropriate if it is in a developing country with high unemployment and scarce energy, raw materials, and capital, because of its effects on employment, local industries, foreign exchange and so on.

These points are evident in most definitions of appropriate technology by practitioners. For example, Darrow and Pam[4] stated:

"Appropriate technology" is a term that represents a particular view of society and technology. It suggests that technology is neither neutral nor does it evolve along a single path. It recognizes that different cultural and geographical groups will have different technologies that are appropriate to their circumstances; that technological self-determination is essential to cultural identity (and political independence). It suspects that the only wise technologies are those which seek to accommodate themselves to the biological environment within which they are used. It assumes that the purpose of economically productive activity is to produce what is determined by need, in an enjoyable, creative process; not what is determined by endless greed, in an alienating, repetitive production process. It stresses that every society has a technological tradition and that new technologies must grow out of this tradition. And it presumes that the only development that makes sense is development of the people and their skills, by the people and for the people.

The key element of appropriateness in the development context according to Darrow and Pam[4] is generating innovation and self-reliance at the village level rather than importing mass produced gadgets. However, Jequier[3] argued that "backyard" appropriate technology has no hope of meeting the potential demand among the world's one billion poorest people, so it is essential to harness the ability of modern industry to produce large quantities cheaply and efficiently. He saw the need for governments to coordinate the transition to mass production by involving development banks, industry, planners, entrepreneurs, and so on. From this viewpoint, appropriate technology consists in providing tools, machines, and products for use in the villages that are of appropriate scale, well designed, well made, and cheap in order to increase economic productivity. As in traditional approaches to economic development, this tends to ignore the contribution that could be made by village craftsmen such as blacksmiths, carpenters, and masons who might otherwise go out of business. It diminishes the importance of developing community self-confidence and self-reliance, and of regional cultural variations that affect appropriateness, but which cannot be accommodated readily in mass production.

This difference between the originators of the appropriate technology idea and the major institutions which have adopted it represents a fundamental philosophic split; as Hoda, head of the Indian Appropriate Technology Association has said: "Disaster may follow if multi-national organizations take up to produce small machines in stainless steel packages for the rural areas of the developing countries. This would be the end of Appropriate Technology" (quoted by Rybczynski).[5] This dispute is related to—but not identical with—that over whether appropriate technology should be an end in itself or a stepping stone to modern western technology. The concepts associated with the former view are essentially those of groups concerned with the ills of western society.

Developed Countries

The term "alternative technology" has been used mainly in developed countries and implies a rejection of modern technology whereas "appropriate technology" permits discrimination between desirable and undesirable aspects of it. Harper (quoted by Darrow in note 4) has also pointed out that "alternative" has connotations of the counterculture in the West: not controlled by dominant institutions, cheap, improvisatory, personalized, and accessible to amateurs. "Radical technology" is similar, having its origins in the alternative lifestyle movement and utopian socialism. "The word 'radical' literally means 'going to the root,' and accordingly 'radical technology' implies a fundamental reexamination of the role of technology in modern societies. It also implies a commitment to the ideals of the political left. Let's say we're into *liberation*" (Introduction to Boyle and Harper).[6] "Power to the People; Decentralisation; Participatory Democracy; Workers Control; Small is Beautiful . . . between the lines are values of self-generated activity, distributed responsibility, control from the bottom upwards. In short, of autonomy" (Harper in note 7).

This is obviously closely linked to the concept of liberatory technology, which is most easily explained by a quotation from *Science for the People:*[8] "Primitive man, who knew no engineering to cross rivers and no medicine to cure disease was not free . . . but neither are the citizens of advanced nations, who cross rivers, are cured of disease and hold jobs, if they do not both understand and control the means by which they are accomplished."

Whether or not it is possible to have a level of technology that is adequate to meet the needs of man in the crowded world of the 20th century and that is also accessible to the understanding of all is highly questionable. Clarke[9] contrasted "hard" modern technology with "soft technology" using 35 characteristics, many of which overlap. In essence, he espoused an environmentally benign technology that is frugal in its use of resources; relatively labor-intensive production in small-scale, craft-based industries; a decentralized, village-based, communal lifestyle that encourages cultural diversity and is

based on participatory democracy; a steady state economy with local barter and a reduction in world trade; satisfying work and a reduction in the distinction between work and leisure; and a popularization and demystification of science and technology. According to Lovins,[10] "soft" energy technology uses renewable energy flows; involves many modest and diverse energy sources matched in scale, quality, and geographic distribution to end-use needs; and is flexible and easily understood. The similarity of terminology to the "hard" and "soft" ego personality types of Taylor[11] is striking. He claims that modern technology is created by—and demands—hard-ego people who are individualistic, selfish, tough, and success-oriented. By contrast, soft-ego types are cooperative, sympathetic and tender, and identify with others.

Rybczynski[5] argued that the concept of nonviolent technology will not withstand rational analysis. In theory, it would not have unintended side effects; would not cause social disruption; could be insinuated alongside traditional techniques without disrupting them; would be completely under human control; and would not destroy, exploit or manipulate the natural world. He asked: "Is a man with a bulldozer more violent than a man with a shovel? or a hundred men with a hundred shovels?" He pointed out that Hitler's death camps were high technology, but Stalin's Gulag Archipelago was low technology. He doubted whether an appropriate technology can be found and introduced that will not have violent social consequences on a "backward" society, and he quoted Hannah Arendt's claim that all technology is violent: cutting down a tree, wrenching a stone out of the ground, melting iron ore, domesticating animals. Nevertheless, although absolute nonviolence may not be achievable, technologies do differ in their degree of disruption. For example, integrated pest control programs in agriculture can be highly effective and yet far less damaging to ecosystems than chemical pest control; house renovation can be much less socially destructive than slum clearance; and public transport systems are generally less destructive of life, health, and community than cars. As McRobie[12] put it: "Non-violence . . . refers to modes of production which respect ecological principles and strive to work with nature instead of attempting to force their way through natural systems."

The concept of "convivial tools" was introduced by Illich,[13] who was careful to state that he was using "convivial" as a technical term to designate a society of "responsibly limited tools." The term "tool" also covered more than just technology, and included social institutions such as factories, education, and health care. A convivial society would "guarantee for each member the most ample and free access to the tools of the community and limit his freedom only in favor of another member's equal freedom." Tools would be limited to those needed to protect survival, justice and self-defined work and would lead to a diversity of lifestyles. Illich argued that people experience joy, rather than mere pleasure, only in creative activities. Up to a certain point, tools extend human creative ability, but beyond that point they lead to regimentation, dependence, exploitation and impotence. "Tools foster conviviality to the extent to which they can be easily used—by anybody—as often or as seldom as desired, for the accomplishment of a purpose chosen by the user." Illich cited the telephone as an example of a convivial tool, since—provided he has the money—the user can call anybody for as long as he likes and communicate anything he chooses. However, others have argued that the current technology is limiting because of its emphasis on two-person, rather than group, communication—a restriction that is not inherent in the device, but stems from the society that developed it.[14]

A Unified Image

There are many differences of approach and opinion, and yet the picture of a society based on appropriate technology that emerges is sufficiently coherent that it is possible to speak of an appropriate technology (AT) movement, provided that those who advocate the mass production of AT gadgetry for developing countries and/or view AT merely as a necessary way station on the road to western-style development are excluded. To a large extent the visions of Third World development then merge with those of the future of the West in a unified image of a desirable society. However, this is portrayed only in outline and significant differences and problems emerge on closer scrutiny.

The society envisaged is decentralized and based mainly on small communities rather than towns and cities. Each community is relatively self-sufficient, using local resources to grow much of its food, produce most of its energy, and make many of its manufactured goods in small, craft-based workshops. Organization is cooperative and based on participatory democracy. Tools are relatively small and simple, so that they can be readily controlled, used, maintained, understood, and modified by people without specialist knowledge and with access only to small workshops. This results in relatively labor-intensive, low-capital techniques, and in an output of products lower in quantity than in developed countries, but higher than in developing countries. Production goals are based on identified needs and environmental constraints within a steady state economy in order to minimize the use of nonrenewable resources. The division between work and leisure is small, so gratification comes through satisfying, creative work rather than through consumption of goods. As far as possible, only renewable energy flows are used, and environmental impacts are minimized.

RATIONALE AND LIMITS

Some writers on appropriate technology are uncompromisingly idealistic, but others recognize that the characteristics sketched above may not be ideal for all types of social and economic activities or in all circumstances. In this section, some of the more perceptive justifications and criticisms of appropriate technology as a basis for society are discussed, but the transitional problems of achieving that state are largely ignored. These have been lucidly dealt with by Jequier,[2] Dickson,[14] Mitchell,[15] and Rybczynski[5] for developing countries and by *The Ecologist*,[16] Dickson,[14] and various contributors to Boyle and Harper[6] for developed countries.

Cultural Diversity and Individual Freedom

One of the basic values of the appropriate technology movement is that cultural diversity is a good thing and, hence, that technologies should be compatible with existing cultures in developing countries and conducive to the evolution of more diversity in developed ones. This belief is justified on the grounds that social systems—like ecosystems—gain stability through complexity, and that variety of physical and social surroundings is essential to the emotional and intellectual development of the individual.[16]

Cultural uniformity is promoted by many aspects of modern technology, but particularly by cheap travel and mass communications. Lowbury[17] linked the generation of community crafts, stories, music, architecture, and rituals to freedom from external domination, and claimed that this "clearly presupposes radical changes in a global communications system whose greatest achievement to date has been to let 10 million Japanese watch Princess Anne's wedding." However, Rybczynski[5] pointed out that it is not television and other media themselves which are political and social shaping tools, but the way in which they are used. This depends on the cultural, economic and political environment rather than vice versa.

Perhaps more fundamentally, this belief in diversity reflects a belief that groups and individuals should be free to shape their own lives, and the recognition that technology is a major determinant of social possibilities. Dickson[14] expressed this idea as follows:

While machines, like words, coincide with possible social actions that the individual is able to carry out, they also implicitly contain constraints on this action. . . . We are unable to carry out those activities for which machines are necessary but are not accessible. . . . Few of us are in the position to devise machines to perform tasks which we have selected or defined ourselves . . . we have to rely on those machines which society makes available to us.

The institutionalization of technology has meant that the choice of particular machines, or . . . control over this choice, remains in the hands of a dominant social class. And since technological innovation . . . is only carried out to the extent that it coincides with and maintains the interests of this class, new machines will only be introduced within the constraints that are imposed on the activities of the individual members of society.

This is very similar to Illich,[13] who stated that "convivial tools are those which give each person who uses them the greatest opportunity to enrich the environment with the fruits of his or her vision. Industrial tools deny this possibility . . . and allow their designers to determine the meaning and expectations of others."

Lovins[10] argued that large-scale technology leads to the mobilization of massive social resources without genuine regard to diverse opinions or circumstances. It results in sweeping, uniform national policies which conflict with local desires and interests and in lifestyles which are shaped by centralized utilities and industrial production. Diversity becomes uneconomic. He pointed out that centralized services are so vulnerable that— for example—a single rifleman could black out a whole city by cutting transmission lines. Similarly, workers in key industries, such as oil transport drivers, can exert considerable pressure to have their demands met. The response to such vulnerability is to increase surveillance and security activities and curtail freedoms such as the right to strike. All these characteristics combine to produce a significant loss of personal freedom.

In a broader context, freedom is curtailed by what Illich[13] called "radical monopolies" in which one type of product rather than one brand dominates (e.g., car versus personal transport) or when "one industrial production process exercises an exclusive control over the satisfaction of a pressing need, and excludes nonindustrial activities from competition." This corresponds quite closely to Bella's[18] concept of "dominating bads." He pointed out that no "goods" are so dominant that their fulfillment guarantees well-being, but that certain "bads," such as hunger, are dominant in the sense that well-being can be precluded by the presence of a single "bad." From this he argued that the more dominant a factor is, the more likely it is to turn out to be a "bad," and, hence, diversity should be encouraged.

In sum, these arguments make a strong case for the need to control, and perhaps reverse, the tendency toward cultural uniformity and loss of certain individual freedoms in the developed nations. However, when applied to developing countries, these ideas can lead to contradictory conclusions. On the one hand, there is the desire to stimulate material development in order to free people from hunger, disease and ignorance, and to do this in such a way that cultural changes will be minimized. On the other hand, there is the widespread recognition that social reform is essential to the success of any development effort. Thus, to quote Rybczynski:[5] "It [was] assumed that development could take place without major cultural changes. Although it is generally accepted that popular education, emancipation of women, and general democratization . . . are required for development to take place, there are traditional values that oppose these. . . . Restrictive religious practices, tribal divisions, or traditional elites may contradict modernization ideas. . . . To start with the assumption that they will not change may preclude development altogether." Elsewhere he argued that "landlordism, powerful rural elites, conservative banks and rapacious moneylenders all conspire to maintain the poverty of the landless peasants. These social and political problems require social and political solutions." He then distinguished these essential social *reforms* from the possibly less desirable social *changes* that technology on its own will produce. Similarly, Dickson[14] argued that political change to achieve liberation from the "economic and political shackles of a dominant class" is a precondition of significant technological change.

Rybczynski[5] doubted whether a new technology can be found and introduced that will not have profound social consequences for a relatively nontechnical society and cited the example of the far-reaching effects of the introduction of the snowmobile to the nomadic Lapps. This small scale and freely chosen machine has changed the relationship between the herdsman and his reindeer, possibly affecting the health and size of herds. Social contacts have been intensified by faster travel; the status of older, experienced men has declined; the cost of maintenance has led to new economic constraints; and social stratification has emerged between those who have adapted to the machine and those who have not. Similarly, "even jobs traditionally classified as 'women's work' are often taken over by men when they are mechanized: palm-oil pressing in Nigeria and rice-milling in Indonesia are two examples" (Newland quoted in note 19). In Singapore, the traditional Chinese extended-family way of life has been broken down by the introduction of western-style, high-rise housing designed for nuclear family units.

In the Sahel, modern medicine led to an expanding population which—coupled with the introduction of cash crops for the farmers and artesian water supplies for the nomadic herdsmen—resulted in the breakdown of the traditional culture and the disastrous ecological consequences of the Sahelian drought.[20] It is unlikely that any of these improvements would have been identified as inappropriate, although the dangers of making pasture, rather than water, the limiting factor might well be identified now. Yet, with hindsight, it is evident that the Sahelian peoples had evolved complex cultural patterns that enabled them to make efficient use of the natural resources of the region while protecting the fragile ecosystem on which they depended. They had developed a deep understanding of the environment in which they lived, and often had good reasons for resisting changes advocated by relatively ignorant western advisers. A policy of minimizing cultural change might have at least reduced the scale of the tragedy, but one is forced to wonder if any development in the western sense would have been possible under such a constraint, or whether the existing technology was most appropriate.

There is also a sense in which successful technological change, where this is seen as desirable, may be dependent on social appropriateness. Cultural beliefs, values, and norms change relatively slowly—certainly more slowly than technology, and often more slowly than organizational structures. Thus, to be successful, innovations must be compatible with these cultural features. For example, the practice of village midwives in parts of Burma of leaving the umbilical cord uncut until the placenta has emerged and then jumping on it is related to the belief that the spirit of life is in the placenta and must be persuaded to move to the infant. Successful modification of this method depended on a sensitive appreciation of this belief and a subtle modification of it, rather than outright condemnation of the practice. This was done by agreeing that the spirit of life is indeed in the placenta, but maintaining that it moves to the infant at the moment of birth.

Similarly, demands made on the operators by the new techniques must be compatible with their educational and cultural background. Sterilization of implements by midwives in Burma was introduced by telling them to leave them in a jar of boiling water until "two fingers" had boiled away. Another example is that the rotary motion of the legs required for "pedal power"—so beloved by many appropriate technologists—is quite foreign to people in some parts of Africa, who find it hard to learn.

Social systems are dynamic and even the most stagnant ones change slowly. Technological change is one of the forces for change, or, viewed from a different perspective, can be one of the consequences of change. To aim to preserve cultures is unrealistic, since even seemingly minor innovations may have unforeseen and far-reaching effects as the ripples due to dynamic interactions spread outwards. Nevertheless, innovation must be of a type and at a rate that can be absorbed by the culture without causing rejection or social breakdown if the goal of development is to be reached.

Decentralization and Self-Sufficiency

Decentralization to relatively self-sufficient village scale units is one of the central themes of the appropriate technology movement. *The Ecologist*[16] envisaged this as a means of easing the transition to a steady state economy, which it regarded as inevitable for resource and environmental reasons, and as a viable organizational form for such an economy. It argued firstly that the stress of rapid change can be handled more easily in small communities, where there can be full participation in decision-making. However, while participatory democracy may be easier to operate in small communities, size alone will not guarantee its existence. Indeed, most small communities have been—and are—far from such ideals, and small size could make autocratic control and even centralized dictatorship easier to impose than does the anonymity of large cities.

Secondly, it maintained that large-scale, energy-intensive agriculture will decline and that small farms and small holdings run by expert teams will increase. Small communities make it easier to return organic wastes to the land and minimize food transport costs.

Thirdly, it stated that small communities can be a source of pleasure and stimulation, leaving the individual free of bureaucratic authority and providing richer human relationships. However, it recognized that inward-looking, closed communities must be avoided if burdensome community constraints are not to be substituted, and hence that good communications with other groups are needed. How successful this strategy could be is debatable. For example, it is hard to envisage means for controlling community size without creating a closed group unless intergroup mobility is fairly high, but mobility is one of the prime factors causing a breakdown of community structure and relationships. Similarly, good communications were factors in the loss of local identity and the mobility that destroyed small communities in developed countries. It is worth noting that one of the few communitarian groups to survive within a modern society, the Hutterites, is essentially closed, has strict rules for subdivision when a community becomes too large, and has norms and mores that few in western countries would regard as providing a satisfactory level of individual freedom.[21]

The fourth advantage *The Ecologist* claimed for a decentralized society is that the total environmental impact would be lower than for an urban one because of reduced problems of servicing, distribution and mobility. Certainly some forms of impact would be reduced in total and the excessive concentrations that occur in large cities might be eliminated, but it is possible that, overall, the nature of the impact would be changed rather than reduced. For example, with regard to community self-sufficiency in services such as energy, water, and waste disposal. Harper[7] concluded that the use of nonrenewable energy sources, such as metals, might be increased, but the consumption of nonrenewable resources reduced. Similarly, experience to date suggests that emissions from a few centralized plants can be controlled more readily than from many small plants so that decentralization might result in lower local concentrations of pollutants, but higher total quantities. Whether or not this would represent a higher or lower impact would depend on the capacity of the environment as a whole to assimilate the pollutants without degradation.

Rybczynski[5] countered the decentralization case by arguing that not all production processes can be successfully decentralized or miniaturized, and that it would be foolish for a small country with good communications, which enable goods to be transported easily, to decentralize production. Certainly, the mining of large mineral deposits cannot be decentralized, and this will continue to be an essential activity for the foreseeable future even with maximum conservation and recycling. Nor would it appear to make sense to decentralize mineral processing because of the costs of transporting the bulk ore, unless local, small-scale energy sources became very much cheaper than alternative centralized supplies. However, this situation could change in the future if the dreams of biological mineral concentration using solar energy come to fruition. On the manufacturing front, it would be possible with computer-controlled machines to produce such items as refrigerators, washing machines, agricultural machinery,

and transport vehicles and replacement parts locally, but it is debatable whether this would be sensible. Costs are still likely to be substantially lower with some degree of specialization, so communities based on certain products rather than self-sufficiency might be more rational. However, this would negate some of the savings in transport and distribution costs envisaged with decentralized production. Also, experience with appropriate technology in developing countries suggests that decentralized production would need protection from competition from mass-produced goods in order to survive.[5]

Probably the strongest argument against decentralization is its sheer impossibility in the foreseeable future. The majority of people in developed countries already live in cities, the developing nations are urbanizing rapidly, and there seems little prospect that this trend can be reversed at least until population growth is controlled. Once established, cities represent a capital stock of housing, industry, commercial premises and services which turns over relatively slowly and cannot simply be abandoned or replaced. They also contain much of the cultural heritage of any civilization that is essential to social identity and cohesion.

A more realistic and immediately worthwhile goal than decentralization would be to ensure that the emerging "ecumenopolis" provides a satisfactory standard of life.[22] One way to do this, certainly, is to devise means of retaining more people in the rural areas and small towns by developing suitable economic activities, but—if it is to succeed—the appropriate technology movement must come to grips with the problems of the cities. In fact, this has been happening to a considerable extent with urban groups developing energy efficient houses, methods for waste disposal, selfhelp cooperative industries, etc. McRobie[12] gave an excellent outline of progress in this field.

The degree of self-sufficiency that is feasible or desirable is also a matter of some contention. One of the most discriminating articles on this topic is by Harper,[7] who recognized that some products are suitable for community production, but others are better produced by modern mass production techniques. In the former category he listed such things as dairying, flour-grinding, and bread-baking; building and furniture-making; printing, weaving, pottery-making and glass-blowing; and tanning and small foundries. In the latter category are materials such as sand, cement, wood, clay, glass, steel, and other metals; products such as nails, screws, paint, string, needles, matches, light bulbs, pencils, spectacles, etc; and machines such as sewing machines and clocks (and, presumably, power tools, tractors, trucks, etc.). He also listed paper and leather as suitable for mass production, although some people would advocate producing these at the community level. These lists are instructive and revealing, indicating a desire for self-sufficiency only in those products which are amenable to craft production with a high degree of creativity on the part of the producer. This aspect will be examined in more detail in the next section of this article.

With regard to services such as energy, water, and waste disposal, Harper[7] recognized that high standards of performance are very expensive to achieve in autonomous systems and that most people in developed countries are not prepared to accept the lower standard of amenity provided by affordable systems. Furthermore, "justifications from the resource point of view are only to be found in the countryside where network costs from central plant are high, ambient resources are abundant and are not feasibly collected, concentrated and redistributed. The communal level would reduce plant costs over the private level, and reduce network costs over the larger public level . . . a group of 20 family-sized units captures most of the economies of scale for autonomous systems. This agrees fairly well with the social criteria that separate cooperation among friends from transactions among buyers and sellers." Interestingly, this size also corresponds quite closely to the 60–150 people regarded as ideal for a Hutterite community—one of the very few successful commune-based social groups.[21]

The final words on self-sufficiency may be taken from a few hardy practitioners:

I moved to a two-hectare blackberry-infested farm with the aim of growing my own food. Suddenly, I was plunged into a world of pests, diseases and weeds; I discovered that all my new-found ideals of using no resources except my own and becoming self-sufficient were orders of magnitude harder to attain than I had imagined. . . . After two years of back-breaking work . . . I was ready to admit it wasn't working out as the blissful, relaxed, wholesome lifestyle I had envisaged. . . ." (Pausacker in note 23).

"Anyone who has actually tried to live in total self-sufficiency . . . knows the mind-numbing labor and loneliness and frustration and real marginless hazard that goes with the attempt" (Stewart Brand, editor of *The Whole Earth Catalog*, quoted in note 5). As Rybczynski said, "Interdependency is the unavoidable fact of the Modern Age."

Work and Alienation

It is generally agreed by appropriate technologists that work is desirable for personal fulfillment. However, they distinguish between "work," which is satisfying and creative, and "toil"[1] or "labor,"[13] which is not. The back-breaking, physically debilitating manual labor of the rural poor in developing countries, due to the absence of modern tools and machines, is toil, as is the psychologically debilitating, alienating employment as an appendage to a machine on an assembly line.

In developing countries, there is generally a pool of under- or unemployed labor available, leading to the idea that appropriate technologies are relatively labor-rather than capital-intensive if they are to improve the employment situation. In extreme cases, major infrastructure works such as roads, dams, and irrigation canals have been built by hard labor—for example, in China[8] or under the Indian Food for Work Program. In a less extreme way, small-scale, relatively labor-intensive plants have been devised for such things as brick, sugar, soap, and egg-carton making.[12] However, there is a limit to this process since, once all labor is absorbed, improvements to living standards can occur only as a result of improved labor productivity, and this requires steady improvement of the tools used. Also, much of the work generated can only be regarded as toil, even if those involved gain some satisfaction from the results. Thus Rybczynski[5] quoted the Chinese peasant who said: "The new agricultural implements make farm work easier. We are hoping for tractors. . . . Life will be much better then."

The problems are quite different in the developed countries, where physical toil has been almost completely eliminated by machines, but alienation and structural unemployment have been substituted. Historically, the concept of alienation has been mainly associated with the manufacturing industry, where mechanization has led to minimal operator involvement in repetitive operations and minimal contact with other workers. It has left the worker no control over the speed or method of work and has removed his satisfaction in the product, since he only makes a small contribution to each. However, the appearance of alienation in many white collar and service industry jobs before widespread mechanization suggests that the organization of work into simple repetitive tasks is the key factor. As the father of scientific management said, this requires that the worker "shall be so stupid and so phlegmatic that he more nearly resembles in his mental make-up the ox than any other type" (Taylor, quoted in note 14). Computers are enabling such job fragmentation and machine-pacing to be extended into ever more areas. For example, Cooley[24] described an industrial dispute at Rolls-Royce in 1971, when the management tried to get design staff to accept "shift work in order to exploit high capital equipment . . . work measurement techniques, the division of work into basic elements, and the setting of times for these elements, such time to be compared with actual performance." New physical problems such as tenosynovitis are also starting to emerge as a result of fast, repetitive operation of keyboards.

Industrial society is founded on the idea that meaningless, frustrating work can be compensated for by increased leisure and consumption of products, but appropriate technologists reject this. For example, Dickson[14] says "we must do away with machines that appear to treat man as mere appendages, and replace them with machines that the individual can operate in a way that is both socially productive and personally fulfilling." And Jungk (in note 6) wondered: "Is it possible to construct machines which actually respond to the human rhythm rather than the human being responding to the . . . machine? . . . The machine picks up signals caused by your movements and actually follows your style of work. If you work slower, then it turns slower, because it has artificial 'senses' which feel, or see that you work in this or that rhythm. . . ."

These concepts still appear to leave little room for the traditional "non-academic" knowledge of many "uneducated" workers and craftsmen. This can be of a high level, and of great economic value, as the following quotations show. More importantly, perhaps, making use of it is a key factor in reducing alienation:

The (Tanzanian) blacksmith's knowledge is entirely based upon accumulated empirical experience, which has been "inherited" from one generation of blacksmiths by the next. The knowledge is part of the blacksmith's senses and cannot be separated from him. If you give a blacksmith a piece of scrap, he will first test it. He weighs it a couple of times in each hand, heats it in the furnace and observes how long it takes to reach a certain colour. Finally, he beats it and looks at the sort of sparks it gives, listens and feels how the iron "responds" and perhaps he will also smell the sparks. Meanwhile he mumbles, as if he is talking to the steel. After testing it, he knows what sort of steel he is working with; furthermore, he even knows for which purpose this steel is best suited. He cannot convert his knowledge into the percentage of carbon content, but he "knows" (Müller, quoted in note 15).

And as Cooley[25] points out:

We have ordinary maintenance fitters who go to London Airport if a generator system is causing a problem. The whole aircraft might perhaps be grounded because of it. One of these fitters can listen to the generator, make a series of apparently simple tests—some of the older fitters will touch it in the way a doctor will touch a patient—and if it is running, will be able to tell you from the vibrations whether a bearing is worn and which one. The fitter will subsequently make decisions about the reliability of that piece of equipment, and upon that decision, the lives of 400 people may directly depend. The decision may be far more profound in many ways than that which a medical practitioner might make, yet if you asked those "ordinary people" to describe how they reached that decision, they could not do so in the usually accepted academic sense . . . yet that conclusion will be right, because they will have spent a lifetime accumulating the skill and knowledge and ability which helps them to arrive at it.

The selection of nonalienating technologies is not as simple as the rejection of alienating ones, however. Dickson[14] noted that "different people will obtain satisfaction from working with different types of tools or machines. It is therefore difficult to write down a list of machines which can be labelled as 'non alienating.' " Similarly, in discussing self-sufficient communities, Harper[7] concluded: "Whether they reduce social alienation in the long run is hard to say, but I would judge the autonomists probably have a case." He elaborated this by assuming that alienation costs are "the sum total of human misery involved in creating and running an autonomous unit. Generally speaking, the running alienation costs . . . fall on the occupants themselves in the form of vigilance, effort, social tensions, discomfort, and so on. The capital alienation costs are those required for building . . . and in making the materials: the unpleasant and ill-rewarded work involved in mining, manufacture of parts, cement, plastics, glass, wood, steel, aluminium, etc., which has to be set against those needed to provide coal, oil, electricity, food, water and sewerage for main services." It is clear that the provision of satisfying creative work is not as simple as the concept of "small is beautiful" would suggest.

DISCUSSION

Perhaps the greatest contribution of the appropriate technology movement to date has been the awakening of a widespread realization that technology is a controllable force for human betterment, rather than an autonomous juggernaut. In order to promote this view it was probably necessary to argue for a technology radically different from the prevailing one, but this paper has shown that, in practice, small may not always be beautiful. In discussing radical forecasts of the future, Ayres[26] said "Visionaries often prescribe what they believe people should have, but consistently fail to inquire deeply enough about how people or institutions would react to the innovations being put forward on their behalf." Despite the aim of a humane technology and an "economics as if people mattered,"[1] there is an element of this failure in the AT movement. The result is the prescription of solutions based on certain values which many people regard as undesirable.

The western philosophical emphasis on the primacy of the individual, which was formalized in the U.S. Declaration of Independence and is now enshrined in the UN Universal Declaration of Human Rights, is central to the values of the AT movement. While the concepts of community and culture are emphasized, these are secondary to the perceived need for individually satisfying and creative work and for autonomy of individuals to shape their own lives and pursue happiness. Historically, however, these are relatively recent ideas that can lay no more claim to being absolutely true than can earlier concepts that have been displaced, despite the fact that Jefferson held them to be self-evident. In many societies, the individual is still subordinate to the group and this is regarded as natural and right by those who are socialized into such traditions. There is little to suggest that the satisfaction or happiness of people in such societies is necessarily any less than that of those in individualistic societies, and, indeed, it may often be greater because of their clearly-defined roles and status and the supportive social structure. In the interests of cultural diversity, which the AT movement generally supports, technology should be adaptive to such radically different values where they occur, rather than be a subversive factor in favor of current western views.

The goal of decentralization in developed

countries to small self-sufficient communities has a long tradition amongst utopian groups, few of which have survived the attempt to turn the dream into reality. Its recent resurgence is rooted in the "back-to-the-land" movement, members of which see themselves as having escaped from the soulless "concrete jungle" to a more meaningful life in contact with nature, and who believe that all could benefit from a similar move. Not everyone agrees. Many who have been raised in the city feel lost and uncomfortable in rural environments, and others born in the country leave for the anonymity of the city to escape the narrowness and limitations of small country towns. However, the creation of a viable rural economy as a counterweight to the cities is a goal that should lead to increased freedom and choice of lifestyles for individuals in the developed world, and should reduce the growth of shanty slums and enhance the prospects for survival of traditional cultures in developing countries.

The emergence of interest in self-sufficiency also seems to be associated with the "back-to-the-land," "do-it-yourself," and "arts-and-crafts" movements of middle-class western suburbia. Many have found satisfaction and cost-savings in manual work as a relief from office and factory toil, and some have projected this into a whole way of life. The reality has often been very different from the dream, as the earlier quotations from Pausacker and Brand show. The mistakes that the protagonists made were to assume that because they enjoyed increased—but partial—self-sufficiency, they would enjoy total self-sufficiency more, and that everyone else would, too. While many like "doing-it-themselves" to a limited extent, few would find it satisfying as a way of life, and some loathe all forms of manual work, whether creative or not. Nevertheless, an increased level of self-sufficiency can be a powerful weapon for the poor in both cities and rural areas throughout the world in their fight for improved living standards.

The definition of what constitutes creative work also seems to be rooted in these same western middle-class movements. For these people, growing, preserving and cooking foods; making furniture and windmills; and generating their own entertainments are all highly satisfying, and hence, by definition, "creative" activities. Yet one wonders if their forebears and those who are still forced to do these things by necessity might not regard them as toil to be given up if and when the opportunity arises? Why else would the country housewife buy factory-preserved foods instead of preserving her own? Why else would the rich of all ages and the masses of today pay professional entertainers to keep them amused? Creative activity is perhaps too personal to be so easily defined.

Production for need, rather than greed, is another goal that tends not to be analyzed. What constitutes basic human need in this sense, and when does the desire for physical comfort and security become material greed? It is evident that material needs beyond sheer physical survival are largely culturally determined. The nomadic herdsman acquires more cattle than he "needs" because they provide social status, but is he greedy? Hi-fi equipment and a record collection may not be "necessary," and yet may be a source of great pleasure and satisfaction—what right has anyone to condemn such "luxuries"?

More seriously, in a society that produces only to satisfy "needs," who would decide what constitutes these needs? "Presumably the state would, in the end, have to undertake to define human 'needs' and to determine whose needs deserve to be met. Such an all-powerful state is, by definition, totalitarian. To me it is curious and ironic that such a program should be advocated by liberal humanitarians (such as Schumacher and Illich) who, in theory, believe strongly in freedom and democracy."[25]

CONCLUSIONS

This analysis has revealed considerable diversity of opinion within the AT movement on a number of issues. Small is not always beautiful; rural self-sufficiency is not always idyllic; not all sectors of economic activity are amenable to craft production; cultural stability is not always desirable; decentralization is not always practicable or good; one person's need may be another person's greed; and so on. It has also shown that, despite the best of intentions, there may be cultural biases in the suggested solutions to problems. The picture of a society based on AT thus turns out to be rather blurred and blotched on closer examination. It is not possible to define simply and clearly what an appropriate technology is.

Maybe the time has come to try to develop a theory of appropriate technology that avoids the worst of these cultural biases and permits a blend of big, small, and middling. Such a theory would have to be built upon a deep understanding of human needs—both individual and social—that could accommodate wide cultural variations. It would have to include sufficiently specific criteria that the appropriateness of any particular technology could be assessed, but avoid the totalitarian implications of state determination of appropriateness or needs.

This is a massive task which may be beyond the bounds of possibility because of the extreme variations of human culture and the ability of individuals to find satisfaction within diverse social systems. Nevertheless, even failure could prove to be very valuable in clarifying the nature of a "technology as if people mattered."

REFERENCES

1. Schumacher, E.F., *Small is Beautiful: Economics As If People Mattered* (London: Blond & Briggs, 1973).

2. Jequier, N., ed., *Appropriate Technology: Problems and Promises* (Paris: OECD, 1976).

3. Jequier, N., "Appropriate Technology: The Transition from First to Second Generation," paper for a joint seminar of the Conselho Nacional de De Servolvimento Cientifico e Tecnologia, and the International Council for Science Policy Studies and the Organisation of American States. Rio de Janeiro, March 6–10, 1978.

4. Darrow, K., and R. Pam, *Appropriate Technology Sourcebook* (Stanford: Volunteers in Asia, Inc., 1976; also 1977).

5. Rybczynski, W., *Paper Heroes: A Review of Appropriate Technology* (Dorchester: Prism Press, 1980).

6. Boyle, G. and P. Harper, eds., *Radical Technology* (London: Wildwood House, 1976)

7. Harper, P., "Autonomy" in Boyle and Harper, eds., op. cit.

8. Science for the People, *China: Science Walks on Two Legs* (New York: Discus Books, 1974).

9. Clarke, R., "Soft Technology: Blueprint for Research Community," *Undercurrents* no. 2 (1972).

10. Lovins, A.B., *Soft Energy Paths: Toward a Durable Peace* (Harmondsworth: Pelican Books, 1977).

11. Taylor, G.R., *Rethink: Radical Proposals to Save a Disintegrating World* (London: Secker and Warbury, 1972).

12. McRobie, G., *Small is Possible* (London: Jonathan Cape, 1981).

13. Illich, I.D., *Tools for Conviviality* (London: Calder and Boyers, 1973).

14. Dickson, D., *Alternative Technology and the Politics of Technical Change* (London: Fontana, 1974).

15. Mitchell, R.J., ed., *Experiences in Appropriate Technology* (Ottawa: Canadian Hunger Foundation, 1980).

16. "A Blueprint for Survival," *The Ecologist* (Hammondsworth: Penguin Books, 1972).

17. Lowbury, E., "Communications" in Boyle and Harper, eds., op. cit.

18. Bella, D. A., *Fundamentals of Comprehensive Environmental Planning* Proceedings of the American Society of Civil Engineers, Engineering Issues, *EI* 100 (1974).

19. Caughman, S. and M.N. Thiam, "Women Finding Suitable Assistance: Soapmaking in Mali," in R.J. Mitchell ed., *Experiences in Appropriate Technology* (Ottawa: The Canadian Hunger Foundation, 1980).

20. Wade, N., "Sahelian Drought: No Victory for Western Aid," *Science* 185 (1974).

21. Hostetler, J.A. and G.E. Huntington, *The Hutterites in North America* (New York: Holt, Rinehart and Winston, 1967).

22. Doxiadis C.A., *Ecology and Ekistics* (London: Elek Press, 1977).

23. Pausacker, I. and J. Andrews, *Living Better with Less* (Ringwood: Penguin Books, Australia, 1981).

24. Cooley, M., "Contradictions of Science and Technology in the Productive Process," in G. Boyle, D. Elliott and R. Roys, eds., *The Politics of Technology* (London: Longmans/Open University Press, 1977).

25. Cooley, M., *Architect or Bee? The Human/Technology Relationship* (Sydney: Trans National Coop., 1980).

26. Ayres, Robert U., *Uncertain Futures: Challenges for Decision-Makers* (New York: Wiley, 1979).

31
Technology Transfer: That's What It's All About

ROBERT R. IRVING

Robert R. Irving discusses a variety of factors that constitute obstacles to the transfer of technology in industry, as well as a number of ways of promoting greater acceptance of such transfers. His view is that technologically conservative individuals, who have the most power, refuse to believe that quality—which would be brought about by technology transfer—plays any role at all in maintaining the financial soundness of their firms.

What are the factors that oppose technological change in industry?

1. The politically powerful industrial empires are afraid of it. The people who manage and work in these empires do not want to see the boat rocked.
2. Companies hesitate to be the guinea pigs. They might read about some new technology or listen to lectures on the subject, but that's it.
3. The NIH factor is still prevalent. "It's a nice process," they will say, "but we can do better than that. We'll roll up our sleeves and show you how to do it."
4. Companies are afraid that the process won't work and or that the material has not been tested thoroughly enough.
5. Word gets around about the failures. Often, they're cases of misuse. What about the successes?

One of the many experts who has addressed this subject is William M. Webster, vice president, RCA Laboratories, Princeton, N.J. In a recent article in *RCA Engineer,* Mr.

Webster stressed the importance of the presence of a receiver, some person or some organization that is sold, if you will, on this new technology.

But the technology will die, he warns, unless the receiver is technically capable of pursuing the project through the next phase. There must also be stability in terms of funding and direction to finish the next phase. In addition, he says, there must also be an "impedance match" for transfer at the other end.

"Most important," claims Dr. Webster, "the project being transferred must have high priority in the eyes of the receiver's management."

Another criterion that must be established is how to know when the technology has been effectively transferred. According to Dr. Webster, the basic condition that must be met is that the receiving organization must be truly and unconditionally comfortable taking on the responsibility for the project.

So, why do things go wrong?

One problem is that the project wasn't right

From *Iron Age* Volume 226 (November 7, 1983), pp. 53, 57, 58, 61, 62. Reprinted with permission from *Iron Age.*

in the first place. No matter how well intended, the originator of the technology did not really understand what the customer needed.

Another problem is that the project was not ready yet to be transferred. The originator couldn't answer questions with respect to reliability, tolerances, and costs. "Perhaps no one asked these questions," Dr. Webster suggests, "but the project was transferred anyway, only to bounce back and forth between the two organizations."

Perhaps there really wasn't a receiver at all. Perhaps the receiver was, in fact, largely committed to other more urgent projects. Then, sometimes the participants thought that the project had been transferred, but it hadn't.

In summary, Dr. Webster observes: "Managers involved in technology transfer must realize that egos exist and that the *natural* tendency for organizations is to drift apart— toward provincialism, the "not-invented-here" syndrome, secrecy and mistrust.

"The only preventative medicine I know of," he points out, "is for the management of each activity to bend over backward to maintain a constructive relationship. Instead of each group being willing to meet the other half-way, each must be willing to go a good deal farther. If the project works, there is always enough glory to go around. And, if it doesn't, everyone has failed."

According to another expert on the subject, technology transfer is not simple. It is not something that can be done by edict. There has to be an identified fit of a need and a capability.

A classic example of a technology in midstream is CAD/CAM. The implementation of CAD/CAM is still being delayed because industry, as a whole, still is not thinking in terms of long-term strategies. Many companies have impressive five-year marketing plans and engineering is even involved in the preparation of these plans, but manufacturing, it seems, has been left out in the cold. This is particularly true in the medium- and small-sized companies.

What does a company have to gain? Im-

proved profitability, improved productivity, the ability to get the product out into the field faster, lower inventory, better quality. For companies making a variety of products, they will be able to go into flexible manufacturing concepts. Thus, they can convert from hard tooling to computer control.

You won't need drawings any more. You won't need duplicate copies of prints. You don't have all these committees set up for production control and material control and in the purchasing department, all handling drawings. The information is available for everyone to see on the cathode ray tube.

At the crux of it all, however, are people. Because of the glamour and the money, many young scientists and engineers have been going into research and development rather than into manufacturing. Nobody over 30 has been educated in the computer. The older people are just not familiar with computer technology. Therefore, they are not going to propose it. Or, if a consultant is involved, the older engineers still feel uncomfortable and tend to shy away from it.

The universities will have to become much more involved in establishing programs in manufacturing engineering.

With some exceptions, the universities have just not recognized the importance of manufacturing engineering. Corporations have to begin to send their people back to college to learn these new technologies.

Fred Michel is with the U.S. Army Development and Readiness Command, Alexandria, Va. He is the director for manufacturing technology.

"We have a new program," explains Mr. Michel, "called producibility engineering and planning. The fundamental aspect of this program is to force, through contractual means, the contractor's manufacturing engineer—early on in the design of a component— to achieve a greatly improved ease of manufacture. This forces the contractor to start making plans for an improved factor during the engineering design phase."

One successful technology transferral mechanism is the Department of Defense's manufacturing technology of ManTech program.

This program is still alive and well. Its main thrusts include metal removal, metal shaping, the application of the computer-aided manufacturing principle, the integrated factory and flexible manufacturing.

With defense budgets in place and contracts about to be announced, the ManTech program is bound to grow in importance.

The objective of this program is to improve the productivity and responsiveness of industry by engaging in various initiatives. Those initiatives are as follows:

1. Aid in insuring the economical production of qualitatively superior weapon systems on a timely basis.
2. Insure that advanced manufacturing processes, techniques and equipment are used to reduce DOD materiel acquisition costs.
3. Continuously advance manufacturing technology to bridge the gap from R&D advances to full-scale production.
4. Foster greater use of computer technology in all elements of manufacturing.
5. Assure that more effective industrial innovation is simulated by reducing the cost and risk of advancing and applying new and improved manufacturing technology.
6. Assure that manufacturing processes are consistent with safety and environment considerations and energy conservation objectives.

The above are the program objectives from the ManTech program's statement of principles. Also in the statement, it is pointed out that implementation and technology transfer of project results are critical elements of manufacturing technology program management.

It has been said that a main aim of the ManTech program is to do what is needed to move existing technology that has been sitting on the shelf onto the production floor. It is really not so simple. Often, several steps, several projects are required.

The importance of technology as a tool for cost reduction is apparent in the philosophy known as near net shapes. This philosophy seems to have been conceived in the U.S. Air Force, where it is still very much alive and kicking. The point of this philosophy is to manufacture components with as little waste or scrap as possible. So, we are hearing more about and seeing more of hot isostatic pressing, isothermal forging, superplastic forming/ diffusion bonding, powder metallurgy, high-quality castings and composite materials.

According to John Williamson, one of the technical managers in Wright-Patterson Air Force Base's Manufacturing Technology Division, the next generation of military fighter plane will probably contain between 60 to 80 pct aluminum-plus-polymer composites, and the aluminum-composite combination will probably be split in half. Needless to say, it has taken polymer composites a long, long time to penetrate the military aircraft field, but it is finally taking place.

Why so long? The main hang-up, says Mr. Williamson, has been price. Here we are talking about a material which had been selling for about $200 per lb about 10 years ago, but the price is now down in the $20 to $30 per lb range. Even though it is still much more expensive than aluminum, it is lighter in weight and it has a few other advantages going for it.

The time factor is best portrayed in the following situation. In a few years, a hot isostatically pressed titanium powder component will make it onto a military aircraft. Researchers have been working on this one for nine years.

As sensible as it sounds, the near net shape philosophy will take a long time before it becomes totally accepted throughout industry. Many, many manufacturers—major aircraft manufacturers included—have heavy investments in machining systems. One just doesn't write off investments like that.

Still, the new company or the new competitor can afford to look into near net shapes.

On the other hand, from the looks of it, we will have to be much more "fleet of foot" technologically than we have ever been in the past. Everyone will have to become much more familiar with any new development that might impinge on his or her area. Revolutionary change may strike without much warning.

And, new competition may take shape quite unexpectedly.

A good example is a ManTech project undertaken for the Navy by the McLean-Anderson, Inc. Laboratory, Menomonee Falls, Wis. The project involved the feasibility of a filament-wound ship hull. Based on the results obtained on scale model size hulls, the concept looked very promising using either E glass or graphite as the reinforcing material.

As reported at the recent SAMPE meeting in Anaheim, Calif., the laboratory noted that only 22 hours of continuous processing would be required to filament wind a full-size hull.

The same SAMPE meeting also produced some interesting developmental projects in the near net shape arena. One was a project in isothermal shape rolling performed by Solar Turbines International, San Diego, for the Naval Air Systems Command. The near net shape titanium components were tested by Grumman Aerospace Corp., Bethpage, N.Y.

Isothermal shape rolling is a process which employs localized electrical resistance heating to produce shapes such as channel beams and custom tees from billet, sheet and plate materials. The test results were positive. The potential savings in machining costs are very high indeed.

In another project, Northrop Corp., Hawthorne, Calif., reported on the hot isostatic pressing of aluminum castings and the opportunity of using such castings in place of components machined out of wrought shapes. It was found that the castings would be adequate structurally and that they would reduce acquisition costs by 30 to 50 pct.

A new material is something else. Recent years have seen the introduction of such materials as the graphite epoxies, metal matrix composites, mechanical alloys, amorphous metals and aluminides. Within the established families of metals, alloy developers have also been hard at work. Witness, for example, the tremendous strides made in the high-strength low-alloy steels, the high-performance stainless steels and the higher-strength aluminum alloys.

Many times, the implementation of a new material is delayed because of safety factors. A new superalloy does not make the transition from the metallurgical laboratory to a jet engine overnight. Thousands of hours of testing are required. The superalloy must prove itself.

The situation is even more frustrating to metals producers in the boiler and pressure field, where promising new steels have had to wait years before receiving the blessing of the ASME code. But here again, the concern is human safety.

However, not all user industries have to be so safety-conscious. You have undoubtedly heard people say: "Competition builds their components out of mild steel. It's a good material. It's cheap. We know how to work it. So, why change?"

Also in the materials field, another badly neglected technology is the use of coatings and/or clads to prevent premature failures due to corrosion or wear. Why specify a premium alloy for an entire component when only the surface of the component will be subjected to some sort of corrosive attack? Why not design the component so 90 pct of its mass will be of steel and the rest will be made out of an appropriate corrosion-resistant material?

One individual who is very hard to convince is the design engineer. The last airplane he designed flew very nicely, thank you. You are asking him to put his reputation on the line and have him gamble on a new material which has never been up in an airplane before. Then, there is the manufacturing engineer. His people, his tools have no learning curve on the material.

On the subject of lasers, David Belforte, president of Belforte Associates, Sturbridge, Mass., sees the metalworking laser as finally catching on. Its main hang-up, until a few years ago, was the question of its reliability in an industrial environment. It was also an expensive instrument, he says.

"I am hearing comments from the automotive industry," he points out, "that the uptime on laser welders is 80 pct, compared to 60 pct with the electron beam. Had it not been for the fact that new automobile transmissions were being developed, it's unlikely that the laser would have been able to crack the market so soon."

The laser also fits in naturally with automated systems. Thanks to the fact that laser pricing has become more stabilized, this technology appears to be a good bet for flexible manufacturing systems as well.

Remember the underbody laser welder which had been proposed for the Ford Motor Co.? It didn't fly at the time, but this kind of application will be of interest again fairly soon. Why? Because there seems to be a strong movement under way in Detroit towards more careful part design, better fixturing, better dies, better control of the stamping operation, better manipulation on the production line to insure that the parts will fit better.

Several key components are already being laser welded at the Northern Ordnance Division of FMC Corp., Minneapolis. In this Navy ManTech project, effective cost reductions are being realized. These particular parts had been welded using the submerged-arc process.

What about laser cutting? There are 80 to 90 laser cutting systems in operation in this country in sheet metal shops. Some are pure laser systems and others are lasers in conjunction with turret punches.

The automobile industry has done a lot with laser heat treating, especially on gears. The main drawback, at this time, is cost of equipment. Here the laser is competing with high-frequency induction heating. Mr. Belforte notes that the costs of these two processes have become quite competitive.

"The laser is a proven process now. I think the business is about ready to take off. In five years," he predicts, "the laser will just be another tool and will no longer be regarded as high technology any more."

Also, in many applications the laser and the robot are bound to become familiar companions.

A great deal is written about lasers and robots, but there aren't that many in operation yet.

In 1977, a group of executives from a number of large American corporations flew to West Germany to attend the Essen Welding Fair. These executives had never been to a welding show in their lives, but they went to this one to see the robots. Welding, apparently, had been a problem in these companies. It was felt that the robot might solve that problem.

Well, here it is six years later and the robot is probably the hottest development to hit the metalworking industry since CAD/CAM. Yes, the automotive industry is making good use of robotic spot welding, but the big plum—robotic arc welding—has not really been tapped as expected.

A possibility here is that the brand new American Welding Technology Application Center can do something to pave the way for better market acceptance of the technology.

Another badly needed technology, but one that is having all kinds of trouble breaking through, is statistical quality control.

Statistical QC is as old as the hills. Painstaking attention to its principles is required to make it go. There are now software packages available from various sources that will collect, analyze and display the appropriate manufacturing data. The basic tools of statistical quality control—the control charts, histograms and scatter diagrams—can now be called up conveniently on the cathode ray tube.

Yet, with all this talk of quality lately, why is it that more companies have not jumped on the statistical QC bandwagon? It's the same old story, the experts point out. The bean counters are very much in control and most of them refuse to believe that quality plays any role at all in the bottom line.

PART VI

GOVERNING TECHNOLOGY: MORALLY ASSESSING APPROACHES TO TECHNOLOGY POLICY MAKING

TECHNOLOGY POLICY MAKING AND TECHNOLOGY CONTROVERSIES

Discussing technology policy making can be rather irritating. It arouses impatience and tends to create conflict, not least because it concerns such urgent and threatening matters as nuclear energy, environmental collapse, the possible catastrophes of genetic engineering, and nuclear weapons and "Star Wars." After all, these matters call for speedy treatment, and talk of policy tends to complicate and slow the process of acting on them. Why not simply get down to business and *do* something? Calls for immediate policy making action, however, are often exercises in naiveté. For though many agree that matters such as these require quick policy making, the selections and discussions above and to follow provide ample evidence of the lack of agreement and even controversy and confrontation regarding *what* the policy making action should be. Technological policy making itself is not a simple, easy-to-manage activity. A major question throughout this book is What policy making actions ought to be performed, and what policies introduced, concerning matters of technology in view of the controversy and confrontation aroused by such matters? Our discussions have sought to develop a viable framework for providing firm guidance in this area. The characteristically political aspects one must reckon with in addressing this question have, however, only been mentioned in Part VI; an attempt will be made to systematically incorporate them into our framework.

INSULATION VERSUS PARALYSIS: A POLICY MAKER'S DILEMMA?

The first selection in Part VI, A Typology of Technological Policymaking in the U.S. Congress, by Patrick W. Hamlett, discusses the problems posed by conflicts and difficulties in technological policy making, and provides an initial taxonomy for dealing with them. This taxonomy has two dimensions. The first, policy discontinuity, is the degree of deviation from established practices and policies on matters thought to require policy making action; the second, technological integration, is the degree of concentration or decentralization in the background network of social, economic, and political institutions that surround a technology associated with an issue thought to require active policy making. Focusing on the U.S. Congress, on the grounds that it contributes greatly to the evolution of technological policy, Hamlett states that, together, these dimensions serve to construct a policy typology that "can . . . be seen as a possible first step toward predicting the outcomes of specific technological policy battles in Congress." This is because the taxonomy is based on dimensions Hamlett considers significant for congressional policy making: "Concentrated infrastructures, because they have fewer participants, offer Congress a greater opportunity to make and implement long-term technology management decisions."

According to Hamlett, this does not mean that the fewer the participants, the smaller the degree of discontinuity in the policies introduced by Congress; nor does it mean that the less concentrated the participants, the greater the degree of discontinuity in congressionally sponsored policies. Hamlett mentions the decisions to develop the atomic and hydrogen bombs, and the decisions leading to the introduction of the intercontinental ballistic missile, the MIRV'd ICBM, and the cruise missile into the U.S. nuclear arsenal as examples of policy decisions involving relatively few participants but a high degree of discontinuity. He also indicates that certainly not all, but doubtless some technology-enforcing environmental protection legislation was brought about by highly decentralized policy making, with only a moderate degree of discontinuity.[1]

This typology raises a number of moral questions, considered in the light of Hamlett's statement about the conditions necessary for Congress to make long-term technology management decisions:

> For Congress, the key to making long-term technology management decisions is to gain a degree of policy insulation from cross-cutting political pressures. Only through insulating such decisions from conflicting and disruptive constituent demands does Congress gain the flexibility to review existing technology policies dispassionately, to determine if they still contribute to (or hinder) the public weal. Relatively free of pressure politics, Congress may be able to create policies more congruent with emerging technical options, policies which may be more beneficial to the majority of people even if temporarily harmful to those attached to the existing policies.

These remarks are no doubt realistic. They also suggest various moral questions worth addressing in further exploring Hamlett's suggestions: When, if ever, should the long-term benefits to the majority of people take precedence over the temporary harm to some people? Does it depend on what the temporary harm is? Granting that Congress sometimes—even often—can sufficiently insulate itself from conflicting and disruptive constituent demands, when, if ever, would it be right for Congress thus to insulate itself? Would Congress, in doing so, ever take upon itself to determine *for* the public what is in the public's interest? What, if any, is the difference between determining for the public what is in its interest and gaining a degree of freedom from pressure politics? In preceding parts, the objections prompted by the first question against prevalent forms of utilitarianism were discussed in some detail and, accordingly, will not be pursued further. Some objections raised by the remaining questions have also been discussed, but deserve further attention. It was previously argued that there are strong reasons to believe that the above-described insulation is morally objectionable, however effective it might be, if it is paternalistic, and thus conflicts with the right of the public to help in establishing what they deem desirable. Hence, any form of policy making insulation needs special justification that shows it is not paternalistic or, if it is paternalistic, the reasons, under certain circumstances, are stronger for than against it. Without such justification, it is morally objectionable. Additional reasons can be added in support of this conclusion: Such insulation may turn out to be ineffective in the long-term as well, in that it may lead to even greater controversy and confrontation than it means to avoid by excluding significant public participation; and the long-term benefits may not be forthcoming after all. Indeed, the current controversies and confrontation regarding the arms race—including heated arguments about the intercontinental ballistic missile, the MIRV'd ICBM, and the cruise missile—provide evidence that the decision to introduce them into the U.S. nuclear arsenal, in significant isolation from public opinion, has not been as successful in the long-term as expected, and may, after all, turn out to be self-frustrating. Hence, without special justification, policy makers' insulation is morally objectionable not only if it conflicts with the public's right to contribute in establishing what is desirable, but also if it turns out to be self-frustrating.

Of course, this does not mean that such policy making is never morally justified. Nor does it indicate that Hamlett's position is unsound. He presents his typology simply "as a possible first step toward predicting the outcomes of specific technological policy battles in Congress," and this leaves room for refinements or additions. Rather, stating that policy making through insulation is morally objectionable without special justification indicates that, if and when it is justified, there must be reasons that establish that the above right does not override other considerations in a given case, and reasons indicating that such policy making will not frustrate its own purpose.[2] This is relevant, for example, when isolating Congress from conflicts frees it to introduce technology policies that disregard them, which could lead to even greater disruption from increased conflict, and even to societal crises.

If, as argued, the degree of conflict and confrontation that impend, not only at policy making time, but also in the future, as a result of isolating Congress from public pressures—whenever this amounts to isolating the public from the policy making process—turns out to be critical in assessing technological policies and policy making actions, then adding a third dimension to Hamlett's two may improve the chances of reliably predicting the outcome of technological policy making battles, and of responsibly assessing technological policies and policy making actions. This third, pragmatic, dimension is in accord with the considerations our approach combines with considerations of consequences and rights. One must make significant room for dialogue and public participation, however heated, and rule it out only for special reasons, for such participation, though often frustrating, involves not only a respect for people, as considerations of rights require, but provides the only sound alternative to simply postponing and increasing conflict through isolation. Indeed, this pragmatic consideration makes it possible for respect for people and foreseeable desirable consequences to become a reality. The valid concern with long-term planning is not only morally, but also politically, justified only when it is addressed within the constraints of the above considerations of rights and consequences, mediated by the pragmatic considerations of what policy will work in the foreseeable future and not simply in the short-run.

TECHNOLOGY LITERACY AND PUBLIC PARTICIPATION

If congressional isolation from constituencies' conflicting or uninformed demands turns out not to be possible or desirable, then providing technological information to the members of those constituencies might be required to ensure that their demands cease to be uninformed and, in some cases, maybe also cease to conflict. Attempts at providing this information are discussed in Rustum Roy's Technological Literacy: An Uphill Battle. The author describes the Science, Technology, and Society programs, launched with the aim of addressing what the National State Teachers Association, in 1982, called "the biggest gap in high-school science education." This gap "is not in physics, biology, or even computer manipulation—but in the relationship of science and technology to society." Rustum Roy states that more such programs are desirable at U.S. secondary high schools and college campuses. Their introduction and successful development, however, face some serious obstacles, which the selection points out.

The Science, Technology, and Society programs were for the most part launched in the late sixties, and there are currently about fifty or sixty substantial university programs that focus on science, technology, and human values in one form or another. But most are limited and faltering. Further, the programs launched did not have much of an effect. Not even 1 percent of the targeted goal of one million technology-literate college students had been reached after about a decade of teaching. Rustum Roy attributes this failure to "the rigidity of the departmental structure in universities," and states that a truly interdisciplinary faculty constituted by engineers and historians, philosophers and biochemists, political scientists and physicists working together is crucial to any effective Science, Technology, and Society program.

These suggestions are no doubt worth pursuing. In doing so, however, some hard, practical questions arise: What does it mean for a program or an approach to be interdisciplinary? Is it interdisciplinary if it simply juxtaposes approaches to one subject matter from the points of view of different disciplines? Or must it join the methods of one or more disciplines in attempting to treat problems that no one discipline's methods can resolve in isolation from others'? Is this not, after all, a way of formulating and dealing with problems within the scope of a new discipline, but just another discipline nonetheless? What is interdisciplinary about it? On what basis can one really assess whether a given combination of concepts and methods from more than one discipline has any moral value and, if it does, what this value is? How should the problem-solving needs be balanced against professional or disciplinary constraints, especially when existent disciplines are embedded in institutional arrangements that strengthen their constraints and cannot be altered overnight? And, what effect are interdisciplinary approaches likely to have on the public's technological literacy? Is it not overly idealistic to expect that the public will be literate about everything, when not even the practitioners of a single discipline are able to keep up with all of the information in their own fields?

WHAT TYPE OF PUBLIC PARTICIPATION?

The problems regarding the very possibility of public technological literacy are discussed in Science for Public Consumption: More Than We Can Chew?, by Samuel Florman. He writes:

> How would I find time to keep abreast of the latest information on acid rain, the greenhouse effect, recombinant DNA, nuclear waste, new drugs, new diets, and a myriad of other technical matters that affect me and the society around me? It is all very well to speak of an informed public, but in truth we spend our lives relying upon experts.
>
> The paradox defies resolution. A wide diffusion of knowledge is good but the uncertainties are awesome, no citizen can be adequately informed, and perplexing technical reports lead to anxiety and erratic political action.

The author concludes that the way in which the public should stay knowledgeable about technology is not by keeping abreast of every field's latest information. It is, rather, by establishing relationships with experts and politicians that combine trust and suspicion, respect and obstinance—all aimed at ensuring that social objectives are best translated into technical decisions.

This suggestion is no doubt worth pursuing further; but what the particular relationship between experts, politicians, and the public ought to be has yet to be worked out. In preceding parts, some such relationships were discussed in rough descriptions of the membership and procedures of hospital teams attempting to establish whether to use certain medical technologies, and when indicating how the public interest could be, to some extent, determined by means of surveys using the willingness-to-sell criterion. Much more, however, needs to be covered in this area, through further, outside reading. The present selection, nonetheless, provides a worthwhile starting point for the critical scrutiny of technological policy making. Some moral questions that promise to be of help in this task are: What is technocracy? Is it ever justified? How can and how should the public be informed about new technological developments and their implications, so that its members can responsibly affect technological policy making under the present circumstances of rapid development? What new institutions ought to be created? What procedures ought these to follow?

HIGHLIGHTS OF THE BOOK'S DISCUSSIONS

As was stated in the Preface and in the Note to the Reader, the aim of this book is to stimulate critical discussion and to help readers develop their reasoning and value-appraising skills when dealing with contemporary moral controversies in technology. The activity involved in pursuing this aim and developing these skills is called, as explained in the General Introduction, "ethics as a branch of inquiry" or, the same thing, for all relevant purposes, "moral philosophy," "ethical theory," "moral theory," and "reflection on morality." This is critical inquiry aimed at soundly dealing with the problems of right and wrong, good and bad, and justified and unjustified, that arise in people's lives. When the inquiry is intended, as ours is, to deal with problems in technology, it is sometimes called "ethics of technology" or "technology ethics."

The General Introduction also explains that ethical problems can be behavioral, institutional, or of character, also called "educational." Though these are not unrelated to each other, they have different subject matters: behavioral problems concern actions or conduct; institutional problems deal with policies, practices or institutions; and problems of character involve such things as a person's character, character traits, and attitudes. The selections and discussions do not entirely disregard behavioral moral problems or moral problems of character; but they do emphasize institutional moral problems in technology.

The introduction to Part I describes how conflicting concerns or considerations about rules, obligations, claims, rights and duties, needs, interests, wants, advantages, desires, attitudes, and traits prompt moral problems. Moral problems have been defined as problems prompted by such conflicting concerns and considerations, and are formulated in questions of right and wrong, good and bad, justified and unjustified. Those addressed in this book are moral problems concerning controversies in technology. In identifying these, however, there has been no rush to define technology and then establish which developments are technological; the question of the nature of technology is left open, and a variety of developments, ordinarily considered technological, which raise moral problems and controversies—thereby having some claim to being matters of moral controversies *in technology*—are discussed.

In attempting to help readers develop their reasoning and value-appraising skills regarding contemporary moral problems in technology, the book develops a basic theoretical approach including the range hypothesis. This is the view that there is a range of ethical problems that, roughly, has the following characteristics: at one end of this range, rights carry the most weight; at the other end of it, consequences (especially collective consequences) carry the most weight; and all along, pragmatic considerations set limits to the alternatives that can actually be applied to problems. Throughout, we have provided reasons indicating why alternative, less flexible, theories—such as some forms of utilitarianism that are not sensitive to pragmatic constraints, and theories of justice or rights that are not sensitive to pragmatic constraints or do not appeal to the desirability of consequences—are not as helpful in dealing well with contemporary moral controversies in technology as is the framework here developed. For one thing, this framework can, while the alternative theories cannot, help answer valid moral questions arising in connection with the problems posed by the controversies. As discussed in Part III, for example, at least some predominant forms of utilitarianism cannot help answer certain questions about the distribution of happiness, and at least some rights-based theories cannot help answer questions on certain war-related issues, in which the very existence of rights is in question. By contrast, the framework partially developed throughout the book provides ways of attempting to answer these questions through procedures that, among other things, involve meaningful dialogue between those affected. It further gives a central role to public participation procedures and the willingness-to-sell criterion, both sensitive to individual rights and dignity in ways that isolated policy making may not be and the willingness-to-pay criterion never is. Hence, by contrast with the alternatives, this framework is less arbitrary, more relevant to and compatible with the concerns expressed in the controversies. It gives more extensive guidance by helping to answer valid questions, that alternative theories cannot address, and by sensitively covering a wider range of technology controversies.

However, this book's theoretical framework does not provide formulas for all controversies. It is, rather, intended to help readers develop a perspective that will enable them to deal more intelligently with current and future moral controversies in technology.

NOTES

1. This type of policy making process fits into what David Braybrooke and Charles E. Lindblom characterized as disjointed incrementalism in their *A Strategy of Decision* (New York: The Free Press, 1963), especially chaps. 4 and 5. The former type of policy making process would not, or not clearly, fit into the disjointed incrementalism category.

2. This position leaves room for strategies other than disjointed incrementalism, but only when there are reasons of the said type. These are likely to involve a reference to such conditions as present or impending crises, to which disjointed incrementalism was not meant to apply. See Braybrooke and Lindblom.

32
A Typology of Technological Policymaking in the U.S. Congress

PATRICK W. HAMLETT

*Patrick W. Hamlett argues that there are two basic dimensions of policy making, policy disconti-
nuity and technological integration. Policy discontinuity is the degree of deviation from established practices and policies in any given area of technological policy. Technological integration is
the degree of concentration or decentralization in the network of social, economic, and political
institutions surrounding a technology. He focuses on the U.S. Congress on the grounds that it
contributed significantly to the development of technological policy in the United States, and
argues that the typology he presents can be seen as a first step towards predicting the outcome of
specific technological policy battles.*

In a rapidly developing research field, broad
theoretical analysis often fails to keep pace
with the growth of independent and unconnected research. At some point, it becomes
fruitful to stop, to reassess what has been
accomplished in the field, and to attempt to
develop the broader conceptual coherence
needed for theory formation. Science and
technology policy studies have grown dramatically in the last few decades, and, as books,
articles, and scholarly journals on this subject
increase, the need for some coherent theoretical grounding grows accordingly.

One initial step in theorizing is the creation
of typologies of phenomena, which can then
be used to generate testable empirical hypotheses. And so, this essay describes a typology
of technological policy decisions made by the
U.S. Congress, a typology that may prove
useful in integrating such decisions into a
theoretically coherent whole.

A typology itself is not an empirical proposition, but a more or less useful "filing
system" for grouping or categorizing similar
phenomena. In consequence, typologies are
judged by their logical coherence and conceptual breadth. If the dimensions selected for a
typology are designed well, then the typology
itself will suggest empirically verifiable hypotheses, the results of which may modify,
extend, or enrich the original classification.

The categorizations presented rest upon an
explicit conception of the scope of technological policymaking which is a good deal broader
than the traditional emphasis upon "high tech"
hardware, moon missions, or new laboratory
products. Technological policies include all of
these, of course, but they also include governmental decisions in other areas. Decisions
affecting national transportation, communications, or energy-production systems, for instance, often involve a large technological
component, or may affect an existing technological system; so also do decisions about

Reprinted from *Science, Technology and Human Values* Volume 8, no. 2 (Spring 1983), pp. 33–40.
Copyright © 1983 by the Massachusetts Institute of Technology and the President and Fellows of Harvard
College. Reprinted by permission of John Wiley & Sons, Inc., and the author.

safety regulations, risk-assessment, resources management, and many other areas. Technology policy analysis assumes that, in all of these diverse policy domains, certain discernible regularities may be attributed to the technological components of the specific policy under consideration. Although the policymakers who are pursuing other goals may have regarded the technology affected by a policy decision as having only secondary importance, in many cases, the technology selected or altered will have affected that decision. Research in technological policymaking, then, often moves through a variety of domains— e.g., energy policy or transportation policy— as it follows the theoretical connections between decisions.

The influence of the U.S. Congress in the creation of new programs, in continuation of funding, and in legislative oversight make it a natural center for research in technological policy analysis.[1] This typology focuses upon two policy dimensions that are especially sensitive to the likelihood of short-term constituent pressures affecting the coherence of long-term technological policies made in Congress. The first dimension of the typology— *policy discontinuity*—assesses the degree of deviation from established practices and policies in the area under consideration. The policy option chosen by Congress may vary from a simple reassertion of existing policies, with no change, to relatively modest modifications of existing policies, to truly radical departure from the established situation. The latter option may occur through the introduction of techniques that either create new technical capacities or improve existing capacities in significant ways, or through a major alteration in the structure, support, or utilization of an established technology. This dimension is a continuum, from moderate change through radical alterations.

The second dimension of the typology attempts to capture certain characteristics of the social, economic, and political environment in which the policy changes will occur. This variable—*technological integration*— assesses the relative degree of concentration or decentralization in the network of social,

economic, and political institutions and relationships surrounding a technology, that is, the "technological infrastructure." Except for a technical breakthrough made by someone unconnected with an existing infrastructure, most technologies will be associated with organizations committed to their production and use. Surrounding each modern technology are networks, small and large, of primary providers—engineering designers, manufacturers, contractors, suppliers, wholesalers, retailers, consumers, and so forth—whose livelihood depends upon the existing technology and the public policies bearing on it. In many cases, a variety of ancillary groups derive considerable income from servicing the primary providers, as in financing, fuels, and parts for the industry, and in housing, food, consumer goods, and services for the workers. Congressional decisions about renewing, altering, or terminating existing policies are of critical importance to all members of the related technological infrastructure. (And, in many cases, the decision may be of greater importance to the service firms than to the primary providers, whose resources and size may permit them to weather policy changes more easily than small, local firms.) An established technological infrastructure thus will support the continuation of favorable public policies affecting their technology, and oppose changes in policy perceived as potentially disruptive.

Technological infrastructures vary across a variety of dimensions. For well-established technologies, in use for years or decades, the infrastructure may include national organizations, such as trade associations, professional councils, lobbyists, or political action committees. As such, these infrastructures are part of the panoply of interest groups participating in American politics. Other infrastructures may lack significant national organization, or any formal organization at all. These tend to be the newer technologies seeking entry into the market, although some older technologies also lack extensive organization.

Of more significance to this analysis is the relative degree of internal concentration or decentralization within the infrastructure. A concentrated infrastructure will have relatively few primary providers and relatively few service firms dependent upon them. Quite often, the primary providers will be large, integrated corporations involved with the manufacture or development of an array of technologies, often applicable in many different businesses. A concentrated infrastructure can also provide a technology for a limited number of customers, as illustrated by the relationship of the civilian nuclear power industry to the public utilities. In some cases, consumers may be scattered throughout the country, as in the communications and computer industries. And in other cases, concentrated infrastructures deal with only one customer, for example, government purchase of large weapons systems.

Decentralized infrastructures are composed of many primary providers, frequently scattered about the country; a large number of service firms are associated with the primary providers; entire communities may be economically dependent on the primary providers. Decentralized infrastructures often develop around mature, standardized, non-exotic technologies and involve a large number of customers also widely scattered around the nation. Railroad transport, both passenger and freight, is an example of a decentralized infrastructure.

The importance of technological integration for Congressional decisions derives from the differing political tactics that characterize decentralized versus concentrated infrastructures. Each kind of infrastructure presents a different set of political opportunities and constraints to Congressional policymakers.

SOME EXAMPLES

The two dimensions of the proposed typology—policy discontinuity and technological integration—intersect to create four major technological policy types (see Table 32.1). Each dimension is a continuum, moving from lesser to greater, rather than a fixed, discrete variable. Thus, the four policy types should be regarded as idealized forms that blend into each other, rather than as rigidly separated constructions.

Table 32.1.

Technological integration	Policy discontinuity	
	Moderate	Radical
Decentralized	Moderate decentralized	Radical decentralized
Concentrated	Moderate concentrated	Radical concentrated

rated constructions. For moderate-decentralized policies, the degree of policy change contemplated by Congress represents only a marginal variation in existing policies, concerning a technology possessing a decentralized infrastructure. Radical-decentralized policies, on the other hand, involve significantly discontinuous changes in an established policy, or significant alterations in the technology itself, affecting a decentralized infrastructure. Likewise, moderate-concentrated policies involve only modest policy changes of concern to a concentrated infrastructure, while radical-concentrated policies represent substantial policy changes affecting a concentrated infrastructure.

Moderate- and Radical-Concentrated Policies

Concentrated infrastructures, because they have fewer participants, offer Congress a greater opportunity to make and implement long-term technology management decisions. Because virtually any decision about an existing technology affects various groups differently, the greater the number of participants in the decision process, the greater the difficulty for Congress in defining technologically responsible policy goals and in structuring programs to achieve those goals. This is especially true when Congress must choose to switch technologies, reducing or eliminating programs favorable to one technology in favor of another. Such decisions become necessary as technical developments and breakthroughs, changes in constituent demands, fiscal constraints, or other political changes press upon existing policies.

Over the years, Congress has sometimes intentionally kept some technological infrastructures concentrated, to maintain close control of technologies considered too important for either broad public dissemination or broad public participation in the policy process. Most weapons procurement decisions, for instance, fall within the concentrated infrastructure categories—that is, few primary providers and service firms and only one primary consumer. Of course, in nearly all cases, executive agencies develop the technologies and recommend them to the legislature, which must then decide about authorizing and appropriating additional production funds. Because of the time and previous funding invested in bringing new weapons technologies to production readiness, there is an inevitable pressure to continue onward with existing plans. In consequence, many weapons decisions made by Congress fall on the moderate end of the policy discontinuity scale. Most are modifications of existing technologies rather than radical changes in design or capabilities. The decision to purchase one kind of wide-body airframe over another, to serve as troop and material transports, is usually not a decision involving radically different technical designs. Most decisions concerning other weapons involve similar predictable technical advances upon existing technologies.

However, truly radical policy decisions have been made regarding weapons systems. The choices to develop the atomic and hydrogen bombs, of course, were radical-concentrated policy decisions—so radical that Congress felt the need to create a new mechanism for monitoring those decisions, the Joint Committee on Atomic Energy (JCAE). Another series of radical-concentrated decisions resulted in the introduction of the intercontinental ballistic missile, the MIRV'd ICBM, and the Cruise missile into the American nuclear arsenal.[2]

Congressional decisions to support physics research using particle accelerators, the development of the civilian nuclear industry, and the development of a domestic synthetic fuels industry are additional examples of both moderate- and radical-concentrated policy decisions. In each case, a small number of primary providers and ancillary concerns are involved, along with relatively small numbers of customers for the technology involved.

Sponsorship for particle accelerator research began with the Manhattan Project to develop the first atomic bomb, and continued after the end of the war. At first, the technology of such research represented a radical departure in physics. However, as the technology standardized, later decisions to support their construction amounted to only moderate alterations of existing policies. In fact, eventually, particle accelerator funding became the target of traditional distributive policy competition, as midwestern research universities organized MURA (Midwestern Universities Research Association) to wrest their "fair share" of accelerator funding away from the control of such institutions as the University of California at Berkeley and the Massachusetts Institute of Technology.[3]

Congressional involvement in the creation of a civilian nuclear power industry is an archetypal example of a radical-concentrated policy decision. The technology of using atomic fuel to generate electricity was surely a radical departure from the standard gas, oil, and hydroelectric generating systems. The technology was in the sole hands of the government, administered by the Atomic Energy Commission (later the Nuclear Regulatory Commission) and overseen by JCAE. Following President Eisenhower's famous "Atoms for Peace" speech in the United Nations, Congress enacted the 1954 amendments to the 1946 Atomic Energy Act, which made the commercial use of atomic power the official policy of the government. Ironically, the technology's prospective customers, the public utilities, at first resisted introduction of the new process. Risks attended the manipulation of radioactive materials, large capital outlays were needed to build the new facilities, and the potential losses from accidents were great. All these aspects served to undermine the utilities' enthusiasm for the new system. Not until Congress promised to provide research and development funding for safety research, and capital assistance in the building of facilities and, most importantly, passed the 1957 Price-Anderson Act limitations on utility accident liabilities, did the public utilities "get on board" the nuclear energy bandwagon.

During the infancy of the new industry, Congress sought to preserve its decisions from too much uninformed public participation. The concentrated nature of the existing nuclear infrastructure, the complexity of the technology itself, and the optimistic projections about "energy too cheap to meter," all contributed to a strictly limited public access to the overall decision process. The commitment to a nuclear future for America meant that the technology had to be managed with long-term goals in mind. To allow short-term needs and pressures to pull the program off track, it was felt, would only waste very valuable resources.[4]

In a similar fashion in 1980, the Congress chose to invest heavily in another energy technology, synthetic fuels. In this case, the government was not the sole possessor of the technology; synfuel processes were known within the private sector. Development costs, however, deterred many companies interested in synfuels from undertaking the capital investments. The 1980 Energy Security Act was aimed at providing investment capital and other incentives to private firms to develop the technologies to a level of commercial readiness. The Act called for a $20 billion investment in synfuels technologies, perhaps as much as $88 billion in time. The technology was to be in the hands of a relatively small group of primary providers, and was intended for a relatively small number of consumers. The technology itself represented a radical departure from conventional natural petroleum recovery techniques. And, just as in the case of nuclear energy, the existing petroleum infrastructure resisted the introduction of such a radical technological process. Even after the passage of the Act, few major petroleum corporations became deeply involved in the program. To manage the program, Congress also created a new administrative agency, the U.S. Synthetic Fuels Corporation.[5]

Moderate- and Radical-Decentralized Policies

There are examples of both moderate- and radical-decentralized policy decisions as well. An example of a radical-decentralized policy was the 1979 effort to cut Federal subsidies for Amtrak passenger rail service by about 43 percent. Although a Federal corporation (Amtrak) coordinates and administers rail passenger services, it must do so through the facilities of the private railroads whose tracks Amtrak trains must use. Moreover, the service companies in the thousands of communities served by Amtrak are numerous and dispersed throughout the United States. The 1979 cutback in Federal subsidies constituted a radical change in transportation technology policy and, not surprisingly, it prompted widespread political opposition from the existing decentralized infrastructure.[6]

Most technology-forcing environmental protection legislation also falls into either moderate- or radical-decentralized policy categories. The "polluter pays" provisions of such enactments as the Clean Air Act (and its 1977 amendments), the Clean Water Act, the Solid Waste Disposal Act, the Toxic Substances Control Act, the Surface Mining Control and Reclamation Act, and several others sometimes require significant initial technical steps on the part of widely scattered manufacturing, public utilities, energy corporations, or city governments. There is no centralized concentration in the provision of the various environmental technologies in question, and a wide dispersion of consumers.

DISCUSSION

For Congress, the key to making long-term technology management decisions is to gain a degree of policy insulation from cross-cutting political pressures. Only through insulating such decisions from conflicting and disruptive constituent demands, does Congress gain the flexibility to review existing technology policies dispassionately, to determine if they still contribute to (or hinder) the broader public weal. Relatively free of pressure politics,

Congress may be able to create policies more congruent with emerging technical options, policies which may be more beneficial to the majority of people even if temporarily harmful to those attached to the existing policies. Dealing with concentrated infrastructures allows a greater—although never absolute—degree of policy insulation. The early years of the civilian nuclear power industry illustrate the extensive efforts of Congress, through a concentrated technological infrastructure, to develop and implement long-range policy. The considerable literature reviewing the early history of nuclear power is unanimous in detailing how both the AEC and the JCAE pursued policy insulation in directing the evolution of nuclear technology, in the support for the light water reactor (LWR) over other reactor designs for both military and civilian uses, and in setting technical standards for reactor siting decisions.[7]

Similar tight controls mediated through concentrated infrastructures was the management mechanism of choice for several other recent technical developments. The authorization and appropriations for chemical and biological warfare systems, for managing nuclear wastes, for developing the neutron "bomb," antiballistic missile systems, and many others demonstrate the utility of concentrated infrastructures in achieving policy goals. Of course, the management of technology through concentrated infrastructures does not always work smoothly. Even moderate policy shifts (e.g., a new tank design based on "normal" extensions of existing designs) can generate intense political pressures as various private manufacturers compete for lucrative contracts. Yet even here the concentrated infrastructure permits relatively efficient management: all parties concerned support the general direction of policy, while they may vie with each other over specifics.

However, concentrated infrastructures sometimes fail to maintain the policy insulation needed to permit long-range technological decisions to proceed. In two recent examples, the supersonic transport funding issue and the proposed antiballistic missile system,[8] the policies seemed at first to be quite ordinary developments within established programs. Each proposed program possessed both Presidential endorsement and extensive public support from the infrastructure members. Both the SST and the ABM represented long-standing commitments to "high tech" solutions to national problems—in the one case, a dwindling private aircraft industry; in the other, national defense. In both cases, a diverse array of non-infrastructure participants—sometimes noted scientific and technological experts, at other times non-expert citizens—were able to penetrate the decision process so successfully that Congress eventually made decisions about each technology which were substantially different from those initially expected. In both cases, the non-infrastructure participants based their objections to Congressional support for the SST and the ABM largely upon scientific and technical arguments, as opposed to, for example, more traditional economic issues. The SST was resisted because of noise and air pollution problems; the ABM, because of doubts about its technical feasibility and the fear of becoming a target for Soviet missiles if ABM facilities were constructed near population centers. Economic arguments were made by the infrastructure supporters who were likely to benefit from Congressional funding.

Another example of a radical-concentrated policy unable to sustain policy insulation was the 1980 Energy Security Act, which created the U.S. Synthetic Fuels Corporation. In this case, a combination of political pressures overcame a concentrated infrastructure's opposition to a radical change in petroleum policy. Heavy Federal investment in the new technologies of synthetic fuels—oil shale, tar sands, and coal gasification, for example—succeeded in 1980, although it had failed as recently as 1975, because of a confluence of gasoline shortages and price increases precipitated by the Iranian crisis and the accompanying public demand that the government do *something* about the energy crisis. Synfuels supporters in the Senate also proved willing to enlarge the original modest bill passed by the House by adding on nine unrelated energy technology programs. The original $3 billion synfuels bill from the House ballooned into a massive $122 billion program, with new initiatives in solar, geothermal, biomass conversion, conservation, and acid rain research technologies added to maintain the fragile coalition. Infrastructure members fought the omnibus bill, and were joined by a variety of environmental groups and affected state governments. But their objections, often backed by extensive scientific analyses, fell on deaf ears.[9]

Although concentrated infrastructures offer greater policy insulation to policymakers interested in long-range technology management, when the policy change is sufficiently radical in nature, the policy insulation may be undone by the concerted efforts of other affected groups. Often, such groups do not have a direct economic stake in the contemplated policy decision, but instead represent larger social values, such as the need for environmental protection. Also, non-infrastructure groups must often resort to unconventional political tactics to penetrate the screen of policy insulation.

Concentrated infrastructures may then, under certain circumstances, fail to provide adequate policy insulation for policymakers. Decentralized infrastructures, however, operate generally through intense political pressures upon policymakers in Congress. Decentralized infrastructures can make long-term technological planning more difficult because of the greatly enlarged roster of affected interests whose concerns must be taken into account in whatever policy emerges. In addition, dispersed infrastructure members can be adept at lobbying the Congressional representatives in their home districts. As John Kingdon and many others have pointed out,[10] no other influence shaping Congressional decisions is more potent than organized home district constituents. It would take a courageous Senator or Representative to vote against the desires of a home district infrastructure while promising that the policy change in question will benefit everyone "in the long run." Getting to the point where "in the long run" extends beyond the next election is often difficult, to say the least.

The existence of decentralized infrastructures creates less policy insulation for Congress, but it does offer many opportunities for individual members of Congress to display their sensitivity to constituent demands. Because the infrastructure members are widely dispersed, and often politically organized, they offer an attractive, attentive constituency for the Congressmen or women to develop and maintain a reputation of protecting local interests. What may be lost in long-range policy coherence may be made up by protecting vocal constituents from what they regard as undesirable policy changes. Short-term electoral security may therefore be purchased through special exceptions, exemptions, exclusions, permissions, licenses, clearances, and so forth, from long-term policies.

Such a case of long-range management upset by localized political opposition from decentralized infrastructure members as the 1979 Amtrak service cutbacks illustrates the problems inherent in choosing to shift from an established but poorly performing technology that possesses a decentralized but attentive infrastructure. In its first nine years, Amtrak's revenues increased by 205 percent, while its expenses grew by 291 percent. In 1977, after a struggle over Amtrak subsidies, Congress ordered the Secretary of Transportation to prepare a thorough "zero-base" study of the entire system. The Secretary's Final Report recommended substantial restructuring; with a 43 percent reduction in passenger miles, and the termination of several long-haul trains. Public response to the Secretary's recommendation was explosive. Amtrak serves thousands of communities throughout the United States, hundreds of which would have been adversely affected by the proposed policy change. Passenger organizations, environmentalists, city and state governments, even businesses that serviced passengers flooded their representatives with demands that the cut-backs be reduced. Most complained that not only were "their" trains being arbitrarily cut, but also most of the remaining service would be concentrated only in the "Northeast corridor," from Boston to Washington, DC. As one person observed:

You see, people in places like Kansas are not going to pay just to run trains in the Northeast. They want their own trains. That's what happened on Capitol Hill.

The clamor to protect regional economic interests eventually affected the Secretary's planned reductions. The 43 percent cutback was reduced to only about 20 percent, "splitting the difference" between supporters and opponents of the plan. Moreover, several poorly performing trains that had been slated for termination but crossed the districts of important Congressmen were given reprieves. Whether or not the Secretary's plan was the best available, the final result did reflect ad hoc policymaking rather than long-term management.[11]

CONCLUSION

The typology I have drawn highlights an important irony in American technology policymaking. Because concentrated infrastructures have fewer participants whose diverse demands must be somehow integrated into a single policy, they are better policy partners for those members of Congress interested in long-term policy management. However, they are also frequently less accountable to the public specifically because they have fewer participants in the decision process. Hence, they often lack safeguards against manipulation by special interests, and sometimes produce policies benefitting only infrastructure members. Their potential for long-term management for the common good may often be subverted by their undemocratic character.

Although decentralized infrastructures are more democratically accountable because they have more participants, they often produce incoherent policies precisely because of that responsiveness. The potential for responsive long-term policies is often subverted by the clash and compromise of so many voices. The demands of technological responsibility and democratic responsiveness clash as Congress makes technological policy decisions. This conflict remains the fundamental problem of science and technology policymaking in our society.

The role of Congress in technological policymaking emphasizes the potential for internal conflicts between the need for long-term, coherent policies in technological areas and the dominant operating style of a national legislature. This operating style suffers from the defects of its virtues: technologically responsible policies can be undermined by Congress' own democratic responsiveness, when individual members of Congress seek to protect local groups. Responsible technological management requires a long view of social change, as well as the willingness to take risks and to accept the inevitable dislocations accompanying technical change. Technological opportunities beneficial to society as a whole must be balanced against the cost of upset individual lives. Constituent demands to be given a special exclusion from such disruptions, if multiplied by all of the members of Congress, would obviously make coherent policies impossible, a situation that is especially true for long-term policies whose rewards may only be visible years or decades later.

The creation of the Congressional Office of Technology Assessment, and greater use of the resources of the General Accounting Office, the Library of Congress Legislative Research Service, and the Congressional Budget Office all contribute to an increased ability to manage technology policy in Congress. Yet Congressional policymaking remains highly complex and, despite improvements in forecasting and analysis, still fraught with crosscutting pressures. Decision-making is fragmented among a multitude of committees and subcommittees, interest group pressures, political debts and deals. The close working relationships between committee members, interest group lobbyists, and bureaucrats—the "cozy triangles"—and the highly constituent-oriented style of many members can contribute to the derailment and derangement of long-term policy coherence for the sake of protecting established policies and privileges.

This conflict, of course, is not unique to technological policymaking. However, the way that Congress resolves the conflicts inherent in the opposing agendas of technological responsibility and democratic responsiveness is fundamentally important for both sets of policy demands. Long-term policies beset by repeated interruptions and alterations to accommodate local demands stand little chance of success. By the same token, long-range policies that ignore their potential impact upon individual lives violate established ethical norms central to our political self-definition. The virtue of the typology I have described in this essay is its direct focus upon this enduring conflict in policymaking.

Designing measures of relative technological integration and of relative policy discontinuity should pose no intractable problems. The existence and strength of a technological infrastructure can be measured through an analysis of firms already engaged in the specific technical field, through investment levels and trends, sales figures and profit levels, distribution networks, even stock market activities. Where technological policies involve governmental contracts instead of market forces, the levels of Congressional appropriations, size and distribution of contracts and subcontracts, and similar measures will serve as good indicators of the existence—or prospective formation—of a technological infrastructure, along with some estimate of its strength. It remains to develop some form of scalar ranking of various technological infrastructures, thereby permitting empirical testing of the impact of different forms of Congressional policymaking.

Levels of policy discontinuity may be more difficult to rank, since the quality of discontinuity can be more elusive. In some cases, the new technology—for instance, wind-generated electricity—may appear to be discontinuous when, in fact, it is more correctly described as the reintroduction of an older technical tradition. In other instances, such as the creation of wholly new life forms through genetic engineering, it is possible to determine a high level of radical discontinuity. One possible approach would involve expert opinion sampling in the relevant field, to develop a consensus concerning the degree of policy discontinuity in a proposed policy change.

This policy typology, therefore, can also be seen as a possible first step toward predicting the outcomes of specific technological policy battles in Congress. Modification and refinement would then emerge through practical application in specific studies, accumulating thereby a set of case studies framed in essentially the same theoretical language. This Congressional policy typology may thus serve to advance the sophistication and rigor of technological policy analysis, and prepare the way for further theoretical developments.

NOTES

1. Congress is the focus of this typology because it contributes greatly to the evolution of technological policy in the United States, in a wide variety of ways. It is ironic that the scholarly literature has tended to neglect Congress' role in technological policymaking, while examining the special influences of the White House and "technoscience" agencies, such as NASA, the Department of Defense, NIH, etc. Dorothy Nelkin et al., *Controversy: Politics of Technical Decisions* (Beverly Hills, CA: Sage Publishing, 1979); David Elliot, *The Control of Technology* (New York: Springer-Verlag, 1976); Ina Spiegel-Rösing, Ed., *Science, Technology and Society: A Cross-Disciplinary Perspective* (Beverly Hills, CA: Sage Publishing, 1977); Thomas J. Kuehn and Alan L. Porter, Eds., *Science, Technology and National Policy* (Ithaca, NY: Cornell University Press, 1981); William T. Golden, Ed., "Science Advice to the President," special issues, Parts 1 and 2 *Presidential Politics and Science Policy* (New York: Praeger Publishers, 1978); Henry Lambright, *Governing Science and Technology* (New York: Oxford University Press, 1976); Joel Primack and Frank Von Hippel, *Advice and Dissent: Scientists in the Political Arena* (New York: Basic Books, 1974).

2. Ted Greenwood, *Making the MIRV: A Study of Defense Decision Making* (Cambridge, MA: Ballinger Publishing Company, 1975); Ronald Huisken, *The Origin of the Strategic Cruise Missile* (New York: Praeger Publishers, 1981).

3. Daniel S. Greenberg, *The Politics of Pure Science* (New York: The New American Library, Inc., 1967), chapters X and XI.

4. There is a considerable literature reviewing the management of civilian nuclear energy. See especially, Steven L. Del Sesto, *Science, Politics and Controversy: Civilian Nuclear Power in the United States, 1946–1974* (Boulder, CO: Westview

Press, 1979); Steven L. Del Sesto, "Nuclear Reactor Safety and the Role of the Congressman: A Content Analysis of Congressional Hearings," Volume 42, Number 1 (February 1980): 227–241; and Dorothy Nelkin, *Nuclear Power and its Critics* (Ithaca, NY: Cornell University Press, 1971).

5. Patrick W. Hamlett, "Technological Policymaking in Congress: The Creation of the U.S. Synthetic Fuels Corporation," paper presented at the Annual Meeting of the American Political Science Association, Denver, CO, 1–5 September 1982.

6. Patrick W. Hamlett, "Technological Policymaking in Congress: The Amtrak Passenger Service Cutbacks of 1979," paper presented at the Annual Meeting of the Midwest Political Science Association, Cincinnati, OH, 17 April 1981.

7. Del Sesto, "Nuclear Reactor Safety and the Role of the Congressman," op. cit.

8. Joel Primack and Frank Von Hippel, op. cit., chapters 2, 5, and 13.

9. Hamlett, "Technological Policymaking in Congress: The Creation of the U.S. Synthetic Fuels Corporation," op. cit.

10. John Kingdon, *Congressman's Voting Decisions* (New York: Harper and Row, 1980); Aage Clausen, *How Congressmen Decide: A Policy Focus* (New York: St. Martin's Press, 1973); John Jackson, *Congress: The Electoral Connection* (New Haven: Yale University Press, 1971); Donald Matthews and James Stimson, *Yeas and Nays: Normal Decision Making in the U.S. House of Representatives* (New York: John Wiley and Sons, 1975).

11. Hamlett, "Technological Policymaking in Congress: The Amtrak Passenger Service Cutbacks of 1979," op. cit.

33

Technological Literacy: An Uphill Battle

RUSTUM ROY

The author discusses the lack of technological literacy in the United States, and suggests that more Science, Technology and Society programs are needed at the high school and college levels. The ones launched in the late sixties, however, have not been very successful. The author attributes this lack of success to the rigidity of the departmental structure of universities, and argues that the suggested programs will work only when they become truly interdisciplinary and entrenched in academic institutions.

Add up, if you will, the cost of all the solutions that have been proposed to curb the decline in math and science education. Dr. Gregg Edwards, formerly of the Science Education Directorate at the National Science Foundation, estimates the sum to be $150 billion. So far, the U.S. House has allocated only $500 million—and the Senate and President have yet to approve that. Since any allocation is likely to be much less than $150 billion, we will clearly have to be innovative in how we use the new funds. Unfortunately, the university world, which sets educational priorities for the country, resists genuine innovations as much as any conservative board of directors or entrenched union.

For the last 30 years, the leaders of academic science and engineering have treated the problem of technological illiteracy with what amounts to benign neglect. In recent months, however, the problem has attracted nationwide attention, and the educational community will no doubt respond to the half-billion federal dollars being dangled out there for "science education." The crucial question that every policymaker and school board or university president must ask is:

science education for whom? Is this crisis merely a way of saying that we have shortages of computer scientists and electrical engineers? Or is it an epidemic affecting the entire population? For whom shall we design the cure—the roughly 1 percent who become professional scientists, engineers, or doctors?

No, I submit that while this may be the group that most scientists and engineers think of first—as we did after Sputnik—it is not what the public and Congress have in mind. No further proof is needed of congressional intent than the "horror stories" that have been cited in testimony to win the passage of recent bills to improve math and science education. The tellers of these stories invariably focus on the problem of math and science illiteracy in the general population, and they offer alarming comparisons with other countries to drive the point home.

It is true that in sheer number of hours, the average student in the United States is exposed to one-fifth to one-third as many hours in science and math as her or his counterpart in Western Europe or Japan. Out of 17,000 school districts in this country, well over half have an inadequate teaching staff to cover

From *Technology Review* (November–December 1983), pp. 18–19. Copyright ©1983. Reprinted with permission from *Technology Review*.

math, science, and technology. And while the Soviet Union has 123,000 physics teachers, the United States has 10,000. Even more striking is the technological illiteracy of college seniors who have already had required science and math courses. According to a National Science Foundation study reported in *Daedalus* last Spring, the vast majority of seniors still can't solve a simple word problem after four years of college. Given the extent of this problem, we in the science and education community would betray the country if we focused once again on just creating more or "better" scientists and engineers. The goal this time should be math and science education for all.

Those who are closest to the problem—the nation's secondary-school science teachers—have pointed to one solution. In a position paper adopted unanimously in 1982, the National State Teachers Association claims that the biggest gap in high-school science education is not in physics, biology, or even computer manipulation—but in the relationship of science and technology to society. Science, technology and society (STS) programs would focus, for example, on technology's relationship to the food-population seesaw, the consequences of genetic engineering, or the effect of computer automation on jobs.

Only by teaching science and technology in this context can we truly expect the American public to become interested in these subjects. By studying acid rain, not only does a citizen become informed about a major policy issue, but she (or he) learns what pH means and how bases neutralize acids. At Pennsylvania State University, discussing the issues of nuclear war and nuclear power has helped our philosophy and English majors grasp the principles of fission in a way that their required science courses in high school and college were never able to. Science teaching has long followed the more elitist European model of teaching pure science first with very little reference to technology. We must turn this sequence around by focusing on experience and teaching technology first, science thereafter.

In implementing what amounts to a basic restructuring of science education in the United States, there are major hurdles to overcome. The first and perhaps most serious is that there is no constituency fighting for institutional reform or the dollars with which to launch STS programs at secondary schools and college campuses. While there is, for instance, an established (and powerful) physics community fighting for financial support of physics research and education, there is no entrenched group of scholars fighting in the interests of STS.

But what, you might ask, happened to all the ambitious STS programs that sprang up on hundreds of college campuses in the late 1960s? Such programs were launched in an effort to educate a generation disoriented and disturbed by the onrush of technological progress. Today, some 50 or 60 substantial university programs focus on science, technology, and society in one form or another. These range from "interdisciplinary" courses team-taught by members of different faculties to rare full-fledged STS departments, such as the one at State University of New York–Stonybrook, where 4,000 students a year take one or more STS courses. At Vassar and Connecticut Wesleyan, students are able to major in STS, and Cornell, Stanford, Penn State, Duke, and Lehigh offer solid interdisciplinary STS programs. But the majority of college programs now available are more limited.

THE PLAGUE OF DEPARTMENTALISM

Furthermore, according to faculty members who spoke at the 1983 meeting of the American Association for the Advancement of Science, most of the interdisciplinary STS programs are faltering. A survey I conducted while at the Brookings Institution this summer reaches the same conclusions. If the goal is technological literacy for a million college students, then in a decade of overwork hundreds of faculty groups have failed to attain even 1 percent of their goal, according to my survey.

The blame for this failure can be laid at the university door, specifically at the rigidity of the departmental structure in universities.

Long after modern science rendered such divisions meaningless, the basic unit of power on almost all college campuses remains the department. Faculty members are well aware that doing specialized work within those departments is their sole avenue for advancement. On most college campuses, STS courses do not have the departmental structure supporting them, and as a result, faculty are not promoted for teaching STS or publishing in that field.

The history of STS programs at Harvard and Columbia—both originally funded to the tune of millions of dollars—speaks volumes. The programs were terminated after just a few years, and this was only the most extreme manifestation of academia's catatonic response to any attempt at restructuring the knowledge pie. The fledgling STS program at M.I.T. is having similar problems: announced with great fanfare as a college a year and a half year ago, it has since been reduced to an interdisciplinary program. But even under that more modest umbrella, it is having trouble bringing the many faculty stars from different departments together and attracting financial resources. Few department heads at any university are willing to allot faculty time or credits to courses taught outside their own departments. At Harvard, for instance, a student earning a Ph.D. in chemistry is discouraged from taking even one course in science and public policy for credit, even though such a course is taught by no less a distinguished scholar than Harvey Brooks, former dean of applied science and engineering.

Despite faculty resistance, some universities are making a concerted effort to restructure their curricula. At Stanford, for example, a large fraction of freshmen are permitted to take a course in "Values, Technology, and Society" as an alternative section within the "History of Western Civilization" course. The three-year-old Harvard core curriculum is another attempt to add societal relevance to standard course material. Titles such as "Dynamics and Energy: Concepts and Development," which includes a discussion of the "concepts underlying modern energy technology"; "Space, Time, and Motion," which includes "intuitive and philosophical views of space and time in the light of modern biology and psychology"; and "Chance, Necessity, and Order," which is billed as an "inquiry into the processes that create and destroy order in physical, astronomical, and biological systems"—all illustrate the effort to broaden the curriculum. Although some Harvard graduates have observed informally that the STS content in the core is little more than "cosmetic," the jury is still out. At the very least, Harvard must be lauded for making an attempt to take the broader view.

National policymakers must recognize the danger of departmentalism on university campuses and legislate accordingly. In allocating millions of dollars to improve the public's grasp of technology and its relevance to society, legislators must make special provisions to ensure that the funding will go specifically into STS programs or departments. If money intended for technological literacy is thrown into existing physics, chemistry, or biology departments, it will only reinforce the plague of fragmentation in science. Only if enough money is explicitly directed into technological literacy or STS efforts will the university system eventually respond with institutional changes. And once the universities begin the process of change, the secondary schools will follow suit rapidly—adapting teaching materials and curricula to the precollege level.

What is crucial to any effective STS program in secondary or higher education is a truly interdisciplinary faculty. Such staffs must have engineers and historians, philosophers and biochemists, political scientists and physicists working together. Indeed, as we have found at Penn State, students find it very enriching when a course is taught by faculty from each of the "two cultures." The divide between those cultures will remain and possibly worsen until the concept of STS is permanently and thoroughly absorbed into the academic bloodstream.

34
Science for Public Consumption: More Than We Can Chew?

SAMUEL FLORMAN

Samuel Florman argues that, although a wide diffusion of knowledge is good, the amount of uncertainty concerning new developments is awesome. No citizen can be adequately informed; and perplexing technical reports can lead to anxiety and erratic political action. He suggests that the public become knowledgeable about technology policy making not by staying abreast of the new information in every field—which is impossible—but by establishing fruitful relationships with experts and politicians, with the aim of ensuring that social objectives are best translated into technical decisions.

Like most people of goodwill, I have always believed that the public should be kept informed about science and technology. Facts for the masses, and the more the better. Only that way, in a democracy, can appropriate decisions be reached.

My faith in this premise, however, is occasionally shaken—most recently in my dentist's office. I asked why a cracked silver filling was to be replaced with a costly gold inlay and was given various structural reasons that were more or less convincing. I agreed to my dentist's recommendation and was about to drift into the trance that I try to attain in such situations when he added something that made me suddenly alert. "Besides," he said, "these so-called silver fillings really are amalgams that contain a lot of mercury, and we're beginning to wonder about the possibility of this mercury leaching into the systems of our patients. I've been following the work of experiments in Colorado, and pending further results I'm being a little cautious about using

the stuff." When I told him that I had never heard of any such danger, he replied that it was not exactly the sort of information that the dental profession wants bandied about. "The research is in very early stages," he explained, "and we don't want to frighten people unduly."

As he proceeded with his work, my mind started to race. A potential catastrophe! Tens of millions of people—one of them me—with insidious mercury leaching from their teeth into their vital organs. And what a scandal! Research was being performed and the findings were not being publicized. By the time I left the dentist's office, my alarm had subsided, but I determined to find out more.

My research consisted of obtaining a newsletter published by the Toxic Element Research Foundation (TERF) of Colorado Springs. Its single urgent message is that toxic elements have no place in the mouth. The four-page leaflet seems to be addressed mainly to dentists, but nothing in it is technically obscure. Unfortunately, I can't tell whether the newsletter is the product of discerning professionals or the fantasy of a group of eccentrics. I suspect the latter, particularly since a section captioned "Strong Testimony" consists of an "unsolicited expression of appreciation" from a young man whose arthritic symptoms disappeared one week after two small amalgams were removed from his teeth. Yet the board [of] TERF includes a D.D.S., an M.D., a biochemist, a psychologist, and the president of a bank. I am feeling healthy at the moment and busy with other concerns, so I guess that I will forget about the whole thing—unless I hear further from my dentist.

ALL EXPERTS, ALL THE TIME?

I could pursue the matter, of course, but then how would I find time to keep abreast of the latest information on acid rain, the greenhouse effect, recombinant DNA, nuclear waste, new drugs, new diets, and a myriad of other technical matters that affect me and the society around me? It is all very well to speak of an informed public, but in truth we spend our lives relying upon experts.

This is not necessarily as distressing as it sounds. Lewis Thomas, writing about his newly implanted pacemaker, reports with surprise and amiable guilt that the theories he held as physician-philosopher have changed completely since he became a patient. "Don't explain it to me," he says. "Go ahead and fix it." A lot of people seem to feel that way.

The conventional wisdom about maintaining a technologically informed public was challenged effectively a couple of years ago by Leon Trachtman of Purdue University. After a quarter-century devoted to studying, teaching, and science writing, Professor Trachtman (in the quarterly *Science, Technology & Human Values*) questioned what he had come to think of as a "glib assumption." Efforts to inform the public about science and technology were rarely effective, he concluded, either in improving individual consumer choices or communal policy decisions. "When there is a scientific consensus," wrote Trachtman,

"there is no need to inform the public except to recommend a proper course of action. When there is no consensus, why innundate the public with ambiguous and contradictory reports?" And further: "Since the important issues are generally the ambiguous ones, more knowledge seems almost calculated to create greater uncertainty."

The argument impressed me very much and brought me to the verge of changing my mind. But when I spoke about it to a few people I respected, they all warned me not to adopt an elitist position.

Even as I write this column, an issue of *The American Scholar* arrives in the mail containing an article by Jeremy Bernstein entitled "Science Education for the Non-Scientist." Here it is again, the warning that unless we learn science, technological decisions will be made on our behalf—and to our regret—by others. (Of course, as Bernstein points out, there are other reasons to study science—not the least for pleasure.) Bernstein is optimistic that a scientifically literate public can learn to make its own decisions, yet what does he offer to support his conviction? He tells of teaching a course to 14 science majors at Princeton and bringing in 4 experts in nuclear power, both pro and con, to address the class. By the end of the term, the class had been converted from unthinking opponents of nuclear power to grudging advocates of nuclear for at least a partial solution to the energy problem.

This is an interesting object lesson, and if science education for the masses could be based on this model, what a fine world it would be. But the trouble is that nuclear power is only one of hundreds of complex technological issues, and none of us can spend a semester on each. Also, there are not enough Jeremy Bernsteins to go around—to say nothing of traveling experts and Princeton science majors.

LEARNING VERSUS KNOWLEDGE

The trouble with letting a few make decisions for the many is that the many might, if they knew more, want to do somethig different.

There is a further concern, however. Some people fear the coming of "a new kind of Dark Age—a time when small cadres of specialists will control knowledge and thus control the decision-making process." (The quote is from *Higher Learning in the Nation's Service,* cited approvingly on the *New York Times* Op-Ed page by the president of Cornell University.)

I do not fear the coming of a sinister technocratic cabal, mainly because on consequential issues the technicians invariably give conflicting advice, and the politicians end up making the decisions whether they want to or not. (Jimmy Carter complained about this, and Ronald Reagan certainly will complain if he hasn't already.) Still, it would be nice to think that people could make choices that intimately affect their own lives.

The paradox defies resolution. A wide diffusion of knowledge is good but the uncertainties are awesome, no citizen can be adequately informed, and perplexing technical reports lead to anxiety and erratic political action. As the saying goes, a little knowledge is a dangerous thing.

Ah, but this is not the saying, at least as Alexander Pope coined it. Pope spoke not of knowledge but of *learning:*

A little learning is a dangerous thing:
Drink deep, or taste not the Pierian spring:
There shallow draughts intoxicate the brain,
And drinking largely sobers us again.

Perhaps the semantic difference between "learning" and "knowledge" can give us a helpful clue. Learning is knowledge acquired by systematic study, and a little of that—a few undigested facts—can indeed "intoxicate the brain." Knowledge in the broad sense, however, implies understanding, discernment, and judgment, and no amount of this, however small, can be a dangerous thing. A knowledgeable public will not expect to resolve each technical issue by analyzing evidence, but will seek to establish a fruitful relationship with its experts—and its politicians—a combination of trust and suspicion, respect and obstinance, calculated to best translate social objective into technical decisions. Science educators and science journalists will have to explore uncharted realms to responsibly assist this process.

I believe that we have been too simplistic in our assumptions about science education and the public. While I'm rethinking the big picture, however, and resigning myself to reliance upon experts, I plan to keep asking my dentist what they're discovering—if anything—about silver fillings.

Glossary

The purpose of this glossary is to provide brief characterizations of terms that may not be altogether clear to some readers, including those used frequently in technology or that have significance in ethics. Words often have more than one use. No attempt has been made to list every use, only those of significance to the discussions in this book and which may be useful to those readers without a background in technology or ethics.

In preparing the glossary, the following publications have proved to be especially useful: Sidney Davidson et al., Financial Accounting *(Hinsdale, IL: The Dryden Press, 1979); Harold P. Ford and Francis X. Winters, S.J.,* Ethics and Nuclear Strategy? *(Maryknoll, NY: Orbis, 1977); Spurgeon M. Keeny, Jr.,* Nuclear Power Issues and Choices *(Cambridge, MA: Ballinger, 1977); David A. Jackson and Stephen Stich,* The Recombinant DNA Debate *(Englewood Cliffs, NJ: Prentice-Hall, 1979); A. R. Lacey,* A Dictionary of Philosophy *(NY: Charles Scribner's Sons, 1976); and National Science Foundation.* Emerging Issues in Science and Technology, 1981 *(Washington, DC: National Science Foundation, 1982).*

ABM Antiballistic missile: 1. a defensive missile designed to intercept and destroy or neutralize an incoming warhead/reentry vehicle; 2. broadly, the whole system of launchers, radars, computers, and missiles designed to defend some specified target or geographic area against ballistic missile attack.

(ABM) Protocol An extension of the initial ABM Treaty that further restrained both the United States and the USSR from deploying more than 100 ABM launchers and interceptors at no more than one site.

ABM Treaty Anti-Ballistic Missile Treaty of May 1972. A treaty between the United States and the USSR limiting each nation to two ABM launching sites at least 1,300 kilometers apart, with no more than 100 ABM launchers and interceptors at each.

ACDA The U.S. Arms Control and Disarmament Agency.

Action The doing of something or what is done. Characteristically, a performance or omission, not merely a reflex movement.

ASM Air-to-surface missile: a missile launched from an airborne carrier against a target on the ground.

Automation The technique, method, or system of operating or controlling machines or processes by highly sophisticated self-moving or self-guiding means, as by electronic devices.

Ballistic missile A missile that does not rely on aerodynamic surfaces to produce lift.

Behavior What an object, especially a living being, does.

Belief Assent to or acceptance of a statement or proposition as true.

Biosphere The part of the earth's crust, waters, and atmosphere where living organisms can subsist.

Breeder reactor A nuclear reactor that produces more fissile material than it consumes.

Clone A group of identical cells or organisms, all of which arose from the same cell by asexual reproduction.

Consequentialism A family of theories according to which the value of such things as actions, policies, and traits is somehow dependent on the value of consequences.

Cost-effective Usually, among alternatives, the one whose expected benefits or payoffs, divided by its expected costs, are the highest. Sometimes, among alternatives, the one whose expected benefits exceed its expected costs whether or not there are other alternatives with larger benefit/cost ratios.

Cost-risk-benefit analysis A procedure used to evaluate alternative courses of action in four basic steps: first, determining what alternative courses of action are open in given circumstances; second, determining what consequences each alternative course of action is likely to lead to; third, assigning a common quantitative measure, usually money, to formulate the costs and benefits of each of the consequences; finally, to adjust the values thus given to costs and benefits in accord with the rule that the earlier a benefit comes, the better, and the later a cost comes, the better.

Cruise missile A missile powered by rocket or jet engines that flies within the atmosphere like an airplane along most of its trajectory.

Disarmament The reduction or elimination of military forces and weapons especially by formal or informal international action.

DNA Deoxyribonucleic acid: the genetic material of all cells and many viruses. Most DNA molecules consist of two interwound chains or strands of four basic units, the nucleotides, or bases.

Duty See Obligation.

Ecology The study of how organisms relate to each other and their environment.

Ecosystem A system formed by the interaction of a network of organisms and their environment.

Egoism A family of theories, some psychological, others ethical. Ethical egoism is itself a family of theories whose basic component is some formulation of the principle of ethical egoism. One such formulation is this: An action is right (or a trait is good, or a policy is justified) if it tends to maximize the balance of desirable over undesirable consequences for the particular person who performs that action (assesses the policy, or has the trait), regardless of how great the overall balance of undesirable consequences might be for any other person or group, unless this would hinder the overall balance of desirable consequences for the said person. Otherwise, the action is wrong (or the policy unjustified, or the trait bad). By contrast with ethical egoism, egoism, as a family of psychological theories, holds that people, as a matter of *fact,* think and act only so as to maximize the overall balance of desirable over undesirable consequences for themselves.

Environmental Protection Agency (EPA) Agency established by Congress in 1970. Its purpose is to control and abate pollution in the areas of air, water, solid waste, noise, radiation, and toxic substances. The EPA conducts research to establish standards and controls of all forms of pollution, and establishes and enforces such standards.

Enzyme A protein molecule that increases the rate of a chemical reaction.

Ethical theory See **Ethics.**

Ethics There are at least three senses of the term "ethics": the personal sense, the group sense, and the branch of inquiry sense. In the personal sense, ethics is a particular individual's beliefs and presuppositions about right and wrong, good and bad, justified and unjustified. In the group sense, ethics is a group's beliefs and presuppositions about right and wrong, good and bad, justified and unjustified. In the branch of inquiry sense, ethics is a critical activity aimed at dealing with problems posed by the fact that some beliefs and presuppositions about right and wrong, good and bad, justified and unjustified appear to conflict with others. Ethics as a branch of inquiry attempts to deal with these problems by developing instruments for establishing whether the conflicts are real, clarifying them, and establishing what beliefs and presuppositions are sound and what to do about the conflicts. These instruments are ethical theories, which are roughly the same as moral theories and moral philosophies. Ethics as a branch of inquiry is roughly the same as moral theory, ethical theory, and moral philosophy.

First use   The launching of an initial nuclear attack against the enemy after a conventional war is in progress.

Fission   The splitting of an atomic nucleus, with the release of energy.

Fissile material   Atoms such as uranium-233, uranium-235, or plutonium-239, whose nucleus splits upon the absorption of a low-energy neutron.

Formal justice   A conception of justice characterized by the principle of formal justice, which says that no one ought to be treated differently from anyone else, despite the various differences between these individuals, except when one or more of these differences constitutes a good reason for doing so.

Formalism   In ethics, the family of theories according to which the value of such things as actions, policies, or traits is somehow dependent on the nature of the actions, policies, or traits, not on the value of consequences.

Fusion   The combining of certain light atomic nuclei to form heavier nuclei, with release of energy.

Gene   A sequence of DNA base pairs that codes for a single species of protein.

Geneva Protocol of 1925   An international agreement prohibiting the use of chemical and biological weapons in warfare.

Genotype   An organism's total array of genes.

Half-life   The period required for the disintegration of half of the atoms in a given amount of a specific radioactive material.

Intercontinental ballistic missile (ICBM)   A multistage rocket capable of delivering nuclear warheads at least 4,000 nautical miles away.

Intermediate-range ballistic missile   A ballistic missile with a range of about 1,500 to 4,000 nautical miles.

Light water reactor   A nuclear reactor that uses ordinary water as a coolant to transfer heat from the fissioning of uranium to a steam turbine and that employs slightly enriched uranium-235 as a fuel.

Medicaid/Medicare   U.S. programs providing funds for the elderly, disabled, and poor for basic health care and treatment.

Medium-range ballistic missile (MRBM)   A ballistic missile with a range of 600 to 1,500 nautical miles.

Megawatt   The unit by which the rate of production of electricity is usually measured.

Moral philosophy   See Ethics.

Moral theory   See Ethics.

Morals   See Ethics.

Multiple independently targetable reentry vehicle (MIRV)   A system in which a single missile carries multiple warheads, each targeted to a different area.

Multiple reentry vehicle (MRV)   A system in which a single missile carries multiple warheads which would be dispersed over a general area.

Mutation   A change in the genetic material of an organism.

National Institutes of Health (NIH)   A medical research center dependent on the U.S. Department of Health and Human Services (HHS).

National Transportation Safety Board (NTSB)   An agency established by the Independent Safety Board Act of 1974. Its purpose is to conduct independent investigations of accidents and safety problems and formulate safety improvement recommendations for transportation of all sorts.

Nuclear deterrence   A strategy aimed at convincing an opponent that any act of aggression on its part would make it face costs and risks that far outweigh whatever benefits it might expect from the aggression.

Nuclear Regulatory Commission (NRC)   The commission formed in 1975 when the Atomic Energy Commission was divided into the NRC and the Energy Research and Development Administration, which afterwards became the Department of Energy. The NRC is responsible for licensing and regulation of the nuclear industry.

Nuclear waste   The radioactive products formed by fission and other nuclear processes in a reactor. Most nuclear waste is initially in the form of spent fuel. If this material is reprocessed, new types of waste result: high-level wastes, low-level wastes, and others.

Obligation   Ordinarily, what we incur because of such specifics as a promise made or a favor received. It is sometimes distinguished from a duty, in that a duty is thought to be longer-standing and less ad hoc than an obligation. Like duties, obligations are kinds of things we morally or legally ought to do except when specifiable considerations override or nullify them.

Occupational Safety and Health Review Commission (OSHRC)   An adjudicatory agency established by the Occupations Safety and Health Act of 1970. Another agency, the Occupational Safety and Health Administration (OSHA), is in charge of enforcing the act. OSHRC's function is to adjudicate cases in which a citation issued by OSHA is contested.

Opinion   See Belief.

Ought   See Obligation.

Preemptive Strike   A first strike against an adversary's offensive forces, population, or industry, in anticipation of a nuclear attack by the adversary.

Principle   In ethics, a generalization which has no exceptions, does not vary with changes in circumstances, and is relevant to a wide range of circumstances (e.g., the principle of utility, the principle of personality).

Rad   A measure of the radiation absorbed in tissue, corresponding to an energy absorption of 100 ergs per gram.

Recombinant DNA   DNA molecules of different origin which have been joined together by biochemical techniques to make a single molecule.

Rem   Roentgen Equivalent Man: the unit of biological dose given by the product of the absorbed dose in rads and the relative biological efficiency of the radiation.

Right   In the weakest sense of the term "right," to say that it is right for someone to perform an action is to say that it is not wrong for that person to perform it. If there is a twenty dollar bill on the ground which someone has lost, it is right for you to pick it up, and it is also right for me to pick it up. You and I are both at liberty to pick it up. If, by contrast with the previous case, the bill is mine and I have dropped it, it is now wrong for you to pick it up and keep it. I am entitled to the bill and to claim it from you. In a stronger sense of the term "right," I have a right to the bill and you do not. These two conditions, an entitlement to something and to claim it, serve to distinguish *a* right from what is right in the weak sense of simply not being wrong.

Risk-cost-benefit analysis   See Cost-risk-benefit analysis

RNA   Ribonucleic acid: RNA is different from DNA in that its sugar is ribose instead of deoxyribose; it is usually single-stranded while DNA is double-stranded; and its base is uracil instead of thymine.

Rules   In ethics, generalizations that may have exceptions, may vary with changes in the circumstances, and may be relevant only to specific areas (e.g., the rule that one generally ought not to lie).

Utilitarianism A family of moral theories whose component is some formulation of the principle of utility. One such formulation says that an action is right (or a policy justified, or a trait good) if it tends to maximize the balance of desirable consequences over undesirable. Otherwise, the action is wrong (or the policy unjustified, or the trait bad).

Virus A DNA or RNA molecule surrounded by a protective protein coat.

Selected Bibliography

This selected bibliography is by no means intended to be exhaustive. Works from which selections in this book have been taken are not listed.

I. TECHNOLOGY, ETHICS, TECHNOLOGY ETHICS

Baier, Kurt, *The Moral Point of View* (New York: Random House, 1965)

Barbour, Ian G., *Technology, Environment, and Human Values* (New York: Praeger Publishers, 1980)

Baum, Robert J., and Albert Flores, eds., *Ethical Problems in Engineering* (New York: Center for the Study of Human Dimensions of Science and Technology, 1978)

Dewey, John, and James H. Tufts, *Ethics* (New York: Henry Holt, 1913)

Dorf, R. C., *Technology and Society* (San Francisco: Boyd and Fraser, 1974)

Ellul, Jacques, *The Technological Society* (New York: Knopf, 1967)

Lacey, A. R., *A Dictionary of Philosophy* (New York: Charles Scribner's Sons, 1976)

Mabbott, J.D., *An Introduction to Ethics* (New York: Doubleday, 1969)

Mesthene, Emmanuel G., *Technological Change* (Cambridge, MA: Harvard U.P., 1970)

Press, Frank, Leon T. Silver et al., *New Pathways in Science and Technology* (New York: Vintage, 1985)

Pytlik, E.C., D.P. Lauda, and D.L. Johnson, *Technology, Change, and Society* (Worcester, MA: Davis, 1978)

Rawls, John, *A Theory of Justice* (Cambridge, MA: Harvard U.P., 1971)

Schuurman, Egbert, *Technology and the Future* (Toronto: Wedge Publishing Foundation, 1980)

Singer, Marcus G., *Generalization in Ethics* (New York: Atheneum, 1971)

Singer, Marcus G., ed., "Theoretical and Practical Ethics," *Morals and Values* (New York: Charles Scribner's Sons, 1977)

Warnock, J.G., *The Object of Morality* (London: Methuen, 1971)

II. MORAL CONTROVERSIES IN TECHNOLOGY ASSESSMENT

Baram, Michael S., "Technology Assessment and Social Control," *Science* 180 (1973)

Baram, Michael, "Cost-Benefit Analysis: An Inadequate Basis for Health, Safety, and Environmental Regulatory Decisionmaking," *Ecology Law Quarterly* 8 (1980)

Bosselman, F. et al., *The Taking Issue* (Washington, DC: U.S. Government Printing Office, 1971)

Coburn R., "Technology Assessment, Human Good, and Freedom," in *Ethics & Problems of the 21st Century,* ed. K.E. Goodpaster and K.M. Sayre, (Notre Dame, IN: Notre Dame U.P., 1979)

Davidson, Sidney et al., *Financial Accounting* (Hinsdale, IL: The Dryden Press, 1979)

Freeman, A., R. Haveman, and A. Kneese, *The Economics of Environmental Policy* (Baltimore, MD: Resources for the Future and Johns Hopkins U.P., 1973)

Kennedy, Duncan, "Cost-Benefit Analysis of Entitlement Problems: A Critique," *Stanford Law Review* 33 (1981)

MacIntyre, Alasdair, "Utilitarianism and Cost-Benefit Analysis: An Essay on the Relevance of Moral Philosophy and Bureaucratic Theory," in *Ethics and the Environment* ed. D. Scherer and T. Attig (Englewood Cliffs, NJ: Prentice-Hall, 1983)

Office of Technology Assessment, *What OTA Is, What OTA Does, How OTA Works* (Washington, DC: Congress of the United States Office of Technology Assessment, 1984)

Sagoff, Mark, "Ethics and Economics in Environmental Law," in *Earthbound,* ed. T. Regan (New York: Random House, 1984)

Smart, J.J.C., and Bernard Williams, *Utilitarianism: For and Against* (New York: Cambridge U.P., 1973)

Socolow, Robert H., "Failures of Discourse: Obstacles to Integration of Environmental Values into Natural Resource Policy," in *Ethics and the Environment,* ed. D. Scherer and T. Attig (Englewood Cliffs, NJ: Prentice-Hall, 1983)

III. MORAL CONTROVERSIES IN TECHNOLOGY MANAGEMENT

Bromberg, Joan Lisa, *Fusion. Science, Politics, and the Invention of a New Energy Source* (Cambridge, MA: MIT, 1982)

Del Sesto, Steven L. *Science, Politics, and Controversy: Civilian Nuclear Power in the United States, 1946–1974* (Boulder, CO: Westview, 1979)

Enos, Darryl D., and Paul Sultan, *The Sociology of Health Care* (New York: Praeger, 1977)

Ford, Harold P., and Francis X. Winters, S.J., eds., *Ethics and Nuclear Strategy?* (Maryknoll, NY: Orbis, 1977)

Hoffman, W. Michael, and Jennifer Mills Moore, eds., *Ethics and the Management of Computer Technology* (Cambridge, MA: Oelgeschlager, Gunn and Hain, 1982)

Jackson, David A., and Stephen P. Stich, eds., *The Recombinant DNA Debate* (Englewood Cliffs, NJ: Prentice-Hall, 1979)

Keeny, Jr., Spurgeon M. et al., *Nuclear Power Issues and Choices* (Cambridge, MA: Ballinger, 1977)

Nash, Hugh, ed., *The Energy Controversy* (San Francisco: Friends of the Earth, 1979)

Nader, Ralph, and John Abbotts, *The Menace of Atomic Energy* (New York: Norton, 1977)

National Science Foundation, *Emerging Issues in Science and Technology, 1981* (Washington, DC: National Science Foundation, 1982)

Office of Technology Assessment, *Automation and the Workplace* (Washington DC: Congress of the United States Office of Technology Assessment, 1983)

Office of Technology Assessment, *Computer-Based National Information Systems* (Washington DC: Congress of the United States Office of Technology Assessment, 1981)

Office of Technology Assessment, *Space Science Research in the United States* (Washington, DC: Congress of the United States Office of Technology Assessment, 1982)

Office of Technology Assessment, *Computerized Manufacturing Automation* (Washington, DC: Congress of the United States Office of Technology Assessment, 1984)

Passmore, John, *Man's Responsibility for Nature* (New York: Charles Scribner's Sons, 1974)

Parker, Donn B., *Ethical Conflicts in Computer Science and Technology* (Arlington, VA: AFIPS, 1977)

Partridge, Ernest, ed., *Responsibilities to Future Generations* (Buffalo, NY: Prometheus, 1981)

Regan, Tom, ed., *Earthbound* (New York: Random House, 1984)

Rescher, Nicholas, *Unpopular Essays on Technological Progress* (Pittsburgh, PA: University of Pittsburgh Press, 1980)

Shrader-Frechette, K.S., *Nuclear Power and Public Policy* (Boston: Reidel, 1980)

Veatch, Robert M., and Roy Branson, eds., *Ethics and Health Policy* (Cambridge, MA: Ballinger, 1976)

IV. MORAL CONTROVERSIES IN TECHNOLOGY RESEARCH AND DEVELOPMENT

Busch, Lawrence, and William B. Lacy, *Science, Agriculture, and the Politics of Research* (Boulder, CO: Westview, 1983)

Kruytbosch, C.E., *Academic-Corporate Research Relationships: Forms, Functions, and Fantasies* (Washington DC: The National Science Foundation, 1981)

Lindblom, Charles E., and David K. Cohen, *Usable Knowledge* (New Haven, CT: Yale U.P., 1979)

National Academy of Sciences, *Scientific Communication and National Security* (Washington DC: National Academy of Sciences, 1982)

Teich, J.L., *Inventory of University-Industry Research Support Agreements in Biomedical Science and Technology* (Bethesda, MD: National Institutes of Health, 1982)

U.S. Congress, House, Subcommittee on Science, Research and Development of the Committee on Science and Astronautics, *National Science Policy.* 91st Congress, 2d session, 1970 (Washington DC: U.S. Government Printing Office, 1970)

U.S. Congress, House, Subcommittee on Science, Research and Development of the Committee on Science and Astronautics, *Teaching and Research in the Field of Science Policy—A Survey.* 92nd Congress, 2d session, 1972 (Washington, DC: U.S. Government Printing Office, 1972)

York, C.M., "Steps Toward a National Policy for Academic Science," *Science* 172 (1971)

V. MORAL CONTROVERSIES IN TECHNOLOGY TRANSFER

Aiken, William, and Hugh La Follette, eds., *World Hunger and Moral Obligation* (Englewood Cliffs, NJ: Prentice-Hall, 1977)

Berry, Wendell, *The Unsettling of America. Culture and Agriculture* (New York: Avon, 1977)

Brandt, Willy et al., *North-South: A Programme for Survival* (Cambridge, MA: MIT Press, 1980)

Dorner, Peter, and Mahmoud A. El-Shafie, *Resources and Development: Natural Resource Policies and Economic Development in an Interdependent World* (Madison, WI: The University of Wisconsin P., 1980)

Hardt, J.P., and G.D. Holliday, *U.S.–Soviet Commercial Relations: The Interplay of Economics, Technology Transfer and Diplomacy* (Washington, DC: United States Government Printing Office, 1973)

Haynes, Richard, and Ray Lanier, eds., *Agriculture, Change, and Human Values* (Gainesville, FL: University of Florida Humanities and Agriculture Program, 1983)

Hopkins, Raymond F., and Donald J. Puchala, eds., *The Global Economy of Food* (Madison, WI: The University of Wisconsin P., 1978)

Kammeyer, Kenneth C.W., *Population Studies: Selected Essays and Research* (Chicago: Rand McNally, 1975)

Kanel, Don, "Power and Property as Issues in Institutional Economics and Economic Development," in *Proceedings of the Wisconsin Seminar on Natural Resource Policies in Relation to Economic Development and International Cooperation* (Madison, WI: Institute for Environmental Studies–University of Wisconsin P., 1978)

Lappe, F.M. et al., *Aid As Obstacle* (San Francisco: Institute for Food and Development Policy, 1980)

Lekachman, Robert, *Economists at Bay* (New York: McGraw-Hill, 1976)

Schumacher, E.F., *Small is Beautiful: Economics As If People Mattered* (New York: Harper & Row, 1973)

Seaborg, G.T., "Science, Technology and Development: A New World Outlook," *Science,* 181 (1973)

VI. GOVERNING TECHNOLOGY: MORALLY ASSESSING APPROACHES TO TECHNOLOGY POLICY MAKING

Anderson, James E. et al., *Public Policy and Politics in America* (Belmont, CA: Duxbury/Wadsworth, 1978)

Barry, Brian, *Political Argument* (London: Routledge & Kegan Paul, 1965)

Braybrooke, David, and Charles E. Lindblom, *A Strategy of Decision* (New York: The Free Press, 1963)

Dye, Thomas R., *Understanding Public Policy* (Englewood Cliffs, NJ: Prentice-Hall, 1972)

Gendron, Bernard, *Technology and the Human Condition* (New York: St. Martin's, 1977)

Jones, Charles O., *An Introduction to the Study of Public Policy* (Belmont, CA: Duxbury/Wadsworth, 1970)

Lineberry, Robert L., *American Public Policy* (New York: Harper & Row, 1977)

Nelkin, Dorothy, ed., *Controversy. Politics of Technical Decisions* (Beverly Hills: Sage, 1979)

Rohr, John, *Ethics for Bureaucrats: An Essay on Law and Values* (New York: Dekker, 1978)

Sayre, Kenneth M. et al., *Regulation, Values and the Public Interest* (Notre Dame, IN: University of Notre Dame P., 1980)